FORD AEROSTAR
1986-97 REPAIR MANUAL

CHILTON'S

Covers all U.S. and Canadian models of Ford Aerostar

by Will Kessler, A.S.E., S.A.E.

CHILTON Automotive Books

PUBLISHED BY HAYNES NORTH AMERICA, Inc.

Manufactured in USA
© 1999 Haynes North America, Inc.
ISBN 0-8019-9132-3
Library of Congress Catalog Card No. 99-80003
2345678901 9876543210

Haynes Publishing Group
Sparkford Nr Yeovil
Somerset BA22 7JJ England

Haynes North America, Inc
861 Lawrence Drive
Newbury Park
California 91320 USA

ABCDE
FGHIJ
KLMNO
PQ

7E1

Contents

Contents

SAFETY NOTICE

Proper service and repair procedures are vital to the safe, reliable operation of all motor vehicles, as well as the personal safety of those performing repairs. This manual outlines procedures for servicing and repairing vehicles using safe, effective methods. The procedures contain many NOTES, CAUTIONS and WARNINGS which should be followed, along with standard procedures to eliminate the possibility of personal injury or improper service which could damage the vehicle or compromise its safety.

It is important to note that repair procedures and techniques, tools and parts for servicing motor vehicles, as well as the skill and experience of the individual performing the work vary widely. It is not possible to anticipate all of the conceivable ways or conditions under which vehicles may be serviced, or to provide cautions as to all possible hazards that may result. Standard and accepted safety precautions and equipment should be used when handling toxic or flammable fluids, and safety goggles or other protection should be used during cutting, grinding, chiseling, prying, or any other process that can cause material removal or projectiles.

Some procedures require the use of tools specially designed for a specific purpose. Before substituting another tool or procedure, you must be completely satisfied that neither your personal safety, nor the performance of the vehicle will be endangered.

Although information in this manual is based on industry sources and is complete as possible at the time of publication, the possibility exists that some car manufacturers made later changes which could not be included here. While striving for total accuracy, the authors or publishers cannot assume responsibility for any errors, changes or omissions that may occur in the compilation of this data.

PART NUMBERS

Part numbers listed in this reference are not recommendations by Haynes North America, Inc. for any product brand name. They are references that can be used with interchange manuals and aftermarket supplier catalogs to locate each brand supplier's discrete part number.

SPECIAL TOOLS

Special tools are recommended by the vehicle manufacturer to perform their specific job. Use has been kept to a minimum, but where absolutely necessary, they are referred to in the text by the part number of the tool manufacturer. These tools can be purchased, under the appropriate part number, from your local dealer or regional distributor, or an equivalent tool can be purchased locally from a tool supplier or parts outlet. Before substituting any tool for the one recommended, read the SAFETY NOTICE at the top of this page.

ACKNOWLEDGMENTS

This publication contains material that is reproduced and distributed under a license from Ford Motor Company. No further reproduction or distribution of the Ford Motor Company material is allowed without the express written permission from Ford Motor Company.

1

GENERAL INFORMATION AND MAINTENANCE

HOW TO USE THIS BOOK

This Chilton's Total Car Care manual is intended to help you learn more about the inner workings of your 1986–97 Ford Aerostar, while saving you money on its upkeep and operation.

The beginning of the book will likely be referred to the most, since that is where you will find information for maintenance and tune-up. The other sections deal with the more complex systems of your vehicle. Systems (from engine through brakes) are covered to the extent that the average do-it-yourselfer can attempt. This book will not explain such things as rebuilding a differential because the expertise required and the special tools necessary make this uneconomical. It will, however, give you detailed instructions to help you change your own brake pads and shoes, replace spark plugs, and perform many more jobs that can save you money and help avoid expensive problems.

A secondary purpose of this book is a reference for owners who want to understand their vehicle and/or their mechanics better.

Where to Begin

Before removing any bolts, read through the entire procedure. This will give you the overall view of what tools and supplies will be required. So read ahead and plan ahead. Each operation should be approached logically and all procedures thoroughly understood before attempting any work.

If repair of a component is not considered practical, we tell you how to remove the part and then how to install the new or rebuilt replacement. In this way, you at least save labor costs.

Avoiding Trouble

Many procedures in this book require you to "label and disconnect . . ." a group of lines, hoses or wires. Don't be think you can remember where everything goes—you won't. If you hook up vacuum or fuel lines incorrectly, the vehicle may run poorly, if at all. If you hook up electrical wiring incorrectly, you may instantly learn a very expensive lesson.

You don't need to know the proper name for each hose or line. A piece of masking tape on the hose and a piece on its fitting will allow you to assign your own label. As long as you remember your own code, the lines can be reconnected by matching your tags. Remember that tape will dissolve in gasoline or solvents; if a part is to be washed or cleaned, use another method of identification. A permanent felt-tipped marker or a metal scribe can be very handy for marking metal parts. Remove any tape or paper labels after assembly.

Maintenance or Repair?

Maintenance includes routine inspections, adjustments, and replacement of parts which show signs of normal wear. Maintenance compensates for wear or deterioration. Repair implies that something has broken or is not working. A need for a repair is often caused by lack of maintenance. for example: draining and refilling automatic transmission fluid is maintenance recommended at specific intervals. Failure to do this can shorten the life of the transmission/transaxle, requiring very expensive repairs. While no maintenance program can prevent items from eventually breaking or wearing out, a general rule is true: MAINTENANCE IS CHEAPER THAN REPAIR.

Two basic mechanic's rules should be mentioned here. First, whenever the left side of the vehicle or engine is referred to, it means the driver's side. Conversely, the right side of the vehicle means the passenger's side. Second, screws and bolts are removed by turning counterclockwise, and tightened by turning clockwise unless specifically noted.

Safety is always the most important rule. Constantly be aware of the dangers involved in working on an automobile and take the proper precautions. Please refer to the information in this section regarding SERVICING YOUR VEHICLE SAFELY and the SAFETY NOTICE on the acknowledgment page.

Avoiding the Most Common Mistakes

Pay attention to the instructions provided. There are 3 common mistakes in mechanical work:

1. Incorrect order of assembly, disassembly or adjustment. When taking something apart or putting it together, performing steps in the wrong order usually just costs you extra time; however, it CAN break something. Read the entire procedure before beginning. Perform everything in the order in which the instructions say you should, even if you can't see a reason for it. When you're taking apart something that is very intricate, you might want to draw a picture of how it looks when assembled in order to make sure you get everything back in its proper position. When making adjustments, perform them in the proper order. One adjustment possibly will affect another.

2. Overtorquing (or undertorquing). While it is more common for overtorquing to cause damage, undertorquing may allow a fastener to vibrate loose causing serious damage. Especially when dealing with aluminum parts, pay attention to torque specifications and utilize a torque wrench in assembly. If a torque figure is not available, remember that if you are using the right tool to perform the job, you will probably not have to strain yourself to get a fastener tight enough. The pitch of most threads is so slight that the tension you put on the wrench will be multiplied many times in actual force on what you are tightening.

There are many commercial products available for ensuring that fasteners won't come loose, even if they are not torqued just right (a very common brand is Loctite®). If you're worried about getting something together tight enough to hold, but loose enough to avoid mechanical damage during assembly, one of these products might offer substantial insurance. Before choosing a threadlocking compound, read the label on the package and make sure the product is compatible with the materials, fluids, etc. involved.

3. Crossthreading. This occurs when a part such as a bolt is screwed into a nut or casting at the wrong angle and forced. Crossthreading is more likely to occur if access is difficult. It helps to clean and lubricate fasteners, then to start threading the bolt, spark plug, etc. with your fingers. If you encounter resistance, unscrew the part and start over again at a different angle until it can be inserted and turned several times without much effort. Keep in mind that many parts have tapered threads, so that gentle turning will automatically bring the part you're threading to the proper angle. Don't put a wrench on the part until it's been tightened a couple of turns by hand. If you suddenly encounter resistance, and the part has not seated fully, don't force it. Pull it back out to make sure it's clean and threading properly.

Be sure to take your time and be patient, and always plan ahead. Allow yourself ample time to perform repairs and maintenance.

TOOLS AND EQUIPMENT

▶ **See Figures 1 thru 15**

Without the proper tools and equipment it is impossible to properly service your vehicle. It would be virtually impossible to catalog every tool that you would need to perform all of the operations in this book. It would be unwise for the amateur to rush out and buy an expensive set of tools on the theory that he/she may need one or more of them at some time.

The best approach is to proceed slowly, gathering a good quality set of those tools that are used most frequently. Don't be misled by the low cost of bargain tools. It is far better to spend a little more for better quality. Forged wrenches, 6 or 12-point sockets and fine tooth ratchets are by far preferable to their less expensive counterparts. As any good mechanic can tell you, there are few worse experiences than trying to work on a vehicle with bad tools. Your monetary savings will be far outweighed by frustration and mangled knuckles.

Begin accumulating those tools that are used most frequently: those associated with routine maintenance and tune-up. In addition to the normal assortment of screwdrivers and pliers, you should have the following tools:

• Wrenches/sockets and combination open end/box end wrenches in sizes ⅛–¾ in. and/or 3mm–19mm ¹³⁄₁₆ in. or ⅝ in. spark plug socket (depending on plug type).

➡ **If possible, buy various length socket drive extensions. Universal-joint and wobble extensions can be extremely useful, but be careful when using them, as they can change the amount of torque applied to the socket.**

• Jackstands for support.
• Oil filter wrench.

- Spout or funnel for pouring fluids.
- Grease gun for chassis lubrication (unless your vehicle is not equipped with any grease fittings)
- Hydrometer for checking the battery (unless equipped with a sealed, maintenance-free battery).
- A container for draining oil and other fluids.
- Rags for wiping up the inevitable mess.

In addition to the above items there are several others that are not absolutely necessary, but handy to have around. These include an equivalent oil absorbent gravel, like cat litter, and the usual supply of lubricants, antifreeze and fluids. This is a basic list for routine maintenance, but only your personal needs and desire can accurately determine your list of tools.

After performing a few projects on the vehicle, you'll be amazed at the other tools and non-tools on your workbench. Some useful household items are: a large turkey baster or siphon, empty coffee cans and ice trays (to store parts), a ball of twine, electrical tape for wiring, small rolls of colored tape for tagging lines or hoses, markers and pens, a note pad, golf tees (for plugging vacuum lines), metal coat hangers or a roll of mechanic's wire (to hold things out of the way), dental pick or similar long, pointed probe, a strong magnet, and a small mirror (to see into recesses and under manifolds).

A more advanced set of tools, suitable for tune-up work, can be drawn up easily. While the tools are slightly more sophisticated, they need not be outrageously expensive. There are several inexpensive tach/dwell meters on the market that are every bit as good for the average mechanic as a professional model. Just be sure that it goes to a least 1200–1500 rpm on the tach scale and that it works on 4, 6 and 8-cylinder engines. The key to these purchases is to make them with an eye towards adaptability and wide range. A basic list of tune-up tools could include:

- Tach/dwell meter.
- Spark plug wrench and gapping tool.
- Feeler gauges for valve adjustment.
- Timing light.

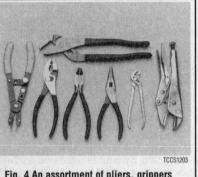

Fig. 1 All but the most basic procedures will require an assortment of ratchets and sockets

TCCS1200

Fig. 2 In addition to ratchets, a good set of wrenches and hex keys will be necessary

TCCS1201

Fig. 3 A hydraulic floor jack and a set of jackstands are essential for lifting and supporting the vehicle

TCCS1202

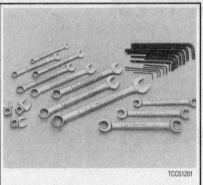

Fig. 4 An assortment of pliers, grippers and cutters will be handy for old rusted parts and stripped bolt heads

TCCS1203

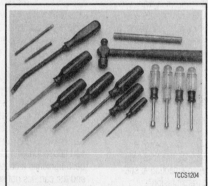

Fig. 5 Various drivers, chisels and prybars are great tools to have in your toolbox

TCCS1204

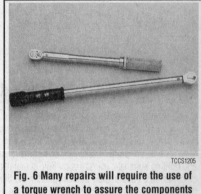

Fig. 6 Many repairs will require the use of a torque wrench to assure the components are properly fastened

TCCS1205

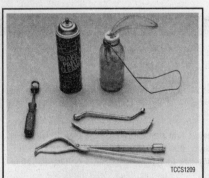

Fig. 7 Although not always necessary, using specialized brake tools will save time

TCCS1209

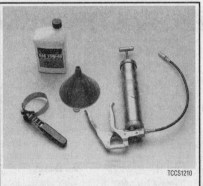

Fig. 8 A few inexpensive lubrication tools will make maintenance easier

TCCS1210

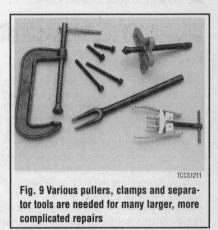

Fig. 9 Various pullers, clamps and separator tools are needed for many larger, more complicated repairs

TCCS1211

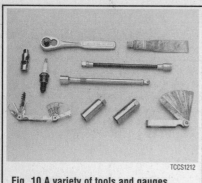

Fig. 10 A variety of tools and gauges should be used for spark plug gapping and installation

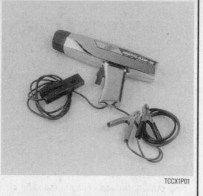

Fig. 11 Inductive type timing light

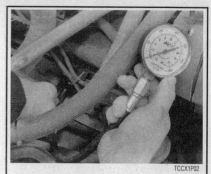

Fig. 12 A screw-in type compression gauge is recommended for compression testing

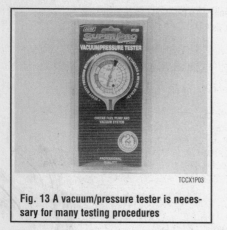

Fig. 13 A vacuum/pressure tester is necessary for many testing procedures

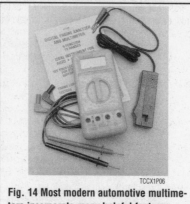

Fig. 14 Most modern automotive multimeters incorporate many helpful features

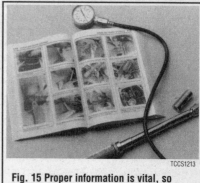

Fig. 15 Proper information is vital, so always have a Chilton Total Car Care manual handy

The choice of a timing light should be made carefully. A light which works on the DC current supplied by the vehicle's battery is the best choice; it should have a xenon tube for brightness. On any vehicle with an electronic ignition system, a timing light with an inductive pickup that clamps around the No. 1 spark plug cable is preferred.

In addition to these basic tools, there are several other tools and gauges you may find useful. These include:

• Compression gauge. The screw-in type is slower to use, but eliminates the possibility of a faulty reading due to escaping pressure.
• Manifold vacuum gauge.
• 12V test light.
• A combination volt/ohmmeter
• Induction Ammeter. This is used for determining whether or not there is current in a wire. These are handy for use if a wire is broken somewhere in a wiring harness.

As a final note, you will probably find a torque wrench necessary for all but the most basic work. The beam type models are perfectly adequate, although the newer click types (breakaway) are easier to use. The click type torque wrenches tend to be more expensive. Also keep in mind that all types of torque wrenches should be periodically checked and/or recalibrated. You will have to decide for yourself which better fits your pocketbook, and purpose.

Special Tools

Normally, the use of special factory tools is avoided for repair procedures, since these are not readily available for the do-it-yourself mechanic. When it is possible to perform the job with more commonly available tools, it will be pointed out, but occasionally, a special tool was designed to perform a specific function and should be used. Before substituting another tool, you should be convinced that neither your safety nor the performance of the vehicle will be compromised.

Special tools can usually be purchased from an automotive parts store or from your dealer. In some cases special tools may be available directly from the tool manufacturer.

SERVICING YOUR VEHICLE SAFELY

▶ See Figures 16, 17 and 18

It is virtually impossible to anticipate all of the hazards involved with automotive maintenance and service, but care and common sense will prevent most accidents.

The rules of safety for mechanics range from "don't smoke around gasoline," to "use the proper tool(s) for the job." The trick to avoiding injuries is to develop safe work habits and to take every possible precaution.

Do's

• Do keep a fire extinguisher and first aid kit handy.
• Do wear safety glasses or goggles when cutting, drilling, grinding or prying, even if you have 20–20 vision. If you wear glasses for the sake of vision, wear safety goggles over your regular glasses.

• Do shield your eyes whenever you work around the battery. Batteries contain sulfuric acid. In case of contact with, flush the area with water or a mixture of water and baking soda, then seek immediate medical attention.
• Do use safety stands (jackstands) for any undervehicle service. Jacks are for raising vehicles; jackstands are for making sure the vehicle stays raised until you want it to come down.
• Do use adequate ventilation when working with any chemicals or hazardous materials. Like carbon monoxide, the asbestos dust resulting from some brake lining wear can be hazardous in sufficient quantities.
• Do disconnect the negative battery cable when working on the electrical system. The secondary ignition system contains EXTREMELY HIGH VOLTAGE. In some cases it can even exceed 50,000 volts.
• Do follow manufacturer's directions whenever working with potentially hazardous materials. Most chemicals and fluids are poisonous.

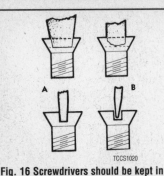

Fig. 16 Screwdrivers should be kept in good condition to prevent injury or damage which could result if the blade slips from the screw

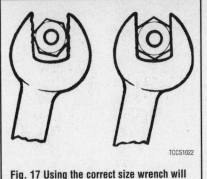

Fig. 17 Using the correct size wrench will help prevent the possibility of rounding off a nut

Fig. 18 NEVER work under a vehicle unless it is supported using safety stands (jackstands)

• Do properly maintain your tools. Loose hammerheads, mushroomed punches and chisels, frayed or poorly grounded electrical cords, excessively worn screwdrivers, spread wrenches (open end), cracked sockets, slipping ratchets, or faulty droplight sockets can cause accidents.

• Likewise, keep your tools clean; a greasy wrench can slip off a bolt head, ruining the bolt and often harming your knuckles in the process.

• Do use the proper size and type of tool for the job at hand. Do select a wrench or socket that fits the nut or bolt. The wrench or socket should sit straight, not cocked.

• Do, when possible, pull on a wrench handle rather than push on it, and adjust your stance to prevent a fall.

• Do be sure that adjustable wrenches are tightly closed on the nut or bolt and pulled so that the force is on the side of the fixed jaw.

• Do strike squarely with a hammer; avoid glancing blows.

• Do set the parking brake and block the drive wheels if the work requires a running engine.

Don'ts

• Don't run the engine in a garage or anywhere else without proper ventilation—EVER! Carbon monoxide is poisonous; it takes a long time to leave the human body and you can build up a deadly supply of it in your system by simply breathing in a little at a time. You may not realize you are slowly poisoning yourself. Always use power vents, windows, fans and/or open the garage door.

• Don't work around moving parts while wearing loose clothing. Short sleeves are much safer than long, loose sleeves. Hard-toed shoes with neoprene soles protect your toes and give a better grip on slippery surfaces. Watches and jewelry is not safe working around a vehicle. Long hair should be tied back under a hat or cap.

• Don't use pockets for toolboxes. A fall or bump can drive a screwdriver deep into your body. Even a rag hanging from your back pocket can wrap around a spinning shaft or fan.

• Don't smoke when working around gasoline, cleaning solvent or other flammable material.

• Don't smoke when working around the battery. When the battery is being charged, it gives off explosive hydrogen gas.

• Don't use gasoline to wash your hands; there are excellent soaps available. Gasoline contains dangerous additives which can enter the body through a cut or through your pores. Gasoline also removes all the natural oils from the skin so that bone dry hands will suck up oil and grease.

• Don't service the air conditioning system unless you are equipped with the necessary tools and training. When liquid or compressed gas refrigerant is released to atmospheric pressure it will absorb heat from whatever it contacts. This will chill or freeze anything it touches.

• Don't use screwdrivers for anything other than driving screws! A screwdriver used as an prying tool can snap when you least expect it, causing injuries. At the very least, you'll ruin a good screwdriver.

• Don't use an emergency jack (that little ratchet, scissors, or pantograph jack supplied with the vehicle) for anything other than changing a flat! These jacks are only intended for emergency use out on the road; they are NOT designed as a maintenance tool. If you are serious about maintaining your vehicle yourself, invest in a hydraulic floor jack of at least a 1½ ton capacity, and at least two sturdy jackstands.

FASTENERS, MEASUREMENTS AND CONVERSIONS

Bolts, Nuts and Other Threaded Retainers

▶ See Figures 19 and 20

Although there are a great variety of fasteners found in the modern car or truck, the most commonly used retainer is the threaded fastener (nuts, bolts, screws, studs, etc.). Most threaded retainers may be reused, provided that they are not damaged in use or during the repair. Some retainers (such as stretch bolts or torque prevailing nuts) are designed to deform when tightened or in use and should not be reinstalled.

Whenever possible, we will note any special retainers which should be replaced during a procedure. But you should always inspect the condition of a retainer when it is removed and replace any that show signs of damage. Check all threads for rust or corrosion which can increase the torque necessary to achieve the desired clamp load for which that fastener was originally selected. Additionally, be sure that the driver surface of the fastener has not been compromised by rounding or other damage. In some cases a driver surface may become only partially rounded, allowing the driver to catch in only one direction. In many of these occurrences, a fastener may be installed and tightened, but the driver would not be able to grip and loosen the fastener again.

If you must replace a fastener, whether due to design or damage, you must ALWAYS be sure to use the proper replacement. In all cases, a retainer of the

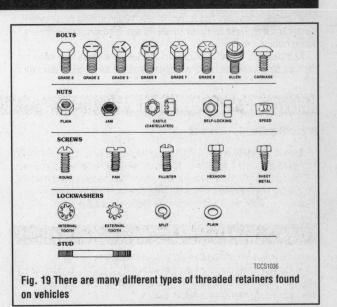

Fig. 19 There are many different types of threaded retainers found on vehicles

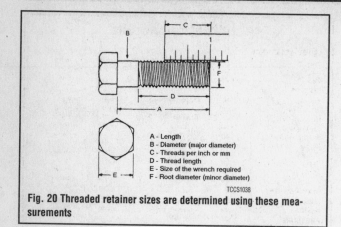

A - Length
B - Diameter (major diameter)
C - Threads per inch or mm
D - Thread length
E - Size of the wrench required
F - Root diameter (minor diameter)

TCCS1038

Fig. 20 Threaded retainer sizes are determined using these measurements

same design, material and strength should be used. Markings on the heads of most bolts will help determine the proper strength of the fastener. The same material, thread and pitch must be selected to assure proper installation and safe operation of the vehicle afterwards.

Thread gauges are available to help measure a bolt or stud's thread. Most automotive and hardware stores keep gauges available to help you select the proper size. In a pinch, you can use another nut or bolt for a thread gauge. If the bolt you are replacing is not too badly damaged, you can select a match by finding another bolt which will thread in its place. If you find a nut which threads properly onto the damaged bolt, then use that nut to help select the replacement bolt.

❊❊ WARNING

Be aware that when you find a bolt with damaged threads, you may also find the nut or drilled hole it was threaded into has also been damaged. If this is the case, you may have to drill and tap the hole, replace the nut or otherwise repair the threads. NEVER try to force a replacement bolt to fit into the damaged threads.

Torque

Torque is defined as the measurement of resistance to turning or rotating. It tends to twist a body about an axis of rotation. A common example of this would be tightening a threaded retainer such as a nut, bolt or screw. Measuring torque is one of the most common ways to help assure that a threaded retainer has been properly fastened.

When tightening a threaded fastener, torque is applied in three distinct areas, the head, the bearing surface and the clamp load. About 50 percent of the measured torque is used in overcoming bearing friction. This is the friction between the bearing surface of the bolt head, screw head or nut face and the base material or washer (the surface on which the fastener is rotating). Approximately 40 percent of the applied torque is used in overcoming thread friction. This leaves only about 10 percent of the applied torque to develop a useful clamp load (the force which holds a joint together). This means that friction can account for as much as 90 percent of the applied torque on a fastener.

TORQUE WRENCHES

♦ See Figure 21

In most applications, a torque wrench can be used to assure proper installation of a fastener. Torque wrenches come in various designs and most automotive supply stores will carry a variety to suit your needs. A torque wrench should be used any time we supply a specific torque value for a fastener. Again, the general rule of "if you are using the right tool for the job, you should not have to strain to tighten a fastener" applies here.

Beam Type

The beam type torque wrench is one of the most popular types. It consists of a pointer attached to the head that runs the length of the flexible beam (shaft) to a scale located near the handle. As the wrench is pulled, the beam bends and the pointer indicates the torque using the scale.

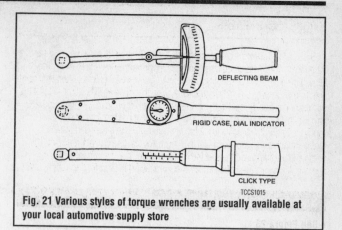

DEFLECTING BEAM

RIGID CASE, DIAL INDICATOR

CLICK TYPE

TCCS1015

Fig. 21 Various styles of torque wrenches are usually available at your local automotive supply store

Click (Breakaway) Type

Another popular design of torque wrench is the click type. To use the click type wrench you pre-adjust it to a torque setting. Once the torque is reached, the wrench has a reflex signaling feature that causes a momentary breakaway of the torque wrench body, sending an impulse to the operator's hand.

Pivot Head Type

♦ See Figure 22

Some torque wrenches (usually of the click type) may be equipped with a pivot head which can allow it to be used in areas of limited access. BUT, it must be used properly. To hold a pivot head wrench, grasp the handle lightly, and as you pull on the handle, it should be floated on the pivot point. If the handle comes in contact with the yoke extension during the process of pulling, there is a very good chance the torque readings will be inaccurate because this could alter the wrench loading point. The design of the handle is usually such as to make it inconvenient to deliberately misuse the wrench.

➡ It should be mentioned that the use of any U-joint, wobble or extension will have an effect on the torque readings, no matter what type of wrench you are using. For the most accurate readings, install the socket directly on the wrench driver. If necessary, straight extensions (which hold a socket directly under the wrench driver) will have the least effect on the torque reading. Avoid any extension that alters the length of the wrench from the handle to the head/driving point (such as a crow's foot). U-joint or wobble extensions can greatly affect the readings; avoid their use at all times.

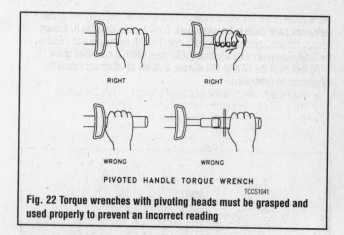

RIGHT

RIGHT

WRONG

WRONG

PIVOTED HANDLE TORQUE WRENCH

TCCS1041

Fig. 22 Torque wrenches with pivoting heads must be grasped and used properly to prevent an incorrect reading

Rigid Case (Direct Reading)

A rigid case or direct reading torque wrench is equipped with a dial indicator to show torque values. One advantage of these wrenches is that they can be held at any position on the wrench without affecting accuracy. These wrenches are often preferred because they tend to be compact, easy to read and have a great degree of accuracy.

TORQUE ANGLE METERS

Because the frictional characteristics of each fastener or threaded hole will vary, clamp loads which are based strictly on torque will vary as well. In most applications, this variance is not significant enough to cause worry. But, in certain applications, a manufacturer's engineers may determine that more precise clamp loads are necessary (such is the case with many aluminum cylinder heads). In these cases, a torque angle method of installation would be specified. When installing fasteners which are torque angle tightened, a predetermined seating torque and standard torque wrench are usually used first to remove any compliance from the joint. The fastener is then tightened the specified additional portion of a turn measured in degrees. A torque angle gauge (mechanical protractor) is used for these applications.

Standard and Metric Measurements

▶ See Figure 23

Throughout this manual, specifications are given to help you determine the condition of various components on your vehicle, or to assist you in their installation. Some of the most common measurements include length (in. or cm/mm), torque (ft. lbs., inch lbs. or Nm) and pressure (psi, in. Hg, kPa or mm Hg). In most cases, we strive to provide the proper measurement as determined by the manufacturer's engineers.

Though, in some cases, that value may not be conveniently measured with what is available in your toolbox. Luckily, many of the measuring devices which are available today will have two scales so the Standard or Metric measurements may easily be taken. If any of the various measuring tools which are available to you do not contain the same scale as listed in the specifications, use the accompanying conversion factors to determine the proper value.

The conversion factor chart is used by taking the given specification and multiplying it by the necessary conversion factor. For instance, looking at the first line, if you have a measurement in inches such as "free-play should be 2 in." but your ruler reads only in millimeters, multiply 2 in. by the conversion factor of 25.4 to get the metric equivalent of 50.8mm. Likewise, if the specification was given only in a Metric measurement, for example in Newton Meters (Nm), then look at the center column first. If the measurement is 100 Nm, multiply it by the conversion factor of 0.738 to get 73.8 ft. lbs.

CONVERSION FACTORS

LENGTH–DISTANCE

Inches (in.)	x 25.4	= Millimeters (mm)	x .0394	= Inches
Feet (ft.)	x .305	= Meters (m)	x 3.281	= Feet
Miles	x 1.609	= Kilometers (km)	x .0621	= Miles

VOLUME

Cubic Inches (in3)	x 16.387	= Cubic Centimeters	x .061	= in3
IMP Pints (IMP pt.)	x .568	= Liters (L)	x 1.76	= IMP pt.
IMP Quarts (IMP qt.)	x 1.137	= Liters (L)	x .88	= IMP qt.
IMP Gallons (IMP gal.)	x 4.546	= Liters (L)	x .22	= IMP gal.
IMP Quarts (IMP qt.)	x 1.201	= US Quarts (US qt.)	x .833	= IMP qt.
IMP Gallons (IMP gal.)	x 1.201	= US Gallons (US gal.)	x .833	= IMP gal.
Fl. Ounces	x 29.573	= Milliliters	x .034	= Ounces
US Pints (US pt.)	x .473	= Liters (L)	x 2.113	= Pints
US Quarts (US qt.)	x .946	= Liters (L)	x 1.057	= Quarts
US Gallons (US gal.)	x 3.785	= Liters (L)	x .264	= Gallons

MASS–WEIGHT

Ounces (oz.)	x 28.35	= Grams (g)	x .035	= Ounces
Pounds (lb.)	x .454	= Kilograms (kg)	x 2.205	= Pounds

PRESSURE

Pounds Per Sq. In. (psi)	x 6.895	= Kilopascals (kPa)	x .145	= psi
Inches of Mercury (Hg)	x .4912	= psi	x 2.036	= Hg
Inches of Mercury (Hg)	x 3.377	= Kilopascals (kPa)	x .2961	= Hg
Inches of Water (H_2O)	x .07355	= Inches of Mercury	x 13.783	= H_2O
Inches of Water (H_2O)	x .03613	= psi	x 27.684	= H_2O
Inches of Water (H_2O)	x .248	= Kilopascals (kPa)	x 4.026	= H_2O

TORQUE

Pounds–Force Inches (in-lb)	x .113	= Newton Meters (N·m)	x 8.85	= in-lb
Pounds–Force Feet (ft-lb)	x 1.356	= Newton Meters (N·m)	x .738	= ft-lb

VELOCITY

Miles Per Hour (MPH)	x 1.609	= Kilometers Per Hour (KPH)	x .621	= MPH

POWER

Horsepower (Hp)	x .745	= Kilowatts	x 1.34	= Horsepower

FUEL CONSUMPTION*

Miles Per Gallon IMP (MPG)	x .354	= Kilometers Per Liter (Km/L)	
Kilometers Per Liter (Km/L)	x 2.352	= IMP MPG	
Miles Per Gallon US (MPG)	x .425	= Kilometers Per Liter (Km/L)	
Kilometers Per Liter (Km/L)	x 2.352	= US MPG	

*It is common to covert from miles per gallon (mpg) to liters/100 kilometers (1/100 km), where mpg (IMP) x 1/100 km = 282 and mpg (US) x 1/100 km = 235.

TEMPERATURE

Degree Fahrenheit (°F) = (°C x 1.8) + 32
Degree Celsius (°C) = (°F – 32) x .56

TCCS1044

Fig. 23 Standard and metric conversion factors chart

SERIAL NUMBER IDENTIFICATION

Vehicle Identification Number (VIN)

▶ See Figures 24, 25 and 26

A 17 digit combination of numbers and letters forms the Vehicle Identification Number (VIN). The VIN is stamped on a metal tab that is riveted to the instrument panel close to the windshield. The VIN plate is visible by looking through the windshield on the driver's side. The VIN number is also found on the Safety Compliance Certification (SCC) label which is described below.

By looking at the 17 digit VIN number, a variety of information about the vehicle can be determined.
• The 1st digit identifies the country of origin. 1 = USA; 2 = Canada.
• The 2nd digit identifies the manufacturer. F = Ford.
• The 3rd digit identifies the type of vehicle.
C = Basic (stripped) chassis

D = Incomplete vehicle
M = Multi-purpose vehicle
T = Truck (complete vehicle)
• The 4th digit identifies the gross vehicle weight rating (GVWR Class) and brake system. For incomplete vehicles, the 4th digit determines the brake system only. All brake systems are hydraulic.
A = up to 3,000 lbs.
B= 3,001–4,000 lbs.
C = 4,001–5,000 lbs.
D = 5,001–6,000 lbs.
E = 6,001–7,000 lbs.
F = 7,001–8,000 lbs.
G = 8,001–8,500 lbs.
H = 8,500–9,000 lbs.
J = 9,001–10,000 lbs.
• The 5th digits identifies the model or line. A = Aerostar.
• The 6th and 7th digits identify chassis and body type.
11 = 2-wheel drive, regular length, passenger van

VIN number plate location

88241GA0

Fig. 24 Location of VIN number at the base of the windshield

1 F T	D	A 1 4	A 5	G Z A	0 0 0 0 1
A	B	C	D E	F G H	I

A. Position 1, 2, and 3—Manufacturer, Make and Type (World Manufacturer Identifier)
B. Position 4—Brake System/GVWR
C. Position 5, 6, and 7—Model or Line, Series, Chassis, Cab Type
D. Position 8—Engine Type
E. Position 9—Check Digit
F. Position 10—Model Year
G. Position 11—Assembly Plant
H. Position 12—Constant "A" until sequence number of 99,999 is reached, then changes to a constant "B" and so on
I. Position 13 through 17—Sequence number—begins at 00001

88241G01

Fig. 25 Explanation of sample VIN number

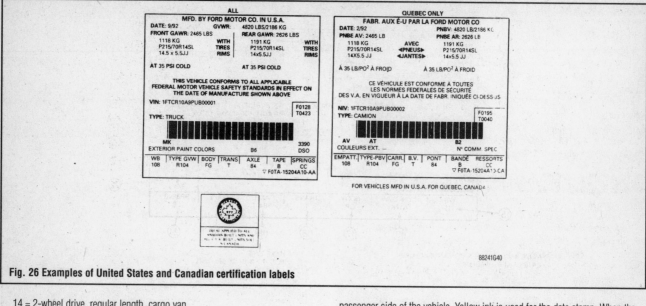

Fig. 26 Examples of United States and Canadian certification labels

14 = 2-wheel drive, regular length, cargo van
15 = 2-wheel drive, regular length, window van
31 = 2-wheel drive, extra length, passenger van
34 = 2-wheel drive, extra length, cargo van
35 = 2-wheel drive, extra length, window van
21 = All wheel drive, regular length, passenger van
24 = All wheel drive, regular length, cargo van
25 = All wheel drive, regular length, window van
41 = All wheel drive, extra length, passenger van
44 = All wheel drive, extra length, cargo van
45 = All wheel drive, extra length, window van
• The 8th digit identifies the engine.
A = 2.3L 4-cylinder
S = 2.8L 4-cylinder
U = 3.0L 6-cylinder
X = 4.0L 6-cylinder
• The 9th digit is a check digit.
• The 10th digit identifies the model year.
G = 1986
H = 1987
J = 1988
K = 1989
L = 1990
M = 1991
N = 1992
P = 1993
R = 1994
S = 1995
T = 1996
V = 1997
• The 11th digit identifies the assembly plant.
C = Ontario, Canada
H = Lorain, OH
K = Claycomo, MO
L = Wayne, MI
N = Norfolk, VA
P = St. Paul, MN
U = Louisville, KY
Z = Hazlewood, MO
• Digits twelve through seventeen make up the sequential serial and warranty number. Digit twelve uses the letter A until the production or sequence of 99,999 units (digits thirteen through seventeen) is reached. Letter A then becomes B for the next production sequence of vehicles.

Build Date Stamp Location

The vehicle build date is stamped on the front of the radiator support on the passenger side of the vehicle. Yellow ink is used for the date stamp. When the marking surface is painted the body color, the date stamp will be marked in red ink. Units from the Ontario truck plant (code C) will be marked with silver ink.

Safety Compliance Certification Label

♦ See Figures 27, 28 and 29

The English Safety Compliance Certification (SCC) label is affixed to the door latch edge on the driver's side door. The French Safety Compliance Certification (SCC) label is affixed to the door latch edge on the passenger's side door.

Fig. 27 Certification label affixed to the door jam

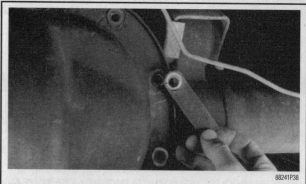

Fig. 28 Rear axle identification plate. If you are removing the cover, do not lose this plate

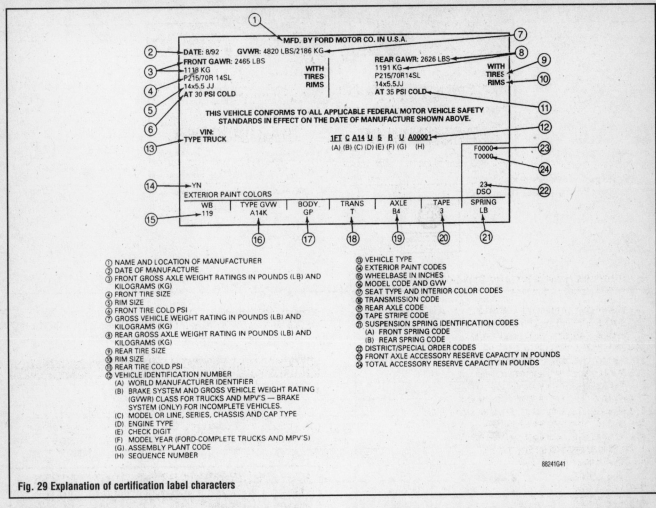

Fig. 29 Explanation of certification label characters

① NAME AND LOCATION OF MANUFACTURER
② DATE OF MANUFACTURE
③ FRONT GROSS AXLE WEIGHT RATINGS IN POUNDS (LB) AND KILOGRAMS (KG)
④ FRONT TIRE SIZE
⑤ RIM SIZE
⑥ FRONT TIRE COLD PSI
⑦ GROSS VEHICLE WEIGHT RATING IN POUNDS (LB) AND KILOGRAMS (KG)
⑧ REAR GROSS AXLE WEIGHT RATING IN POUNDS (LB) AND KILOGRAMS (KG)
⑨ REAR TIRE SIZE
⑩ RIM SIZE
⑪ REAR TIRE COLD PSI
⑫ VEHICLE IDENTIFICATION NUMBER
  (A) WORLD MANUFACTURER IDENTIFIER
  (B) BRAKE SYSTEM AND GROSS VEHICLE WEIGHT RATING (GVWR) CLASS FOR TRUCKS AND MPV'S — BRAKE SYSTEM (ONLY) FOR INCOMPLETE VEHICLES.
  (C) MODEL OR LINE, SERIES, CHASSIS AND CAP TYPE
  (D) ENGINE TYPE
  (E) CHECK DIGIT
  (F) MODEL YEAR (FORD-COMPLETE TRUCKS AND MPV'S)
  (G) ASSEMBLY PLANT CODE
  (H) SEQUENCE NUMBER

⑬ VEHICLE TYPE
⑭ EXTERIOR PAINT CODES
⑮ WHEELBASE IN INCHES
⑯ MODEL CODE AND GVW
⑰ SEAT TYPE AND INTERIOR COLOR CODES
⑱ TRANSMISSION CODE
⑲ REAR AXLE CODE
⑳ TAPE STRIPE CODE
㉑ SUSPENSION SPRING IDENTIFICATION CODES
  (A) FRONT SPRING CODE
  (B) REAR SPRING CODE
㉒ DISTRICT/SPECIAL ORDER CODES
㉓ FRONT AXLE ACCESSORY RESERVE CAPACITY IN POUNDS
㉔ TOTAL ACCESSORY RESERVE CAPACITY IN POUNDS

88241G41

The label contains the following information: name of manufacturer, the month and year of manufacture, the certification statement, and the Vehicle Identification Number (VIN). The label also contains information on Gross Vehicle (GVW) weight ratings, wheel and tire data, and additional vehicle data information codes.

Emission Calibration Label

The emission calibration number label is attached to the left side door or the left door post pillar. This label plate identifies the engine calibration number, engine code number and the revision level. These numbers are used to determine if parts are unique to specific engines. The engine codes and calibration are necessary for ordering parts and asking questions related to the engine.

Engine

The engine ID code is a letter located in the eighth digit of the Vehicle Identification Number (VIN). Specific engine data is located on a label attached to the timing cover.

Transmission

The transmission code may be found in two places on the vehicle. One is on the SSC label attached to the left driver's side door lock post. The code appears as a letter in the "Trans" column of the label. M = 5-speed manual transmission; T or V = 4-speed automatic transmission, D = 5-speed automatic transmission.

The other location is on the transmission body itself. On manual transmissions, the ID number is located on a plate attached to the main transmission case. On the plate you find Ford's assigned part number, the serial number and a bar code used for inventory purposes. On automatic transmissions, the ID number is stamped on a plate that hangs from the lower left extension housing bolt. The plate identifies when the transmission was built, the code letter and model number.

Transfer Case

The 1990–97 Aerostar can be equipped with all wheel drive, utilizing a Dana/Spicer 28 transfer case. The identification number is stamped on a plate on the side of the case.

Front Drive Axle

The 1990–97 Aerostar can be equipped with all wheel drive, utilizing a Dana/Spicer 28-2 front drive axle. The identification number is stamped on a plate on the differential housing.

Rear Axle

▶ **See Figure 28**

The rear axle code may be found in two places on the vehicle. One is on the SCC label attached to the left driver's side door lock post. The code appears as a number or letter/number combination in the "Axle" column of the label. The rear axle ID code is also stamped on a metal tag hanging from the axle cover-to-carrier bolt at the 2 o'clock bolt position.

Four rear axles are used on the Aerostar.
- 1986–97: Ford 7.5 in. (190mm) ring gear
- 1987–89: Dana 30, 7 in. (181mm) ring gear
- 1990–96: Dana 35-1A, 7 in. (181mm) ring gear
- 1990–97: Ford 8.8 in. (223mm) ring gear

The Ford 7.5 inch is available in both standard and Traction-Lok versions. All axles are integral carrier type.

ENGINE AND VEHICLE IDENTIFICATION

Code ①	Liters	Cu. In.	Cyl.	Fuel Sys.	Type	Eng. Mfg.
A	2.3	140	4	MFI	OHC	Ford
S	2.8	173	6	2 BBL	OHV	Ford
U	3.0	182	6	MFI	OHV	Ford
X	4.0	241	6	MFI	OHV	Ford

Engine

Model Year	
Code ②	Year
G	1986
H	1987
J	1988
K	1989
L	1990
M	1991
N	1992
P	1993
R	1994
S	1995
T	1996
U	1997

EFI - Electronic Fuel Injection
2 BBL- 2 Barrel Carburetor
OHC- Overhead Camshaft
OHV- Overhead Valve
① 8th digit of the Vehicle Identification Number (VIN)
② 10th digit of the Vehicle Identification Number (VIN)

91321C01

ENGINE IDENTIFICATION

All measurements are given in inches.

Year	Model	Engine Displacement Liters (cc)	Engine Series (ID/VIN)	Fuel System	No. of Cylinders	Engine Type
1986	Aerostar	2.3 (2300)	A	1 BBL	4	SOHC
	Aerostar	2.8 (2835)	S	2 BBL	6	OHV
	Aerostar	3.0 (2983)	U	MFI	6	OHV
1987	Aerostar	2.3 (2300)	A	1 BBL	4	SOHC
	Aerostar	2.8 (2835)	S	2 BBL	6	OHV
	Aerostar	3.0 (2983)	U	MFI	6	OHV
1988	Aerostar	3.0 (2983)	U	MFI	6	OHV
1989	Aerostar	3.0 (2983)	U	MFI	6	OHV
1990	Aerostar	3.0 (2983)	U	MFI	6	OHV
	Aerostar	4.0 (3950)	X	MFI	6	OHV
1991	Aerostar	3.0 (2999)	U	MFI	6	OHV
	Aerostar	4.0 (3998)	X	MFI	6	OHV
1992	Aerostar	3.0 (2999)	U	MFI	6	OHV
	Aerostar	4.0 (3998)	X	MFI	6	OHV
1993	Aerostar	3.0 (2999)	U	MFI	6	OHV
	Aerostar	4.0 (3998)	X	MFI	6	OHV
1994	Aerostar	3.0 (2999)	U	MFI	6	OHV
	Aerostar	4.0 (3998)	X	MFI	6	OHV
1995	Aerostar	3.0 (2882)	U	MFI	6	OHV
	Aerostar	4.0 (3998)	X	MFI	6	OHV
1996-97	Aerostar	3.0 (2882)	U	MFI	6	OHV
	Aerostar	4.0 (3998)	X	MFI	6	OHV

BBL - Barrel carburetor
MFI - Multiport fuel injection
OHV - Overhead valve
SOHC - Single overhead camshaft

91321C02

GENERAL ENGINE SPECIFICATIONS

Year	Engine ID/VIN	Engine Displacement Liters (cc)	Fuel System Type	Net Horsepower @ rpm	Net Torque @ rpm (ft. lbs.)	Bore x Stroke (in.)	Compression Ratio	Oil Pressure @ rpm
1986	A	2.3 (2294)	MFI	90@4000	134@2000	3.78x3.13	9.5:1	40-60@2000
	S	2.8 (2787)	2 BBL	115@4600	150@2600	3.65x2.70	8.7:1	40-60@2000
	U	3.0 (2999)	MFI	145@4800	165@3600	3.50x3.14	9.3:1	40-60@2000
1987	A	2.3 (2294)	MFI	90@4000	134@2000	3.78x3.13	9.5:1	40-60@2000
	S	2.8 (2787)	2 BBL	115@4600	150@2600	3.65x2.70	8.7:1	40-60@2000
	U	3.0 (2999)	MFI	145@4800	165@3600	3.50x3.14	9.3:1	40-60@2000
1988	U	3.0 (2999)	MFI	145@4800	165@3600	3.50x3.14	9.3:1	40-60@2500
1989	U	3.0 (2999)	MFI	145@4800	165@3600	3.50x3.14	9.3:1	40-60@2500
1990	U	3.0 (2999)	MFI	145@4800	165@3600	3.50x3.14	9.3:1	40-60@2500
	X	4.0 (3998)	MFI	155@4200	215@2400	3.95x3.32	9.0:1	40-60@2000
1991	U	3.0 (2999)	MFI	145@4800	165@3600	3.50x3.14	9.3:1	40-60@2500
	X	4.0 (3998)	MFI	155@4200	215@2400	3.95x3.32	9.0:1	40-60@2000
1992	U	3.0 (2999)	MFI	145@4800	165@3600	3.50x3.14	9.3:1	40-60@2500
	X	4.0 (3998)	MFI	155@4200	215@2400	3.95x3.32	9.0:1	40-60@2000
1993	U	3.0 (2999)	MFI	145@4800	165@3600	3.50x3.14	9.3:1	40-60@2500
	X	4.0 (3998)	MFI	155@4200	215@2400	3.95x3.32	9.0:1	40-60@2000
1994	U	3.0 (2999)	MFI	135@4600	160@2800	3.50x3.14	9.3:1	40-60@2500
	X	4.0 (3998)	MFI	160@4000	225@2500	3.95x3.32	9.0:1	40-60@2000
1995	U	3.0 (2999)	MFI	135@4600	160@2800	3.50x3.14	9.3:1	40-60@2500
	X	4.0 (3998)	MFI	160@4000	225@2500	3.81x3.39	9.0:1	40-60@2000
1996	U	3.0 (2982)	MFI	147@5000	162@3250	3.50x3.14	9.3:1	40-60@2500
	X	4.0 (3950)	MFI	160@4000	225@2500	3.81x3.39	9.0:1	40-60@2000
1997	U	3.0 (2982)	MFI	147@5000	162@3250	3.50x3.14	9.3:1	40-60@2500
	X	4.0 (3950)	MFI	160@4000	225@2500	3.81x3.39	9.0:1	40-60@2000

91321C03

ROUTINE MAINTENANCE AND TUNE-UP

Proper maintenance and tune-up is the key to long and trouble-free vehicle life, and the work can yield its own rewards. Studies have shown that a properly tuned and maintained vehicle can achieve better gas mileage than an out-of-tune vehicle. As a conscientious owner and driver, set aside a Saturday morning, say once a month, to check or replace items which could cause major problems later. Keep your own personal log to jot down which services you performed, how much the parts cost you, the date, and the exact odometer reading at the time. Keep all receipts for such items as engine oil and filters, so that they may be referred to in case of related problems or to determine operating expenses. As a do-it-yourselfer, these receipts are the only proof you have that the required maintenance was performed. In the event of a warranty problem, these receipts will be invaluable.

The literature provided with your vehicle when it was originally delivered includes the factory recommended maintenance schedule. If you no longer have this literature, replacement copies are usually available from the dealer. A maintenance schedule is provided later in this section, in case you do not have the factory literature.

Air Cleaner (Element)

REMOVAL & INSTALLATION

2.3L Engine

♦ See Figure 30

1. Disconnect the tube and idle bypass tubes from the air cleaner cover.
2. Disconnect the electrical harness attached to the throttle air bypass valve.
3. Remove the air cleaner cover by loosening the wing nuts holding the air cleaner case together.
4. Lift the element out of the air cleaner case and wipe the interior of the case clean with a rag.
   To install:
5. Install a new air cleaner element into the case, making sure it is seated properly.

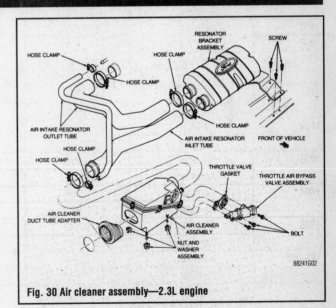

Fig. 30 Air cleaner assembly—2.3L engine

6. Install the case cover and tighten the wing nuts until they are finger-tight.
7. Reconnect the electrical harness attached to the throttle air bypass valve.
8. Fasten the inlet and idle air bypass tubes to the air cleaner cover.

2.8L Engine

♦ See Figure 31

1. Remove the center wing nut on the cleaner cover.
2. Lift the air cleaner cover off.
3. Lift out the old air filter element. If the inside of the housing is dirty, the

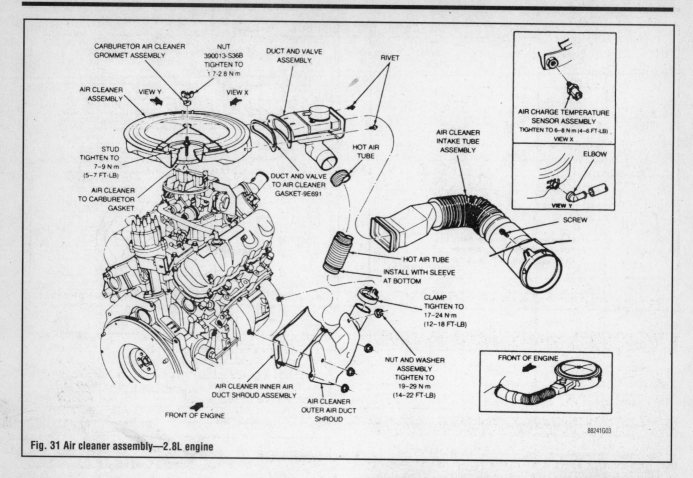

Fig. 31 Air cleaner assembly—2.8L engine

entire air cleaner assembly should be wiped clean to prevent any dirt from entering the carburetor.

To install:

4. Install a new air cleaner element into the air cleaner assembly, making sure it is seated properly.

5. Install the cover and tighten the wing nut until it is finger-tight.

3.0L and 4.0L Engines

▶ See Figures 32, 33 and 34

1. Disconnect the hose clamps from the air cleaner and the intake manifold.

2. Remove the resonator assembly from the air cleaner and engine compartment.

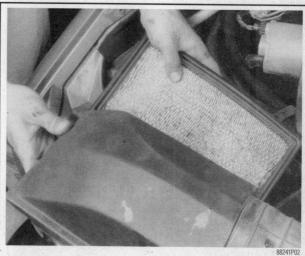

Fig. 33 Raise the top of the cleaner housing and lift the filter element out

3. Remove the retaining screws from the air cleaner cover and lift the cover off the air cleaner housing.

4. Remove the old air cleaner element.

5. Wipe out the inside of the air cleaner assembly with a clean, dry rag.

To install:

6. Install a new air cleaner element into the case, making sure it is seated properly.

7. Install the case cover and secure with the retaining screws.

8. Connect the resonator assembly to the intake manifold and the air cleaner.

9. Install and tighten the hose clamps.

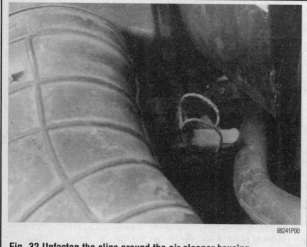

Fig. 32 Unfasten the clips around the air cleaner housing

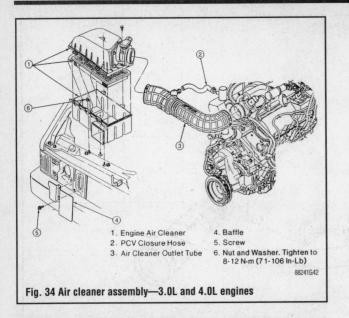

1. Engine Air Cleaner
2. PCV Closure Hose
3. Air Cleaner Outlet Tube
4. Baffle
5. Screw
6. Nut and Washer. Tighten to 8-12 N·m (71-106 In-Lb)

88241G42

Fig. 34 Air cleaner assembly—3.0L and 4.0L engines

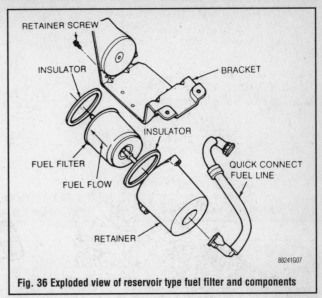

88241G07

Fig. 36 Exploded view of reservoir type fuel filter and components

Fuel Filter

LOCATION

▶ See Figures 35 and 36

※ CAUTION

On fuel injected engines, the fuel system is under constant pressure, even when the engine is turned OFF. Follow the instructions for relieving fuel system pressure before attempting any service to the fuel system. Whenever working on or around any open fuel system, take precautions to avoid the risk of fire and use clean rags to catch any fuel spray while disconnecting fuel lines.

Depending on the model year, engine and fuel delivery system, the fuel filter could be located in several different locations. Also, some models have more than one fuel filter. Before removing any fuel filter, identify the type of engine in the vehicle, and whether the engine utilizes one or more fuel filters.

The fuel filter on carbureted engines is located on the carburetor where the fuel inlet line is attached. These fuel filters are one piece units that cannot be cleaned.

On fuel injected engines available between 1986–88, there are three fuel filters: one inside the inline reservoir, one at the electric fuel pump mounted on the chassis and a third on the low pressure electric fuel pump mounted inside the fuel tank itself. On these models the fuel filter is part of a modular assembly

which also contains the fuel supply pump. Normally, only the filters at the chassis mounted pump and fuel reservoir are replaced as part of normal maintenance.

On all 1989–97 models, fuel is filtered at two locations: one maintenance-free type on the inlet (suction) of the electric fuel pump inside the fuel tank and the other through an in-line fuel filter located on the left hand frame side rail downstream from the fuel pump.

REMOVAL & INSTALLATION

Carbureted Engine

▶ See Figure 37

1. Remove the air cleaner assembly.
2. Using two flare or open ended wrenches, one on the fuel line and one holding the filter body, loosen and disconnect the fuel inlet line from the filter. Use a clean rag under the fitting to catch any fuel.
3. Unscrew the fuel filter from the carburetor fuel inlet.
To install:
4. Apply one drop of Loctite® (or equivalent) hydraulic sealant to the external threads of the new fuel filter, then thread the filter into the carburetor inlet port.
5. Tighten the fuel filter to 6–8 ft. lbs. (9–11 Nm). Do not overtighten.
6. Thread the fuel supply line into the filter and, using two wrenches as before, tighten the fuel supply line nut to 15–18 ft. lbs. (20–24 Nm).
7. Start the engine and check for any fuel leaks. Correct any fuel leak immediately.
8. Install the air cleaner assembly. Dispose of any gasoline soaked rags properly.

Fuel Injected Engine

▶ See Figures 38, 39, 40, 41 and 42

1. Remove the fuel tank cap to vent tank pressure.
2. Relieve the fuel system pressure by:
   a. Detach the electrical connector from the inertia switch and crank the engine for 15–30 seconds until it runs out of fuel and dies. The inertia switch is located on the toe board to the right of the transmission hump or the kick panel to the right of the passenger's seat below the heater duct. After the fuel pressure is relieved, remember to re-connect it.
3. Raise the vehicle and support it safely on jackstands.
4. Locate the fuel filter mounted to the underbody, on the left frame bracket.
5. Clean all dirt and/or grease from the fuel filter fittings. "Quick-Connect" fittings are used on all models. These fittings must be disconnected using the proper procedure or the fittings may be damaged. The fuel filter uses a "hairpin" clip retainer. To remove the clip;

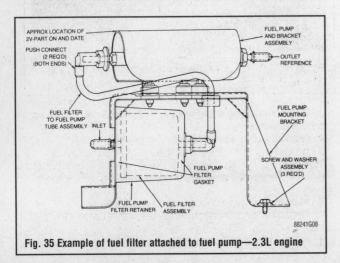

88241G08

Fig. 35 Example of fuel filter attached to fuel pump—2.3L engine

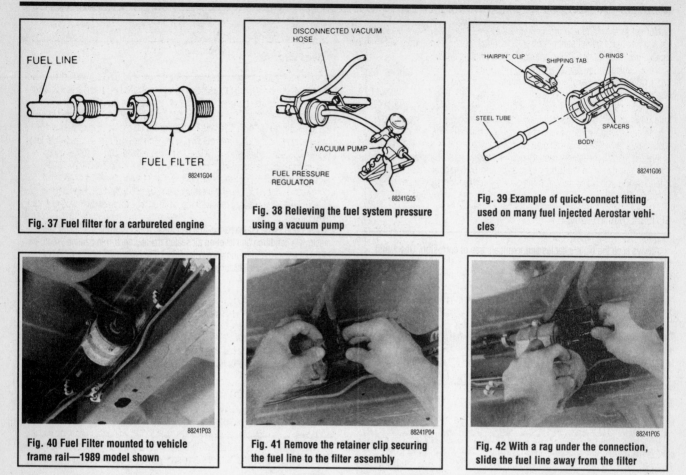

Fig. 37 Fuel filter for a carbureted engine

Fig. 38 Relieving the fuel system pressure using a vacuum pump

Fig. 39 Example of quick-connect fitting used on many fuel injected Aerostar vehicles

Fig. 40 Fuel Filter mounted to vehicle frame rail—1989 model shown

Fig. 41 Remove the retainer clip securing the fuel line to the filter assembly

Fig. 42 With a rag under the connection, slide the fuel line away from the filter

a. Spread the two hairpin clip legs about ⅛ in. (3mm) each to disengage it from the fitting, then pull the clip outward. Use finger pressure only; do not use any tools. Disconnect both fittings from the fuel filter.

➡**Ford recommends that the retaining clips be replaced whenever removed.**

6. Place a container below the fuel filter to capture any fuel which may spill out.

7. Remove the fuel filter and retainer from the metal mounting bracket.

8. Remove the rubber insulator rings from the filter and the filter retainer. Note that the direction of fuel flow (arrow on the filter) points to the open end of the retainer.

To install:

9. Place the new filter into the retainer with the flow arrow pointing toward the open end.

10. Install the insulator rings.

11. Install the retainer on the metal bracket and tighten the mounting bolts.

12. Fasten the quick-connect fittings onto the filter ends. A click will be heard when the hairpin clip snaps into its proper position. Pull on the lines with moderate pressure to ensure proper connection.

13. Cycle the ignition switch from the **OFF** to **ON** position several times to re-charge the fuel system before attempting to start the engine. Start the engine and check for any fuel leaks.

14. Lower the vehicle.

PCV Valve

REMOVAL & INSTALLATION

All models use a closed crankcase ventilation system with a sealed breather cap connected to the air cleaner by a rubber hose. The PCV valve is usually mounted in the valve cover and connected to the intake manifold by a rubber hose. The system is used to regulate the amount of crankcase (blow-by) gases

which are recycled into the combustion chambers for burning with the normal fuel charge.

The only maintenance required on the PCV system is to replace the PCV valve and/or air filter element in the air cleaner at the intervals specified in the maintenance chart. Replacement involves removing the valve from the grommet in the valve cover and installing a new valve. No attempt should be made to clean an old PCV valve; it should be replaced.

Evaporative Emissions Canister

SERVICING

The canister functions to direct evaporating fuel (vapor) from the fuel tank and engine fuel system into the intake manifold and eventually into the cylinders for combustion with the normal fuel charge. The activated charcoal within the canister acts as a storage device for the fuel vapor at times when the engine is not operating or when the engine operating condition will not permit fuel vapor to burn efficiently. All Aerostars are equipped with engine compartment mounted, activated carbon canisters. The canister is mounted on the bottom of the right hand fender apron.

The only required service for the evaporative canister is inspection at the interval specified in the maintenance chart. If the charcoal element is saturated with fuel, the entire canister should be replaced. Disconnect the canister purge hose(s), loosen the canister retaining bracket and lift up the canister to disengage the tab on the back side. Installation is the reverse of removal.

Battery

PRECAUTIONS

Always use caution when working on or near the battery. Never allow a tool to bridge the gap between the negative and positive battery terminals. Also, be careful not to allow a tool to provide a ground between the positive cable/terminal and any metal component on the vehicle. Either of these conditions will cause a short circuit, leading to sparks and possible personal injury.

Do not smoke or all open flames/sparks near a battery; the gases contained in the battery are very explosive and, if ignited, could cause severe injury or death.

All batteries, regardless of type, should be carefully secured by a battery hold-down device. If not, the terminals or casing may crack from stress during vehicle operation. A battery which is not secured may allow acid to leak, making it discharge faster. The acid can also eat away at components under the hood.

Always inspect the battery case for cracks, leakage and corrosion. A white corrosive substance on the battery case or on nearby components would indicate a leaking or cracked battery. If the battery is cracked, it should be replaced immediately.

GENERAL MAINTENANCE

Always keep the battery cables and terminals free of corrosion. Check and clean these components about once a year.

Keep the top of the battery clean, as a film of dirt can help discharge a battery that is not used for long periods. A solution of baking soda and water may be used for cleaning, but be careful to flush this off with clear water. DO NOT let any of the solution into the filler holes. Baking soda neutralizes battery acid and will de-activate a battery cell.

Batteries in vehicles which are not operated on a regular basis can fall victim to parasitic loads (small current drains which are constantly drawing current from the battery). Normal parasitic loads may drain a battery on a vehicle that is in storage and not used for 6–8 weeks. Vehicles that have additional accessories such as a phone or an alarm system may discharge a battery sooner. If the vehicle is to be stored for longer periods in a secure area and the alarm system is not necessary, the negative battery cable should be disconnected to protect the battery.

Remember that constantly deep cycling a battery (completely discharging and recharging it) will shorten battery life.

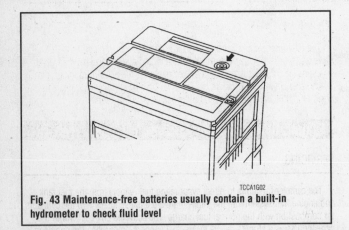

Fig. 43 Maintenance-free batteries usually contain a built-in hydrometer to check fluid level

BATTERY FLUID

▶ **See Figure 43**

Check the battery electrolyte level at least once a month, or more often in hot weather or during periods of extended vehicle operation. On non-sealed batteries, the level can be checked either through the case (if translucent) or by removing the cell caps. The electrolyte level in each cell should be kept filled to the split ring inside each cell, or the line marked on the outside of the case.

If the level is low, add only distilled water through the opening until the level is correct. Each cell must be checked and filled individually. Distilled water should be used, because the chemicals and minerals found in most drinking water are harmful to the battery and could significantly shorten its life.

If water is added in freezing weather, the vehicle should be driven several miles to allow the water to mix with the electrolyte. Otherwise, the battery could freeze.

Although some maintenance-free batteries have removable cell caps, the electrolyte condition and level on all sealed maintenance-free batteries must be checked using the built-in hydrometer "eye." The exact type of eye will vary. But, most battery manufacturers, apply a sticker to the battery itself explaining the readings.

➡ **Although the readings from built-in hydrometers will vary, a green eye usually indicates a properly charged battery with sufficient fluid level. A dark eye is normally an indicator of a battery with sufficient fluid, but which is low in charge. A light or yellow eye usually indicates that electrolyte has dropped below the necessary level. In this last case, sealed batteries with an insufficient electrolyte must usually be discarded.**

Checking the Specific Gravity

▶ **See Figures 44, 45 and 46**

A hydrometer is required to check the specific gravity on all batteries that are not maintenance-free. On batteries that are maintenance-free, the specific gravity is checked by observing the built-in hydrometer "eye" on the top of the battery case.

✳✳ CAUTION

Battery electrolyte contains sulfuric acid. If you should splash any on your skin or in your eyes, flush the affected area with plenty of clear water. If it lands in your eyes, get medical help immediately.

The fluid (sulfuric acid solution) contained in the battery cells will tell you many things about the condition of the battery. Because the cell plates must be kept submerged below the fluid level in order to operate, the fluid level is extremely important. And, because the specific gravity of the acid is an indication of electrical charge, testing the fluid can be an aid in determining if the battery must be replaced. A battery in a vehicle with a properly operating charging system should require little maintenance, but careful, periodic inspection should reveal problems before they leave you stranded.

At least once a year, check the specific gravity of the battery. It should be between 1.20 and 1.26 on the gravity scale. Most auto stores carry a variety of

Fig. 44 On non-sealed batteries, the fluid level can be checked by removing the cell caps

Fig. 45 If the fluid level is low, add only distilled water until the level is correct

Fig. 46 Check the specific gravity of the battery's electrolyte with a hydrometer

inexpensive battery hydrometers. These can be used on any non-sealed battery to test the specific gravity in each cell.

The battery testing hydrometer has a squeeze bulb at one end and a nozzle at the other. Battery electrolyte is sucked into the hydrometer until the float is lifted from its seat. The specific gravity is then read by noting the position of the float. If gravity is low in one or more cells, the battery should be slowly charged and checked again to see if the gravity has come up. Generally, if after charging, the specific gravity between any two cells varies more than 50 points (0.50), the battery should be replaced, as it can no longer produce sufficient voltage to guarantee proper operation.

CABLES

▶ See Figures 47, 48, 49 and 50

Once a year (or as necessary), the battery terminals and the cable clamps should be cleaned. Loosen the clamps and remove the cables, negative cable first. On top post batteries, the use of a puller specially made for this purpose is recommended. These are inexpensive and available in most parts stores. Side terminal battery cables are secured with a small bolt.

Clean the cable clamps and the battery terminal with a wire brush, until all corrosion, grease, etc., is removed and the metal is shiny. It is especially important to clean the inside of the clamp thoroughly (an old knife is useful here), since a small deposit of oxidation there will prevent a sound connection and inhibit starting or charging. Special tools are available for cleaning these parts, one type for conventional top post batteries and another type for side terminal batteries. It is also a good idea to apply some dielectric grease to the terminal, as this will aid in the prevention of corrosion.

After the clamps and terminals are clean, reinstall the cables, negative cable last; DO NOT hammer the clamps onto battery posts. Tighten the clamps securely, but do not distort them. Give the clamps and terminals a thin external coating of grease after installation, to retard corrosion.

Check the cables at the same time that the terminals are cleaned. If the cable insulation is cracked or broken, or if the ends are frayed, the cable should be replaced with a new cable of the same length and gauge.

CHARGING

A battery should be charged at a slow rate to keep the plates inside from getting too hot. However, if some maintenance-free batteries are allowed to discharge until they are almost "dead," they may have to be charged at a high rate to bring them back to "life." Always follow the charger manufacturer's instructions on charging the battery.

REPLACEMENT

When it becomes necessary to replace the battery, select one with an amperage rating equal to or greater than the battery originally installed. Deterioration and just plain aging of the battery cables, starter motor, and associated wires makes the battery's job harder in successive years. This makes it prudent to install a new battery with a greater capacity than the old.

Belts

INSPECTION

▶ See Figures 51, 52, 53, 54 and 55

Inspect the belts for signs of glazing or cracking. A glazed belt will be perfectly smooth from slippage, while a good belt will have a slight texture of fabric visible. Cracks will usually start at the inner edge of the belt and run outward.

Fig. 47 The underside of this special battery tool has a wire brush to clean post terminals

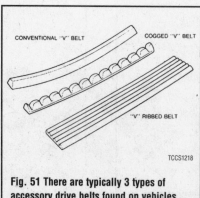
Fig. 48 Place the tool over the battery posts and twist to clean until the metal is shiny

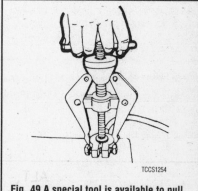
Fig. 49 A special tool is available to pull the clamp from the post

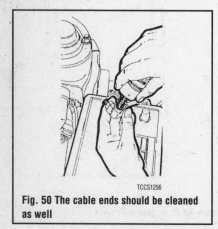
Fig. 50 The cable ends should be cleaned as well

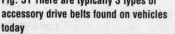
Fig. 51 There are typically 3 types of accessory drive belts found on vehicles today

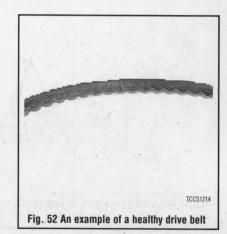
Fig. 52 An example of a healthy drive belt

Fig. 53 Deep cracks in this belt will cause flex, building up heat that will eventually lead to belt failure

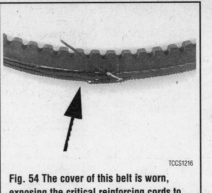

Fig. 54 The cover of this belt is worn, exposing the critical reinforcing cords to excessive wear

Fig. 55 Installing too wide a belt can result in serious belt wear and/or breakage

All worn or damaged drive belts should be replaced immediately. It is best to replace all drive belts at one time, as a preventive maintenance measure, during this service operation.

ADJUSTING

All V-ribbed belts are normally adjusted by loosening the bolts of the accessory being driven and moving that accessory on its pivot points until the proper tension is applied to the belt. The accessory is held in this position while the bolts are tightened. To determine proper belt tension, you can purchase a belt tension gauge or simply use the deflection method. If you are using a belt tension gauge, make sure to position the instrument so that it is not contacting the belt pulley when checking tension. To determine deflection, press inward on the belt at the mid-point of its longest straight run. The belt should deflect (move inward) 0.39–0.5 in. (10–13mm). Some engines, such as the 2.8L and 3.0L equipped with power steering, have idler pulleys which are used for adjusting purposes. Just loosen the idler pulley and move it to take up tension on the belt.

All serpentine belts are adjusted automatically by a spring-loaded belt tensioner pulley. No periodic adjustment is possible.

REMOVAL & INSTALLATION

▶ **See Figures 56 thru 69**

To remove a drive belt, simply loosen the accessory being driven and move it on its pivot point to free the belt. Then, remove the belt. If an idler pulley is used, it is often necessary to loosen the idler pulley only to provide enough slack to slip the belt from the pulley.

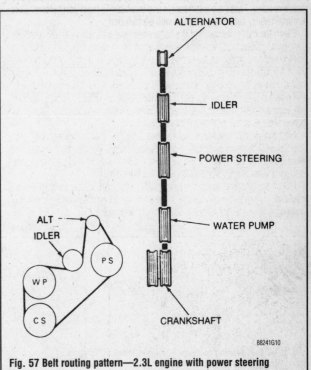

Fig. 57 Belt routing pattern—2.3L engine with power steering

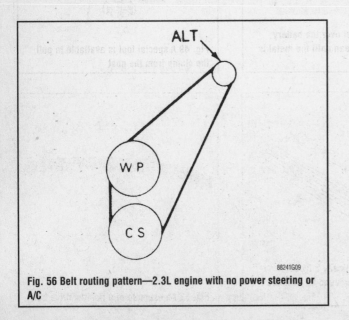

Fig. 56 Belt routing pattern—2.3L engine with no power steering or A/C

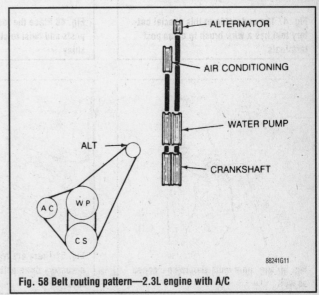

Fig. 58 Belt routing pattern—2.3L engine with A/C

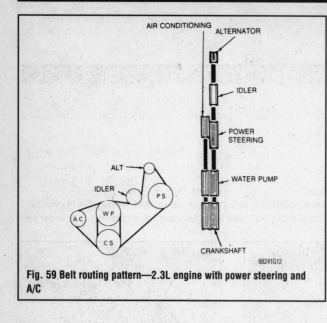

Fig. 59 Belt routing pattern—2.3L engine with power steering and A/C

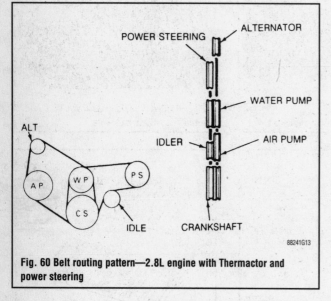

Fig. 60 Belt routing pattern—2.8L engine with Thermactor and power steering

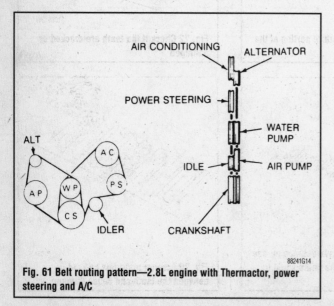

Fig. 61 Belt routing pattern—2.8L engine with Thermactor, power steering and A/C

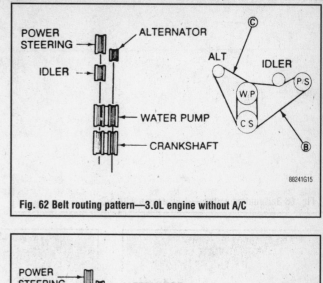

Fig. 62 Belt routing pattern—3.0L engine without A/C

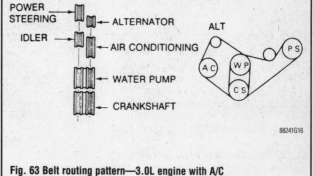

Fig. 63 Belt routing pattern—3.0L engine with A/C

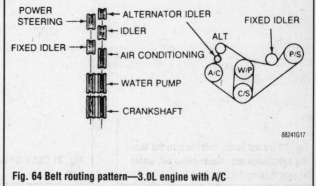

Fig. 64 Belt routing pattern—3.0L engine with A/C

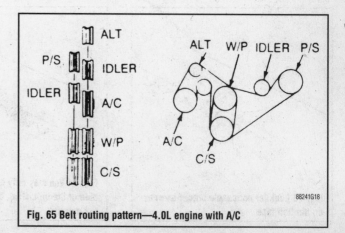

Fig. 65 Belt routing pattern—4.0L engine with A/C

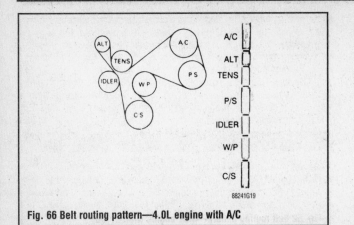

Fig. 66 Belt routing pattern—4.0L engine with A/C

It is important to note however, that on engines with many driven accessories, several or all of the belts may have to be removed to get at the one to be replaced.

Timing Belt

INSPECTION

▶ See Figures 70 thru 75

Timing belts are constructed in a similar manner as V-ribbed belts, therefore, they do not easily show wear and some people cannot distinguish between a good belt and one that is in need of replacement. It is a good idea to visually inspect the timing belt once a year and replace them in accordance with the intervals specified in the maintenance interval chart. Although this requires the removal of part or all of the timing belt cover, this inspection may prevent driver

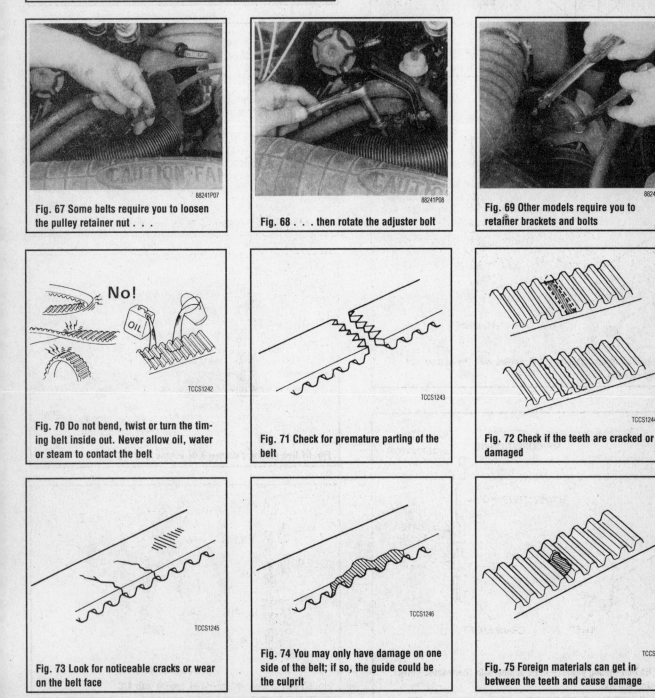

Fig. 67 Some belts require you to loosen the pulley retainer nut . . .

Fig. 68 . . . then rotate the adjuster bolt

Fig. 69 Other models require you to retainer brackets and bolts

Fig. 70 Do not bend, twist or turn the timing belt inside out. Never allow oil, water or steam to contact the belt

Fig. 71 Check for premature parting of the belt

Fig. 72 Check if the teeth are cracked or damaged

Fig. 73 Look for noticeable cracks or wear on the belt face

Fig. 74 You may only have damage on one side of the belt; if so, the guide could be the culprit

Fig. 75 Foreign materials can get in between the teeth and cause damage

and passenger inconvenience and or serve engine damage. The timing belt must always be properly adjusted or severe engine damage could occur.

Inspect the timing belt for signs of glazing or cracking. Cracks will usually start at the inner edge of the belt and run outward. All worn or damaged drive belts should be replaced immediately.

Hoses

INSPECTION

♦ See Figures 76, 77, 78 and 79

Upper and lower radiator hoses, along with the heater hoses, should be checked for deterioration, leaks and loose hose clamps at least every 15,000 miles (24,000 km). It is also wise to check the hoses periodically in early spring and at the beginning of the fall or winter when you are performing other maintenance. A quick visual inspection could discover a weakened hose which might have left you stranded if it had remained unrepaired.

Whenever you are checking the hoses, make sure the engine and cooling system are cold. Visually inspect for cracking, rotting or collapsed hoses, and replace as necessary. Run your hand along the length of the hose. If a weak or swollen spot is noted when squeezing the hose wall, the hose should be replaced.

REMOVAL & INSTALLATION

1. Remove the radiator pressure cap.

✳ CAUTION

Never remove the pressure cap while the engine is running, or personal injury from scalding hot coolant or steam may result. If possible, wait until the engine has cooled to remove the pressure cap. If this is not possible, wrap a thick cloth around the pressure cap

Fig. 76 The cracks developing along this hose are a result of age-related hardening

and turn it slowly to the stop. Step back while the pressure is released from the cooling system. When you are sure all the pressure has been released, use the cloth to turn and remove the cap.

2. Position a clean container under the radiator and/or engine draincock or plug, then open the drain and allow the cooling system to drain to an appropriate level. For some upper hoses, only a little coolant must be drained. To remove hoses positioned lower on the engine, such as a lower radiator hose, the entire cooling system must be emptied.

✳ CAUTION

When draining coolant, keep in mind that cats and dogs are attracted by ethylene glycol antifreeze, and are quite likely to drink any that is left in an uncovered container or in puddles on the ground. This will prove fatal in sufficient quantity. Always drain coolant into a sealable container.

3. Loosen the hose clamps at each end of the hose requiring replacement. Clamps are usually either of the spring tension type (which require pliers to squeeze the tabs and loosen) or of the screw tension type (which require screw or hex drivers to loosen). Pull the clamps back on the hose away from the connection.
4. Twist, pull and slide the hose off the fitting, taking care not to damage the neck of the component from which the hose is being removed.

➡ If the hose is stuck at the connection, do not try to insert a screwdriver or other sharp tool under the hose end in an effort to free it, as the connection and/or hose may become damaged. Heater connections especially may be easily damaged by such a procedure. If the hose is to be replaced, use a single-edged razor blade to make a slice along the portion of the hose which is stuck on the connection, perpendicular to the end of the hose. Do not cut too deep so as to prevent damaging the connection. The hose can then be peeled from the connection and discarded.

5. Clean both hose mounting connections. Inspect the condition of the hose clamps and replace them, if necessary.
   To install:
6. Dip the ends of the new hose into clean engine coolant to ease installation.
7. Slide the clamps over the replacement hose, then slide the hose ends over the connections into position.
8. Position and secure the clamps at least ¼ in. (6.35mm) from the ends of the hose. Make sure they are located beyond the raised bead of the connector.
9. Close the radiator or engine drains and properly refill the cooling system with the clean drained engine coolant or a suitable mixture of coolant and water.
10. If available, install a pressure tester and check for leaks. If a pressure tester is not available, run the engine until normal operating temperature is reached (allowing the system to naturally pressurize), then check for leaks.

✳ CAUTION

If you are checking for leaks with the system at normal operating temperature, BE EXTREMELY CAREFUL not to touch any moving or hot engine parts. Once temperature has been reached, shut the engine OFF, and check for leaks around the hose fittings and connections which were removed earlier.

Fig. 77 A hose clamp that is too tight can cause older hoses to separate and tear on either side of the clamp

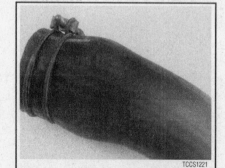

Fig. 78 A soft spongy hose (identifiable by the swollen section) will eventually burst and should be replaced

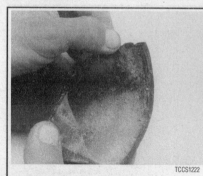

Fig. 79 Hoses are likely to deteriorate from the inside if the cooling system is not periodically flushed

Heater Hose Snap-Lock Fittings

Some heater hoses are joined by snap-lock fittings. There is a special tool for disconnecting these fittings. Since there are both ⅝ in. and ¾ in. lines, there are 2 different tools: T85T-18539-AH1 (⅝ in.) and T85T-18539-AH2 (¾ in.). Both are used with extension handle T85T-18539-AH3. There are also equivalent tools on the market.

To disconnect the fitting, use the tool to depress the plastic tabs and pull on the hose until the plastic connector clears the tabs.

To connect the hose, simply push the ends together until they snap tightly.

CV-Boots

INSPECTION

▶ See Figures 80 and 81

The CV (Constant Velocity) boots should be checked for damage each time the oil is changed and any other time the vehicle is raised for service. These boots keep water, grime, dirt and other damaging matter from entering the CV-joints. Any of these could cause early CV-joint failure which can be expensive to repair. Heavy grease thrown around the inside of the front wheel(s) and on the brake caliper/drum can be an indication of a torn boot. Thoroughly check the boots for missing clamps and tears. If the boot is damaged, it should be replaced immediately. Please refer to Section 7 for procedures.

Spark Plugs

▶ See Figures 82 and 83

A typical spark plug consists of a metal shell surrounding a ceramic insulator. A metal electrode extends downward through the center of the insulator and protrudes a small distance. Located at the end of the plug and attached to the side of the outer metal shell is the side electrode. The side electrode bends in at a 90° angle so that its tip is just past and parallel to the tip of the center electrode. The distance between these two electrodes (measured in thousandths of an inch or hundredths of a millimeter) is called the spark plug gap.

The spark plug does not produce a spark, but instead provides a gap across which the current can arc. The coil produces anywhere from 20,000 to 50,000 volts (depending on the type and application) which travels through the wires to the spark plugs. The current passes along the center electrode and jumps the gap to the side electrode, and in doing so, ignites the air/fuel mixture in the combustion chamber.

SPARK PLUG HEAT RANGE

▶ See Figure 84

Spark plug heat range is the ability of the plug to dissipate heat. The longer the insulator (or the farther it extends into the engine), the hotter the plug will operate; the shorter the insulator (the closer the electrode is to the block's cooling passages) the cooler it will operate. A plug that absorbs little heat and remains too cool will quickly accumulate deposits of oil and carbon since it is not hot enough to burn them off. This leads to plug fouling and consequently to misfiring. A plug that absorbs too much heat will have no deposits but, due to the excessive heat, the electrodes will burn away quickly and might possibly lead to preignition or other ignition problems. Preignition takes place when plug tips get so hot that they glow sufficiently to ignite the air/fuel mixture before the actual spark occurs. This early ignition will usually cause a pinging during low speeds and heavy loads.

The general rule of thumb for choosing the correct heat range when picking a spark plug is: if most of your driving is long distance, high speed travel, use a colder plug; if most of your driving is stop and go, use a hotter plug. Original equipment plugs are generally a good compromise between the 2 styles and most people never have the need to change their plugs from the factory-recommended heat range.

REMOVAL & INSTALLATION

▶ See Figures 85, 86 and 87

A set of spark plugs usually requires replacement after about 20,000–30,000 miles (32,000–48,000 km), depending on your style of driving. In normal operation plug gap increases about 0.001 in. (0.025mm) for every 2500 miles (4000

Fig. 80 CV-boots must be inspected periodically for damage

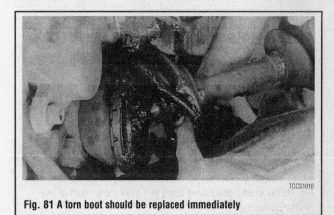

Fig. 81 A torn boot should be replaced immediately

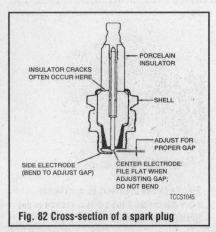

Fig. 82 Cross-section of a spark plug

Fig. 83 A variety of tools and gauges are needed for spark plug service

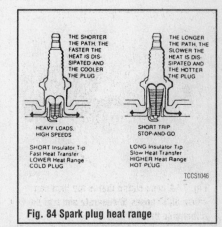

Fig. 84 Spark plug heat range

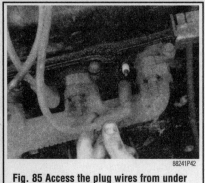

Fig. 85 Access the plug wires from under the hood or engine cover. Remove the wire with a twisting motion

Fig. 86 Using the correct sized spark plug socket, remove the plug from the engine cylinder head

Fig. 87 When the plug is removed, examine it carefully. It can tell you a lot about the condition of your engine

km). As the gap increases, the plug's voltage requirement also increases. It requires a greater voltage to jump the wider gap and about two to three times as much voltage to fire the plug at high speeds than at idle. The improved air/fuel ratio control of modern fuel injection combined with the higher voltage output of modern ignition systems will often allow an engine to run significantly longer on a set of standard spark plugs, but keep in mind that efficiency will drop as the gap widens (along with fuel economy and power).

When you're removing spark plugs, work on one at a time. Don't start by removing the plug wires all at once, because, unless you number them, they may become mixed up. Take a minute before you begin and number the wires with tape.

1. Disconnect the negative battery cable, and if the vehicle has been run recently, allow the engine to thoroughly cool.

2. Carefully twist the spark plug wire boot to loosen it, then pull upward and remove the boot from the plug. Be sure to pull on the boot and not on the wire, otherwise the connector located inside the boot may become separated.

3. Using compressed air, blow any water or debris from the spark plug well to assure that no harmful contaminants are allowed to enter the combustion chamber when the spark plug is removed. If compressed air is not available, use a rag or a brush to clean the area.

➡Remove the spark plugs when the engine is cold, if possible, to prevent damage to the threads. If removal of the plugs is difficult, apply a few drops of penetrating oil or silicone spray to the area around the base of the plug, and allow it a few minutes to work.

4. Using a spark plug socket that is equipped with a rubber insert to properly hold the plug, turn the spark plug counterclockwise to loosen and remove the spark plug from the bore.

✼ WARNING

Be sure not to use a flexible extension on the socket. Use of a flexible extension may allow a shear force to be applied to the plug. A shear force could break the plug off in the cylinder head, leading to costly and frustrating repairs.

To install:

5. Inspect the spark plug boot for tears or damage. If a damaged boot is found, the spark plug wire must be replaced.

6. Using a wire feeler gauge, check and adjust the spark plug gap. When using a gauge, the proper size should pass between the electrodes with a slight drag. The next larger size should not be able to pass while the next smaller size should pass freely.

7. Carefully thread the plug into the bore by hand. If resistance is felt before the plug is almost completely threaded, back the plug out and begin threading again. In small, hard to reach areas, an old spark plug wire and boot could be used as a threading tool. The boot will hold the plug while you twist the end of the wire and the wire is supple enough to twist before it would allow the plug to crossthread.

✼ WARNING

Do not use the spark plug socket to thread the plugs. Always carefully thread the plug by hand or using an old plug wire to prevent the possibility of crossthreading and damaging the cylinder head bore.

8. Carefully tighten the spark plug. If the plug you are installing is equipped with a crush washer, seat the plug, then tighten about ¼ turn to crush the washer. If you are installing a tapered seat plug, tighten the plug to specifications provided by the vehicle or plug manufacturer.

9. Apply a small amount of silicone dielectric compound to the end of the spark plug lead or inside the spark plug boot to prevent sticking, then install the boot to the spark plug and push until it clicks into place. The click may be felt or heard, then gently pull back on the boot to assure proper contact.

INSPECTION & GAPPING

▸ **See Figures 88, 89, 90 and 91**

Check the plugs for deposits and wear. If they are not going to be replaced, clean the plugs thoroughly. Remember that any kind of deposit will decrease the efficiency of the plug. Plugs can be cleaned on a spark plug cleaning machine,

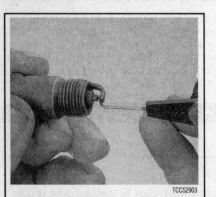

Fig. 88 Checking the spark plug gap with a feeler gauge

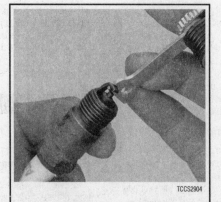

Fig. 89 Adjusting the spark plug gap

Fig. 90 If the standard plug is in good condition, the electrode may be filed flat—WARNING: do not file platinum plugs

A **normally worn** spark plug should have light tan or gray deposits on the firing tip.

A **carbon fouled** plug, identified by soft, sooty, black deposits, may indicate an improperly tuned vehicle. Check the air cleaner, ignition components and engine control system.

This spark plug has been **left in the engine too long,** as evidenced by the extreme gap- Plugs with such an extreme gap can cause misfiring and stumbling accompanied by a noticeable lack of power.

An **oil fouled** spark plug indicates an engine with worn poston rings and/or bad valve seals allowing excessive oil to enter the chamber.

A **physically damaged** spark plug may be evidence of severe detonation in that cylinder. Watch that cylinder carefully between services, as a continued detonation will not only damage the plug, but could also damage the engine.

A **bridged or almost bridged** spark plug, identified by a build-up between the electrodes caused by excessive carbon or oil build-up on the plug.

TCCA1P40

Fig. 91 Inspect the spark plug to determine engine running conditions

which can sometimes be found in service stations, or you can do an acceptable job of cleaning with a stiff brush. If the plugs are cleaned, the electrodes must be filed flat. Use an ignition points file, not an emery board or the like, which will leave deposits. The electrodes must be filed perfectly flat with sharp edges; rounded edges reduce the spark plug voltage by as much as 50%.

Check spark plug gap before installation. The ground electrode (the L-shaped one connected to the body of the plug) must be parallel to the center electrode and the specified size wire gauge (please refer to the Tune-Up Specifications chart for details) must pass between the electrodes with a slight drag.

➡**NEVER adjust the gap on a used platinum type spark plug.**

Always check the gap on new plugs as they are not always set correctly at the factory. Do not use a flat feeler gauge when measuring the gap on a used plug, because the reading may be inaccurate. A round-wire type gapping tool is the best way to check the gap. The correct gauge should pass through the electrode gap with a slight drag. If you're in doubt, try one size smaller and one larger.

The smaller gauge should go through easily, while the larger one shouldn't go through at all. Wire gapping tools usually have a bending tool attached. Use that to adjust the side electrode until the proper distance is obtained. Absolutely never attempt to bend the center electrode. Also, be careful not to bend the side electrode too far or too often as it may weaken and break off within the engine, requiring removal of the cylinder head to retrieve it.

Spark Plug Wires

TESTING

♦ **See Figures 92 and 93**

At every tune-up/inspection, visually check the spark plug cables for burns cuts, or breaks in the insulation. Check the boots and the nipples on the distributor cap and/or coil. Replace any damaged wiring.

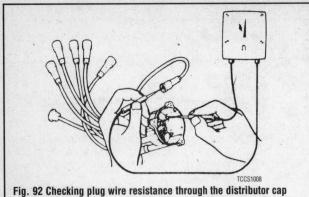

Fig. 92 Checking plug wire resistance through the distributor cap with an ohmmeter

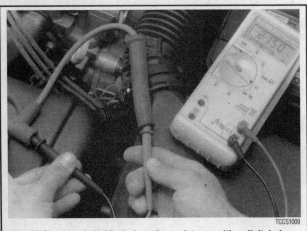

Fig. 93 Checking individual plug wire resistance with a digital ohmmeter

Every 50,000 miles (80,000 Km) or 60 months, the resistance of the wires should be checked with an ohmmeter. Wires with excessive resistance will cause misfiring, and may make the engine difficult to start in damp weather.

To check resistance;

1. Disconnect the negative battery cable.
2. If equipped, remove the distributor cap from the distributor assembly.
3. If equipped, remove the wire from the coil pack.
4. Visually inspect the spark plug wires for burns, cuts or breaks in the insulation. Check the spark plug boots and the nipples on all attached components. Replace any damaged wiring.
5. Inspect the spark plug wires to insure that they are firmly seated on the distributor cap or coil pack.
6. Disconnect the spark plug wire(s) thought to be defective at the spark plug.
7. Using an ohmmeter, measure the resistance between the terminal ends.

➡ Make certain that a good connection exists between the distributor cap or coil pack and the spark terminal. Never, under any circumstances, measure resistance by puncturing the spark plug wire.

8. If the measured resistance is less than 7000 ohms per foot of wire, the wire is good. If the measured resistance is greater than 7000 ohms per foot, the wire is defective and should be replaced.
9. Connect the negative battery cable.

REMOVAL & INSTALLATION

➡ Because of the design of the electronics, the 4.0L engine uses a distributorless ignition system.

1. Disconnect the negative battery cable.

➡ To prevent possible incorrect spark plug wire installation, remove and install spark plug wires one at a time.

2. Grasp the ignition wire with spark plug removal tool T74P-6666-A or equivalent, then twist the boot back and forth several times while pulling upward to free it from the plug.

❈❈ CAUTION

DO NOT tug on the wire to remove it.

To install:

3. Before reconnecting the spark plug wire, lubricate the entire inside surface of the boot with Motorcraft Silicone Dielectric Compound D7AZ-19A331-A or equivalent.
4. When installing a new set of spark plug wires, make sure the boot is installed firmly over the spark plug and distributor cap tower. Route the wire exactly the same way as the original and make sure the wire loom clips are fastened securely when done. Starting with the number one wire which is marked on the distributor cap, install the spark plug wires in sequence making sure that the following firing orders and rotations are observed.

Distributor Cap and Rotor

➡ The 4.0L engine has an ignition system which does not use a distributor.

REMOVAL & INSTALLATION

▶ **See Figures 94, 95 and 96**

1. Disconnect the negative battery cable.
2. Tag all spark plug wires and distributor cap terminals with a piece of tape according to cylinder number for reference when installing the wires, then remove them from the distributor cap. Note the position of No. 1 spark plug tower.
3. Unclip the distributor cap and lift it straight up and off the distributor.
4. Using a screwdriver, loosen the adapter attaching screws and remove.
5. Loosen the screws attaching the rotor to the distributor and remove the rotor.
6. Wipe the distributor cap and rotor with a clean, damp cloth. Inspect the cap.

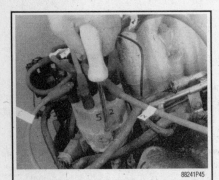

Fig. 94 With the wire and/or cap clearly marked, remove the distributor cap retainer screws

Fig. 95 Lift the cap off and remove the spark plug wires—3.0L engine shown

Fig. 96 Lift the rotor cap off

To install:

7. Position the distributor rotor with the square and round locator pins matched to the rotor mounting plate. Tighten the screws to 24–36 inch lbs. (2–4 Nm).

8. Install the adapter and tighten the attaching screws to 18–23 inch lbs. (2–3 Nm).

9. Install the cap, noting the square alignment locator, then tighten the hold-down screws to 18–23 inch lbs. (2–3 Nm).

10. Install the spark plug wires in firing order, starting from No. 1 tower and working in sequence around the cap. Refer to the firing order illustrations in Section 2, if necessary. Make sure the ignition wires are installed correctly and are firmly seated in the distributor cap towers.

11. Connect the negative battery cable.

INSPECTION

With the rotor and or distributor cap removed, inspect all the surfaces of the components for sign of cracking, corrosion or possible water leakage, and replace if any of these conditions are found.

Inspect the metal contact surfaces of both the rotor and distributor cap for burning, grooves or pieces of metal missing. If any of these examples exist, replace the component.

Ignition Timing

GENERAL INFORMATION

Periodic adjustment of the ignition timing is not necessary for any engine covered by this manual. If ignition timing is not within specification, there is a fault in the engine control system. Diagnose and repair the problem as necessary.

Ignition timing is the measurement, in degrees of crankshaft rotation, of the point at which the spark plugs fire in each of the cylinders. It is measured in degrees before or after Top Dead Center (TDC) of the compression stroke.

Ideally, the air/fuel mixture in the cylinder will be ignited by the spark plug just as the piston passes TDC of the compression stroke. If this happens, the piston will be at the beginning of the power stroke just as the compressed and ignited air/fuel mixture forces the piston down and turns the crankshaft. Because it takes a fraction of a second for the spark plug to ignite the mixture in the cylinder, the spark plug must fire a little before the piston reaches TDC. Otherwise, the mixture will not be completely ignited as the piston passes TDC and the full power of the explosion will not be used by the engine.

The timing measurement is given in degrees of crankshaft rotation before the piston reaches TDC (BTDC). If the setting for the ignition timing is 10 BTDC, each spark plug must fire 10 degrees before each piston reaches TDC. This only holds true, however, when the engine is at idle speed. The combustion process must be complete by 23° ATDC to maintain proper engine performance, fuel mileage, and low emissions.

As the engine speed increases, the pistons go faster. The spark plugs have to ignite the fuel even sooner if it is to be completely ignited when the piston reaches TDC. On all engines covered in this manual, spark timing changes are accomplished electronically by the Powertrain Control Module (PCM), based on input from engine sensors.

If the ignition is set too far advanced (BTDC), the ignition and expansion of the fuel in the cylinder will occur too soon and tend to force the piston down while it is still traveling up. This causes pre ignition or "knocking and pinging". If the ignition spark is set too far retarded, or after TDC (ATDC), the piston will have already started on its way down when the fuel is ignited. The piston will be forced down for only a portion of its travel, resulting in poor engine performance and lack of power.

Timing marks or scales can be found on the rim of the crankshaft pulley and the timing cover. The marks on the pulley correspond to the position of the piston in the No. 1 cylinder. A stroboscopic (dynamic) timing light is hooked onto the No. 1 cylinder spark plug wire. Every time the spark plug fires, the timing light flashes. By aiming the light at the timing marks while the engine is running, the exact position of the piston within the cylinder can be easily read (the flash of light makes the mark on the pulley appear to be standing still). Proper timing is indicated when the mark and scale are in specified alignment.

✶✶ WARNING

When checking timing with the engine running, take care not to get the timing light wires tangled in the fan blades and/or drive belts.

INSPECTION

1. Place the vehicle in **P** or **N** with the parking brake applied and the drive wheels blocked.

2. Connect a suitable tachometer and timing light to the engine, as per the manufacturer's instructions.

3. Remove the **SPOUT** (Spark Output) connector.

4. Start the engine and allow it reach normal operating temperature. Make sure all accessories are off.

5. Check that the idle speed is within the specified rpm range.

6. Following the timing light manufacturer's instructions, aim the timing light and check the ignition timing. As the light flashes, note the position of the mark on the crankshaft pulley against the scale on the timing cover. Timing should be 8–12 degrees BTDC.

7. If the ignition timing is not within specification, refer to ADJUSTMENT, in this Section.

8. Install the **SPOUT** connector.

9. Stop the engine and remove the tachometer and timing light.

ADJUSTMENT

If the ignition timing is not within specification, loosen the distributor hold-down bolt and carefully rotate the distributor in the correct direction to achieve the desired advance/retard required to correct the timing. Recheck the timing as you rotate the distributor and when the desired timing is reached, tighten the hold-down bolt.

Valve Lash

GENERAL INFORMATION

Valve adjustment can affect how far the valves enter the cylinder and how long they stay open and closed.

If the valve clearance is too large, part of the lobe of the camshaft will be used to removing the excessive clearance. Consequently, the valve will not be opening as far as it should. This condition has two effects: the valve train components will emit a tapping sound as they take up the excessive clearance and the engine will perform poorly because the valves don't open fully and allow the proper amount of gases to flow into and out of the engine.

If the valve clearance is too small, the intake valve and the exhaust valves will open too far and they will not fully seat on the cylinder head when they close. When a seat on the cylinder head when they close. When a valve seats itself on the cylinder head, it does two things: it seals the combustion chamber so that none of the gases in the cylinder escape and it cools itself by transferring some of the heat it absorbs from the combustion in the cylinder to the cylinder head and to the engine's cooling system. If the valve clearance is too small, the engine will run poorly because of the gases escaping from the combustion chamber. The valves will also become overheated and will warp, since they cannot transfer heat unless they are touching the valve seat in the cylinder head.

➡**While all valve adjustments must be made as accurately as possible, it is better to have the valve adjustment slightly loose than slightly tight as a burned valve may result from overly tight adjustments.**

ADJUSTMENT

2.3L Engine

▸ **See Figure 97**

➡**The 4-cylinder gasoline engine in this vehicle is equipped with hydraulic valve lash adjusters. Adjustment is not necessary.**

To check the valve lash use the following procedure.

➡**The allowable collapsed tappet gap is 0.035–0.055 in. (0.9–1.4mm) at the camshaft. The desired collapsed tappet gap is 0.040–0.050 in. (0.04–0.06mm) at the camshaft.**

1. Disconnect the negative battery cable.

2. Remove the rocker arm cover. Refer to Section 3 if needed.

3. Position the camshaft so that the base circle of the lobe is facing the cam follower of the valve to be checked.

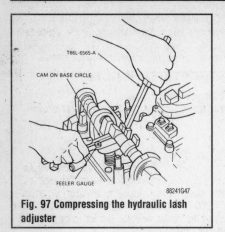

Fig. 97 Compressing the hydraulic lash adjuster

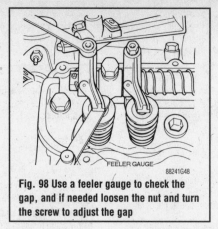

Fig. 98 Use a feeler gauge to check the gap, and if needed loosen the nut and turn the screw to adjust the gap

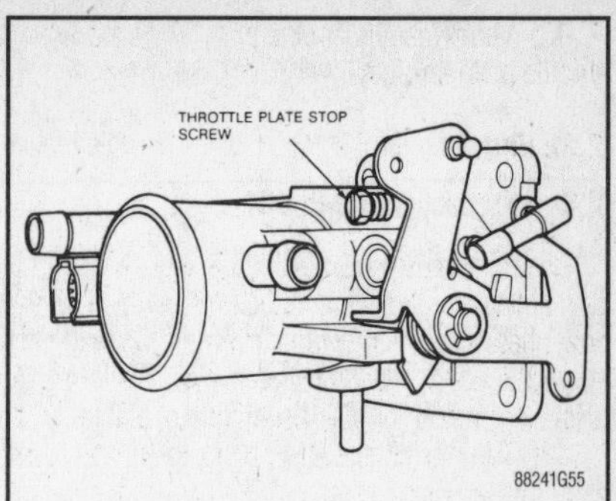

Fig. 99 Idle adjusting screw on throttle body—2.3L engine

4. Using tool T74P-6565-A or equivalent, slowly apply pressure to the cam follower until the lash adjuster is completely collapsed. Hold the follower in this position and insert the proper size feeler gauge between the base circle of the cam and the follower.

5. If the clearance is excessive, remove the cam follower and inspect for damage.

6. If the cam follower appears to be intact, and not excessively worn, measure the valve spring damper assembly height to be sure that the valve is not sticking.

7. If the valve spring height is correct, check the dimensions of the camshaft.

8. If the camshaft dimensions are to specifications, remove, clean and test the lash adjuster.

9. Reinstall the lash adjuster and check the clearance. Replace any damaged or worn parts as necessary.

10. When complete, connect the negative battery cable.

2.8L Engine

◆ See Figure 98

➡This procedure should be performed on a cold engine.

1. Disconnect the negative battery cable.
2. Remove the rocker arm cover. Refer to Section 3 if needed.
3. Place your finger on the adjusting screw of the intake valve rocker arm for the number 5 cylinder. You should be able to feel any movement in the rocker arm.
4. Using a remote starter switch or equivalent, bump the engine over until the intake valve for the number 5 cylinder just begins to open. The valves on the number 1 cylinder may now be adjusted.
5. Adjust the number 1 intake valve so that a 0.013 in. (0.35mm) feeler gauge has a light drag and a 0.015 in. (0.38mm) feeler gauge is very tight. Turn the adjusting screw clockwise to decrease the gap and counterclockwise to increase the gap. The adjusting screws are self-locking and will stay in position once they are set.

➡When checking the valve lash, be sure to insert the feeler gauge between the rocker arm and the valve tip at the front edge of the valve and move it toward the opposite edge with a forward motion.

6. Using the same method, adjust the number 1 exhaust valve lash so that a 0.016 in.(0.40mm) feeler gauge has a light drag and a 0.0.017 in. (0.43mm) feeler gauge is very tight.

7. Adjust the remaining valves in the same manner, in the firing order (1–4–2–5–3–6) by positioning the camshaft according to the chart.

8. When all the valves have been adjusted, install the rocker arm cover. Refer to Section 3 if needed.

9. Connect the negative battery cable.

10. Start the engine and check for oil and vacuum leaks as well as a smooth sounding engine.

3.0L and 4.0L Engines

The intake and exhaust valves installed in the 3.0L and 4.0L engines are driven by the camshaft. The energy created by the turning force of the camshaft drives a series of hydraulic lash adjusters and stamped steel rocker arms. As these rockers arms move back and forth, the individual valve attached to the

rocker arm opens and closes. These lash adjusters eliminate the need for any periodic valve lash adjustment.

Although there is no periodic adjustment needed, it is not uncommon for vehicles equipped with these hydraulic valve lifters to develop a valve tapping noise from time to time at the top of the engine. Usually this noise is created due to air in the hydraulic assembly. In the event the noise continues, more involved mechanical repairs may be needed.

To eliminate the valve tap noise, try this procedure;

1. Park the vehicle on a level surface. Engage the parking brake fully and place blocks behind the rear wheels.
2. Make sure the vehicle is in **PARK**. Start the engine and allow to reach normal operating temperature.
3. Once normal operating temperature is reached, run the engine for 20 minutes at 2000 rpm.
4. After 20 minutes, shut the engine **OFF** for 2 minutes, then restart and allow it to idle for one to two minutes. If this procedure was effective, there should no longer be any tapping noise.

Idle Speed and Mixture

ADJUSTMENT

2.3L Engine

◆ See Figure 99

The curb idle speed and mixture is controlled by the EEC-IV processor and idle speed control bypass valve.

➡This procedure should be performed only if the curb idle speed is not within 625–700 rpm for automatic equipped models, or 575–650 rpm for manually equipped models and all necessary repairs to the system have been made.

1. Park the vehicle on a level surface and place block behind the wheels.
2. Place the transmission in NEUTRAL and make sure the A/C-Heat selector is off.
3. Start the engine and allow it to reach normal operating temperature, then turn the ignition off.
4. Disconnect the idle speed control air bypass valve power lead.
5. Start the engine and operate at 1,500 rpm for approximately 20 seconds.
6. Allow the engine to idle and check that the idle speed is 550–600 rpm.

➡The engine may stall when the idle speed air bypass valve is disconnected. This is acceptable as long as the throttle plate is not stuck in the throttle body assembly bore.

7. If the idle speed requires adjustment, disconnect the throttle cable and adjust the engine rpm by turning the throttle plate stop screw on the throttle body assembly.
8. Reconnect the throttle cable, then recheck the idle speed and adjust, if needed.
9. Once the idle speed is set, turn the engine **OFF** and reconnect the power lead to the idle speed control air bypass valve.

10.   Verify that the throttle plate is not stuck in the bore by moving the throttle plate linkage.

2.8L Engine

♦ See Figures 100 and 101

The mixture is controlled by the EEC-IV processor and engine sensors. There is no manual adjustment. If the mixture is suspected of being either too high or low, check the electronic fuel controls. Consult Section 4 for testing procedures.

1.   Place the transmission in PARK or NEUTRAL then start the engine and allow it to reach normal operating temperature.

2.   Turn the engine **OFF**, block the drive wheels and set the parking brake firmly. Turn all accessories OFF.

3.   Remove the Air Charge Temperature (ACT) sensor and adapter from the air cleaner tray by disengaging the retainer clip. Do not unfasten the connector. Remove the air cleaner, then disconnect and plug the vacuum line at the cold weather duct and valve motor.

4.   Start the engine, then turn **OFF** and verify that the Idle Speed Control (ISC) plunger moves out to its maximum extension within 10 seconds of key **OFF**.

5.   Disconnect the idle speed control. Disconnect and plug the EGR vacuum hose.

6.   Start the engine and manually open the throttle, then set the fast idle adjusting screw on the high step of the fast idle cam.

7.   Adjust the fast idle speed to specifications listed on the underhood sticker.

8.   Open the throttle manually to release the fast idle cam, allowing the throttle lever to rest on the ISC plunger.

9.   Loosen the ISC bracket lock screw. Adjust the ISC bracket screw to 2,000 rpm, then retighten the bracket lock screw.

10.   Reconnect the ISC connector. The engine rpm should automatically be adjusted to curb idle.

11.   Simultaneously:
   a.   Manually hold the throttle above 1,000 rpm

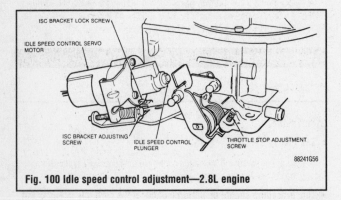

Fig. 100 Idle speed control adjustment—2.8L engine

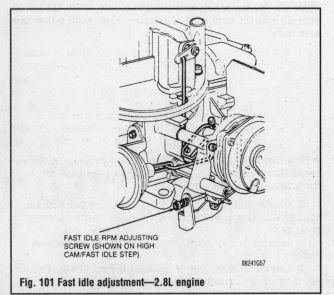

Fig. 101 Fast idle adjustment—2.8L engine

   b.   Push the ISC plunger until it retracts fully
   c.   After the plunger retracts, release the throttle and quickly unplug the connection.

12.   Adjust the anti-dieseling speed throttle stop screw to 750 rpm.

➡**The anti-dieseling speed is NOT the curb idle speed.**

13.   Reconnect the ISC and EGR vacuum hose.

14.   Stop the engine, then restart it to verify that curb idle speed is within specifications.

3.0L Engine

Curb idle speed is controlled by the EEC processor and the idle speed control air bypass valve assembly. The throttle plate stop screw is factory set and does not directly control idle speed. Adjustments to this setting should be performed only as part of a full EEC-IV diagnosis of irregular idle conditions or idle speed. Failure to accurately set the throttle plate stop position to the procedure below could result in erroneous idle speed control.

The mixture is controlled by the EEC processor and engine sensors. There is no manual adjustment. If the mixture is suspected of being either too high or low, check the electronic fuel controls. Consult

1.   Place the transmission in NEUTRAL (MT) or PARK (AT), turn the A/C-heat selector to OFF, apply the parking brake firmly and block the drive wheels.

2.   Bring the engine up to normal operating temperature and check for vacuum leaks downstream of the throttle plates.

3.   Unplug the single wire, inline spout connector near the distributor and verify that ignition timing is 8–12° BTDC. If not, reset the ignition timing.

4.   Turn **OFF** the engine and disconnect the air bypass valve assembly connector.

5.   Remove the PCV entry line at the PCV valve.

6.   Install Orifice Tool T86P-9600-A or equivalent (0.200 in. orifice diameter) in the PCV entry line.

7.   Start the engine. The vehicle should be idling in DRIVE(AT) or in NEUTRAL (MT). Make sure the drive wheels are blocked and the parking brake is firmly set.

➡**If the electric cooling fan comes on during idle set, unplug the fan motor power leads or wait until the fan switches OFF.**

8.   Check the idle speed. It should be 820–870 rpm on models with an automatic transmission or 1,015–1,065 rpm on models with manual transmission. If the idle speed is not within this range, adjust by turning the throttle plate stop screw.

9.   Turn **OFF** the engine after the idle speed is set.

10.   Restart the engine and confirm the idle speed is within specifications after 3 to 5 minutes. If not, repeat setting procedure.

11.   If the idle speed is correct, turn **OFF** the engine, remove the orifice and reconnect the PCV entry line.

12.   Reconnect the distributor spout line, the ISC motor and the cooling fan power supply, if unfastened. Verify that the throttle plate is not stuck in the bore.

4.0L Engine

Idle speed and mixture are completely controlled by the EEC and EDIS system. No routine adjustments are required or possible. If idle speed or mixture is not within specification, consult an authorized dealer with the proper diagnostic equipment as soon as possible.

Air Conditioning System

SYSTEM SERVICE & REPAIR

➡**It is recommended that the A/C system be serviced by an EPA Section 609 certified automotive technician utilizing a refrigerant recovery/recycling machine.**

The do-it-yourselfer should not service his/her own vehicle's A/C system for many reasons, including legal concerns, personal injury, environmental damage and cost.

According to the U.S. Clean Air Act, it is a federal crime to service or repair (involving the refrigerant) a Motor Vehicle Air Conditioning (MVAC) system for money without being EPA certified. It is also illegal to vent R-12 and R-134a refrigerants into the atmosphere. State and/or local laws may be more strict than the federal regulations, so be sure to check with your state and/or local authorities for further information.

➡ **Federal law dictates that a fine of up to $25,000 may be levied on people convicted of venting refrigerant into the atmosphere.**

When servicing an A/C system you run the risk of handling or coming in contact with refrigerant, which may result in skin or eye irritation or frostbite. Although low in toxicity (due to chemical stability), inhalation of concentrated refrigerant fumes is dangerous and can result in death; cases of fatal cardiac arrhythmia have been reported in people accidentally subjected to high levels of refrigerant. Some early symptoms include loss of concentration and drowsiness.

➡ **Generally, the limit for exposure is lower for R-134a than it is for R-12. Exceptional care must be practiced when handling R-134a.**

Also, some refrigerants can decompose at high temperatures (near gas heaters or open flame), which may result in hydrofluoric acid, hydrochloric acid and phosgene (a fatal nerve gas).

It is usually more economically feasible to have a certified MVAC automotive technician perform A/C system service on your vehicle.

R-12 Refrigerant Conversion

If your vehicle still uses R-12 refrigerant, one way to save A/C system costs down the road is to investigate the possibility of having your system converted to R-134a. The older R-12 systems can be easily converted to R-134a refrigerant by a certified automotive technician by installing a few new components and changing the system oil.

The cost of R-12 is steadily rising and will continue to increase, because it is no longer imported or manufactured in the United States. Therefore, it is often possible to have an R-12 system converted to R-134a and recharged for less than it would cost to just charge the system with R-12.

If you are interested in having your system converted, contact local automotive service stations for more details and information.

PREVENTIVE MAINTENANCE

Although the A/C system should not be serviced by the do-it-yourselfer, preventive maintenance should be practiced to help maintain the efficiency of the vehicle's A/C system. Be sure to perform the following:

• The easiest and most important preventive maintenance for your A/C system is to be sure that it is used on a regular basis. Running the system for five minutes each month (no matter what the season) will help ensure that the seals and all internal components remain lubricated.

➡ **Some vehicles automatically operate the A/C system compressor whenever the windshield defroster is activated. Therefore, the A/C system would not need to be operated each month if the defroster was used.**

• In order to prevent heater core freeze-up during A/C operation, it is necessary to maintain proper antifreeze protection. Be sure to properly maintain the engine cooling system.

• Any obstruction of or damage to the condenser configuration will restrict air flow which is essential to its efficient operation. Keep this unit clean and in proper physical shape.

➡ **Bug screens which are mounted in front of the condenser (unless they are original equipment) are regarded as obstructions.**

• The condensation drain tube expels any water which accumulates on the bottom of the evaporator housing into the engine compartment. If this tube is obstructed, the air conditioning performance can be restricted and condensation buildup can spill over onto the vehicle's floor.

SYSTEM INSPECTION

Although the A/C system should not be serviced by the do-it-yourselfer, system inspections should be performed to help maintain the efficiency of the vehicle's A/C system. Be sure to perform the following:

The easiest and often most important check for the air conditioning system consists of a visual inspection of the system components. Visually inspect the system for refrigerant leaks, damaged compressor clutch, abnormal compressor drive belt tension and/or condition, plugged evaporator drain tube, blocked condenser fins, disconnected or broken wires, blown fuses, corroded connections and poor insulation.

A refrigerant leak will usually appear as an oily residue at the leakage point in the system. The oily residue soon picks up dust or dirt particles from the surrounding air and appears greasy. Through time, this will build up and appear to be a heavy dirt impregnated grease.

For a thorough visual and operational inspection, check the following:

• Check the surface of the radiator and condenser for dirt, leaves or other material which might block air flow.

• Check for kinks in hoses and lines. Check the system for leaks.

• Make sure the drive belt is properly tensioned. During operation, make sure the belt is free of noise or slippage.

• Make sure the blower motor operates at all appropriate positions, then check for distribution of the air from all outlets.

➡ **Remember that in high humidity, air discharged from the vents may not feel as cold as expected, even if the system is working properly. This is because moisture in humid air retains heat more effectively than dry air, thereby making humid air more difficult to cool.**

Windshield Wipers

ELEMENT (REFILL) CARE & REPLACEMENT

▶ **See Figures 102, 103 and 104**

For maximum effectiveness and longest element life, the windshield and wiper blades should be kept clean. Dirt, tree sap, road tar and so on will cause streaking, smearing and blade deterioration if left on the glass. It is advisable to wash the windshield carefully with a commercial glass cleaner at least once a month. Wipe off the rubber blades with the wet rag afterwards. Do not attempt to move wipers across the windshield by hand; damage to the motor and drive mechanism will result.

To inspect and/or replace the wiper blade elements, place the wiper switch in the **LOW** speed position and the ignition switch in the **ACC** position. When the wiper blades are approximately vertical on the windshield, turn the ignition switch to **OFF**.

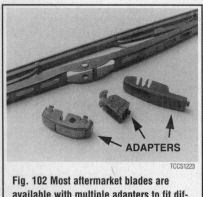

TCCS1223

Fig. 102 Most aftermarket blades are available with multiple adapters to fit different vehicles

TCCS1224

Fig. 103 Choose a blade which will fit your vehicle, and that will be readily available next time you need blades

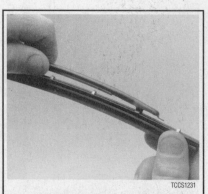

TCCS1231

Fig. 104 When installed, be certain the blade is fully inserted into the backing

Examine the wiper blade elements. If they are found to be cracked, broken or torn, they should be replaced immediately. Replacement intervals will vary with usage, although ozone deterioration usually limits element life to about one year. If the wiper pattern is smeared or streaked, or if the blade chatters across the glass, the elements should be replaced. It is easiest and most sensible to replace the elements in pairs.

If your vehicle is equipped with aftermarket blades, there are several different types of refills and your vehicle might have any kind. Aftermarket blades and arms rarely use the exact same type blade or refill as the original equipment.

Regardless of the type of refill used, be sure to follow the part manufacturer's instructions closely. Make sure that all of the frame jaws are engaged as the refill is pushed into place and locked. If the metal blade holder and frame are allowed to touch the glass during wiper operation, the glass will be scratched.

Tires and Wheels

Common sense and good driving habits will afford maximum tire life. Fast starts, sudden stops and hard cornering are hard on tires and will shorten their useful life span. Make sure that you don't overload the vehicle or run with incorrect pressure in the tires. Both of these practices will increase tread wear.

➡️ **For optimum tire life, keep the tires properly inflated, rotate them often and have the wheel alignment checked periodically.**

Inspect your tires frequently. Be especially careful to watch for bubbles in the tread or sidewall, deep cuts or under-inflation. Replace any tires with bubbles in the sidewall. If cuts are so deep that they penetrate to the cords, discard the tire. Any cut in the sidewall of a radial tire renders it unsafe. Also look for uneven tread wear patterns that may indicate the front end is out of alignment or that the tires are out of balance.

TIRE ROTATION

▶ **See Figures 105, 106 and 107**

Tires must be rotated periodically to equalize wear patterns that vary with a tire's position on the vehicle. Tires will also wear in an uneven way as the front

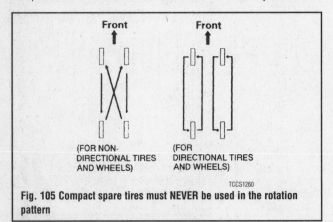

Fig. 105 Compact spare tires must NEVER be used in the rotation pattern

steering/suspension system wears to the point where the alignment should be reset.

Rotating the tires will ensure maximum life for the tires as a set, so you will not have to discard a tire early due to wear on only part of the tread. Regular rotation is required to equalize wear.

When rotating "unidirectional tires," make sure that they always roll in the same direction. This means that a tire used on the left side of the vehicle must not be switched to the right side and vice-versa. These tires are marked on the sidewall as to the direction of rotation; observe the mark when reinstalling the tire(s).

Some styled or "mag" wheels may have different offsets front to rear. In these cases, the rear wheels must not be used up front and vice-versa. Furthermore, if these wheels are equipped with unidirectional tires, they cannot be rotated unless the tire is remounted for the proper direction of rotation.

➡️ **The compact or space-saver spare is strictly for emergency use. It must never be included in the tire rotation or placed on the vehicle for everyday use.**

TIRE DESIGN

▶ **See Figure 108**

For maximum satisfaction, tires should be used in sets of four. Mixing of different types (radial, bias-belted, fiberglass belted) must be avoided. In most cases, the vehicle manufacturer has designated a type of tire on which the vehicle will perform best. Your first choice when replacing tires should be to use the same type of tire that the manufacturer recommends.

When radial tires are used, tire sizes and wheel diameters should be selected to maintain ground clearance and tire load capacity equivalent to the original specified tire. Radial tires should always be used in sets of four.

✳✳ **CAUTION**

Radial tires should never be used on only the front axle.

When selecting tires, pay attention to the original size as marked on the tire. Most tires are described using an industry size code sometimes referred to as P-Metric. This allows the exact identification of the tire specifications, regardless of the manufacturer. If selecting a different tire size or brand, remember to check the installed tire for any sign of interference with the body or suspension while the vehicle is stopping, turning sharply or heavily loaded.

Snow Tires

Good radial tires can produce a big advantage in slippery weather, but in snow, a street radial tire does not have sufficient tread to provide traction and control. The small grooves of a street tire quickly pack with snow and the tire behaves like a billiard ball on a marble floor. The more open, chunky tread of a snow tire will self-clean as the tire turns, providing much better grip on snowy surfaces.

To satisfy municipalities requiring snow tires during weather emergencies, most snow tires carry either an M + S designation after the tire size stamped on the sidewall, or the designation "all-season." In general, no change in tire size is necessary when buying snow tires.

Fig. 106 Unidirectional tires can only be rotated on the same side of the vehicle (front-to-rear). Such tires are identified by an arrow or the word "rotation"

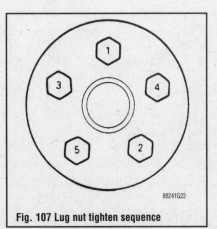

Fig. 107 Lug nut tighten sequence

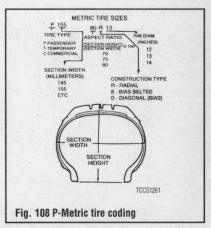

Fig. 108 P-Metric tire coding

Most manufacturers strongly recommend the use of 4 snow tires on their vehicles for reasons of stability. If snow tires are fitted only to the drive wheels, the opposite end of the vehicle may become very unstable when braking or turning on slippery surfaces. This instability can lead to unpleasant endings if the driver can't counteract the slide in time.

Note that snow tires, whether 2 or 4, will affect vehicle handling in all non-snow situations. The snow tires will noticeably change the turning and braking characteristics of the vehicle. Once the snow tires are installed, you must re-learn the behavior of the vehicle and drive accordingly.

➡**Consider buying extra wheels on which to mount the snow tires. Once done, the "snow wheels" can be installed and removed as needed. This eliminates the potential damage to tires or wheels from seasonal removal and installation. Even if your vehicle has styled wheels, see if inexpensive steel wheels are available. Although the look of the vehicle will change, the expensive wheels will be protected from salt, curb hits and pothole damage.**

Fig. 109 Tires should be checked frequently for any sign of puncture or damage

TIRE STORAGE

If they are mounted on wheels, store the tires at proper inflation pressure. All tires should be kept in a cool, dry place. If they are stored in the garage or basement, do not let them stand on a concrete floor; set them on strips of wood, a mat or a large stack of newspaper. Keeping them away from direct moisture is of paramount importance. Tires should not be stored upright, but in a flat position.

INSPECTION

▶ See Figures 109 thru 116

The importance of proper tire inflation cannot be overemphasized. A tire employs air as part of its structure. It is designed around the supporting strength of the air at a specified pressure. For this reason, improper inflation drastically reduces the tire's ability to perform as intended. A tire will lose some air in day-to-day use; having to add a few pounds of air periodically is not necessarily a sign of a leaking tire.

Two items should be a permanent fixture in every glove compartment: an accurate tire pressure gauge and a tread depth gauge. Check the tire pressure (including the spare) regularly with a pocket type gauge. Too often, the gauge on the end of the air hose at your corner garage is not accurate because it suffers too much abuse. Always check tire pressure when the tires are cold, as pressure increases with temperature. If you must move the vehicle to check the tire inflation, do not drive more than a mile before checking. A cold tire is generally one that has not been driven for more than three hours.

A plate or sticker is normally provided somewhere in the vehicle (door post, hood or tailgate) which shows the proper pressure for the tires. Never counter-act excessive pressure build-up by bleeding off air pressure (letting some air out). This will cause the tire to run hotter and wear quicker.

Fig. 110 Tires with deep cuts, or cuts which show bulging should be replaced immediately

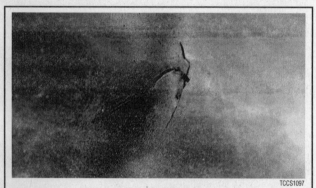

- DRIVE WHEEL HEAVY ACCELERATION
- OVERINFLATION

- HARD CORNERING
- UNDERINFLATION
- LACK OF ROTATION

Fig. 111 Examples of inflation-related tire wear patterns

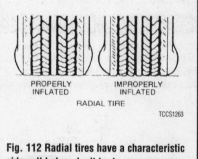

PROPERLY INFLATED   IMPROPERLY INFLATED

RADIAL TIRE

TCCS1263

Fig. 112 Radial tires have a characteristic sidewall bulge; don't try to measure pressure by looking at the tire. Use a quality air pressure gauge

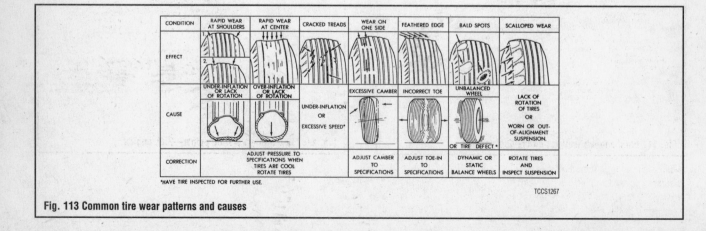

CONDITION	RAPID WEAR AT SHOULDERS	RAPID WEAR AT CENTER	CRACKED TREADS	WEAR ON ONE SIDE	FEATHERED EDGE	BALD SPOTS	SCALLOPED WEAR
EFFECT							
CAUSE	UNDER-INFLATION OR LACK OF ROTATION	OVER-INFLATION OR LACK OF ROTATION	UNDER-INFLATION OR EXCESSIVE SPEED*	EXCESSIVE CAMBER	INCORRECT TOE	UNBALANCED WHEEL OR TIRE DEFECT*	LACK OF ROTATION OF TIRES OR WORN OR OUT-OF-ALIGNMENT SUSPENSION.
CORRECTION		ADJUST PRESSURE TO SPECIFICATIONS WHEN TIRES ARE COOL ROTATE TIRES		ADJUST CAMBER TO SPECIFICATIONS	ADJUST TOE-IN TO SPECIFICATIONS	DYNAMIC OR STATIC BALANCE WHEELS	ROTATE TIRES AND INSPECT SUSPENSION

*HAVE TIRE INSPECTED FOR FURTHER USE.

TCCS1267

Fig. 113 Common tire wear patterns and causes

Fig. 114 Tread wear indicators will appear when the tire is worn

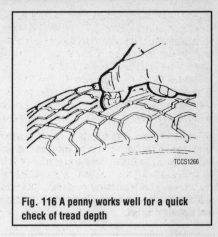

Fig. 115 Accurate tread depth indicators are inexpensive and handy

Fig. 116 A penny works well for a quick check of tread depth

✳✳ CAUTION

Never exceed the maximum tire pressure embossed on the tire! This is the pressure to be used when the tire is at maximum loading, but it is rarely the correct pressure for everyday driving. Consult the owner's manual or the tire pressure sticker for the correct tire pressure.

Once you've maintained the correct tire pressures for several weeks, you'll be familiar with the vehicle's braking and handling personality. Slight adjustments in tire pressures can fine-tune these characteristics, but never change the cold pressure specification by more than 2 psi. A slightly softer tire pressure will give a softer ride but also yield lower fuel mileage. A slightly harder tire will give crisper dry road handling but can cause skidding on wet surfaces.

Unless you're fully attuned to the vehicle, stick to the recommended inflation pressures.

All tires made since 1968 have built-in tread wear indicator bars that show up as ½ in. (13mm) wide smooth bands across the tire when 1/16 in. (1.5mm) of tread remains. The appearance of tread wear indicators means that the tires should be replaced. In fact, many states have laws prohibiting the use of tires with less than this amount of tread.

You can check your own tread depth with an inexpensive gauge or by using a Lincoln head penny. Slip the Lincoln penny (with Lincoln's head upside-down) into several tread grooves. If you can see the top of Lincoln's head in 2 adjacent grooves, the tire has less than 1/16 in. (1.5mm) tread left and should be replaced. You can measure snow tires in the same manner by using the "tails" side of the Lincoln penny. If you can see the top of the Lincoln memorial, it's time to replace the snow tire(s).

FLUIDS AND LUBRICANTS

▶ **See Figures 117, 118 and 119**

Fluid Disposal

Used fluids such as engine oil, transmission fluid, antifreeze and brake fluid are hazardous wastes and must be disposed of properly. Before draining any fluids, consult with your local authorities; in many areas waste oil, etc. is being accepted as a part of recycling programs. A number of service stations and auto parts stores are also accepting waste fluids for recycling.

Be sure of the recycling center's policies before draining any fluids, as many will not accept different fluids that have been mixed together.

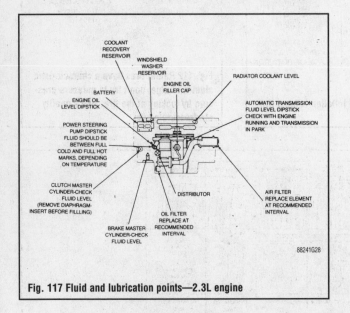

Fig. 117 Fluid and lubrication points—2.3L engine

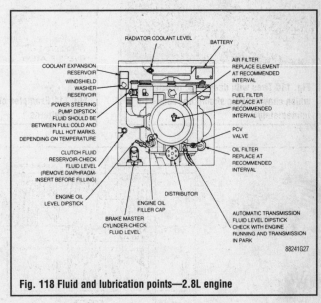

Fig. 118 Fluid and lubrication points—2.8L engine

CLUTCH MASTER CYLINDER RESERVOIR

BATTERY

WINDSHIELD WASHER FLUID RESERVOIR

BRAKE FLUID RESERVOIR

RADIATOR FILLER CAP

OIL LEVEL DIPSTICK

POWER STEERING RESERVOIR

TRANSMISSION FLUID LEVEL DIPSTICK

OIL FILL CAP

AIR CLEANER

88241P12

Fig. 119 Vehicle fluid check and fill locations

Fuel Recommendations

▶ See Figure 120

The Aerostar is equipped with a catalytic converter and must use unleaded fuel only. The use of leaded fuel or additives containing lead will result in damage to the catalytic converter, oxygen sensor and EGR valve. Both the 4 and 6 cylinder engines are designed to operate using gasoline with a minimum octane rating of 87. Use of gasoline with a rating lower than 87 can cause persistent, heavy spark knock which can lead to engine damage.

You may notice occasional, light spark knock when accelerating or driving up hills. This is normal and should not cause concern because the maximum fuel economy is obtained under conditions of occasional light spark knock. Gasoline with an octane rating higher than 87 may be used, but it is not necessary for proper operation.

Gasohol, a mixture of gasoline and ethanol (grain alcohol) is available in some areas. Your Aerostar should operate satisfactorily on gasohol blends containing no more than 10% ethanol by volume and having an octane rating of 87 or higher. In some cases, methanol (wood alcohol) or other alcohols may be added to gasoline. Again, your Aerostar should operate satisfactorily on blends containing up to 5% methanol by volume when co-solvents and other necessary additives are used. If not properly formulated with appropriate co-solvents and corrosion inhibitors, such blends may cause driveability problems or damage emission and fuel system materials. If you are uncertain as to the presence of alcohols in the gasoline you are purchasing, check the label on the pump or ask the attendant.

➡ Discontinue use of any gasohol or alcohol/gasoline blend if driveability or fuel system problems occur. Do not use such fuels unless they are unleaded.

Some models are equipped with a remote fuel filler door release, located between the driver seat and the door. If the filler door cannot be opened by pulling the release lever, there is a manual over-ride cord located on the left side of the jack stowage compartment. The manual release is a cord attached to a handle marked "Fuel Filler Door Manual Release."

Engine Oil Recommendations

▶ See Figure 121

To insure proper engine performance and durability, the proper quality engine oil is essential. Using the proper grade of oil for your engine will not only prolong its life, it will improve fuel economy. Ford recommends that you use Motorcraft® oil or an equivalent that meets Ford Specification ESE-M2C153-C and American Petroleum Institute (API) categories of at least SG, SG/CC or SG/CD.

Engine oils with improved fuel economy properties are currently available. They offer the potential for small improvements in fuel economy by reducing the amount of fuel burned by the engine to overcome friction. These improvements are often difficult to measure in everyday driving, but over the course of a year can offer significant savings. These oils are recommended to be used in conjunction with the recommended API Category.

A symbol has been developed by the API to help consumers select the proper grade of engine oil. It should be printed on top of the oil container to show oil performance by the API designation. This symbol should match the manufacturer recommendation. The center section will show the Society of Automotive Engineers (SAE) rating, while the top outer ring contains the API rating. The bottom outer ring will have the words "Energy Conserving" only if the oil has proven fuel saving capabilities.

SYNTHETIC OIL

There are excellent synthetic and fuel-efficient oils available that, under the right circumstances, can help provide better fuel mileage and better engine protection. However, these advantages come at a price, which can be three or four times the price per quart of conventional motor oils.

Before pouring any synthetic oils into your vehicle's engine, you should consider the condition of the engine and the type of driving you do. Also, check the truck's warranty conditions regarding the use of synthetics.

Generally, it is best to avoid the use of synthetic oil in both brand new and older, high mileage engines. New engines require a proper break-in, and the synthetics can prevent this. Most manufacturers recommend that you wait at least 5,000 miles (8,000 km) before switching to a synthetic oil. Conversely, older engines are looser and tend to use more oil. Some synthetics may not adhere properly and may slip past worn parts more readily than regular oil. If your vehicle already leaks and/or uses oil (due to worn parts and bad seals or gaskets), it may leak and use more with a slippery synthetic inside.

Consider your type of driving. If most of your accumulated mileage is on the highway at higher, steadier speeds, a synthetic oil will reduce friction and probably help deliver fuel mileage. Under such ideal highway conditions, the oil change interval can be extended, as long as the oil filter will operate effectively for the extended life of the oil. If the filter can't do its job for this extended period, dirt and sludge will build up in your engine's crankcase, sump, oil pump and lines, no matter what type of oil is used. If using synthetic oil in this manner, you should continue to change the oil filter at the recommended intervals.

Vehicles used under harder, stop-and-go, short hop circumstances should always be serviced more frequently, and for these vehicles, synthetic oil may not be a wise investment. Because of the necessary shorter change interval needed for this type of driving, you cannot take advantage of the long recommended change interval of most synthetic oils.

OIL LEVEL CHECK

▶ See Figures 122, 123, 124 and 125

It is normal to add some oil between oil changes. The engine oil level should be checked ideally at the same time you get gas and or at least every 500 miles (800 km).

1. Park the vehicle on a level surface and turn the engine OFF. Open the hood.
2. Wait a few minutes to allow the oil to drain back into the crankcase.
3. Pull the dipstick out and wipe it clean with a clean rag.
4. Reinsert the dipstick. Make sure it is pushed all the way down and seated on the tube, then remove the dipstick again and look at the oil level scale on the end of the dipstick. The oil level should fall within the safe range on the dipstick scale.
5. If necessary, add oil to the engine to bring the level up. Be careful not to overfill the crankcase and wipe the dipstick off before checking the oil level again.

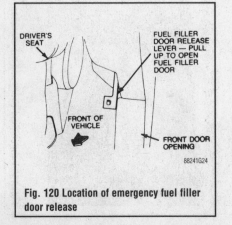

Fig. 120 Location of emergency fuel filler door release

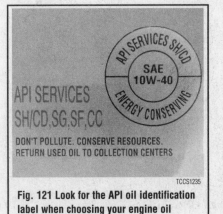

Fig. 121 Look for the API oil identification label when choosing your engine oil

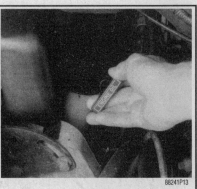

Fig. 122 Remove the oil dipstick from the driver's side of the engine

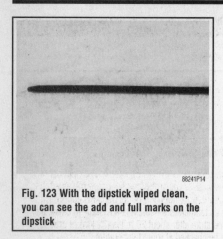

Fig. 123 With the dipstick wiped clean, you can see the add and full marks on the dipstick

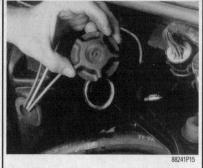

Fig. 124 If oil is needed, remove the oil tube cap at the center rear of the engine compartment

Fig. 125 Use a funnel inserted into the tube to add clean oil into the engine

OIL & FILTER CHANGE

▶ See Figures 126, 127, 128, 129 and 130

The engine oil and filter should be changed at the recommended intervals on the maintenance schedule chart or sooner. The oil filter protects the engine by removing harmful, abrasive or sludgy particles from the system without blocking the flow of oil to vital engine parts. It is recommended that the filter be changed along with the oil at the specified intervals.

➡Changing the oil requires the use of an oil filter wrench to remove the filter. It's also a good idea to have some Oil Dry® (or kitty litter) handy to absorb any oil that misses the drain pan.

1. Start the engine and allow it to reach normal operating temperature. Park the truck on a level surface and shut the engine **OFF**.
2. Set the parking brake firmly and block the rear wheels.
3. Raise the vehicle and support safely on jackstands.

4. Place a drip pan of at least five quart capacity beneath the oil pan.
5. Loosen the oil pan drain plug with a socket wrench, then finish threading it out by hand while pressing in slightly until it is free. Be careful, the oil will be hot.
6. Allow the oil to drain completely before installing the drain plug. Clean the drain plug threads and inspect the plug gasket. If the gasket is worn, replace it. Tighten the plug securely, but do not overtighten.
7. Position the drain pan under the oil filter, then use an oil filter removal wrench or equivalent to loosen the filter. Once the filter is loose, finish removing it by hand. Again, be careful, the oil and filter will be hot.
8. Clean the filter mounting base on the engine block and lightly coat the gasket of the new filter with a thin film of oil. Install the new filter by hand and tighten it another ½–¾ turn after the gasket contacts the filter base. Tighten the filter by hand, do not use the filter wrench.
9. Fill the crankcase with the recommended grade of oil and start the engine to check for leaks. It is normal for the oil warning light to remain on for a few

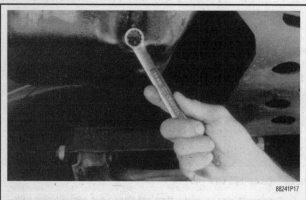

Fig. 126 Loosen the oil pan drain plug

Fig. 127 With a suitable drain pan underneath, remove the drain plug and allow the oil to drain out

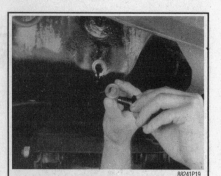

Fig. 128 Oil drain plug and washer. Replace the washer each time the oil is drained out

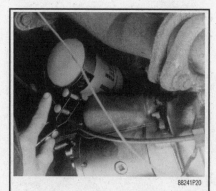

Fig. 129 Use a suitable filter removal tool to remove the filter from the engine

Fig. 130 Before installing a new oil filter, lightly coat the rubber gasket with clean oil

seconds after start-up until the oil filter fills up. Once the oil light goes out, check for leaks from the filter mounting and drain plug. If no leaks are noticed, stop the engine and check the oil level on the dipstick. Add additional oil, if necessary.

Manual Transmission

FLUID RECOMMENDATIONS

Use only Dexron® or Mercon® automatic transmission fluid.

FLUID LEVEL CHECK

▶ **See Figure 131**

To check the fluid level, the vehicle should be raised slightly to access the plug. Place jackstand under the jacking points at all four tires, then remove the filler plug on the side of the transmission case. Clean the plug and remove it. The fluid should be up to the bottom of the filler plug hole.

If additional fluid is required, add it through the filler plug hole to bring the level up. Use only Dexron® or Mercon® automatic transmission fluid. Install the filler plug when the fluid level is correct, making sure it is fully seated.

DRAIN & REFILL

▶ **See Figure 131**

The fluid can be drained from the manual transmission simply by removing the drain plug on the side of the transmission case. Use a suitable container to catch the old fluid, then install the plug and remove the filler plug on the side of the transmission to add new fluid. Add fluid until the level is at the base of the filler plug hole.

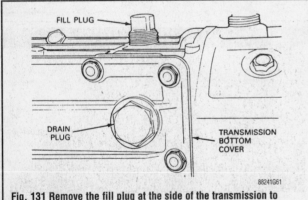

Fig. 131 Remove the fill plug at the side of the transmission to check the fluid level or the drain plug at the bottom of the transmission to empty fluid

Automatic Transmission

FLUID RECOMMENDATIONS

Fill the automatic transmission with Ford Motocraft Mercon® or Dexron®II fluid except on 1997 models. On 1997 models, use Mercon V® fluid.

LEVEL CHECK

▶ **See Figures 132, 133 and 134**

Correct automatic transmission fluid level is important for proper operation of the vehicle. Low fluid level causes transmission slippage, while overfilling can cause foaming, loss of fluid or malfunction of the transmission. Since transmission fluid expands as temperature rises, it is advisable to check the fluid level at operating temperature after about 20 miles (32 km) of driving, however, the fluid level can be checked at room temperature.

To check the fluid level, park the vehicle on a level surface and apply the parking brake. Start the engine and hold the foot brake while moving the transmission shift lever through all the gear positions, allowing sufficient time for each gear to engage. Return the shifter to the PARK position and leave the engine running.

Secure all loose clothing and remove any jewelry, then open the hood. While protecting yourself against engine heat, wipe the dipstick cap clean, then remove the dipstick. Wipe the dipstick clean then reinsert it into the tube, making sure it is fully seated. Remove the dipstick again and read the fluid level on the dipstick scale. At normal operating temperature, the level on the dipstick should be within the crosshatched area or between the arrows. At room temperature, the level should be between the middle and top hole on the dipstick.

➡ **If the vehicle was operated a long period of time at high speeds, in city traffic or hot weather, or was used to pull a trailer, to obtain an accurate reading, allow the vehicle to cool for approximately 30 minutes before checking the fluid level.**

If fluid has to be added, use a small necked funnel to add the necessary amount of Dexron® or Mercon® type fluid through the dipstick tube to bring the level up to normal. Do not bring the level above the crosshatched area on the dipstick. If overfilled, the excess transmission fluid must be removed. Once the fluid level is correct, reinsert the dipstick and make sure it is fully seated.

✳✳ WARNING

Do not operate the vehicle if the fluid level is at the "DO NOT DRIVE" mark on the dipstick. Serious damage to the transmission could result.

PAN & FILTER SCREEN SERVICE

▶ **See Figures 135 thru 141**

1. Park the vehicle on a level surface and place a drip pan under the transmission to catch the fluid.

Fig. 132 Remove the transmission fluid dipstick from the center portion of the engine compartment

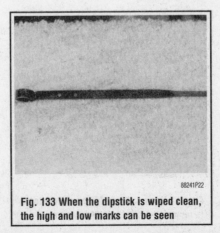

Fig. 133 When the dipstick is wiped clean, the high and low marks can be seen

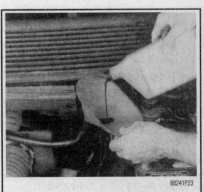

Fig. 134 Use a funnel attached to the dipstick tube to add transmission fluid

Fig. 135 Loosen and remove all the pan retainer bolts except for on one side

Fig. 136 Once the fluid has drained out, remove the remaining bolts and lower the pan down

Fig. 137 With the pan removed, the filter is clearly visible. Make sure the replacement filter is alike

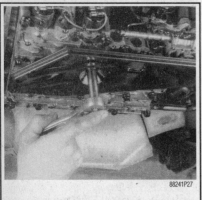

Fig. 138 Loosen the filter retainer bolt

Fig. 139 Lower the filter down. Be careful, some remaining fluid may spill out

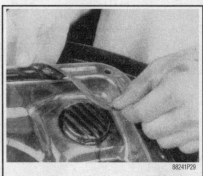

Fig. 140 With the pan on a clean surface. remove the gasket, and clean the gasket mating surface

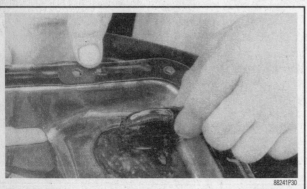

Fig. 141 Remove the magnet from the pan and clean any metal particles off it

2. Slowly loosen the pan attaching bolts. When all the bolts are loose, gradually remove all the bolts except for two at one end to allow the pan to tilt down and the fluid to drain out.

3. When the fluid has drained from the transmission oil pan, remove the remaining mounting bolts and lower the pan. Some fluid may still be in the pan, therefore lower it carefully and pour out any remaining fluid.

4. Thoroughly clean the pan and filter screen with suitable solvent and remove any old gasket material from the pan or transmission housing. Clean all gasket mating surfaces thoroughly, but be careful not to scratch any aluminum surfaces. Do not attempt to reuse an old pan gasket.

5. Place a new gasket on the pan, then install the pan on the transmission. Install the pan bolts and tighten them evenly in a crisscross pattern to 8–10 ft. lbs. (11–14 Nm). Do not overtighten the pan bolts.

6. Add three quarts of fluid to the transmission through the filler tube, then check the transmission fluid level as described earlier and add additional fluid, if necessary.

Transfer Case

FLUID LEVEL CHECK

♦ See Figure 142

The transfer case fluid level is checked at the filler plug hole at the side of the transfer case. Raise the vehicle level with jackstands. The case should be cold. Remove the filler plug. The fluid level should be filled just to the bottom of the hole.

The proper fluid is Mercon® or Dexron® automatic transmission fluid.

If additional fluid is required, add it through the filler plug hole to bring the level up. Install the filler plug when the fluid level is correct, making sure it is fully seated.

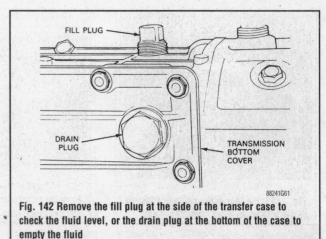

Fig. 142 Remove the fill plug at the side of the transfer case to check the fluid level, or the drain plug at the bottom of the case to empty the fluid

DRAIN & REFILL

▶ **See Figure 142**

The fluid can be drained from the transfer case by removing the drain plug on the side of the case. Use a suitable container to catch the old fluid, then replace the plug and remove the filler plug on the side of the transfer case to add new fluid. Add fluid until the level is at the base of the filler plug hole.

Front Drive Axle

The Dana 28 axle fluid level is checked at the filler plug hole. The fluid level should just reach the bottom of the hole with the axle cold.

The proper fluid is SAE 80W-90 gear oil.

Rear Drive Axle

FLUID RECOMMENDATIONS

The ability of any axle to deliver quiet, trouble free operation over a period of years is largely dependent upon the use of a good quality gear lubricant. Ford recommends the use of hypoid gear lubricant part number E0AZ-19580-A, E0AZ-19580-AA or any equivalent lubricant meeting Ford specification ESP-M2C154-A in their conventional or Traction-Lok® axles. Aerostar equipped with Dana axles should use hypoid gear lubricant part number C6AZ-19580-E or any equivalent lubricant meeting Ford specification ESW-M2C105-A.

Traction-Lok® limited slip rear axles also require approximately four ounces of friction modifier part number C8AZ-19B546-A or equivalent fluid meeting EST-M2C118-A specifications whenever the fluid is changed. This amount is added to the normal fluid capacity.

LEVEL CHECK

▶ **See Figures 143, 144 and 145**

To check the fluid level in the rear axle, remove the filler plug located on the side of the axle housing and make sure the axle fluid is within ¼ in. (6mm) below the bottom of the filler hole. If not, top up by adding lubricant through the filler hole. Do not overfill.

➡ **If any water is noted in the axle when checking the fluid level, the axle lubricant should be drained and replaced. Change the axle lubricant if the axle is submerged in water, especially if the water covers the vent hole.**

DRAIN & REFILL

▶ **See Figures 146 thru 151**

1. Drive the vehicle for 10–15 miles (16–24 km) at highway speeds to warm the axle lubricant to operating temperature to maximize the fluids' ability to flow.
2. Raise the vehicle and support it safely with jackstands. Place a drain pan under the axle.
3. From the rear of the vehicle, unfasten the brake line attached to the rear axle gear cover.
4. Use a wire brush and clean around the axle gear cover.
5. Loosen and remove all the cover plate retainer bolts EXCEPT two. These two you will loosen but not remove at this time.
6. With a suitable pan under the rear axle, pry the cover away from the gear and axle assembly to allow the fluid to drain.
7. Once most of the fluid has drained, remove the remaining bolts and lift the cover away.
8. Remove all gasket material from both mating surfaces.

Fig. 143 Use a suitable socket or wrench to loosen the rear axle fill plug

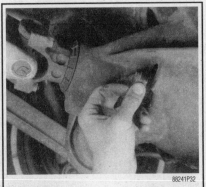
Fig. 144 Remove the fill plug and check the fluid level

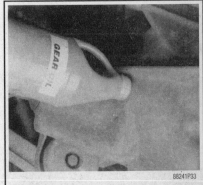
Fig. 145 Add fluid if needed. Make sure you add the correct grade fluid

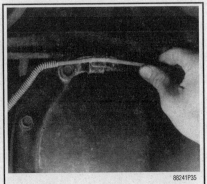
Fig. 146 If the rear brake cable is attached to the axle cover plate, unfasten it now

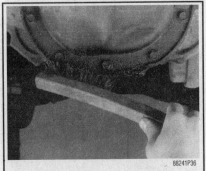
Fig. 147 Use a brush to remove debris from the cover plate (this will help keep dirt out of the case)

Fig. 148 Loosen and remove all (but 2) cover retaining bolts, then pry the cover away and drain the fluid

Fig. 149 Remove the remaining bolts. Do not loose the axle identification plate

Fig. 150 Remove all gasket material from the cover and axle housing

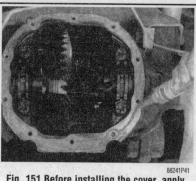

Fig. 151 Before installing the cover, apply a bead of sealant to the axle housing surface

To install:

9. Apply a ¼ in. (4mm) wide bead of silicone gasket sealant around the inside circumference of the axle housing.

10. Install the cover with the retainer bolts. Tighten the bolts in a crisscross pattern to 25–35 ft. lbs. (34–47 Nm).

11. Fill the axle housing with 3.5 pints of the specified hypoid gear lubricant (3.6 pints on Dana axles), then check the fluid level. On Traction-Lok® limited slip rear axles, in addition to the specified lubricant amount, add approximately four ounces of friction modifier part number C8AZ-19B546-A or equivalent fluid meeting EST-M2C118-A specifications. Top off if necessary, but do not overfill.

12. Install the filler plug and tighten it to 15–30 ft. lbs. (20–40 Nm).

Cooling System

▶ See Figure 152

FLUID RECOMMENDATIONS

At the factory, the cooling system is filled with a 45–55% mixture (50–50% for Canada, Seattle, Salt Lake City and Twin Cities) of Ford Cooling System Fluid part number E2FZ-19549-A and distilled water. The Aerostar is equipped with an aluminum radiator and the factory coolant has a special corrosion inhibiting formula to prevent damage to the radiator. If the Ford type coolant is not available, a good quality antifreeze meeting ESE-M97B44-A standards should be used. Do not use alcohol or methanol based antifreeze in any quantity or mixture. The use of the wrong coolant may result in radiator and engine damage. The 45–55 and 50–50 mixtures should be maintained at all times. A coolant mixture of less than 30% will result in corrosion of the engine block and overheating.

LEVEL CHECK

▶ See Figures 153, 154, 157 and 158

The coolant level is checked at either the radiator, if the vehicle is not equipped with a coolant recovery system, or at the coolant recovery tank, if equipped.

The coolant level should be checked in both the radiator and recovery reservoir at least once a month and then only when the engine is cool. Never, under any circumstances, attempt to check the coolant level in the radiator when the engine is hot or operating. On a full system, it is normal to have coolant in the expansion reservoir when the engine is hot.

Whenever coolant level checks of the radiator are made, check the condition of the radiator cap rubber seal. Make sure it is clean and free of any dirt particles. Rinse with water, if necessary, and make sure the radiator filler neck seat is clean. Check that the overflow hose is not kinked and is attached to the reservoir. If you have to add coolant more than once a month, or if you have to add more than one quart at a time, check the cooling system for leaks.

DRAIN & REFILLING

▶ See Figures 155 and 156

✷✷ CAUTION

Never attempt to check the radiator coolant level while the engine is hot. Use extreme care when removing the radiator cap. Wrap a thick towel around the cap and turn it slowly to the first stop. Step back while the pressure is released from the cooling system. When all pressure has vented, press down on the cap (still wrapped in the towel) and remove it. Failure to follow this procedure may result in serious personal injury from hot coolant or steam blowout and/or damage to the cooling system.

A standard ethylene glycol hydrometer is used to check the coolant concentration. It is available at all automotive parts stores and most supermarkets for about a buck. No tool box should be without one.

On systems with a coolant recovery tank, maintain the coolant level at the level marks on the recovery bottle. The coolant should be at the base of the filler neck in the radiator. The Aerostar uses an aluminum radiator and requires coolant with corrosion inhibitors to prevent radiator damage. Use only a perma-

Fig. 152 Read the coolant caution label before performing any service on the cooling system

Fig. 153 Carefully remove the radiator cap if checking the fluid level in the radiator

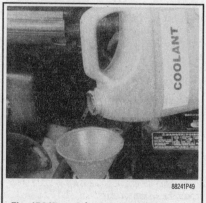

Fig. 154 Use a funnel to add coolant

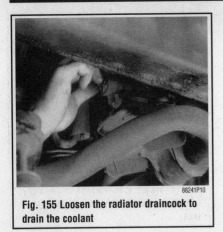

Fig. 155 Loosen the radiator draincock to drain the coolant

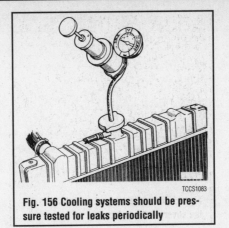

Fig. 156 Cooling systems should be pressure tested for leaks periodically

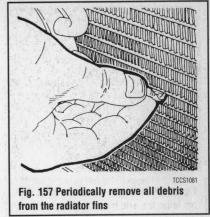

Fig. 157 Periodically remove all debris from the radiator fins

nent type coolant that meets Ford specification ESE-M97B44-A. Do not use alcohol or methanol antifreeze.

For best protection against freezing and overheating, maintain an approximate 45–55% water and 45–55% ethylene glycol antifreeze mixture in the cooling system. Do not mix different brands of antifreeze to avoid possible chemical damage to the cooling system. Avoid using water that is known to have a high alkaline content or is very hard, except in emergency situations. Drain and flush the cooling system as soon as possible after using such water.

➡️Never add cold water to an overheated engine while the engine is not running.

After filling the radiator, run the engine until it reaches normal operating temperature, to make sure that the thermostat has opened and all the air is bled from the system.

FLUSHING & CLEANING THE SYSTEM

▶ See Figure 157

✳✳ CAUTION

When draining the coolant, keep in mind that cats and dogs are attracted to ethylene glycol antifreeze, and could drink any that is left in an uncovered container or in puddles on the ground. This will prove fatal in sufficient quantity. Always drain the coolant into a sealable container. Coolant should be reused unless it is contaminated or several years old.

To drain the cooling system, allow the engine to cool down **BEFORE ATTEMPTING TO REMOVE THE RADIATOR CAP**. Then turn the cap slowly in case any pressure remains. If there is any remaining pressure, wait until all pressure is relieved before removing the cap completely. To avoid burns and scalding, always handle a warm radiator cap with a heavy rag.

1. At the dash, set the heater **TEMP** control lever to the fully **HOT** position.
2. With the radiator cap removed, drain the radiator by loosening the petcock at the bottom of the radiator. Flush the radiator with water until the fluid runs clear. Disconnect the lower radiator hose from the radiator and drain any remaining coolant from the engine block.
3. Close the petcock and reconnect the lower radiator hose, then refill the system with a 50/50 mix of ethylene glycol antifreeze and water. Fill the system to the bottom of the radiator filler neck, then reinstall the radiator cap after allowing several minutes for trapped air to bubble out. Back the radiator cap off to the first stop (pressure relief position).

➡️Fill the fluid reservoir tank up to the MAX COLD level.

4. Operate the engine at 2000 rpm for a few minutes with the heater control lever in the **MAX HEAT** position.
5. Turn the engine **OFF**, then wrap a rag around the radiator cap and remove it. Be careful, the coolant will be hot. Top off the radiator coolant level, if necessary, then reinstall the radiator cap to its down and locked position.
6. Start the engine and allow it to reach normal operating temperature, then check the system for leaks.

RADIATOR CAP INSPECTION

▶ See Figure 158

Allow the engine to cool sufficiently before attempting to remove the radiator cap. Use a rag to cover the cap, then remove by pressing down and turning counterclockwise to the first stop. If any hissing is noted (indicating the release of pressure), wait until the hissing stops completely, then press down again and turn counterclockwise until the cap can be removed.

✳✳ WARNING

DO NOT attempt to remove the radiator cap while the engine is hot. Severe personal injury from steam burns can result.

Check the condition of the radiator cap gasket and seal inside of the cap. The radiator cap is designed to seal the cooling system under normal operating conditions which allows the build up of a certain amount of pressure (this pressure rating is stamped or printed on the cap). The pressure in the system raises the boiling point of the coolant to help prevent overheating. If the radiator cap does not seal, the boiling point of the coolant is lowered and overheating will occur. If the cap must be replaced, purchase the new cap according to the pressure rating which is specified for your vehicle.

Prior to installing the radiator cap, inspect and clean the filler neck. If you are reusing the old cap, clean it thoroughly with clear water. After turning the cap on, make sure the arrows align with the overflow hose.

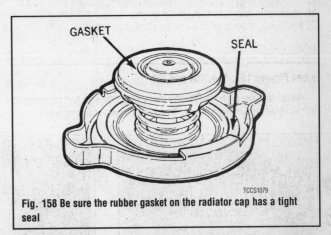

Fig. 158 Be sure the rubber gasket on the radiator cap has a tight seal

Clutch Master Cylinder

FLUID RECOMMENDATIONS

Fill the clutch fluid reservoir with brake fluid that meets DOT 3 or DOT 4 specifications.

LEVEL CHECK

▶ **See Figure 159**

The clutch system in the Aerostar does not have free-play. It is automatically self-adjusting and should not require any routine service throughout the life of the clutch. The fluid level in the clutch reservoir will slowly increase as the clutch wears. As long as the fluid is visible at or above the step in the translucent reservoir body, top-off is not recommended and should be avoided. This will help prevent overflow and possible contamination of the fluid while the diaphragm and cap are removed. If it becomes necessary to remove the reservoir cap, thoroughly clean the reservoir cap before removing it to prevent dirt or water from entering the reservoir.

Brake Master Cylinder

FLUID RECOMMENDATIONS

Fill the brake master cylinder with DOT 3 or DOT 4 brake fluid meeting Ford specification ESA-M6C25-A.

LEVEL CHECK

▶ **See Figures 160 and 161**

To check the brake fluid level, visually inspect the translucent master cylinder reservoir. The fluid level should be at the maximum level line of the reservoir. If the level is low, top it off using DOT 3 or DOT 4 brake fluid meeting Ford specification ESA-M6C25-A. It is normal for the brake fluid level to decrease as the brake linings wear. If the level is excessively low, inspect the brake linings for wear and/or the brake system for leaks.

Power Steering Pump

FLUID RECOMMENDATIONS

Fill the power steering pump reservoir with Motorcraft Type F automatic transmission, or power steering fluid that meets ESW-M2C33-F specifications.

LEVEL CHECK

▶ **See Figures 162, 163, 164 and 165**

Before attempting to check the fluid level, first clean all dirt from the outside of the power steering pump reservoir before removing the cap. Start the engine and allow it to reach normal operating temperature, then turn the steering wheel from lock-to-lock several times to bleed any air out of the system. Turn the engine **OFF** and check the fluid level on the power steering pump dipstick. The level should be within the FULL HOT scale on the dipstick. If necessary, top the reservoir up with fluid that meets Ford specification ESW-M2C33-F, such as Motorcraft Automatic Transmission or power steering fluid Type F. Do not overfill.

Chassis Greasing

The front ball joints should be lubricated at 30,000 mile (48,000 km) intervals. Locate the ball joint grease fittings, wipe them clean, then use a grease gun to lubricate the ball joints. Inspect the ball joints for any obvious wear or damage and replace parts as necessary. Although there are no lubrication requirements, all suspension bushings should be inspected at this time for wear or damage and replaced as required. If equipped with grease fittings, the universal joints should be greased at this time also. U-joints without grease fittings require no lubrication.

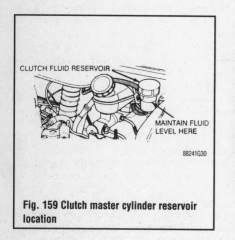

Fig. 159 Clutch master cylinder reservoir location

Fig. 160 Remove the filler cap from the brake reservoir. This fluid level is low

Fig. 161 Add brake fluid slowly. Do not spill any. Brake fluid will damage painted surfaces

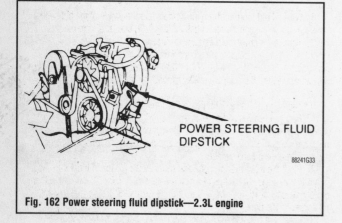

Fig. 162 Power steering fluid dipstick—2.3L engine

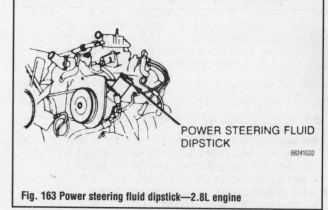

Fig. 163 Power steering fluid dipstick—2.8L engine

Fig. 164 Remove the dipstick and compare the fluid level mark on the hash marks

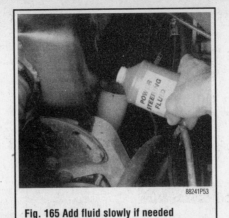

Fig. 165 Add fluid slowly if needed

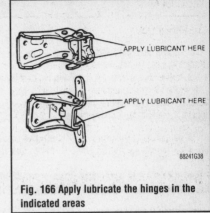

Fig. 166 Apply lubricate the hinges in the indicated areas

Body Lubrication

LOCK CYLINDERS

Apply graphite lubricant sparingly thought the key slot. Insert the key and operate the lock several times to be sure that the lubricant is worked into the lock cylinder.

LATCHES

Lubricate the hood, rear liftgate and door latches with polyethylene grease, then operate the mechanism several times to be sure the lubricant is worked into the latch assembly. A small brush is very helpful in getting the grease to those hard to reach places.

DOOR HINGES & HINGE CHECKS

▶ **See Figure 166**

Spray a silicone lubricant or apply white lithium grease on the hinge pivot points to eliminate any binding conditions. Open and close the door several times to be sure that the lubricant is evenly and thoroughly distributed.

REAR LIFTGATE

Spray a silicone lubricant or apply white lithium grease on all of the pivot and friction surfaces to eliminate any squeaks or binds. Work the tailgate to distribute the lubricant.

Front Wheel Bearings

REMOVAL, PACKING & INSTALLATION

The front wheel bearings on all models except All Wheel Drive (AWD) equipped models should be inspected and repacked with grease every 30, 000 miles (48,000 km). A good quality, high temperature wheel bearing grease should be used. The procedure involves removing the front brake rotors.

➡**AWD equipped models do not require regular front wheel bearing service.**

Before handling the bearings, there are a few things that you should remember to do and not to do.
Remember to DO the following:
• Remove all outside dirt from the housing before exposing the bearing.
• Treat a used bearing as gently as you would a new one.
• Work with clean tools in clean surroundings.
• Use clean, dry canvas gloves, or at least clean, dry hands.
• Clean solvents and flushing fluids are a must.
• Use clean paper when laying out the bearings to dry.
• Protect disassembled bearings from rust and dirt. Cover them up.

• Use clean rags to wipe bearings.
• Keep the bearings in oil-proof paper when they are to be stored or are not in use.
• Clean the inside of the housing before replacing the bearing.
Do NOT do the following:
• Don't work in dirty surroundings.
• Don't use dirty, chipped or damaged tools.
• Try not to work on wooden work benches or use wooden mallets.
• Don't handle bearings with dirty or moist hands.
• Do not use gasoline for cleaning; use a safe solvent.
• Do not spin-dry bearings with compressed air. They will be damaged.
• Do not spin dirty bearings.
• Avoid using cotton waste or dirty cloths to wipe bearings.
• Try not to scratch or nick bearing surfaces.
• Do not allow the bearing to come in contact with dirt or rust at any time.

2-Wheel Drive Models

1. Raise the vehicle until the tire clears the ground. Install a jackstand for safety, then remove the front tire(s).
2. Remove the brake caliper from the spindle as described in Section 9, then wire it to the underbody. Do not let the caliper hang by the brake hose.
3. Remove the grease cup from the hub. Remove the cotter pin, castellated retainer, adjusting nut and flat washer from the spindle. Remove the outer bearing cone and roller assembly.
4. Pull the hub and rotor assembly off the spindle.
5. Place the hub and rotor on a clean workbench, with the back side facing up, and remove the grease seal using a suitable seal remover or small prybar. Discard the grease seal.
6. Remove the inner bearing cone and roller assembly from the hub.
7. Clean the inner and outer bearing cups with solvent. Inspect the cups for scratches, pits, excessive wear and other damage. If the cups are worn or damaged, remove them with a bearing cup puller (T77F-1102-A or equivalent).
8. Wipe all old lubricant from the spindle and the inside of the hub with a clean rag. Cover the spindle and brush all loose dirt and dust from the dust shield. Remove the cover cloth carefully to prevent dirt from falling on it.
9. If the inner or outer bearing cups were removed, install replacement cups using a suitable driver tool (T80T-4000-W or equivalent) and bearing cup replacer. Make sure the cups are seated properly in the hub and not cocked in the bore.
10. Thoroughly clean all old grease from the surrounding surfaces.
11. Pack the bearing and cone assemblies with a suitable wheel bearing grease using a bearing packer tool. If a packer tool is not available, work as much grease as possible between the top and bottom of the roller cage assembly, then grease the cone surfaces.
12. Place the inner bearing cone and roller assembly in the inner cup. Apply a light film of grease to the lips of a new grease seal and install the seal with an appropriate seal driver tool. Make sure the grease seal is properly seated and not cocked in the bore.
13. Install the hub and rotor assembly on the spindle. Keep the hub centered on the spindle to prevent damage to the retainer and the spindle threads.

14. Install the outer bearing cone and roller assembly along with the flat-washer on the spindle, then install the adjusting nut finger tight.

15. Adjust the wheel bearing(s) as described in this section.

16. Install the caliper on the spindle as described in Section 9.

17. Install the front tire(s), then lower the vehicle and tighten the lug nuts to 85–115 ft. lbs. (115–155 Nm). Install the wheel cover.

18. Before moving the vehicle, pump the brake pedal several times to restore normal brake travel.

❊❊ CAUTION

After 500 miles of driving, re-tighten the wheel lug nuts to 85–115 ft. lbs. (115–155 Nm). If this is not done, the wheel may come off.

All Wheel Drive Models

The front hub and bearing is an integral assembly and is not serviceable or adjustable. See

ADJUSTMENT

→The front hubs and bearings on AWD equipped models are an integral assembly. No adjustment is possible.

2-Wheel Drive Models

1. Raise the vehicle and support safely on jackstands.

2. Remove the hub or wheel cover.

3. Remove the grease cap.

4. Wipe any excess grease from the end of the spindle. Remove the cotter pin and retainer. Discard the cotter pin.

5. Loosen the adjusting nut 3 turns. Obtain a running clearance between the rotor and brake surface by rocking the rotor assembly back and forth. If running clearance cannot be maintained, then remove the caliper and hand aside with wire. Never allow a caliper to hang free.

6. While rotating the rotor assembly, tighten the adjusting nut to 17–25 ft. lbs. (23–24 Nm) to seat the bearing.

7. Loosen the nut ½ turn. Retighten the nut to 18–20 ft. lbs. (23–26 Nm).

8. Place the retainer on the adjusting nut. The castellations on the retainer must be aligned with the cotter pin hole in the spindle. Do not turn the adjusting nut to make the castellation nut line up. Remove the retainer from the nut and re-index the retainer without moving the nut.

9. Install a new cotter pin, and bend the ends in opposite directions.

10. Check the front wheel rotation. If the wheels rotate freely, install the grease cap, then the hub or cover. If the wheel rotates with a noise or rough motion, then remove the bearing cones and cups. Inspect the components and lubricate and or replace.

11. Lower the vehicle, and pump the brake before driving.

TRAILER TOWING

General Recommendations

Your vehicle was primarily designed to carry passengers and cargo. It is important to remember that towing a trailer will place additional loads on your vehicles engine, drive train, steering, braking and other systems. However, if you decide to tow a trailer, using the prior equipment is a must.

Local laws may require specific equipment such as trailer brakes or fender mounted mirrors. Check your local laws.

Trailer Weight

The weight of the trailer is the most important factor. A good weight-to-horsepower ratio is about 35:1, 35 lbs. of Gross Combined Weight (GCW) for every horsepower your engine develops. Multiply the engine's rated horsepower by 35 and subtract the weight of the vehicle passengers and luggage. The number remaining is the approximate ideal maximum weight you should tow, although a numerically higher axle ratio can help compensate for heavier weight.

Hitch (Tongue) Weight

▸ **See Figure 167**

Calculate the hitch weight in order to select a proper hitch. The weight of the hitch is usually 9–11% of the trailer gross weight and should be measured with the trailer loaded. Hitches fall into various categories: those that mount on the frame and rear bumper, the bolt-on type, or the weld-on distribution type used for larger trailers. Axle mounted or clamp-on bumper hitches should never be used.

Check the gross weight rating of your trailer. Tongue weight is usually figured as 10% of gross trailer weight. Therefore, a trailer with a maximum gross weight of 2000 lbs. will have a maximum tongue weight of 200 lbs. Class I trailers fall into this category. Class II trailers are those with a gross weight rating of 2000–3000 lbs., while Class III trailers fall into the 3500–6000 lbs. category. Class IV trailers are those over 6000 lbs. and are for use with fifth wheel trucks, only.

When you've determined the hitch that you'll need, follow the manufacturer's installation instructions, exactly, especially when it comes to fastener torques. The hitch will subjected to a lot of stress and good hitches come with hardened bolts. Never substitute an inferior bolt for a hardened bolt.

Cooling

ENGINE

Aftermarket engine oil coolers are helpful for prolonging engine oil life and reducing overall engine temperatures. Both of these factors increase engine life. While not absolutely necessary in towing Class I and some Class II trailers, they are recommended for heavier Class II and all Class III towing. Engine oil cooler systems usually consist of an adapter, screwed on in place of the oil filter, a remote filter mounting and a multi-tube, finned heat exchanger, which is mounted in front of the radiator or air conditioning condenser.

Transmission

An automatic transmission is usually recommended for trailer towing. Modern automatics have proven reliable and, of course, easy to operate, in trailer towing. The increased load of a trailer, however, causes an increase in the temperature of the transmission fluid. Heat is the worst enemy of an automatic transmission. As the temperature of the fluid increases, the life of the fluid decreases.

It is essential, therefore, that you install an automatic transmission cooler and that you pay close attention to transmission fluid changes. The cooler, which consists of a multi-tube, finned heat exchanger, is usually installed in front of the radiator or air conditioning compressor, and hooked in-line with the transmission cooler tank inlet line. Follow the cooler manufacturer's installation instructions.

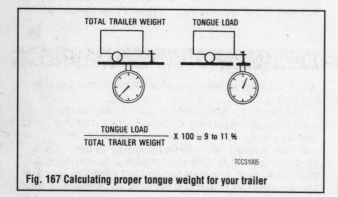

$$\frac{\text{TONGUE LOAD}}{\text{TOTAL TRAILER WEIGHT}} \times 100 = 9 \text{ to } 11 \text{ %}$$

TCCS1005

Fig. 167 Calculating proper tongue weight for your trailer

JUMP STARTING A DEAD BATTERY

▶ See Figure 168

Whenever a vehicle is jump started, precautions must be followed in order to prevent the possibility of personal injury. Remember that batteries contain a small amount of explosive hydrogen gas which is a by-product of battery charging. Sparks should always be avoided when working around batteries, especially when attaching jumper cables. To minimize the possibility of accidental sparks, follow the procedure carefully.

❊❊❊ CAUTION

NEVER hook the batteries up in a series circuit or the entire electrical system will go up in smoke, including the starter!

Vehicles equipped with a diesel engine may utilize two 12 volt batteries. If so, the batteries are connected in a parallel circuit (positive terminal to positive terminal, negative terminal to negative terminal). Hooking the batteries up in parallel circuit increases battery cranking power without increasing total battery voltage output. Output remains at 12 volts. On the other hand, hooking two 12 volt batteries up in a series circuit (positive terminal to negative terminal, positive terminal to negative terminal) increases total battery output to 24 volts (12 volts plus 12 volts).

Jump Starting Precautions

- Be sure that both batteries are of the same polarity (have the same terminal, in most cases NEGATIVE grounded).
- Be sure that the vehicles are not touching or a short could occur.
- On non-sealed batteries, be sure the vent cap holes are not obstructed.
- Do not smoke or allow sparks anywhere near the batteries.
- In cold weather, make sure the battery electrolyte is not frozen. This can occur more readily in a battery that has been in a state of discharge.
- Do not allow electrolyte to contact your skin or clothing.

Jump Starting Procedure

1. Make sure that the voltages of the 2 batteries are the same. Most batteries and charging systems are of the 12 volt variety.
2. Pull the jumping vehicle (with the good battery) into a position so the jumper cables can reach the dead battery and that vehicle's engine. Make sure that the vehicles do NOT touch.
3. Place the transmissions/transaxles of both vehicles in **Neutral** (MT) or **P** (AT), as applicable, then firmly set their parking brakes.

➡️**If necessary for safety reasons, the hazard lights on both vehicles may be operated throughout the entire procedure without significantly increasing the difficulty of jumping the dead battery.**

4. Turn all lights and accessories OFF on both vehicles. Make sure the ignition switches on both vehicles are turned to the **OFF** position.
5. Cover the battery cell caps with a rag, but do not cover the terminals.
6. Make sure the terminals on both batteries are clean and free of corrosion for good electrical contact.
7. Identify the positive (+) and negative (−) terminals on both batteries.
8. Connect the first jumper cable to the positive (+) terminal of the dead battery, then connect the other end of that cable to the positive (+) terminal of the booster (good) battery.

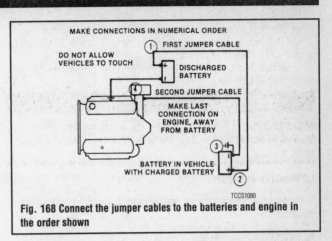

Fig. 168 Connect the jumper cables to the batteries and engine in the order shown

9. Connect one end of the other jumper cable to the negative (−) terminal on the booster battery and the final cable clamp to an engine bolt head, alternator bracket or other solid, metallic point on the engine with the dead battery. Try to pick a ground on the engine that is positioned away from the battery in order to minimize the possibility of the 2 clamps touching should one loosen during the procedure. DO NOT connect this clamp to the negative (−) terminal of the bad battery.

❊❊❊ CAUTION

Be very careful to keep the jumper cables away from moving parts (cooling fan, belts, etc.) on both engines.

10. Check to make sure that the cables are routed away from any moving parts, then start the donor vehicle's engine. Run the engine at moderate speed for several minutes to allow the dead battery a chance to receive some initial charge.
11. With the donor vehicle's engine still running slightly above idle, try to start the vehicle with the dead battery. Crank the engine for no more than 10 seconds at a time and let the starter cool for at least 20 seconds between tries. If the vehicle does not start in 3 tries, it is likely that something else is also wrong or that the battery needs additional time to charge.
12. Once the vehicle is started, allow it to run at idle for a few seconds to make sure that it is operating properly.
13. Turn ON the headlights, heater blower and, if equipped, the rear defroster of both vehicles in order to reduce the severity of voltage spikes and subsequent risk of damage to the vehicles' electrical systems when the cables are disconnected. This step is especially important to any vehicle equipped with computer control modules.
14. Carefully disconnect the cables in the reverse order of connection. Start with the negative cable that is attached to the engine ground, then the negative cable on the donor battery. Disconnect the positive cable from the donor battery and finally, disconnect the positive cable from the formerly dead battery. Be careful when disconnecting the cables from the positive terminals not to allow the alligator clips to touch any metal on either vehicle or a short and sparks will occur.

JACKING

▶ See Figures 169, 170, 171 and 172

Your vehicle was supplied with a jack for emergency road repairs. This jack is fine for changing a flat tire or other short term procedures not requiring you to go beneath the vehicle. If it is used in an emergency situation, carefully follow the instructions provided either with the jack or in your owner's manual. Do not attempt to use the jack on any portions of the vehicle other than specified by the vehicle manufacturer. Always block the diagonally opposite wheel when using a jack.

A more convenient way of jacking is the use of a garage or floor jack. When raising the front of the vehicle, place the jack under the front frame support, with blocks placed behind the rear wheels. When raising the rear of the vehicle,

place the jack below the center of rear differential with blocks in front of the front wheels.

Never place the jack under the radiator, engine or transmission components. Severe and expensive damage will result when the jack is raised. Additionally, never jack under the floorpan or bodywork; the metal will deform.

Whenever you plan to work under the vehicle, you must support it on jackstands or ramps. Never use cinder blocks or stacks of wood to support the vehicle, even if you're only going to be under it for a few minutes. Never crawl under the vehicle when it is supported only by the tire-changing jack or other floor jack.

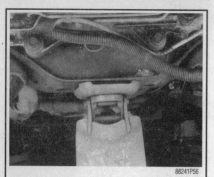

Fig. 169 To lift the front of the vehicle, place a jack under the front frame support, below the transmission

Fig. 170 When lifting the rear of the vehicle, place the jack below the center of the rear axle

Fig. 171 Place the jackstand under a portion of the frame, like this frame rail at the front of the vehicle . . .

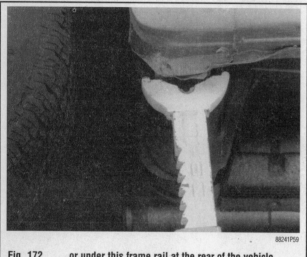

Fig. 172 . . . or under this frame rail at the rear of the vehicle

➡Always position a block of wood or small rubber pad on top of the jack or jackstand to protect the lifting point's finish when lifting or supporting the vehicle.

Small hydraulic, screw, or scissors jacks are satisfactory for raising the vehicle. Drive-on trestles or ramps are also a handy and safe way to both raise and support the vehicle. Be careful though, some ramps may be too steep to drive your vehicle onto without scraping the front bottom panels. Never support the vehicle on any suspension member (unless specifically instructed to do so by a repair manual) or by an underbody panel.

Jacking Precautions

The following safety points cannot be overemphasized:
• Always block the opposite wheel or wheels to keep the vehicle from rolling off the jack.
• When raising the front of the vehicle, firmly apply the parking brake.
• When the drive wheels are to remain on the ground, leave the vehicle in gear to help prevent it from rolling.
• Always use jackstands to support the vehicle when you are working underneath. Place the stands beneath the vehicle's jacking brackets. Before climbing underneath, rock the vehicle a bit to make sure it is firmly supported.

MANUFACTURER RECOMMENDED MAINTENANCE INTERVALS (1994-97)

TO BE SERVICED	TYPE OF SERVICE	5	10	15	20	25	30	35	40	45	50	55	60
Engine oil & filter	R	✓	✓	✓	✓	✓	✓	✓	✓	✓	✓	✓	✓
Rotate tires	S/I	✓	✓	✓	✓	✓	✓	✓	✓	✓	✓	✓	✓
Inspect exhaust system	S/I	✓	✓	✓	✓	✓	✓	✓	✓	✓	✓	✓	✓
Lube steering linkage, U-joints, slip yoke	S/I	✓	✓	✓	✓	✓	✓	✓	✓	✓	✓	✓	✓
Check clutch reservoir fluid	S/I	✓	✓	✓	✓	✓	✓	✓	✓	✓	✓	✓	✓
Lube automatic transmission shift linkage	S/I	✓	✓	✓	✓	✓	✓	✓	✓	✓	✓	✓	✓
Inspect cooling system	S/I			✓			✓			✓			✓
Inspect brakes	S/I			✓			✓			✓			✓
Parking brake for damage & operation	S/I			✓			✓			✓			✓
Brake lines, hoses & connections	S/I			✓			✓			✓			✓
Spark plugs	R						✓						✓
Air filter element	R						✓						✓
Engine coolant	R						✓						✓
Fuel filter	R						✓						✓
Lube throttle kick-down or TV lever ball studs	S/I			✓			✓			✓			✓
Lube front axle & RH axle shaft slip yoke (4WD)	S/I			✓			✓			✓			✓
Lube spindle needle & spindle thrust bearings (4WD)	S/I						✓						✓
Lube hub locks (4WD)	S/I						✓						✓
Lube front wheel bearings	S/I						✓						✓
Lube suspension	S/I						✓						✓
Lube transfer case	S/I						✓						✓
Lube caliper slide rails	S/I						✓						✓
Check manual transmission fluid level	S/I						✓						✓
Transfer case oil (4WD)	S/I						✓						✓
Accessory drive belts	R												✓
PCV valve	R												✓
Lube underbody grease fittings	S/I												✓

FREQUENT OPERATION MAINTENANCE (SEVERE SERVICE)
3000 mile intervals (or every 3 months) – change engine oil and filter
30,000 mile intervals – change automatic transmission fluid
Inspect more often than scheduled intervals – air cleaner & crankcase ventilation filters (in dusty conditions)
– brake pads, rotors, linings & drums (mountainous areas or continuous stop & go)

91321C06

MANUFACTURER RECOMMENDED MAINTENANCE INTERVALS (1986-93)

TO BE SERVICED	TYPE OF SERVICE	7.5	15	22.5	30	37.5	45	52.5	60
Engine oil & filter	R	✓	✓	✓	✓	✓	✓	✓	✓
Rotate tires	S/I	✓	✓	✓	✓	✓	✓	✓	✓
Check valve clearance (2.8L)	S/I	✓	✓				✓		✓
Disc & drum brakes, lubricate caliper slide rails	S/I						✓		✓
Parking brake system	S/I				✓				✓
Spark plugs (2.3L & 2.8L)	R				✓				✓
Spark plugs (all engines)	R				✓				✓
Air filter element	R				✓				✓
Crankcase emission filter	R				✓				✓
Engine coolant	R				✓				✓
Cooling system, hoses & clamps	S/I				✓				✓
Exhaust system	S/I				✓				✓
Exhaust heat shields	S/I				✓				✓
Clean choke linkage & carburetor components (2.8L)	S/I				✓				✓
Accessory drive belts	S/I				✓				✓
Throttle/kick-down cable ball stud	S/I				✓				✓
Suspension bushings, springs, arms, rear jounce bumpers & front suspension ball joints	S/I				✓				✓
Front suspension ball joints	S/I				✓				✓
Repack front wheel bearings	S/I				✓				✓
Clean injector tips (2.3L EFI)	S/I				✓				✓
Check manual transmission fluid level	S/I				✓				✓
Transfer case oil (E-4WD)	R				✓				✓
EGR valve assembly	R								✓
EGR vacuum solenoid & filter (2.3L & 2.8L)	R								✓
Ignition wires	R								✓
Camshaft timing belt	R								✓
Brake hoses	S/I				✓				✓
Ignition wires	R								✓
Oxygen sensor (2.3L & 2.8L)	R								✓
Camshaft timing belt (2.3L)	R								✓

R – Replace
S/I – Service or Inspect
NOTE: For complete warranty coverage, consult individual vehicle manufacturer's warranty maintenance guide.

91321C05

CAPACITIES

Year	Model	Engine ID/VIN	Engine Displacement Liters (cc)	Engine Oil with Filter (qts.)	Transmission		Transfer Case (pts.)	Drive Axle		Fuel Tank (gal.)	Cooling System	
					Man. ①	Auto. ②		Front (pts.)	Rear (pts.)		wo/AC (qts.)	w/AC (qts.)
1986	Aerostar	A	2.3 (2294)	5.0	3.0	9.7	-	-	5.0	17.0	7.0	7.0
		S	2.8 (2803)	5.0	3.0	9.7	-	-	5.0	17.0	8.0	8.0
		U	3.0 (2999)	5.0	3.0	9.7	-	-	5.0	17.0	9.0	9.0
1987	Aerostar	A	2.3 (2294)	5.0	3.0	9.7	-	-	5.0	17.0	7.0	7.0
		S	2.8 (2803)	5.0	3.0	9.7	-	-	5.0	17.0	8.0	8.0
		U	3.0 (2999)	5.0	3.0	9.7	-	-	5.0	17.0	9.0	9.0
1988	Aerostar	U	3.0 (2999)	5.0	3.0	9.7	-	-	5.0	17.0	9.0	9.0
1989	Aerostar	U	3.0 (2999)	5.0	5.6	9.7	-	-	5.5	21.0	9.0	11.8
1990	Aerostar	U	3.0 (2999)	5.0	5.6	9.7 ③	2.5	3.5	5.5	21.0	9.0	11.8
		X	4.0 (3949)	5.0	5.6	9.7 ③	2.5	3.5	5.5	21.0	7.8	8.5
1991	Aerostar	U	3.0 (2999)	5.0	5.6	9.7 ③	2.5	3.5	5.5	21.0	9.0	11.8
		X	4.0 (3949)	5.0	5.6	9.7 ③	2.5	3.5	5.5	21.0	7.8	8.5
1992	Aerostar	U	3.0 (2999)	5.0	5.6	9.7 ③	2.5	3.5	5.5	21.0	9.0	11.8
		X	4.0 (3949)	5.0	5.6	9.7 ②	2.5	3.5	5.5	21.0	7.8	8.5
1993	Aerostar	U	3.0 (2999)	4.5	5.6	9.7 ③	2.5	3.5	5.5	21.0	9.0	11.8
		X	4.0 (3949)	5.0	5.6	9.7 ③	2.5	3.5	5.5	21.0	7.8	12.6
1994	Aerostar	U	3.0 (2999)	4.5	5.6	9.7 ③	2.5	3.5	5.5	21.0	9.0	11.8
		X	4.0 (3949)	5.0	5.6	9.7 ③	2.5	3.5	5.5	21.0	7.8	12.6
1996	Aerostar	U	3.0 (2999)	4.5	5.6	9.7 ③	2.5	3.5	5.5	21.0	9.0	11.8
		X	4.0 (3949)	5.0	5.6	9.7 ③	2.5	3.5	5.5	21.0	7.8	12.6
1997	Aerostar	U	3.0 (2999)	4.5	5.6	9.7 ③	2.5	3.5	5.5	21.0	9.0	11.8
		X	4.0 (3949)	5.0	5.6	9.7 ③	2.5	3.5	5.5	21.0	7.8	12.6

Note: All capacities are approximate. Fill slowly and check fluid level often.

① All measurements given are in pints (pts.)
② All meaurements given are in quarts (qts.)
③ Measurement given is for 4x2 vehicles
for 4x4 vehicles, add 0.3 pts.

91321C07

ENGLISH TO METRIC CONVERSION: MASS (WEIGHT)

Current mass measurement is expressed in pounds and ounces (lbs. & ozs.). The metric unit of mass (or weight) is the kilogram (kg). Even although this table does not show conversion of masses (weights) larger than 15 lbs, it is easy to calculate larger units by following the data immediately below.

To convert ounces (oz.) to grams (g): multiply th number of ozs. by 28
To convert grams (g) to ounces (oz.): multiply the number of grams by .035

To convert pounds (lbs.) to kilograms (kg): multiply the number of lbs. by .45
To convert kilograms (kg) to pounds (lbs.): multiply the number of kilograms by 2.2

lbs	kg	lbs	kg	oz	kg	oz	kg
0.1	0.04	0.9	0.41	0.1	0.003	0.9	0.024
0.2	0.09	1	0.4	0.2	0.005	1	0.03
0.3	0.14	2	0.9	0.3	0.008	2	0.06
0.4	0.18	3	1.4	0.4	0.011	3	0.08
0.5	0.23	4	1.8	0.5	0.014	4	0.11
0.6	0.27	5	2.3	0.6	0.017	5	0.14
0.7	0.32	10	4.5	0.7	0.020	10	0.28
0.8	0.36	15	6.8	0.8	0.023	15	0.42

ENGLISH TO METRIC CONVERSION: TEMPERATURE

To convert Fahrenheit (°F) to Celsius (°C): take number of °F and subtract 32; multiply result by 5; divide result by 9
To convert Celsius (°C) to Fahrenheit (°F): take number of °C and multiply by 9; divide result by 5; add 32 to total

°F	°C	°C	°F	°F	°C	°C	°F	°F	°C	°C	°F
−40	−40	−38	−36.4	80	26.7	18	64.4	215	101.7	80	176
−35	−37.2	−36	−32.8	85	29.4	20	68	220	104.4	85	185
−30	−34.4	−34	−29.2	90	32.2	22	71.6	225	107.2	90	194
−25	−31.7	−32	−25.6	95	35.0	24	75.2	230	110.0	95	202
−20	−28.9	−30	−22	100	37.8	26	78.8	235	112.8	100	212
−15	−26.1	−28	−18.4	105	40.6	28	82.4	240	115.6	105	221
−10	−23.3	−26	−14.8	110	43.3	30	86	245	118.3	110	230
−5	−20.6	−24	−11.2	115	46.1	32	89.6	250	121.1	115	239
0	−17.8	−22	−7.6	120	48.9	34	93.2	255	123.9	120	248
1	−17.2	−20	−4	125	51.7	36	96.8	260	126.6	125	257
2	−16.7	−18	−0.4	130	54.4	38	100.4	265	129.4	130	266
3	−16.1	−16	3.2	135	57.2	40	104	270	132.2	135	275
4	−15.6	−14	6.8	140	60.0	42	107.6	275	135.0	140	284
5	−15.0	−12	10.4	145	62.8	44	112.2	280	137.8	145	293
10	−12.2	−10	14	150	65.6	46	114.8	285	140.6	150	302
15	−9.4	−8	17.6	155	68.3	48	118.4	290	143.3	155	311
20	−6.7	−6	21.2	160	71.1	50	122	295	146.1	160	320
25	−3.9	−4	24.8	165	73.9	52	125.6	300	148.9	165	329
30	−1.1	−2	28.4	170	76.7	54	129.2	305	151.7	170	338
35	1.7	0	32	175	79.4	56	132.8	310	154.4	175	347
40	4.4	2	35.6	180	82.2	58	136.4	315	157.2	180	356
45	7.2	4	39.2	185	85.0	60	140	320	160.0	185	365
50	10.0	6	42.8	190	87.8	62	143.6	325	162.8	190	374
55	12.8	8	46.4	195	90.6	64	147.2	330	165.6	195	383
60	15.6	10	50	200	93.3	66	150.8	335	168.3	200	392
65	18.3	12	53.6	205	96.1	68	154.4	340	171.1	205	401
70	21.1	14	57.2	210	98.9	70	158	345	173.9	210	410
75	23.9	16	60.8	212	100.0	75	167	350	176.7	215	414

TCCS1C01

ENGLISH TO METRIC CONVERSION: LENGTH

To convert inches (ins.) to millimeters (mm): multiply number of inches by 25.4

To convert millimeters (mm) to inches (ins.): multiply number of millimeters by .04

Inches		Decimals	Milli-meters	Inches to millimeters inches	mm	Inches		Decimals	Milli-meters	Inches to millimeters inches	mm
	1/64	0.051625	0.3969	0.0001	0.00254		33/64	0.515625	13.0969	0.6	15.24
1/32		0.03125	0.7937	0.0002	0.00508	17/32		0.53125	13.4937	0.7	17.78
	3/64	0.046875	1.1906	0.0003	0.00762		35/64	0.546875	13.8906	0.8	20.32
1/16		0.0625	1.5875	0.0004	0.01016	9/16		0.5625	14.2875	0.9	22.86
	5/64	0.078125	1.9844	0.0005	0.01270		37/64	0.578125	14.6844	1	25.4
3/32		0.09375	2.3812	0.0006	0.01524	19/32		0.59375	15.0812	2	50.8
	7/64	0.109375	2.7781	0.0007	0.01778		39/64	0.609375	15.4781	3	76.2
1/8		0.125	3.1750	0.0008	0.02032	5/8		0.625	15.8750	4	101.6
	9/64	0.140625	3.5719	0.0009	0.02286		41/64	0.640625	16.2719	5	127.0
5/32		0.15625	3.9687	0.001	0.0254	21/32		0.65625	16.6687	6	152.4
	11/64	0.171875	4.3656	0.002	0.0508		43/64	0.671875	17.0656	7	177.8
3/16		0.1875	4.7625	0.003	0.0762	11/16		0.6875	17.4625	8	203.2
	13/64	0.203125	5.1594	0.004	0.1016		45/64	0.703125	17.8594	9	228.6
7/32		0.21875	5.5562	0.005	0.1270	23/32		0.71875	18.2562	10	254.0
	15/64	0.234375	5.9531	0.006	0.1524		47/64	0.734375	18.6531	11	279.4
1/4		0.25	6.3500	0.007	0.1778	3/4		0.75	19.0500	12	304.8
	17/64	0.265625	6.7469	0.008	0.2032		49/64	0.765625	19.4469	13	330.2
9/32		0.28125	7.1437	0.009	0.2286	25/32		0.78125	19.8437	14	355.6
	19/64	0.296875	7.5406	0.01	0.254		51/64	0.796875	20.2406	15	381.0
5/16		0.3125	7.9375	0.02	0.508	13/16		0.8125	20.6375	16	406.4
	21/64	0.328125	8.3344	0.03	0.762		53/64	0.828125	21.0344	17	431.8
11/32		0.34375	8.7312	0.04	1.016	27/32		0.84375	21.4312	18	457.2
	23/64	0.359375	9.1281	0.05	1.270		55/64	0.859375	21.8281	19	482.6
3/8		0.375	9.5250	0.06	1.524	7/8		0.875	22.2250	20	508.0
	25/64	0.390625	9.9219	0.07	1.778		57/64	0.890625	22.6219	21	533.4
13/32		0.40625	10.3187	0.08	2.032	29/32		0.90625	23.0187	22	558.8
	27/64	0.421875	10.7156	0.09	2.286		59/64	0.921875	23.4156	23	584.2
7/16		0.4375	11.1125	0.1	2.54	15/16		0.9375	23.8125	24	609.6
	29/64	0.453125	11.5094	0.2	5.08		61/64	0.953125	24.2094	25	635.0
15/32		0.46875	11.9062	0.3	7.62	31/32		0.96875	24.6062	26	660.4
	31/64	0.484375	12.3031	0.4	10.16		63/64	0.984375	25.0031	27	690.6
1/2		0.5	12.7000	0.5	12.70						

ENGLISH TO METRIC CONVERSION: TORQUE

To convert foot-pounds (ft. lbs.) to Newton-meters: multiply the number of ft. lbs. by 1.3

To convert inch-pounds (in. lbs.) to Newton-meters: multiply the number of in. lbs. by .11

in lbs	N-m	in lbs	N-m	in lbs	N-m	in lbs	N-m	in lbs	N-m
0.1	0.01	1	0.11	10	1.13	19	2.15	28	3.16
0.2	0.02	2	0.23	11	1.24	20	2.26	29	3.28
0.3	0.03	3	0.34	12	1.36	21	2.37	30	3.39
0.4	0.04	4	0.45	13	1.47	22	2.49	31	3.50
0.5	0.06	5	0.56	14	1.58	23	2.60	32	3.62
0.6	0.07	6	0.68	15	1.70	24	2.71	33	3.73
0.7	0.08	7	0.78	16	1.81	25	2.82	34	3.84
0.8	0.09	8	0.90	17	1.92	26	2.94	35	3.95
0.9	0.10	9	1.02	18	2.03	27	3.05	36	4.0

ENGLISH TO METRIC CONVERSION: TORQUE

Torque is now expressed as either foot-pounds (ft./lbs.) or inch-pounds (in./lbs.). The metric measurement unit for torque is the Newton-meter (Nm). This unit—the Nm—will be used for all SI metric torque references, both the present ft./lbs. and in./lbs.

ft lbs	N-m	ft lbs	N-m	ft lbs	N-m	ft lbs	N-m
0.1	0.1	33	44.7	74	100.3	115	155.9
0.2	0.3	34	46.1	75	101.7	116	157.3
0.3	0.4	35	47.4	76	103.0	117	158.6
0.4	0.5	36	48.8	77	104.4	118	160.0
0.5	0.7	37	50.7	78	105.8	119	161.3
0.6	0.8	38	51.5	79	107.1	120	162.7
0.7	1.0	39	52.9	80	108.5	121	164.0
0.8	1.1	40	54.2	81	109.8	122	165.4
0.9	1.2	41	55.6	82	111.2	123	166.8
1	1.3	42	56.9	83	112.5	124	168.1
2	2.7	43	58.3	84	113.9	125	169.5
3	4.1	44	59.7	85	115.2	126	170.8
4	5.4	45	61.0	86	116.6	127	172.2
5	6.8	46	62.4	87	118.0	128	173.5
6	8.1	47	63.7	88	119.3	129	174.9
7	9.5	48	65.1	89	120.7	130	176.2
8	10.8	49	66.4	90	122.0	131	177.6
9	12.2	50	67.8	91	123.4	132	179.0
10	13.6	51	69.2	92	124.7	133	180.3
11	14.9	52	70.5	93	126.1	134	181.7
12	16.3	53	71.9	94	127.4	135	183.0
13	17.6	54	73.2	95	128.8	136	184.4
14	18.9	55	74.6	96	130.2	137	185.7
15	20.3	56	75.9	97	131.5	138	187.1
16	21.7	57	77.3	98	132.9	139	188.5
17	23.0	58	78.6	99	134.2	140	189.8
18	24.4	59	80.0	100	135.6	141	191.2
19	25.8	60	81.4	101	136.9	142	192.5
20	27.1	61	82.7	102	138.3	143	193.9
21	28.5	62	84.1	103	139.6	144	195.2
22	29.8	63	85.4	104	141.0	145	196.6
23	31.2	64	86.8	105	142.4	146	198.0
24	32.5	65	88.1	106	143.7	147	199.3
25	33.9	66	89.5	107	145.1	148	200.7
26	35.2	67	90.8	108	146.4	149	202.0
27	36.6	68	92.2	109	147.8	150	203.4
28	38.0	69	93.6	110	149.1	151	204.7
29	39.3	70	94.9	111	150.5	152	206.1
30	40.7	71	96.3	112	151.8	153	207.4
31	42.0	72	97.6	113	153.2	154	208.8
32	43.4	73	99.0	114	154.6	155	210.2

TCCS1C03

ENGLISH TO METRIC CONVERSION: FORCE

Force is presently measured in pounds (lbs.). This type of measurement is used to measure spring pressure, specifically how many pounds it takes to compress a spring. Our present force unit (the pound) will be replaced in SI metric measurements by the Newton (N). This term will eventually see use in specifications for electric motor brush spring pressures, valve spring pressures, etc.

To convert pounds (lbs.) to Newton (N): multiply the number of lbs. by 4.45

lbs	N	lbs	N	lbs	N	oz	N
0.01	0.04	21	93.4	59	262.4	1	0.3
0.02	0.09	22	97.9	60	266.9	2	0.6
0.03	0.13	23	102.3	61	271.3	3	0.8
0.04	0.18	24	106.8	62	275.8	4	1.1
0.05	0.22	25	111.2	63	280.2	5	1.4
0.06	0.27	26	115.6	64	284.6	6	1.7
0.07	0.31	27	120.1	65	289.1	7	2.0
0.08	0.36	28	124.6	66	293.6	8	2.2
0.09	0.40	29	129.0	67	298.0	9	2.5
0.1	0.4	30	133.4	68	302.5	10	2.8
0.2	0.9	31	137.9	69	306.9	11	3.1
0.3	1.3	32	142.3	70	311.4	12	3.3
0.4	1.8	33	146.8	71	315.8	13	3.6
0.5	2.2	34	151.2	72	320.3	14	3.9
0.6	2.7	35	155.7	73	324.7	15	4.2
0.7	3.1	36	160.1	74	329.2	16	4.4
0.8	3.6	37	164.6	75	333.6	17	4.7
0.9	4.0	38	169.0	76	338.1	18	5.0
1	4.4	39	173.5	77	342.5	19	5.3
2	8.9	40	177.9	78	347.0	20	5.6
3	13.4	41	182.4	79	351.4	21	5.8
4	17.8	42	186.8	80	355.9	22	6.1
5	22.2	43	191.3	81	360.3	23	6.4
6	26.7	44	195.7	82	364.8	24	6.7
7	31.1	45	200.2	83	369.2	25	7.0
8	35.6	46	204.6	84	373.6	26	7.2
9	40.0	47	209.1	85	378.1	27	7.5
10	44.5	48	213.5	86	382.6	28	7.8
11	48.9	49	218.0	87	387.0	29	8.1
12	53.4	50	224.4	88	391.4	30	8.3
13	57.8	51	226.9	89	395.9	31	8.6
14	62.3	52	231.3	90	400.3	32	8.9
15	66.7	53	235.8	91	404.8	33	9.2
16	71.2	54	240.2	92	409.2	34	9.4
17	75.6	55	244.6	93	413.7	35	9.7
18	80.1	56	249.1	94	418.1	36	10.0
19	84.5	57	253.6	95	422.6	37	10.3
20	89.0	58	258.0	96	427.0	38	10.6

TCCS1C04

2

ENGINE ELECTRICAL

ELECTRONIC DISTRIBUTOR IGNITION SYSTEM

➡For information on understanding electricity and troubleshooting electrical circuits, please refer to Section 6 of this manual.

General Description

▶ See Figures 1, 2 and 3

All 1986–95 2.3L, 2.8L and 3.0L engines used in the Aerostar utilize one electronic distributor ignition system, which is referred to by two different names: the Thick Film Integrated (TFI-IV) ignition system for 1986–92 models and the Distributor Ignition (DI) system for 1993–95 models. The different names are based entirely upon the years of manufacture. Therefore the ignition system from 1986–92 is known as the TFI-IV system, and the ignition system from 1993–96 is referred to as the DI system. Through-out this section, the ignition system will be referred to as the TFI-IV system.

➡The 1996–97 3.0L engine utilizes a distributorless ignition system like that of the 4.0L engine which is covered later in this section.

The ignition system utilizes a controlling computer (known as the EEC-IV computer for 1986–92 models or as the PCM for 1993–97 models), an ignition module (TFI-IV module or Ignition Control Module), a distributor and an ignition coil (E-Core Coil for 1986–92 models/ignition coil for the 1993–96 models).

There are two TFI-IV type sub-systems: Push Start and Computer Controlled Dwell (CCD). The first system features a push-start mode that will allow manual transmission vehicles to be push started. Do not attempt to push start automatic transmission vehicles. The second system, CCD, features EEC-IV controlled ignition coil charge times.

The operation of the universal distributor is accomplished through the Hall effect vane switch assembly, causing the ignition coil to be switched on and off by the EEC-IV and TFI-IV modules. The vane switch is an encapsulated package consisting of a Hall sensor on one side and a permanent magnet on the other side. A rotary vane cup, made of ferrous (magnetic) metal is used to trigger the Hall Effect switch.

When the window of the vane cup is between the magnet and Hall Effect device, a magnetic flux field is completed from the magnet through the Hall Effect device and back to the magnet. As the vane passes through this opening, the flux lines are shunted through the vane and back to the magnet. As the vane passes through this opening, the flux lines are shunted through the vane and back to the magnet. A voltage is produced while the vane passes through the opening. When the vane clears the opening, the window causes the signal to go to zero volts. The signal is then used by the EEC-IV system, along with the signal from the crankshaft position sensor, for crankshaft position sensing and the computation of the desired spark advance based on engine demand and calibration. The conditioned spark advance and voltage distribution is accomplished through a conventional rotor, cap and ignition wires.

➡The ignition timing is preset at the factory and computer controlled. No attempt should be made to alter the ignition timing from the factory specifications.

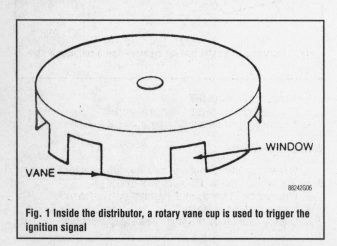

Fig. 1 Inside the distributor, a rotary vane cup is used to trigger the ignition signal

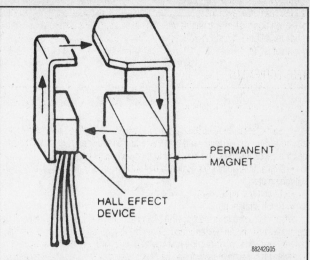

Fig. 2 As a ferrous metal disc rotates between the magnets and the Hall effect device, a voltage signal is created and sent to the EEC-IV

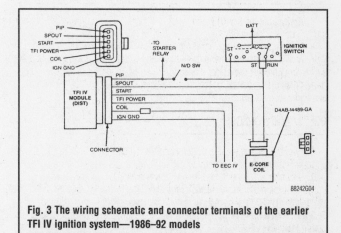

Fig. 3 The wiring schematic and connector terminals of the earlier TFI IV ignition system—1986–92 models

Diagnosis and Testing

▶ See Figures 4, 5, 6 and 7

Many times a quick test can locate the cause of a problem without going into full system checkout. Included are tests which may isolate the cause of the problem. The first step is to verify that a problem exists and then to make some preliminary tests to determine if the problem is in the ignition system, a related system or a completely unrelated system. The following procedures are intended to provide tests to identify and locate some of the more frequently encountered problems.

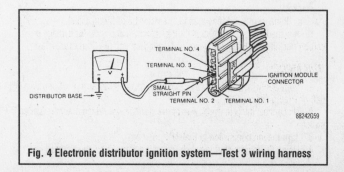

Fig. 4 Electronic distributor ignition system—Test 3 wiring harness

Intermittent faults are the hardest faults to identify simply because they alternately appear and disappear. Intermittent faults, which may be the result of corroded terminals, cracked or broken wires, voltage leakage and heat related failures, can drive even the most experienced technician crazy. Verify the mode of the ignition system and engine when the malfunction occurs and relate to this mode for failure indications. (examples = engine hot or cold, acceleration or deceleration, etc.).

TEST EQUIPMENT

The following test equipment, or equivalents, are necessary to diagnose the ignition system:
• Spark Tester D81P–6666–A, which resembles a spark plug with the side electrode removed. A spark plug with the side electrode removed **IS NOT** sufficient to check for spark and may lead to incorrect results.
• Digital Volt/Ohmmeter (Rotunda 014–00407, or any good digital volt/ohmmeter).
• 12 volt test light.
• Small straight pin.
When instructed to inspect a wiring harness, both a visual inspection and a continuity test should be performed. When making measurements on a wiring harness or connector, it is good practice to wiggle the wires while measuring. The following tests are designed to be performed in order to gradually narrow down the cause of a problem in the ignition system.

SERVICE PRECAUTIONS

• Always turn the key **OFF** and isolate both ends of a circuit whenever testing for shorts or continuity.
• Never measure voltage or resistance directly at the processor connector.
• Always disconnect solenoids and switches from the harness before measuring for continuity, resistance or energizing by way of a 12-volt source.
• When disconnecting connectors, inspect for damaged or pushed-out pins, corrosion, loose wires, etc. Service if required.

PRELIMINARY CHECKS

1. Visually inspect the engine compartment to ensure that all vacuum lines and spark plug wires are properly routed and securely connected.
2. Examine all wiring harnesses and connectors for insulation damage, burned, overheated, loose or broken conditions. Check the TFI module is securely fastened to the side of the distributor.
3. Be certain that the battery is fully charged and that all accessories are off during the diagnosis.

TFI–IV AND TFI–IV WITH CCD

Ignition Coil Secondary Voltage Test

CRANK MODE

1. Connect a spark tester between the ignition coil wire and a good engine ground.
2. Crank the engine and check for spark at the tester.
3. Turn the ignition switch **OFF.**
4. If no spark occurs, check the following:
    a. Inspect the ignition coil for damage or carbon tracking.
    b. Check that the distributor shaft is rotating when the engine is being cranked.
    c. If the results in Steps a and b are okay, go to Module Test.
5. If a spark did occur, check the distributor cap and rotor for damage or carbon tracking. Go to the Ignition Coil Secondary Voltage (Run Mode) Test

RUN MODE

1. Fully apply the parking brake. Place the gear shift lever in neutral (manual) or **P**(automatic).
2. Disconnect the S terminal wire at the starter relay. Attach a remote starter switch.
3. Turn the ignition switch to the **RUN** position.
4. Using the remote starter switch, crank the engine and check for spark.

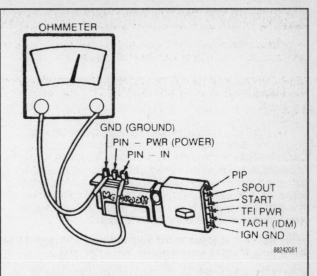

Fig. 5 Electronic distributor ignition system—Test 5 stator

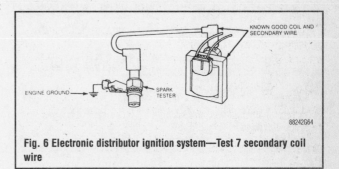

Fig. 6 Electronic distributor ignition system—Test 7 secondary coil wire

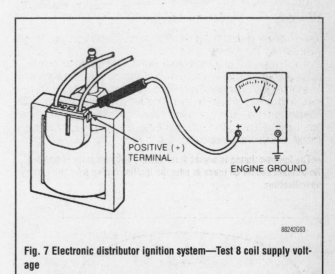

Fig. 7 Electronic distributor ignition system—Test 8 coil supply voltage

5. Turn the ignition switch **OFF.**
6. If no spark occurred, go to the Wiring Harness test.
7. If a spark did occur, the problem is not in the ignition system.

Wiring Harness Test

1. Push the connector tabs and separate the wiring harness connector from the ignition module. Check for dirt, corrosion or damage.
2. Check that the S terminal wire at the starter relay is disconnected.
3. Measure the battery voltage.
4. Carefully insert a small, straight pin in the appropriate terminal.

➡**Do not allow the straight pin to contact electrical ground while performing this test.**

5. Measure the voltage at the following points:

    a. TFI without CCD: Terminal No. 3 (Run circuit) with the ignition switch in **START** and **RUN**.

    b. TFI without CCD: Terminal No. 4 (Start circuit) with the ignition switch in **START**.

    c. TFI with CCD: Terminal No. 3 (Run circuit) with the ignition switch in **START** and **RUN**.

6. Turn the ignition switch **OFF** and remove the straight pin.

7. Reconnect the S terminal wire at the starter relay.

8. If the results are within 90% of battery voltage, replace the TFI module.

9. If the results are not within 90% of battery voltage, inspect the wiring harness and connectors in the faulty circuit. Also, check for a faulty ignition switch.

Module Test

1. Remove the distributor from the engine. Remove the TFI module from the distributor.

2. Measure the resistance between the TFI module terminals as shown below:

    a. GID terminal to PIP IN terminal—should be greater than 500 ohms.

    b. PIP PWR terminal to PIP IN terminal—should be less than 2,000 ohms.

    c. PIP PWR terminal to TFI PWR terminal—should be less than 200 ohms.

    d. GND terminal to IGN GND terminal—should be less than 2 ohms.

    e. PIP IN terminal to PIP terminal—should be less than 200 ohms.

Coil Wire and Coil Test

➡**The test should be performed only if the ignition system is producing no spark with its current ignition coil.**

1. Detach the ignition coil connector and check for dirt, corrosion or damage.

2. Substitute a known-good coil and check for spark using a spark tester.

➡**Dangerous high voltage may be present when performing this test. Do not hold the coil while performing this test.**

3. Crank the engine and check for spark.

4. Turn the ignition switch **OFF**.

5. If a spark did occur, measure the resistance of the ignition coil wire, replace it if the resistance is greater than 7000 ohms per foot (7000 ohms per 25.4cm). If the readings are within specification, replace the ignition coil.

6. If no spark occurs, the problem is not the coil. Go to the EEC-IV and TFI-IV system test.

EEC–IV and TFI–IV System Test

1. Disconnect the pin-in-line connector near the distributor.

2. Crank the engine

3. Turn the ignition switch **OFF**.

4. If a spark did occur during the coil wire and coil test, check the PIP and ignition ground wires for continuity. If okay, the problem is not in the ignition system.

5. If no spark occurred, check the voltage at the positive (+) terminal of the ignition coil with the ignition switch in **RUN**.

6. If the reading is not within current battery voltage, check for a worn or damaged ignition switch.

7. If the reading is within battery voltage, check for faults in the wiring between the coil and TFI module terminal No. 2 or any additional wiring or components connected to that circuit.

Spark Timing Advance Test

Spark timing advance is controlled by the EEC system. This procedure checks the capability of the ignition module to receive the spark timing command from the EEC module. The use of a volt/ohmmeter is required.

1. Turn the ignition switch **OFF**.

2. Disconnect the pin-in-line connector (SPOUT connector) near the TFI module.

3. Start the engine and measure the voltage, at idle, from the SPOUT connector to the distributor base. The reading should equal battery voltage.

4. If the result is okay, the problem lies within the EEC-IV system.

5. If the result was not satisfactory, separate the wiring harness connector from the ignition module. Check for damage, corrosion or dirt. Service as necessary.

6. Measure the resistance between terminal No. 5 and the pin-in-line connector. This test is done at the ignition module connector only. The reading should be less than 5 ohms.

7. If the reading is okay, replace the TFI module.

8. If the result was not satisfactory, service the wiring between the pin inline connector and the TFI connector.

Ignition Coil

TESTING

▶ **See Figure 8**

Ignition Coil Secondary Voltage Test

Connect the spark tester (D81P–6666–A or equivalent) between the ignition coil wire and engine ground, then crank the engine. If spark is present, the secondary voltage is sufficient. If there is no spark, measure the resistance of the ignition coil wire and replace the wire if the resistance is greater than 7,000 ohms per foot (30.4cm) of wire length. Inspect the ignition coil for damage or carbon tracking, then crank the engine with the distributor cap removed to verify distributor rotation. All Aerostar distributors rotate in the **CLOCKWISE** direction.

Ignition Coil Primary Circuit Switching Test

➡**This test applies only to 1986–88 models.**

Push the connector tabs to separate the wiring harness connector from the ignition module and check for dirt, corrosion or damage, then reconnect the harness. Do not remove the lubricant compound from inside the connector. Attach a 12 volt test light between the coil tach terminal and the engine ground, then crank the engine. If the light is on steadily or flashes, continue to the Ignition Coil Primary Resistance Test. If the light is off or on very dimly, go to the Primary Circuit Continuity Test.

Ignition Coil Primary Resistance Test

Turn the ignition switch off, then disconnect the ignition coil connector. Check for dirt, corrosion or damage. Use an ohmmeter to measure the resistance from the positive (+) to negative (-) terminals of the ignition coil. If the

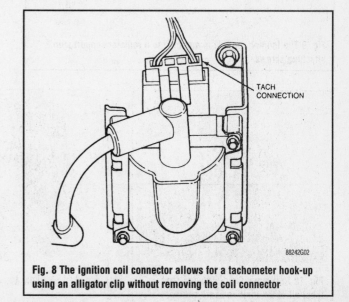

TACH CONNECTION

88242G02

Fig. 8 The ignition coil connector allows for a tachometer hook-up using an alligator clip without removing the coil connector

reading is between 0.3–1.0 ohm, the ignition coil is OK; continue on to the Ignition Coil Secondary Resistance Test. If the reading is less than 0.3 ohm or greater than 1.0 ohm, replace the ignition coil with a new one.

Ignition Coil Secondary Resistance Test

Use an ohmmeter to measure the resistance between the negative (-) terminal to the high voltage terminal of the ignition coil. If the reading is between 6,500–11,500 ohms, the ignition coil is OK; progress to the Wiring Harness Test. If the reading is less than 6,500 or more than 11,500 ohms, replace the ignition coil.

REMOVAL & INSTALLATION

1. Disconnect the negative battery cable.
2. Disconnect the two small and one large wires from the coil.
3. Detach the condenser connector from the coil, if equipped.
4. Unbolt and remove the coil.

To install:
5. Position the coil in place and install the retaining bolts.
6. Attach the condenser connector to the coil, if applicable.
7. Attach the 2 small wires and 1 large wire to the coil.
8. Connect the negative battery cable.

Ignition Module

REMOVAL & INSTALLATION

▶ **See Figure 9**

➥The Ignition Control Modules (ICM) are located on one of the radiator vertical supports.

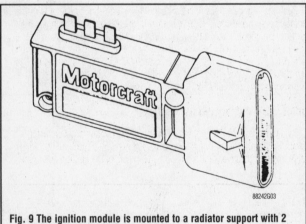

Fig. 9 The ignition module is mounted to a radiator support with 2 attaching screws

1. Disconnect the negative battery cable.
2. Remove the 2 retaining screws holding the ICM onto the radiator support.
3. Remove the harness connector from the ICM.
4. Remove the 2 retaining screws holding the ICM to the ICM heat sink, if applicable.

To install:
5. Coat the metal base of the ICM uniformly with silicone compound (Silicone Dielectric Compound WA-10 D7AZ-19A331-A ESE-M1C171-A or equivalent), approximately 1/32 in. (0.8mm) thick.
6. Position the ICM onto the heat sink, then install the 2 retaining screws to 15–35 inch lbs. (2–4 Nm).
7. Install the ICM/heat sink assembly onto the radiator support using the 2 mounting screws.
8. Attach the wiring harness connector to the ICM.
9. Connect the battery cable.

Distributor

REMOVAL & INSTALLATION

▶ **See Figures 10 thru 17**

➥Except for the cap, adapter, rotor, Hall effect stator, TFI module (if applicable) and O-ring, no other distributor assembly parts are replaceable. There is no calibration required with the universal distributor. The distributor assembly can be identified by the part number information printed on a decal attached to the side of the distributor base.

1. Disconnect the negative battery cable.
2. Set the No. 1 cylinder at TDC on the compression stroke with the timing marks aligned. To set the engine to TDC on No. 1 cylinder compression stroke, perform the following:

   a. Remove the rocker arm cover over the valves of cylinder No. 1.

   b. Rotate the crankshaft until the timing mark aligns with the TDC mark. While rotating the crankshaft watch the valves of cylinder No. 1. Since the crankshaft timing mark can align with the TDC mark on both the exhaust stroke and compression stroke, it is imperative that both the intake and exhaust valves are closed when cylinder No. 1 reaches TDC. If this is the case, cylinder No. 1 is at TDC on the compression stroke. If the exhaust valve is still not completely closed, or if the intake valve has opened some what, Cylinder No. 1 is on the exhaust stroke and must be rotated another 360°.

3. Disconnect the primary wiring connector from the distributor.
4. Mark the position of the No. 1 spark plug wire tower on the distributor base for future reference before removing the distributor cap.
5. Use a screwdriver to remove the distributor cap and adapter. Position the distributor cap and any attached ignition wires to the side.
6. Remove the rotor.
7. For vehicles with the TFI IV ignition system (1986–92 models), remove the TFI wiring connector, if applicable.
8. Remove the distributor hold-down bolt and clamp. Some engines may be equipped with a security type hold-down bolt, requiring a Torx® bit of the proper size to remove it.

Fig. 10 To remove the distributor, first label all of the ignition spark cables, . . .

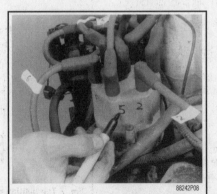

Fig. 11 . . . mark the distributor cap and . . .

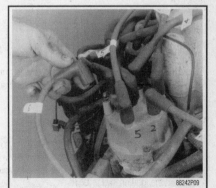

Fig. 12 . . . remove the spark plug ignition wires from the distributor cap

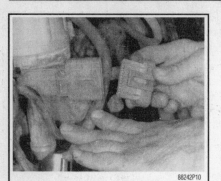

Fig. 13 Detach the ignition wiring harness connector from the distributor, then remove the distributor cap

Fig. 14 Without rotating or moving the distributor, remove the distributor hold-down bolt . . .

Fig. 15 . . . then matchmark the distributor housing to the engine block

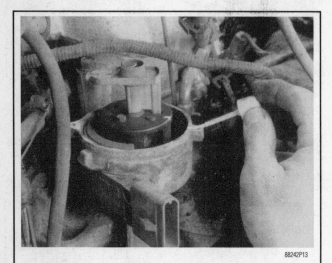

Fig. 16 Matchmark the distributor rotor to the distributor housing, then . . .

Fig. 17 . . . lift the distributor out of the engine block—3.0L engine shown, other engines similar

9. Remove the distributor by lifting it straight up.

To install:

10. If the engine was rotated while the distributor was removed, once again set the No. 1 cylinder at TDC on the compression stroke with the timing marks aligned for correct initial timing.

11. Rotate the distributor shaft so that the rotor tip is pointing toward the mark previously made on the distributor base (No. 1 spark plug tower). Continue rotating slightly so that the leading edge of the vane is centered in the vane switch stator assembly.

12. Rotate the distributor in the engine block to align the leading edge of the vane and the vane switch and verify that the rotor is pointing at No. 1 cap terminal.

➡️ If the vane and vane switch stator cannot be aligned by rotating the distributor in the engine block, pull the distributor out of the block enough to disengage the distributor and rotate the distributor to engage a different distributor gear tooth. Repeat Steps 9 and 10 if necessary.

13. Install the distributor hold-down bolt and clamp, but do not tighten yet.

14. Connect the distributor TFI and primary wiring harnesses.

15. Install the distributor rotor and tighten the attaching screws to 24–36 inch lbs. (3–4 Nm).

16. Install the distributor cap and tighten the attaching screws to 18–23 inch lbs. (2–3 Nm). Check that the ignition wires are securely attached to the cap towers.

17. Install the ignition wires to the spark plugs, making sure they are in the correct firing order and tight on the spark plugs.

18. Check and adjust the initial timing to specifications with a timing light. Refer to the tune-up chart or the underhood emission control sticker for initial timing specifications. The ignition timing procedure is outlined in Section 1. No attempt should be made to alter the timing from factory specifications.

19. Once the initial timing is set, tighten the distributor hold-down bolt to 17–25 ft. lbs. (23–34 Nm). Recheck the timing, then remove the timing light.

Crankshaft Position Sensor

For service procedures of the Crankshaft Position Sensor, please refer to Electronic Engine Controls in Section 4.

Camshaft Position Sensor

For service procedures concerning the Camshaft Position Sensor, please refer to Electronic Engine Controls in Section 4.

ELECTRONIC DISTRIBUTORLESS IGNITION SYSTEM

General Information

In the Distributorless Ignition System (DIS), known as Electronic Ignition (EI) on 1993–97 vehicles and used on all 4.0L and 1996–97 3.0L engines, all engine timing and spark distribution is handled electronically with no moving parts. This system has fewer parts, which require replacement, and provides a more accurately timed spark. The system does not change from 1990 to 1997 with only two exceptions. The first exception is that on all 1996–97 engines, the ignition system does not use a separate Ignition Control Module (ICM) to regulate the firing of the spark system. These engines use the Powertrain Control Module (PCM) to handle this task. The second exception is only in the names of the various components of the ignition system. The following components' names were changed with the 1993 model year:

• The EEC-IV Module became the Powertrain Control Module (PCM)
• The EDIS module became the Ignition Control Module (ICM)
• Variable Reluctance Sensor became the Crankshaft Position (CKP) Sensor
• The EEC system became the Electronic Ignition (EI) system

➟Through-out the EI system procedures, the newer names for the components will be used, unless there is a difference between the earlier (pre-1993) and later (1993 and newer) components.

The EI ignition system consists of a Crankshaft Position (CKP) sensor, an Ignition Control Module (only on 1990–95 models), a Powertrain Control Module (PCM) and one 6-tower coil pack.

The EI system operates by sending crankshaft position information from the CKP sensor to the ICM (PCM in 1996–97 models). The ICM generates a Profile Ignition Pick-up (PIP) signal and sends it to the PCM. The PCM responds with a Spark OUT (SPOUT) signal containing advance or retard timing information that is sent back to the ICM. The ICM processes the CKP and SPOUT signals and decides which coils to fire. In addition, the ICM generates an Ignition Diagnostic Monitor (IDM) signal to the PCM, which is used to indicate a failure mode and also provide a tachometer output signal.

IGNITION CONTROL MODULE (ICM)

The ICM is a microprocessor-based device with coil drivers which make decisions about spark timing and coil firing. The ICM turns the coils on and off at the correct time and in the proper sequence based on information from the CKP sensor and a pulse width modulated signal (SPOUT) generated from the PCM. The module receives CKP sensor and SPOUT signals and produces PIP and IDM output signals, which are sent to the PCM.

➟On the 1996–97 models, the PCM performs the ICM tasks.

POWERTRAIN CONTROL MODULE (PCM)

The PCM receives IGN, GND and PIP signals from the ICM, then generates a SPOUT signal based upon engine speed, load, temperature and other sensor information. An IDM signal is received from the ICM to determine if an ignition failure mode should be recorded.

COIL PACK

▶ See Figure 18

The coil is turned on (coil charging) by the ICM, then turned off, thus firing two spark plugs at once. One is for the cylinder which is to be fired (on compression stroke) and the other to the mating cylinder which is on the exhaust stroke. The next time the coil is fired the situation is reversed, The next pair of spark plugs will fire according to the engine firing order.

Diagnosis and Testing

▶ See Figures 19 thru 27

➟For the testing procedures, please refer to the applicable diagnostic flowcharts in this section.

PRELIMINARY INSPECTION

Before testing the ignition coil pack, perform this preliminary checkout:
1. Visually inspect the engine compartment to ensure that all vacuum hoses and spark plug wires are properly and securely connected.

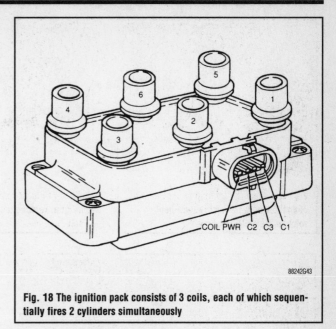

Fig. 18 The ignition pack consists of 3 coils, each of which sequentially fires 2 cylinders simultaneously

2. Examine all wiring harnesses and connectors for damaged, burned or overheated insulation, damaged pins and loose or broken conditions. Check the sensor shield connector.
3. Be certain the battery is fully charged.
4. All accessories should be off during the diagnosis.

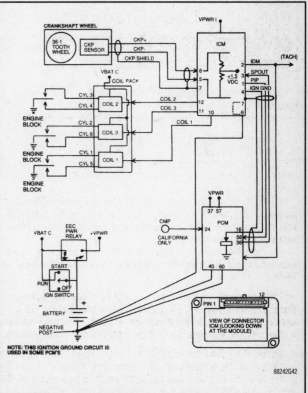

Fig. 19 Wiring schematic diagram of the EI system

Fig. 20 Electronic Ignition (EI) system No Start/Coil Failure test

	TEST STEP	RESULT	ACTION TO TAKE
D1	**CHECK FOR SPARK DURING CRANK** • Using a Neon Bulb Spark Tester (Special Service Tool D89P-6666-A) or Air Gap Spark Tester (D81P-6666-A), check for spark at all spark plug wires while cranking. • **Was spark consistent on all spark plug wires (one spark per crankshaft revolution)?**	Yes No	▲ Ignition System OK. REFER to Section 2A. ▲ GO to **D2**. Spark fault.
D2	**CHECK PLUGS AND WIRES** • Check spark plug wires for insulation damage, looseness, shorting or other damage. • Remove and check spark plugs for damage, wear, carbon deposits and proper plug gap. • **Are spark plugs and wires OK?**	Yes No	▲ REINSTALL plugs and wires. GO to **D3**. ▲ SERVICE or REPLACE damaged component. REMOVE all test equipment. RECONNECT all components. CLEAR Continuous Memory. RERUN Quick Test.
D3	**CHECK FOR COIL PWR AT COIL** **WARNING: NEVER CONNECT PCM TO THE EEC BREAKOUT BOX WHEN PERFORMING EI DIAGNOSTICS.** • Key off. • Install EI diagnostic harness to breakout box. • Connect negative lead to battery. • Set EI diagnostic harness type switch to 4/6 position. • Install the coil tee (The tee is blue with 4 pins). • Use EI (High Data Rate) 6 overlay. • DVOM on 40 volt DC scale. • Key on, engine off. • Measure voltage between (+)J5 (COIL PWR) and (-)J7 (B-) at breakout box. • **Is DC voltage greater than 10.0 volts?**	Yes No	▲ GO to **D4**. ▲ CHECK connectors, SERVICE or REPLACE harness. COIL PWR is open. REMOVE all test equipment. RECONNECT all components. CLEAR Continuous Memory. RERUN Quick Test.
D4	**CHECK FOR C1 HIGH AT COIL PACK—KOEO** • Key on, engine off. • Measure voltage between (+)J3 (C1C) and (-)J7 (B-) at breakout box. • **Is DC voltage reading greater than 10.0 volts?**	Yes No	▲ GO to **D5**. ▲ GO to **D16**. C1 low fault.
D5	**CHECK FOR C2 HIGH AT COIL PACK—KOEO** • Key on, engine off. • Measure voltage between (+)J6 (C2C) and (-)J7 (B-) at breakout box. • **Is DC voltage reading greater than 10.0 volts?**	Yes No	▲ GO to **D6**. ▲ GO to **D18**. C2 low fault.

88242G44

Fig. 20 Electronic Ignition (EI) system No Start/Coil Failure test

Fig. 21 (continued)

	TEST STEP	RESULT	ACTION TO TAKE
D6	**CHECK FOR C3 HIGH AT COIL PACK—KOEO** • Key on, engine off. • Measure voltage between (+)J10 (C3C) and (-)J7 (B-) at breakout box. • **Is DC voltage reading greater than 10.0 volts?**	Yes No	▲ GO to **D7**. ▲ GO to **D20**. C3 low fault.
D7	**CHECK FOR C1 HIGH AT ICM—KOEO** • Key off. • Connect ICM tee to ICM and vehicle harness connector. • DVOM on 40 volt DC scale. • Key on, engine off. • Measure voltage between (+)J53 (C1I) and (-)J7 (B-) at breakout box. • **Is DC voltage reading greater than 10.0 volts?**	Yes No	▲ GO to **D8**. ▲ CHECK connectors, SERVICE or REPLACE harness. C1 is open. REMOVE all test equipment. RECONNECT all components. CLEAR Continuous Memory. RERUN Quick Test.
D8	**CHECK FOR C2 HIGH AT ICM—KOEO** • Key on, engine off. • Measure voltage between (+)J55 (C2I) and (-)J7 (B-) at breakout box. • **Is DC voltage reading greater than 10.0 volts?**	Yes No	▲ GO to **D9**. ▲ CHECK connectors, SERVICE or REPLACE harness. C2 is open. REMOVE all test equipment. RECONNECT all components. CLEAR Continuous Memory. RERUN Quick Test.
D9	**CHECK FOR C3 HIGH AT ICM—KOEO** • Key on, engine off. • Measure voltage between (+)J54 (C3I) and -J7 (B-) at breakout box. • **Is DC voltage reading greater than 10.0 volts?**	Yes No	▲ GO to **D10**. ▲ CHECK connectors, SERVICE or REPLACE harness. C3 is open. REMOVE all test equipment. RECONNECT all components. CLEAR Continuous Memory. RERUN Quick Test.

88242G45

Fig. 21 Electronic Ignition (EI) system No Start/Coil Failure test—continued

	TEST STEP		RESULT	ACTION TO TAKE
D15	CHECK C3 AT COIL CONNECTOR WHILE CRANKING ENGINE—COIL DISCONNECTED—KOEC			
	• Connect test lamp between J1 (B+) and J10 (C3C). • Crank engine. • **Does lamp blink consistently and brightly (one blink per engine revolution)?**	▸	Yes	▸ REPLACE right coil pack. Input to coil pack is OK, but no high voltage output. REMOVE all test equipment. RECONNECT all components. CLEAR Continuous Memory. RERUN Quick Test.
			No	▸ REPLACE ICM. C3 open in ICM. REMOVE all test equipment. RECONNECT all components. CLEAR Continuous Memory. RERUN Quick Test.
D16	CHECK FOR C1 SHORT LOW—COIL DISCONNECTED—KEY OFF			
	• Key off. • DVOM on 20K ohm scale. • Disconnect coil from coil tee, leave EI diagnostic harness connected to vehicle harness coil connector. • Measure resistance between J7 (B-) and J3 (C1C) at breakout box. • **Is resistance reading greater than 2K ohms?**	▸	Yes	▸ REPLACE coil pack. C1 open in coil. REMOVE all test equipment. RECONNECT all components. CLEAR Continuous Memory. RERUN Quick Test.
			No	▸ GO to **D17**.

88242G47

Fig. 23 Electronic Ignition (EI) system No Start/Coil Failure test—continued

	TEST STEP		RESULT	ACTION TO TAKE
D10	CHECK FOR C1 LOW AT COIL CONNECTOR—COIL DISCONNECTED—KOEO			
	• Key off. • Disconnect the coil from the coil tee, leave EI diagnostic harness coil tee connected to vehicle harness coil connector. • DVOM on 40 volt DC scale. • Key on, engine off. • Measure voltage between (+)J3 (C1C) and (-)J7 (B-) at breakout box. • **Is DC voltage reading less than 0.5 volts?**	▸	Yes	▸ GO to **D11**.
			No	▸ GO to **D22**. C1 high fault.
D11	CHECK FOR C2 LOW AT COIL CONNECTOR—COIL DISCONNECTED—KOEO			
	• Key on, engine off. • Measure voltage between (+)J6 (C2C) and (-)J7 (B-) at breakout box. • **Is DC voltage reading less than 0.5 volts?**	▸	Yes	▸ GO to **D12**.
			No	▸ GO to **D23**. C2 high fault.
D12	CHECK FOR C3 LOW AT COIL CONNECTOR—COIL DISCONNECTED			
	• Key on, engine off. • Measure voltage between (+)J10 (C3C) and (-)J7 (B-) at breakout box. • **Is DC voltage reading less than 0.5 volts?**	▸	Yes	▸ GO to **D13**.
			No	▸ GO to **D24**. C3 high fault.
D13	CHECK C1 AT COIL CONNECTOR WHILE CRANKING ENGINE—COIL DISCONNECTED—KOEC			
	• Connect EI diagnostic harness positive lead to battery. • Connect incandescent test lamp between J1 (B+) and J3 (C1C). • Crank engine. • **Does lamp blink consistently and brightly (one blink per engine revolution)?**	▸	Yes	▸ GO to **D14**.
			No	▸ REPLACE ICM. C1 open in ICM. REMOVE all test equipment. RECONNECT all components. CLEAR Continuous Memory. RERUN Quick Test.
D14	CHECK C2 AT COIL CONNECTOR WHILE CRANKING ENGINE—COIL DISCONNECTED—KOEC			
	• Connect incandescent test lamp between J1 (B+) and J6 (C2C). • Crank engine. • **Does lamp blink consistently and brightly (one blink per engine revolution)?**	▸	Yes	▸ GO to **D15**.
			No	▸ REPLACE ICM. C3 open in ICM. REMOVE all test equipment. RECONNECT all components. CLEAR Continuous Memory. RERUN Quick Test.

88242G46

Fig. 22 Electronic Ignition (EI) system No Start/Coil Failure test—continued

TEST STEP	RESULT	ACTION TO TAKE
D19 CHECK FOR C2 LOW—ICM AND COIL DISCONNECTED—KEY OFF • Key off. • Disconnect ICM from vehicle harness connector. • DVOM on 20K ohm scale. • Measure resistance between J6 (C2C) and J7 (B-) at breakout box. • Is resistance reading greater than 10K ohms?	Yes	REPLACE ICM. C2 shorted low. REMOVE all test equipment. RECONNECT all components. CLEAR Continuous Memory. RERUN Quick Test.
	No	CHECK connectors. SERVICE or REPLACE harness. C2 is shorted low. REMOVE all test equipment. RECONNECT all components. CLEAR Continuous Memory. RERUN Quick Test. NOTE: A C2 short to ground may have damaged the coil.
D20 CHECK FOR C3 SHORT LOW—COIL DISCONNECTED—KEY OFF • Key off. • DVOM on 20K ohm scale. • Disconnect coil from coil tee, leave EI diagnostic harness connected to vehicle harness coil connector. • Measure resistance between J7 (B-) and J10 (C3C) at breakout box. • Is resistance reading greater than 2K ohms?	Yes	REPLACE coil pack. C3 open in coil. REMOVE all test equipment. RECONNECT all components. CLEAR Continuous Memory. RERUN Quick Test.
	No	GO to D21.

Fig. 25 Electronic Ignition (EI) system No Start/Coil Failure test—continued

TEST STEP	RESULT	ACTION TO TAKE
D17 CHECK FOR C1 SHORT LOW—ICM AND COIL DISCONNECTED—KEY OFF • Key off. • Disconnect ICM from vehicle harness connector. • DVOM on 20K ohm scale. • Measure resistance between J7 (B-) and J3 (C1C) at breakout box. • Is resistance reading greater than 10K ohms?	Yes	REPLACE ICM. C1 is shorted low. REMOVE all test equipment. RECONNECT all components. CLEAR Continuous Memory. RERUN Quick Test.
	No	CHECK connectors. SERVICE or REPLACE harness. C1 is shorted low. REMOVE all test equipment. RECONNECT all components. CLEAR Continuous Memory. RERUN Quick Test. NOTE: A C1 short to ground may have damaged the coil.
D18 CHECK FOR C2 SHORT LOW—COIL—KEY OFF • Key off. • DVOM on 20K ohm scale. • Disconnect coil from coil tee, leave EI diagnostic harness connected to vehicle harness coil connector. • Measure resistance between J7 (B-) and J6 (C2C) at breakout box. • Is resistance reading greater than 2K ohms?	Yes	REPLACE coil pack. C2 open in coil. REMOVE all test equipment. RECONNECT all components. CLEAR Continuous Memory. RERUN Quick Test.
	No	GO to D19.

Fig. 24 Electronic Ignition (EI) system No Start/Coil Failure test—continued

	TEST STEP	RESULT	ACTION TO TAKE
D23	CHECK FOR C2 LOW—ICM AND COIL DISCONNECTED		
	• Key off. • Disconnect ICM from the ICM tee, leave EI diagnostic harness connected to vehicle harness connector. • DVOM on 40 volt DC scale. • Key on, engine off. • Measure voltage between (+)J6 (C2C) and (-)J7 (B-) at breakout box. • Is DC voltage reading less than 0.5 volts?	Yes ▲	REPLACE ICM. C2 is shorted high. REMOVE all test equipment. RECONNECT all components. CLEAR Continuous Memory. RERUN Quick Test.
		No ▲	CHECK connectors, SERVICE or REPLACE harness. C2 is shorted high. REMOVE all test equipment. RECONNECT all components. CLEAR Continuous Memory. RERUN Quick Test.
D24	CHECK FOR C3 LOW—ICM AND COIL DISCONNECTED		
	• Key off. • Disconnect ICM from the ICM tee, leave EI diagnostic harness connected to vehicle harness connector. • DVOM on 40 volt DC scale. • Key on, engine off. • Measure voltage between (+)J10 (C3C) and (-)J7 (B-) at breakout box. • Is DC voltage reading less than 0.5 volts?	Yes ▲	REPLACE ICM. C3 is shorted high. REMOVE all test equipment. RECONNECT all components. CLEAR Continuous Memory. RERUN Quick Test.
		No ▲	CHECK connectors, SERVICE or REPLACE harness. C3 is shorted high. REMOVE all test equipment. RECONNECT all components. CLEAR Continuous Memory. RERUN Quick Test.

Fig. 27 Electronic Ignition (EI) system No Start/Coil Failure test—continued

	TEST STEP	RESULT	ACTION TO TAKE
D21	CHECK FOR C3 SHORT LOW—ICM AND COIL DISCONNECTED—KEY OFF		
	• Key off. • Disconnect ICM from vehicle harness connector. • DVOM on 20K ohm scale. • Measure resistance between J7 (B-) and J10 (C3C) at breakout box. • Is resistance greater than 10K ohms?	Yes ▲	REPLACE ICM. C3 is shorted low. REMOVE all test equipment. RECONNECT all components. CLEAR Continuous Memory. RERUN Quick Test.
		No ▲	CHECK connectors, SERVICE or REPLACE harness. C3 is shorted low. REMOVE all test equipment. RECONNECT all components. CLEAR Continuous Memory. RERUN Quick Test. NOTE: A C3 short to ground may have damaged the coil.
D22	CHECK FOR C1 LOW—ICM AND COIL DISCONNECTED—KOEO		
	• Key off. • Disconnect ICM from the ICM tee, leave EI diagnostic harness connected to vehicle harness connector. • DVOM on 40 volt DC scale. • Key on, engine off. • Measure voltage between (+)J3 (C1C) and (-)J7 (B-) at breakout box. • Is DC voltage reading less than 0.5 volts?	Yes ▲	REPLACE ICM. C1 is shorted high. REMOVE all test equipment. RECONNECT all components. CLEAR Continuous Memory. RERUN Quick Test.
		No ▲	CHECK connectors, SERVICE or REPLACE harness. C1 is shorted high. REMOVE all test equipment. RECONNECT all components. CLEAR Continuous Memory. RERUN Quick Test.

Fig. 26 Electronic Ignition (EI) system No Start/Coil Failure test—continued

Ignition Coil Pack

TESTING

♦ **See Figures 28 and 29**

➡ **For the testing procedures, please refer to the applicable diagnostic flowcharts in this section.**

Preliminary Inspection

Before testing the ignition coil pack, perform this preliminary checkout:

1. Visually inspect the engine compartment to ensure that all vacuum hoses and spark plug wires are properly and securely connected.

2. Examine all wiring harnesses and connectors for damaged, burned or overheated insulation, damaged pins and loose or broken conditions. Check the sensor shield connector.

3. Be certain the battery is fully charged.

4. All accessories should be off during the diagnosis.

Test Equipment

♦ **See Figure 30**

To correctly test the ignition coil pack an DIST EI-High Data Rate HOOKUP, or equivalent, is necessary. Install the tester as follows:

1. Turn the ignition key **OFF**. All accessories should be off during testing.

2. Select the proper Overlay and Program Cartridge to match the ignition system to be tested.

3. Install the overlay on the front panel of the tester.

TEST STEP		RESULT	▶	ACTION TO TAKE
A1	VBATC CHECK			
	• Key off. • Disconnect ignition coil pack(s). • Key on, engine off. • Measure the voltage from VBATC pin in the coil pack harness connector to IGN GND jack. • **Is the voltage between 10 and 14 volts?**	Yes No	▶ ▶	GO to A2. SERVICE VBATC line(s) to the pack(s).
A2	CHECK FOR SHORTS			
	• Key off. • Measure the resistance from COIL jacks to IGN GND jack. • Measure the resistance from COIL jacks to VPWR jack. • **Is each resistance less than 6K ohms?**	Yes No	▶ ▶	GO to A7. GO to A3.
A3	COIL LINE CONTINUITY			
	• Measure the resistance from each COIL JACK to its pin in the coil pack harness connector. • **Is each resistance less than 5 ohms?**	Yes No	▶ ▶	GO to A4. SERVICE coil signal line.
A4	COIL CHECK			
	• Reconnect coil pack(s). • Key on, engine off. • Press the tester reset button. • **Any COIL fault memory LEDs on?**	Yes No	▶ ▶	GO to A9. GO to A5.
A5	WIGGLE TEST			
	• Place WIGGLE TEST switch to ON. • Place MODE switch to B. • Press RESET button and wait 5 seconds for initialization. • Wiggle Test. • **Any fault memory LEDs on?** •	Yes No	▶ ▶	PRESS RESET button. CONTINUE to test until intermittent is isolated. GO to A6.
A6	WIGGLE TEST			
	• Key off. • Disconnect coil pack(s). • Key on, engine off. • Press RESET button and wait 5 seconds for initialization. • Wiggle Test. • **Any fault memory LEDs on?**	Yes No	▶ ▶	PRESS RESET button. CONTINUE to test until intermittent is isolated. REPLACE ICM.
A7	DISCONNECT ICM - RECHECK FOR SHORTS			
	• Disconnect ICM. • Measure the resistance from COIL jacks to IGN GND jack. • Measure the resistance from COIL jacks to VPWR jack. • **Is any resistance less than 10K ohms?**	Yes No	▶ ▶	SERVICE coil signal line(s). GO to A8.

88242G52

Fig. 28 Ignition coil pack test procedure—4.0L and 1996–97 3.0L engines

TEST STEP		RESULT	►	ACTION TO TAKE
A8	CHECK COIL LINES SHORTED TO EACH OTHER			
	• Measure the resistance from each COIL jack to all other COIL jacks. • Is any resistance less than 10K ohms?	Yes No	► ►	SERVICE coil signal line(s). REPLACE ICM.
A9	KEY OFF			
	• Check the ignition system connectors for corrosion. • Any corrosion found?	Yes No	► ►	SERVICE corroded connectors. REPLACE ignition coil pack(s).

88242G53

Fig. 29 Ignition coil pack test procedure (continued)—4.0L and 1996–97 3.0L engines

4. Insert the Program Cartridge into the cartridge slot (marked on the right hand side of the front panel). Make sure the module is fully inserted.

➡The DIST may be damaged or cause driveability problems if the Program Cartridge is not inserted or is improperly inserted.

5. Select and install the EI High Data Rate harness adapter to the DIST tester.

6. Verify that the tester switches, CKP SIMULATION and WIGGLE TEST, are in the OFF position.

7. Disconnect the vehicle wiring harnesses from the ICM.

a. Depress the tab on the connector clip to remove the ignition harness.

b. Inspect the connectors for dirt, corrosion, moisture, and bent or broken pins.

8. Hook the tester to the ICM.

a. Plug the male connector of the tester into the engine harness connector.

b. Plug the Female connector of the tester into the ICM.

9. Key On, Engine Off (KOEO). Press the RESET button on the tester. The tester will perform a Self-Test every time it is reset or powered up. During the Self-Test, all LEDs will light and a beep will be heard. If the tester fails to perform the Self-Test and VPWR LED is off, complete the following test sequence:

a. Turn the ignition key OFF.

b. Disconnect the tester from the vehicle.

c. Connect a jumper wire from the VPWR jack to the vehicle battery positive (+) terminal.

d. Connect a jumper wire from the PWR GND jack to the vehicle battery negative (-) terminal.

e. If the tester performs the Self-Test at this time, there is a malfunction of the VPWR circuit or a related component. Have the vehicle diagnosed by a professional automotive mechanic.@S1:f.   If the tester does not perform a Self-Test, the tester is defective.

REMOVAL & INSTALLATION

▶ See Figure 31

1. Disconnect the negative battery cable.
2. Disconnect the electrical harness connector from the ignition coil pack.
3. Remove the spark plug wires by squeezing the locking tabs to release the coil boot retainers.
4. Remove the coil pack mounting screws and remove the coil pack.

➡On vehicle equipped with power steering it may be necessary to remove the intake (left hand) coil and bracket as an assembly.

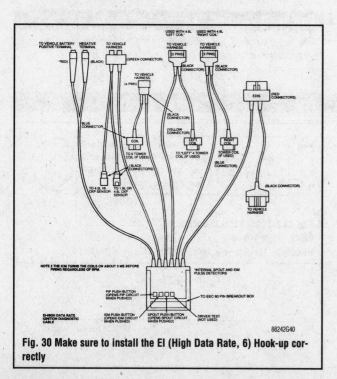

Fig. 30 Make sure to install the EI (High Data Rate, 6) Hook-up correctly

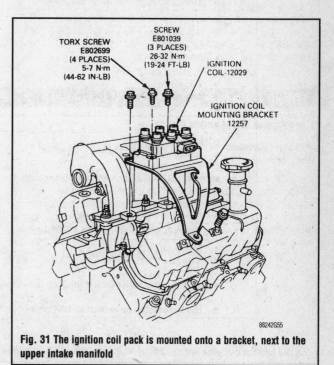

Fig. 31 The ignition coil pack is mounted onto a bracket, next to the upper intake manifold

To install:

5. Install the coil pack and the retaining screws. Tighten the retaining screws to 40–62 inch lbs. (5–7 Nm)

➡Be sure to place some dielectric compound into each spark plug boot prior to installation of the spark plug wire.

6. Attach the spark plug wires and electrical connector to the coil pack.
7. Reconnect the negative battery cable.

➡When the battery has been disconnected and reconnected, some abnormal drive symptoms may occur while the ignition control module relearns its adaptive strategy. The vehicle may need to be driven 10 miles (16 km) or more to relearn the strategy.

Ignition Control Module (ICM)

➡The ignition modules in earlier Aerostar models are known as EDIS modules.

REMOVAL & INSTALLATION

1990–92 Models

1. Disconnect the negative battery cable.
2. Disconnect each electrical connector of the EDIS ignition module assembly by pushing down the connector locking tabs where it is stamped **PUSH**, then pull it away from the module.
3. Remove the 3 retaining screws, then remove the ignition module assembly from the lower intake manifold.
   To install:
4. Apply an even coat (approximately 1/32 in./ 0.8mm) of a suitable silicone dielectric compound to the mounting surface of the EDIS module.
5. Mount the EDIS module assembly onto the intake assembly and install the retaining screws. Tighten the screws to 22–31 inch lbs. (2–3 Nm).
6. Install the electrical connectors to the EDIS ignition module assembly.
7. Reconnect the negative battery cable.

1993–95 Models

▶ See Figure 32

➡The Ignition Control Module (ICM) is located on the inner right-side fender.

1. Disconnect the negative battery cable.
2. Detach the electrical connector at the Ignition Control Module (ICM).
3. Remove the mounting bolt, then remove the ICM from the right-side fender. Slide the ICM toward the front of the vehicle to release the ICM from the teardrop hole in the fender sheet metal.

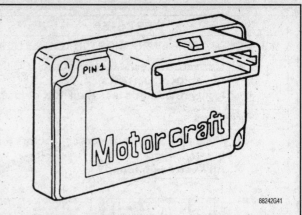

Fig. 32 The ignition control module fires the coils based on signals from the CKP sensor and the PCM

To install:

4. Insert the rivet of the ICM into the teardrop mounting hole in the fender sheet metal, then push the ICM into position.
5. Install the mounting bolt to 27–35 inch lbs. (3–4 Nm).
6. Attach the electrical connector to the ICM.

➡When the battery has been disconnected and reconnected, some abnormal drive symptoms may occur while the ignition control module relearns its adaptive strategy. The vehicle may need to be driven 10 miles (16 km) or more to relearn the strategy.

7. Connect the negative battery cable.

1996–97 Models

The 1996–97 models do not have an individual ignition module. The Powertrain Control Module (PCM) regulates the spark timing without the need of a separate module.

Crankshaft Position Sensor

For the testing or removal and installation procedures of the crankshaft timing sensor, please refer to Electronic Engine Controls in Section 4.

Camshaft Position Sensor

For the testing or removal and installation procedures of the camshaft timing sensor, please refer to Electronic Engine Controls in Section 4.

FIRING ORDERS

▶ See Figures 33, 34 and 35

➡To avoid confusion, remove and tag the spark plug wires one at a time, for replacement.

If a distributor is not keyed for installation with only one orientation, it could have been removed previously and rewired. The resultant wiring would hold the correct firing order, but could change the relative placement of the plug towers in relation to the engine. For this reason it is imperative that you label all wires before disconnecting any of them. Also, before removal, compare the current wiring with the accompanying illustrations. If the current wiring does not match, make notes in your book to reflect how your engine is wired.

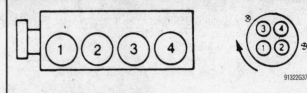

Fig. 33 2.3L (140 cid) I4 engine
Firing order: 1–3–4–2
Distributor rotation: clockwise

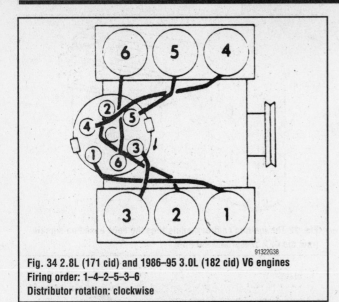

Fig. 34 2.8L (171 cid) and 1986–95 3.0L (182 cid) V6 engines
Firing order: 1–4–2–5–3–6
Distributor rotation: clockwise

Fig. 35 4.0L (244 cid) and 1996–97 3.0L (182 cid) V6 engines
Firing order: 1–4–2–5–3–6
Distributor rotation: distributorless

CHARGING SYSTEM

Alternator Precautions

To prevent damage to the alternator and regulator, the following precautionary measures must be taken when working with the electrical system.
• Never reverse battery connections. Always check the battery polarity visually. This should be done before any connections are made to be sure that all of the connections correspond to the battery ground polarity of the truck.
• Booster batteries for starting must be connected properly. Make sure that the positive cable of the booster battery is connected to the positive terminal of the battery that is getting the boost. The same applies to the negative cables.
• Disconnect the battery cables before using a fast charger; the charger has a tendency to force current through the diodes in the opposite direction for which they were designed. This burns out the diodes.
• Never use a fast charger as a booster for starting the vehicle.
• Never disconnect the voltage regulator while the engine is running.
• Do not ground the alternator output terminal.
• Do not operate the alternator on an open circuit with the field energized.
• Do not attempt to polarize an alternator.

Alternator

TESTING

Voltage Test

1. Make sure the engine is **OFF**, and turn the headlights on for 15–20 seconds to remove any surface charge from the battery.
2. Using a DVOM set to volts DC, probe across the battery terminals.
3. Measure the battery voltage.
4. Write down the voltage reading and proceed to the next test.

No-Load Test

1. Connect a tachometer to the engine.

✴ CAUTION

Ensure that the transmission is in PARK and the emergency brake is set. Blocking a wheel is optional and an added safety measure.

2. Turn off all electrical loads (radio, blower motor, wipers, etc.)
3. Start the engine and increase engine speed to approximately 1500 rpm.
4. Measure the voltage reading at the battery with the engine holding a

steady 1500 rpm. Voltage should have raised at least 0.5 volts, but no more than 2.5 volts.
5. If the voltage does not go up more than 0.5 volts, the alternator is not charging. If the voltage goes up more than 2.5 volts, the alternator is overcharging.

➥Usually under and overcharging is caused by a defective alternator, or its related parts (regulator), and replacement will fix the problem; however, faulty wiring and other problems can cause the charging system to malfunction. Further testing, which is not covered by this book, will reveal the exact component failure. Many automotive parts stores have alternator bench testers available for use by customers. An alternator bench test is the most definitive way to determine the condition of your alternator.

6. If the voltage is within specifications, proceed to the next test.

Load Test

1. With the engine running, turn on the blower motor and the high beams (or other electrical accessories to place a load on the charging system).
2. Increase and hold engine speed to 2000 rpm.
3. Measure the voltage reading at the battery.
4. The voltage should increase at least 0.5 volts from the voltage test. If the voltage does not meet specifications, the charging system is malfunctioning.

➥Usually under and overcharging is caused by a defective alternator, or its related parts (regulator), and replacement will fix the problem; however, faulty wiring and other problems can cause the charging system to malfunction. Further testing, which is not covered by this book, will reveal the exact component failure. Many automotive parts stores have alternator bench testers available for use by customers. An alternator bench test is the most definitive way to determine the condition of your alternator.

REMOVAL & INSTALLATION

External Fan Type

▶ See Figures 36, 37, 38 and 39

1. Disconnect the negative (-) battery cable.
2. Disconnect the wiring harness attachments to the voltage regulator assembly.
3. Remove the wiring connector bracket.
4. On 1986–90 models, loosen the alternator pivot bolt and remove the

Fig. 36 To remove the alternator, first remove the support brackets, then loosen the idler assembly

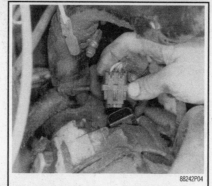

Fig. 37 Detach the right hand electrical connector, then . . .

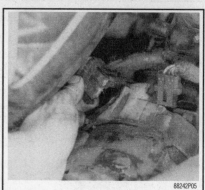

Fig. 38 . . . the left hand connector from the alternator housing

Fig. 39 Remove the alternator mounting bolts, then lift the alternator off of the engine

Fig. 40 The internal fan type alternator and voltage regulator terminal identification—newer 3.0L and 4.0L engines

adjustment arm bolt from the alternator. Disengage the alternator drive belt from the alternator pulley.

5. Remove the alternator pivot bolt and carefully lift the alternator/regulator assembly from the engine.

6. Remove the alternator fan shield from the old alternator, if equipped.

To install:

7. Position the new alternator/regulator assembly on the engine.

8. Install the alternator pivot and adjuster arm bolts, but do not tighten the bolts until the belt is tensioned.

9. Install the drive belt over the alternator pulley.

10. Adjust the belt tension, then tighten the adjuster and pivot bolts.

➡Apply pressure to alternator front housing only when adjusting belt tension

11. Connect the wiring harness to the alternator/regulator assembly. Push the two connectors straight in.

12. Attach the alternator fan shield to the alternator, if equipped.

13. Reconnect the ground cable to the battery.

Internal Fan Type

▶ See Figures 40, 41 and 42

1. Disconnect the negative battery cable.
2. Remove the snow/ice shield from the alternator.
3. Remove the engine air cleaner intake tube.
4. Disconnect the alternator wiring at the voltage regulator.
5. Remove the attaching nut and wire from the alternator.
6. Remove the wiring connector bracket.

7. Loosen the drive belt tensioner and remove the drive belt.

8. Remove the bolts holding the voltage regulator to the alternator bracket.

9. Remove the generator brace and bolt attaching the generator to the drive belt tensioner bracket.

To install:

10. Position the alternator onto the alternator mounting bracket.

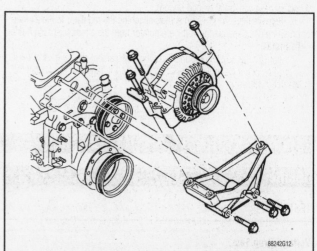

Fig. 41 Once the alternator is removed, the alternator bracket can be removed from the engine block—1992–97 3.0L engines equipped with the internal fan type alternator

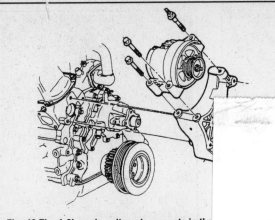

Fig. 42 The 4.0L engine alternator mounts in the [...]
the 3.0L engine—1993 models

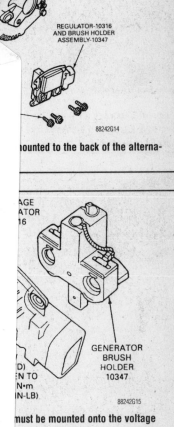

[...]ounted to the back of the alterna-

11. Install the attaching bolts and tighten them to 30[...]
12. Install the drive belt over the generator pulley.
13. Adjust the drive belt tensioner as outlined in Se[...]
14. Connect the wiring to the voltage regulator.
15. Tighten the attaching nut to 7–9 ft. lbs. (9–12 N[...]
16. Install the wiring terminal and attaching nut on [...]
minal.
17. Install the wiring connector bracket.
18. Install the engine air cleaner intake tube and the[...]

➡ **When the battery is disconnected and reconnec[...]
drive symptoms may occur while the Powertrain C[...]
relearns its adaptive strategy. The vehicle may ne[...]
miles (16 km) or more for the PCM to relearn the [...]**

19. Connect the negative battery cable.

Regulator

REMOVAL & INSTALLATION

◆ **See Figures 43 and 44**

The regulator is attached to the back of the alternat[...]
1. Disconnect the negative battery cable.
2. Detach the wiring connector.
3. Remove the regulator mounting screws.
4. Remove the regulator with the brush holder att[...]
5. Hold the voltage regulator in one hand and pr[...]
"A" screw head with a flat bladed prytool.
6. Remove the 2 Torx® (T20) screws attaching th[...]
tor brush holder. Separate the voltage regulator from t[...]
To install:
7. Transfer the brush components to the replacer[...]
   a. Position the alternator brush holder onto the[...]
attaching screws.
   b. Install the cap on the head of the "A" termin[...]
   c. Depress the alternator brushes into the alter[...]

[...]position by inserting a standard size
[...] both the location hole in the voltage
[...] the alternator brush holder.

[...]ors are clean and tight.
[...]e back of the alternator, then install the

[...]uivalent) from the voltage regulator, if

[...]nnector to the regulator.

[...]**ed and reconnected, some abnormal
[...] the Powertrain Control Module (PCM)
[...]he vehicle may need to be driven 10
[...]PCM to relearn the strategy.**

[...]attery cable.

STARTING SYSTEM

Starter

TESTING

Voltage Drop Test

➡ **The battery must be in good condition and fully charged prior to performing this test.**

[...]tion system by unplugging the coil pack. Verify that the
vehicle will not start.
2. Connect a voltmeter between the positive terminal of the battery and the
starter **B+** circuit.
3. Turn the ignition key to the **START** position and note the voltage on the
meter.
4. If voltage reads 0.5 volts or more, there is high resistance in the starter
cables or the cable ground, repair as necessary. If the voltage reading is ok,
proceed to the next step.

Fig. 45 Detach the wiring connectors from the starter motor, . . .

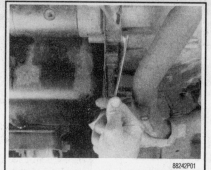

Fig. 46 . . . then, while supporting the starter motor, remove the starter mounting bolts

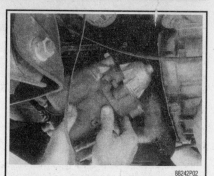

Fig. 47 Lower the starter motor out from under the engine—1991 3.0L engine shown, other engines similar

5. Connect a voltmeter between the positive terminal of the battery and the starter **M** circuit.

6. Turn the ignition key to the **START** position and note the voltage on the meter.

7. If voltage reads 0.5 volts or more, there is high resistance in the starter. Repair or replace the starter as necessary.

➡️**Many automotive parts stores have starter bench testers available for use by customers. A starter bench test is the most definitive way to determine the condition of your starter.**

REMOVAL & INSTALLATION

▶ **See Figures 45, 46 and 47**

1. Disconnect the negative battery cable.
2. Raise the vehicle and support it safely on jackstands.
3. Disconnect all cables and wires at the starter solenoid on the starter motor.
4. Remove the starter mounting bolts and lower the starter from the engine.
To install:
5. Position the new starter assembly to the engine block and start the mounting bolts in by hand.
6. Snug all bolts while holding the starter squarely against its mounting surface and fully inserted into the pilot hole. Tighten the mounting bolts to 15–20 ft. lbs. (21–27 Nm).
7. Reconnect the starter cables and wires to the starter motor. Tighten the screw and washer assemblies to 70–130 inch lbs. (8–15 Nm).
8. Lower the vehicle, then connect the negative battery cable.

➡️**When the battery is disconnected and reconnected, some abnormal drive symptoms may occur while the Powertrain Control Module (PCM) relearns its adaptive strategy. The vehicle may need to be driven 10 miles (16 km) or more for the PCM to relearn the strategy.**

RELAY REPLACEMENT

▶ **See Figure 48**

The starter relay is mounted to the inner fender, next to the battery, in the engine compartment.
1. Disconnect the negative battery cable.
2. Remove the starter relay terminal cover.
3. Remove the 2 starter relay terminal nuts.
4. Pull off the push-on wire assembly.

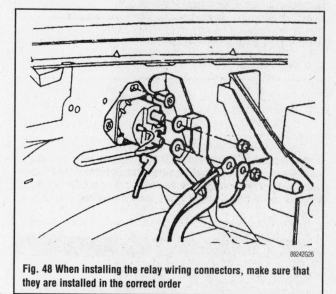

Fig. 48 When installing the relay wiring connectors, make sure that they are installed in the correct order

➡️**To aid installation, note the wire assembly orientation.**

5. Remove the wiring connectors from the starter relay terminals.
6. Remove the 2 starter relay-to-inner fender screws.
To install:
7. Position the starter relay onto the inner fender, then install the 2 mounting screws to 91–122 inch lbs. (11–13 Nm).
8. Install the wiring onto the starter relay in the same orientation as when removed.
9. Install the push-on wire terminal connector.
10. Install the 2 starter relay terminal nuts to 61–81 inch lbs. (7–9 Nm).
11. Install the starter relay terminal cover.
12. Attach the negative battery cable.

➡️**When the battery is disconnected and reconnected, some abnormal drive symptoms may occur while the Powertrain Control Module (PCM) relearns its adaptive strategy. The vehicle may need to be driven 10 miles (16 km) or more for the PCM to relearn the strategy.**

SENDING UNITS AND SENSORS

➡️**This section describes the operating principles of sending units, warning lights and gauges. Sensors which provide information to the Electronic Control Module (ECM) are covered in Section 4 of this manual.**

Instrument panels contain a number of indicating devices (gauges and warning lights). These devices are composed of two separate components. One is the sending unit, mounted on the engine or other remote part of the vehicle, and the other is the actual gauge or light in the instrument panel.

Several types of sending units exist, however most can be characterized as being either a pressure type or a resistance type. Pressure type sending units convert liquid pressure into an electrical signal which is sent to the gauge. Resistance type sending units are most often used to measure temperature and use variable resistance to control the current flow back to the indicating device. Both types of sending units are connected in series by a wire to the battery (through the ignition switch). When the ignition is turned **ON**, current flows from the battery through the indicating device and on to the sending unit.

Coolant Temperature Sending Unit

OPERATION

▶ See Figure 49

The coolant temperature sender (also known as water temperature indicator sender) is a thermistor, which means that as the coolant temperature increases, the resistance inside the sender unit changes accordingly. The coolant temperature senders' resistance in the models covered by this manual changes inversely from the temperature of the coolant. The resistance in the sender unit increases as the fluid temperature decreases and vice versa. When the engine is cold, the resistance of the sender unit is approximately 74 ohms. As the engine warms up to operating temperature, the resistance inside the sender gradually and smoothly decreases until the engine is completely warmed up. At this point the resistance of the sender is around 10 ohms.

TESTING

1. Remove the coolant temperature sender from the engine block.
2. Attach an ohmmeter to the sender unit as follows:
   a. Attach one lead to the metal body of the sender unit (near the sender unit's threads).
   b. Attach the other lead to the sender unit's wiring harness connector terminal.
3. With the leads still attached, place the sender unit in a pot of cold water so that neither of the leads is immersed in the water. The portion of the sender unit which normally makes contact with the engine coolant should be submerged.
4. Measure the resistance. The resistance should be on, or near, 74 ohms.
5. Slowly heat the pot up (on the stove) and observe the resistance of the sender unit. The resistance should evenly and steadily decrease as the water temperature increases. The resistance should not jump drastically or decrease erratically.
6. When the water reaches 190–210° F (88–99° C) the resistance of the sender unit should be on, or near, 9.7 ohms.
7. If the sender unit did not function exactly as described above, replace the sender unit with a new one.

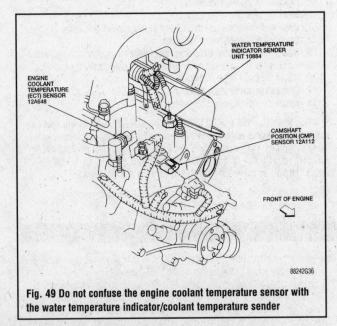

Fig. 49 Do not confuse the engine coolant temperature sensor with the water temperature indicator/coolant temperature sender

88242G36

WATER TEMPERATURE INDICATOR SENDER UNIT 10884

ENGINE COOLANT TEMPERATURE (ECT) SENSOR 12A648

CAMSHAFT POSITION (CMP) SENSOR 12A112

FRONT OF ENGINE

REMOVAL & INSTALLATION

The unit is located as follows:
- 2.3L—Left rear of the engine block
- 2.8L—Below water outlet housing
- 3.0L—Front of the intake manifold
- 4.0L—Front of the left cylinder head
1. Disconnect the wire at the sending unit.
2. Drain the cooling system to a level below the sending unit.

✳✳ CAUTION

When draining the coolant, keep in mind that cats and dogs are attracted by the ethylene glycol antifreeze, and are quite likely to drink any that is left in an uncovered container or in puddles on the ground. This will prove fatal in sufficient quantity. Always drain the coolant into a sealable container. Coolant should be reused unless it is contaminated or several years old.

3. Unscrew the sender.
4. Coat the threads of the new sender with sealer and screw it into place. Tighten the sender to 15 ft. lbs.
5. Connect the wire.
6. Fill the cooling system.

Oil Pressure Sending Unit

TESTING

This test should be performed if the oil pressure gauge does not show correct oil pressure and the cause is thought to be the sender.
1. Turn the ignition to the **ON** position (do not start the engine). Observe the oil pressure gauge.
   a. If the gauge reads **L** or below, proceed to Step 2.
   b. If the gauge reads anything but **L** or below, the problem lies in the wiring, the gauge itself or the instrument cluster.
2. Disconnect the oil pressure switch/sender and short the lead to an engine ground.
   a. If the gauge indicates approximately mid-scale or slightly above mid-scale (around the "MAL" in NORMAL), replace the oil pressure switch/sender. Retest the system after repairs are complete.
   b. If the gauge does not perform as described above, the problem lies in the wiring, the gauge itself or the instrument cluster.

REMOVAL & INSTALLATION

The sending unit is located as follows:
- 2.3L—Left rear of cylinder head
- 2.8L—Next to fuel pump
- 3.0L—In block behind right cylinder head
- 4.0L—Low left side of block near front

➡The pressure switch-type unit used with the indicator lamp system is not interchangeable with the variable resistance-type unit called a sender, which is used with the gauge system. Installation of the wrong part will result in an inoperative oil pressure indicating system and a damaged switch unit or gauge.

1. Disconnect the negative battery cable.
2. Remove the inside engine cover.
3. Disconnect the wire at the sending/switch unit.
4. Remove the sending unit from the engine block.
To install:
5. Wrap the threads of the new sending unit with Teflon® tape and carefully screw it into place. Make sure not to cross-thread the sending unit.
6. Tighten the sending unit to 15 ft. lbs. (20 Nm).
7. Attach the wire to the sending unit.
8. Connect the negative battery cable.

Oil Level Sensor

OPERATION

The low oil level sensor is mounted to the side of the oil pan.

When the oil level is at 1.5 qt. (1.4L), or lower, the sensor closes the electrical circuit to ground and the oil level warning lamp illuminates. When the oil level rises above 1.5 qt. (1.4L), the low oil level sensor opens the circuit to ground, thereby shutting the warning lamp off.

TESTING

Before commencing with the tests, determine if the oil level indicator lamp (in the instrument cluster) is always or never on. If the indicator lamp is always on, proceed to Test 1, otherwise skip to Test 2.

Test 1

1. Disconnect the low oil level sensor at the engine oil pan. Start the engine and observe the indicator lamp in the instrument panel.
   a. If the indicator lamp turned off, continue to Step 2.
   b. If the indicator lamp remained illuminated, skip to Step 3.
2. Using an ohmmeter connected to a known good ground, connect the second lead to the oil level sensor terminal. Measure the sensor's resistance.
   a. If the oil level sensor's resistance was lower than 8 kilohms, replace the oil level sensor. Retest the system after replacing the old sensor.
   b. If the resistance was 8 kilohms or more, proceed to Step 3.
3. Using an ohmmeter connected to a known good ground, connect the second lead to the terminal corresponding to the white wire with a pink tracer at the sensor connector. Measure the resistance.
   a. If the resistance of the circuit is less than 8 kilohms, repair the circuit for a short to ground. After the repairs, retest the system.
   b. If the resistance was 8 kilohms or greater, replace the low oil level sensor with a new one. After the repairs, retest the system.

Test 2

♦ **See Figure 50**

1. Make sure that the engine has been **OFF** for at least 5 minutes. Ensure that the oil level in the oil pan is at least 1.5 qt. (1.4L) low.
2. Disconnect the wiring harness from the oil level sensor at the oil pan.
3. Using a jumper wire, connect one end to a known good ground. Attach the other end to the terminal corresponding to the white wire with a pink tracer at the sensor connector.
4. Start the engine and observe the warning light in the instrument panel.
   a. If the oil level warning light turns off, replace the low oil level sensor with a new one. Retest the system after repairs.
   b. If the oil level warning light remains illuminated, proceed to the next step.
5. Leave the jumper wire attached between the ground and the sensor connector. Gain access to the low oil level relay at the instrument panel. Using an ohmmeter connected to a good ground, connect the second lead to the terminal corresponding to the white/pink wire at the relay connector. Measure the circuit's resistance.
   a. If the resistance is 5 ohms or less, proceed to Step 6.
   b. If the resistance was greater than 5 ohms, service the white/pink wire for an open circuit condition. Retest the system after repairs are completed.
6. Remove the ohmmeter lead from the white with pink tracer terminal of the sensor connector. Attach the lead to the terminal corresponding to the black wire with the white tracer at the relay connector. Read the resistance.
   a. If the resistance is greater than 5 ohms, repair the open in the circuit (black wire with white tracer). Retest the system after repairs are completed.
   b. If the resistance is 5 ohms or less, proceed to the next step.

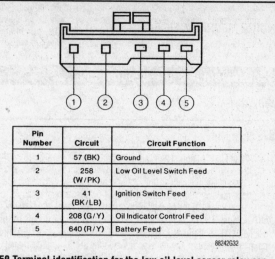

Pin Number	Circuit	Circuit Function
1	57 (BK)	Ground
2	258 (W/PK)	Low Oil Level Switch Feed
3	41 (BK/LB)	Ignition Switch Feed
4	208 (G/Y)	Oil Indicator Control Feed
5	640 (R/Y)	Battery Feed

88242G32

Fig. 50 Terminal identification for the low oil level sensor relay connector—all late model Aerostars

7. Using a test light connected to a good ground, connect the test light probe to the terminal corresponding to the gray/yellow wire at the relay connector.
   a. If the test light illuminates, proceed to Step 9.
   b. If the test light does not illuminate, proceed to Step 8.
8. Using the test light, check for power on the output side of Fuse 9 (10A).
   a. If the test light turns on, service the gray/yellow circuit for an open condition. Retest the system after repairs are complete.
   b. If the test light does not turn on, replace Fuse 9 (10A). Retest the system after repairs are complete.
9. Remove the low oil level warning indicator bulb. Inspect the bulb for any damage.
   a. If the bulb exhibits damage, replace it with a new one, then retest the system.
   b. If the bulb is not damaged or blown out, replace the instrument cluster printed circuit. Retest the system once repairs are complete.

REMOVAL & INSTALLATION

All 1991–97 production engines are equipped with an oil level sensor screwed into the side of the oil pan.

1. Disconnect the negative battery cable.
2. Block the rear wheels of the Aerostar.
3. Raise and safely support the front of the vehicle on jackstands.
4. Drain the engine oil into a large pan.
5. Detach the wiring connector from the sensor.
6. Remove the oil level sensor from the oil pan using a 26mm wrench or socket.
7. Discard the old sensor gasket.

To install:

➡**When installing the low oil level sensor, always use a new metal gasket with a rubber O-ring.**

8. Install the new sensor with a new gasket into the oil pan.
9. Tighten the sensor to 15–25 ft. lbs. (20–34 Nm).
10. Install the oil pan drain plug.
11. Attach the low oil level sensor wiring connector to the sensor.
12. Lower the vehicle.
13. Fill the engine oil with the correct amount of new oil.
14. Connect the negative battery cable.

3

ENGINE AND ENGINE OVERHAUL

ENGINE MECHANICAL

ENGINE REBUILDING SPECIFICATIONS

	2.3L Engine	2.8L Engine	3.0L Engine	4.0L Engine
General Specifications				
Displacement	140 cid	171 cid	183 cid	244 cid
Number of cylinders	4	6	6	6
Bore and stroke	3.780 x 3.126 in.	3.65 x 2.70 in.	3.50 x 3.14 in.	3.94 x 3.31 in.
Firing order	1-3-4-2	1-4-2-5-3-6	1-4-2-5-3-6	1-4-2-5-3-6
Cylinder Head and Valve Train				
Combustion chamber volume	3.65-3.83 ci	2.61-2.70 ci	3.75-3.93 ci ①	2.83-2.95 ci
Valve guide bore diameter	0.3433-0.3443 in.	0.3174-0.3184 in.	0.3443-0.3433 in.	0.3174-0.3184 in.
Valve seat width				
Intake	0.60-0.80 in.	0.060-0.079 in.	0.060-0.080 in.	0.060-0.079 in.
Exhaust	0.070-0.090 in.	0.060-0.079 in.	0.060-0.080 in.	0.060-0.079 in.
Gasket surface flatness	NA	0.006 in. overall	0.007 in. overall	0.006 in. overall
Valve lash adjuster bore diameter	0.8430-0.9449 in.	NA	NA	NA
Valve head diameter				
Intake	1.723-1.747 in.	1.562-1.577 in.	1.57 in.	1.71 in.
Exhaust	1.49-1.51 in.	1.261-1.276 in.	1.30 in.	1.36 in.
Valve face runout limit	0.002 in.	0.002 in.	0.002 in.	0.002 in.
Valve spring free length	1.877 in.	1.91 in.	1.86 in.	1.91 in.
Valve spring service limit (pressure loss@spec. length)	5%	10%	10%	10%
Valve spring out-of-square service limit	0.078 in.	0.078 in.	NA	0.078 in.
Rocker arm ratio	1.64:1	1.46:1	1.61:1	1.46:1
Push rod runout	NA	0.020 in.	0.020 in.	0.020 in.
Valve tappet, lifter or adjuster				
Diameter	0.8422-0.8427 in.	0.8736-0.8741 in.	0.874 in.	0.8742-0.8755 in.
Clearance-to-bore	0.0007-0.0027 in.	0.0009-0.0024 in.	0.0007-0.0027 in.	0.0005-0.0022 in.
Collapsed tappet gap				
Intake	0.035-0.055 in.	0.014 in.	0.088-0.189 in.	—
Exhaust	0.035-0.055 in.	0.016 in.	0.088-0.189 in.	—
Camshaft				
Intake lobe lift	0.238 in.	0.255 in.	0.260 in.	0.276 in.
Exhaust lobe lift	0.238 in.	0.255 in.	0.260 in.	0.276 in.
Theoretical intake valve lift	0.39 in.	0.373 in.	0.419 in.	0.4024 in.
Theoretical exhaust valve lift	0.39 in.	0.373 in.	0.419 in.	0.4024 in.
Allowable lobe lift loss	0.005 in.	0.005 in.	0.005 in.	0.005 in.
Journal runout limit	0.005 in.	0.005 in.	0.002 in.	0.05 in.
Journal out-of-round limit	0.0003 in.	0.0003 in.	0.001 in.	0.0003 in.
Crankshaft, Flywheel and Connecting Rods				
Main bearing journal				
Out-of-round limit	0.0006 in.	0.0006 in.	0.0003 in.	0.0006 in.
Taper limit	0.0006 in. per in.	0.0006 per in.	0.0003 per in.	0.0006 per in.
Runout limit	0.002 in.	0.005 in.	0.002 in.	0.005 in.
Thrust bearing journal				
Length	1.201-1.199 in.	1.039-1.041 in.	1.0148-1.0670 in.	1.039-1.041 in.
Connecting rod journal				
Out-of-round limit	0.0006 in.	0.0006 in.	0.0006 in.	0.0006 in.
Taper limit	0.0006 in. per in.	0.0006 per in.	0.0006 per in.	0.0006 per in.
Main bearing thrust face				
Runout limit	0.001 in.	0.001 in.	0.001 in.	0.001 in.
Flywheel clutch face				
Runout limit	0.005 in.	0.005 in.	0.005 in.	0.005 in.

ENGINE REBUILDING SPECIFICATIONS

	2.3L Engine	2.8L Engine	3.0L Engine	4.0L Engine
Crankshaft, Flywheel and Connecting Rods (cont.)				
Flywheel/Flexplate ring gear lateral runout				
Standard transmission	0.025 in.	0.025 in.	0.025 in.	0.025 in.
Automatic transmission	0.06 in.	0.060 in.	0.070 in.	0.060 in.
Auxiliary shaft				
End-play	0.001-0.007 in.	—	—	—
Bearing clearance to shaft	0.0006-0.0026 in.	—	—	—
Connecting rod				
Piston pin bore diameter	0.9123-0.9126 in.	0.9450-0.9452 in.	0.9096-0.9112 in.	0.9432-1.0439 in.
Crank. bearing bore diameter	2.1720-2.1728 in.	2.2370-2.2378 in.	2.250-2.251 in.	2.250-2.251 in.
Out-of-round limit	0.0004 in.	0.0004 in.	0.0004 in.	0.0004 in.
Taper limit	0.0004 in.	0.0004 in.	0.0004 in.	0.0004 in.
Length (center-to-center)	5.2031-5.2063 in.	5.1386-5.1413 in.	5.530-5.533 in.	5.1386-5.1413 in.
Alignment (bore-to-bore)				
Twist	0.024 in.	0.006 in.	0.003 per in.	0.006 in.
Bend	0.012 in.	0.002 in.	0.0016 per in.	0.002 in.
Pistons and Rings				
Piston diameter	3.7780-3.7786 in.	3.6605-3.6615 in.	3.5024-3.5031 in.	3.9524-3.9531 in.
Piston pin				
Length	3.01-3.04 in.	2.835-2.866 in.	3.012-3.039 in.	2.835-2.866 in.
Diameter	0.9119-0.9124 in.	0.9446-0.9450 in. ②	0.9119-0.9124 in.	0.9119-0.9124 in.
Piston-to-pin clearance	0.0002-0.0004 in.	0.0003-0.0006 in.	0.0002-0.0005 in.	0.0003-0.0006 in.
Piston-to-rod clearance	Interference fit	Interference fit	Interference fit	Interference fit
Piston ring width				
Top compression	0.0770-0.0780 in.	0.0778-0.0783 in.	0.0575-0.0587 in.	0.0778-0.0783 in.
Bottom compression	0.0770-0.0780 in.	0.1172-0.1177 in.	0.0575-0.0587 in.	0.1172-0.1177 in.
Lubrication System				
Oil pump				
Relief valve spring tension	15.2-17.2 lbs. @ 1.20 in.	13.6-14.7 lbs. @ 1.39 in.	9.1-10.1 lbs. @ 1.11 in.	13.6-14.7 lbs. @ 1.39 in.
Drive shaft-to-housing bearing clearance	0.0015-0.0030 in.	0.0015-0.0030 in.	0.0005-0.0019 in.	0.0015-0.0030 in.
Relief valve-to-bore clearance	0.0015-0.0030 in.	0.0015-0.0030 in.	0.0017-0.0029 in.	0.0015-0.0030 in.
Rotor assembly end clearance	0.004 in.	0.004 in.	0.004 in.	0.004 in.
Outer race-to-housing clearance	0.001-0.013 in.	0.001-0.013 in.	0.001-0.013 in.	0.001-0.013 in.
Oil capacity (US quarts)				
Without filter	4	4	4	4
With filter	5	5	4.5	1
Cylinder Block				
Head gasket surface flatness (warpage)	0.003 per 6 in. ③	0.003 per 6 in. ③	0.003 per 6 in. ③	0.003 per 6 in. ③
Cylinder bore				
Diameter	3.7795-3.7825 in.	3.6614-3.6630 in.	3.504 in.	3.9527-3.9543 in.
Out-of-round limit	0.0015 in.	0.0015 in.	0.001 in.	0.0015 in.
Taper limit	0.01 in.	0.01 in.	0.002 in.	0.01 in.
Main bearing bore diameter	2.5902-2.5910 in.	2.3866-2.3874 in.	2.713 in.	2.3866-2.3874 in.
Distributor shaft bearing bore diameter	0.5155-0.5170 in.	0.4534-0.4549 in.	0.8767-0.8752 in.	—

Notes:
① For 1986-87 Models, 1988-97 Models have 2.87-3.06 ci combustion chambers.
② Red piston pin – 0.9446-0.9448 in. Blue piston pin – 0.9448-0.9449 in.
③ 0.006 in. overall

91323C02

91323C01

Engine

REMOVAL & INSTALLATION

♦ **See Figures 1 thru 10**

In the process of removing the engine, you will come across a number of steps which call for the removal of a separate component or system, such as "disconnect the exhaust system" or "remove the radiator." In most instances, a detailed removal procedure can be found elsewhere in this manual.

It is virtually impossible to list each individual wire and hose which must be disconnected, simply because so many different model and engine combinations have been manufactured. Careful observation and common sense are the best possible approaches to any repair procedure.

Removal and installation of the engine can be made easier if you follow these basic points:

• If you have to drain any of the fluids, use a suitable container.
• Always tag any wires or hoses and, if possible, the components they came from before disconnecting them.
• Because there are so many bolts and fasteners involved, store and label the retainers from components separately in muffin pans, jars or coffee cans. This will prevent confusion during installation.
• After unbolting the transmission or transaxle, always make sure it is properly supported.
• If it is necessary to disconnect the air conditioning system, have this service performed by a qualified technician using a recovery/recycling station. If the system does not have to be disconnected, unbolt the compressor and set it aside.
• When unbolting the engine mounts, always make sure the engine is properly supported. When removing the engine, make sure that any lifting devices are properly attached. It is recommended that if your engine is supplied with lifting hooks, your lifting apparatus be attached to them.

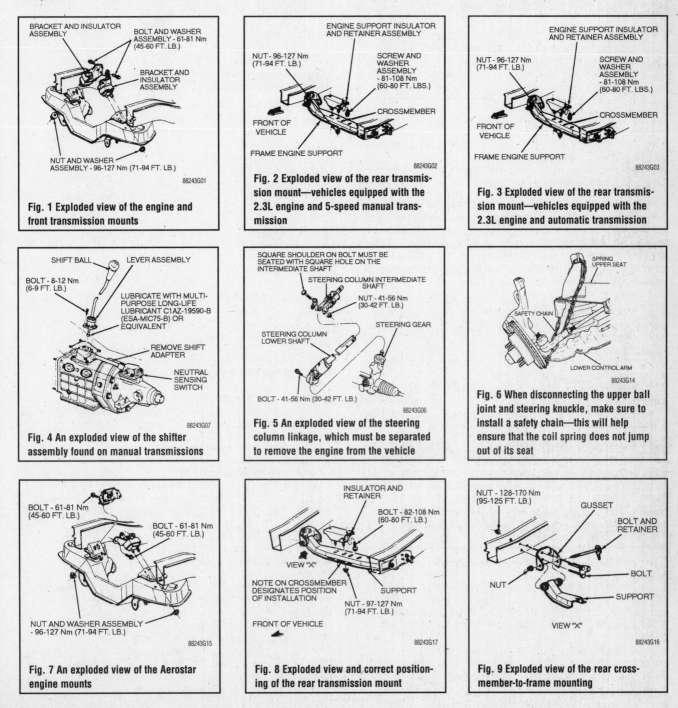

Fig. 1 Exploded view of the engine and front transmission mounts

Fig. 2 Exploded view of the rear transmission mount—vehicles equipped with the 2.3L engine and 5-speed manual transmission

Fig. 3 Exploded view of the rear transmission mount—vehicles equipped with the 2.3L engine and automatic transmission

Fig. 4 An exploded view of the shifter assembly found on manual transmissions

Fig. 5 An exploded view of the steering column linkage, which must be separated to remove the engine from the vehicle

Fig. 6 When disconnecting the upper ball joint and steering knuckle, make sure to install a safety chain—this will help ensure that the coil spring does not jump out of its seat

Fig. 7 An exploded view of the Aerostar engine mounts

Fig. 8 Exploded view and correct positioning of the rear transmission mount

Fig. 9 Exploded view of the rear crossmember-to-frame mounting

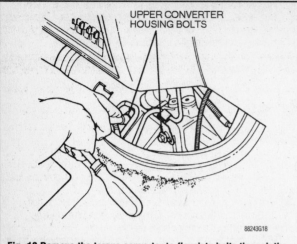

UPPER CONVERTER
HOUSING BOLTS

88243G18

Fig. 10 Remove the torque converter-to-flexplate bolts through the opening of the floor—use a 22mm socket and breaker bar to turn the engine during this procedure

- Lift the engine from its compartment slowly, checking that no hoses, wires or other components are still connected.
- After the engine is clear of the compartment, place it on an engine stand or workbench.
- After the engine has been removed, you can perform a partial or full teardown of the engine using the procedures outlined in this manual.

2.3L, 2.8L, and 3.0L Engines

➡The engine removal procedure requires that the engine and front suspension subframe be removed from beneath the van. Unless provisions can be made to safely raise the body enough to allow the engine to be removed from the bottom, this procedure should not be attempted. Tag all electrical and vacuum connections before disconnection to make installation easier. A piece of masking tape on each connector end with matching numbers is the easiest way to do this.

1. Relieve the fuel system pressure. For more information, refer to Section 5.
2. For vehicles equipped with air conditioning, have the A/C system discharged by a reputable, qualified automotive technician utilizing a recovery/recycling machine.
3. Disconnect the negative battery cable, then the positive battery cable. Remove the retaining bolt from the battery cable-to-frame bracket at the left front of the engine. Secure the cables to the engine.
4. Remove the engine access cover inside the vehicle by unfastening the clamps and pulling away from the floor.
5. Loosen the draincock and drain the coolant from the radiator into a suitable container.

✳✳ CAUTION

When draining coolant, keep in mind that cats and dogs are attracted by ethylene glycol antifreeze, and are quite likely to drink any that is left in an uncovered container or in puddles on the ground. This will prove fatal in sufficient quantity. Always drain the coolant into a sealable container. Coolant should be reused unless it is contaminated or several years old.

6. Disconnect the air cleaner outlet tube at the throttle body and the idle speed control hose.
7. Remove the vacuum supply hoses from the power brake booster, cruise control at the check valve near the throttle linkage (if equipped), the Manifold Absolute Pressure (MAP) sensor and the heater and air conditioner supply hose at the A/C vacuum check valve (located near the A/C vacuum reservoir tank and bracket).
8. Disconnect the upper and lower hoses at the radiator.
9. Disconnect the wiring harness from the power steering pressure switch. Remove the power steering pressure hose from the clips in the fan shroud, if so equipped.

10. Detach the electrical connector for the Idle Speed Control (ISC) motor.
11. On the 2.3L engine:
  a. If equipped with air conditioning, disconnect the suction and discharge hoses from the compressor. Detach the air conditioning compressor clutch electrical connector from the compressor. Plug the A/C lines to prevent contamination of the A/C system.
  b. From the lower left front of the engine, detach the electrical connector for the coil.
  c. From beneath the lower intake manifold, detach the electrical connector for the TFI module on the distributor.
  d. Separate the electrical connector from the knock sensor on the side of the upper intake manifold.
12. On the 2.8L engine:
  a. Tag and remove the electrical connectors for the throttle position sensor on the carburetor choke shield, canister purge valve solenoid and the solenoid valve carburetor bowl vent. Detach the electrical connector to the variable voltage choke cap. Disconnect the evaporative emission hose from the solenoid valve carburetor bowl vent to the vapor storage canister. Route the wiring harness out of the engine compartment.
  b. Disconnect the hose from the air control valve to the catalytic converter.
  c. Remove the electrical connector from the feedback control solenoid at the rear of the carburetor.

✳✳ WARNING

The fan clutch mounting nut has a left-hand thread. It must be turned counterclockwise in order to tighten.

13. Remove the engine fan.
14. Remove the fan shroud retaining bolts and remove the shroud.
15. Remove the electrical connector and vacuum hose from the Exhaust Gas Recirculation (EGR) valve at the rear of the upper intake manifold.
16. Detach the electrical connector for the Throttle Position Sensor (TPS) at the rear of the throttle body.
17. Remove the electrical connector from the Air Charge Temperature (ACT) sensor at the rear side of the lower intake manifold.
18. On manual transmissions, separate the electrical connector for the shift indicator sender.
19. Disconnect the manifold absolute pressure (MAP) sensor electrical connector from the sensor, located on the dash panel.
20. Remove the shroud covering the throttle linkage and disconnect the linkage at the throttle body.
21. Loosen the idler pulley adjustment bolt and alternator mounting arm bolt and remove the drive belts.
22. Disconnect the injector wiring harness at the main EEC connector.
23. Detach the electrical connectors for the engine coolant temperature sensor and the water temperature sender switch, located in the thermostat housing.
24. Disconnect the canister purge valve solenoid hoses.
25. Matchmark the inlet and outlet heater hoses and disconnect them from the engine side of the ballast tube.
26. Remove the engine breather tube.
27. If equipped with an automatic transmission, disconnect the 4 fluid lines at the radiator.
28. Remove the radiator.
29. If equipped with air conditioning, detach the air conditioning clutch electrical connector from the compressor, then remove the compressor mounting bolts and position the compressor out of the way. Tie it to the crossmember, to be safe.
30. Remove the oil filler tube-to-alternator bracket nut.
31. If equipped with an automatic transmission, remove the oil fill tube retaining bolt from the top of the manifold and gently pull the tube out of the transmission.
32. If equipped, disconnect the throttle and kickdown cable from the transmission lever. Route the kickdown cable out of the engine compartment and remove the cable.
33. Unplug the alternator wiring.
34. Disconnect the brake booster vacuum hose.
35. Make sure the steering wheel and front wheels are straight ahead (centered), then remove the bolt retaining the intermediate steering column shaft to the steering gear and disconnect the shaft from the gear.
36. Disconnect the radio frequency suppressor.

37. On earlier models, detach the electrical connector for the thick film ignition (TFI) module at the distributor.

38. Disconnect the oil pressure sender.

39. Depressurize the fuel system, as described in Section 1, then disconnect the nylon fuel delivery from the fuel supply manifold at the engine.

40. If equipped with a manual transmission, place the shift lever in Neutral and remove the bolts retaining the shift lever to the floor. Remove the bolts retaining the shift lever assembly to the transmission and remove the lever assembly.

41. Raise and support the van on jackstands.

42. Disconnect the oil level sensor at the oil pan.

43. Matchmark the driveshaft-to-flange position. Remove the nuts and U-bolts retaining the driveshaft to the rear axle and carefully pull the driveshaft from the transmission. Insert a plug in the extension housing to prevent fluid leakage.

44. Disconnect the speedometer cable from the transmission. Detach the electrical connector from the backup lamp switch.

45. Remove the bolts, then disconnect the starter cable and ground cable from the starter. Route the ground and starter cables out from the crossmember.

46. On vehicles with manual transmission, remove the lockpin retaining the hydraulic hose to the slave cylinder in the clutch housing. Remove and plug the hose.

47. With manual transmissions, detach the back-up lamp switch and neutral position switch connectors at the transmission.

48. On automatic transmissions, separate the electrical connector for the neutral start switch and 3rd/4th shift solenoid connector. Disconnect the selector and kickdown cable from the transmission lever.

49. Disconnect the vacuum hose at the transmission vacuum modulator.

50. With automatic transmissions, remove the torque converter access plate cover and adapter plate bolts from the bottom of the converter housing.

51. With automatic transmissions, remove the flywheel-to-converter nuts. To rotate the engine, use a breaker bar with a 22mm socket on the crankshaft pulley bolt.

52. Detach the electrical connector for the exhaust gas oxygen sensor from the left exhaust manifold.

53. Remove the heater hoses from the bracket underneath the engine at the front of the crossmember.

54. Disconnect the elbow connector from the oil pressure sender beneath the fuel pump.

55. Disconnect and plug the inlet hose on the fuel pump from the lines on the frame.

56. Remove the retaining bolt, then remove the bracket and accelerator cable and transmission kickdown linkage.

57. If equipped with cruise control, disconnect the cruise control cable from the throttle linkage.

58. If equipped with power steering, disconnect the power steering hoses from the pump to the gear and plug the hose ends.

59. With lifting tension applied, loosen the nuts retaining the motor mounts to the crossmember and lift the engine off the crossmember.

60. Remove the necessary components to attach the engine to a suitable engine stand. Make sure the engine is securely bolted to the stand before releasing tension on the hoist. Continue disassembly as desired.

61. Disconnect the transmission cooler lines at the transmission.

62. Position a transmission jack under the transmission and slightly raise the transmission. Remove the nuts and bolts retaining the crossmember to the frame and the nuts retaining the transmission to the crossmember. Remove the crossmember.

63. Remove the bell-housing-to-engine bolts.

64. Roll the transmission rearward until it is free of the engine and remove it from under the van.

65. Remove the exhaust manifold stud nuts.

66. Remove the bolts and nuts retaining the catalytic converter pipe to the muffler and outlet pipe.

67. Disconnect and remove the exhaust pipe and catalytic converter.

68. Remove the front wheels.

69. Remove the engine block ground straps. One is located on the cylinder head behind the power steering pump; the other at the junction of the exhaust manifold and exhaust pipe.

70. Remove the bar nuts and disconnect the stabilizer bar from the lower control arms. Discard the stabilizer bar nuts.

71. Disconnect and plug the brake lines at the bracket on the frame behind the spindles.

72. Position a jack under the lower control arm and raise the arm until tension is applied to the coil spring. Remove the bolt and nut retaining the spindle to the upper control arm ball joint. Slowly lower the jack under the lower control arm to disconnect the spindle from the ball joint.

✳✳ CAUTION

Place safety chains around the lower control arms and spring upper seat.

73. Position a wheeled dolly under the crossmember and engine assembly.

74. Slowly lower the vehicle until the crossmember rests on the dolly. Place wood blocks under the front crossmember and the rear of the engine block (or transmission, if installed), to keep the engine and crossmember assembly level. Install safety chains around the crossmember and dolly.

75. With the engine and crossmember securely supported on the dolly, remove the 3 nuts from the bolts that retain the engine and crossmember assembly to the frame on each side of the vehicle.

76. Slowly raise the body off the engine and crossmember assembly on the dolly and/or lower the engine and crossmember assembly. Make sure that any wiring or hoses do not snag, or interfere with the removal process.

77. When the engine and crossmember assembly are clear of the van body, roll the dolly out from under the vehicle.

78. Install lifting eyes to the rear of the left cylinder head. There should already be a lifting eye at the front of the right cylinder head. If not, install one.

✳✳ WARNING

The support hook or chain must angle rearward toward the rear attaching point! Damage will result if the chain runs across the throttle cable or throttle valve mechanism.

To install:

79. Attach the shop crane to the engine assembly.

80. Lower the engine onto the crossmember assembly, so that the engine mount studs are piloted into the crossmember holes. Install the engine-to-crossmember retaining nuts. Tighten the retaining nuts to 71–94 ft. lbs. (96–127 Nm). Install safety chains.

81. Position the engine rear plate onto the engine.

82. Roll the engine assembly under the vehicle.

83. Slowly lower the body and/or raise the engine and crossmember assembly. Make sure that any wiring or hoses do not snag or interfere with the installation process.

84. Install the 3 nuts that retain the engine and crossmember assembly to the frame on each side of the vehicle. Tighten the nuts to 145–195 ft. lbs. (196–264 Nm).

85. Remove the dolly and safety chains.

86. The balance of the installation is the reverse of removal.

87. Note any applicable torque specifications in the torque spec charts at the end of the Section.

88. If applicable, have the A/C system evacuated and recharged by a reputable, qualified automotive technician using a recovery/recycling machine.

4.0L Engine

➡The engine assembly can be removed through the front of the engine compartment without the transmission attached.

1. Relieve the fuel system pressure. For more information, refer to Section 5.

2. For vehicles equipped with air conditioning, have the A/C system discharged by a reputable, qualified automotive technician utilizing a recovery/recycling machine.

3. Disconnect the negative battery cable, then the positive battery cable. Remove the retaining bolt from the battery cable-to-frame bracket at the left front of the engine. Secure the cables to the engine.

4. Remove the engine access cover inside the vehicle by unfastening the clamps and pulling away from the floor.

5. Loosen the draincock and drain the coolant from the radiator into a suitable container.

6. Remove the grille. For more information, refer to Section 10.
7. Remove the air cleaner and intake duct assembly.
8. If equipped with air conditioning, detach the air conditioning clutch electrical connector from the compressor. Remove the A/C compressor. Cap all openings at once to keep dirt or other contaminants from entering the A/C system.
9. Remove the air conditioning condenser.
10. Drain the engine oil.
11. Remove the power steering cooler.
12. Remove the front bumper cover. For more information, refer to Section 10.
13. Remove the transmission oil cooler.
14. Remove the fan shroud retaining bolts and position the shroud over the fan.
15. Remove the upper and lower radiator hoses.
16. Remove the engine fan and shroud.
17. Remove the radiator.
18. Remove the accessory drive belt(s).
19. Remove the right front air diverter flap.
20. Remove the center hood latch support and the hood.
21. Remove the alternator.
22. Remove the engine oil filler tube.
23. Remove the engine cover from inside the van.
24. Remove the weather shield.
25. Disconnect the power steering pump hoses, then remove the pump and bracket.
26. If equipped with an automatic transmission, remove the oil fill tube.
27. Remove the engine oil dipstick and tube.
28. Raise and safely support the front of the vehicle on jackstands.
29. Disconnect the exhaust pipes at the manifolds.
30. Remove the bolts, then disconnect the starter cable and ground cable from the starter. Remove the starter.
31. Reach through the starter opening and remove the flywheel-to-converter nuts. To rotate the engine, use a breaker bar with a socket on the crankshaft pulley bolt.
32. Remove the automatic transmission oil cooler line bracket bolt.
33. Remove the right and left side engine mount-to-frame bolts.
34. Remove all the converter housing-to-engine bolts except the upper 2 bolts.
35. Remove the left engine mount.
36. Support the transmission with a floor jack.
37. Remove the 2 upper converter housing-to-engine bolts.
38. Tag and disconnect all wires at the transmission and transfer case (if applicable).
39. Depressurize the fuel system, as described in Section 1, then disconnect the fuel delivery and return lines from the fuel supply manifold at the engine.
40. Disconnect the throttle linkage.
41. Matchmark, then disconnect the inlet and outlet heater hoses.
42. Tag and disconnect all vacuum lines at the engine.
43. Tag and remove the spark plug wires.
44. Remove the ignition coil assembly and bracket.
45. Disconnect the throttle position sensor wire.
46. Remove the throttle body from the upper intake manifold. For the precise removal and installation procedures of the throttle body unit, refer to Section 5.
47. Tag and separate the wiring harness main connectors.
48. Install lifting eyes on the right front and left rear of the cylinder heads. Connect a shop crane with hoisting chain to the engine. Raise the engine enough to allow movement. Carefully roll the engine forward, then lift it from the van.
To install:

➡**Failure to use the correct spacers will result in damage to the oil pan and oil leakage!**

49. On earlier models, there are 2 spacers on the rear of the oil pan to allow proper mating of the transmission and oil pan. If these spacers were lost, or the block and/or oil pan were replaced, you must determine the proper spacers to install. To do this:
   a. With the oil pan installed, place a straightedge across the machined mating surface of the rear of the block, extending over the oil pan-to-transmission mounting surface.
   b. Using a feeler gauge, measure the gap between the oil pan mounting pad and the straightedge.
   c. Repeat the procedure for the other side.
   d. Select the spacers as follows:
   • Gap = 0.011–0.020 in.; spacer = 0.010 in.
   • Gap = 0.021–0.029 in.; spacer = 0.020 in.
   • Gap = 0.031–0.039 in.; spacer = 0.030 in.

➡**To facilitate engine-to-transmission installation and to prevent clutch hub damage on manual transmission vehicles, make two guide studs by cutting the heads off of two M10x70mm bolts. Then grind a screwdriver slot in the end of each bolt on the unthreaded end.**

50. Connect the shop crane or hoist to the engine, then position the engine into the engine compartment of the van. Make sure that the converter-to-flywheel pins align with the holes.
51. Install the left engine mount. Tighten the bolt to 64 ft. lbs. (87 Nm).
52. Install the converter housing-to-engine bolts. Tighten the bolts to 38 ft. lbs. (52 Nm).
53. Install the right and left side engine mount-to-frame bolts. Tighten the bolts to 75 ft. lbs. (102 Nm).
54. Reach through the starter opening and install the flywheel-to-converter nuts. Tighten the nuts to 34 ft. lbs. (46 Nm). To rotate the engine, use a breaker bar with a socket on the crankshaft pulley bolt.
55. Remove the crane and floor jack.
56. The balance of the installation is the reverse of removal.
57. Note any applicable torque specifications in the torque spec charts at the end of the Section.
58. If applicable, have the A/C system evacuated and recharged by a reputable, qualified automotive technician using a recovery/recycling machine.

Rocker Arm (Valve) Cover

REMOVAL & INSTALLATION

➡**Although Ford suggests that this component is removable while the engine is installed in the vehicle, depending on the particular options with which your Aerostar is equipped, working clearance may be extremely tight and this procedure may be much easier to perform with the engine removed. Before commencing, read through this procedure and make certain enough clearance, or working room, exists with the engine in the vehicle; if there is not enough space, the engine should be removed.**

2.3L Engine

♦ See Figure 11

1. Disconnect the negative battery cable.
2. Remove the engine cover inside the cab.
3. Remove the air cleaner and intake ducts from the throttle body assembly.

➡**The throttle body and upper intake manifold are a one piece assembly and, therefore, must be removed together.**

4. Remove the throttle body. For more details, refer to Section 5.
5. Tag and disconnect the spark plug wires from the plugs, then position the wires out of the way. Leave the spark plug wires in their looms to make installation easier.
6. Loosen the seven screw and washer assemblies along the outside of the rocker cover, then remove them along with their retainers. Loosen and remove the one stud on the right side of the rocker cover.
7. Tap the rocker cover lightly with a rubber mallet to break it loose, then lift the rocker arm cover straight up off the engine.
8. Remove and discard the rocker cover gasket.
To install:
9. Carefully clean all gasket mating surfaces, being careful not to scratch the rocker cover or cylinder head surfaces.

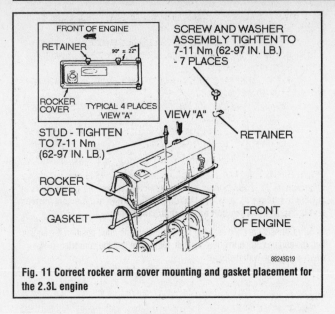

Fig. 11 Correct rocker arm cover mounting and gasket placement for the 2.3L engine

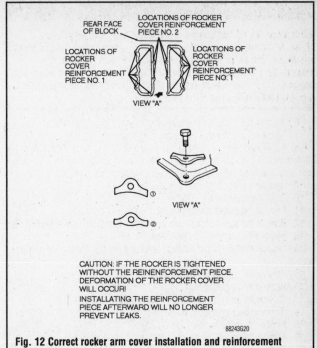

CAUTION: IF THE ROCKER IS TIGHTENED WITHOUT THE REINENFORCEMENT PIECE, DEFORMATION OF THE ROCKER COVER WILL OCCUR!

INSTALLING THE REINFORCEMENT PIECE AFTERWARD WILL NO LONGER PREVENT LEAKS.

Fig. 12 Correct rocker arm cover installation and reinforcement piece positioning for the 2.8L engine

10. Set the new gasket in the rocker arm cover, then lower the cover straight down onto the cylinder head. Make sure the gasket is seated properly all the way around the cover.

11. Install the screw and washer assemblies with their retainers and tighten them to 62–97 inch lbs. (7–11 Nm). The retainers should be gripping the edge of the rocker cover, 90° from the bolt holes. Install the stud and tighten to 62–97 inch lbs. (7–11 Nm).

12. Install the ignition cables, throttle body and air cleaner assembly.

13. Install the interior engine cover. Set the cover in place on the floor and engage the hold-down clamps.

14. Connect the negative battery cable, start the engine and check for leaks.

2.8L Engine

▶ See Figure 12

1. Remove the engine access cover inside the vehicle by unfastening the clamps and pulling away from the floor.

2. Remove the air cleaner and air duct assembly.

3. Tag, then remove the spark plug wires from the plugs, but leave them attached to their wire loom. Lay the wires out of the way.

4. Remove the PCV valve and hose.

5. Remove the two screws attaching the throttle position sensor connector to the carburetor choke air shield, then route the connector forward to clear the valve cover area.

6. Remove the carburetor choke air deflector plate (shield).

7. Remove the air conditioning compressor and brackets, if equipped, and move it aside without disconnecting any refrigerant lines.

8. Remove the rocker arm cover attaching screws and load distribution washers. Lay the washers out in order so they may be installed in their original positions.

9. If equipped with an automatic transmission, remove the transmission fluid level indicator tube and bracket, which is attached to the rocker cover.

10. Disconnect the kickdown linkage from the carburetor on automatic transmission models.

11. Position the thermactor air hose and wiring harness away from the right-hand rocker cover.

12. Remove the engine oil filler tube and bracket assembly from the valve cover and exhaust manifold stud.

13. Disconnect the vacuum line at the canister purge solenoid and disconnect the line routed from the canister to purge solenoid. Detach the power brake booster hose, if equipped.

14. Tap the rocker arm cover lightly with a rubber mallet to break it loose. Remove the rocker arm cover by lifting it up and off the cylinder head.

To install:

15. Clean all gasket material from the rocker arm cover and cylinder head mating surfaces.

16. Install the rocker arm cover, using a new gasket. Install the attaching screws and rocker cover reinforcement pieces.

17. If equipped with an automatic transmission, install the transmission fluid level indictor tube and bracket to the rocker cover.

18. Connect the kickdown linkage (automatic transmission only).

19. Make sure all rocker cover load distribution washers are installed in their original positions, then tighten the rocker arm cover screws to 36–60 inch lbs. (4–7 Nm).

20. Install the spark plug wires, PCV valve and hose.

21. Install the carburetor choke air deflector plate (shield).

22. Install the two screws retaining the throttle position sensor connector to the choke air deflector shield.

23. Reposition the thermactor air hose and wiring harness in their original locations.

24. Install the engine oil filler tube and bracket to the valve cover and exhaust manifold studs.

25. Connect the vacuum line at the canister purge solenoid and connect the line routed from the canister to the purge solenoid. Connect the power brake hose, if equipped.

26. Install the air conditioning compressor and brackets, if equipped.

27. Install the interior engine cover. Set the cover in place on the floor and engage the hold-down clamps.

28. Install the air cleaner assembly, start the engine and check for leaks.

3.0L Engine

▶ See Figure 13, 14, 15, 16, and 17

1986–90 MODELS

1. Disconnect the negative battery cable.

2. Remove the engine access cover inside the vehicle by unfastening the clamps and pulling away from the floor.

3. Remove the air cleaner outlet tube.

4. Remove the engine cover in the cab. Disconnect the ignition wires from the spark plugs, but leave them attached to their wire looms.

5. Remove the ignition wire separators from the rocker arm cover attaching bolt studs and the spark plugs with the wires attached, then lay the wires out of the way. Make sure to label the spark plug wires.

6. If the left-hand cover is being removed, perform the following:

    a. Remove the oil filler cap.

    b. Remove the PCV system hose.

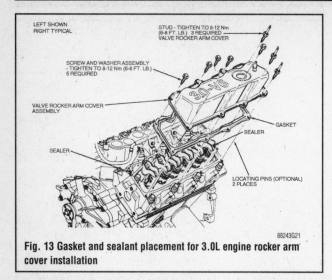

Fig. 13 Gasket and sealant placement for 3.0L engine rocker arm cover installation

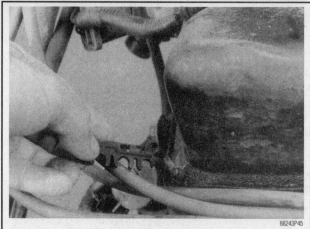

Fig. 14 To remove the rocker arm cover, detach the ignition spark plug wires from the cover, then . . .

Fig. 15 . . . remove the hold-down bolts

Fig. 16 Lift the rocker arm cover off . . .

Fig. 17 . . . then remove the old gasket from the cylinder head

7. If the right-hand cover is being removed, remove the PCV valve and disconnect the EGR tube and heater hoses.

8. Remove the rocker arm cover attaching screws and lift the cover off the engine. Tap the cover lightly with a rubber mallet to break it loose, if necessary.

To install:

9. Clean all gasket mating surfaces and remove any traces of the old gasket material and dirt.

10. To install, lightly oil all bolts and stud threads. Apply a bead of RTV sealant at the cylinder head to intake manifold rail step (two places per rail). Position a new cover gasket into place.

11. Place the rocker cover on the cylinder head and install five attaching bolts and three attaching studs. Note the location of the ignition wire separator clip stud bolts. Tighten the attaching bolts to 80–106 inch lbs. (9–12 Nm).

12. Install the oil filler cap and PCV hose (left-hand), or the PCV valve and EGR tube (right-hand). Tighten the EGR tube to 25–36 ft. lbs. (35–50 Nm).

13. Install the ignition wire separators.

14. Connect the ignition wires to the spark plugs.

15. Install the interior engine cover. Set the cover in place on the floor and engage the hold-down clamps.

16. Start the engine and check for leaks.

1991–97 MODELS

➡ The rocker arm covers installed on the 1991–97 3.0L engines incorporate integral gaskets which should last the life of the vehicle. Be sure to adhere to the following steps when removing and replacing the rocker arm covers. Replacement gaskets are available, however, if required.

1. Disconnect the negative battery cable.

2. Remove the air cleaner outlet tube.

3. Disconnect the spark plug wire sets from the spark plugs with a twisting motion.

4. Remove the spark plug wire assembly from the rocker arm cover retaining studs and move them aside.

5. If the left rocker arm cover is to be removed, perform the following:

a. Remove the throttle body. For more details, refer to Section 5 in this manual.

b. Remove the PCV valve.

c. Remove the fuel injection wiring standoffs from the inboard rocker arm cover studs. Move the harness aside.

6. If the right side rocker arm cover is to be removed, perform the following:

a. Remove the oil filler tube.

b. Remove the fuel injection wiring standoffs from the inboard rocker arm cover studs. Move the harness out of the way.

c. Remove the PCV closure hose from the oil fill adapter.

7. Completely loosen all rocker arm cover retaining bolts (they are captive by the gasket).

8. Using extreme caution, slide a sharp, thin-bladed knife between the cylinder head surface and the rocker arm cover gasket at the two RTV sealant junctions. Cut only the RTV sealant and avoid cutting the integral gasket. Lift the rocker arm cover off of the cylinder head while making sure that the RTV sealant is not pulling the gasket from the rocker arm cover.

9. If the gasket needs to be replaced because of damage or the rocker arm cover is going to be cleaned, note the bolt/stud locations before removing the gasket from the cover, since the fasteners are held in place by the gasket. Remove the integral gasket by pulling it from the gasket channel.

To install:

10. If the gasket was removed earlier, perform the following:

a. Clean the gasket channel with a soft cloth to remove all dirt and grease.

b. Clean off any remaining RTV sealant using a suitable solvent.

c. Lay the gasket onto the rocker arm cover gasket channel, while aligning the fastener holes. Using a finger, install the gasket into the channel.

d. Install the gasket to each fastener by securing the fastener head with a nut driver or socket. Seat the fastener against the rocker arm cover and, at the same time, roll the gasket around the fastener collar. If installed correctly, all fasteners will be secured by the gasket and will not fall out.

11. Check the rocker arm cover gasket for correct installation. New gaskets should lay flat against the rocker arm cover in both the channel and fastener areas. If the gasket is installed incorrectly, oil leakage will occur.

➡**Lightly oil all bolt and stud threads before installation. using solvent, clean the cylinder head and rocker arm cover sealing surfaces to remove all silicone sealer and dirt. Do not allow the solvent to come in contact with the rocker arm cover gasket.**

12. Apply a bead of silicone sealant or equivalent meeting Ford specification ESE-M4G 195-B at the cylinder head-to-intake manifold rail step (two places per rail) as illustrated.

➡**When positioning the rocker arm cover onto the cylinder head, lower the rocker arm cover straight-down onto the cylinder head to align the bolt holes. Once the cover is in contact with the RTV sealant, any adjustment for the bolt alignment can roll the gasket out of the channel, which will result in oil leaks.**

13. Position the rocker arm cover onto the cylinder head and hand-tighten the retaining bolts. Then tighten the retainers to 7–10 ft. lbs. (10–14 Nm).

14. If the left rocker arm cover is being installed, perform the following:
   a. Install the fuel injection wiring standoffs onto the inboard rocker arm cover studs.
   b. Install the PCV valve, then connect the hoses to it.
   c. Install the throttle body assembly. For more information, refer to Section 5.

15. If the right side rocker arm cover is being installed, perform the following:
   a. Install the engine harness connectors to the rocker arm cover retainer.
   b. Install the fuel injection harness standoffs to the inboard rocker arm cover studs.
   c. Install the oil filler tube assembly.
   d. Install the PCV closure hose to the oil fill adapter.

16. Connect the spark plug wires to the spark plugs.

➡**When the battery has been disconnected and reconnected, some abnormal drive symptoms may occur while the Powertrain Control Module (PCM) relearns its adaptive strategy. The vehicle may need to be driven about 10 miles (16 km) or more to relearn the strategy.**

17. Connect the negative battery cable.
18. Install the air cleaner outlet tube.
19. Install the interior engine cover. Set the cover in place on the floor and engage the hold-down clamps.
20. Start the engine and check for oil, gasoline and vacuum leaks.

4.0L Engine

▸ **See Figure 18**

1. Disconnect the negative battery cable and remove the intake shield. Remove the air cleaner outlet tube.
2. Remove the inside engine cover.
3. For right rocker arm cover removal, remove the oil fill pipe, oil level indicator tube and transmission oil filler tube (automatic models).
4. Remove the alternator and ignition coil. For more details, refer to Section 2 in this manual.
5. Tag and remove the spark plug wires.
6. For left rocker cover removal, remove the upper intake manifold, as described later in this section.
7. Remove the PCV valve hose and breather.
8. Remove the A/C compressor from the A/C compressor mounting bracket, then set it out of the way. Do not disconnect the hoses from the A/C compressor.
9. Remove the rocker cover bolts and rocker arm cover flange plate. The washers must be installed in their original positions, so keep track of them.
10. Remove the rocker cover. It will probably be necessary to tap the cover loose with a plastic or rubber mallet.

To install:

11. Clean all gasket material from the cover and head.
12. Position the rocker arm cover gaskets onto the rocker arm covers.

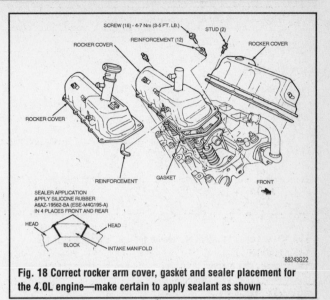

Fig. 18 Correct rocker arm cover, gasket and sealer placement for the 4.0L engine—make certain to apply sealant as shown

➡**Since silicone rubber will set within 15 minutes, if both covers are being installed, only apply the silicone sealant to one cover at a time.**

13. Apply Silicone Rubber D6AZ-19562-BA or equivalent meeting Ford specifications ESB-M4G92-A and ESE-M4G195-A, to the left intake manifold-to-cylinder head parting seam and an ⅛ in. (8mm) ball of sealant to the valve cover bolt holes on the exhaust side of the cylinder head.

14. Install the right side rocker arm cover, rocker arm cover flange plates and bolts. Snug the bolts starting from the center bolts working in a crisscross pattern to 5–6 ft. lbs. (6–8 Nm).

15. Install the A/C air register impingement screen on the A/C compressor mounting bracket, then tighten the compressor bolts to 18–23 ft. lbs. (24–30 Nm).

16. Snap the spark plug wires into the clips on the right side rocker arm cover.

17. If applicable, install the upper intake manifold, as described later in this section.

18. Apply Silicone Rubber D6AZ-19562-BA or equivalent meeting Ford specifications ESB-M4G92-A and ESE-M4G195-A, to the right intake manifold-to-cylinder head parting seam and an ⅛ in. (8mm) ball of sealant to the valve cover bolt holes on the exhaust side of the cylinder head.

19. Install the left side rocker arm cover, rocker arm cover flange plates and bolts. Snug the bolts starting from the center bolts working in a crisscross pattern to 5–6 ft. lbs. (6–8 Nm).

20. Install the ignition coil and assembled bracket. Install the alternator. For more information, refer to Section 2 in this manual.

21. Snap the spark plug wires into the clips on the left side rocker arm cover.

22. Install the oil fill pipe, oil level indicator tube, and the transmission filler tube (automatic models).

23. Install the air cleaner outlet tube and shield.

➡**When the battery has been disconnected and reconnected, some abnormal drive symptoms may occur while the Powertrain Control Module (PCM) relearns its adaptive strategy. The vehicle may need to be driven about 10 miles (16 km) or more to relearn the strategy.**

24. Connect the negative battery cable. Start the engine and check for oil, fuel or vacuum leaks.

25. Install the engine cover and close the hood.

Rocker Arms/Shafts

➡**Although Ford suggests that this component is removable while the engine is installed in the vehicle, depending on the particular options with which your Aerostar is equipped, working clearance may be extremely tight and this procedure may be much easier to perform with the engine removed. Before commencing, read through this procedure and make certain enough clearance, or working room, exists with the engine in the vehicle; if there is not enough space, the engine should be removed.**

REMOVAL & INSTALLATION

2.3L Engine

♦ **See Figure 19**

1. Disconnect the negative battery cable.
2. Remove the upper intake manifold with throttle body attached and associated parts as required.
3. Remove the rocker arm cover, as described earlier in this section.
4. Rotate the camshaft so that the base circle of the camshaft is facing the applicable camshaft follower of the rocker arm which is to be removed.
5. Using a valve spring compressor lever (T74P–6565–A or equivalent), collapse the valve spring and slide the camshaft follower over the lash adjuster and out.
6. Lift out the hydraulic lash adjuster.

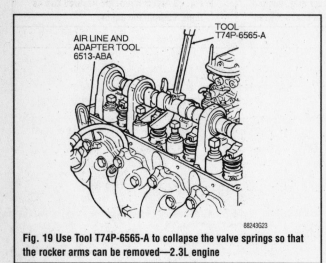

Fig. 19 Use Tool T74P-6565-A to collapse the valve springs so that the rocker arms can be removed—2.3L engine

To install:

7. Rotate the camshaft so that the base circle of the camshaft is facing the applicable camshaft follower.
8. Place the hydraulic lash adjuster in position in the bore.
9. Collapse the valve spring using the compressor lever and position the camshaft follower over the lash adjuster and the valve stem.
10. Install the upper and lower intake manifolds, as described later in this section.
11. Install the rocker arm cover. Refer to the procedures described earlier in this section.
12. Connect the negative battery cable.
13. Install any remaining components removed earlier. Run the engine at fast idle and check for oil, gasoline and vacuum leaks.

2.8L Engine

1. Disconnect the negative battery cable.
2. Remove the rocker arm cover, as described earlier in this section.
3. Remove the rocker arm shaft stand attaching bolts by loosening the bolts two turns at a time in sequence. Lift off the rocker arm and shaft assembly and oil baffle. The assembly may then be transferred to a workbench for disassembly as necessary.

To install:

4. Loosen the valve lash adjusting screws a few turns, then apply clean engine oil to the assembly to provide initial lubrication.
5. Install the oil baffle and rocker arm shaft assembly to the cylinder head and guide the adjusting screws on to the pushrods.
6. Install and tighten the rocker arm stand attaching bolts to 43–50 ft. lbs. (59–67 Nm), two turns at a time, in sequence.
7. Adjust the valve clearance, as described in Section 1.
8. Install the rocker arm covers, as described earlier in this section, then start the engine and check for leaks.

3.0L Engine

♦ **See Figure 20, 21, 22, 23, and 24**

1. Disconnect the negative battery cable.
2. Remove the rocker arm covers, as described earlier in this section.

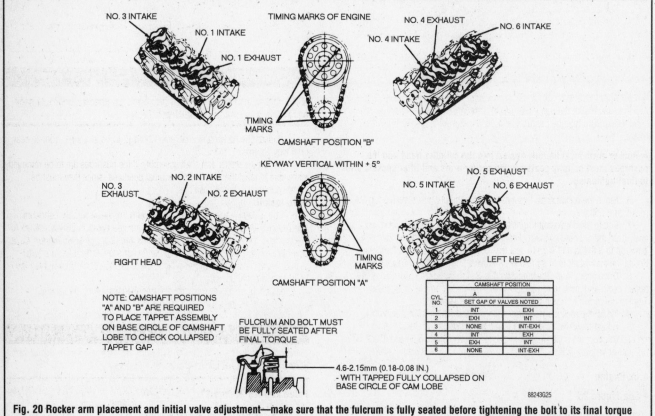

CYL. NO.	CAMSHAFT POSITION	
	A	B
	SET GAP OF VALVES NOTED	
1	INT	EXH
2	EXH	INT
3	NONE	INT-EXH
4	INT	EXH
5	EXH	INT
6	NONE	INT-EXH

Fig. 20 Rocker arm placement and initial valve adjustment—make sure that the fulcrum is fully seated before tightening the bolt to its final torque value

Fig. 21 After removing the rocker arm cover, remove the rocker arm retaining bolt, then . . .

Fig. 22 . . . pull the rocker arm, fulcrum and retaining bolt from the cylinder head

Fig. 23 At this point, the pushrod can be removed from the engine

Fig. 24 When removing multiple pushrods, make sure to note the positions of each pushrod for installation

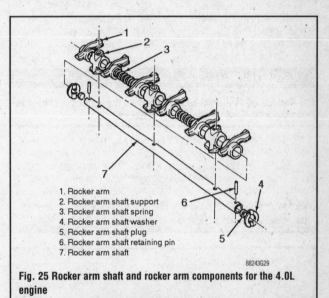

1. Rocker arm
2. Rocker arm shaft support
3. Rocker arm shaft spring
4. Rocker arm shaft washer
5. Rocker arm shaft plug
6. Rocker arm shaft retaining pin
7. Rocker arm shaft

Fig. 25 Rocker arm shaft and rocker arm components for the 4.0L engine

3. Removing the single retaining bolt at each rocker arm.

4. The rocker arm and pushrod may then be removed from the engine. Keep all rocker arms and pushrods in order so they may be installed in their original locations.

To install:

➡Lightly oil all bolt and stud threads before installation.

5. Apply ESE-M2C39-F oil, or equivalent, to the removed pushrods and rocker arms. Install the pushrods into their respective holes of the cylinder head. Make sure that the pushrods are seated correctly against the valve lifters.

➡Rocker arms must be fully seated into the cylinder head and the pushrods must be fully seated in the rocker arms and lifter sockets prior to final tightening.

6. Move the rocker arms into position with the pushrods, then snug the rocker arm bolts.

7. Rotate the crankshaft to position the camshaft lobes straight down and away from the pushrod of the rocker arm being tightened. Tighten the rocker arm bolt to 8 ft. lbs. (11 Nm) to seat the rocker arm into the cylinder block. Rotate the crankshaft until all rocker arms have been initially tightened.

8. Once again rotate the crankshaft so that the camshaft lobes are positioned down and away from the pushrod of the rocker arm to be tightened. Tighten the rocker arm bolt to 19–28 ft. lbs. (26–38 Nm).

9. Install the rocker arm covers, as described earlier in this section.

10. Adjust the valve lash according to the procedure in Section 1.

11. Connect the negative battery cable, then run the engine and check for oil, fuel or vacuum leaks.

4.0L Engine

⬧ See Figure 25

1. Disconnect the negative battery cable.

2. Remove the rocker arm cover, as described earlier in this section.

❄❄ CAUTION

If the rocker arm shafts are not loosened gradually, the shaft may become bent or damaged during removal.

3. Loosen the rocker arm shaft stand bolts, 2 turns at a time, front-to-rear, until they are free.

4. Lift off the rocker arm shaft assembly. If the pushrods are to be removed, make sure to label them as to their original positions, since they must be installed in their original positions.

To install:

5. Lubricate all rocker arm assemblies with Engine Assembly Lubricant D9AZ-19579-D, or the equivalent meeting Ford specification ESR-M99C80-A.

6. Install the rocker arm shaft assemblies and draw the shaft support bolts down evenly, two turns at a time, until the rocker shaft assemblies are fully seated. Tighten the shaft support bolts to 24 ft. lbs. (32 Nm), then tighten the bolts an additional 90°.

7. Install the rocker arm covers, as described earlier in this section.

8. Connect the negative battery cable.

Thermostat

REMOVAL & INSTALLATION

⬧ See Figures 26 thru 31

1. Disconnect the negative battery cable.

2. Drain the cooling system with the engine cold.

☀ CAUTION

When draining coolant, keep in mind that cats and dogs are attracted by ethylene glycol antifreeze, and are quite likely to drink any that is left in an uncovered container or in puddles on the ground. This will prove fatal in sufficient quantity. Always drain the coolant into a sealable container. Coolant should be reused unless it is contaminated or several years old.

3. On the 4.0L engine, remove the air cleaner duct assembly.

4. On the 3.0L and 4.0L engines, remove the upper radiator hose.

5. Remove the retaining bolts for the thermostat housing.

6. On the 2.3L and 2.8L engines, lift the housing clear and remove the thermostat. It may be easier to clean the gasket mating surfaces with the heater and radiator hoses removed from the thermostat housing.

7. On the 3.0L engine, remove the water outlet connection and thermostat as an assembly. Turn the thermostat counterclockwise to remove it from the housing.

To install:

8. Clean all gasket material from the housing and engine with a gasket scraper. Gouges in aluminum could form leak paths. Use care when scraping the thermostat-to-gasket mating surfaces. Always use a new gasket.

9. On the 4.0L engine:

☀ CAUTION

The thermostat seal must be positioned on the water outlet connection before the water thermostat is installed.

10. Make sure that the sealing ring is properly installed on the thermostat rim. Position the thermostat in the housing making sure that the air release valve is in the **UP** (12 o'clock) position. It is critical that the correct water thermostat installation alignment be made to provide coolant flow to the heater. Insert and rotate the thermostat to the left or right until it stops in the water outlet connection housing, then visually check for full width of heater outlet tube opening to be visible within the thermostat port in assembly. This port alignment at assembly is required to provide maximum coolant flow to the heater.

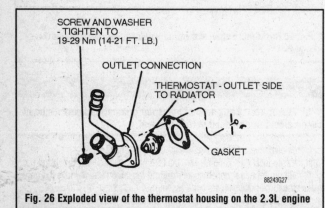

Fig. 26 Exploded view of the thermostat housing on the 2.3L engine

a. To prevent incorrect installation of the water thermostat, the water outlet connection casting on the 4.0L engine contains a locking recess into which the water thermostat is turned and locked. Install the water thermostat with the bridge section in the outlet casting. Turn the water thermostat clockwise to lock it in position on the flats cast into the water outlet connection.

11. On the 3.0L engine, turn the thermostat clockwise into the housing until the thermostat bridge is perpendicular to the mounting holes.

12. Tighten the thermostat housing retaining bolts to the proper torque for the engine. Refer to the torque specification charts in the back of this Section.

13. If removed, install the upper radiator hose. Tighten the hose clamp securely.

14. Refill the cooling system, start the engine and check for leaks.

Intake Manifold

➡**Although Ford suggests that this component is removable while the engine is installed in the vehicle, depending on the particular options with which your Aerostar is equipped, working clearance may be extremely tight and this procedure may be much easier to perform with the engine removed. Before commencing, read through this procedure and make certain enough clearance, or working room, exists with the engine in the vehicle; if there is not enough space, the engine should be removed.**

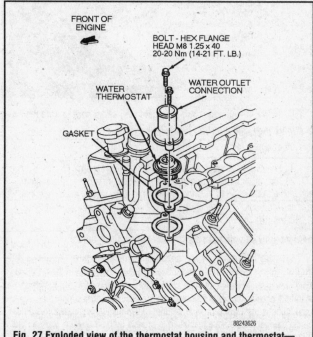

Fig. 27 Exploded view of the thermostat housing and thermostat—3.0L engine

Fig. 28 After draining the coolant system, remove the water neck housing retaining bolts, then . . .

Fig. 29 . . . lift the housing off of the engine block

Fig. 30 Remove the thermostat, then scrape off any remaining gasket material from the thermostat housing

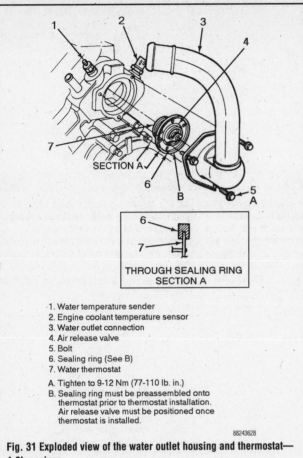

1. Water temperature sender
2. Engine coolant temperature sensor
3. Water outlet connection
4. Air release valve
5. Bolt
6. Sealing ring (See B)
7. Water thermostat
A. Tighten to 9-12 Nm (77-110 lb. in.)
B. Sealing ring must be preassembled onto thermostat prior to thermostat installation. Air release valve must be positioned once thermostat is installed.

Fig. 31 Exploded view of the water outlet housing and thermostat—4.0L engines

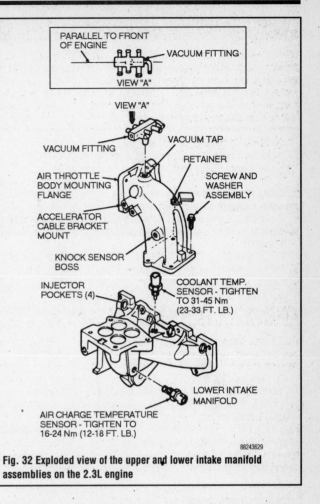

Fig. 32 Exploded view of the upper and lower intake manifold assemblies on the 2.3L engine

REMOVAL & INSTALLATION

2.3L Engine

▶ **See Figures 32 thru 38**

The intake manifold is a two-piece (upper and lower) aluminum casting. Runner lengths are tuned to optimize engine torque and power output. The manifold provides mounting flanges for the air throttle body assembly, fuel supply manifold, accelerator control bracket and the EGR valve and supply tube. A vacuum fitting is installed to provide vacuum to various engine accessories. Pockets for the fuel injectors are machined to prevent both air and fuel leakage. The following procedure is for the removal of the intake manifold with the fuel charging assembly attached.

1. Make sure the ignition is **OFF**, then drain the coolant from the radiator with the engine cold.

✳✳ CAUTION

When draining coolant, keep in mind that cats and dogs are attracted by ethylene glycol antifreeze, and are quite likely to drink any that is left in an uncovered container or in puddles on the ground. This will prove fatal in sufficient quantity. Always drain the coolant into a sealable container. Coolant should be reused unless it is contaminated or several years old.

2. Disconnect the negative battery cable and secure it out of the way.
3. Remove the fuel filler cap to vent tank pressure. Release the pressure from the fuel system. For more details, refer to Section 5.
4. Detach the electrical connectors at the Throttle Position Sensor (TPS), knock sensor, injector wiring harness, air charge temperature sensor and Engine Coolant Temperature (ECT) sensor.

5. Tag and disconnect the vacuum lines at the upper intake manifold vacuum tree, at the EGR valve and at the fuel pressure regulator.
6. Remove the throttle linkage shield and disconnect the throttle linkage and speed control cable (if equipped). Unbolt the accelerator cable from the bracket and position the cable out of the way.
7. Disconnect the air intake hose, air bypass hose and crankcase vent hose.
8. Disconnect the PCV hose from the fitting on the underside of the upper intake manifold.
9. Loosen the clamp on the coolant bypass line at the lower intake manifold, then disconnect the hose.
10. Disconnect the EGR tube from the EGR valve by removing the flange nut.
11. Remove the four upper intake manifold retaining nuts. Remove the upper intake manifold and air throttle body assembly.
12. Disengage the push connect fitting at the fuel supply manifold and fuel return lines. Disconnect the fuel return line from the fuel supply manifold.
13. Remove the engine oil dipstick bracket retaining bolt.
14. Detach the electrical connectors from all four fuel injectors and move the harness aside.
15. Remove the two fuel supply manifold retaining bolts, then carefully remove the fuel supply manifold and injectors. Remove the injectors by exerting a slight twisting/pulling motion.
16. Remove the four bottom retaining bolts from the lower manifold. The front two bolts also secure an engine lifting bracket. Once the bolts are removed, remove the lower intake manifold.
17. Clean and inspect the mounting faces of the lower intake manifold and cylinder head. Both surfaces must be clean and flat.

To install:

➡ **If the intake manifold upper or lower section is being replaced, it will be necessary to transfer components from the old to the new part.**

18. Clean and oil the manifold bolt threads. Install a new lower manifold gasket.

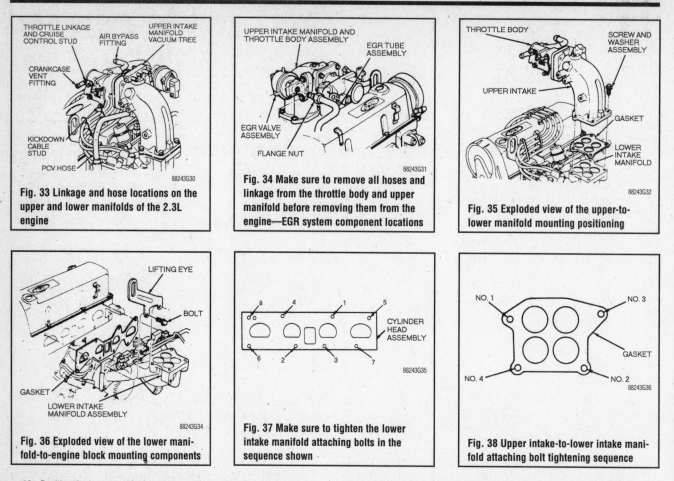

Fig. 33 Linkage and hose locations on the upper and lower manifolds of the 2.3L engine

Fig. 34 Make sure to remove all hoses and linkage from the throttle body and upper manifold before removing them from the engine—EGR system component locations

Fig. 35 Exploded view of the upper-to-lower manifold mounting positioning

Fig. 36 Exploded view of the lower manifold-to-engine block mounting components

Fig. 37 Make sure to tighten the lower intake manifold attaching bolts in the sequence shown

Fig. 38 Upper intake-to-lower intake manifold attaching bolt tightening sequence

19. Position the lower manifold assembly to the head and install the engine lifting bracket. Install the four top manifold retaining bolts finger-tight. Install the four remaining manifold bolts and tighten all bolts to 12–15 ft. lbs. (16–20 Nm), following the sequence illustrated.

20. Install the fuel supply manifold and injectors with two retaining bolts. Tighten the retaining bolts to 12–15 ft. lbs. (16–20 Nm).

21. Attach the four electrical connectors to the injectors.

22. Make sure the gasket surfaces of the upper and lower intake manifolds are clean. Place a gasket on the lower intake manifold assembly, then place the upper intake manifold in position.

23. Install the four retaining bolts and tighten in sequence to 15–22 ft. lbs. (20–30 Nm).

24. The balance of the installation is the reverse of removal.

25. Reconnect the negative battery cable. Refill the cooling system to specifications and pressurize the fuel system by turning the ignition switch on and off (without starting the engine) at least six times, leaving the ignition on for at least five seconds each time.

26. Start the engine and let it idle while checking for fuel, coolant and vacuum leaks. Correct as necessary.

2.8L Engine

▶ See Figure 39

1. Disconnect the negative battery cable.
2. Remove the air cleaner assembly.
3. Disconnect the throttle transmission cable and remove the bracket from the left cylinder head.
4. Drain the cooling system with the engine cold, then disconnect and remove the hose from the water outlet to the radiator and bypass hose from the intake manifold-to-thermostat housing rear cover.

✳✳ CAUTION

When draining coolant, keep in mind that cats and dogs are attracted by ethylene glycol antifreeze, and are quite likely to drink

any that is left in an uncovered container or in puddles on the ground. This will prove fatal in sufficient quantity. Always drain the coolant into a sealable container. Coolant should be reused unless it is contaminated or several years old.

5. Tag the spark plug wires, then detach them from the spark plugs. Remove the distributor cap and spark plug wires as an assembly. Disconnect the distributor wiring harness.

6. Observe and mark the location of the distributor rotor and housing so ignition timing can be maintained at reassembly. Remove the distributor hold-down screw and clamp and lift out the distributor.

➡ Make certain not to turn the crankshaft once the distributor is removed, otherwise the ignition timing will have to be completely reset, as described in Section 1.

7. Remove the rocker arm covers as outlined previously.
8. Remove the fuel line from the fuel filter.

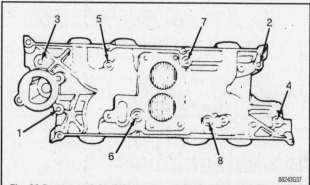

Fig. 39 Be sure to tighten the intake manifold attaching bolts in the correct sequence, as shown

9. Remove the carburetor and EGR spacer.

10. Remove the intake manifold attaching bolts and nuts. Note the length of the manifold attaching bolts during removal so that they may be installed in their original positions. Tap the manifold lightly with a plastic mallet to break the gasket seal, then lift off the manifold.

To install:

11. Remove all traces of old gasket material and sealing compound from all gasket mating surfaces. Be careful not to scratch the intake manifold or cylinder head mating surfaces.

12. To install the intake manifold; first apply sealing compound to the joining surfaces. Place the intake manifold gasket in position, making sure that the tab on the right bank cylinder head gasket fits into the cutout on the manifold gasket.

13. Apply sealing compound to the attaching bolt bosses on the intake manifold and position the intake manifold on the engine. Follow the illustrated tightening sequence and tighten the manifold mounting bolts in five steps:

    a. Install the bolts finger-tight.
    b. Tighten to 36–72 inch lbs. (4–8 Nm).
    c. Tighten to 6–11 ft. lbs. (8–15 Nm).
    d. Tighten to 11–15 ft. lbs. (15–21 Nm).
    e. Tighten to 15–18 ft. lbs. (21–25 Nm).

14. The balance of the installation is the reverse of removal.

15. Connect the negative battery cable.

16. Refill and bleed the cooling system. Check the ignition timing and idle speed and reset to specifications, if necessary. Run the engine at fast idle and check for coolant or oil leaks.

3.0L Engine

▶ **See Figures 40 thru 47**

➡ **The upper intake manifold is integral with the throttle body. For procedures regarding this component, refer to Section 5.**

1. Drain the cooling system with the engine cold.

✳✳ CAUTION

When draining coolant, keep in mind that cats and dogs are attracted by ethylene glycol antifreeze, and are quite likely to drink any that is left in an uncovered container or in puddles on the ground. This will prove fatal in sufficient quantity. Always drain the coolant into a sealable container. Coolant should be reused unless it is contaminated or several years old.

2. Disconnect the negative battery cable.

3. Remove the wiring harnesses from the following components:
- Intake Air Temperature (IAT) sensor
- Idle Air Control (IAC) valve
- Engine Coolant Temperature (ECT) sensor
- Distributor
- Ignition coil
- Radio ignition interference capacitor
- Water temperature indicator sender unit
- EGR pressure sensor, if equipped
- EGR vacuum regulator control, if equipped

4. Depressurize the fuel system and remove the throttle body. For more details, refer to Section 5.

5. Disconnect the fuel return and supply lines.

6. Disconnect the fuel injection wiring retaining standoffs from the inboard rocker arm cover studs. Carefully remove the fuel injector wiring harness from each the fuel injectors.

7. Disconnect the upper radiator hose.

8. Disconnect the water outlet heater hose.

9. Remove the spark plug from cylinder No. 1, then bring the No. 1 piston to top dead center on the compression stroke.

10. Tag and detach the spark plug wires from the spark plugs, then remove the distributor cap with the spark plug wires attached. Matchmark and remove the distributor assembly. For more information, refer to Section 2.

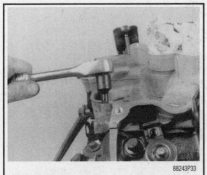

Fig. 40 After removing the throttle body and related components, remove the manifold retaining bolts, . . .

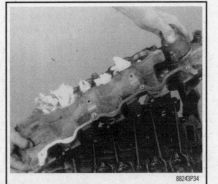

Fig. 41 . . . then lift the intake manifold off the engine block

Fig. 42 Remove the old intake manifold-to-cylinder head gaskets

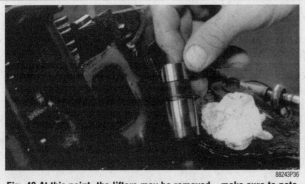

Fig. 43 At this point, the lifters may be removed—make sure to note the original locations of the lifters

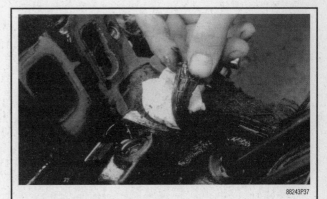

Fig. 44 Remove the rubber end gaskets from the engine block

11. Remove the rocker arm covers, as described earlier in this section.

12. Loosen the No. 3 intake valve rocker arm bolt and rotate the rocker arm off of the pushrod and away from the top of the valve stem. Remove the pushrod from the engine.

13. Remove the intake manifold attaching bolts and studs using a Torx® head socket.

14. Lift the intake manifold off the engine. Use a plastic mallet to tap lightly around the intake manifold to break it loose, if necessary. Do not pry between the manifold and cylinder head with any sharp instrument. The manifold can be removed with the fuel rails and injectors in place.

To install:

➡When cleaning the engine surfaces, lay a clean cloth or shop rag in the lifter valley to catch any gasket material. After scraping, carefully lift the cloth from the lifter valley preventing any particles from entering oil drain holes or cylinder head.

15. Remove the manifold side gaskets and end seals and discard. If the manifold is being replaced, transfer the fuel injector and fuel rail components to the new manifold on a clean workbench. Clean all gasket mating surfaces.

16. Lightly oil all attaching bolts and stud threads. The intake manifold, cylinder head and cylinder block mating surfaces should be clean and free of old silicone rubber sealer or old gasket material. Use a suitable solvent to clean these areas.

17. If installing a new intake manifold, transfer the fuel injectors, fuel injection supply manifold, ECT sensor, water thermostat, thermostat housing, hot water heater elbow connection, and the coolant temperature sending unit to the new manifold.

18. Apply silicone rubber sealer (D6AZ–19562–A or equivalent) to the intersection of the cylinder block assembly and head assembly at four corners as illustrated.

➡When using silicone rubber sealer, assembly must occur within 15 minutes after sealer application. After this time, the sealer may start to set and its sealing effectiveness may be reduced. In high temperature/humidity conditions, the RTV will start to skin over in about 5 minutes.

19. Install the front intake manifold seal and rear intake manifold seal, then secure them with retaining features.

20. Position the intake manifold gaskets in place and insert the locking tabs over the tabs on the cylinder head gaskets.

21. Apply silicone rubber sealer over the gasket in the same places as in Step 17.

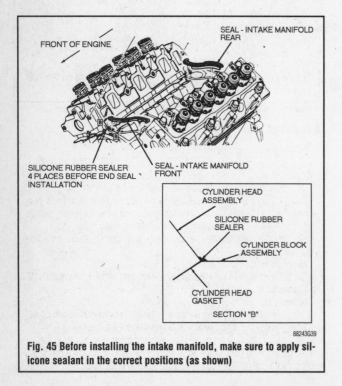

Fig. 45 Before installing the intake manifold, make sure to apply silicone sealant in the correct positions (as shown)

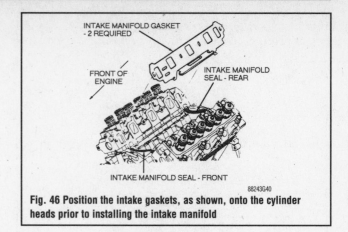

Fig. 46 Position the intake gaskets, as shown, onto the cylinder heads prior to installing the intake manifold

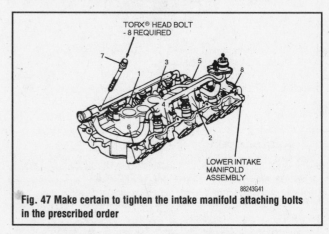

Fig. 47 Make certain to tighten the intake manifold attaching bolts in the prescribed order

22. Carefully lower the intake manifold into position on the cylinder block and cylinder heads to prevent smearing the silicone sealer and causing gasket leaks.

23. Install the retaining bolts and tighten in two stages, in the sequence illustrated, first to 11 ft. lbs. (15 Nm) and then to 18 ft. lbs. (24 Nm).

24. The balance of the installation is the reverse of removal.

25. Reconnect the negative battery cable and refill the cooling system.

26. Run the engine and check for coolant, fuel, oil and vacuum leaks.

4.0L Engine

▶ **See Figures 48 and 49**

The intake manifold is a 4-piece assembly, consisting of the upper intake manifold, the throttle body, the fuel supply manifold, and the lower intake manifold. For servicing of the throttle body and fuel injection supply manifold, refer to Section 5.

1. Relieve the fuel system pressure, as described in Section 5 of this manual.

2. Disconnect the negative battery cable.

3. Remove the air cleaner and intake duct.

4. Remove the weather shield.

5. Disconnect the throttle cable and bracket.

6. Tag and disconnect all vacuum lines attached to the manifold.

7. Tag and disconnect all electrical wires attached to the manifold assemblies.

8. Tag and remove the spark plug wires.

9. Remove the ignition coil and bracket.

10. Remove the throttle body. For more information, refer to Section 5.

11. Remove the 6 attaching nuts and lift off the upper manifold.

12. Remove the rocker arm covers, as described earlier in this section.

13. Remove the lower intake manifold bolts. Tap the manifold lightly with a plastic mallet to break the seal, then remove it from the engine.

14. Clean all surfaces of old gasket material.

To install:

15. Apply Silicone Rubber D6AZ-19562-BA or equivalent to the block and cylinder head mating surfaces at the four corners shown. Install the intake manifold gasket and again apply sealer to the four corner locations.

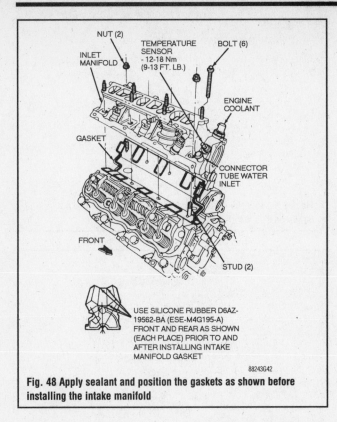

Fig. 48 Apply sealant and position the gaskets as shown before installing the intake manifold

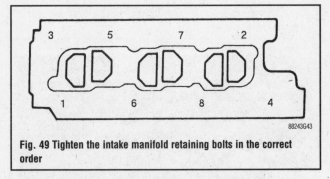

Fig. 49 Tighten the intake manifold retaining bolts in the correct order

➡ This material will set within 15 minutes, so work quickly!

16. Position the lower manifold onto the engine block, then install the nuts hand-tight. Tighten the nuts, in 3 stages, in the sequence shown, to 18 ft. lbs. (25 Nm).

   a. 6 ft. lbs. (8 Nm).
   b. 11 ft. lbs. (15 Nm).
   c. 16 ft. lbs. (22 Nm).

17. Once again, apply RTV material to the manifold/head joints as before.
18. Install the rocker arm covers.
19. Install the upper manifold. Tighten the nuts to 15–18 ft. lbs. (20–25 Nm).
20. The balance of the installation is the reverse of removal.
21. Connect the negative battery cable.
22. Fill and bleed the cooling system. For more information, refer to Section 1.
23. Check for coolant leaks.

Exhaust Manifold

➡ Although Ford suggests that this component is removable while the engine is installed in the vehicle, depending on the particular options with which your Aerostar is equipped, working clearance may be extremely tight and this procedure may be much easier to perform with the engine removed. Before commencing, read through this procedure

and make certain enough clearance, or working room, exists with the engine in the vehicle; if there is not enough space, the engine should be removed.

REMOVAL & INSTALLATION

2.3L Engine

▶ See Figure 50

1. Remove the air cleaner ducts, if necessary to gain working clearance.
2. Disconnect the EGR line at the exhaust manifold, then loosen it at the EGR tube.
3. Detach electrical connector from the oxygen sensor.
4. Remove the screw attaching the heater hoses on the valve cover.
5. Remove the eight exhaust manifold mounting bolts, then move the exhaust manifold away from the cylinder head and remove the gasket.
6. Raise the van and support it safely on jackstands.
7. Remove the two exhaust pipe bolts and separate the exhaust pipe from the exhaust manifold.
8. Carefully lower the exhaust manifold down and out of the engine compartment. Be careful not to damage the oxygen sensor during removal.

To install:

9. Clean all gasket mating surfaces. If the exhaust manifold is being replaced, the oxygen sensor will have to be transferred to the new manifold.
10. Place a new gasket on the exhaust manifold, then position the manifold on the cylinder head.
11. Install the eight exhaust manifold bolts and tighten them in two stages, first to 60–84 inch lbs. (7–9 Nm) and then to 16–23 ft. lbs. (22–31 Nm).
12. Install the two exhaust pipe bolts and tighten them to 25–34 ft. lbs. (34–46 Nm).
13. The balance of the installation is the reverse of removal.

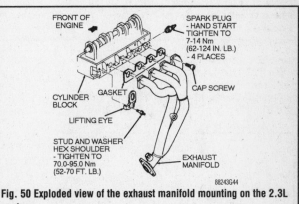

Fig. 50 Exploded view of the exhaust manifold mounting on the 2.3L engine

2.8L Engine

1. Remove the air cleaner.
2. Remove the attaching nuts from the exhaust manifold shroud on the right side.
3. Raise the van and support it safely on jackstands.
4. Working under the van, disconnect the attaching nuts from the Y-pipe. Remove the thermactor upstream crossover tube and other thermactor components, as necessary, to allow removal of the exhaust manifold(s).
5. Detach the exhaust gas oxygen sensor connector on the left exhaust manifold.
6. Remove the manifold attaching nuts.
7. Lift the manifold from the cylinder head, then remove the manifold to head gaskets.

To install:

8. Clean all gasket mating surfaces. If the left exhaust manifold is being replaced, the oxygen sensor will have to be transferred to the new part.
9. Position the new gasket and the manifold on the engine studs, then install the attaching bolts to 20–30 ft. lbs. (27–37 Nm). Start at the center and work outward, alternating sides during the tightening sequence.

10. Install a new inlet pipe gasket, then install the inlet pipe attaching bolts to 25–34 ft. lbs. (34–36 Nm).

11. The balance of the installation is the reverse of removal.

3.0L Engine

▶ See Figure 51

✳✳ CAUTION

Allow the engine to cool sufficiently before removing the manifolds. Serious injury can result from contact with hot exhaust manifolds.

1986–91 MODELS

▶ See Figures 52, 53, 54 and 55

1. Remove the air cleaner assembly, if necessary to gain working clearance.

2. Remove the oil level indicator tube support bracket. Remove the power steering pump pressure and return hoses if the left-hand manifold is being removed. If the right-hand manifold is being removed, disconnect the EGR tube from the exhaust manifold and the oxygen sensor connector.

3. Raise the vehicle and support it safely.

4. Remove the manifold-to-exhaust pipe attaching nuts, then separate the exhaust pipe from the manifold.

5. Remove the exhaust manifold attaching bolts and the manifold.

To install:

6. Clean all gasket mating surfaces.

7. Lightly oil all bolt and stud threads before installation. If a new manifold is being installed, the oxygen sensor will have to be transferred to the new part.

8. Position the exhaust manifold on the cylinder head and install the manifold attaching bolts. Tighten them to 15–22 ft. lbs. (20–30 Nm).

9. Connect the exhaust pipe to the manifold, then tighten the attaching nuts to 16–24 ft. lbs. (21–32 Nm). Lower the vehicle.

10. The balance of the installation is the reverse of removal.

1992–97 MODELS

1. Disconnect the negative battery cable.

➡Spray retaining fasteners with rust penetrant prior to loosening in order to prevent removal of the stud when the nut is loosened.

2. Raise and safely support the vehicle on jackstands.

3. Loosen and remove the muffler inlet pipe retaining nuts from the exhaust manifolds.

4. Lower the vehicle.

5. To remove the right-hand side manifold, perform the following:
   a. Remove the spark plugs.
   b. Remove the exhaust manifold retaining bolts and studs.

6. To remove the left-hand side manifold, perform the following:
   a. Remove the two hoses from the EGR valve to the exhaust manifold tube.
   b. Loosen the EGR tube flare nut at the EGR valve.
   c. Remove the EGR tube bolt at the exhaust manifold.
   d. Remove the engine oil level indicator dipstick tube retaining nut. Rotate or remove the tube out of the way.
   e. Remove the spark plugs.
   f. Remove the exhaust manifold retaining bolts and studs.

7. Remove the exhaust manifolds.

To install:

8. Clean the mating surfaces of the exhaust manifolds and cylinder heads of carbon deposits.

9. Position the right or left exhaust manifold in place to the cylinder head, then hand-tighten the retaining bolts and studs. Tighten to 15–22 ft. lbs. (20–30 Nm).

10. Install the oil level indicator tube to the appropriate exhaust stud and install the retaining nut if the exhaust manifold was removed. Tighten the nut to 12–15 ft. lbs. (16–20 Nm). Apply ESE-M4G217-A sealer to the tube prior to installation if the tube was removed.

11. The balance of the installation is the reverse of removal.

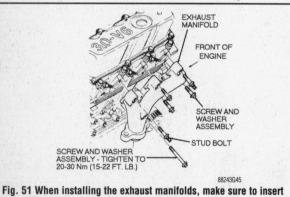

Fig. 51 When installing the exhaust manifolds, make sure to insert the long bolt into the correct hole—left-hand side exhaust manifold

Fig. 52 Disconnect the exhaust pipe from the manifold and remove the manifold attaching bolts, then . . .

Fig. 53 . . . pull the exhaust manifold off of the engine block

Fig. 54 Make sure to remove all of the old gasket material, which . . .

Fig. 55 . . . may require scraping to remove all of the hardened gasket material

4.0L Engine

LEFT SIDE

1. Raise and safely support the vehicle on jackstands so that access can be gained from both the top and the bottom of the engine compartment.
2. Remove the oil level indicator tube bracket.
3. Remove the power steering pump hoses.
4. Remove the exhaust pipe-to-manifold bolts.
5. Unbolt and remove the manifold.
   To install:

➡**Clean and lightly oil all fastener threads prior to installation.**

6. Clean the mating surfaces on the exhaust manifold, cylinder head and exhaust pipe.
7. Position the exhaust manifold on the cylinder head and install manifold attaching bolts. Tighten the bolts to 19 ft. lbs. (25 Nm).
8. The balance of the installation is the reverse of removal.

RIGHT SIDE

1. Raise and safely support the vehicle on jackstands so that access can be gained from both the top and the bottom of the engine compartment.
2. Drain the cooling system.

✳✳ CAUTION

When draining coolant, keep in mind that cats and dogs are attracted by ethylene glycol antifreeze, and are quite likely to drink any that is left in an uncovered container or in puddles on the ground. This will prove fatal in sufficient quantity. Always drain the coolant into a sealable container. Coolant should be reused unless it is contaminated or several years old.

3. Remove the heater hose support bracket.
4. Disconnect the heater hoses.
5. Remove the exhaust pipe-to-manifold nuts.

6. Unbolt and remove the manifold.
   To install:

➡**Lightly oil all bolt and stud threads before installation.**

7. Clean the mating surfaces on the exhaust manifold cylinder head and exhaust inlet pipe.
8. Position the exhaust manifold on the cylinder head and install the manifold attaching bolts. Tighten the bolts to 18 ft. lbs. (25 Nm).
9. Connect the exhaust inlet pipe to the exhaust manifold. Tighten the attaching nuts to 20 ft. lbs. (27 Nm).
10. The balance of the installation is the reverse of removal.

Radiator

REMOVAL & INSTALLATION

▶ **See Figures 56 thru 62**

1. With the engine cold, drain the cooling system by removing the radiator cap, attaching a ⅜ in. (9.5mm) inside diameter hose to the draincock nipple, then opening the draincock at the lower rear corner of the radiator tank. Drain the coolant out of the radiator, through the hose, and into a suitably sized container.

✳✳ CAUTION

When draining coolant, keep in mind that cats and dogs are attracted by ethylene glycol antifreeze, and are quite likely to drink any that is left in an uncovered container or in puddles on the ground. This will prove fatal in sufficient quantity. Always drain the coolant into a sealable container. Coolant should be reused unless it is contaminated or several years old.

2. Remove the rubber overflow tube from the radiator and store it out of the way.

Fig. 56 After draining the radiator, disconnect the transmission cooling lines from the radiator

Fig. 57 Disconnect the fan and clutch assembly from the water pump pulley, . . .

Fig. 58 . . . remove all of the radiator shroud-to-radiator retaining bolts, then . . .

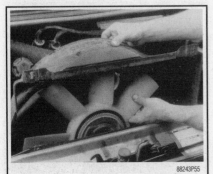

Fig. 59 . . . lift the radiator shroud and fan/clutch assembly from the engine compartment

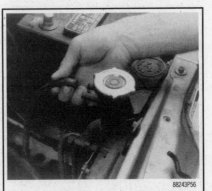

Fig. 60 Detach any remaining lines from the radiator

Fig. 61 Remove the radiator-to-body attaching bolts, then . . .

Fig. 62 . . . lift the radiator out of the engine bay—do not damage the cooling fins on any sharp edges

3. Remove the cooling fan and clutch assembly from the water pump pulley. For more details, refer to the cooling fan procedures later in this section.

4. Remove the radiator fan shroud upper attaching screws, then lift the shroud out of the lower retaining clips. Lift it and the cooling fan/clutch out of the engine compartment.

5. Loosen the upper and lower hose clamps at the radiator and remove the hoses from the radiator connections.

6. If equipped with an automatic transmission, disconnect the transmission cooling lines from the radiator fittings. Disconnect the transmission cooler tube support bracket from the bottom flange of the radiator by removing the screw.

7. Remove the two radiator upper attaching screws.

8. Tilt the radiator back (rearward) about 1 in. (25mm) and lift it directly upward, clear of the radiator support and the cooling fan.

9. If either hose is being replaced, loosen the clamp at the engine end and slip the hose off the connection with a twisting motion.

10. Lift the fan shroud off of the fan, then remove it from the vehicle.

11. Remove the radiator lower support rubber insulators.

To install:

12. Install the coolant hose(s) to the engine connections, making sure any bends are oriented exactly as the old hose for alignment purposes.

13. If the radiator is being replaced, transfer the lower support rubber insulators to the new part. The radiator cooling fins should be cleaned of any dirt or debris and any bent fins should be CAREFULLY straightened.

14. Install the radiator into the engine compartment, making sure the lower rubber insulators are properly positioned in the radiator support. Be careful to clear the fan with the radiator to avoid damage to the cooling fins.

15. Connect the upper attaching bolts to the radiator support and tighten them to 12–20 ft. lbs. (17–27 Nm).

16. The balance of the installation is the reverse of removal.

17. Fill and bleed the cooling system.

Engine Fan

REMOVAL & INSTALLATION

2.3L Engine

1. Unbolt and remove the fan guard.

2. Disconnect the overflow tube from the shroud, remove the mounting screws and lift the shroud off the brackets.

3. Place the shroud behind the fan.

4. Remove the 4 clutch/fan assembly-to-pulley screws and remove the clutch/fan assembly.

5. Remove the 4 fan-to-clutch screws.

To install:

6. Position the fan onto the clutch assembly, then install the retaining screws to 55–70 inch lbs. (6–8 Nm).

7. Position the clutch/fan assembly onto the pulley. Install the mounting screws to 12–18 ft. lbs. (16–24 Nm).

8. Position the fan onto the radiator. Install the shroud mounting screws until snug.

9. Install the fan guard.

2.8L, 3.0L and 4.0L Engines

▸ See Figures 63 and 64

1. Remove the accessory drive belt. For more information, refer to Section 1.

2. If necessary for added clearance, remove the fan shroud retaining screws.

✳✳ CAUTION

On some engines, the fan clutch nut is a left-hand thread. Remove by turning the nut clockwise. Check the fan shroud for identification.

3. Using the Fan Clutch Holding tool T84T-6312-C and Fan Clutch Nut Wrench T84T-6312-D, or their equivalents, loosen the large nut attaching the fan clutch to the water pump pulley.

4. Remove the fan/clutch assembly.

5. Remove the fan-to-clutch bolts, then separate the fan from the clutch assembly.

To install:

6. Position the fan onto the clutch assembly, then install the fan-to-clutch mounting bolts to 53–71 inch lbs. (6–8 Nm).

7. Position the lower edge of the fan shroud in the lower retaining clips, then install the fan shroud attaching screws until snug.

8. Using the holding tool and clutch nut wrench, or equivalent, install the fan/clutch assembly onto the water pump pulley. Remember, the fan/clutch nut has a reverse thread and must be turned counterclockwise to tighten. Tighten the nut to 30–100 ft. lbs. (41–135 Nm).

9. Install the accessory drive belt.

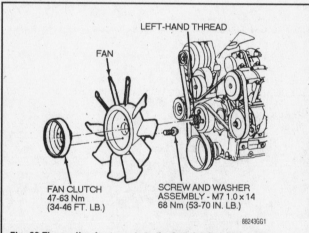

Fig. 63 The cooling fan mounts to the fan clutch, which in turn attaches to the water pump pulley—3.0L and 4.0L engines

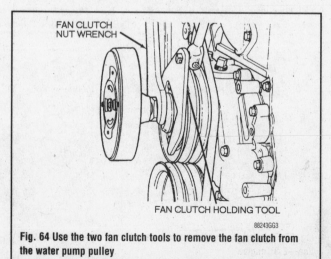

Fig. 64 Use the two fan clutch tools to remove the fan clutch from the water pump pulley

Water Pump

REMOVAL & INSTALLATION

2.3L Engine

▶ See Figure 65

➡Provision for wrench clearance has been made in the timing belt inner cover, so only the outer cover must be removed in order to replace the water pump.

1. Raise a safely support the van on jackstands so that access to the engine can be gained from both the top or the bottom of the engine compartment.
2. Disconnect the negative battery cable.
3. Drain the cooling system with the engine cold.

❊❊ CAUTION

When draining coolant, keep in mind that cats and dogs are attracted by ethylene glycol antifreeze, and are quite likely to drink any that is left in an uncovered container or in puddles on the ground. This will prove fatal in sufficient quantity. Always drain the coolant into a sealable container. Coolant should be reused unless it is contaminated or several years old.

4. Remove the two bolts retaining the fan shroud and position the shroud over the fan.
5. Remove the four bolts retaining the fan assembly to the water pump shaft, then remove the fan and shroud.
6. If applicable, loosen the air conditioning compressor adjusting idler pulley, then remove the drive belt.
7. Loosen the power steering bolts, if equipped, then remove the alternator and power steering belts.
8. Remove the water pump pulley and the vent tube to the canister.
9. Remove the heater hose to the water pump.
10. Remove the outer timing belt cover, as described later in this section.
11. Remove the lower radiator hose from the water pump.
12. Remove the water pump retaining bolts, then remove the water pump from the engine.

To install:

13. Clean the water pump gasket surface at the engine block. Remove all traces of old gasket and/or sealer.
14. Use contact cement to position the new gasket onto the water pump. Position the water pump to the engine block and install three retaining bolts. Apply sealer (D8AZ–19554–A or equivalent) to the water pump bolts prior to installation, then tighten the bolts to 14–21 ft. lbs. (19–29 Nm).
15. The balance of the installation is the reverse of removal.
16. Refill the cooling system, then start the engine and check for leaks.

2.8L Engine

▶ See Figures 66, 67 and 68

➡This procedure requires the use of special tools to remove the fan and clutch assembly.

1. Raise and safely support the vehicle on jackstands so that access to the engine can be gained from both the top and the bottom of the engine compartment.
2. Drain the cooling system with the engine cold into a clean container and save the coolant for reuse.

❊❊ CAUTION

When draining coolant, keep in mind that cats and dogs are attracted by ethylene glycol antifreeze, and are quite likely to drink any that is left in an uncovered container or in puddles on the ground. This will prove fatal in sufficient quantity. Always drain the coolant into a sealable container. Coolant should be reused unless it is contaminated or several years old.

3. Loosen the hose clamps, then detach the lower radiator hose and heater return hose from the water inlet housing.

❊❊ CAUTION

On some engines, the fan clutch nut is a left-hand thread. Remove by turning the nut clockwise. Check the fan shroud for identification.

4. Remove the clutch and fan assembly using a Fan Clutch Pulley Holder (tool no. T83T–6312–A) and Fan Clutch Nut Wrench (tool no. T83T–6312–B).
5. Loosen the alternator mounting bolts and remove the belt. If equipped with air conditioning, remove the alternator and bracket.
6. Remove the water pump pulley.
7. Remove the water pump assembly attaching bolts, then remove the water pump assembly and water inlet housing from the front cover. Note the position of the different length bolts when removing them so they may be installed in their original locations.

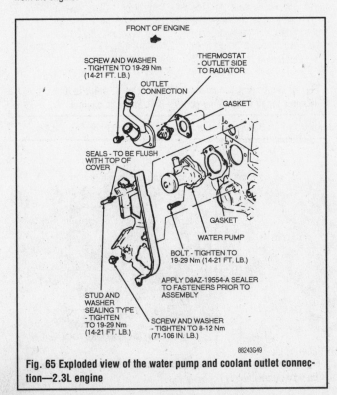

FRONT OF ENGINE

SCREW AND WASHER - TIGHTEN TO 19-29 Nm (14-21 FT. LB.)

THERMOSTAT - OUTLET SIDE TO RADIATOR

OUTLET CONNECTION

GASKET

SEALS - TO BE FLUSH WITH TOP OF COVER

GASKET

WATER PUMP

BOLT - TIGHTEN TO 19-29 Nm (14-21 FT. LB.)

APPLY D8AZ-19554-A SEALER TO FASTENERS PRIOR TO ASSEMBLY

STUD AND WASHER SEALING TYPE - TIGHTEN TO 19-29 Nm (14-21 FT. LB.)

SCREW AND WASHER - TIGHTEN TO 8-12 Nm (71-106 IN. LB.)

88243G49

Fig. 65 Exploded view of the water pump and coolant outlet connection—2.3L engine

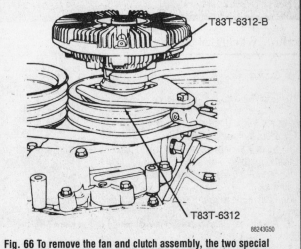

T83T-6312-B

T83T-6312

88243G50

Fig. 66 To remove the fan and clutch assembly, the two special tools (T83T-6312-B and T83T-6312 or their equivalents) should be used to avoid damaging the assembly—2.8L and 3.0L engines

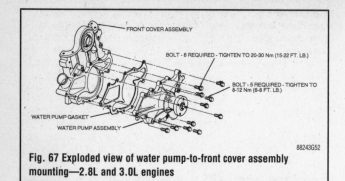

Fig. 67 Exploded view of water pump-to-front cover assembly mounting—2.8L and 3.0L engines

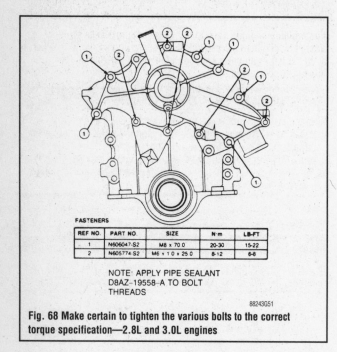

NOTE: APPLY PIPE SEALANT D8AZ-19558-A TO BOLT THREADS

REF NO.	PART NO.	SIZE	N·m	LB-FT
1	N606047-S2	M8 x 70.0	20-30	15-22
2	N605774-S2	M6 x 1.0 x 25.0	8-12	6-8

Fig. 68 Make certain to tighten the various bolts to the correct torque specification—2.8L and 3.0L engines

To install:

8. Clean all gasket material and/or sealer from all gasket mating surfaces on the front cover and water pump assembly.

9. Apply sealer to both sides of the new gasket and place the gasket on the water pump.

10. Position the water pump assembly to the front cover and install two bolts finger-tight to hold it in position.

11. Clean all gasket material and/or sealer from the mating surfaces of the water inlet housing. Apply sealer to both sides of a new gasket and place it on the water inlet housing.

12. Position the water inlet housing and install the attaching bolts. Note the different length bolts. Tighten the water inlet bolts to 12–15 ft. lbs. (17–21 Nm).

13. Install and tighten the water pump attaching bolts to 7–9 ft. lbs. (9–12 Nm).

14. The balance of the installation is the reverse of removal.

15. Refill the cooling system, then start the engine and check for leaks.

3.0L Engine

♦ **See Figures 66 thru 72**

1. Disconnect the negative battery cable.
2. Drain the cooling system.

✱✱ CAUTION

When draining coolant, keep in mind that cats and dogs are attracted by ethylene glycol antifreeze, and are quite likely to drink any that is left in an uncovered container or in puddles on the ground. This will prove fatal in sufficient quantity. Always drain the coolant into a sealable container. Coolant should be reused unless it is contaminated or several years old.

3. Remove the engine air cleaner outlet tube.

4. Remove the engine fan and radiator shield, as described earlier in this section.

➡The fan/clutch-to-water pump pulley nut has left-hand threads. It is removed by turning it clockwise.

5. Loosen, but do not remove at this time, the 4 water pump pulley bolts.

6. Remove the accessory drive belts. For more information, refer to Section 1.

7. Remove the 4 water pump pulley retaining screws, then remove the pulley itself.

8. Disconnect the engine wiring harness from the alternator.

9. Remove the oil fill tube retaining nut at the alternator stud, then lift the tube from the stud.

10. Remove the alternator adjusting arm and throttle body brace.

11. Using a Torx® 50 driver, remove the engine drive belt tensioner assembly.

12. If equipped with an auxiliary heater, remove the screw retaining the auxiliary heater tube bracket at the power steering pump support bracket.

13. Remove the lower radiator hose.

14. Disconnect the heater hose at the water pump.

15. For vehicles equipped with power steering, remove the 5 screws retaining the power steering pump support bracket to the engine, then secure the power steering pump and bracket assembly near the battery tray. Do not disconnect the power steering hoses from the pump.

16. Remove the water pump attaching bolts. Note their location for reinstallation.

17. Remove the pump from the engine and discard the old gasket.

To install:

➡Lightly oil all bolts and stud threads before installation except those retaining special sealant.

Fig. 69 While the accessory drive belts are still installed, loosen the water pump pulley bolts

Fig. 70 Remove the drive belts, water pump pulley and detach the hose from the pump

Fig. 71 Remove the water pump mounting bolts, then . . .

88243P03

Fig. 72 . . . remove the pump from the front cover

18. Thoroughly clean the pump and engine mating surfaces.
19. Using an adhesive type sealer (Trim Adhesive D7AZ-19B508-B or equivalent), position a new gasket on the timing cover.
20. Position the water pump onto the engine, then install the retaining bolts. When all the bolts are started, tighten them to 84 inch lbs. (9 Nm).
21. The balance of the installation is the reverse of removal.
22. Connect the negative battery cable.
23. Fill and bleed the cooling system.
24. Run the engine and check for leaks.

4.0L Engine

1. Raise and safely support the vehicle on jackstands so that access to the engine can be gained from both the top and the bottom of the engine compartment.
2. Drain the cooling system.

> **✴✴ CAUTION**
>
> When draining coolant, keep in mind that cats and dogs are attracted by ethylene glycol antifreeze, and are quite likely to drink any that is left in an uncovered container or in puddles on the ground. This will prove fatal in sufficient quantity. Always drain the coolant into a sealable container. Coolant should be reused unless it is contaminated or several years old.

3. Remove the lower radiator hose and heater return hose from the water pump.
4. Remove the fan and fan clutch assembly, as described earlier in this section.
5. Loosen the alternator mounting bolts and remove the belt. On vans with air conditioning, remove the compressor and bracket without disconnecting the A/C lines. Support the compressor from the vehicle frame rail with strong cord or wire.
6. If equipped with power steering, remove the power steering pump. Set it aside as with the A/C compressor.
7. Remove the water pump pulley.
8. Remove the water pump attaching bolts, then remove the water pump.

To install:

9. Clean the mounting surfaces of the pump and front cover thoroughly. Remove all traces of gasket material.
10. Apply adhesive gasket sealer to both sides of a new gasket and place the gasket on the pump.
11. Position the pump on the cover and install the bolts finger-tight. When all bolts are in place, tighten them to 6–9 ft. lbs. (9–12 Nm).
12. The balance of the installation is the reverse of removal.
13. Refill the cooling system, then start the engine and check for leaks.

Cylinder Head

➡Although Ford suggests that this component is removable while the engine is installed in the vehicle, depending on the particular options with which your Aerostar is equipped, working clearance may be extremely tight and this procedure may be much easier to perform with

the engine removed. Before commencing, read through this procedure and make certain enough clearance, or working room, exists with the engine in the vehicle; if there is not enough space, the engine should be removed.

REMOVAL & INSTALLATION

2.3L Engine

▶ **See Figure 73**

1. Disconnect the negative battery cable.
2. Drain the cooling system, with the engine cold, into a clean container and save the coolant for reuse.

> **✴✴ CAUTION**
>
> When draining coolant, keep in mind that cats and dogs are attracted by ethylene glycol antifreeze, and are quite likely to drink any that is left in an uncovered container or in puddles on the ground. This will prove fatal in sufficient quantity. Always drain the coolant into a sealable container. Coolant should be reused unless it is contaminated or several years old.

3. Raise the vehicle and support it safely on jackstands.
4. Remove the resonator assembly.
5. Lower the vehicle.
6. Tag and disconnect the spark plug wires from the plugs, then remove the distributor cap and spark plug wires as an assembly. Remove the distributor. For more details, refer to Section 2.
7. Remove the spark plugs.
8. Tag and disconnect all vacuum hoses.
9. Remove the dipstick and tube from the engine block.
10. Remove the rocker arm cover, as described earlier in this section.
11. Remove the intake manifold, as described earlier in this section.
12. Loosen the alternator retaining bolts, remove the belt from the pulley and remove the mounting bracket retaining bolts from the cylinder head.
13. Remove the upper radiator hose.

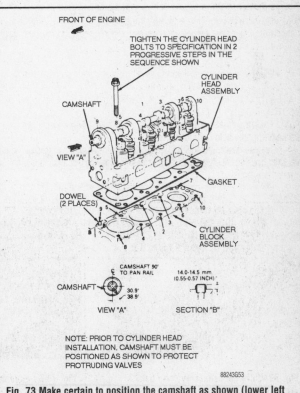

88243G53

Fig. 73 Make certain to position the camshaft as shown (lower left in the illustration) when installing the cylinder head—2.3L engine

14. Remove the timing belt cover, belt and tensioner/idler assembly, as described later in this section.
15. Remove the exhaust manifold, as described earlier in this section.
16. Disconnect the oil sending unit lead wire.
17. Remove the cylinder head retaining bolts in reverse of the tightening sequence.
18. Carefully lift the cylinder head off the engine.

To install:
19. Clean the cylinder head gasket surface at the block.
20. Clean the intake manifold gasket surface at the intake manifold and the exhaust manifold gasket surface at the exhaust manifold and cylinder head.
21. Clean the cylinder head gasket surface at the cylinder head and the intake manifold gasket surface at the cylinder head.
22. Blow oil out of the cylinder head bolt block holes with compressed air.
23. Clean the rocker cover gasket surface on the cylinder head and check the head for flatness.
24. Position the head gasket on the block, then carefully lower the cylinder head down into place. Refer to the illustration to make sure the camshaft is positioned correctly to protect the valves when installing the cylinder head.
25. Install the cylinder head retaining bolts and tighten them in sequence in two steps, first to 50–60 ft. lbs. (68–81 Nm) and then to 80–90 ft. lbs. (108–122 Nm).
26. Connect the oil sending unit lead wires.
27. Install the timing belt idler spring stop to the cylinder head.
28. Position the timing belt idler onto the cylinder head, then install the retaining bolts.
29. Position the exhaust manifold onto the cylinder head, then install the eight exhaust manifold retaining bolts.
30. Align the distributor rotor with the No. 1 plug location in the distributor cap.
31. Align the camshaft gear with the timing pointer.
32. Align the crankshaft pulley TDC mark with the pointer on the timing belt cover.
33. Install the timing belt to the pulleys (camshaft and auxiliary).
34. Loosen the idler retaining bolts and allow it to tension the timing belt, then rotate the engine by hand and check the timing alignment. For more information, refer to the timing belt procedure later in this section.
35. Adjust the belt tensioner and tighten the retaining bolts. Install the timing belt cover and tighten the retaining bolts.
36. The balance of the installation is the reverse of removal.
37. Refill the cooling system, as described in Section 1.
38. Install the resonator assembly, then start the engine and check for leaks. Adjust the ignition timing and idle speed, if necessary.

2.8L Engine

▶ See Figure 74

1. Disconnect the negative battery cable.
2. Drain the cooling system, with the engine cold, into a clean container and save the coolant for reuse.

⁂ CAUTION

When draining coolant, keep in mind that cats and dogs are attracted by ethylene glycol antifreeze, and are quite likely to drink any that is left in an uncovered container or in puddles on the ground. This will prove fatal in sufficient quantity. Always drain the coolant into a sealable container. Coolant should be reused unless it is contaminated or several years old.

3. Remove the air cleaner from the carburetor and disconnect the throttle linkage. Remove the linkage bracket.
4. Tag and disconnect the spark plug wires from the spark plugs. Remove the distributor cap and wires as an assembly. Disconnect the distributor wiring harness.
5. Matchmark the location of the distributor rotor and housing so the ignition timing can be maintained at reassembly. Remove the distributor hold-down screw and clamp, then lift out the distributor. Note the rotor movement as the distributor is installed so it may be positioned correctly on installation.
6. Remove the radiator and bypass hoses from the thermostat and intake manifold.

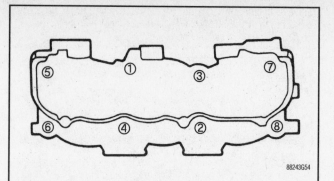

Fig. 74 Tighten the cylinder head bolts in the sequence shown to provide proper gasket sealing—2.8L engine

7. Remove the rocker arm covers and rocker arm shafts as previously described in this section.
8. Disconnect the fuel line from the carburetor, then remove the carburetor.
9. Remove the intake manifold, as described earlier in this section.
10. Remove the pushrods, keeping them in order so they may be installed in their original locations.
11. Remove the exhaust manifold(s) as previously described in this section.
12. Loosen the cylinder head attaching bolts in reverse of the tightening sequence, then remove the bolts and lift off the cylinder head. Remove and discard the head gasket.

To install:
13. Clean the cylinder heads, intake manifold, valve rocker arm cover and cylinder block gasket surfaces of all traces of old gasket material and/or sealer.
14. Place the cylinder head gasket(s) in position on the cylinder block. Gaskets are marked with the words **Front** and **Top** for correct positioning. Left and right head gaskets are NOT interchangeable.
15. Install fabricated alignment dowels (used head bolts with the heads cut off) in the cylinder block and install the cylinder head assembly.
16. Remove the alignment dowels and install the cylinder head attaching bolts. Tighten the bolts in sequence, in three stages:
   a. Step 1—29–40 ft. lbs. (39–54 Nm)
   b. Step 2—40–51 ft. lbs. (54–69 Nm)
   c. Step 3—70–85 ft. lbs. (95–115 Nm)
17. Install the intake and exhaust manifolds, as described earlier in this section.
18. Apply heavy SG or SH or SH engine oil to both ends of the pushrods and install the pushrods. Install the oil baffles and rocker arms, as described earlier in this section.
19. Install the distributor using the matchmarks made earlier to insure correct rotor alignment. For more information, refer to Section 2. Install the distributor wiring harness and vacuum hose, then install the hold-down clamp and bolt and tighten.
20. Adjust the valve clearance. For more details, refer to Section 1, then install the rocker arm covers, as described earlier in this section.
21. The balance of the installation is the reverse of removal.
22. Refill the cooling system, then start the engine and check for leaks.
23. Connect the negative battery cable.
24. Fill and bleed the cooling system, as described earlier in this section.
25. Check for leaks. Adjust the idle speed and ignition timing, if necessary.

3.0L Engine

1987–88 MODELS

▶ See Figure 75

1. Drain the cooling system (engine cold) into a clean container and save the coolant for reuse.

⁂ CAUTION

When draining coolant, keep in mind that cats and dogs are attracted by ethylene glycol antifreeze, and are quite likely to drink any that is left in an uncovered container or in puddles on the

ground. This will prove fatal in sufficient quantity. Always drain the coolant into a sealable container. Coolant should be reused unless it is contaminated or several years old.

2. Disconnect the negative battery cable.

3. Remove the air cleaner and intake manifold, as described earlier in this section.

4. Loosen the accessory drive belt idler and remove the belt.

5. If the left-hand cylinder head is being removed, remove the alternator adjusting arm.

6. If the right-hand head is being removed, remove the accessory belt idler.

7. If equipped with power steering, remove the pump mounting bracket attaching bolts. Leaving the hoses connected, place the pump/bracket assembly aside in a position to prevent the fluid from leaking out. Secure the pump with wire or string during service.

8. If the left-hand head is being removed, remove the coil bracket and dipstick tube.

9. If the right-hand cylinder head is being removed, remove the ground strap and throttle cable support bracket.

10. Remove the exhaust manifold(s), PCV valve and rocker arm covers, as described earlier in this section.

11. Loosen the rocker arm fulcrum attaching bolts enough to allow the rocker arm to be lifted off the pushrod and rotated to one side. Remove the pushrods, keeping them in order so that they may be installed in their original locations.

12. Loosen the cylinder head attaching bolts in reverse of the tightening sequence, then remove the bolts and lift off the cylinder head(s). Remove and discard the old cylinder head gasket(s).

To install:

13. Clean the cylinder heads, intake manifold, rocker arm cover and cylinder block gasket surfaces of all traces of old gasket material and/or sealer.

14. Lightly oil all bolt and stud threads, except for the threads of bolts passing through water passages in the cylinder head. For the bolts installed into the cylinder head passages, apply an RTV sealant to the threads. Position the new head gasket(s) on the cylinder block, using the dowels for alignment. The dowels should be replaced if damaged.

15. Position the cylinder head(s) on the block and install the attaching bolts. Tighten the head bolts in sequence, in two stages: first to 48–54 ft. lbs. (65–75 Nm), then to 63–80 ft. lbs. (85–110 Nm).

16. Dip each pushrod in heavy engine oil, then install the pushrods in their original locations.

17. For each valve, rotate the crankshaft until the lifter rests on the heel (base circle) of the camshaft lobe before tightening the fulcrum attaching bolts. Position the rocker arms over the pushrods, install the fulcrums, then tighten the fulcrum attaching bolts to 19–29 ft. lbs. (26–38 Nm).

✶✶ CAUTION

Fulcrums must be fully seated in the cylinder head and pushrods must be seated in the rocker arm and lifter sockets prior to final tightening.

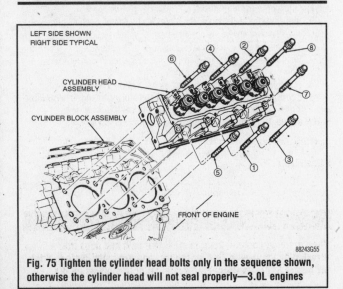

Fig. 75 Tighten the cylinder head bolts only in the sequence shown, otherwise the cylinder head will not seal properly—3.0L engines

18. Lubricate all rocker arm assemblies with heavy engine oil. If the original valve train components are being installed, a valve clearance check is not required. If, however, a component has been replaced, the valve clearance should be checked. For more information, refer to Section 1.

19. The balance of the installation is the reverse of removal.

20. Refill the cooling system, then start the engine and check for leaks.

21. Start the engine and check for leaks. If necessary, adjust the transmission throttle and cruise control linkage and ignition timing.

1989–91 MODELS

▶ **See Figures 75 thru 80**

1. Have the air conditioning system discharged by a qualified, professional mechanic utilizing a refrigerant recovery/recycling machine. For more information regarding A/C precautions, refer to Section 1.

2. Drain the cooling system (engine cold) into a clean container and save the coolant for reuse.

✶✶ CAUTION

When draining coolant, keep in mind that cats and dogs are attracted by ethylene glycol antifreeze, and are quite likely to drink any that is left in an uncovered container or in puddles on the ground. This will prove fatal in sufficient quantity. Always drain the coolant into a sealable container. Coolant should be reused unless it is contaminated or several years old.

3. Disconnect the negative battery cable.

4. Remove the air cleaner, air cleaner outlet tube and PCV closure hose.

5. Remove the throttle body. Refer to Section 5 for more information.

6. Remove the accessory drive belt. For more information, refer to Section 1.

7. Disconnect the fuel lines from the fuel injection fuel manifold. For more information on disconnecting the fuel lines, refer to Section 5.

8. Tag and remove all vacuum lines from the engine.

9. Remove the upper radiator and heater water hoses.

10. Remove the spark plugs and bring No. 1 piston to Top Dead Center of the compression stroke.

11. Mark the distributor housing to the block and note the rotor position. Remove the ignition wires from the locating studs. Remove the distributor. For more information, refer to Section 2.

12. If the left-hand cylinder head is being removed:

a. Remove the accessory drive belt.

b. Remove the power steering pump and bracket assembly. DO NOT disconnect the hoses. Tie the assembly out of the way.

c. Remove the ignition coil and bracket.

d. Remove the engine oil dipstick and tube.

13. If the right-hand head is being removed:

a. Remove the accessory drive belt.

b. Remove the alternator and bracket.

14. Remove the exhaust manifold(s).

15. Remove the rocker arm covers, as described earlier in this section.

16. Remove the intake manifold, as described earlier in this section.

17. If equipped with A/C, disconnect the liquid line at the A/C condenser

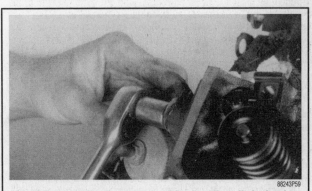

Fig. 76 Remove any components or wiring from the cylinder head to be removed, then . . .

Fig. 77 . . . remove the cylinder head mounting bolts

Fig. 78 Lift the cylinder head off of the engine block

Fig. 79 Remove the old gasket from the engine block and . . .

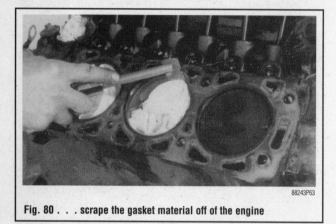

Fig. 80 . . . scrape the gasket material off of the engine

and the suction hose from the accumulator. Remove the bolt securing the air conditioning hose assembly to the compressor housing, then remove the hose assembly from the vehicle. Plug or cap all openings in the air conditioning system to keep dirt, foreign material and excess moisture out of the system.

18. Remove the exhaust inlet pipe and exhaust manifolds, as described earlier in this section.

19. Loosen the rocker arm fulcrum attaching bolts enough to allow the rocker arm to lifted off the pushrod and rotated to one side. Remove the pushrods, keeping them in order so they may be installed in their original locations.

20. Loosen the cylinder head attaching bolts in reverse of the tightening sequence, then remove the bolts and lift off the cylinder head(s). Remove and discard the old cylinder head gasket(s).

To install:

21. Clean the cylinder heads, intake manifold, valve rocker arm cover and cylinder block gasket surfaces of all traces of old gasket material and/or sealer. Refer to the following overhaul procedures for cylinder head component removal, valve replacement, resurfacing, etc.

22. Lightly oil all bolt and stud bolt threads except those specifying special sealant. Position the new head gasket(s) on the cylinder block, using the dowels for alignment. The dowels should be replaced if damaged.

23. Set the cylinder head onto the engine block.

24. Install NEW cylinder head retaining bolts hand-tight.

25. Tighten the retaining bolts, in sequence, to 60 ft. lbs. (80 Nm). Then back off all bolts a minimum of one full rotation (360°).

➡When the cylinder head retaining bolts have been tightened using this procedure, it is not necessary to retighten the bolts after extended engine operation. However, the bolts can be checked for tightness if desired.

26. Retighten the head bolts in sequence, in two stages: first step to 33–41 ft. lbs. (45–55 Nm), second step to 63–73 ft. lbs. (85–99 Nm).

27. Install the intake manifold, as described earlier in this section.

⁂ CAUTION

If a new distributor or camshaft position sensor is installed, be sure to add the rest of the pint of Engine Assembly Lubricant D9AZ-19579-D or equivalent to the engine oil by pouring it through the distributor hole onto the camshaft drive gear. Once the engine is completely reassembled, run the engine at idle for five minutes before driving the vehicle.

28. Dip the entire distributor or camshaft position sensor drive gear in Engine Assembly Lubricant D9AZ-19579-D or equivalent.

29. Install the distributor. For more information, refer to Section 2.

30. Install the camshaft position sensor. For more information, refer to Section 4.

31. Install the spark plugs. Then install the distributor cap and wires.

32. Dip each pushrod in heavy engine oil or Engine Assembly Lubricant, then install the pushrods in their original locations.

33. Install the rocker arms, as described earlier in this section.

⁂ CAUTION

The fulcrums must be fully seated in the cylinder head and pushrods must be seated in the rocker arm sockets prior to final tightening.

34. For each valve, tighten the fulcrum attaching bolts to 24 ft. lbs. (32 Nm).

35. Lubricate all rocker arm assemblies with heavy engine oil. If the original valve train components are being installed, a valve clearance check is not required. If, however, a component has been replaced, the valve clearance should be checked.

36. The balance of the installation is the reverse of removal.

37. Fill the cooling system. Refer to Section 1 for more information.

➡At this point, it is recommended to change the engine oil. Coolant contamination of the engine oil often occurs during cylinder head removal.

➡When the battery has been disconnected and reconnected, some abnormal drive symptoms may occur while the Powertrain Control Module (PCM) relearns its adaptive strategy. The vehicle may need to be driven about 10 miles (16 km) or more to relearn the strategy.

38. Connect the negative battery cable.

39. Start the engine and check for leaks. Adjust the throttle linkage and speed control, as necessary.

40. Have the A/C system evacuated and recharged by a qualified, professional mechanic utilizing a recovery/recycling machine as soon as possible.

4.0L Engine

◗ See Figures 81 and 82

➡New cylinder head bolts must be used when installing the cylinder head on the 4.0L engine.

1. Relieve the fuel system pressure. For more information, refer to Section 5.
2. Disconnect the negative battery cable.
3. Drain the cooling system (engine cold) into a clean container and save the coolant for reuse.

✳✳ CAUTION

When draining coolant, keep in mind that cats and dogs are attracted by ethylene glycol antifreeze, and are quite likely to drink any that is left in an uncovered container or in puddles on the ground. This will prove fatal in sufficient quantity. Always drain the coolant into a sealable container. Coolant should be reused unless it is contaminated or several years old.

4. Remove the upper and lower intake manifolds, as described earlier in this section.
5. Remove the accessory drive belt. Refer to Section 1 for more information.
6. If the left cylinder head is being removed, perform the following:
   a. Remove the air conditioning compressor. Remove the screw securing the A/C manifold tube to the upper intake manifold. Set the compressor aside without disconnecting the A/C refrigerant lines.
   b. Remove the power steering pump and bracket assembly. DO NOT disconnect the hoses. Tie the assembly out of the way.
7. If the right head is being removed, perform the following:
   a. Remove the alternator and bracket.
   b. Remove the ignition coil and bracket.
8. Remove the spark plugs.
9. Remove the exhaust manifold(s), as described earlier in this section.
10. Remove the rocker arm covers, as described earlier in this section.
11. Remove the rocker arm shaft assemblies, as described earlier in this section.
12. Remove the pushrods, keeping them in order so they may be installed in their original locations.

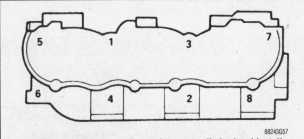

Fig. 81 To ensure proper sealing and correct cylinder head installation, tighten the retaining bolts in the sequence shown—4.0L engine

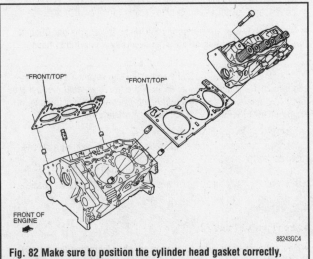

Fig. 82 Make sure to position the cylinder head gasket correctly, otherwise the cylinders will not seal properly—4.0L engine

13. Loosen the cylinder head attaching bolts in reverse of the tightening sequence, then remove the bolts and discard them. They cannot be re-used.
14. Lift the cylinder head(s) off of the engine block. Do not pry between the cylinder head and engine block.
15. Remove and discard the old cylinder head gasket(s).

To install:

16. Clean the cylinder heads, intake manifolds, valve rocker arm cover and cylinder block gasket surfaces of all traces of old gasket material and/or sealer.

➡ **The 4.0L engine should always be assembled using new cylinder head bolts.**

17. Lightly oil all bolt and stud bolt threads except those specifying special sealant. Position the new head gasket(s) on the cylinder block, using the dowels for alignment. The installation arrows on the head gaskets must be pointing to the front of the engine. The alignment dowels should be replaced if damaged.
18. Position the cylinder head(s) on the block.
19. Install and tighten the cylinder head bolts in the sequence shown, in the following steps:
   - Step 1—22–26 ft. lbs. (30–35 Nm)
   - Step 2—52–56 ft. lbs. (70–75 Nm)
   - Step 3—tighten bolts an additional 90°

➡ **Once applied, the silicone sealer will set in approximately 15 minutes. The intake manifold must be installed immediately after the sealer is applied.**

20. Apply a bead of RTV silicone gasket material to the mating joints of the head and block at the 4 corners. Install the intake manifold gasket and again apply the sealer in the same locations.
21. Position the intake manifold with the aid of two guide studs located in tightening sequence positions 3 and 4. Hand-tighten the retaining bolts. Remove the 2 guide studs, then replace them with bolts.
22. Tighten the intake manifold bolts in three stages following the sequence shown.
   - Step 1—6 ft. lbs. (8 Nm)
   - Step 2—11 ft. lbs. (15 Nm)
   - Step 3—16 ft. lbs. (22 Nm)
23. Install the valve lifters, if removed.
24. Dip each pushrod in heavy engine oil then install the pushrods in their original locations.
25. Install the rocker shaft assemblies, as described earlier in this section.
26. Apply another bead of RTV sealer at the 4 corners where the intake manifold and heads meet.
27. Install the rocker arm covers, as described earlier in this section.
28. The balance of the installation is the reverse of removal.
29. Fill the cooling system. See Section 1.

➡ **At this point, it is recommended to change the engine oil. Coolant contamination of the engine oil often occurs during cylinder head removal.**

30. Connect the negative battery cable.

➡ **When the battery has been disconnected and reconnected, some abnormal drive symptoms may occur while the Powertrain Control Module (PCM) relearns its adaptive strategy. The vehicle may need to be driven about 10 miles (16 km) or more to relearn the strategy.**

31. Start the engine and check for leaks. Adjust the throttle linkage and speed control, as necessary.

Valve Lifters (Tappets)

REMOVAL & INSTALLATION

◆ **See Figure 83**

2.3L Engine

The 2.3L engine uses valve lifters mounted directly under the camshaft, between the camshaft and the valves. These lifters are referred to as camshaft followers by the manufacturer. The camshaft followers are covered under the rocker arm removal and installation procedure, located earlier in this section.

2.8L Engine

1. Disconnect the negative battery cable.
2. Remove the cylinder heads.
3. Lift out the tappets with a magnet. If they are to be re-used, mark them for reinstallation. They must be inserted in their original locations lifter bores.

➡️**If the tappets are stuck in their bores, you'll need a claw-type removal tool.**

To install:

4. Coat the new tappets with clean engine oil and insert them in their bores.
5. Install the cylinder heads.
6. Connect the negative battery cable.

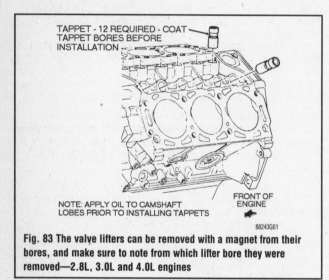

Fig. 83 The valve lifters can be removed with a magnet from their bores, and make sure to note from which lifter bore they were removed—2.8L, 3.0L and 4.0L engines

3.0L Engine

♦ **See Figures 84, 85, 86, 87 and 88**

1. Disconnect the negative battery cable.
2. Remove the rocker arm covers, as described earlier in this section.
3. Remove the intake manifold, as described earlier in this section.
4. Loosen the rocker arm nuts and pivot the rocker arm out of the way. Remove and mark the pushrods for reinstallation.
5. Remove the tappets with a magnet. If they are to be re-used, identify them.

➡️**If the tappets are stuck in their bores, you'll need a claw-type removal tool.**

To install:

6. Coat the new tappets with clean engine oil and insert them in their bores.
7. Coat the pushrods with heavy engine oil and insert them into the bores from which they came.
8. Install the rocker arms, as described earlier in this section.
9. Install the intake manifold.
10. Install the rocker arm covers.
11. Connect the negative battery cable.

4.0L Engine

1. Disconnect the negative battery cable.
2. Remove the upper and lower intake manifolds.
3. Remove the rocker arm covers.
4. Remove the rocker arm shaft assembly.
5. Remove and mark the pushrods for installation.
6. Remove the tappets with a magnet. If they are to be re-used, identify them.

➡️**If the tappets are stuck in their bores, you'll need a claw-type removal tool.**

Fig. 84 After removing the throttle body, remove the intake manifold retaining bolts, . . .

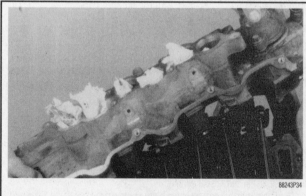

Fig. 85 . . . then lift the intake manifold off the engine block

Fig. 86 Remove the old intake manifold-to-cylinder head gaskets

Fig. 87 At this point, the lifters may be removed, if necessary

Fig. 88 Remove the rubber end gaskets from the engine block

To install:

7. Coat the new tappets with clean engine oil and insert them in their bores.

8. Coat the pushrods with heavy engine oil and insert them into the bores from which they came.

9. Install the rocker arm shaft assembly.

10. Install the rocker arm covers.

11. Install the upper and lower intake manifolds.

12. Disconnect the negative battery cable.

Oil Pan

REMOVAL & INSTALLATION

2.3L Engine

♦ See Figure 89

➟For vehicles equipped with automatic transmissions, the oil pans are removed from the front of the engine compartment, while manual transmission equipped vehicles should have their oil pans removed from the rear.

1. Disconnect the negative battery cable. Remove the oil dipstick and tube from the engine.

2. Remove the engine mount retaining nuts.

3. If equipped with an automatic transmission, disconnect the transmission fluid cooler lines from the radiator.

4. Remove the two bolts retaining the fan shroud to the radiator and remove the shroud.

5. On automatic transmissions vehicles only, remove the radiator retaining bolts, position the radiator upward and safety wire it to the hood.

6. Raise the van and support it safely on jackstands.

7. Drain the crankcase oil into a suitable container and dispose of it properly.

8. Disconnect the starter cable from the starter, then remove the starter from the engine.

9. Disconnect the exhaust manifold tube to the inlet pipe bracket at the thermactor check valve.

10. Remove the transmission mount retaining nuts from the crossmember.

11. On automatic transmissions vehicles, remove the bell crank from the converter housing. Disconnect the transmission oil cooler lines from the retainer at the block.

12. Remove the front crossmember (automatic only).

13. Disconnect the right front lower shock absorber mount (manual transmission only).

14. Position a hydraulic jack under the engine, then raise the engine and insert a wood block approximately 2½ in. (63.5mm) high. Carefully lower the jack until the engine is resting securely on the wood block.

15. On automatic transmissions vehicles, position the hydraulic jack under the transmission and raise it slightly.

16. Remove the oil pan retaining bolts and lower the pan to the chassis.

17. Remove the oil pump drive and pick-up tube assembly.

18. Remove the oil pan from the front on automatics, or from the rear on manual transmissions.

To install:

19. Clean the oil pan and inspect it for damage. Remove the spacers, if any, attached to the oil pan transmission mounting pad.

20. Clean the oil pan gasket surface at the pan and engine block. Remove all traces of old gasket and/or sealer. Clean the oil pump exterior and oil pump pick-up tube screen.

21. Position the one-piece oil pan gasket in the oil pan channel and press it into place.

22. Position the oil pan on the crossmember.

23. Install the oil pump and pick-up tube assembly. Prime the oil pump with engine oil when making final installation.

24. Install the oil pan to the cylinder block with retaining bolts. Install the retaining bolts by hand, just enough to start the two oil pan-to-transmission bolts.

25. Tighten the two pan-to-transmission bolts to 29–40 ft. lbs. (40–54 Nm) to align the pan with the rear face of the block, then loosen them ½ turn.

26. Tighten the oil pan-to-cylinder block bolts to 7–10 ft. lbs. (10–14 Nm), then tighten the remaining two transmission bolts to 29–40 ft. lbs. (40–54 Nm).

➟If the oil pan is being installed on the engine with the engine removed from the van, the transmission or a special fixture must be bolted to the block to insure the oil pan is installed flush with the rear face of the block.

27. On automatic transmissions models, lower the jack under the transmission. Position the jack under the engine, then raise the engine slightly and remove the wood block installed earlier.

28. Replace the oil filter.

29. The balance of the installation is the reverse of removal.

30. Refill the crankcase with engine oil.

31. Start the engine and check for leaks.

2.8L Engine

1. Disconnect the negative battery cable.

2. Raise the van and support it safely on jackstands.

3. Remove the starter motor from the engine.

4. Remove the nuts attaching the engine front insulators to the crossmember.

5. Drain the engine oil from the crankcase into a suitable container and dispose of it properly.

6. Position a hydraulic jack under the engine and, protecting the engine from the floor jack with a piece of wood, raise the engine enough to install wooden blocks between the front insulator mounts and No. 2 crossmember.

7. Carefully lower the engine onto the blocks and remove the jack.

8. Remove the oil pan attaching bolts, then lower and remove the pan from the engine block.

9. Clean all gasket surfaces on the engine and oil pan. Remove all traces of old gasket and/or sealer.

To install:

10. Apply adhesive to the gasket mating surfaces and install oil pan gaskets. Install the oil pan to the engine block.

11. Position a hydraulic jack under the engine and raise the engine to remove the wooden blocks. Lower the engine and remove the jack.

12. Install the starter motor.

13. Lower the van.

14. Install the nuts attaching the engine front insulators to the crossmember and tighten them to 71–94 ft. lbs. (96–127 Nm).

15. Fill the engine with the correct amount and type of engine oil. Refer to Section 1 for more information.

✳✳ WARNING

Do not start the engine without first filling it with the proper amount and type of engine oil.

16. Connect the negative battery cable.

17. Start the engine and check for leaks.

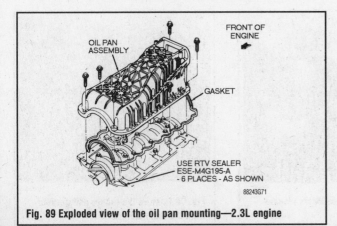

Fig. 89 Exploded view of the oil pan mounting—2.3L engine

3.0L Engine

1987–88 MODELS

1. Disconnect the negative battery cable.
2. Remove the oil level dipstick.
3. Raise and safely support the front of the vehicle on jackstands.
4. Remove the oil level sensor wire.
5. Drain the engine oil from the crankcase into a suitable container and dispose of it properly.
6. Remove the starter motor from the engine.
7. Remove the lower flywheel housing cover.
8. Support the transmission on a jack, loosen the transmission-to-engine bolts, and slide the transmission back about ¼ in. (6mm).
9. Remove the oil pan attaching bolts, then lower and remove the pan from the engine block.
10. Clean all gasket surfaces on the engine and oil pan. Remove all traces of old gasket and/or sealer.

To install:

11. Apply a 0.16 in. (4mm) bead of RTV sealer to the junctions of the rear main bearing cap and block, and the front cover and block.

➡**The sealer sets in 15 minutes, so work quickly.**

12. Apply adhesive to the gasket mating surfaces and install oil pan gasket.
13. Install the oil pan on the engine block.
14. Tighten the pan bolts to 71–106 inch lbs. (8–12 Nm).
15. Slide the transmission forward and tighten the bolts to 38 ft. lbs. (51 Nm).
16. The balance of the installation is the reverse of removal.
17. Connect the negative battery cable.
18. Fill the engine with new engine oil to the correct level.
19. Start the engine and check for leaks.

1989–97 MODELS

▶ See Figures 90, 91, 92, 93 and 94

1. Disconnect the negative battery cable.
2. Remove the oil level dipstick.
3. Raise and support the front end on jackstands.
4. Remove the oil level sensor wire.
5. Drain the engine oil from the crankcase into a suitable container and dispose of it properly.
6. Remove the starter motor from the engine.
7. Remove the transmission from the vehicle. For more details, refer to Section 7.
8. Remove the oil pan attaching bolts, then lower and remove the pan from the engine block.

To install:

9. Clean all gasket surfaces on the engine and oil pan. Remove all traces of old gasket and/or sealer.
10. Apply a 0.16–0.24 in. (4–6mm) bead of Silicone Sealer D6AZ-19562-AA or -BA, or the equivalent, to the junctions of the rear main bearing cap and block, and the front cover and block. Refer to the illustration of the exploded view of the oil pan mounting.

➡**The sealer sets in 15 minutes, so work quickly.**

11. Apply Gasket and Trim Adhesive D7AZ-19B508-B or equivalent to the gasket mating surfaces and install oil pan gasket to the engine block.
12. Install the oil pan on the engine block.
13. Tighten the oil pan bolts to 7–10 ft. lbs. (10–14 Nm).
14. Install the transmission to the vehicle. For more information, refer to Section 7.
15. The balance of the installation is the reverse of removal.
16. Fill the oil pan with clean engine oil to the correct level.
17. Connect the negative battery cable.

➡**When the battery has been disconnected and reconnected, some abnormal drive symptoms may occur while the Powertrain Control Module (PCM) relearns its adaptive strategy. The vehicle may need to be driven about 10 miles (16 km) or more to relearn the strategy.**

18. Start the engine and check for leaks.

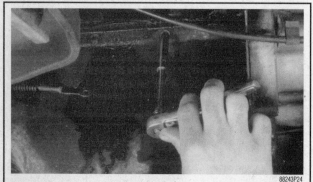

Fig. 90 Support the vehicle on jackstands, then remove the oil pan retaining bolts

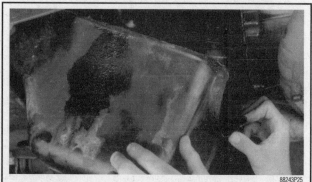

Fig. 91 Lower the rear of the oil pan, then pull the oil pan off the engine block

Fig. 92 Once the oil pan is removed, access to the crankshaft baffle and oil pan can be gained

Fig. 93 Remove the crankshaft oil baffle retaining bolts, then . . .

Fig. 94 . . . pull the baffle down from the engine block

4.0L Engine

1990–92 MODELS

1. Disconnect the negative battery cable. Disconnect the oil level sensor wire at the pan.
2. Remove the engine cover.
3. Raise the van and support it safely on jackstands.
4. Remove the starter motor from the engine.
5. Drain the engine oil from the crankcase into a suitable container and dispose of it properly.
6. You may find that there is insufficient clearance to remove the oil pan. If so, perform the following steps. If there is sufficient clearance, skip to Step 7.
    a. Remove the nuts attaching the engine front insulators to the cross-member.
    b. Position a hydraulic jack under the engine and raise the engine enough to install wooden blocks between the front insulator mounts and No. 2 crossmember.
    c. Carefully lower the engine onto the blocks and remove the jack.
    d. Support the transmission on a floor jack, remove the transmission-to-engine/oil pan bolts and force the transmission back about ¼ in. (6mm).
7. Remove the oil pan attaching bolts, then lower and remove the pan from the engine block. Take note of the spacers on the back of the oil pan. Do not lose them.
8. Remove the crankshaft baffle, if necessary.

To install:

9. Clean all gasket surfaces on the engine and oil pan. Remove all traces of old gasket and/or sealer.
10. If removed, install the baffle. Tighten the nuts to 15 ft. lbs. (20 Nm).
11. Apply adhesive to the gasket mating surfaces and install the oil pan gasket. Position the oil pan on the engine block. Torque the bolts to 60–84 inch lbs. Do NOT forget the spacers.
12. There are 2 spacers on the rear of the oil pan to allow proper mating of the transmission and oil pan. If these spacers were lost, or the oil pan was replaced, you must determine the proper spacers to install. To do this:
    a. With the oil pan installed, place a straightedge across the machined mating surface of the rear of the block, extending over the oil pan-to-transmission mounting surface.
    b. Using a feeler gauge, measure the gap between the oil pan mounting pad and the straightedge.
    c. Repeat the procedure for the other side.
    d. Select the spacers as follows:
    • Gap = 0.011–0.020 in. (0.28–0.51mm)—spacer = 0.010 in. (0.25mm)
    • Gap = 0.021–0.029 in. (0.53–0.74mm)—spacer = 0.020 in. (0.51mm)
    • Gap = 0.031–0.039 in. (0.79–0.99mm)—spacer = 0.030 in. (0.76mm)

➡**Failure to use the correct spacers will result in damage to the oil pan and oil leakage!**

13. If the engine was raised, lift the engine to remove the wooden blocks. Lower the engine and remove the jack. Install the nuts attaching the engine front insulators to the crossmember and tighten them to 60 ft. lbs. (82 Nm).
14. Slide the transmission forward and tighten the bolts to 38 ft. lbs. (52 Nm).
15. Install the starter motor.
16. Connect the oil level sensor wire.
17. Lower the van.
18. Fill the engine with the proper amount and type of engine oil.
19. Connect the negative battery cable.

➡**When the battery has been disconnected and reconnected, some abnormal drive symptoms may occur while the Powertrain Control Module (PCM) relearns its adaptive strategy. The vehicle may need to be driven about 10 miles (16 km) or more to relearn the strategy.**

20. Start the engine and check for leaks.

1993–97 MODELS

1. Disconnect the negative battery cable.
2. Remove the engine cover.
3. Raise and safely support the front of the vehicle on jackstands.
4. Remove the rear engine support, as described earlier in this section.
5. Remove the transmission and, if equipped, the transfer case. For more information, refer to Section 7.

6. Once the transmission is out of the vehicle, remove the flywheel, as described later in this section.
7. Remove the starter motor.
8. For vehicles with four wheel drive (E-4WD), perform the following steps:
    a. Support the left front suspension lower arm with a hydraulic floor jack.
    b. Note the bolt arm position, then remove both left control arm pivot bolts.
    c. Remove the floor jack and allow the control arm to hang. It is retained by the shock absorber and ball joint.
    d. Support the right front suspension lower arm with a hydraulic floor jack.
    e. Note the bolt arm position, then remove both right control arm pivot bolts.
    f. Remove the floor jack and allow the control arm to hang. It is retained by the shock absorber and ball joint.
    g. Support the front carrier assembly with the floor jack.
    h. Remove the bolts and rear pivot crossmember.
    i. Remove the bolts and nuts securing the front carrier assembly to the front drive axle crossmember.
    j. Lower the front carrier assembly enough to access the oil pan.
9. Drain the engine oil and remove the oil bypass filter.
10. Disconnect the low oil level sensor from the oil pan.
11. Remove the engine oil pan retaining bolts and nuts.
12. Remove the oil pan.
13. Remove the crankshaft oil windage baffle and oil pump assembly, if necessary.
14. Remove the oil pan gasket and the crankshaft rear main bearing cap.

To install:

✳✳ CAUTION

Prevent engine contamination. Always use necessary precautions to prevent old sealer or gasket material from falling into the engine.

15. Thoroughly clean all the oil and the old sealer from the oil pan, taking special care to remove all of the old sealer from the oil pan gasket in the oil pan. Thoroughly wash the oil pan.

➡**Thoroughly clean all exposed areas with metal surface cleaner F4AZ-19536-RA or denatured alcohol. Place special attention on removing the remains of the integral rubber wedge seal. the tabs on the wedge seal tear away from the oil pan gasket when the oil pan is removed. They remain lodged between the block and the rear main bearing cap.**

16. Thoroughly clean all of the old sealer from the rear main bearing cap using a scraper and wire wheel. The original sealer used during production assembly becomes extremely hard after it has cured. It is extremely important that all old sealer is removed from all joining faces and grooves.
17. Thoroughly clean all oil and old sealer from the cylinder block oil pan sealing area and the rear main bearing cap joint area. Also clean the oil pan sealing area.
18. After all parts have been thoroughly cleaned and washed, it is necessary and extremely important that they be wiped down with Extra Strength Spot and Stain Remover B7A-19521-AA or denatured alcohol.
19. Thoroughly clean the transmission bell-housing area and the rear of the cylinder block.
20. Place a bead of Ford Gasket Eliminator E1FZ-19562-A, Loctite 515®, or equivalent sealer to the block along the corners of the rear main bearing cap joint area, and on the joint face approximately ½ in. (13mm) from the rear of the engine block.

➡**New main bearing cap bolts must be used during assembly.**

21. Verify that the lower rear main bearing insert is in place, then install the rear main bearing cap and snug the bolts.

➡**The rear main bearing cap MUST be aligned and installed properly to seal correctly. Misalignment will cause an oil leak.**

22. Align the rear main bearing cap to block by moving the bearing cap fore or aft so that the rear seal stop (approximately ½ in./13mm inward in the rear oil seal bore) of the block and cap line up. This will ensure the crankshaft rear oil seal will seat properly when installed in the bore.
23. Tighten the bolts evenly to 66–77 ft. lbs. (90–104 Nm).

Use a NEW oil seal. Failure to install a new seal, or incorrect installation will result in an oil leak after the vehicle is returned to service.

24. Fill the cavities on both sides of the rear main cap with Gasket Eliminator E1FZ-19562-A or equivalent sealer.

25. Clean and inspect the oil inlet tube. prime the oil pump by filling the inlet opening with oil while rotating he shaft until oil emerges from the outlet opening. Install the pump and screen, then tighten the bolts to 13–15 ft. lbs. (17–21 Nm).

26. Install the crankshaft oil windage baffle, then tighten the retaining bolts to 13–15 ft. lbs. (17–21 Nm).

➡The transmission bolts to the engine and oil pan when installed, so it is important to measure the gap between the surface of the rear face of the oil pan (at the spacer locations) and the rear face of the cylinder block.

27. Determine if oil pan spacers will be required at installation.

Failure to measure the required spacer thickness can result in insufficient or excessive clearance between the oil pan and the transmission when installed in the vehicle. This can result in oil pan damage, and/or an oil leak.

➡If the same oil pan that was removed is to be installed, the existing spacers may be used. If a new oil pan is being installed, measure the pan-to-transmission gap as detailed in the following steps.

28. If a new oil pan is being installed, determine the correct spacer thickness as follows:

a. Position the oil pan on the engine without the spacers, then install the retaining nuts on the four locating studs.

b. Measure the gap between the locating pads on the pan and the transmission converter housing using a feeler gauge.

c. Select oil pan spacers of the required thickness from the following:
  * 0.000–0.010 in. (0.000–0.254mm)—no shim
  * 0.011–0.020 in. (0.27–0.51mm)—yellow shim (0.010 in./0.254mm)
  * 0.021–0.029 in. (0.52–0.76mm)—blue shim (0.020 in./0.508mm)
  * 0.030–0.039 in. (0.77–1.00mm)—pink shim (0.030 in./0.762mm)

29. Remove the oil pan and position the correct spacers for pan installation.

30. Place a bead of Ford Silicone Sealer F1AZ-19562-A, Loctite® 598 or equivalent in the oil pan gasket groove at the radius areas at the front.

31. Place the oil pan gasket on the flange on the oil pan.

32. Place a bead of Ford Silicone Sealer F1AZ-19562-A, Loctite® 598 or equivalent on top of the oil pan gasket at the radius areas at the front and rear of the oil pan. Also apply sealant on the cylinder block at the cylinder block-to-front cover joint area.

➡The wedge seal is an integral part of the oil pan gasket and must be placed in position when the oil pan is set in place.

33. Set the oil pan in place. Install and snug four oil pan nuts tightly enough to align the bolt holes, but lose enough that the oil pan may be pushed backwards.

34. Align the rear face of the oil pan with the rear face of the cylinder.

35. Install the remaining oil pan bolts finger-tight.

36. Tighten the oil pan bolts and nuts evenly to 62–89 inch lbs. (7–10 Nm). Tighten the transmission-to-oil pan bolts to 28–38 ft. lbs. (38–51 Nm).

37. Always use a new crankshaft rear oil seal. Coat the rear main seal-to-cylinder block surface of the oil seal with oil XO-5W30-QSP or equivalent SAE 5W-30 service SG or SH oil. Install the rear oil seal, as described later in this section.

38. Connect the low oil level sensor to the oil pan.

39. Install the oil pan drain plug and the oil filter.

40. On four wheel drive vehicles (E-4WD), perform the following:

a. Raise the front carrier assembly into place.

b. Install the front carrier assembly to front drive axle crossmember bolts, then tighten to 70–80 ft. lbs. (95–108 Nm).

c. Install the rear pivot crossmember, then tighten the bolts.

d. Remove the hydraulic floor jack. Use it to raise the right front suspension lower arm into place.

e. Install the right lower control arm pivot bolts with the bolt arm in original position. Install the nuts and tighten them to 100–140 ft. lbs. (136–190 Nm).

f. Remove the hydraulic floor jack. Use it to raise the left front suspension lower arm into place.

g. Install the left lower control arm pivot bolts with the bolt arm in original position. Install the nuts and tighten them to 100–140 ft. lbs. (136–190 Nm).

h. Remove the floor jack.

41. Install the starter motor.

42. Lower the vehicle.

➡It is important to adhere to the following step exactly.

43. After letting the vehicle sit overnight, fill the crankcase with the quantity and quality of engine oil recommended in Section 1. A good method to prevent you from forgetting to fill the engine the next day is to leave the hood unlatched and put a bottle of oil on the driver's seat in the van, or put the van keys in an envelope and seal it. Write a message on the envelope reminding yourself to fill the engine with oil on the next day.

Make sure to fill the engine the next day; do NOT start the engine without first filling it with oil.

➡When the battery has been disconnected and reconnected, some abnormal drive symptoms may occur while the Powertrain Control Module (PCM) relearns its adaptive strategy. The vehicle may need to be driven about 10 miles (16 km) or more to relearn the strategy.

44. Connect the negative battery cable.

45. Start the engine and check for leaks. Fix as needed.

Oil Pump

REMOVAL

▶ **See Figures 95 thru 100**

1. Remove the oil pan, as described in the previous procedure.

2. Remove the oil pump retainer bolts, then remove the oil pump along with the drive shaft.

3. Prime the oil pump with clean engine oil by filling either the inlet or outlet port with engine oil. Rotate the pump shaft to distribute the oil within the pump body.

4. Insert the oil pump intermediate shaft into the block with the pointed end facing inward. The pointed end is closest to the pressed-on flange.

5. Install the pump and tighten the mounting bolts to 14–21 ft. lbs. (19–28

Fig. 95 Once the oil pan is removed, access to the oil pump is gained

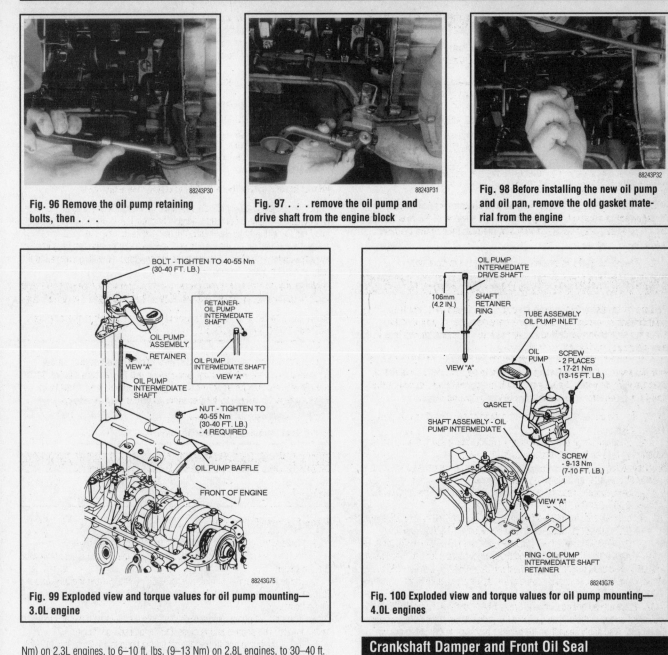

Fig. 96 Remove the oil pump retaining bolts, then . . .

Fig. 97 . . . remove the oil pump and drive shaft from the engine block

Fig. 98 Before installing the new oil pump and oil pan, remove the old gasket material from the engine

Fig. 99 Exploded view and torque values for oil pump mounting—3.0L engine

Fig. 100 Exploded view and torque values for oil pump mounting—4.0L engines

Nm) on 2.3L engines, to 6–10 ft. lbs. (9–13 Nm) on 2.8L engines, to 30–40 ft. lbs. (40–55 Nm) on 3.0L engines, and to 13–15 ft. lbs. on 4.0L engines.

6. Clean and install the oil pump screen cover and tube with an oil pump inlet tube gasket. Tighten the bolts to 7–10 ft. lbs. (9–13 Nm).

7. Install the oil pan, as described in the previous procedure.

Oil Pump Drive

REMOVAL & INSTALLATION

4.0L and 1996–97 3.0L Engines

Since this engine has no ignition distributor, the oil pump driveshaft engages an oil pump drive unit which installs in the same way and same position as a conventional distributor.

To remove the drive unit, located at the rear of the block, behind the intake manifold, simply remove the hold-down clamp and pull the unit from the engine.

When installing the unit, coat the gear and O-ring with clean engine oil, insert it in the block and torque the hold-down clamp bolt to 15 ft. lbs. (20 Nm).

Crankshaft Damper and Front Oil Seal

REMOVAL & INSTALLATION

2.3L Engine

The 2.3L engine does not have a seal mounted in the front timing belt cover since the timing belt is run dry, which means that no oil is allowed into the timing belt cover.

1. Disconnect the negative battery cable.

2. Remove the engine fan and the water pump pulley bolts.

3. Loosen the alternator retaining bolts and remove the drive belt from the pulleys. Remove the water pump pulley.

4. Loosen and position the power steering pump mounting bracket and position it aside.

5. Remove the crankshaft pulley bolts and remove the pulley.

6. Remove the hub/damper bolt from the end of the crankshaft.

7. Remove the four timing belt outer cover retaining bolts and remove the cover.

8. Using a crankshaft damper puller, remove the crankshaft hub/damper assembly.

To install:

9. Position the crankshaft damper onto the crankshaft so that the key way in the damper is aligned with the key on the crankshaft.

10. Install the hub/damper bolt. On vehicles equipped with manual transmissions, position transmission in first gear and apply the parking brake (this will hold the engine from turning while tightening the hub/damper bolt). On automatic equipped vehicles, the vehicle will have to be raised and safely supported on jackstands. Remove the torque converter cover. Have an assistant hold the driveplate (with a wrench on one of the torque converter-to-driveplate bolts) while tightening the hub/damper bolt to 150 ft. lbs. (204 Nm).

11. The balance of the installation is the reverse of removal.

12. Connect the negative battery cable.

3.0L Engine

♦ See Figures 101 thru 106

1. Disconnect the negative battery cable.
2. Remove the air cleaner outlet tube assembly.
3. Remove the accessory drive belts.
4. Remove the 4 pulley-to-damper bolts, then lift off the crankshaft pulley.
5. Remove the crankshaft vibration damper bolt and washer.
6. Using a puller, remove the damper from the crankshaft. The seal can now be pried from the cover, if necessary.

To install:

7. If the seal was removed, check the opening for roughness and smooth it as needed.

8. Coat the lip of the new seal with clean engine oil and drive it into place in the cover using Vibration Damper and Seal Replacer T82L-6316-A and Front Cover Seal Replacer T7OP-6B070-A.

9. Coat the outer surface of the damper neck with clean engine oil. Apply RTV gasket material to the keyway of the damper and position the damper on the crankshaft.

10. Install the damper bolt and washer. Torque the bolt to 92–122 ft. lbs. (125–165 Nm).

11. Install the pulley. Tighten the bolts to 24 ft. lbs. (32 Nm).

12. Install and adjust the accessory belts. For more information, refer to Section 1.

13. Install air cleaner outlet tube.

➡When the battery has been disconnected and reconnected, some abnormal drive symptoms may occur while the Powertrain Control Module (PCM) relearns its adaptive strategy. The vehicle may need to be driven about 10 miles (16 km) or more to relearn the strategy.

14. Connect the negative battery cable.
15. Start the engine and check for oil leaks.

2.8L and 4.0L Engines

♦ See Figure 107

1. Remove the accessory drive belts.
2. Remove the damper bolt.
3. Using a puller, remove the damper from the crankshaft.
4. The seal can now be pried from the cover, if necessary. Use a flat-bladed prytool to remove the seal. Be careful not to damage the front cover and crankshaft.

To install:

5. If the seal was removed, check the opening for roughness and smooth it as needed.

6. Coat the lip of the new seal with clean engine oil and drive it into place in the cover using Front cover Aligner T74P–6019–A, and installer T90T–6701–A, or equivalent.

7. Coat the outer surface of the damper neck with clean engine oil. Apply RTV gasket material to the keyway of the damper and position the damper on the crankshaft.

CAUTION

Do not drive damper on with a hammer.

Fig. 101 Remove the crankshaft pulley retaining bolts, then . . .

Fig. 102 . . . remove the pulley from the crankshaft damper

Fig. 103 Loosen the crankshaft damper center retaining bolt, then . . .

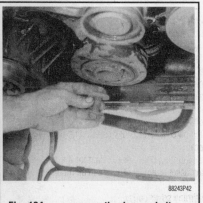
Fig. 104 . . . remove the damper bolt

Fig. 105 Use a steering wheel/damper puller to pull the damper off of the end of the crankshaft

Fig. 106 Remove the crankshaft damper from the crankshaft

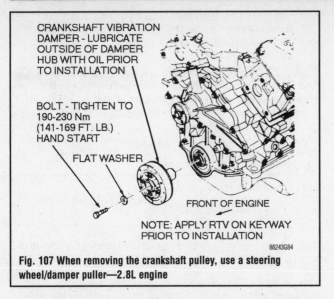

Fig. 107 When removing the crankshaft pulley, use a steering wheel/damper puller—2.8L engine

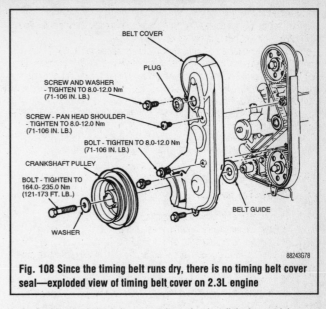

Fig. 108 Since the timing belt runs dry, there is no timing belt cover seal—exploded view of timing belt cover on 2.3L engine

8. Install the damper using Installer T74P–6316–B, or equivalent. Install the damper bolt and torque it to 37 ft. lbs. (50 Nm) plus an additional ¼ turn (90°).
9. Install and adjust the accessory belts.
10. Start the engine and check for oil leaks.

Timing Belt Cover

REMOVAL & INSTALLATION

For the recommended timing belt replacement intervals, refer to Section 1.

> ❈❈ **CAUTION**

It is extremely important to change the timing belt at the recommended intervals. The 2.3L engine is an interference engine, which means that if the timing belt breaks, or the engine is rotated without the timing belt in place, the pistons and valves will come in contact. This can easily lead to extensive damage to either of these components.

2.3L Engine

▶ **See Figure 108**

1. Rotate the engine so that No. 1 cylinder is at TDC on the compression stroke. Check that the timing marks are aligned on the camshaft and crankshaft pulleys. An access plug is provided in the timing belt cover so that the camshaft timing can be checked without removal of the cover or any other parts. Set the crankshaft to TDC by aligning the timing mark on the crankshaft pulley with the TDC mark on the belt cover. Look through the access hole in the belt cover to make sure that the timing mark on the camshaft drive sprocket is aligned with the pointer on the inner belt cover.

➡**Always turn the engine in the normal direction of rotation. Backward rotation may cause the timing belt to jump teeth, due to the arrangement of the belt tensioner.**

2. Remove the fan blade and water pump pulley bolts.
3. Loosen the alternator retaining bolts and remove the drive belt from the pulleys. Remove the water pump pulley.
4. Loosen and position the power steering pump mounting bracket, then position it aside.
5. Remove the four timing belt outer cover retaining bolts, then remove the cover.
To install:

➡**Since the timing belt runs dry, there is no seal in the timing belt cover to be replaced. The crankshaft seal is mounted in the front of the engine block.**

6. Position the timing belt cover on the engine. Install the four retaining bolts until snug.
7. Install the water pump pulley and fan blades, as described earlier in this section.
8. Position the alternator and drive belts, then adjust and tighten it to specifications. For more information on the correct tensioning techniques, refer to Section 1.
9. Start the engine and check the ignition timing. Adjust the timing, if necessary.

Timing Chain Cover and Seal

REMOVAL & INSTALLATION

3.0L Engine

▶ **See Figure 109**

1. Disconnect the negative battery cable.
2. Turn the crankshaft until the No. 1 cylinder is at TDC on the compression stroke with the timing marks aligned. Remove the idler pulley and bracket assembly.
3. Remove the drive and accessory belts.
4. Remove the radiator and water pump, as described earlier in this section.
5. Remove the crankshaft pulley and damper, as described in this section.
6. Remove the lower radiator hose.
7. Remove the oil pan-to-timing cover bolts.
8. Remove the front cover bolts and the front cover. Tap the cover lightly with a plastic mallet, if necessary, to break it loose.
To install:
9. Carefully clean all gasket mating surfaces on the cover and replace the crankshaft damper oil seal as follows:
 a. Coat the lip of the new seal with clean engine oil and drive it into place in the cover using Vibration Damper and Seal Replacer T82L-6316-A and Front Cover Seal Replacer T70P-6B070-A.
10. Carefully cut and remove exposed portion of the oil pan gasket. To install, coat the gasket surface of the oil pan with sealing compound (B5A–19554–A or equivalent), then cut and position the required sections of a new gasket on the oil pan and apply more sealing compound at the corners. Coat the gasket surfaces of the block and cover with sealing compound and position the cover on the block.
11. Install the front cover mounting bolts. Use sealant for the front cover bolt which goes into the water jacket of the block. Tighten all mounting bolts to 15–22 ft. lbs. (20–30 Nm).
12. Install the oil pan-to-timing cover bolts.

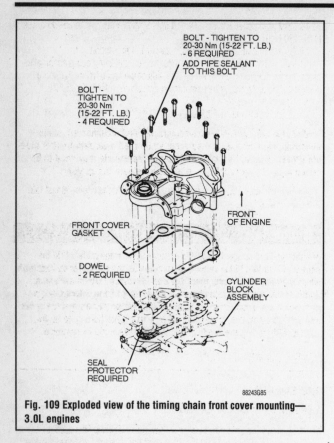

BOLT - TIGHTEN TO
20-30 Nm (15-22 FT. LB.)
- 6 REQUIRED
ADD PIPE SEALANT
TO THIS BOLT

BOLT -
TIGHTEN TO
20-30 Nm
(15-22 FT. LB.)
- 4 REQUIRED

FRONT
OF ENGINE

FRONT COVER
GASKET

DOWEL
- 2 REQUIRED

CYLINDER
BLOCK
ASSEMBLY

SEAL
PROTECTOR
REQUIRED

88243G85

Fig. 109 Exploded view of the timing chain front cover mounting—3.0L engines

13. Install the lower radiator hose.

14. Lubricate the neck of the crankshaft damper with clean engine oil. Install the crankshaft damper and pulley. Tighten the damper bolt to 141–169 ft. lbs. (190–230 Nm) and the pulley bolts to 19–26 ft. lbs. (26–38 Nm).

15. Install the water pump and radiator, as described earlier in this section.

16. Install the idler pulley and drive belt(s). Refill the cooling system. For more information, refer to Section 1.

➡ When the battery has been disconnected and reconnected, some abnormal drive symptoms may occur while the Powertrain Control Module (PCM) relearns its adaptive strategy. The vehicle may need to be driven about 10 miles (16 km) or more to relearn the strategy.

17. Connect the negative battery cable.

18. Start the engine and check for leaks.

4.0L Engine

▸ See Figure 110

➡ It will be necessary to remove the oil pan to properly reseal the front cover to oil pan. It will also be necessary to remove the transmission to reseal the oil pan.

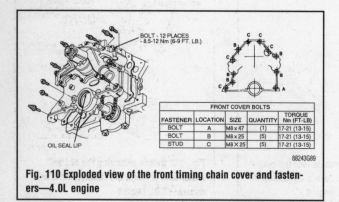

BOLT - 12 PLACES
- 8.5-12 Nm (6-9 FT. LB.)

OIL SEAL LIP

FRONT COVER BOLTS				
FASTENER	LOCATION	SIZE	QUANTITY	TORQUE Nm (FT-LB)
BOLT	A	M8 x 47	(1)	17-21 (13-15)
BOLT	B	M8 x 25	(5)	17-21 (13-15)
STUD	C	M8 X 25	(5)	17-21 (13-15)

88243G89

Fig. 110 Exploded view of the front timing chain cover and fasteners—4.0L engine

1. Disconnect the negative battery cable.
2. Remove the oil pan, as described earlier in this section.
3. Remove the air cleaner outlet tube.
4. Drain the cooling system.

✳✳ CAUTION

When draining coolant, keep in mind that cats and dogs are attracted by ethylene glycol antifreeze, and are quite likely to drink any that is left in an uncovered container or in puddles on the ground. This will prove fatal in sufficient quantity. Always drain the coolant into a sealable container. Coolant should be reused unless it is contaminated or several years old.

5. Remove the accessory drive belt.

6. Remove the air conditioning compressor and position it out of the way. DO NOT disconnect the refrigerant lines.

7. Remove the power steering pump and position it out of the way. DO NOT disconnect the hoses.

8. Remove the alternator. For more information, refer to Section 2.

9. Remove the cooling fan, as described earlier in this section.

➡ The engine front cover may be removed with the water pump attached.

10. Remove the water pump, as described earlier in this section, if desired.

11. Remove the drive pulley/damper from the crankshaft, as described earlier in this section.

12. Remove the crankshaft position sensor. For more information, refer to Section 4.

13. Remove the radiator, as described earlier in this section.

➡ While removing the front cover retaining bolts, make sure to note which bolt goes where. The bolts have different lengths and must be reinstalled in the original locations.

14. Remove the front cover attaching bolts. It may be necessary to tap the cover loose with a plastic mallet.

15. At this time the timing chain cover oil seal can be tapped out of the cover. Make sure not to distort the cover.

To install:

16. Remove the gasket material and sealer from the gasket surfaces. Inspect the engine front cover and damper seal surface for nicks, burns, or other roughness which could cause a gasket or seal to fail.

17. Apply sealing compound to the cylinder block sealing surfaces.

18. Apply sealing compound to the front cover gasket surface and position the front cover gasket onto the front cover.

19. If necessary, install a new oil seal using the Crankshaft Front Seal Replacer T90T-6701-A. Carefully tap the new seal in place. Lubricate the lip of the seal with new engine oil.

20. Install the front cover and attaching bolts. Tighten the bolts 2 or 3 turns. Make sure to install the correct bolts in their respective positions.

21. Tighten the retaining bolts to 13–15 ft. lbs. (17–21 Nm).

22. Install the radiator, as described earlier in this section.

23. Install the crankshaft position sensor. For more information, refer to Section 4.

24. Install the drive pulley/damper, as described earlier in this section.

25. Install the water pump, as described earlier in this section.

26. Install the cooling fan.

27. Install the alternator.

28. Install the power steering pump.

29. Install the air conditioning compressor.

30. Fill the cooling system.

31. Install the oil pan, as described earlier in this section.

32. Fill the crankcase to the proper level with clean engine oil.

33. Connect the negative battery cable.

➡ When the battery has been disconnected and reconnected, some abnormal drive symptoms may occur while the Powertrain Control Module (PCM) relearns its adaptive strategy. The vehicle may need to be driven about 10 miles (16 km) or more to relearn the strategy.

34. Start the vehicle and check for leaks.

Timing Gear Cover and Seal

REMOVAL & INSTALLATION

2.8L Engine

♦ See Figures 111 and 112

1. Disconnect the negative battery cable.
2. Remove the oil pan, as described earlier in this section.
3. Drain the cooling system and remove the radiator, as described in this section.

✳✳ CAUTION

When draining coolant, keep in mind that cats and dogs are attracted by ethylene glycol antifreeze, and are quite likely to drink any that is left in an uncovered container or in puddles on the ground. This will prove fatal in sufficient quantity. Always drain the coolant into a sealable container. Coolant should be reused unless it is contaminated or several years old.

4. Remove the air conditioning compressor and power steering bracket, if equipped.
5. Remove the alternator, thermactor pump and drive belt(s).
6. Remove the cooling fan.
7. Remove the water pump, heater hoses and radiator hoses.
8. Remove the crankshaft pulley, as described earlier in this section.
9. Remove the front cover retaining bolts. If necessary, tap the cover lightly with a plastic mallet to break the gasket seal, then remove the front cover. If the front cover plate gasket needs replacement, remove the two screws and remove the plate. If necessary, remove the guide sleeves from the cylinder block.

To install:

10. Clean the front cover mating surfaces of all gasket material and/or sealer. If the front cover seal is being replaced, support the cover to prevent damage and drive out the seal using tool T74P–6700–A or equivalent. Coat the new seal with heavy SG or SH engine oil and install it in the cover, making sure it is not cocked.
11. Install the timing gears, if removed, making sure the timing marks are correctly aligned. Tighten the camshaft gear bolt to 30–36 ft. lbs. (41–49 Nm).
12. Apply sealing compound to the gasket surfaces on the cylinder block and back side of the front cover plate. Install the guide sleeves with new seal rings lubricated with engine oil to prevent cutting the rings, with the chamfered end toward the front cover. Position the gasket and front cover plate on the cylinder block. Temporarily install four front cover screws to position the gasket and front cover plate in place. Install and tighten two cover plate attaching bolts, then remove the four screws that were temporarily installed.
13. Apply sealing compound to the front cover gasket surface, then place the gasket in position on the front cover.
14. Place the front cover on the engine and start all retaining screws two or three turns. Center the cover by inserting an alignment tool (T74P–6019–A or equivalent) in the oil seal.
15. Tighten the front cover attaching screws to 13–16 ft. lbs. (17–21 Nm).

16. Install the crankshaft pulley and tighten the center bolt to 85–96 ft. lbs. (115–130 Nm).
17. Install the oil pan, as described earlier in this section.
18. Install the water pump, heater hose, air conditioning compressor, alternator, thermactor pump and drive belt(s). Adjust the belt tension. For more details on the correct drive belt tensioning procedure, refer to Section 1.
19. Install the radiator.
20. Connect the negative battery cable.

➡ **When the battery has been disconnected and reconnected, some abnormal drive symptoms may occur while the Powertrain Control Module (PCM) relearns its adaptive strategy. The vehicle may need to be driven about 10 miles (16 km) or more to relearn the strategy.**

21. Fill and bleed the cooling system, then operate the engine at fast idle and check for leaks.

Timing Belt

➡ **Although Ford suggests that this component is removable while the engine is installed in the vehicle, depending on the particular options with which your Aerostar is equipped, working clearance may be extremely tight and this procedure may be much easier to perform with the engine removed. Before commencing, read through this procedure and make certain enough clearance, or working room, exists with the engine in the vehicle; if there is not enough space, the engine should be removed.**

REMOVAL & INSTALLATION

2.3L Engine

♦ See Figures 113, 114 and 115

1. Remove the timing belt cover, as described earlier in this section.
2. Turn the crankshaft until the crankshaft timing marks and the camshaft timing marks align with those found on the front of the engine block—make sure that ALL of the timing marks are aligned simultaneously, otherwise the internal engine components will not correctly positioned. The engine should be at Top Dead Center (TDC) when these marks are aligned.
3. Remove the crankshaft pulley and belt guide.
4. Loosen the belt tensioner pulley assembly, then position a camshaft belt adjuster tool (T74P–6254–A or equivalent) on the tension spring rollpin and retract the belt tensioner away from the timing belt. Tighten the adjustment bolt to lock the tensioner in the retracted position.
5. Remove the timing belt.

To install:

6. Install the new belt over the crankshaft sprocket and then counterclockwise over the auxiliary and camshaft sprockets, making sure the lugs on the belt properly engage the sprocket teeth on the pulleys. Be careful not to rotate the pulleys when installing the belt.
7. Release the timing belt tensioner pulley, allowing the tensioner to take up the belt slack. If the spring does not have enough tension to move the roller against the belt (belt hangs loose), it might be necessary to manually push the roller against the belt and tighten the bolt.

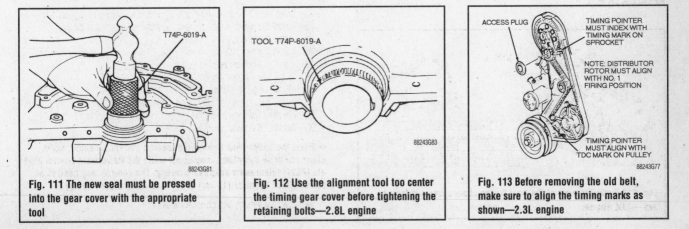

Fig. 111 The new seal must be pressed into the gear cover with the appropriate tool

Fig. 112 Use the alignment tool too center the timing gear cover before tightening the retaining bolts—2.8L engine

Fig. 113 Before removing the old belt, make sure to align the timing marks as shown—2.3L engine

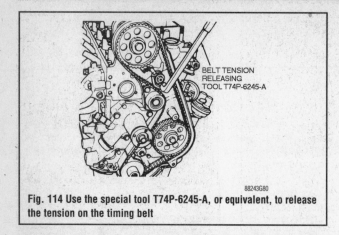

Fig. 114 Use the special tool T74P-6245-A, or equivalent, to release the tension on the timing belt

➡ The spring cannot be used to set belt tension; a wrench must be used on the tensioner assembly.

8. Rotate the crankshaft two complete turns by hand (in the normal direction of rotation) to remove the slack from the belt, then tighten the tensioner adjustment and pivot bolts to specifications. Make sure the belt is seated properly on the pulleys and that the timing marks are still in alignment when No. 1 cylinder is again at TDC/compression.

9. Install the crankshaft pulley and belt guide.

10. Install the timing belt cover, as described earlier in this section.

Timing Chain

➡ Although Ford suggests that this component is removable while the engine is installed in the vehicle, depending on the particular options with which your Aerostar is equipped, working clearance may be extremely tight and this procedure may be much easier to perform with the engine removed. Before commencing, read through this procedure and make cer-

tain enough clearance, or working room, exists with the engine in the vehicle; if there is not enough space, the engine should be removed.

REMOVAL & INSTALLATION

3.0L Engines

◆ See Figures 116 thru 127

1. Disconnect the negative battery cable.
2. Remove the timing chain cover, as described earlier in this section.
3. Turn the crankshaft until the crankshaft timing marks and the camshaft timing marks are aligned. The timing marks should be in a straight up and down line with each other, they should also be at their closest positions to each other as possible (the crankshaft mark should be at the 12 o'clock position and the camshaft timing mark should be at the 6 o'clock position). The engine should be at Top Dead Center (TDC) when these marks are aligned.
4. Remove the camshaft sprocket attaching bolt and washer. Slide both sprockets and the timing chain forward and remove them as an assembly.
5. After both sprockets and the chain are removed from the engine, the chain can be removed from the two sprockets.

To install:

6. Clean the timing cover and oil pan sealing surfaces of all gasket material and silicone sealer.

➡ The timing chain sprocket bolt has a drilled oil passage for timing chain lubrication. Clean the oil passage with solvent. If damaged, do not replace with a standard bolt.

7. Slide the new timing chain with sprockets on the shafts as an assembly with the timing marks aligned as illustrated. Install the camshaft bolt and washer and tighten it to 41–51 ft. lbs. (55–70 Nm). Apply oil to the timing chain and sprockets after installation.

8. Install the timing chain cover and a new front oil seal, as described earlier in this section.

9. Connect the negative battery cable.

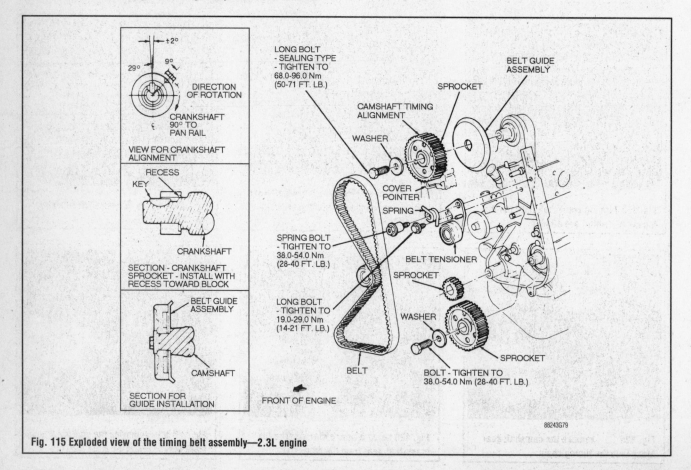

Fig. 115 Exploded view of the timing belt assembly—2.3L engine

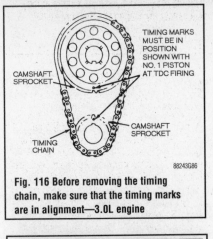

Fig. 116 Before removing the timing chain, make sure that the timing marks are in alignment—3.0L engine

Fig. 117 Remove the A/C compressor mounting bracket retaining bolts on the side and . . .

Fig. 118 . . . on the front of the engine, then . . .

Fig. 119 . . . remove the bracket from the engine

Fig. 120 Remove the water pump from the front cover, then . . .

Fig. 121 . . . remove the front cover

Fig. 122 Turn the crankshaft until the timing marks (white) are aligned

Fig. 123 While holding the crankshaft from turning, loosen the camshaft gear mounting bolt

Fig. 124 Remove the camshaft retaining bolt, then . . .

Fig. 125 . . . remove the camshaft gear along with the timing chain

Fig. 126 Using a gear puller, remove the crankshaft gear from the crankshaft

Fig. 127 After removing the crankshaft gear, make sure to retain the crankshaft key

4.0L Engine

▶ **See Figure 128**

1. Remove the timing chain cover, as described earlier in this section.
2. Remove the radiator.
3. Rotate the engine by hand until the No.1 cylinder is at TDC compression, and the timing marks are aligned.

➡**A packaging clip from a new automatic tensioner can be used to hold the tensioner in a retracted position. If a packaging clip is not available, fabricate a clip to hold the tensioner in a retracted position.**

4. Push the timing chain tensioner into the retracted position, then install the retaining clip.
5. Remove the camshaft sprocket bolt and crankshaft sprocket retaining key.
6. Remove the camshaft and crankshaft sprockets with the timing chain.
7. If necessary, remove the timing chain guide.

To install:

8. Install the timing chain guide. Make sure the pin of the guide is in the hole in the block. Tighten the bolts to 7–9 ft. lbs. (10–12 Nm).
9. Align the timing marks on the crankshaft and camshaft sprockets and install the sprockets and chain.

➡**Make sure that the tensioner side of the timing chain is held inward, and that the guide side of the chain is straight and tight.**

10. Install the camshaft sprocket bolt and sprocket retaining key. Make sure that the timing marks are still aligned.
11. Install the tensioner with the clip in place to keep it retracted.
12. Make sure the tensioner side of the chain is held inward and the other side is straight and tight.
13. Install the camshaft sprocket bolt and tighten it to 50 ft. lbs. (68 Nm).
14. Remove the tensioner clip.
15. Check camshaft end-play.
16. Install the radiator, as described earlier in this section.
17. Install the timing chain cover and oil seal, as described earlier.
18. Connect the negative battery cable.

➡**When the battery has been disconnected and reconnected, some abnormal drive symptoms may occur while the Powertrain Control Module (PCM) relearns its adaptive strategy. The vehicle may need to be driven about 10 miles (16 km) or more to relearn the strategy.**

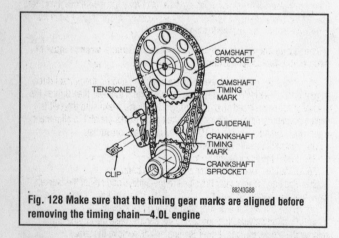
Fig. 128 Make sure that the timing gear marks are aligned before removing the timing chain—4.0L engine

Timing Gears

➡Although Ford suggests that this component is removable while the engine is installed in the vehicle, depending on the particular options with which your Aerostar is equipped, working clearance may be extremely tight and this procedure may be much easier to perform with the engine removed. Before commencing, read through this procedure and make certain enough clearance, or working room, exists with the engine in the vehicle; if there is not enough space, the engine should be removed.

REMOVAL & INSTALLATION

2.8L Engine

▶ **See Figure 129**

1. Remove the front timing gear cover, as described earlier in this section.
2. Temporarily install the crankshaft pulley nut and rotate the engine by hand until the timing marks are in alignment as illustrated.
3. Remove the timing gear bolts and slide the gears off the crankshaft and camshaft using a suitable gear puller.

To install:

4. Position the gears onto the camshaft and crankshaft with the timing marks aligned.
5. Install the crankshaft pulley nut. Draw the crankshaft gear onto the crankshaft by tightening the pulley nut. Make sure that the gear is correctly seated. Perform the same with the camshaft timing gear.
6. Tighten the camshaft gear bolt to 30–36 ft. lbs. (41–49 Nm).
7. Install the timing gear cover, as described earlier in this section.

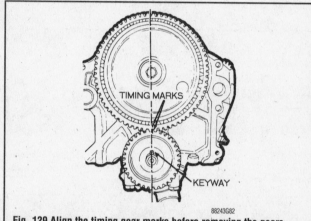
Fig. 129 Align the timing gear marks before removing the gears from the engine—2.8L engine

Camshaft and Bearings

➡Although Ford suggests that this component is removable while the engine is installed in the vehicle, depending on the particular options with which your Aerostar is equipped, working clearance may be extremely tight and this procedure may be much easier to perform with the engine removed. Before commencing, read through this procedure and make certain enough clearance, or working room, exists with the engine in the vehicle; if there is not enough space, the engine should be removed.

REMOVAL & INSTALLATION

2.3L Engine

▶ **See Figures 130 and 131**

1. Drain the cooling system (engine cold).
2. Remove the engine cover from the inside of the van by unfastening the hold-down clamps and lifting the cover from the floor in the passenger's compartment.

✵✵✵ CAUTION

When draining coolant, keep in mind that cats and dogs are attracted by ethylene glycol antifreeze, and are quite likely to drink any that is left in an uncovered container or in puddles on the ground. This will prove fatal in sufficient quantity. Always drain the coolant into a sealable container. Coolant should be reused unless it is contaminated or several years old.

3. Remove the air cleaner assembly.

4. Disconnect the spark plug wires at the plugs, then disconnect the harness at the rocker cover and position it aside.

5. Tag and disconnect the vacuum hoses as required.

6. Remove the rocker cover retaining bolts and remove the cover.

7. Loosen the alternator retaining bolts and remove the belt from the pulley.

8. Remove the alternator mounting bracket-to-cylinder head retaining bolts and position it aside.

9. Disconnect the upper radiator hose at both ends, then remove it from the vehicle.

10. Remove the four timing belt cover bolts and remove the cover. If equipped with power steering, remove the power steering pump bracket.

11. Turn the engine clockwise until the timing marks on the crankshaft pulley and the camshaft sprocket are aligned with the timing marks on the engine block; this should position the engine at TDC of the No. 1 cylinder's compression stroke.

12. Loosen the idler camshaft retaining bolts, position the idler in the unloaded position and tighten the retaining bolts.

13. Remove the timing belt from the camshaft pulley and auxiliary pulley.

14. Using valve spring compressor tool T74P-6565-A or equivalent, depress the valve springs and remove the camshaft followers.

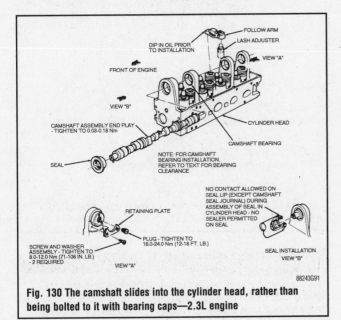

Fig. 130 The camshaft slides into the cylinder head, rather than being bolted to it with bearing caps—2.3L engine

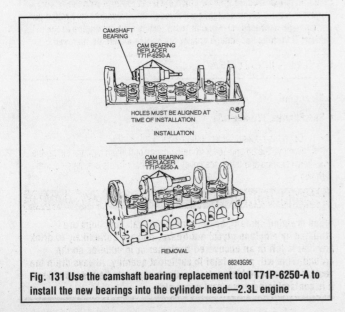

Fig. 131 Use the camshaft bearing replacement tool T71P-6250-A to install the new bearings into the cylinder head—2.3L engine

15. Remove the camshaft gear, as described previously in this section.

16. Remove the seal using the front cover seal remover tool, as described earlier in this section.

17. Remove the two camshaft rear retainer bolts.

18. Raise the vehicle and support it safely on jackstands.

19. Remove the right and left engine support bolts and nuts.

20. Position a hydraulic floor jack under the engine. Position a block of wood on the jack and raise the engine as high as it will go. Place blocks of wood between the engine mounts and chassis bracket, then remove the jack.

21. Carefully slide the camshaft out of the cylinder head, being careful to avoid damaging journals and camshaft lobes.

22. Using a tool such as Bearing Replacer T71P-6250-A, remove the bearings.

To install:

23. Coat the new bearings with clean 50W engine oil and install them with the Bearing Replacer tool, or its equivalent.

24. Make sure the threaded plug is in the rear of the camshaft. If not, remove it from the old camshaft and install it. Coat the camshaft lobes with polyethylene grease (part no. DOAZ-19584-A or equivalent) and lubricate the journals with heavy SG or SH engine oil before installation. Carefully slide the camshaft through the bearings.

25. Install the two camshaft rear retainer screws.

26. Install the camshaft seal using the seal replacer T74P-6150-A or equivalent.

27. Install the belt deflector and sprocket to the camshaft.

28. Install the retaining bolt, using the sprocket tool previously described, to hold the sprocket while the center bolt is tightened to 50-71 ft. lbs. (68-96 Nm).

29. Remove the distributor cap screws and lift off the cap with the wires attached.

30. Remove the spark plugs.

31. Align the distributor rotor with the No. 1 spark plug terminal location in the distributor cap.

32. If not already done, align the camshaft gear timing mark with the timing mark pointer on the engine block. Align the crankshaft pulley timing mark with the pointer on the timing belt cover; this should position the engine at TDC on cylinder No. 1's compression stroke.

33. Install the timing belt over the crankshaft sprocket and then counterclockwise over the auxiliary and camshaft sprockets, making sure the lugs on the belt properly engage the sprocket teeth on the pulleys. Be careful not to rotate the pulleys when installing the belt.

34. Release the timing belt tensioner pulley, allowing the tensioner to take up the belt slack. If the spring does not have enough tension to move the roller against the belt (belt hangs loose), it may be necessary to manually push the roller against the belt and tighten the bolt.

➡The spring should not be used to set belt tension; a wrench must be used on the tensioner assembly.

35. Rotate the crankshaft two complete turns by hand (in the normal direction of rotation—clockwise) to remove the slack from the belt, then tighten the tensioner adjustment and pivot bolts to specifications. Make sure the belt is seated properly on the pulleys and that the timing marks are still in alignment when No. 1 cylinder is again at TDC on the compression stroke.

36. Install the distributor cap.

37. Install the spark plugs.

38. Install the timing belt cover and retaining bolts.

39. Position the alternator drive belt to the pulleys and adjust the belt tension, as described in Section 1.

40. Raise the vehicle and support it safely on jackstands.

41. Position a hydraulic floor jack to the engine, raise the engine and remove the blocks of wood. Lower the engine and remove the jack.

42. Install the engine support bolts and nuts.

43. Lower the vehicle.

44. Using a valve spring compressor tool (T74P-6565-A or equivalent), depress the valve spring and install camshaft followers.

➡For any repair that requires the removal of the camshaft follower arm, each affected lash adjuster should be collapsed approximately half way after the installation of the camshaft follower and then released. This step must be taken prior to any rotation of the camshaft is attempted.

45. Clean and install the rocker arm cover, as described earlier in this section.

46. Reconnect the vacuum hoses and wiring. Install the spark plug wires to the plugs.

47. Connect the upper radiator hose to the engine and radiator and tighten the retaining clamps.

48. Refill the cooling system, start the engine and check for leaks.

2.8L Engine

♦ See Figure 132

1. Disconnect the negative battery cable.
2. Drain the engine oil into a suitable container and dispose of it properly.
3. Remove the fan and spacer, drive belt and pulley and the radiator, as described earlier in this section.
4. Disconnect the spark plug wires from the plugs.
5. Remove the distributor cap with the spark plug wires as an assembly.
6. Disconnect the distributor wiring harness and remove the distributor. For more information, refer to Section 2.
7. Remove the alternator.
8. Remove the thermactor pump.
9. Remove the fuel lines, fuel filter and carburetor.
10. Remove the intake manifold, as described earlier in this section.
11. Remove the rocker arm covers and rocker arm shaft assemblies, as described earlier in this section.
12. Remove the tappets from the engine block using a magnet or suitable tappet removal tool. Keep the tappets in order so that they may be installed in their original locations.
13. Remove the oil pan, as described in this section.
14. Remove the crankshaft damper bolt and remove the damper with a suitable gear pulley.
15. Remove the engine front cover and water pump as an assembly.
16. Remove the camshaft gear attaching bolt and washer, then slide the gear off the camshaft.
17. Remove the camshaft thrust plate.
18. Carefully slide the camshaft out of the engine block, using caution to avoid any damage to the camshaft bearings.
19. Remove the camshaft drive gear and spacer ring.
20. Remove the flywheel.
21. Using a sharp punch and hammer, drive a hole in the rear bearing bore plug and pry it out.
22. Using the special tools and instructions in Cam Bearing Replacer Kit T71P–6250–A, or their equivalents, remove the bearings.
23. To remove the front and rear bearings, use the special adapter tube T72C–6250, or equivalent.

To install:

24. Following the instructions in the tool kit, install the bearings. Make sure that you follow the instructions carefully. Failure to use the correct expanding collets can cause severe bearing damage!

➥**Make sure that the oil holes in the camshaft bearings and engine block are aligned!**

25. Install a new bearing bore plug coated with sealer.
26. Install the flywheel.
27. Oil the camshaft journals and camshaft lobes with heavy SG or SH engine oil (50W). Install the spacer ring with the chamfered side toward the camshaft, then insert the camshaft key.
28. Install the camshaft in the block, using caution to avoid any damage to the camshaft bearings.

29. Install the thrust plate so that it covers the main oil gallery. Tighten the attaching screws to 13–16 ft. lbs. (17–21 Nm).

30. Rotate the camshaft and crankshaft as necessary to align the timing marks. Install the camshaft gear and tighten the attaching bolt to 30–36 ft. lbs. (41–49 Nm).

31. Check the camshaft end-play with a dial indicator. The spacer ring and/or thrust plate are available in two available thickness to permit adjustment of the end play.

32. Align the keyway in the crankshaft gear with the key in the crankshaft. Align the timing marks and install the gear.

33. Install the engine front cover and water pump assembly.

34. Install the crankshaft pulley and tighten the retaining bolt to 85–96 ft. lbs. (115–130 Nm).

35. Install the oil pan.

36. Position the tappets in their original locations, then apply heavy SG or SH engine oil (50W) to both ends of the pushrods. Install the pushrods in their original locations.

37. Install the intake manifold and tighten the mounting bolts to the specifications and in the sequence described under the intake manifold removal and installation procedure in this section.

38. Install the oil baffles, rocker arm and shaft assemblies. For more information, refer to the rocker arm procedures earlier in this section.

39. Adjust the valves to the specified cold clearance, then install the rocker arm covers. For more information on valve adjusting, refer to Section 1.

40. Install the fan, spacer and drive belt.

41. Install the carburetor, fuel filter and fuel line.

42. Install the thermactor pump.

43. Install the alternator.

44. Install the distributor, distributor wiring harness, distributor cap and spark plug wires. Reconnect the spark plug wires to the spark plugs.

➥**Before installing the spark plug wires to the plugs, coat the inside of each boot with silicone lubricant using a small wooden or plastic tool.**

45. Install the radiator.

46. Refill the cooling system.

47. Replace the oil filter and refill the crankcase with the specified amount of engine oil.

48. Reconnect the negative battery cable.

49. Start the engine and check the ignition timing and idle speed. Adjust if necessary. Run the engine at fast idle and check for coolant, fuel, vacuum or oil leaks.

3.0L Engine

♦ See Figures 132 and 133

1987–88 MODELS

1. Remove the engine from the vehicle.
2. Remove the timing cover.
3. Remove the intake manifold.
4. Remove the tappets. Keep them in order for installation.

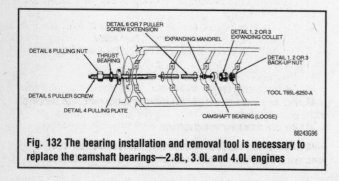

Fig. 132 The bearing installation and removal tool is necessary to replace the camshaft bearings—2.8L, 3.0L and 4.0L engines

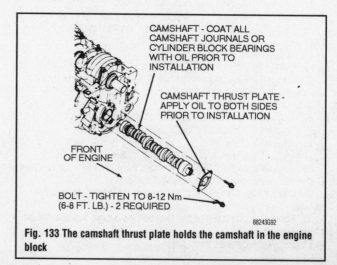

Fig. 133 The camshaft thrust plate holds the camshaft in the engine block

5. Check the camshaft end-play. If excessive, you'll have to replace the thrust plate.

6. Remove the timing chain and sprockets.

7. Remove the thrust plate.

8. Carefully and slowly, pull the camshaft from the block. Take great care to avoid damaging the bearings or lobes!

To install:

9. Coat the camshaft lobes and journals with SG or SH 50W engine oil. Carefully slide the camshaft into the block.

10. Install the thrust plate. Torque the bolts to 72–96 inch lbs. (8.0–10.8 Nm).

11. Install the timing chain and sprockets.

12. Install the tappets.

13. Install the intake manifold.

14. Install the timing cover.

15. Install the engine.

1989–97 MODELS

1. Have the A/C system discharged by a qualified, professional mechanic utilizing a recovery/recycling machine.

2. Disconnect the negative battery cable.

3. Rotate the crankshaft so that No. 1 piston is at TDC on the compression stroke.

4. Remove the air cleaner hoses.

5. Remove the fan and spacer, and shroud.

6. Drain the cooling system. Remove the radiator.

❋❋ CAUTION

When draining coolant, keep in mind that cats and dogs are attracted by ethylene glycol antifreeze, and are quite likely to drink any that is left in an uncovered container or in puddles on the ground. This will prove fatal in sufficient quantity. Always drain the coolant into a sealable container. Coolant should be reused unless it is contaminated or several years old.

7. Remove the A/C system condenser.

8. Relieve the fuel system pressure. Refer to Section 5 for the fuel system pressure release procedure.

9. Remove the fuel lines at the fuel supply manifold.

10. Tag and disconnect all vacuum hoses in the way.

11. Tag and disconnect all wires in the way.

12. Remove the engine front cover and water pump.

13. Remove the alternator.

14. Remove the power steering pump and secure it out of the way. DO NOT disconnect the hoses!

15. Remove the air conditioning compressor and secure it out of the way. DO NOT disconnect the hoses!

16. Remove the throttle body and fuel injection harness. For more information, refer to Section 5.

17. Drain the engine oil into a suitable container and dispose of it properly.

18. Disconnect the spark plug wires from the plugs.

19. Remove the distributor cap with the spark plug wires as an assembly.

20. Matchmark the rotor, distributor body and engine. Disconnect the distributor wiring harness and remove the distributor.

21. Remove the rocker arm covers.

22. Remove the intake manifold, as described earlier in this section.

23. Loosen the rocker arm bolts enough to pivot the rocker arms out of the way and remove the pushrods. Identify them for installation. They must be installed in their original positions!

24. Remove the lifters. Identify them for installation.

25. Remove the crankshaft pulley/damper.

26. Remove the starter motor.

27. Remove the oil pan, as described in this section.

28. If not already performed, turn the engine by hand until the timing marks align at TDC of the power stroke on the No.1 cylinder.

29. Check the camshaft end-play. If excessive, the thrust plate must be replaced.

30. Remove the camshaft gear attaching bolt and washer, then slide the gear off the camshaft.

31. Remove the camshaft thrust plate.

32. Carefully slide the camshaft out of the engine block, using caution to avoid any damage to the camshaft bearings.

➡**The manufacturer recommends that the engine be removed from the vehicle to remove the camshaft bearings.**

33. New camshaft bearings must be installed if a new camshaft is to be installed, or if the old bearings are damaged in any way. To remove the camshaft bearings, perform the following:

   a. The Camshaft Bearing Set T65L-6250-A tool will be needed to remove the camshaft bearings.

   b. Install the puller from the rear of the cylinder block.

   c. Select the proper size expanding collet and back up nut, then assemble it on the expanding mandrel. With the expanding collet collapsed, install the collet assembly in camshaft bearing, then tighten the back up nut on the expanding mandrel until the collet fits the camshaft bearing.

   d. Assemble the puller screw and extension, if necessary, then install on the expanding mandrel. Wrap a cloth around the threads of the puller screw to protect the bearing or journal. Tighten the puller nut against the thrust bearing and pulling plate to remove the camshaft bearing. Be sure to hold the end of the puller screw to prevent it from turning.

   e. Repeat the above steps for each bearing.

To install:

34. Clean the mating gasket surfaces of the intake manifold and cylinder head. Lay a clean cloth or shop rag in the tappet valley to catch any gasket material. After scraping, carefully lift the cloth from the tappet valley preventing any particles from entering the oil drain holes or cylinder head. Use a suitable solvent to remove the old rubber sealant. Clean the gasket mating surfaces of the engine front cover to cylinder block and oil pan to cylinder block.

35. Oil the camshaft journals and camshaft lobes with heavy SG or SH engine oil (50W). Install the spacer ring with the chamfered side toward the camshaft, then insert the camshaft key.

❋❋ CAUTION

Failure to use the correct expanding collet can cause severe bearing damage.

36. Install new camshaft bearings as follows:

   a. The camshaft bearings are available pre-finished to size and require no reaming for standard and 0.015 in. (0.38mm) undersize journal diameters.

➡**Align the oil holes in the bearings with the oil holes in the cylinder block before pressing the new bearings in place. Make sure the front bearing is installed 0.020–0.035 in. (0.51–0.89mm) recessed below the front face of the cylinder block.**

   b. Position the new bearings at the bearing bores, then press them in place with the Camshaft Bearing Set T65L-6520-A, or equivalent. Be sure to center the pulling plate and puller screw to avoid damage to the bearing.

   c. Install the camshaft rear bearing bore plug.

37. Install the camshaft in the block, using caution to avoid any damage to the camshaft bearings.

38. Install the thrust plate. Tighten the attaching bolts to 6–8 ft. lbs. (8–12 Nm).

39. Rotate the camshaft and crankshaft as necessary to align the timing marks. Install the camshaft gear and chain. Tighten the attaching bolt to 37–52 ft. lbs. (50–70 Nm).

40. Coat the tappets with 50W engine oil and place them in their original locations.

41. Apply 50W engine oil to both ends of the pushrods. Install the pushrods in their original locations.

42. Pivot the rocker arms into position. Tighten the fulcrum bolts, as described in the rocker arm procedures earlier in this section.

43. Turn the engine by hand to 0 degrees BTDC of the power stroke on the No. 1 cylinder.

44. The balance of the installation is the reverse of removal.

45. Refill the cooling system.

46. Replace the oil filter and refill the crankcase with the specified amount of engine oil.

47. Reconnect the negative battery cable.

➡**When the battery has been disconnected and reconnected, some abnormal drive symptoms may occur while the Powertrain Control Mod-**

ule (PCM) relearns its adaptive strategy. The vehicle may need to be driven about 10 miles (16 km) or more to relearn the strategy.

48. Start the engine and check the ignition timing and idle speed; adjust if necessary. Run the engine at fast idle and check for coolant, fuel, vacuum or oil leaks.

4.0L Engine

▶ See Figures 132 and 134

➡The manufacturer recommends that the engine be removed from the vehicle to remove the camshaft bearings.

New camshaft bearings must be installed if a new camshaft is to be installed, or if the old bearings are damaged in any way.

➡It is necessary to replace the oil pan gasket when removing and installing the engine front cover. It will also be necessary to remove the transmission to properly reseal the oil pan.

1. If the vehicle is equipped with an Air Conditioning (A/C) system, have the system discharged by a qualified, reputable automotive technician utilizing a refrigerant recovery/recycling machine OR do not disconnect the A/C refrigerant lines from the condenser or from the compressor.
2. Disconnect the negative battery cable.
3. Drain the engine oil into a suitable container and dispose of it properly.
4. Drain the cooling system.

❊❊ CAUTION

When draining coolant, keep in mind that cats and dogs are attracted by ethylene glycol antifreeze, and are quite likely to drink any that is left in an uncovered container or in puddles on the ground. This will prove fatal in sufficient quantity. Always drain the coolant into a sealable container. Coolant should be reused unless it is contaminated or several years old.

5. Remove the radiator, as described in this section.
6. Remove the A/C condenser from the engine. If the A/C was not discharged, remove the A/C compressor from its mounting bracket and secure it aside with the refrigerant lines still attached.
7. Remove the fan and spacer, and shroud.
8. Remove the air cleaner hoses.
9. Tag and remove the spark plug wires.
10. Remove the ignition coil and bracket.
11. Remove the crankshaft pulley/damper.
12. Remove the clamp, bolt and oil pump drive from the rear of the block.
13. Remove the alternator.
14. Relieve the fuel system pressure. For more information, refer to Section 5.
15. Remove the fuel lines at the fuel supply manifold.
16. Remove the upper and lower intake manifolds, as described earlier in this section.
17. Remove the rocker arm covers, as described earlier in this section.
18. Remove the rocker arm shaft assemblies.
19. Remove the pushrods. Identify them for installation. They must be installed in their original positions!
20. Remove the lifters. Identify them for installation.
21. Remove the oil pan, as described in this section.
22. Remove the engine front cover and water pump.
23. Turn the engine by hand until the timing marks align at TDC of the power stroke on No.1 piston.
24. Place the timing chain tensioner in the retracted position and install the retaining clip.
25. Check the camshaft end-play. If excessive, you'll have to replace the thrust plate.
26. Remove the camshaft gear attaching bolt and washer, then slide the gear off the camshaft.
27. Remove the camshaft thrust plate.
28. Carefully slide the camshaft out of the engine block, using caution to avoid any damage to the camshaft bearings.
To remove the camshaft bearings, perform the following:
a. The Camshaft Bearing Set T65L-6250-A tool, or its equivalent, will be needed to remove the camshaft bearings.

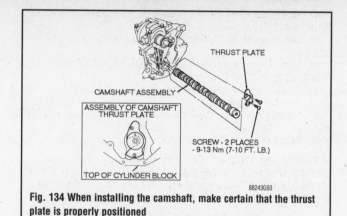

Fig. 134 When installing the camshaft, make certain that the thrust plate is properly positioned

b. Install the puller from the rear of the cylinder block.
c. Select the proper size expanding collet and back up nut, then assemble it on the expanding mandrel. With the expanding collet collapsed, install the collet assembly in camshaft bearing, then tighten the back up nut on the expanding mandrel until the collet fits the camshaft bearing.
d. Assemble the puller screw and extension, if necessary, then install on the expanding mandrel. Wrap a cloth around the threads of the puller screw to protect the bearing or journal. Tighten the puller nut against the thrust bearing and pulling plate to remove the camshaft bearing. Be sure to hold the end of the puller screw to prevent it from turning.
e. Repeat the above steps for each bearing.
To install:
29. Clean the mating gasket surfaces of the intake manifold and cylinder head. Lay a clean cloth or shop rag in the tappet valley to catch any gasket material. After scraping, carefully lift the cloth from the tappet valley preventing any particles from entering the oil drain holes or cylinder head. Use a suitable solvent to remove the old rubber sealant. Clean the gasket mating surfaces of the engine front cover-to-cylinder block and oil pan-to-cylinder block.
30. Oil the camshaft journals and camshaft lobes with heavy SG or SH engine oil (50W). Install the spacer ring with the chamfered side toward the camshaft, then insert the camshaft key.

❊❊ CAUTION

Failure to use the correct expanding collet can cause severe bearing damage.

31. If necessary, install new camshaft bearings as follows:
a. The camshaft bearings are available pre-finished to size and require no reaming for standard and 0.015 in. (0.38mm) undersize journal diameters.

➡Align the oil holes in the bearings with the oil holes in the cylinder block before pressing the new bearings in place. Make sure the front bearing is installed 0.020–0.035 in. (0.51–0.89mm) below the front face of the cylinder block.

b. Position the new bearings at the bearing bores, then press them in place with the Camshaft Bearing Set T65L-6520-A. Be sure to center the pulling plate and puller screw to avoid damage to the bearing.
c. Install the camshaft rear bearing bore plug.
32. Install the camshaft in the block, using caution to avoid any damage to the camshaft bearings.
33. Oil the camshaft journals and camshaft lobes with heavy SG or SH engine oil (50W).
34. Install the camshaft in the block, using caution to avoid any damage to the camshaft bearings.
35. Install the thrust plate. Make sure that it covers the main oil gallery. Tighten the attaching screws to 7–10 ft. lbs. (9–13 Nm).
36. Rotate the camshaft and crankshaft, as necessary, to align the timing marks. Install the camshaft gear and chain. Tighten the attaching bolt to 44–50 ft. lbs. (60–68 Nm).
37. Remove the clip from the chain tensioner.
38. Install the engine front cover and water pump assembly.
39. Install the crankshaft damper/pulley and tighten the retaining bolt to 107 ft. lbs. (146 Nm).

40. Install the oil pan. It is important to adhere to the procedures given earlier in this section.

41. Coat the tappets with 50W engine oil and place them in their original locations.

42. Apply 50W engine oil to both ends of the pushrods. Install the pushrods in their original locations.

43. The balance of the installation is the reverse of removal.

44. Refill the cooling system.

45. Replace the oil filter and refill the crankcase with the specified amount of engine oil.

46. Reconnect the negative battery cable.

➡**When the battery has been disconnected and reconnected, some abnormal drive symptoms may occur while the Powertrain Control Module (PCM) relearns its adaptive strategy. The vehicle may need to be driven about 10 miles (16 km) or more to relearn the strategy.**

47. Start the engine and check the ignition timing and idle speed; adjust if necessary. Run the engine at fast idle and check for coolant, fuel, vacuum or oil leaks.

CAMSHAFT INSPECTION

Completely clean the camshaft with solvent, paying special attention to cleaning the oil holes. Visually inspect the camshaft lobes and bearing journals for excessive wear. If a lobe is questionable, check the camshaft lobe with a micrometer and compare your measurements with the specifications in the Engine Rebuilding Specification charts; replace the camshaft if unevenly or excessively worn on the lobes or journals. Also, check the camshaft for straightness with a dial indicator.

➡**If a camshaft journal is worn, there is a good chance that the bearings are also worn.**

Auxiliary Shaft

REMOVAL & INSTALLATION

2.3L Engine

1. Rotate the engine so that No. 1 cylinder is at TDC on the compression stroke. Check that the timing marks are aligned on the camshaft and crankshaft pulleys. An access plug is provided in the camshaft belt cover so that the camshaft timing can be checked without removal of the cover or any other parts. Set the crankshaft to TDC by aligning the timing mark on the crank pulley with the TDC mark on the belt cover. Look through the access hole in the belt cover to make sure that the timing mark on the camshaft drive sprocket is lined up with the pointer on the inner belt cover.

➡**Always turn the engine in the normal direction of rotation. Backward rotation may cause the timing belt to jump time, due to the arrangement of the belt tensioner.**

2. Remove the fan blade and water pump pulley bolts.

3. Loosen the alternator retaining bolts and remove the drive belt from the pulleys. Remove the water pump pulley.

4. Remove the radiator.

5. Loosen and position the power steering pump mounting bracket aside.

6. Remove the four timing belt outer cover retaining bolts and remove the cover.

7. Remove the auxiliary shaft cover.

8. Remove the crankshaft pulley and belt guide.

9. Loosen the belt tensioner pulley assembly, then position a camshaft belt adjuster tool (T74P–6254–A or equivalent) on the tension spring rollpin and retract the belt tensioner away from the timing belt. Tighten the adjustment bolt to lock the tensioner in the retracted position.

10. Remove the timing belt.

11. Remove the fuel pump. For more information, refer to Section 5.

12. Remove the retaining pin and slide off the auxiliary shaft sprocket.

13. Remove the auxiliary shaft retaining plate.

14. Using a slide hammer and puller attachment, remove the auxiliary shaft from the block. The bearings can be removed with a driver.

To install:

15. Coat the new bearings in 50W engine oil and drive them into place. Make sure the oil holes in the bearings align with the oil holes in the block.

16. Completely dip the auxiliary shaft in 50W engine oil and install it in the block.

17. Install the retaining plate. Tighten the bolts to 6–9 ft. lbs. (8–12 Nm).

18. Install the sprocket and pin.

19. Install the fuel pump.

20. Make certain that the crankshaft timing mark and the camshaft sprocket timing mark are aligned with the engine block timing marks.

21. Install the new timing belt over the crankshaft sprocket and then counterclockwise over the auxiliary and camshaft sprockets, making sure the lugs on the belt properly engage the sprocket teeth on the pulleys. Be careful not to rotate the pulleys when installing the belt.

22. Release the timing belt tensioner pulley, allowing the tensioner to take up the belt slack. If the spring does not have enough tension to move the roller against the belt (belt hangs loose), it might be necessary to manually push the roller against the belt and tighten the bolt.

➡**The spring should not be used to set belt tension; a wrench must be used on the tensioner assembly.**

23. Rotate the crankshaft two complete turns by hand (in the normal direction of rotation) to remove the slack from the belt, then tighten the tensioner adjustment and pivot bolts to specifications. Make sure the belt is seated properly on the pulleys and that the timing marks are still in alignment when No. 1 cylinder is again at TDC of the No. 1 cylinder's compression stroke.

24. The balance of the installation is the reverse of removal.

25. Connect the negative battery cable.

26. Start the engine and check the ignition timing. Adjust the timing, if necessary.

Rear Main Seal

➡**Although Ford suggests that this component is removable while the engine is installed in the vehicle, depending on the particular options with which your Aerostar is equipped, working clearance may be extremely tight and this procedure may be much easier to perform with the engine removed. Before commencing, read through this procedure and make certain enough clearance, or working room, exists with the engine in the vehicle; if there is not enough space, the engine should be removed.**

REMOVAL & INSTALLATION

2.3L and 3.0L Engines

▶ **See Figures 135 and 136**

1. Raise the van and support it safely on jackstands.

2. Remove the transmission. For more details, refer to Section 7.

3. If equipped with a manual transmission, remove the bell housing and clutch assembly.

4. Remove the flywheel or flexplate.

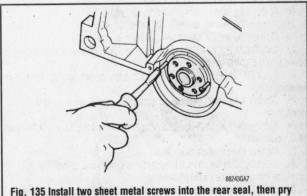

Fig. 135 Install two sheet metal screws into the rear seal, then pry the old seal out of the seal bore—2.3L and 3.0L engines

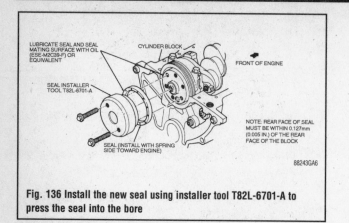

Fig. 136 Install the new seal using installer tool T82L-6701-A to press the seal into the bore

5. Using a sharp awl, punch one hole into the seal metal surface between the seal lip and the engine block.

6. Screw in the threaded end of a slide hammer tool (T77L-9533-B or equivalent), then use the slide hammer to remove the seal. Use caution to avoid scratching or damaging the oil seal surface of the engine block.

To install:

7. Apply clean engine oil to the outer lips and inner seal edge.

8. Position the oil seal on the Rear Main Seal Installer tool (T82L-6701-A or equivalent), then position the tool and seal on the rear of the engine. Alternately tighten the bolts to properly seat the seal.

9. Install the flywheel or flexplate, then tighten the retaining bolts to 56-64 ft. lbs. (73-87 Nm).

10. Install the clutch and bell housing assemblies, if equipped with a manual transmission.

11. Install the transmission. For more details, refer to Section 7.

2.8L and 4.0L Engines

♦ **See Figures 135 and 137**

1. Raise the van and support it safely on jackstands.

2. Remove the transmission, as described in Section 7.

3. If equipped with a manual transmission, remove the bell housing and clutch assembly.

4. Remove the flywheel/flexplate and rear plate.

5. Use a sharp awl to punch two holes in the crankshaft rear oil seal on opposite sides of the crankshaft and just above the bearing cap-to-cylinder block split line.

6. Install a sheet metal screw in each hole, then use two small prytools to pry against both screws at the same time to remove the crankshaft rear oil seal. It may be necessary to place small blocks of wood against the cylinder block to provide a fulcrum point for the pry bars.

✷✷ CAUTION

Exercise care throughout this procedure to avoid scratching or otherwise damaging the crankshaft oil seal surface.

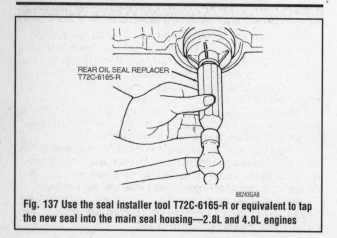

Fig. 137 Use the seal installer tool T72C-6165-R or equivalent to tap the new seal into the main seal housing—2.8L and 4.0L engines

To install:

7. Clean the oil seal recesses in the cylinder block and main bearing cap. Inspect and clean the oil seal contact surface on the crankshaft.

8. Coat the oil seal-to-cylinder block surface of the oil seal with oil. Coat the seal contact surface of the oil seal and crankshaft with heavy SG or SH engine oil.

9. For installing a seal with a metal sleeve, perform the following:

a. Attach the rear crankshaft adapter to the rear of the crankshaft using the supplied mounting screws.

b. Apply a few drops of clean engine oil to the inboard side of the seal/sleeve at the area where the seal contacts the sleeve.

c. Apply a very light film of clean engine oil on the inner diameter of the sleeve and outer diameter of the seal.

d. Slide the seal/sleeve over the rear crankshaft seal adapter with the flange to the rear of the engine.

➡**It is normal for the seal to sit approximately 0.030 in. (0.76mm) deeper than the sleeve flange. DO NOT ADJUST.**

e. Use the rear crankshaft seal replacer and supplied bolt to push the rear seal into the cylinder block. Remove the rear crankshaft seal adapter.

10. For installing a seal without a metal sleeve, perform the following:

a. Attach the rear crankshaft adapter to the rear of the crankshaft using the supplied mounting screws.

b. Slide the rear crankshaft seal protector over the rear crankshaft seal adapter and over the end of the crankshaft.

c. Start the crankshaft rear oil seal over the rear crankshaft seal protector.

d. Use the rear crankshaft seal replacer and supplied bolt to push the seal into the cylinder block.

e. Remove the rear crankshaft seal protector and rear crankshaft seal adapter.

11. Install the flywheel/flexplate. Tighten the retaining bolts as follows:

a. First step—tighten to 9-11 ft. lbs. (12-15 Nm).

b. Second step—tighten to 50-55 ft. lbs. (68-74 Nm).

12. Install the clutch and bell housing assembly on manual transmission models.

13. Install the transmission, as described in Section 7.

Flywheel and Ring Gear

REMOVAL & INSTALLATION

All Engines

♦ **See Figures 138, 139 and 140**

1. Raise the vehicle and support it safely on jackstands.

2. Remove the transmission, as outlined in Section 7.

3. On manual transmission models, remove the bell housing, clutch pressure plate and clutch disc.

4. On automatic transmission models, remove the torque converter.

5. Install a dial indicator, so that the indicator rests against the face of the ring gear adjacent to the gear teeth (automatic), or against the flywheel face (manual). Hold the flywheel and crankshaft forward or backward as far as possible to prevent crankshaft end-play from being indicated as flywheel runout. Zero the dial indicator, then turn the flywheel one complete revolution by hand while observing the total dial indicator reading. If the runout exceeds 0.001 in. (0.025mm) on 2.3L engines; 0.025 in. (0.635mm) for manual, or 0.060 in. (1.5mm) for automatic on 2.8L engines; 0.070 in. (1.8mm) on 3.0L engines; and 0.005 in. (0.127mm) on 4.0L engines, the flywheel/flexplate will have to be replaced. On manual transmissions, the flywheel clutch surface can be machined true, if the runout is not excessive.

6. Remove the flywheel/flexplate mounting bolts and remove the flywheel/flexplate and ring gear assembly.

7. On automatic transmissions models, inspect the flexplate for cracks or other indications that would make it unfit for further use. Check the ring gear for worn, chipped or cracked teeth and replace, if any damage is found.

8. On manual transmissions models, inspect the flywheel for cracks, heat damage or other problems that would make it unfit for further use. Machine the clutch friction surface if it is scored or worn. If it is necessary to remove more than 0.045 in. (1.14mm) of stock from the original thickness, replace the flywheel. Check the ring gear for worn, chipped or cracked teeth and replace, if any damage is found.

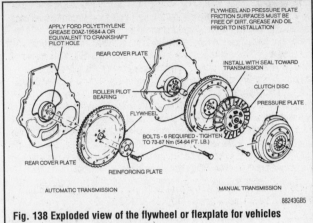

Fig. 138 Exploded view of the flywheel or flexplate for vehicles equipped with the 2.3L engine

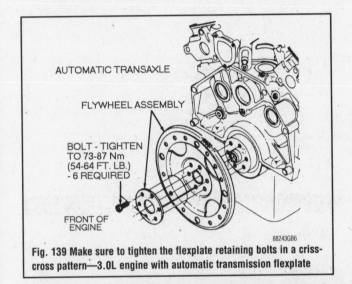

Fig. 139 Make sure to tighten the flexplate retaining bolts in a criss-cross pattern—3.0L engine with automatic transmission flexplate

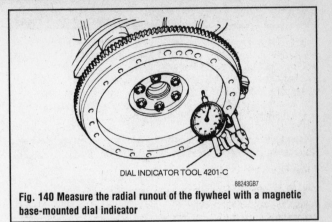

Fig. 140 Measure the radial runout of the flywheel with a magnetic base-mounted dial indicator

To install:

➡**All major rotating components including the flexplate/flywheel are individually balanced. Do not attempt to install balance weights on a new flywheel.**

9. Position the flywheel/flexplate on the crankshaft flange and apply oil resistant sealer to the mounting bolts. Install and tighten the bolts in a criss-cross pattern to the specifications given in the Torque Specifications Chart.

10. On manual transmissions models, install the clutch disc and pressure plate as outlined in Section 7. On automatic transmissions models, install the torque converter.

11. Install the transmission, as outlined in Section 7, then lower the vehicle.

RING GEAR REPLACEMENT

To replace a damaged ring gear on a manual transmission flywheel, perform the following:

1. Heat the ring gear with a blow torch on the engine side of the gear and knock it off the flywheel. Do not hit the flywheel when removing the gear.

2. Heat the new ring gear evenly until the gear expands enough to slip onto the flywheel. Make sure the gear is seated properly against the shoulder. Do not heat any portion of the gear more than 500°F (260°C) or the temper will be removed from the ring gear teeth.

EXHAUST SYSTEM

General Information

➡**Safety glasses should be worn at all times when working on or near the exhaust system. Older exhaust systems will almost always be covered with loose rust particles which will shower you when disturbed. These particles are more than a nuisance and could injure your eye.**

Whenever working on the exhaust system always keep the following in mind:
• Check the complete exhaust system for open seams, holes, loose connections, or other deterioration which could permit exhaust fumes to seep into the passenger compartment.
• The exhaust system is usually supported by free-hanging rubber mounts which permit some movement of the exhaust system, but does not permit transfer of noise and vibration into the passenger compartment. Do not replace the rubber mounts with solid ones.
• Before removing any component of the exhaust system, ALWAYS squirt a liquid rust dissolving agent onto the fasteners for ease of removal. A lot of knuckle skin will be saved by following this rule. It may even be wise to spray the fasteners and allow them to sit overnight.

✳✳ CAUTION

Allow the exhaust system to cool sufficiently before spraying a solvent on the exhaust fasteners. Some solvents are highly flammable and could ignite when sprayed on hot exhaust components.

• Annoying rattles and noise vibrations in the exhaust system are usually caused by misalignment of the parts. When aligning the system, leave all bolts and nuts loose until all parts are properly aligned, then tighten, working from front to rear.
• When installing exhaust system parts, make sure there is enough clearance between the hot exhaust parts and pipes and hoses that would be adversely affected by excessive heat. Also make sure there is adequate clearance from the floor pan to avoid possible overheating of the floor.

Safety Precautions

For a number of reasons, exhaust system work can be the most dangerous type of work you can do on your van. Always observe the following precautions:
• Support the van extra securely. Not only will you often be working directly under it, but you'll frequently be using a lot of force, such as heavy hammer blows, to dislodge rusted parts. This can cause a van that's improperly supported to shift and possibly fall.
• Wear goggles. Exhaust system parts are always rusty. Metal chips can be dislodged, even when you're only turning rusted bolts. Attempting to pry pipes apart with a chisel makes the chips fly even more frequently.
• If you're using a cutting torch, keep it a great distance from either the fuel tank or lines. Stop what you're doing and feel the temperature of the fuel bearing pipes on the tank frequently. Even slight heat can expand and/or vaporize fuel, resulting in accumulated vapor, or even a liquid leak, near your torch.
• Watch where your hammer blows fall. You could easily tap a brake or fuel line when you hit an exhaust system part with a glancing blow. Inspect all lines and hoses in the area where you've been working.

Special Tools

A number of special exhaust system tools can be rented from auto supply houses or local stores that rent special equipment. A common one is a tail pipe expander, designed to enable you to join pipes of identical diameter.

It may also be quite helpful to use solvents designed to loosen rusted bolts or flanges. Soaking rusted parts the night before you do the job can speed the work of freeing rusted parts considerably. Remember that these solvents are often flammable. Apply only to parts after they are cool!

Inspection

▶ **See Figures 141, 142 and 143**

Inspect inlet pipes, outlet pipes and mufflers for cracked joints, broken welds and corrosion damage that would result in a leaking exhaust system. It is normal for a certain amount of moisture and staining to be present around the muffler seams. The presence of soot, light surface rust or moisture does not indicate a faulty muffler. Inspect the clamps, brackets and insulators for cracks and stripped or badly corroded bolt threads. When flat joints are loosened and/or disconnected to replace a shield pipe or muffler, replace the bolts and flange nuts if there is reasonable doubt that their service life is limited.

The exhaust system, including brush shields, must be free of leaks, binding, grounding and excessive vibrations. These conditions are usually caused by loose or broken flange bolts, shields, brackets or pipes. If any of these conditions exist, check the exhaust system components and alignment. Align or replace as necessary. Brush shields are positioned on the underside of the catalytic converter and should be free from bends which would bring any part of the shield in contact with the catalytic converter or muffler. The shield should also be clear of any combustible material such as dried grass or leaves.

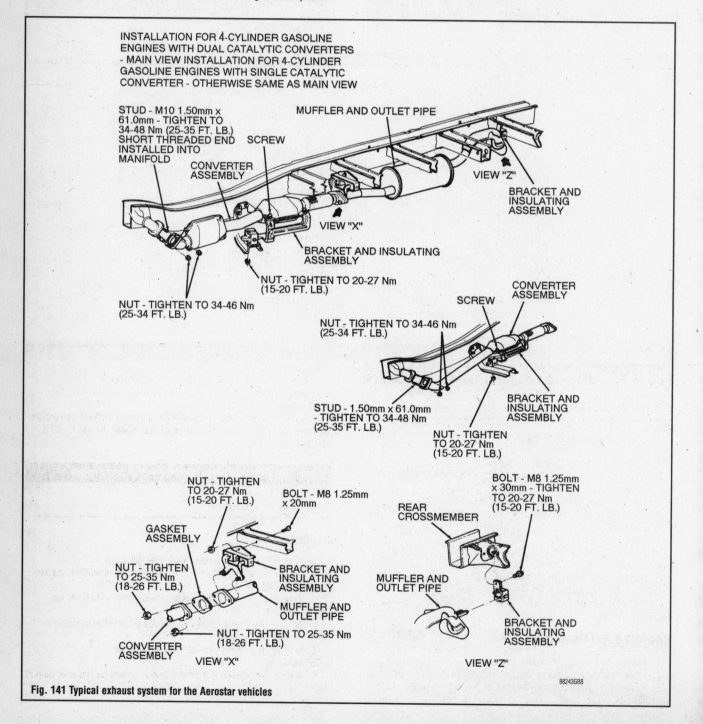

Fig. 141 Typical exhaust system for the Aerostar vehicles

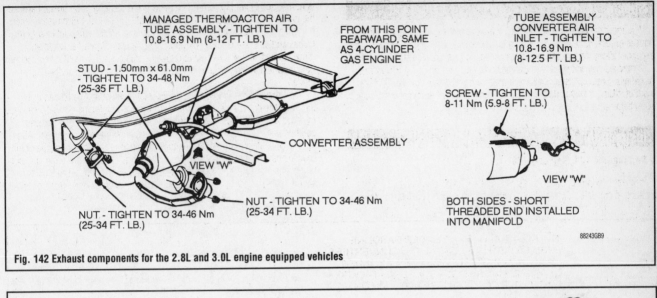

Fig. 142 Exhaust components for the 2.8L and 3.0L engine equipped vehicles

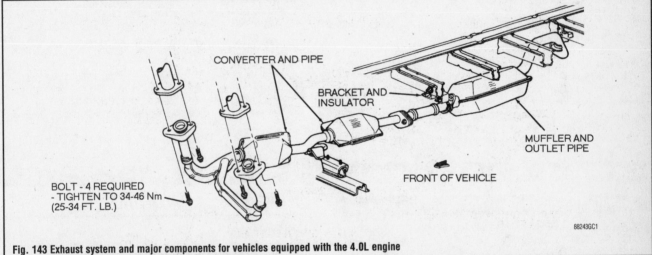

Fig. 143 Exhaust system and major components for vehicles equipped with the 4.0L engine

Muffler and Outlet Pipe Assembly

REMOVAL & INSTALLATION

2.3L, 2.8L and 1987–88 3.0L Engines

1. Remove the two nuts at the muffler flange.
2. Apply a soap solution to the surface of the exhaust hanger slides at the support insulators.
3. Force the support slides out of the rubber insulators.
4. Remove the muffler and outlet pipe assembly by sliding forward, out over the axle housing.

To install:

5. Position the muffler and outlet pipe assembly to the converter and inlet pipe assembly by sliding it in over the axle housing.
6. Apply a soap solution to the metal support slides.
7. Force the metal support slides through the rubber insulators.
8. Install the two nuts to the muffler flange and tighten them to 18–26 ft. lbs. (25–35 Nm).

1989–97 3.0L and 4.0L Engines

1. Remove the 2 nuts at the muffler flange.
2. While supporting the muffler, remove the bolt from the outlet pipe hanger.
3. Remove the nut and bolt from the front hanger, and remove the muffler and outlet pipe.

To install:

4. Install the muffler and outlet pipe over the rear axle.
5. Install the front and rear hangers. Tighten the bolts to 15–20 ft. lbs. (20–27 Nm).
6. Place a new non-asbestos gasket between the muffler/outlet pipe and the converter/inlet pipe. Install the bolts and nuts, then tighten them to 15–20 ft. lbs. (20–27 Nm).

Catalytic Converter(s) and/or Pipe Assembly

REMOVAL & INSTALLATION

2.3L Engine

1. Raise the vehicle and support it safely on jackstands.
2. Remove the two nuts attaching the converter pipe assembly to the muffler and outlet pipe.
3. Remove the two nuts attaching the converter pipe assembly to the exhaust manifold.
4. Apply a soap solution to the support slide of the converter support bracket at the support insulator.
5. Remove the converter pipe assembly from the van.

To install:

6. Apply a soap solution to the metal support slide of the converter support bracket.

7. Install the converter onto the exhaust manifold studs and loosely secure it in place.

8. Install a new, non-asbestos gasket between the converter pipe, muffler and outlet pipe assembly. Loosely secure the flanges and gasket with two nuts.

9. Tighten the exhaust manifold connection by alternately tightening the manifold bolts to 25–34 ft. lbs. (34–46 Nm).

10. Tighten the converter-to-muffler flange to 18–26 ft. lbs. (25–35 Nm).

11. Start the engine and check for exhaust leaks. Correct as necessary. Lower the vehicle.

2.8L and 1986–87 3.0L Engines

1. Raise the vehicle and support it safely on jackstands.

2. Remove the two nuts attaching the converter pipe assembly to the muffler and outlet pipe.

3. On carbureted engines, remove the clamp securing the managed thermactor air tube to the catalytic converter. Remove the screw holding the tube bracket to the forward converter and separate the tube from the converter.

4. Disconnect the hose from the top of the managed thermactor air tube and check valve. Heat may be required to pry the tube from the nipple on the converter. Remove the tube and check valve by rotating the assembly as it is lowered.

5. Loosen and remove the exhaust manifold stud nuts. Slide the muffler and outlet pipe rearward. Remove the gasket, then move the converter assembly rearward and rotate it to clear the studs for removal.

To install:

6. Position the Y-pipe on the exhaust manifold studs and loosely secure it in place with the retaining nuts.

7. Install a new, non-asbestos gasket between the converter and muffler/outlet pipe assembly. Secure the flange gasket and hanger bracket with two nuts and tighten to 18–26 ft. lbs. (25–35 Nm).

8. Tighten the exhaust manifold connections by alternately tightening the manifold bolts to 25–34 ft. lbs. (34–46 Nm).

9. Install the managed thermactor air tube and check valve. Tighten the tube-to-catalytic converter clamp to 8–12 ft. lbs. (10–17 Nm).

10. Attach the tube bracket to the Y-pipe and tighten the fastener to 5–8 ft.

lbs. (8–11 Nm). Attach the rubber hose to the check valve and tighten the clamp.

11. Lower the vehicle, start the engine and check for exhaust leaks. Correct as necessary.

1988 3.0L Engine

1. Remove the 2 nuts attaching the converter assembly to the muffler and outlet pipe.

2. Remove the screw holding the managed thermactor air tube bracket to the forward converter and separate the tube from the converter.

3. Remove the exhaust manifold stud nuts.

4. Slide the muffler and outlet pipe rearward. Remove the gasket.

5. Move the converter rearward and rotate it to clear the studs. Remove it.

To install:

6. Install the Y-pipe on the manifold studs and loosely install the nuts.

7. Using a new, non-asbestos gasket, join the muffler and converter assemblies. Tighten the nuts to 18–26 ft. lbs. (24–35 Nm). Install the hangers.

8. Tighten the manifold nuts, alternately and evenly, to 30 ft. lbs. (40 Nm).

1989–97 3.0L and 4.0L Engines

1. Remove the 2 nuts attaching the converter assembly to the flexible link, muffler and outlet pipe.

2. Remove the exhaust manifold stud nuts.

3. Slide the flexible link, muffler and outlet pipe rearward. Remove the gasket.

4. Move the converter rearward and rotate it to clear the studs. Remove it.

To install:

5. Install the Y-pipe on the manifold studs and loosely install the nuts.

6. Using a new, non-asbestos gasket, join the muffler and converter assemblies. Torque the nuts to 18–26 ft. lbs. (24–35 Nm). Install the hangers.

7. Secure the flexible link/muffler assembly to the bracket and insulator. Tighten the nuts to 18–26 ft. lbs. (24–35 Nm).

8. Tighten the manifold nuts, alternately and evenly, to 30 ft. lbs. (40 Nm).

ENGINE RECONDITIONING

Determining Engine Condition

Anything that generates heat and/or friction will eventually burn or wear out (for example, a light bulb generates heat, therefore its life span is limited). With this in mind, a running engine generates tremendous amounts of both; friction is encountered by the moving and rotating parts inside the engine and heat is created by friction and combustion of the fuel. However, the engine has systems designed to help reduce the effects of heat and friction and provide added longevity. The oiling system reduces the amount of friction encountered by the moving parts inside the engine, while the cooling system reduces heat created by friction and combustion. If either system is not maintained, a break-down will be inevitable. Therefore, you can see how regular maintenance can affect the service life of your vehicle. If you do not drain, flush and refill your cooling system at the proper intervals, deposits will begin to accumulate in the radiator, thereby reducing the amount of heat it can extract from the coolant. The same applies to your oil and filter; if it is not changed often enough it becomes laden with contaminates and is unable to properly lubricate the engine. This increases friction and wear.

There are a number of methods for evaluating the condition of your engine. A compression test can reveal the condition of your pistons, piston rings, cylinder bores, head gasket(s), valves and valve seats. An oil pressure test can warn you of possible engine bearing, or oil pump failures. Excessive oil consumption, evidence of oil in the engine air intake area and/or bluish smoke from the tailpipe may indicate worn piston rings, worn valve guides and/or valve seals. As a general rule, an engine that uses no more than one quart of oil every 1000 miles is in good condition. Engines that use one quart of oil or more in less than 1000 miles should first be checked for oil leaks. If any oil leaks are present, have them fixed before determining how much oil is consumed by the engine, especially if blue smoke is not visible at the tailpipe.

COMPRESSION TEST

▶ **See Figure 144**

A noticeable lack of engine power, excessive oil consumption and/or poor fuel mileage measured over an extended period are all indicators of internal engine wear. Worn piston rings, scored or worn cylinder bores, blown head gaskets, sticking or burnt valves, and worn valve seats are all possible culprits. A check of each cylinder's compression will help locate the problem.

➡**A screw-in type compression gauge is more accurate than the type you simply hold against the spark plug hole. Although it takes slightly longer to use, it's worth the effort to obtain a more accurate reading.**

1. Make sure that the proper amount and viscosity of engine oil is in the crankcase, then ensure the battery is fully charged.

2. Warm-up the engine to normal operating temperature, then shut the engine **OFF**.

3. Disable the ignition system.

4. Label and disconnect all of the spark plug wires from the plugs.

5. Thoroughly clean the cylinder head area around the spark plug ports, then remove the spark plugs.

6. Set the throttle plate to the fully open (wide-open throttle) position. You can block the accelerator linkage open for this, or you can have an assistant fully depress the accelerator pedal.

7. Install a screw-in type compression gauge into the No. 1 spark plug hole until the fitting is snug.

✳✳ WARNING

Be careful not to crossthread the spark plug hole.

Fig. 144 A screw-in type compression gauge is more accurate and easier to use without an assistant

8. According to the tool manufacturer's instructions, connect a remote starting switch to the starting circuit.

9. With the ignition switch in the **OFF** position, use the remote starting switch to crank the engine through at least five compression strokes (approximately 5 seconds of cranking) and record the highest reading on the gauge.

10. Repeat the test on each cylinder, cranking the engine approximately the same number of compression strokes and/or time as the first.

11. Compare the highest readings from each cylinder to that of the others. The indicated compression pressures are considered within specifications if the lowest reading cylinder is within 75 percent of the pressure recorded for the highest reading cylinder. For example, if your highest reading cylinder pressure was 150 psi (1034 kPa), then 75 percent of that would be 113 psi (779 kPa). So the lowest reading cylinder should be no less than 113 psi (779 kPa).

12. If a cylinder exhibits an unusually low compression reading, pour a tablespoon of clean engine oil into the cylinder through the spark plug hole and repeat the compression test. If the compression rises after adding oil, it means that the cylinder's piston rings and/or cylinder bore are damaged or worn. If the pressure remains low, the valves may not be seating properly (a valve job is needed), or the head gasket may be blown near that cylinder. If compression in any two adjacent cylinders is low, and if the addition of oil doesn't help raise compression, there is leakage past the head gasket. Oil and coolant in the combustion chamber, combined with blue or constant white smoke from the tailpipe, are symptoms of this problem. However, don't be alarmed by the normal white smoke emitted from the tailpipe during engine warm-up or from cold weather driving. There may be evidence of water droplets on the engine dipstick and/or oil droplets in the cooling system if a head gasket is blown.

OIL PRESSURE TEST

Check for proper oil pressure at the sending unit passage with an externally mounted mechanical oil pressure gauge (as opposed to relying on a factory installed dash-mounted gauge). A tachometer may also be needed, as some specifications may require running the engine at a specific rpm.

1. With the engine cold, locate and remove the oil pressure sending unit.

2. Following the manufacturer's instructions, connect a mechanical oil pressure gauge and, if necessary, a tachometer to the engine.

3. Start the engine and allow it to idle.

4. Check the oil pressure reading when cold and record the number. You may need to run the engine at a specified rpm, so check the specifications.

5. Run the engine until normal operating temperature is reached (upper radiator hose will feel warm).

6. Check the oil pressure reading again with the engine hot and record the number. Turn the engine **OFF**.

7. Compare your hot oil pressure reading to specification. If the reading is low, check the cold pressure reading against the chart. If the cold pressure is well above the specification, and the hot reading was lower than the specification, you may have the wrong viscosity oil in the engine. Change the oil, making sure to use the proper grade and quantity, then repeat the test.

Low oil pressure readings could be attributed to internal component wear, pump related problems, a low oil level, or oil viscosity that is too low. High oil pressure readings could be caused by an overfilled crankcase, too high of an oil viscosity or a faulty pressure relief valve.

Buy or Rebuild?

Now if you have determined that your engine is worn out, you must make some decisions. The question of whether or not an engine is worth rebuilding is largely a subjective matter and one of personal worth. Is the engine a popular one, or is it an obsolete model? Are parts available? Will it get acceptable gas mileage once it is rebuilt? Is the car it's being put into worth keeping? Would it be less expensive to buy a new engine, have your engine rebuilt by a pro, rebuild it yourself or buy a used engine from a salvage yard? Or would it be simpler and less expensive to buy another car? If you have considered all these matters, and have still decided to rebuild the engine, then it is time to decide how you will rebuild it.

➡The editors at Chilton feel that most engine machining should be performed by a professional machine shop. Think of it as an assurance that the job has been done right the first time. There are many expensive and specialized tools required to perform such tasks as boring and honing an engine block or having a valve job done on a cylinder head. Even inspecting the parts requires expensive micrometers and gauges to properly measure wear and clearances. A machine shop can deliver to you clean, and ready to assemble parts, saving you time and aggravation. Your maximum savings will come from performing the removal, disassembly, assembly and installation of the engine and purchasing or renting only the tools required to perform these tasks.

A complete rebuild or overhaul of an engine involves replacing all of the moving parts (pistons, rods, crankshaft, camshaft, etc.) with new ones and machining the non-moving wearing surfaces of the block and heads. Unfortunately, this may not be cost effective. For instance, your crankshaft may have been damaged or worn, but it can be machined undersize for a minimal fee.

So although you can replace everything inside the engine, it is usually wiser to replace only those parts which are really needed, and, if possible, repair the more expensive ones. Later in this section, we will break the engine down into its two main components: the cylinder head and the engine block. We will discuss each component, and the recommended parts to replace during a rebuild on each.

Engine Overhaul Tips

Most engine overhaul procedures are fairly standard. In addition to specific parts replacement procedures and specifications for your individual engine, this section is also a guide to acceptable rebuilding procedures. Examples of standard rebuilding practice are given and should be used along with specific details concerning your particular engine.

Competent and accurate machine shop services will ensure maximum performance, reliability and engine life. In most instances it is more profitable for the do-it-yourself mechanic to remove, clean and inspect the component, buy the necessary parts and deliver these to a shop for actual machine work.

Much of the assembly work (crankshaft, bearings, piston rods, and other components) is well within the scope of the do-it-yourself mechanic's tools and abilities. You will have to decide for yourself the depth of involvement you desire in an engine repair or rebuild.

TOOLS

The tools required for an engine overhaul or parts replacement will depend on the depth of your involvement. With a few exceptions, they will be the tools found in a mechanic's tool kit (see Section 1 of this manual). More in-depth work will require some or all of the following:

- A dial indicator (reading in thousandths) mounted on a universal base
- Micrometers and telescope gauges
- Jaw and screw-type pullers
- Scraper
- Valve spring compressor
- Ring groove cleaner
- Piston ring expander and compressor
- Ridge reamer
- Cylinder hone or glaze breaker
- Plastigage®
- Engine stand

The use of most of these tools is illustrated in this section. Many can be rented for a one-time use from a local parts jobber or tool supply house specializing in automotive work.

Occasionally, the use of special tools is called for. See the information on Special Tools and the Safety Notice in the front of this book before substituting another tool.

Ford Specialty Tools

▶ **See Figures 145, 146 and 147**

When servicing the engines covered by this manual, often a special Ford tool, or its generic equivalent, is necessary for the particular job at hand. Before starting a procedure make sure to read the entire procedure to ascertain whether special tools will be needed.

Tool Number	Description
T59L-100-B	Impact Slide Hammer
T58L-101-A	Puller Attachment
T74P-6000-LA	2.3L Engine Service Tool Kit
T74P-6015-A	Engine Plug Replacer
T74P-6019-B	Front Cover Alignment Tool
T68P-6135-A	Piston Pin Remover/Replacer
T71P-6135-P	Piston Pin Remover/Replacer
T74P-6150-A	Cam and Auxiliary Shaft Seal Replacer
T71P-6250-A	Cam Bearing Replacer
T74P-6254-A	Camshaft Belt Tension Adjusting Tool
T74P-6256-B	Cam and Auxiliary Shaft Sprocket Tool
T74P-6306-A	Crank Timing Gear Tool
T74P-6312-A	Crankshaft Damper Remover
T74P-6375-A	Flywheel Holding Tool
D81L-6500-A	Blind Hole Puller 5/8 Inch
Tool-6513-ABA	Valve Holdup Air Adapter
T86L-6565-A	Valve Spring Compressor Lever
T73P-6571-A — 1986	Valve Seal Installer
T74P-6700-A	Front Cover Seal Remover
T74P-6700-B	Front Cover Seal Remover
T82L-6701-A	2.3L Crankshaft Seal Installer
D79L-6731-B	Oil Filter Wrench
T71P-7137-C	Pilot Bearing Replacer
T71P-7137-H	Clutch Aligner
T63L-8620-A	Belt Tension Gauge
T74P-9510-A	Carburetor/Throttle Body Wrench

88243GF2

Fig. 145 These special Ford tools, or their generic equivalents, are necessary to completely service the 2.3L engine

Tool Number	Description
109	Removal Table
D81L-6002-C	Piston Ring Compressor
T59L-100-B	Impact Slide Hammer
T58L-101-A	Puller Attachment
TOOL-1175-AC	Seal Remover
T74P-6000-V	2.8L V-6 Engine Service Tool Kit
T74P-6019-A	Front Cover Aligner
T68P-6135-A	Piston Pin Tool Set
T72C-6165-R	Crankshaft Rear Oil Seal Replacer
T71P-6250-A	Cam Bearing Replacer
T72C-6250	Cam Bearing Remover and Replacer Adapter Tube
T72C-6266	Cam Bearing Bore Plug Replacer
T83T-6312-A	Fan Clutch Pulley Holder
T83T-6312-B	Fan Clutch Nut Wrench
TOOL-6331-E	Main Bearing Insert Tool
T86L-6565-A	Valve Spring Compressor Lever
T74P-6565-B	Valve Spring Compressor Bar
T74P-6666-A	Spark Plug Wire Remover
T74P-6700-A	Front Cover Seal Remover
T71P-7137-H	Clutch Aligner
T85T-7137-A	Pilot Bearing Replacer
T63L-8620-A	Belt Tension Gauge
T71P-19703-B	Pulley Remover

88243GF1

Fig. 146 When working on the 2.8L engine, some of these special Ford tools, or equivalents, may be necessary

Tool Number	Description	Tool Number	Description
T50T-100-A	Impact Slide Hammer	T83P-19623-C	Spring Lock Coupling Tool
T59L-100-B	Impact Slide Hammer	TOOL-6331-E	Upper Main Bearing Insert Remover and Replacer
D81L-4201-A	Feeler Gauge	T74P-6375-A	Flywheel Locking Tool
TOOL-4201-C	Dial Indicator	T70L-6500-A	Hydraulic Lifter Puller
D81L-600-A	In-Lb Torque Wrench	T82L-6500-A	Tappet Collapser
D81L-600-B	Ft-Lb Torque Wrench	TOOL-6500-E	Hydraulic Leakdown Tester
T75T-6000-A	Engine Lifting Plate	T81P-6513-A	Valve Spring Compressor
D81L-6002-C	Piston Ring Compressor	TOOL-6513-DD	Valve/Clutch Spring Tester
T68P-6135-A	Piston Pin Remover and Replacer	T74P-6666-A	Spark Plug Wire Remover
T65L-6250-A	Camshaft Bearing Set	T82L-6701-A	Rear Main Seal Installer
T81P-6254-A	Belt Tensioner Adapter	T70P-6B070-A	Front Cover Seal Installer
T58P-6316-D	Crankshaft Damper Remover	T81P-9425-A	Intake Manifold Torque Adapter
T82L-6316-A	Damper/Front Cover Seal Installer	T78P-9481-A	Manual Clamp Cutter
T82L-6316-B	Damper Remover	T77L-9533-B	Slide Hammer
D81L-6001-D	Engine Lifting Eyes		

88243GF0

Fig. 147 To service the 3.0L engine, some of these tools may be necessary—the tools necessary for the 4.0L are similar to these tools

OVERHAUL TIPS

Aluminum has become extremely popular for use in engines, due to its low weight. Observe the following precautions when handling aluminum parts:
• Never hot tank aluminum parts (the caustic hot tank solution will eat the aluminum.)
• Remove all aluminum parts (identification tag, etc.) from engine parts prior to the tanking.
• Always coat threads lightly with engine oil or anti-seize compounds before installation, to prevent seizure.
• Never overtighten bolts or spark plugs especially in aluminum threads.

When assembling the engine, any parts that will be exposed to frictional contact must be prelubed to provide lubrication at initial start-up. Any product specifically formulated for this purpose can be used, but engine oil is not recommended as a prelube in most cases.

When semi-permanent (locked, but removable) installation of bolts or nuts is desired, threads should be cleaned and coated with Loctite® or another similar, commercial non-hardening sealant.

CLEANING

▶ **See Figures 148, 149, 150 and 151**

Before the engine and its components are inspected, they must be thoroughly cleaned. You will need to remove any engine varnish, oil sludge and/or carbon deposits from all of the components to insure an accurate inspection. A crack in the engine block or cylinder head can easily become overlooked if hidden by a layer of sludge or carbon.

Most of the cleaning process can be carried out with common hand tools and readily available solvents or solutions. Carbon deposits can be chipped away using a hammer and a hard wooden chisel. Old gasket material and varnish or sludge can usually be removed using a scraper and/or cleaning solvent. Extremely stubborn deposits may require the use of a power drill with a wire brush. If using a wire brush, use extreme care around any critical machined surfaces (such as the gasket surfaces, bearing saddles, cylinder bores, etc.). Use of a wire brush is NOT

RECOMMENDED on any aluminum components. Always follow any safety recommendations given by the manufacturer of the tool and/or solvent.

✳✳ CAUTION

Always wear eye protection during any cleaning process involving scraping, chipping or spraying of solvents.

An alternative to the mess and hassle of cleaning the parts yourself is to drop them off at a local garage or machine shop. They should have the necessary equipment to properly clean all of the parts for a nominal fee.

Remove any oil galley plugs, freeze plugs and/or pressed-in bearings and carefully wash and degrease all of the engine components including the fasteners and bolts. Small parts such as the valves, springs, etc., should be placed in a metal basket and allowed to soak. Use pipe cleaner type brushes, and clean all passageways in the components.

Use a ring expander and remove the rings from the pistons. Clean the piston ring grooves with a special tool or a piece of broken ring. Scrape the carbon off of the top of the piston. You should never use a wire brush on the pistons. After preparing all of the piston assemblies in this manner, wash and degrease them again.

✳✳ WARNING

Use extreme care when cleaning around the cylinder head valve seats. A mistake or slip may cost you a new seat.

When cleaning the cylinder head, remove carbon from the combustion chamber with the valves installed. This will avoid damaging the valve seats.

REPAIRING DAMAGED THREADS

▶ **See Figures 152, 153, 154, 155 and 156**

Several methods of repairing damaged threads are available. Heli-Coil® (shown here), Keenserts® and Microdot® are among the most widely used. All involve basically the same principle—drilling out stripped threads, tapping the

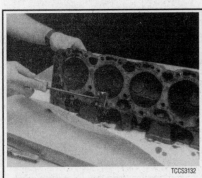

Fig. 148 Use a gasket scraper to remove the old gasket material from the mating surfaces

Fig. 149 Before cleaning and inspection, use a ring expander tool to remove the piston rings

Fig. 150 Clean the piston ring grooves using a ring groove cleaner tool, or . . .

Fig. 151 . . . use a piece of an old ring to clean the grooves. Be careful, the ring can be quite sharp

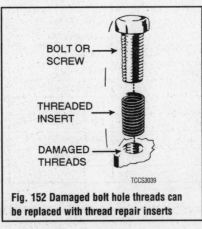

BOLT OR SCREW

THREADED INSERT

DAMAGED THREADS

Fig. 152 Damaged bolt hole threads can be replaced with thread repair inserts

TANG
NOTCH

Fig. 153 Standard thread repair insert (left), and spark plug thread insert

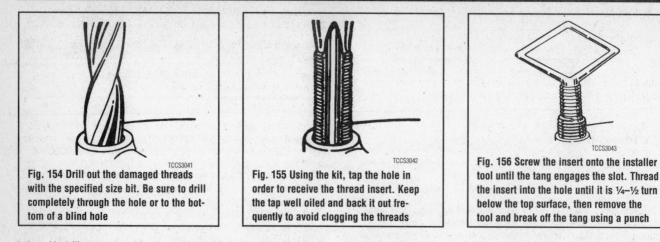

Fig. 154 Drill out the damaged threads with the specified size bit. Be sure to drill completely through the hole or to the bottom of a blind hole

Fig. 155 Using the kit, tap the hole in order to receive the thread insert. Keep the tap well oiled and back it out frequently to avoid clogging the threads

Fig. 156 Screw the insert onto the installer tool until the tang engages the slot. Thread the insert into the hole until it is ¼–½ turn below the top surface, then remove the tool and break off the tang using a punch

hole and installing a prewound insert—making welding, plugging and oversize fasteners unnecessary.

Two types of thread repair inserts are usually supplied: a standard type for most inch coarse, inch fine, metric course and metric fine thread sizes and a spark lug type to fit most spark plug port sizes. Consult the individual tool manufacturer's catalog to determine exact applications. Typical thread repair kits will contain a selection of prewound threaded inserts, a tap (corresponding to the outside diameter threads of the insert) and an installation tool. Spark plug inserts usually differ because they require a tap equipped with pilot threads and a combined reamer/tap section. Most manufacturers also supply blister-packed thread repair inserts separately in addition to a master kit containing a variety of taps and inserts plus installation tools.

Before attempting to repair a threaded hole, remove any snapped, broken or damaged bolts or studs. Penetrating oil can be used to free frozen threads. The offending item can usually be removed with locking pliers or using a screw/stud extractor. After the hole is clear, the thread can be repaired as shown in the kit manufacturer's instructions.

Engine Preparation

To properly rebuild an engine, you must first remove it from the vehicle, then disassemble and diagnose it. Ideally you should place your engine on an engine stand. This affords you the best access to the engine components. Remove the flywheel or flexplate before installing the engine to the stand.

Now that you have the engine on a stand, and assuming that you have drained the oil and coolant from the engine, it's time to strip it of all but the necessary components. Before you start disassembling the engine, you may want to take a moment to draw some pictures, or fabricate some labels or containers to mark the locations of various components and the bolts and/or studs which fasten them. Modern day engines use a lot of little brackets and clips which hold wiring harnesses and such, and these holders are often mounted on studs and/or bolts that can be easily mixed up. The manufacturer spent a lot of time and money designing your vehicle, and they wouldn't have wasted any of it by haphazardly placing brackets, clips or fasteners on the vehicle. If it's present when you disassemble it, put it back when you assemble, you will regret not remembering that little bracket which holds a wire harness out of the path of a rotating part.

You should begin by unbolting any accessories still attached to the engine, such as the water pump, power steering pump, alternator, etc. Then, unfasten any manifolds (intake or exhaust) which were not removed during the engine removal procedure. Finally, remove any covers remaining on the engine such as the rocker arm, front or timing cover and oil pan. Some front covers may require the vibration damper and/or crank pulley to be removed beforehand. The idea is to reduce the engine to the bare necessities of cylinder head(s), valve train, engine block, crankshaft, pistons and connecting rods, plus any other 'in block' components such as oil pumps, balance shafts and auxiliary shafts.

Finally, remove the cylinder head(s) from the engine block and carefully place on a bench. Disassembly instructions for each component follow later in this section.

Cylinder Head

There are two basic types of cylinder heads used on today's automobiles: the Overhead Valve (OHV) and the Overhead Camshaft (OHC). The latter can also be

broken down into two subgroups: the Single Overhead Camshaft (SOHC) and the Dual Overhead Camshaft (DOHC). Generally, if there is only a single camshaft on a head, it is just referred to as an OHC head. Also, an engine with an OHV cylinder head is also known as a pushrod engine.

Most cylinder heads these days are made of an aluminum alloy due to its light weight, durability and heat transfer qualities. However, cast iron was the material of choice in the past, and is still used on many vehicles. Whether made from aluminum or iron, all cylinder heads have valves and seats. Some use two valves per cylinder, while the more hi-tech engines will utilize a multi-valve configuration using 3, 4 and even 5 valves per cylinder. When the valve contacts the seat, it does so on precision machined surfaces, which seals the combustion chamber. All cylinder heads have a valve guide for each valve. The guide centers the valve to the seat and allows it to move up and down within it. The clearance between the valve and guide can be critical. Too much clearance and the engine may consume oil, lose vacuum and/or damage the seat. Too little, and the valve can stick in the guide causing the engine to run poorly if at all, and possibly causing severe damage. The last component all automotive cylinder heads have are valve springs. The spring holds the valve against its seat. It also returns the valve to this position when the valve has been opened by the valve train or camshaft. The spring is fastened to the valve by a retainer and valve locks (sometimes called keepers). Aluminum heads will also have a valve spring shim to keep the spring from wearing away the aluminum.

An ideal method of rebuilding the cylinder head would involve replacing all of the valves, guides, seats, springs, etc. with new ones. However, depending on how the engine was maintained, often this is not necessary. A major cause of valve, guide and seat wear is an improperly tuned engine. An engine that is running too rich, will often wash the lubricating oil out of the guide with gasoline, causing it to wear rapidly. Conversely, an engine which is running too lean will place higher combustion temperatures on the valves and seats allowing them to wear or even burn. Springs fall victim to the driving habits of the individual. A driver who often runs the engine rpm to the redline will wear out or break the springs faster then one that stays well below it. Unfortunately, mileage takes it toll on all of the parts. Generally, the valves, guides, springs and seats in a cylinder head can be machined and re-used, saving you money. However, if a valve is burnt, it may be wise to replace all of the valves, since they were all operating in the same environment. The same goes for any other component on the cylinder head. Think of it as an insurance policy against future problems related to that component.

Unfortunately, the only way to find out which components need replacing, is to disassemble and carefully check each piece. After the cylinder head(s) are disassembled, thoroughly clean all of the components.

DISASSEMBLY

2.8L, 3.0L and 4.0L Engines

♦ See Figures 157 thru 162

Before disassembling the cylinder head, you may want to fabricate some containers to hold the various parts, as some of them can be quite small (such as keepers) and easily lost. Also keeping yourself and the components organized will aid in assembly and reduce confusion. Where possible, try to maintain a components original location; this is especially important if there is not going to be any machine work performed on the components.

1. If you haven't already removed the rocker arms and/or shafts, do so now.

2. Position the head so that the springs are easily accessed.

3. Use a valve spring compressor tool, and relieve spring tension from the retainer.

➡ Due to engine varnish, the retainer may stick to the valve locks. A gentle tap with a hammer may help to break it loose.

4. Remove the valve locks from the valve tip and/or retainer. A small magnet may help in removing the locks.

5. Lift the valve spring, tool and all, off of the valve stem.

6. If equipped, remove the valve seal. If the seal is difficult to remove with the valve in place, try removing the valve first, then the seal. Follow the steps below for valve removal.

7. Position the head to allow access for withdrawing the valve.

➡ Cylinder heads that have seen a lot of miles and/or abuse may have mushroomed the valve lock grove and/or tip, causing difficulty in removal of the valve. If this has happened, use a metal file to carefully remove the high spots around the lock grooves and/or tip. Only file it enough to allow removal.

8. Remove the valve from the cylinder head.

9. If equipped, remove the valve spring shim. A small magnetic tool or screwdriver will aid in removal.

10. Repeat Steps 3 though 9 until all of the valves have been removed.

2.3L Engine

▶ See Figures 163 and 164

Whether it is a single or dual overhead camshaft cylinder head, the disassembly procedure is relatively unchanged. One aspect to pay attention to is careful labeling of the parts on the dual camshaft cylinder head. There will be an intake camshaft and followers as well as an exhaust camshaft and followers and they must be labeled as such. In some cases, the components are identical and could easily be installed incorrectly. DO NOT MIX THEM UP! Determining which is which is very simple; the intake camshaft and components are on the same side of the head as was the intake manifold. Conversely, the exhaust camshaft and components are on the same side of the head as was the exhaust manifold.

Rocker Arm Type Camshaft Followers

▶ See Figures 165 thru 173

Most cylinder heads with rocker arm-type camshaft followers are easily disassembled using a standard valve spring compressor. However, certain models may not have enough open space around the spring for the standard tool and may require you to use a C-clamp style compressor tool instead.

1. If not already removed, remove the rocker arms and/or shafts and the camshaft. If applicable, also remove the hydraulic lash adjusters. Mark their positions for assembly.

2. Position the cylinder head to allow access to the valve spring.

3. Use a valve spring compressor tool to relieve the spring tension from the retainer.

➡ Due to engine varnish, the retainer may stick to the valve locks. A gentle tap with a hammer may help to break it loose.

4. Remove the valve locks from the valve tip and/or retainer. A small magnet may help in removing the small locks.

5. Lift the valve spring, tool and all, off of the valve stem.

6. If equipped, remove the valve seal. If the seal is difficult to remove with the valve in place, try removing the valve first, then the seal. Follow the steps below for valve removal.

7. Position the head to allow access for withdrawing the valve.

➡ Cylinder heads that have seen a lot of miles and/or abuse may have mushroomed the valve lock grove and/or tip, causing difficulty in removal of the valve. If this has happened, use a metal file to carefully remove the high spots around the lock grooves and/or tip. Only file it enough to allow removal.

Fig. 157 When removing an OHV valve spring, use a compressor tool to relieve the tension from the retainer

Fig. 158 A small magnet will help in removal of the valve locks

Fig. 159 Be careful not to lose the small valve locks (keepers)

Fig. 160 Remove the valve seal from the valve stem—O-ring type seal shown

Fig. 161 Removing an umbrella/positive type seal

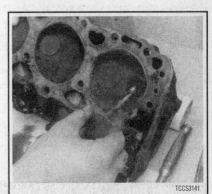

Fig. 162 Invert the cylinder head and withdraw the valve from the valve guide bore

Fig. 163 Exploded view of a valve, seal, spring, retainer and locks from an OHC cylinder head

Fig. 164 Example of a multi-valve cylinder head. Note how it has 2 intake and 2 exhaust valve ports

Fig. 165 Example of the shaft mounted rocker arms on some OHC heads

Fig. 166 Another example of the rocker arm type OHC head. This model uses a follower under the camshaft

Fig. 167 Before the camshaft can be removed, all of the followers must first be removed . . .

Fig. 168 . . . then the camshaft can be removed by sliding it out (shown), or unbolting a bearing cap (not shown)

Fig. 169 Compress the valve spring . . .

Fig. 170 . . . then remove the valve locks from the valve stem and spring retainer

Fig. 171 Remove the valve spring and retainer from the cylinder head

Fig. 172 Remove the valve seal from the guide. Some gentle prying or pliers may help to remove stubborn ones

Fig. 173 All aluminum and some cast iron heads will have these valve spring shims. Remove all of them as well

8. Remove the valve from the cylinder head.
9. If equipped, remove the valve spring shim. A small magnetic tool or screwdriver will aid in removal.
10. Repeat Steps 3 though 9 until all of the valves have been removed.

INSPECTION

Now that all of the cylinder head components are clean, it's time to inspect them for wear and/or damage. To accurately inspect them, you will need some specialized tools:

- A 0–1 in. micrometer for the valves
- A dial indicator or inside diameter gauge for the valve guides
- A spring pressure test gauge

If you do not have access to the proper tools, you may want to bring the components to a shop that does.

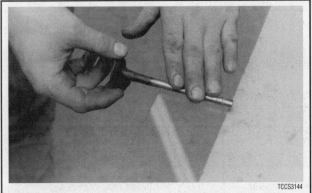

Fig. 174 Valve stems may be rolled on a flat surface to check for bends

Valves

▶ **See Figures 174 and 175**

The first thing to inspect are the valve heads. Look closely at the head, margin and face for any cracks, excessive wear or burning. The margin is the best place to look for burning. It should have a squared edge with an even width all around the diameter. When a valve burns, the margin will look melted and the edges rounded. Also inspect the valve head for any signs of tulipping. This will show as a lifting of the edges or dishing in the center of the head and will usually not occur to all of the valves. All of the heads should look the same, any that seem dished more than others are probably bad. Next, inspect the valve lock grooves and valve tips. Check for any burrs around the lock grooves, especially if you had to file them to remove the valve. Valve tips should appear flat, although slight rounding with high mileage engines is normal. Slightly worn valve tips will need to be machined flat. Last, measure the valve stem diameter with the micrometer. Measure the area that rides within the guide, especially towards the tip where most of the wear occurs. Take several measurements along its length and compare them to each other. Wear should be even along the length with little to no taper. If no minimum diameter is given in the specifications, then the stem should not read more than 0.001 in. (0.025mm) below the unworn portion of the stem. Any valves that fail these inspections should be replaced.

Springs, Retainers and Valve Locks

▶ **See Figures 176 and 177**

The first thing to check is the most obvious, broken springs. Next check the free length and squareness of each spring. If applicable, insure to distinguish between intake and exhaust springs. Use a ruler and/or carpenter's square to measure the length. A carpenter's square should be used to check the springs for squareness. If a spring pressure test gauge is available, check each springs rating and compare to the specifications chart. Check the readings against the specifications given. Any springs that fail these inspections should be replaced.

The spring retainers rarely need replacing, however they should still be

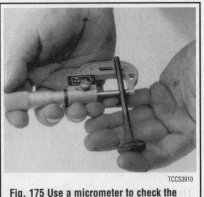

Fig. 175 Use a micrometer to check the valve stem diameter

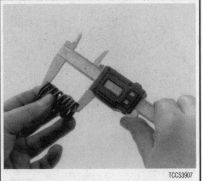

Fig. 176 Use a caliper to check the valve spring free-length

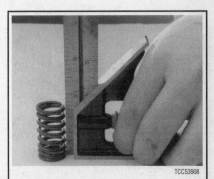

Fig. 177 Check the valve spring for squareness on a flat surface; a carpenter's square can be used

checked as a precaution. Inspect the spring mating surface and the valve lock retention area for any signs of excessive wear. Also check for any signs of cracking. Replace any retainers that are questionable.

Valve locks should be inspected for excessive wear on the outside contact area as well as on the inner notched surface. Any locks which appear worn or broken and its respective valve should be replaced.

Cylinder Head

There are several things to check on the cylinder head: valve guides, seats, cylinder head surface flatness, cracks and physical damage.

VALVE GUIDES

▶ See Figure 178

Now that you know the valves are good, you can use them to check the guides, although a new valve, if available, is preferred. Before you measure anything, look at the guides carefully and inspect them for any cracks, chips or breakage. Also if the guide is a removable style (as in most aluminum heads), check them for any looseness or evidence of movement. All of the guides should appear to be at the same height from the spring seat. If any seem lower (or higher) from another, the guide has moved. Mount a dial indicator onto the spring side of the cylinder head. Lightly oil the valve stem and insert it into the cylinder head. Position the dial indicator against the valve stem near the tip and zero the gauge. Grasp the valve stem and wiggle towards and away from the dial indicator and observe the readings. Mount the dial indicator 90 degrees from the initial point and zero the gauge and again take a reading. Compare the two readings for an out of round condition. Check the readings against the specifications given. An Inside Diameter (I.D.) gauge designed for valve guides will give you an accurate valve guide bore measurement. If the I.D. gauge is used, compare the readings with the specifications given. Any guides that fail these inspections should be replaced or machined.

VALVE SEATS

A visual inspection of the valve seats should show a slightly worn and pitted surface where the valve face contacts the seat. Inspect the seat carefully for severe pitting or cracks. Also, a seat that is badly worn will be recessed into the cylinder head. A severely worn or recessed seat may need to be replaced. All cracked seats must be replaced. A seat concentricity gauge, if available, should be used to check the seat run-out. If run-out exceeds specifications the seat must be machined (if no specification is available given use 0.002 in. or 0.051mm).

CYLINDER HEAD SURFACE FLATNESS

▶ See Figures 179 and 180

After you have cleaned the gasket surface of the cylinder head of any old gasket material, check the head for flatness.

Place a straightedge across the gasket surface. Using feeler gauges, determine the clearance at the center of the straightedge and across the cylinder head at several points. Check along the centerline and diagonally on the head surface. If the warpage exceeds 0.003 in. (0.076mm) within a 6.0 in. (15.2cm) span, or 0.006 in. (0.152mm) over the total length of the head, the cylinder

head must be resurfaced. After resurfacing the heads of a V-type engine, the intake manifold flange surface should be checked, and if necessary, milled proportionally to allow for the change in its mounting position.

CRACKS AND PHYSICAL DAMAGE

Generally, cracks are limited to the combustion chamber, however, it is not uncommon for the head to crack in a spark plug hole, port, outside of the head or in the valve spring/rocker arm area. The first area to inspect is always the hottest: the exhaust seat/port area.

A visual inspection should be performed, but just because you don't see a crack does not mean it is not there. Some more reliable methods for inspecting for cracks include Magnaflux®, a magnetic process or Zyglo®, a dye penetrant. Magnaflux® is used only on ferrous metal (cast iron) heads. Zyglo® uses a spray on fluorescent mixture along with a black light to reveal the cracks. It is strongly recommended to have your cylinder head checked professionally for cracks, especially if the engine was known to have overheated and/or leaked or consumed coolant. Contact a local shop for availability and pricing of these services.

Physical damage is usually very evident. For example, a broken mounting ear from dropping the head or a bent or broken stud and/or bolt. All of these defects should be fixed or, if unrepairable, the head should be replaced.

Camshaft and Followers

Inspect the camshaft(s) and followers as described earlier in this section.

REFINISHING & REPAIRING

Many of the procedures given for refinishing and repairing the cylinder head components must be performed by a machine shop. Certain steps, if the inspected part is not worn, can be performed yourself inexpensively. However, you spent a lot of time and effort so far, why risk trying to save a couple bucks if you might have to do it all over again?

Valves

Any valves that were not replaced should be refaced and the tips ground flat. Unless you have access to a valve grinding machine, this should be done by a machine shop. If the valves are in extremely good condition, as well as the valve seats and guides, they may be lapped in without performing machine work.

It is a recommended practice to lap the valves even after machine work has been performed and/or new valves have been purchased. This insures a positive seal between the valve and seat.

LAPPING THE VALVES

➡**Before lapping the valves to the seats, read the rest of the cylinder head section to insure that any related parts are in acceptable enough condition to continue. Also, remember that before any valve seat machining and/or lapping can be performed, the guides must be within factory recommended specifications.**

1. Invert the cylinder head.
2. Lightly lubricate the valve stems and insert them into the cylinder head in their numbered order.

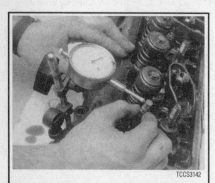

TCCS3142

Fig. 178 A dial gauge may be used to check valve stem-to-guide clearance; read the gauge while moving the valve stem

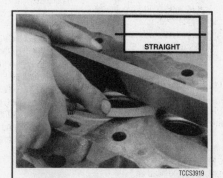

STRAIGHT

TCCS3919

Fig. 179 Check the head for flatness across the center of the head surface using a straightedge and feeler gauge

DIAGONAL

TCCS3918

Fig. 180 Checks should also be made along both diagonals of the head surface

3. Raise the valve from the seat and apply a small amount of fine lapping compound to the seat.

4. Moisten the suction head of a hand-lapping tool and attach it to the head of the valve.

5. Rotate the tool between the palms of both hands, changing the position of the valve on the valve seat and lifting the tool often to prevent grooving.

6. Lap the valve until a smooth, polished circle is evident on the valve and seat.

7. Remove the tool and the valve. Wipe away all traces of the grinding compound and store the valve to maintain its lapped location.

✳✳ WARNING

Do not get the valves out of order after they have been lapped. They must be put back with the same valve seat with which they were lapped.

Springs, Retainers and Valve Locks

There is no repair or refinishing possible with the springs, retainers and valve locks. If they are found to be worn or defective, they must be replaced with new (or known good) parts.

Cylinder Head

Most refinishing procedures dealing with the cylinder head must be performed by a machine shop. Read the sections below and review your inspection data to determine whether or not machining is necessary.

VALVE GUIDE

➡If any machining or replacements are made to the valve guides, the seats must be machined.

Unless the valve guides need machining or replacing, the only service to perform is to thoroughly clean them of any dirt or oil residue.

There are only two types of valve guides used on automobile engines: the replaceable-type (all aluminum heads) and the cast-in integral-type (most cast iron heads). There are four recommended methods for repairing worn guides.

- Knurling
- Inserts
- Reaming oversize
- Replacing

Knurling is a process in which metal is displaced and raised, thereby reducing clearance, giving a true center, and providing oil control. It is the least expensive way of repairing the valve guides. However, it is not necessarily the best, and in some cases, a knurled valve guide will not stand up for more than a short time. It requires a special knurlizer and precision reaming tools to obtain proper clearances. It would not be cost effective to purchase these tools, unless you plan on rebuilding several of the same cylinder head.

Installing a guide insert involves machining the guide to accept a bronze insert. One style is the coil-type which is installed into a threaded guide. Another is the thin-walled insert where the guide is reamed oversize to accept a split-sleeve insert. After the insert is installed, a special tool is then run through the guide to expand the insert, locking it to the guide. The insert is then reamed to the standard size for proper valve clearance.

Reaming for oversize valves restores normal clearances and provides a true valve seat. Most cast-in type guides can be reamed to accept an valve with an oversize stem. The cost factor for this can become quite high as you will need to purchase the reamer and new, oversize stem valves for all guides which were reamed. Oversizes are generally 0.003–0.030 in. (0.076–0.762mm), with 0.015 in. (0.381mm) being the most common.

To replace cast-in type valve guides, they must be drilled out, then reamed to accept replacement guides. This must be done on a fixture which will allow centering and leveling off of the original valve seat or guide, otherwise a serious guide-to-seat misalignment may occur making it impossible to properly machine the seat.

Replaceable-type guides are pressed into the cylinder head. A hammer and a stepped drift or punch may be used to install and remove the guides. Before removing the guides, measure the protrusion on the spring side of the head and record it for installation. Use the stepped drift to hammer out the old guide from the combustion chamber side of the head. When installing, determine whether or not the guide also seals a water jacket in the head, and if it does, use the rec-

ommended sealing agent. If there is no water jacket, grease the valve guide and its bore. Use the stepped drift, and hammer the new guide into the cylinder head from the spring side of the cylinder head. A stack of washers the same thickness as the measured protrusion may help the installation process.

VALVE SEATS

➡Before any valve seat machining can be performed, the guides must be within factory recommended specifications. If any machining occurred or if replacements were made to the valve guides, the seats must be machined.

If the seats are in good condition, the valves can be lapped to the seats, and the cylinder head assembled. See the valves section for instructions on lapping.

If the valve seats are worn, cracked or damaged, they must be serviced by a machine shop. The valve seat must be perfectly centered to the valve guide, which requires very accurate machining.

CYLINDER HEAD SURFACE

If the cylinder head is warped, it must be machined flat. If the warpage is extremely severe, the head may need to be replaced. In some instances, it may be possible to straighten a warped head enough to allow machining. In either case, contact a professional machine shop for service.

➡Any OHC cylinder head that shows excessive warpage should have the camshaft bearing journals align bored after the cylinder head has been resurfaced.

✳✳ WARNING

Failure to align bore the camshaft bearing journals could result in severe engine damage including but not limited to: valve and piston damage, connecting rod damage, camshaft and/or crankshaft breakage.

CRACKS AND PHYSICAL DAMAGE

Certain cracks can be repaired in both cast iron and aluminum heads. For cast iron, a tapered threaded insert is installed along the length of the crack. Aluminum can also use the tapered inserts, however welding is the preferred method. Some physical damage can be repaired through brazing or welding. Contact a machine shop to get expert advice for your particular dilemma.

ASSEMBLY

The first step for any assembly job is to have a clean area in which to work. Next, thoroughly clean all of the parts and components that are to be assembled. Finally, place all of the components onto a suitable work space and, if necessary, arrange the parts to their respective positions.

2.8L, 3.0L and 4.0L Engines

1. Lightly lubricate the valve stems and insert all of the valves into the cylinder head. If possible, maintain their original locations.

2. If equipped, install any valve spring shims which were removed.

3. If equipped, install the new valve seals, keeping the following in mind:

- If the valve seal presses over the guide, lightly lubricate the outer guide surfaces.
- If the seal is an O-ring type, it is installed just after compressing the spring but before the valve locks.

4. Place the valve spring and retainer over the stem.

5. Position the spring compressor tool and compress the spring.

6. Assemble the valve locks to the stem.

7. Relieve the spring pressure slowly and insure that neither valve lock becomes dislodged by the retainer.

8. Remove the spring compressor tool.

9. Repeat Steps 2 through 8 until all of the springs have been installed.

2.3L Engine

CAMSHAFT FOLLOWERS

1. Lightly lubricate the valve stems and insert all of the valves into the cylinder head. If possible, maintain their original locations.

2. If equipped, install any valve spring shims which were removed.

3. If equipped, install the new valve seals, keeping the following in mind:

• If the valve seal presses over the guide, lightly lubricate the outer guide surfaces.

• If the seal is an O-ring type, it is installed just after compressing the spring but before the valve locks.

4. Place the valve spring and retainer over the stem.

5. Position the spring compressor tool and compress the spring.

6. Assemble the valve locks to the stem.

7. Relieve the spring pressure slowly and insure that neither valve lock becomes dislodged by the retainer.

8. Remove the spring compressor tool.

9. Repeat Steps 2 through 8 until all of the springs have been installed.

10. Install the camshaft(s), rockers, shafts and any other components that were removed for disassembly.

Engine Block

GENERAL INFORMATION

A thorough overhaul or rebuild of an engine block would include replacing the pistons, rings, bearings, timing belt/chain assembly and oil pump. For OHV engines also include a new camshaft and lifters. The block would then have the cylinders bored and honed oversize (or if using removable cylinder sleeves, new sleeves installed) and the crankshaft would be cut undersize to provide new wearing surfaces and perfect clearances. However, your particular engine may not have everything worn out. What if only the piston rings have worn out and the clearances on everything else are still within factory specifications? Well, you could just replace the rings and put it back together, but this would be a very rare example. Chances are, if one component in your engine is worn, other components are sure to follow, and soon. At the very least, you should always replace the rings, bearings and oil pump. This is what is commonly called a "freshen up".

Cylinder Ridge Removal

Because the top piston ring does not travel to the very top of the cylinder, a ridge is built up between the end of the travel and the top of the cylinder bore.

Pushing the piston and connecting rod assembly past the ridge can be difficult, and damage to the piston ring lands could occur. If the ridge is not removed before installing a new piston or not removed at all, piston ring breakage and piston damage may occur.

➡️It is always recommended that you remove any cylinder ridges before removing the piston and connecting rod assemblies. If you know that new pistons are going to be installed and the engine block will be bored oversize, you may be able to forego this step. However, some ridges may actually prevent the assemblies from being removed, necessitating its removal.

There are several different types of ridge reamers on the market, none of which are inexpensive. Unless a great deal of engine rebuilding is anticipated, borrow or rent a reamer.

1. Turn the crankshaft until the piston is at the bottom of its travel.

2. Cover the head of the piston with a rag.

3. Follow the tool manufacturers instructions and cut away the ridge, exercising extreme care to avoid cutting too deeply.

4. Remove the ridge reamer, the rag and as many of the cuttings as possible. Continue until all of the cylinder ridges have been removed.

DISASSEMBLY

▸ **See Figures 181 and 182**

The engine disassembly instructions following assume that you have the engine mounted on an engine stand. If not, it is easiest to disassemble the engine on a bench or the floor with it resting on the bell housing or transmission mounting surface. You must be able to access the connecting rod fasteners and turn the crankshaft during disassembly. Also, all engine covers (timing, front, side, oil pan, whatever) should have already been removed. Engines which are seized or locked up may not be able to be completely disassembled, and a core (salvage yard) engine should be purchased.

2.8L, 3.0L, and 4.0L Engines

If not done during the cylinder head removal, remove the pushrods and lifters, keeping them in order for assembly. Remove the timing gears and/or timing chain assembly, then remove the oil pump drive assembly and withdraw the camshaft from the engine block. Remove the oil pick-up and pump assembly. If equipped, remove any balance or auxiliary shafts. If necessary, remove the cylinder ridge from the top of the bore. See the cylinder ridge removal procedure earlier in this section.

2.3L Engine

If not done during the cylinder head removal, remove the timing chain/belt and/or gear/sprocket assembly. Remove the oil pick-up and pump assembly and, if necessary, the pump drive. If equipped, remove any balance or auxiliary shafts. If necessary, remove the cylinder ridge from the top of the bore. See the cylinder ridge removal procedure earlier in this section.

All Engines

Rotate the engine over so that the crankshaft is exposed. Use a number punch or scribe and mark each connecting rod with its respective cylinder number. The cylinder closest to the front of the engine is always number 1. However, depending on the engine placement, the front of the engine could either be the flywheel or damper/pulley end. Generally the front of the engine faces the front of the vehicle. Use a number punch or scribe and also mark the main bearing caps from front to rear with the front most cap being number 1 (if there are five caps, mark them 1 through 5, front to rear).

✳︎✳︎ WARNING

Take special care when pushing the connecting rod up from the crankshaft because the sharp threads of the rod bolts/studs will score the crankshaft journal. Insure that special plastic caps are installed over them, or cut two pieces of rubber hose to do the same.

Again, rotate the engine, this time to position the number one cylinder bore (head surface) up. Turn the crankshaft until the number one piston is at the bottom of its travel, this should allow the maximum access to its connecting rod. Remove the number one connecting rods fasteners and cap and place two lengths of rubber hose over the rod bolts/studs to protect the crankshaft from damage. Using a sturdy wooden dowel and a hammer, push the connecting rod up about 1 in. (25mm) from the crankshaft and remove the upper bearing insert. Continue pushing or tapping the connecting rod up until the piston rings are out of the cylinder bore. Remove the piston and rod by hand, put the upper half of the bearing insert back into the rod, install the cap with its bearing insert installed, and hand-tighten the cap fasteners. If the parts are kept in order in this manner, they will not get lost and you will be able to tell which bearings came form what cylinder if any problems are discovered and diagnosis is necessary. Remove all the other piston assemblies in the same manner. On V-style engines, remove all of the pistons from one bank, then reposition the engine with the other cylinder bank head surface up, and remove that banks piston assemblies.

The only remaining component in the engine block should now be the crankshaft. Loosen the main bearing caps evenly until the fasteners can be turned by

Fig. 181 Place rubber hose over the connecting rod studs to protect the crankshaft and cylinder bores from damage

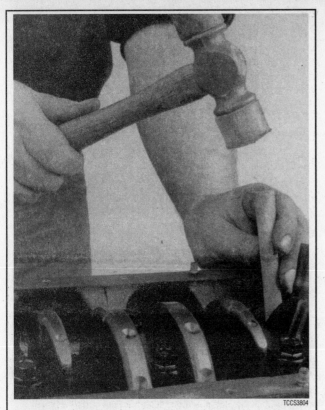

Fig. 182 Carefully tap the piston out of the bore using a wooden dowel

hand, then remove them and the caps. Remove the crankshaft from the engine block. Thoroughly clean all of the components.

INSPECTION

Now that the engine block and all of its components are clean, it's time to inspect them for wear and/or damage. To accurately inspect them, you will need some specialized tools:

- Two or three separate micrometers to measure the pistons and crankshaft journals
- A dial indicator
- Telescoping gauges for the cylinder bores
- A rod alignment fixture to check for bent connecting rods

If you do not have access to the proper tools, you may want to bring the components to a shop that does.

Generally, you shouldn't expect cracks in the engine block or its components unless it was known to leak, consume or mix engine fluids, it was severely overheated, or there was evidence of bad bearings and/or crankshaft damage. A visual inspection should be performed on all of the components, but just because you don't see a crack does not mean it is not there. Some more reliable methods for inspecting for cracks include Magnaflux®, a magnetic process or Zyglo®, a dye penetrant. Magnaflux® is used only on ferrous metal (cast iron). Zyglo® uses a spray on fluorescent mixture along with a black light to reveal the cracks. It is strongly recommended to have your engine block checked professionally for cracks, especially if the engine was known to have overheated and/or leaked or consumed coolant. Contact a local shop for availability and pricing of these services.

Engine Block

ENGINE BLOCK BEARING ALIGNMENT

Remove the main bearing caps and, if still installed, the main bearing inserts. Inspect all of the main bearing saddles and caps for damage, burrs or high spots. If damage is found, and it is caused from a spun main bearing, the block will need to be align-bored or, if severe enough, replacement. Any burrs or high spots should be carefully removed with a metal file.

Place a straightedge on the bearing saddles, in the engine block, along the centerline of the crankshaft. If any clearance exists between the straightedge and the saddles, the block must be align-bored.

Align-boring consists of machining the main bearing saddles and caps by means of a flycutter that runs through the bearing saddles.

DECK FLATNESS

The top of the engine block where the cylinder head mounts is called the deck. Insure that the deck surface is clean of dirt, carbon deposits and old gasket material. Place a straightedge across the surface of the deck along its centerline and, using feeler gauges, check the clearance along several points. Repeat the checking procedure with the straightedge placed along both diagonals of the deck surface. If the reading exceeds 0.003 in. (0.076mm) within a 6.0 in. (15.2cm) span, or 0.006 in. (0.152mm) over the total length of the deck, it must be machined.

CYLINDER BORES

▶ See Figure 183

The cylinder bores house the pistons and are slightly larger than the pistons themselves. A common piston-to-bore clearance is 0.0015–0.0025 in. (0.0381mm–0.0635mm). Inspect and measure the cylinder bores. The bore should be checked for out-of-roundness, taper and size. The results of this inspection will determine whether the cylinder can be used in its existing size and condition, or a rebore to the next oversize is required (or in the case of removable sleeves, have replacements installed).

The amount of cylinder wall wear is always greater at the top of the cylinder than at the bottom. This wear is known as taper. Any cylinder that has a taper of 0.0012 in. (0.305mm) or more, must be rebored. Measurements are taken at a number of positions in each cylinder: at the top, middle and bottom and at two points at each position; that is, at a point 90 degrees from the crankshaft centerline, as well as a point parallel to the crankshaft centerline. The measurements are made with either a special dial indicator or a telescopic gauge and micrometer. If the necessary precision tools to check the bore are not available, take the block to a machine shop and have them mike it. Also if you don't have the tools to check the cylinder bores, chances are you will not have the necessary devices to check the pistons, connecting rods and crankshaft. Take these components with you and save yourself an extra trip.

For our procedures, we will use a telescopic gauge and a micrometer. You will need one of each, with a measuring range which covers your cylinder bore size.

1. Position the telescopic gauge in the cylinder bore, loosen the gauges lock and allow it to expand.

➡Your first two readings will be at the top of the cylinder bore, then proceed to the middle and finally the bottom, making a total of six measurements.

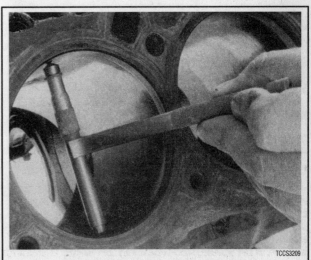

Fig. 183 Use a telescoping gauge to measure the cylinder bore diameter—take several readings within the same bore

2. Hold the gauge square in the bore, 90 degrees from the crankshaft centerline, and gently tighten the lock. Tilt the gauge back to remove it from the bore.

3. Measure the gauge with the micrometer and record the reading.

4. Again, hold the gauge square in the bore, this time parallel to the crankshaft centerline, and gently tighten the lock. Again, you will tilt the gauge back to remove it from the bore.

5. Measure the gauge with the micrometer and record this reading. The difference between these two readings is the out-of-round measurement of the cylinder.

6. Repeat steps 1 through 5, each time going to the next lower position, until you reach the bottom of the cylinder. Then go to the next cylinder, and continue until all of the cylinders have been measured.

The difference between these measurements will tell you all about the wear in your cylinders. The measurements which were taken 90 degrees from the crankshaft centerline will always reflect the most wear. That is because at this position is where the engine power presses the piston against the cylinder bore the hardest. This is known as thrust wear. Take your top, 90 degree measurement and compare it to your bottom, 90 degree measurement. The difference between them is the taper. When you measure your pistons, you will compare these readings to your piston sizes and determine piston-to-wall clearance.

Crankshaft

Inspect the crankshaft for visible signs of wear or damage. All of the journals should be perfectly round and smooth. Slight scores are normal for a used crankshaft, but you should hardly feel them with your fingernail. When measuring the crankshaft with a micrometer, you will take readings at the front and rear of each journal, then turn the micrometer 90 degrees and take two more readings, front and rear. The difference between the front-to-rear readings is the journal taper and the first-to-90 degree reading is the out-of-round measurement. Generally, there should be no taper or out-of-roundness found, however, up to 0.0005 in. (0.0127mm) for either can be overlooked. Also, the readings should fall within the factory specifications for journal diameters.

If the crankshaft journals fall within specifications, it is recommended that it be polished before being returned to service. Polishing the crankshaft insures that any minor burrs or high spots are smoothed, thereby reducing the chance of scoring the new bearings.

Pistons and Connecting Rods

PISTONS

♦ See Figure 184

The piston should be visually inspected for any signs of cracking or burning (caused by hot spots or detonation), and scuffing or excessive wear on the skirts. The wrist pin attaches the piston to the connecting rod. The piston should move freely on the wrist pin, both sliding and pivoting. Grasp the connecting rod securely, or mount it in a vise, and try to rock the piston back and forth along the centerline of the wrist pin. There should not be any excessive play evident between the piston and the pin. If there are C-clips retaining the pin in the piston then you have wrist pin bushings in the rods. There should not be any excessive play between the wrist pin and the rod bushing. Normal clearance for the wrist pin is approx. 0.001–0.002 in. (0.025mm–0.051mm).

TCCS3210

Fig. 184 Measure the piston's outer diameter, perpendicular to the wrist pin, with a micrometer

Use a micrometer and measure the diameter of the piston, perpendicular to the wrist pin, on the skirt. Compare the reading to its original cylinder measurement obtained earlier. The difference between the two readings is the piston-to-wall clearance. If the clearance is within specifications, the piston may be used as is. If the piston is out of specification, but the bore is not, you will need a new piston. If both are out of specification, you will need the cylinder rebored and oversize pistons installed. Generally if two or more pistons/bores are out of specification, it is best to rebore the entire block and purchase a complete set of oversize pistons.

CONNECTING ROD

You should have the connecting rod checked for straightness at a machine shop. If the connecting rod is bent, it will unevenly wear the bearing and piston, as well as place greater stress on these components. Any bent or twisted connecting rods must be replaced. If the rods are straight and the wrist pin clearance is within specifications, then only the bearing end of the rod need be checked. Place the connecting rod into a vice, with the bearing inserts in place, install the cap to the rod and torque the fasteners to specifications. Use a telescoping gauge and carefully measure the inside diameter of the bearings. Compare this reading to the rods original crankshaft journal diameter measurement. The difference is the oil clearance. If the oil clearance is not within specifications, install new bearings in the rod and take another measurement. If the clearance is still out of specifications, and the crankshaft is not, the rod will need to be reconditioned by a machine shop.

➡**You can also use Plastigage® to check the bearing clearances. The assembling section has complete instructions on its use.**

Camshaft

Inspect the camshaft and lifters/followers as described earlier in this section.

Bearings

All of the engine bearings should be visually inspected for wear and/or damage. The bearing should look evenly worn all around with no deep scores or pits. If the bearing is severely worn, scored, pitted or heat blued, then the bearing, and the components that use it, should be brought to a machine shop for inspection. Full-circle bearings (used on most camshafts, auxiliary shafts, balance shafts, etc.) require specialized tools for removal and installation, and should be brought to a machine shop for service.

Oil Pump

➡**The oil pump is responsible for providing constant lubrication to the whole engine and so it is recommended that a new oil pump be installed when rebuilding the engine.**

Completely disassemble the oil pump and thoroughly clean all of the components. Inspect the oil pump gears and housing for wear and/or damage. Insure that the pressure relief valve operates properly and there is no binding or sticking due to varnish or debris. If all of the parts are in proper working condition, lubricate the gears and relief valve, and assemble the pump.

REFINISHING

♦ See Figure 185

Almost all engine block refinishing must be performed by a machine shop. If the cylinders are not to be rebored, then the cylinder glaze can be removed with a ball hone. When removing cylinder glaze with a ball hone, use a light or penetrating type oil to lubricate the hone. Do not allow the hone to run dry as this may cause excessive scoring of the cylinder bores and wear on the hone. If new pistons are required, they will need to be installed to the connecting rods. This should be performed by a machine shop as the pistons must be installed in the correct relationship to the rod or engine damage can occur.

Pistons and Connecting Rods

♦ See Figure 186

Only pistons with the wrist pin retained by C-clips are serviceable by the home-mechanic. Press fit pistons require special presses and/or heaters to remove/install the connecting rod and should only be performed by a machine shop.

All pistons will have a mark indicating the direction to the front of the engine

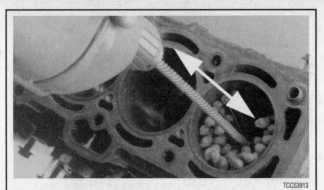

Fig. 185 Use a ball type cylinder hone to remove any glaze and provide a new surface for seating the piston rings

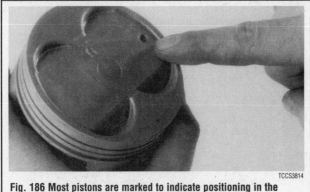

Fig. 186 Most pistons are marked to indicate positioning in the engine (usually a mark means the side facing the front)

and the must be installed into the engine in that manner. Usually it is a notch or arrow on the top of the piston, or it may be the letter F cast or stamped into the piston.

ASSEMBLY

Before you begin assembling the engine, first give yourself a clean, dirt free work area. Next, clean every engine component again. The key to a good assembly is cleanliness.

Mount the engine block into the engine stand and wash it one last time using water and detergent (dishwashing detergent works well). While washing it, scrub the cylinder bores with a soft bristle brush and thoroughly clean all of the oil passages. Completely dry the engine and spray the entire assembly down with an anti-rust solution such as WD-40® or similar product. Take a clean lint-free rag and wipe up any excess anti-rust solution from the bores, bearing saddles, etc. Repeat the final cleaning process on the crankshaft. Replace any freeze or oil galley plugs which were removed during disassembly.

Crankshaft

▶ See Figures 187, 188, 189 and 190

1. Remove the main bearing inserts from the block and bearing caps.
2. If the crankshaft main bearing journals have been refinished to a definite undersize, install the correct undersize bearing. Be sure that the bearing inserts and bearing bores are clean. Foreign material under inserts will distort bearing and cause failure.
3. Place the upper main bearing inserts in bores with tang in slot.

➡The oil holes in the bearing inserts must be aligned with the oil holes in the cylinder block.

4. Install the lower main bearing inserts in bearing caps.
5. Clean the mating surfaces of block and rear main bearing cap.
6. Carefully lower the crankshaft into place. Be careful not to damage bearing surfaces.

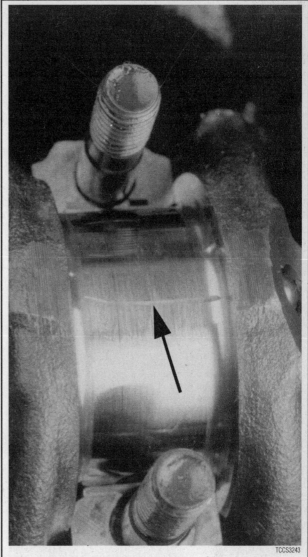

Fig. 187 Apply a strip of gauging material to the bearing journal, then install and torque the cap

7. Check the clearance of each main bearing by using the following procedure:

a. Place a piece of Plastigage® or its equivalent, on bearing surface across full width of bearing cap and about ¼ in. off center.

b. Install cap and tighten bolts to specifications. Do not turn crankshaft while Plastigage® is in place.

c. Remove the cap. Using the supplied Plastigage® scale, check width of Plastigage® at widest point to get maximum clearance. Difference between readings is taper of journal.

d. If clearance exceeds specified limits, try a 0.001 in. or 0.002 in. undersize bearing in combination with the standard bearing. Bearing clearance must be within specified limits. If standard and 0.002 in. undersize bearing does not bring clearance within desired limits, refinish crankshaft journal, then install undersize bearings.

8. After the bearings have been fitted, apply a light coat of engine oil to the journals and bearings. Install the rear main bearing cap. Install all bearing caps except the thrust bearing cap. Be sure that main bearing caps are installed in original locations. Tighten the bearing cap bolts to specifications.

9. Install the thrust bearing cap with bolts finger-tight.

10. Pry the crankshaft forward against the thrust surface of upper half of bearing.

11. Hold the crankshaft forward and pry the thrust bearing cap to the rear. This aligns the thrust surfaces of both halves of the bearing.

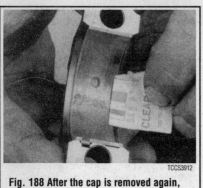

Fig. 188 After the cap is removed again, use the scale supplied with the gauging material to check the clearance

Fig. 189 A dial gauge may be used to check crankshaft end-play

Fig. 190 Carefully pry the crankshaft back and forth while reading the dial gauge for end-play

12. Retain the forward pressure on the crankshaft. Tighten the cap bolts to specifications.

13. Measure the crankshaft end-play as follows:

14. Install the rear main seal.

   a. Mount a dial gauge to the engine block and position the tip of the gauge to read from the crankshaft end.

   b. Carefully pry the crankshaft toward the rear of the engine and hold it there while you zero the gauge.

   c. Carefully pry the crankshaft toward the front of the engine and read the gauge.

   d. Confirm that the reading is within specifications. If not, install a new thrust bearing and repeat the procedure. If the reading is still out of specifications with a new bearing, have a machine shop inspect the thrust surfaces of the crankshaft, and if possible, repair it.

15. Rotate the crankshaft so as to position the first rod journal to the bottom of its stroke.

Pistons and Connecting Rods

♦ **See Figures 191, 192, 193 and 194**

1. Before installing the piston/connecting rod assembly, oil the pistons, piston rings and the cylinder walls with light engine oil. Install connecting rod bolt protectors or rubber hose onto the connecting rod bolts/studs. Also perform the following:

   a. Select the proper ring set for the size cylinder bore.

   b. Position the ring in the bore in which it is going to be used.

   c. Push the ring down into the bore area where normal ring wear is not encountered.

   d. Use the head of the piston to position the ring in the bore so that the ring is square with the cylinder wall. Use caution to avoid damage to the ring or cylinder bore.

   e. Measure the gap between the ends of the ring with a feeler gauge. Ring gap in a worn cylinder is normally greater than specification. If the ring gap is greater than the specified limits, try an oversize ring set.

   f. Check the ring side clearance of the compression rings with a feeler

gauge inserted between the ring and its lower land according to specification. The gauge should slide freely around the entire ring circumference without binding. Any wear that occurs will form a step at the inner portion of the lower land. If the lower lands have high steps, the piston should be replaced.

2. Unless new pistons are installed, be sure to install the pistons in the cylinders from which they were removed. The numbers on the connecting rod and bearing cap must be on the same side when installed in the cylinder bore. If a connecting rod is ever transposed from one engine or cylinder to another, new bearings should be fitted and the connecting rod should be numbered to correspond with the new cylinder number. The notch on the piston head goes toward the front of the engine.

3. Install all of the rod bearing inserts into the rods and caps.

4. Install the rings to the pistons. Install the oil control ring first, then the second compression ring and finally the top compression ring. Use a piston ring expander tool to aid in installation and to help reduce the chance of breakage.

5. Make sure the ring gaps are properly spaced around the circumference of the piston. Fit a piston ring compressor around the piston and slide the piston and connecting rod assembly down into the cylinder bore, pushing it in with the wooden hammer handle. Push the piston down until it is only slightly below the top of the cylinder bore. Guide the connecting rod onto the crankshaft bearing journal carefully, to avoid damaging the crankshaft.

6. Check the bearing clearance of all the rod bearings, fitting them to the crankshaft bearing journals. Follow the procedure in the crankshaft installation above.

7. After the bearings have been fitted, apply a light coating of assembly oil to the journals and bearings.

8. Turn the crankshaft until the appropriate bearing journal is at the bottom of its stroke, then push the piston assembly all the way down until the connecting rod bearing seats on the crankshaft journal. Be careful not to allow the bearing cap screws to strike the crankshaft bearing journals and damage them.

9. After the piston and connecting rod assemblies have been installed, check the connecting rod side clearance on each crankshaft journal.

10. Prime and install the oil pump and the oil pump intake tube.

11. Install the auxiliary/balance shaft(s)/assembly(ies).

Fig. 191 Checking the piston ring-to-ring groove side clearance using the ring and a feeler gauge

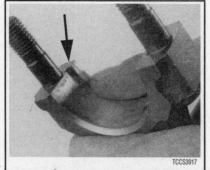

Fig. 192 The notch on the side of the bearing cap matches the tang on the bearing insert

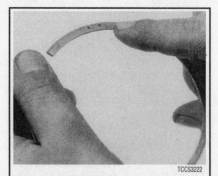

Fig. 193 Most rings are marked to show which side of the ring should face up when installed to the piston

Fig. 194 Install the piston and rod assembly into the block using a ring compressor and the handle of a hammer

2.8L, 3.0L, and 4.0L Engines

CAMSHAFT, LIFTERS AND TIMING ASSEMBLY

1. Install the camshaft.
2. Install the lifters/followers into their bores.
3. Install the timing gears/chain assembly.

CYLINDER HEAD(S)

1. Install the cylinder head(s) using new gaskets.
2. Assemble the rest of the valve train (pushrods and rocker arms and/or shafts).

2.3L Engine

CYLINDER HEAD(S)

1. Install the cylinder head(s) using new gaskets.
2. Install the timing sprockets/gears and the belt/chain assemblies.

Engine Covers and Components

Install the timing cover(s) and oil pan. Refer to your notes and drawings made prior to disassembly and install all of the components that were removed. Install the engine into the vehicle.

Engine Start-up and Break-in

STARTING THE ENGINE

Now that the engine is installed and every wire and hose is properly connected, go back and double check that all coolant and vacuum hoses are connected. Check that your oil drain plug is installed and properly tightened. If not already done, install a new oil filter onto the engine. Fill the crankcase with the proper amount and grade of engine oil. Fill the cooling system with a 50/50 mixture of coolant/water.

1. Connect the vehicle battery.
2. Start the engine. Keep your eye on your oil pressure indicator; if it does not indicate oil pressure within 10 seconds of starting, turn the vehicle **OFF**.

✳✳ WARNING

Damage to the engine can result if it is allowed to run with no oil pressure. Check the engine oil level to make sure that it is full. Check for any leaks and if found, repair the leaks before continuing. If there is still no indication of oil pressure, you may need to prime the system.

3. Confirm that there are no fluid leaks (oil or other).
4. Allow the engine to reach normal operating temperature (the upper radiator hose will be hot to the touch).
5. At this point any necessary checks or adjustments can be performed, such as ignition timing.
6. Install any remaining components or body panels which were removed.

BREAKING IT IN

Make the first miles on the new engine, easy ones. Vary the speed but do not accelerate hard. Most importantly, do not lug the engine, and avoid sustained high speeds until at least 100 miles. Check the engine oil and coolant levels frequently. Expect the engine to use a little oil until the rings seat. Change the oil and filter at 500 miles, 1500 miles, then every 3000 miles past that.

KEEP IT MAINTAINED

Now that you have just gone through all of that hard work, keep yourself from doing it all over again by thoroughly maintaining it. Not that you may not have maintained it before, heck you could have had one to two hundred thousand miles on it before doing this. However, you may have bought the vehicle used, and the previous owner did not keep up on maintenance. Which is why you just went through all of that hard work. See?

TORQUE SPECIFICATIONS

Engine	Component	Ft. Lbs.	Nm
2.3L (140 cid)			
	Auxiliary shaft cover bolt	71-106 inch lbs.	8-12
	Auxiliary shaft gear bolt	28-40	38-54
	Auxiliary shaft thrust plate bolt	71-106 inch lbs.	8-12
	Camshaft gear bolt	50-71	68-96
	Camshaft thrust plate bolt	71-106 inch lbs.	8-12
	Crankshaft pulley bolt	100-120	136-162
	Main bearing cap bolts		
	Step 1	50-60	68-80
	Step 2	80-85	108-115
	Connecting rod nuts		
	Step 1	25-30	33-40
	Step 2	30-36	40-48
	Cylinder front cover bolt	71-106 inch lbs.	8-12
	Distributor clamp bolt	14-21	19-29
	Distributor vacuum tube-to-manifold adapter	62-97 inch lbs.	7-11
	EGR tube nut	18-28	25-35
	EGR tube-to-exhaust manifold connector	18-28	25-35
	EGR valve-to-spacer bolt	15-22	19-29
	Exhaust manifold-to-cylinder head bolt, stud or nut	20-30	27-46
	Fuel pump-to-cylinder block bolt	15-22	19-29
	Inner timing belt cover stud	15-22	19-29
	Oil filter-to-engine	- ①	- ①
	Oil pan drain plug	15-25	19-34
	Oil pan-to-block bolt	8-10	10-14
	Oil pan-to-transmission bolt	30-40	40-54
	Oil pressure sending wire-to-block	8-18	11-24
	Oil pump pick-up tube-to-pump bolt	15-22	19-29
	Oil pump-to-block bolt	15-22	19-29
	Outer timing belt cover bolt	71-106 inch lbs.	8-12
	Rocker arm cover shield bolt	28-40	38-54
	Rocker arm cover-to-cylinder head bolt	62-97 inch lbs.	7-11
	Temperature sending unit-to-block	8-18	11-24
	Thermactor check valve-to-manifold	17-20	24-27
	Timing belt tensioner adjusting bolt	14-21	19-29
	Timing belt tensioner pivot bolt	28-40	38-54
	Water jacket drain plug-to-block	23-28	32-37
	Water outlet connection bolt	15-22	19-29
	Water pump-to-block bolt	15-22	19-29
2.8L (171 cid)			
	Air conditioning pulley-to-crank pulley bolts	19-28	26-38
	Alternator adjustment arm-to-alternator bolt	60-70	70-95
	Alternator adjustment arm-to-front cover bolt	60-70	70-95
	Alternator mounting bracket-to-cylinder head bolt—M10 bolt	29-40	40-55
	Alternator mounting bracket-to-cylinder head bolt—M8 bolts (2)	14-22	20-30
	Alternator mounting bracket-to-engine block bolt	29-40	40-55
	Alternator pivot bolt	45-61	61-82
	Camshaft gear bolt	30-36	41-49
	Camshaft thrust plate bolt	13-16	17-21
	Carburetor spacer-to-carburetor (nut)	12-14	16-20
	Carburetor spacer-to-carburetor (stud)	53 inch lbs.	8 (max.)
	Carburetor spacer-to-intake socket head screw	14-22	20-30
	Cooling fan-to-fan clutch bolts	71-97 inch lbs.	8-11
	Crankshaft pulley bolt	85-96	115-130
	Connecting rod nuts	19-24	25-32
	Main bearing cap bolts	65-75	88-101
	EGR-to-carburetor spacer (nut)—M10	14-22	20-30
	EGR-to-carburetor spacer (nut)—M8	14-22	20-30

TORQUE SPECIFICATIONS

Engine	Component	Ft. Lbs.	Nm
2.8L (171 cid) continued			
	EGR-to-carburetor spacer (stud)—M10	18-88 inch lbs.	3-10
	EGR-to-carburetor spacer (stud)—M8	18-88 inch lbs.	3-10
	Exhaust manifold-to-cylinder head bolt, stud or nut	20-30	27-40
	Exhaust gas oxygen sensor-to-exhaust manifold	28-32	39-43
	Front cover-to-cylinder block bolt	13-16	17-21
	Front plate-to-cylinder block bolt	10-13	13-17
	Fuel line-to-fuel pump and filter	14-18	20-24
	Fuel pump-to-cylinder block bolt	- ②	- ②
	Heat shroud inner-to-heat shroud outer	50-65 inch lbs.	5-7
	Heat shroud-to-exhaust manifold stud (nut)	14-22	19-30
	Knock sensor assembly-to-engine block	30-40	40-54
	Oil filter	- ①	- ①
	Oil filter adapter-to-engine block bolt	15-30	20-40
	Oil level indicator tube-to-block	30-40	40-55
	Oil pan drain plug	15-21	20-28
	Oil pan-to-engine block bolts	62-88 inch lbs.	7-10
	Oil pump case bolts	80-115 inch lbs.	9-13
	Oil pump pick-up support-to-main cap bolt	12-15	17-21
	Oil pump pick-up tube-to-pump bolt	80-115 inch lbs.	9-13
	Rocker arm cover-to-cylinder head bolts	35-62 inch lbs.	4-7
	Rocker arm shaft support bolt	43-50	59-67
	Thermactor pump adjustment arm (pump and front cover) bolts	30-40	40-55
	Thermactor pump pivot bolt	30-40	40-55
	Thermactor pump pulley bolts	12-18	17-25
	Thermactor tube assembly-to-exhaust manifold bolt	14-22	20-30
	Timing pointer-to-front cover bolt	62-80 inch lbs.	7-9
	Water jacket drain plug	14-18	20-25
	Water outlet connection	12-15	17-21
	Water pump pulley bolts	14-22	20-30
	Water pump-to-front cover bolts	80-106 inch lbs.	9-12
3.0L (183 cid)			
	Air conditioner compressor front plate nuts-to-engine studs	30-45	40-61
	Air conditioner compressor front plate-to-lower A/C mounting bracket bolt	30-45	40-61
	Air conditioning brace-to-engine block nut	14-22	20-30
	Air conditioning compressor mounting bolt	30-45	40-61
	Air conditioning compressor support-to-bracket assembly bolt	30-45	40-61
	Air conditioning front brace nut-to-engine stud	14-22	20-30
	Air conditioning front brace-to-engine brace bolt	30-45	40-61
	Air conditioning lower mounting bracket-to-engine block nuts	30-45	40-61
	Air pump pivot bolt	30-40	40-55
	Air pump-to-support bracket bolt	30-40	40-55
	Alternator pivot bolt	45-57	61-75
	Camshaft sprocket-to-camshaft bolt	40-51	55-70
	Coolant temperature switch	8-12	11-16
	Crankshaft damper-to-crankshaft bolt	141-169	190-230
	Crankshaft pulley-to-crankshaft damper bolt	20-28	27-38
	Connecting rod nuts	26	35

	Main bearing cap bolts
	   1988 and earlier
	   1989 through 1992
	   1993 and later
		
		65-81
		66
		59
			
			88-109
			89
			79

	Distributor hold-down bolt	20-29	27-40
	Engine bracket reinforcement brace-to-engine bracket bolt	35-50	47-67
	Engine bracket reinforcement brace-to-engine bracket nut	60-80	80-107

TORQUE SPECIFICATIONS

Engine / Component	Ft. Lbs.	Nm
3.0L (183 cid) continued		
Engine Coolant Temperature (ECT) sensor	12-17	16-24
Front cover-to-engine block bolt	14-22	20-30
Fuel pump-to-front cover bolt	14-22	20-30
Fuel rail-to-intake manifold nut	70 inch lbs.	8
Heater tube-to-intake manifold stud nut	14-22	20-30
Idler bracket-to-alternator top attaching flange bolt	24-34	33-46
Idler front lower bracket attaching bolt	30-40	40-55
Idler front upper bracket attaching bolt	52-70	70-95
Idler pulley adjustment bolts	30-40	40-55
Idler top bracket bolt	30-40	40-55
Low oil level sensor	26-35	34-48
Oil filter adapter-to-front cover bolt	18-22	25-30
Oil filter-to-adapter	- ①	- ①
Oil inlet tube-to-engine block bolt	14-22	20-30
Oil inlet tube-to-main bearing cap nut	30-40	40-55
Oil pan-to-engine block bolt	80-106 inch lbs.	9-12
Rocker arm cover-to-cylinder head bolt	80-106 inch lbs.	9-12
Rocker arm fulcrum-to-cylinder head bolt	- ③	- ③
Thermactor check valve-to-intake manifold	17-19	22-26
Thermostat housing-to-intake manifold	14-22	20-30
Vacuum fitting-to-intake manifold	26-33	35-45
Vacuum tree-to-intake manifold	71-115 inch lbs.	8-13
Water pump-to-front cover bolt	71-106 inch lbs.	8-12
4.0L (244 cid)		
Camshaft sprocket bolt	44-50	60-68
Camshaft thrust plate screws	80-115 inch lbs.	9-13
Coolant temperature sender	44-62 inch lbs.	5-7
Coolent temperature sensor	12	16
Crankshaft oil baffle nuts	13-15	17-21
Crankshaft Position Sensor (CPS)	80-106 inch lbs.	9-12
Crankshaft pulley/vibration damper bolt	30-37	40-50
Main bearing cap bolts	66-77	90-104
Connecting rod cap nuts	18-24	24-32
Cylinder front cover bolts	13-15	17-21
Ignition coil bracket-to-engine bolts	19-24	26-32
Oil filter adapter through bolt	26-30	35-40
Oil pan mounting bolts and nuts	62-88 inch lbs.	7-10
Oil pressure switch	13-16	18-22
Oil pump drive assembly hold-down bolt	13-15	17-21
Oil pump pick-up-to-pump bolts	80-115 inch lbs.	9-13
Oil pump-to-engine block bolts	13-15	17-21
Rocker arm cover bolts	53-71 inch lbs.	6-8
Rocker arm stand bolts	46-52	62-70
Thermostat housing bolts	80-115 inch lbs.	9-13
Timing chain guide bolts	88-106 inch lbs.	10-12
Timing chain tensioner bolts	80-97 inch lbs.	9-11
Water pump-to-front cover bolts	71-106 inch lbs.	8-12

Notes:
① 1/2 turn after the gasket contacts teh engine block surface. Make sure to oil the gasket before installation.
② Step 1: Finger-tighten
   Step 2: 2-6 ft. lbs. (2-8 Nm).
   Step 3: 12-14 ft. lbs. (16-18 Nm).
   Step 4: 15-18 ft. lbs. (21-25 Nm).
③ Step 1: 5-11 ft. lbs. (7-15 Nm).
   Step 2: 18-26 ft. lbs. (25-35 Nm).

4

DRIVEABILITY AND EMISSION CONTROLS

EMISSION CONTROLS

Positive Crankcase Ventilation (PCV) System

OPERATION

The Positive Crankcase Ventilation (PCV) system incorporated into the gasoline engine cycles crankcase gases back through the engine where they are burned. The PCV valve regulates the amount of ventilating air and blow-by gas to the intake manifold and also prevents backfire from traveling into the crankcase. The PCV valve should always be mounted in a vertical position. On some engine applications, the PCV system is connected with the evaporative emission system.

TESTING

▶ See Figure 1

If any of the following operating problems occur, inspect the PCV system:
• Rough idle, not explained by an ordinary vacuum leakage, or fuel delivery problem.
• Oil leaks past the valve cover, oil pan seals or even front and rear crankshaft seals not explainable by age, high mileage or lack of basic maintenance.
• Excessive dirtiness of the air cleaner cartridge at low mileage.
• Noticeable dirtiness in the engine oil due to fuel dilution well before normal oil change interval.

➡An engine with badly worn piston rings and/or valve seals may produce so much blow-by that even a normally functioning PCV system cannot deal with it. A compression test should be performed if extreme wear is suspected.

The PCV system is easily checked with the engine running at normal idle speed (warmed up). Remove the PCV valve, but leave it connected to its hose. Place your thumb over the end of the valve to check for vacuum. If there is no vacuum, check for plugged hoses or ports. If these are open, the valve is faulty. With the engine **OFF**, remove the PCV valve completely. Shake it end to end, listening for the rattle of the needle inside the valve. Generally, if no rattle is heard, the needle is jammed (probably with oil sludge) and the valve should be replaced. If no motion is felt, replace the valve.

An engine which is operated without crankcase ventilation can be damaged very quickly. It is important to check and change the PCV valve at regular maintenance intervals.

PCV VALVE REPLACEMENT

▶ See Figures 2, 3 and 4

Do not attempt to clean an old PCV valve using solvent or any other cleaning material. If the valve is suspect, it should be replaced.

Remove the PCV valve from the valve cover. Depending on the model year,

some valves are pressed into the valve cover and others are threaded into the cover. Remove the hose from the valve. Take note of which end of the valve installed. This one-way valve must be reinstalled correctly or it will not function correctly. While the valve is removed, the hoses should be checked for splits, kinks and blockages.

Remember that the correct function of the PCV system is based on a sealed engine. An air leak at the oil filler cap and/or around the oil pan can defeat the design of the system.

Evaporative Emission Controls

▶ See Figure 5

When liquid gasoline is subjected to heat, it expands and vaporizes. If this expansion and vaporization takes place in a conventional fuel tank, the fuel vapor escapes and pollutes the atmosphere. To control this source of pollution, all models are equipped with an evaporative emission control system that collects gasoline vapors from the fuel tank and carburetor float bowl, if equipped.

The major components of this system are an expansion area in the fuel tank, an orifice valve which is mounted on the fuel tank, a carbon (charcoal) canister

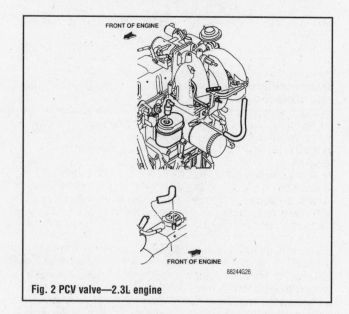

FRONT OF ENGINE

FRONT OF ENGINE

88244G26

Fig. 2 PCV valve—2.3L engine

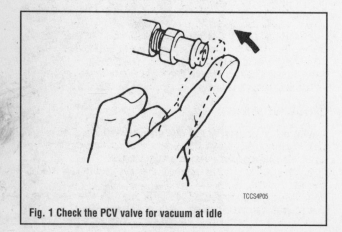

TCCS4P05

Fig. 1 Check the PCV valve for vacuum at idle

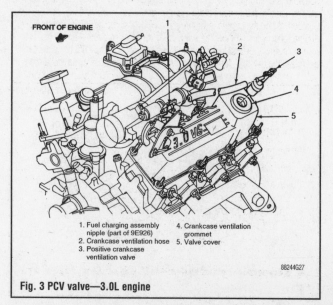

FRONT OF ENGINE

1. Fuel charging assembly nipple (part of 9E926)
2. Crankcase ventilation hose
3. Positive crankcase ventilation valve
4. Crankcase ventilation grommet
5. Valve cover

88244G27

Fig. 3 PCV valve—3.0L engine

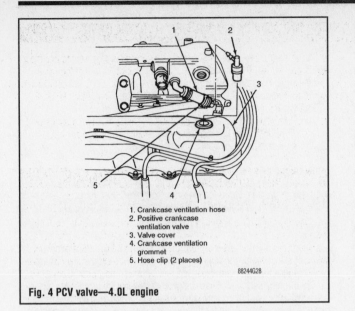

1. Crankcase ventilation hose
2. Positive crankcase ventilation valve
3. Valve cover
4. Crankcase ventilation grommet
5. Hose clip (2 places)

88244G28

Fig. 4 PCV valve—4.0L engine

which stores the fuel vapors and the hoses which connect all this equipment together.

As the gasoline in the fuel tank of a parked vehicle begins to expand due to heat, the vapor that forms moves to the top of the tank. It leaves the fuel tank through the orifice valve, a liquid/vapor separator which permits fuel vapors to leave, but prevents liquid gasoline from escaping. The fuel vapor enters the vapor separator outlet hose and passes through the hose to the carbon canister, which is mounted in the engine compartment. The vapor enters the canister, passes through a charcoal filter, then exits from the canister through its grated bottom. As the fuel vapor passes through the carbon, the hydrocarbons are removed so that the air that passes out of the canister is free of atmospheric pollutants.

When the engine is started, vacuum from the carburetor or throttle body draws fresh air into the carbon canister. Flow of these vapors from the carburetor bowl into the canister is controlled by the fuel bowl vent valve and thermal vent valve on the 2.8L engine. As the entering air passes through the carbon in the canister, it picks up the hydrocarbons that were deposited there and this gas mixture is then carried through a hose to the air cleaner or intake manifold, where it combines with the air/fuel mixture and is burned in the combustion chambers.

On the 2.8L engine only, a canister purge solenoid is installed. The canister purge solenoid is a normally closed valve that is connected inline between the carburetor spacer nipple and the carburetor bowl vent hose. The operation of the solenoid is controlled by the EEC-IV on-board computer. When the engine is off, the canister purge solenoid is not energized and is in a closed, non-flowing position. When the engine is running, the EEC-IV computer reads engine rpm, engine load, engine temperature and other variables to decide the proper time for the engine to accept fuel vapors. When this occurs, the EEC-IV computer energizes the canister purge solenoid to open, allowing flow from the carbon

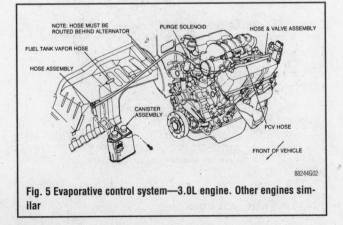

NOTE: HOSE MUST BE ROUTED BEHIND ALTERNATOR

PURGE SOLENOID

HOSE & VALVE ASSEMBLY

FUEL TANK VAPOR HOSE

HOSE ASSEMBLY

CANISTER ASSEMBLY

PCV HOSE

FRONT OF VEHICLE

88244G02

Fig. 5 Evaporative control system—3.0L engine. Other engines similar

canister into the intake manifold through the carburetor spacer. This action purges the carbon canister of fuel vapors as fresh air is drawn into the carbon canister under the fresh air inlet cap of the canister.

➡**Fuel injected engines do not use a canister purge solenoid. The carbon canister is connected directly to the throttle body, so purging of the canister is controlled directly by the throttle plate position, engine load and vacuum level.**

Two other valves are used in the evaporative control system of the 2.8L engine, a fuel bowl thermal vent valve and a fuel bowl solenoid vent valve. The fuel bowl thermal vent valve is inserted in the carburetor-to-canister vent line. The fuel bowl thermal vent valve works in conjunction with the fuel bowl solenoid vent valve to control the opening and closing of the hose between the carburetor fuel bowl vent and the carbon canister. The fuel bowl thermal vent valve is simply an open/close valve that depends only on temperature to open or close the flow path. It does not require any vacuum or electrical input to function. The valve is closed at temperatures below 90°F (32°C) and open at all temperatures above 120°F (49°C). At temperatures between these limits, the valve may be open or closed because the valve operates by an internal disc of thermostatic material whose exact temperature switch point cannot be predicted.

➡**If a valve that has been exposed to temperatures of 120°F (49°C) for one half hour or more is being tested for being open by blowing through it, note that the valve will remain open only for about 15 seconds or less. The air being blown through it will cool the thermostatic disc and cause it to snap shut.**

The fuel bowl solenoid vent valve is a normally open valve located in the carburetor-to-canister vent line. The solenoid vent valve closes off the fuel bowl vent line when the engine is running and returns to the normally open condition when the ignition switch is turned off.

The evaporative emission control system also uses one of two types of ported vacuum switch (PVS). This PVS can be either a 3-port electric or a 4-port type. The 3-port electric type is the same as the EGR system PVS, while the 4-port type consists of two 2-port vacuum valves built into one body. The 4-port type performs the same function as two 2-port PVS valves. The PVS used in the evaporative emission control system turns the purge valve vacuum on as the engine warms up and allows the purge valve to close when the engine is turned off and vacuum is lost.

The final component of the evaporative emission control system is the fuel filler cap. This is a sealed cap with a built-in pressure/vacuum relief valve. Fuel system vacuum relief (necessary as the fuel is used by the engine) is provided after negative 0.50 psi and pressure relief is provided when the fuel tank pressure reaches 1.8 psi. Under normal operating conditions, the fill cap operates as a check valve, allowing air to enter the tank as gasoline is used, while preventing vapors from escaping the tank through the cap. The use of an aftermarket fuel filler cap other than the original factory equipment type could result in damage to the fuel system or improper system operation if not designed for pressure/vacuum relief as described.

TESTING

Canister Purge Control Solenoid

1. Have the key in the **OFF** position.
2. Apply vacuum to the manifold port side of the valve. This should indicate no flow. If flow occurs, replace the valve.
3. Apply vacuum to the canister port side of the valve. This should indicate no flow. The valve should be closed. If flow occurs, replace the valve.
4. Turn the key to the **ON** position.
5. Apply and maintain 16 in. Hg (54 kPa) vacuum to the manifold port side of the valve, and apply vacuum to the canister port. Air should pass through.

Thermal Vent Valve

1. Check for vacuum at the vent valve when the engine is at a normal operating temperature. Air should flow between the engine port and canister port, when no vacuum is applied to the vacuum signal nipple.
2. When vacuum is applied to the vent valve, air should not pass between the ports.
3. At an engine temperature of 90°F (32°C) or less, the valve should not flow air, or be restrictive to air flow.

Vacuum Bowl Vent Valve

The vacuum bowl vent valve should allow an air flow between the engine port and the canister port when no vacuum is applied to the vacuum signal nipple. No air flow should occur air with a vacuum applied at the vacuum signal nipple.

Fuel Bowl Vent Solenoid Valve

Apply 9–14 volts DC power to the fuel bowl vent valve solenoid. With the presence of voltage, the valve should close, not allowing air to pass. If the valve does not close, or leaks when voltage and 1 in. Hg (3.4 kPa) of vacuum is applied to the port, replace the valve.

REMOVAL & INSTALLATION

Periodically check all hoses and connections for leaks and deterioration. Replace any hoses which are found to be damaged in any way. Under normal circumstances, the charcoal canister is expected to last the life of the vehicle, but it should be periodically inspected for any damage or contamination by raw gasoline. Replace any gasoline soaked canister found. Refer to the illustrations for canister mounting and evaporative hose routing on the various engines. Filler cap damage or contamination that clogs the pressure/vacuum valve may result in deformation of the fuel tank.

Carbon Canister

1. Raise vehicle and support safely with jackstands.
2. Loosen the retaining screws securing the mud shield above the front tire. Remove the shield
3. Remove any retaining bolts securing the canister to vehicle.
4. Identify and tag any hoses which are attached to canister. Check the hoses for cracks or damage. Replace if necessary.
To install:
5. Apply engine oil to the hose end on canister.
6. Attach each hose to the respective end of the assembly.
7. Secure the canister to vehicle with retaining bolts.
8. Position and attach the screws to mud shield.
9. Lower the vehicle.

Canister Purge Control Solenoid

1. Disconnect the negative battery cable.
2. Unfasten the wire harness attached to the solenoid.
3. Loosen any hose clamps securing the valve. Identify and tag the hoses attached to the valve.
4. Rotate each hose, and carefully separate it from the assembly.
To install:
5. Apply a small amount of engine oil to the hose ends of the vent valve.
6. Attach each hose to the respective nipple of the assembly.
7. Tighten any hose clamps.
8. Fasten the wire harness to the solenoid.
9. Connect the negative battery cable.

Thermal Vent Valve

1. Loosen any hose clamps securing the valve. Identify and tag the hoses attached to the vent valve.
2. Rotate each hose, and carefully separate it from the assembly.
To install:
3. Apply a small amount of engine oil to the hose ends of the vent valve.
4. Attach each hose to the respective nipple of the assembly.
5. Tighten any hose clamps.

Vacuum Bowl Vent Valve

1. Loosen any hose clamps securing the valve. Identify and tag the hoses attached to the vent valve.
2. Rotate each hose, and carefully separate it from the assembly.
To install:
3. Apply a small amount of engine oil to the hose ends of the vent valve.
4. Attach each hose to the respective nipple of the assembly.
5. Tighten any hose clamps.

Fuel Bowl Vent Solenoid Valve

1. Disconnect the negative battery cable.
2. Disconnect the wire harness attached to the assembly.
3. Loosen any hose clamps.
4. Identify and tag all hoses.
5. Rotate each hose, and carefully separate the assembly.
To install:
6. Apply a small amount of engine oil to the hose ends of the assembly.
7. Attach each hose to the respective end of the assembly.
8. Tighten any equipped hose clamps.
9. Connect wire harness to assembly.
10. Connect the negative battery cable.

Exhaust Gas Recirculation (EGR) System

▶ **See Figure 6**

The exhaust gas recirculation (EGR) system is designed to reintroduce inert exhaust gas into the combustion chamber, thereby lowering peak combustion temperatures and reducing the formation of Nitrous Oxide (NOx). The amount of exhaust gas recirculated and the timing of the cycle varies by calibration and is controlled by various factors, such as engine speed, engine vacuum, exhaust system backpressure, coolant temperature and throttle angle depending on the calibration. All EGR valves are vacuum actuated, but controlled by the EEC-IV on-board computer. The electronic EGR valve is not serviceable, however the EGR valve position (EVP) sensor and EGR valve can be replaced as individual components.

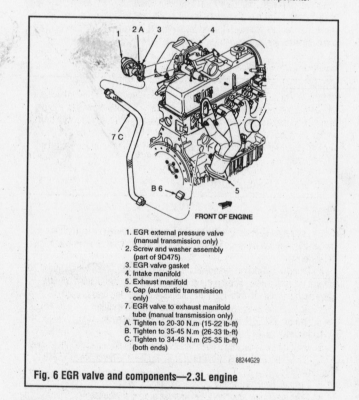

FRONT OF ENGINE

1. EGR external pressure valve (manual transmission only)
2. Screw and washer assembly (part of 9D475)
3. EGR valve gasket
4. Intake manifold
5. Exhaust manifold
6. Cap (automatic transmission only)
7. EGR valve to exhaust manifold tube (manual transmission only)
A. Tighten to 20-30 N.m (15-22 lb-ft)
B. Tighten to 35-45 N.m (26-33 lb-ft)
C. Tighten to 34-48 N.m (25-35 lb-ft) (both ends)

88244G29

Fig. 6 EGR valve and components—2.3L engine

TESTING

▶ **See Figure 7**

1. Check that all vacuum lines are properly routed, all connections are secured and the vacuum hoses are not cracked, crimped or broken.
2. With the EGR valve at rest, air should flow freely when vacuum is applied to the signal vacuum nipple of the valve. Also the valve should not hold any vacuum at this time. If the valve does holds vacuum, clean or replace it, and perform the test again.
3. With the vehicle at idle, there should be no vacuum going to the EGR valve. If there is, check for correct hose routing.

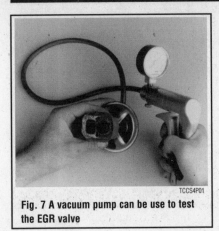

Fig. 7 A vacuum pump can be use to test the EGR valve

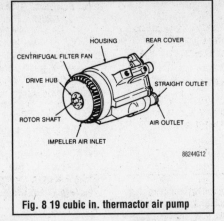

Fig. 8 19 cubic in. thermactor air pump

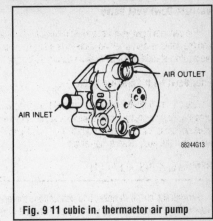

Fig. 9 11 cubic in. thermactor air pump

4. With the engine at normal operating temperature, and the engine running at 3000 rpm, there should be vacuum going to the EGR valve. If there in no vacuum, check back through the vacuum lines from the EGR to source. Replace, as necessary.

EGR SYSTEM SERVICE

The EGR valve assembly should be replaced every 60,000 miles (96,000 km). When replacing the EGR valve, the exhaust gas passages should be cleaned of carbon deposits. Excessive carbon deposits may require the removal of the mounting plate or intake manifold for cleaning. Excessive carbon deposits should not be pushed into the intake manifold where they can be drawn into the combustion chambers when the engine is started.

EGR SUPPLY PASSAGE CLEANING

Remove the EGR supply tube from the engine compartment. Clean the supply tube with a small power-driven rotary type wire brush or blast cleaning equipment. Clean the exhaust gas passages in the spacer using a suitable wire brush and/or scraper. The machined holes in the spacer can be cleaned by using a suitable round wire brush. Hard encrusted material should be probed loose first, then brushed out.

REMOVAL & INSTALLATION

▶ See Figure 6

1. Locate the EGR valve in the engine compartment. Depending on the model, the EGR can be found by the firewall, bolted to the engine or next to the brake booster.
2. Using a suitable open-ended or adjustable wrench, loosen the connection at the base of the valve. Loosen the collar, and push the fitting down. Do not bend the tube. In most vehicles, this tube is thin metal and breaks easily.
3. Remove the nuts/studs securing the valve to the engine.
4. Remove the EGR valve and gasket. Discard the gasket.

To install:

5. Position the valve with a new gasket to the mounting surface on the engine.
6. Secure the EGR valve with nuts/studs. Tighten the hardware to 15–18 ft. lbs. (20–24 Nm).
7. Position the collar to the valve and tighten.
8. Start the engine and check for air leaks around the fittings.

Thermactor (Air Pump) System

▶ See Figures 8 and 9

The thermactor air injection system reduces carbon monoxide and hydrocarbon content of exhaust gases by injecting fresh air into the exhaust gas stream as it leaves the combustion chambers. A belt driven air pump supplies air to the exhaust port near the exhaust valve, by either an external manifold or internal drilled passages. The oxygen in the fresh air plus the heat of the exhaust gases causes burning which converts exhaust gases to carbon dioxide and water vapor.

The air supply pump is a positive displacement, vane type that is available in 11 cu. in. and 19 cu. in. sizes, either of which may be driven with different pulley ratios

for different applications. The 11 cu. in. pump receives its air through a remote filter attached to the air inlet nipple or through an impeller type centrifugal air filter fan. The 19 cu. in. pump uses an impeller type centrifugal air filter fan which separates dirt, dust and other contaminants from the intake air by centrifugal force. The air supply pump does not have a pressure relief valve, a function performed by the bypass valve. There are two general groups of air bypass valves, normally closed and normally open. Each group is available in remote (inline) versions or pump mounted versions. The bypass valves are part of the thermactor system.

Normally closed valves supply air to the exhaust system with medium and high applied vacuum signals during normal operating modes, short idles and some accelerations. With low or no vacuum applied, the pump air is dumped through the silencer ports of the valve. Normally open air bypass valves are available with or without vacuum vents and testing procedures are different for each type. Normally open valve with a vacuum vent provide a timed air dump during decelerations and also dump when a vacuum pressure difference is maintained between the signal port and the vent port. The signal port must have 3 in. Hg more vacuum than the vent port to hold the dump. This mode is used to protect the catalyst from overheating. Normally open valves without a vacuum vent provide a timed dump of air for 1–3 seconds when a sudden high vacuum of about 20 in. Hg is applied to the signal port to prevent backfire during deceleration.

In addition the bypass valves, an air supply control valve is used to direct air pump output to the exhaust manifold or downstream to the catalyst system depending upon the engine control strategy. A combination air bypass/air control valve combines the functions of the air bypass valve and the air control valve into a single unit. There are two normally closed valves, the non-bleed type and the bleed type, all of which look alike. One distinguishing feature will be that the bleed type will have the percent of bleed molded into the plastic case.

Finally, the air check valve is a one-way valve that allows thermactor air to pass into the exhaust system while preventing exhaust gases from passing in the opposite direction. The pulse air valve replaces the air pump application in some thermactor systems. It permits air to be drawn into the exhaust system on vacuum exhaust pulses and blocks the backflow of high pressure exhaust pulses. The fresh air completes the oxidation of exhaust gas components. Although the two valves share the same basic part number and have the same appearance, they are not interchangeable.

TESTING

Air Pump Functional Check

Check the air pump belt tension and adjust it, if necessary. Disconnect the air supply hose from the bypass control valve. The pump is operating properly if air flow is felt at the pump outlet and the flow increases as the engine speed is increased. Do not pry on the pump to adjust the belt as the aluminum housing is likely to collapse.

Normally Closed Bypass Valve Check

1. Disconnect the air supply hose at the valve outlet.
2. Remove the vacuum line to check to see that a vacuum signal is present at the vacuum nipple. Remove or bypass any restrictors or delay valves in the vacuum line. There must be a vacuum present at the nipple before proceeding.
3. With the engine at 1,500 rpm and the vacuum line connected to the vac-

uum nipple, air pump supply air should be heard and felt at the air bypass valve outlet.

4. With the engine at 1,500 rpm, disconnect the vacuum line. Air at the outlet should be significantly decreased or shut off. Air pump supply air should be heard or felt at the silencer ports.

5. If the normally closed air bypass valve does not successfully complete the above tests, check the air pump. If the pump is operating properly, replace the air bypass valve.

Normally Open Bypass Valve Check

1. Disconnect the air pump supply line at the outlet.
2. Disconnect all vacuum lines from the vacuum nipple and the vacuum vent.
3. Start the engine and raise the engine speed to 1,500 rpm. The air pump supply air should be heard and felt at the outlet.
4. Using a length of vacuum hose with no restrictors or devices, connect the vacuum nipple to one of the manifold vacuum fittings on the intake manifold. With the vacuum vent open to the atmosphere and the engine at 1,500 rpm, virtually no air should be felt at the valve outlet and virtually all air should be bypassed through the silencer ports.
5. Using the same direct vacuum line to an intake manifold vacuum source, cap the vacuum vent. Accelerate the engine speed to 2,000 rpm and suddenly release the throttle. A momentary interruption of air pump supply air should be felt at the valve outlet.
6. Reconnect all vacuum and thermactor lines. If any of the above tests are not satisfactorily completed, check the air pump. If the air pump is operating properly, replace the bypass valve.

Normally Open Bypass Valve Without Vacuum Vent

1. Disconnect the air supply line at the valve outlet.
2. Disconnect the vacuum line at the vacuum nipple.
3. With the engine at 1,500 rpm, air should be heard and felt at the valve outlet.
4. Connect a direct vacuum line that is free from restrictions from any manifold vacuum source to the vacuum nipple on the air bypass valve. Air at the outlet should be momentarily decreased or shut off.
5. Air pump supply air should be heard or felt at the silencer ports during the momentary dump. Restore all original connections. If any of the above tests are not as described, check the air pump. If the air pump is operating properly, replace the bypass valve.

Air Supply Control Valve Check

▶ See Figure 10

1. Verify that air flow is being supplied to the valve inlet by disconnecting the air supply hose at the inlet and verifying the presence of air flow with the engine at 1,500 rpm. Reconnect the air supply hose to the valve inlet.
2. Disconnect the air supply hoses at outlets **A** and **B**.
3. Remove the vacuum line at the vacuum nipple.
4. Accelerate the engine speed to 1,500 rpm. Air flow should be heard and felt at outlet **B** with little or no air flow at outlet **A**.
5. With the engine at 1,500 rpm, connect a direct vacuum line from any

manifold vacuum fitting to the air control valve vacuum nipple. Air flow should be heard and felt at outlet **A** with little or no air flow at outlet **B**.

6. If the valve is the bleed type, less air will flow from outlet **A** or **B** and the main discharge will change when vacuum is applied to the vacuum nipple.

7. Restore all connections. If the test results are not as described, replace the air control valve.

Combination Air Bypass/Air Control Valve

The combination air bypass/air control valve combines the functions of the air bypass and air control valve into a single unit. There are two normally closed valves; the non-bleed and bleed type, both of which look alike. One distinguishing feature will be that the bleed type will have the percent of bleed molded into the plastic case.

1. Disconnect the hoses from outlets **A** and **B**.
2. Disconnect and plug the vacuum line to port **D**.
3. With the engine operating at 1,500 rpm, air flow should be noted coming out of the bypass vents.
4. Reconnect the vacuum line to port **D** and disconnect and plug the vacuum line to port **S**. Make sure vacuum is present in the line to vacuum port **D**.
5. With the engine operating at 1,500 rpm, air flow should be noted coming out of outlet **B** and no air flow should be coming from outlet **A**.
6. With the engine at 1,500 rpm, apply 8–10 in.Hg of vacuum to port **S**. Air should now flow from outlet **A**.
7. If the valve is the bleed type, some lesser amount of air will flow from outlet **A** or **B** and the main discharge will change when vacuum is applied to port **S**.

➡ **If there is a small air tap attached to the inlet tube from the air pump, air flow should be present during engine operation.**

Air Check Valve/Pulse Air Valve Test

▶ See Figures 11 and 12

1. Inspect all hoses, tubes and the air valve for leaks.
2. Disconnect the hose on the inlet side if the air valve and attempt to blow through the valve. Air should pass freely.
3. Repeat the test, only this time attempt to suck air through the valve. No air should pass.
4. If any other results are obtained, replace the check valve.

REMOVAL & INSTALLATION

Thermactor Air Pump

1. Disconnect the negative battery cable.
2. Tag or mark the hoses attached to the air pump.
3. Loosen the hose clamps and remove the hoses attached to the pump assembly. Inspect the hoses for cracks tears or any sign of wear and replace the hose(s) if needed.
4. Remove the air pump drive belt. Inspect for excessive wear and replace if needed.
5. Loosen and remove the air pump adjuster bracket bolt. Rotate the adjuster bracket out of the way.
6. Loosen and remove the air pump retainer nut and bolt. With the bolt

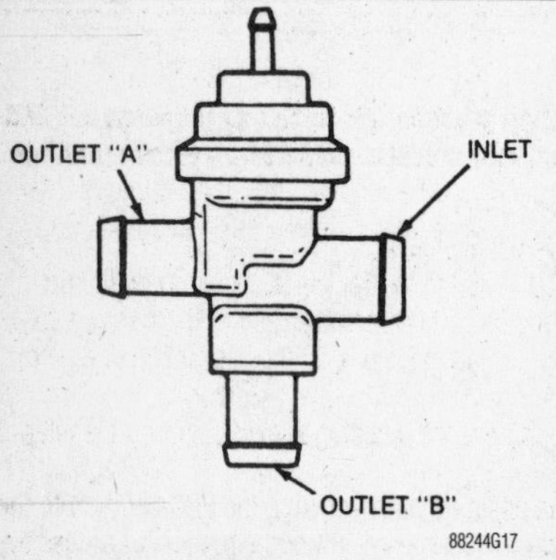

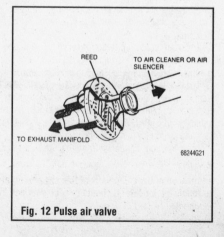

OUTLET "A"   INLET

OUTLET "B"

88244G17

Fig. 10 Air supply control valve

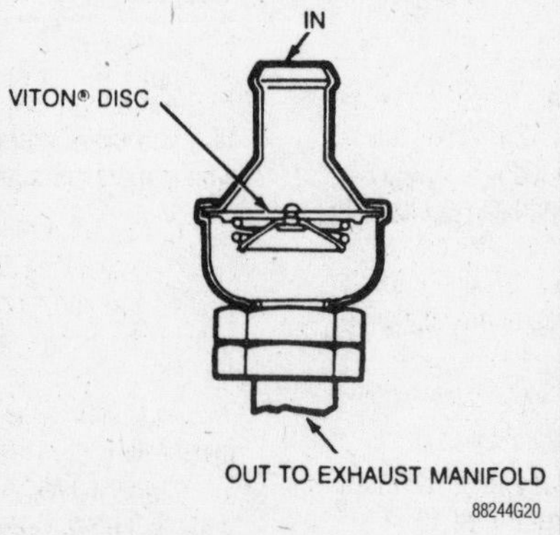

IN

VITON® DISC

OUT TO EXHAUST MANIFOLD

88244G20

Fig. 11 Air check valve

REED   TO AIR CLEANER OR AIR SILENCER

TO EXHAUST MANIFOLD

88244G21

Fig. 12 Pulse air valve

removed, carefully remove the air pump from the engine compartment. Depending on the age of the engine, a small prytool may be needed to aid in removing the pump assembly from the engine.

To Install:

7. Position the air pump into the engine compartment and secure in place with the retainer nut and bolt. Tighten the nut only hand-tight at this time.

8. Rotate the air pump bracket into position on the pump body and secure in place with the retainer bolt. Install the drive belt on the pump pulley, Tension the belt, and tighten the bracket bolt to 22–32 ft. lbs. (29–42 Nm).

9. Connect the hoses to the air pump and secure with the hose clamps.

10. Connect the negative battery cable.

Air Valves

1. Tag or mark each hose attached to the air valve to be removed.

2. If the hose is secured to the valve with a hose clamp, loosen the clamp before removing. Remove the hoses from the air valve and inspect for wear. Replace the hose if needed.

3. Remove the air valve from the engine.

To install;

4. If installing a new air valve, compare the replacement valve with the original valve to make sure they are similar.

5. Position the air valve in the engine compartment and attach the hoses to the valve in the correct order. If equipped, secure the hose in place using the hose clamp removed earlier.

6. Start the engine and check for any vacuum leaks.

Emission Maintenance Warning Light

OPERATION

The emission maintenance warning light system consists of an instrument panel mounted amber lens (with EGR or EMISS printed on it) that is electrically connected to a module located under the instrument panel. The purpose of the system is to alert the driver that emission system maintenance is required. Specific maintenance requirements are listed in the Emission System Scheduled Maintenance Chart.

The system actually measures accumulated vehicle ignition key on-time and is designed to continuously close an electrical circuit to the amber lens after 2000 hours of vehicle operation. Assuming an average vehicle speed of 30 mph, the 2000 hours equates to approximately 60,000 miles (96,000 km) of vehicle operation. Actual vehicle mileage intervals will vary considerably as individual driving habits vary.

Every time the ignition is switched **ON**, the warning light will glow for 2–5 seconds as a bulb check and to verify that the system is operating properly. When approximately 60,000 miles (96,000 km) is reached, the warning light will remain on continuously to indicate that service is required. After the required maintenance is performed, the module must be reset for another 60,000 (96,000 km) mile period. The module is located under the dashboard, on a bracket below the EEC-IV computer.

RESETTING PROCEDURE

1. Make sure the ignition key is in the **OFF** position.

2. Locate the sensor under the dashboard, on a bracket below the EEC-IV computer, and lightly push a Phillips screwdriver or equivalent through the 0.2 in. (5mm) diameter hole with the sticker labeled "RESET" and lightly press down and hold.

3. While lightly holding the screwdriver down, turn the ignition switch to the **RUN** position. The emission warning light will then light and should remain on for as long as the screwdriver is held down. Hold the screwdriver down for approximately five seconds.

4. Remove the screwdriver. The lamp should go out within 2–5 seconds, indicating that a reset has occurred. If the light remains on, begin again at Step 1. If the light goes out, turn the ignition **OFF** and go to the next step.

5. Turn the ignition to the **RUN** position. The warning light should illuminate for 2–5 seconds and then go out. This verifies that a proper reset of the module has been accomplished. If the light remains on, repeat the reset procedure.

ELECTRONIC ENGINE CONTROLS

Control Systems

OPERATION

Micro-processor Control Unit (MCU) System

The Micro-processor Control Unit (MCU) system is used on the 2.8L carbureted 6-cylinder engine. The heart of the system is the fuel control unit. This is necessary to keep the air-fuel ratio at the proper balance (14.7 to 1) to obtain maximum catalyst efficiency. The fuel control loop consists of an Exhaust Gas Oxygen (EGO) sensor, Micro-processor Control Unit (MCU), and Fuel Control Solenoid (FCU).

The EGO sensor senses whether the exhaust gas is rich or lean of proper chemical balance. This signal is sent to the MCU module, which sends a varying signal to the fuel control solenoid to move the air-fuel ratio back to the proper chemical balance. The operation is called a closed loop operation.

The other mode of operation is called an open loop. In this mode, the MCU module sends out a fixed signal to the fuel control solenoid. During this time the input from the EGO sensor is ignored, thus opening the loop.

The factor which determines when the system goes into an open or closed loop is based upon information from the switch inputs, such as the coolant temperature, manifold vacuum, and throttle position switches. Generally, the vehicle will be in closed loop when the vehicle is at operating normal temperature and at a steady part throttle cruise.

Other functions controlled by the MCU module include charcoal canister purge and the spark retard.

➡**Because of the complexity of this system, no attempt should be made to repair the module. It should only be serviced by a qualified mechanic.**

Electronic Engine Control IV (EEC-IV) System

The Electronic Engine Control IV system is used on the 2.3L EFI, 3.0L and 4.0L fuel injected engines. Minimal variations may occur between years and models. This system is designed to improve emission control, fuel economy, driveability, and engine performance. This is achieved by the means of an onboard control assembly which reads the inputs from various sensors and makes computations based on these inputs and then sends controlling outputs to various engine components in order to provide the optimum air/fuel ratio.

The electronic control assembly is calibrated to optimize emissions, fuel economy and driveability. The system controls the fuel injectors for air fuel mixture, spark timing, deceleration fuel cut-off, EGR function, curb and fast idle speed, evaporative emission purge, air condition cut-off during wide open throttle, cold engine start and enrichment, electric fuel pump and self test engine diagnostics.

REMOVAL & INSTALLATION

▶ **See Figure 13**

➡**The removal and installation procedure is basically the same for EEC-IV and MCU modules, except that different modules may have multiple wire harnesses attached.**

1. Disconnect the negative battery cable.

2. Locate the EEC-IV/MCU model in the vehicle. Depending on the production year and model, the module is located to the right of the steering column on the driver's side, or next to the glove box on the passenger side. The module is roughly the size of a cigar box and is silver in color.

3. To access the module, remove the retaining screws securing the interior panel over the assembly.

4. Loosen and remove the retaining bolts securing the EEC-IV/MCU to the bracket or body. Once the hardware is removed, lower the module to access the wire harness.

Fig. 13 EEC-IV module under steering column—1990 model shown

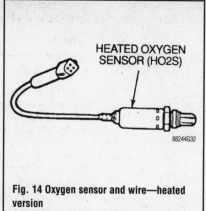

Fig. 14 Oxygen sensor and wire—heated version

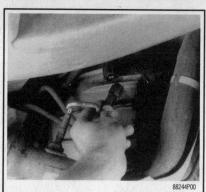

Fig. 15 Disconnect the oxygen sensor wire harness

5. Determine whether the module has multiple wire harnesses attached. If it does, mark or tag each harness to identify its relative position.

6. Disconnect the wire harness(s) from the module.

7. Inspect the connectors for signs of corrosion and clean if needed.

To install:

8. Plug the wire harness (s) into the module. If the plug does not fit in easily, remove and start again. NEVER force a harness into the module assembly.

9. Position the EEC-IV/MCU module to the mounting bracket or body, and secure in place using the mounting bolts. Tighten the bolts to 15–18 ft. lbs. (19–23 Nm).

10. Install the interior panel over the module and secure in place using the retaining screws.

11. Connect the negative battery cable.

➡ **When the battery cable has been disconnected and reconnected, some abnormal drive symptoms may occur while the powertrain control module relearns its adaptive strategy. The vehicle may need to be driven 10 miles (16 km) or more to relearn the adaptive strategy.**

Oxygen Sensor

OPERATION

▶ **See Figure 14**

The exhaust gas oxygen sensor supplies the electronic control assembly with a signal which indicates either a rich or lean mixture condition, during the engine operation. This sensor is screwed into the exhaust manifold before the catalytic converter.

TESTING

Because of the complexity of the electronic control system and this component, no attempt should be made to repair or test the oxygen sensor. It should only be tested by a qualified mechanic utilizing the correct machines and equipment.

In general, the oxygen sensor is maintenance free, and only requires service during the change interval. Refer to the maintenance schedule for the correct change interval for the vehicle.

REMOVAL & INSTALLATION

▶ **See Figures 15, 16 and 17**

1. Disconnect the negative battery cable.

2. Raise and safely support the vehicle on jackstands.

3. Locate the oxygen sensor between the exhaust manifold and the catalytic converter.

4. Disconnect the electrical connector from the sensor. Depending on the production year and electronic control system install on the vehicle, the oxygen sensor could be a two or three wire type. Make sure that all the wires are unfastened.

5. Spray a commercial solvent onto the sensor threads and allow it to soak in for about 5 minutes.

6. Carefully remove the oxygen sensor.

To install:

7. Coat the sensor's threads with an appropriate oxygen sensor anti-seize compound or equivalent. Do not apply the compound too thick. You must coat ONLY the threads with the anti-seize compound.

8. Install the sensor and tighten to 30 ft. lbs. (39 Nm). Be careful not to damage the electrical connector.

9. Fasten the oxygen sensor connector.

10. Connect the negative battery cable.

Air Bypass Solenoid Valve

OPERATION

▶ **See Figure 18**

The air bypass solenoid or idle air control valve is used to control the engine idle speed. This component is operated by the electronic control module. The

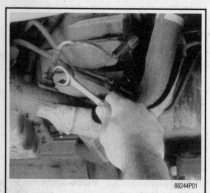

Fig. 16 Use a suitable wrench to loosen the oxygen sensor

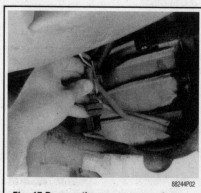

Fig. 17 Remove the oxygen sensor from the exhaust tube

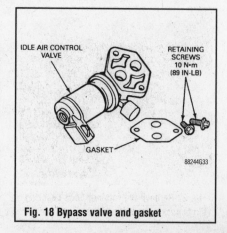

Fig. 18 Bypass valve and gasket

valve allows air to pass around the throttle plates in order to control cold engine idle and promote easier starting and dashpot operation.

TESTING

1. With the ignition in the **ON** position, use a multimeter and check for current at the valve. The meter should register approximately one volt.
2. Connect a tachometer using the manufacturer's instructions.
3. With the engine running at normal operating temperature, apply 12 volts to the valve and watch the tachometer.
4. If the bypass valve is functioning correctly, the idle speed will increase 700–1000 rpm. If the idle speed does not change, or increases less than 500 rpm, replace the bypass valve.

REMOVAL & INSTALLATION

▶ **See Figures 19 thru 24**

➡**When the battery cable has been disconnected and reconnected, some abnormal drive symptoms may occur while the powertrain control module relearns its adaptive strategy. The vehicle may need to be driven 10 miles (16 km) or more to relearn the adaptive strategy.**

1. Disconnect the negative battery cable.
2. Access the idle air control valve on the side of the throttle body, and disconnect the wire harness attached to it.
3. Remove the two Torx® bolts securing the bypass valve into position. Lift the valve off and remove the gasket from the base of the bypass valve. Clean any excess gasket material from both mating surfaces.
   To install:
4. Position a new gasket on the base of the bypass valve and attach to the throttle body using the two Torx® bolts. Tighten the bolts to 8–10 ft. lbs. (10–13 Nm).
5. Fasten the wire harness to the bypass valve.
6. Connect the negative battery cable.

Air Charge Temperature Sensor

OPERATION

▶ **See Figure 25**

The air charge temperature sensor provides the electronic fuel injection system with air/fuel mixture information. This sensor is used as both a density corrector to calculate air flow and to proportion cold enrichment fuel flow. This sensor is similar in construction to the engine coolant temperature sensor.

TESTING

To test the air charge temperature sensor requires the use of expensive specialized equipment. If you suspect a faulty or defective sensor, consult an authorized mechanic whose has access to this equipment.

REMOVAL & INSTALLATION

➡**When the battery cable has been disconnected and reconnected, some abnormal drive symptoms may occur while the powertrain control module relearns its adaptive strategy. The vehicle may need to be driven 10 miles (16 km) or more to relearn the adaptive strategy.**

This sensor is located in the engine cylinder runner of the intake manifold.
1. Disconnect the negative battery cable.
2. Unfasten the wire harness attached to the charge sensor.
3. Using a suitable wrench or equivalent, remove the sensor from the manifold or cylinder runner. Remove the washer from the sensor and discard.
   To install:
4. Install the sensor, using a new washer into the hole in the cylinder runner or intake manifold. Tighten the sensor to 15–18 ft. lbs. (19–23 Nm).
5. Fasten the wire harness to the rear of the charge sensor.
6. Connect the negative battery cable.

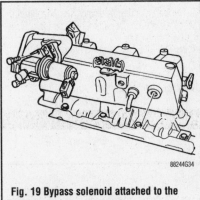

Fig. 19 Bypass solenoid attached to the throttle body—4.0L shown

Fig. 20 Remove the plastic cover over the throttle linkage and bypass solenoid, if equipped

Fig. 21 Unfasten the wire harness attached to the bypass solenoid

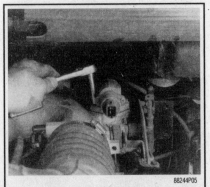

Fig. 22 Remove the retainer bolts securing the bypass solenoid in place

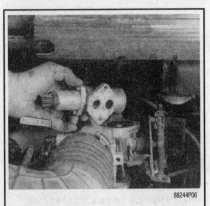

Fig. 23 Lift the bypass solenoid off . . .

Fig. 24 . . . and remove the gasket

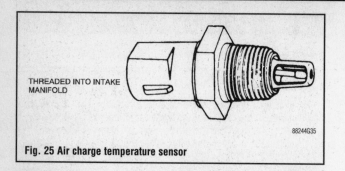

Fig. 25 Air charge temperature sensor

Coolant Temperature Switch

OPERATION

▶ **See Figure 26**

This component detects the temperature of the engine coolant and relays the information to the electronic control assembly. The sensor is located by the heater outlet fitting or in a cooling passage on the engine, depending upon the particular type vehicle. The function of the sensor is to modify ignition timing, control EGR flow and regulate the air/fuel mixture. On vehicles equipped with the electronic instrument cluster, the sensor is also used to control the coolant temperature indicator.

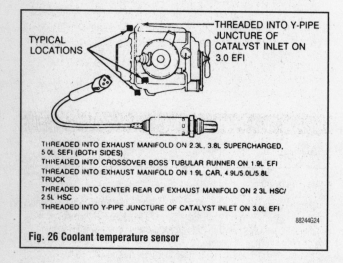

Fig. 26 Coolant temperature sensor

TESTING

Under correct operating conditions, the coolant switch is closed in the normal operating temperature range above 180°F. The switch remains open below the 180°F range. If a switch is defective, the electronic control module is able to determine this and alert the driver.

This switch can also be tested as follows;
1. Remove the switch from the engine while the engine is cool.
2. Using a multimeter, test for continuity at the switch. If the switch is functioning correctly, the meter will register open.
3. Place the probe end of the switch into boiling water for at least two minutes. Use the meter and check for continuity. If the switch is function correctly, there should be continuity.

REMOVAL & INSTALLATION

▶ **See Figure 27**

➡ **When the battery cable has been disconnected and reconnected, some abnormal drive symptoms may occur while the powertrain control module relearns its adaptive strategy. The vehicle may need to be driven 10 miles (16 km) or more to relearn the adaptive strategy.**

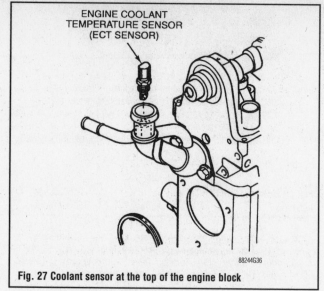

Fig. 27 Coolant sensor at the top of the engine block

1. Disconnect the negative battery cable.
2. Unfasten the wire harness attached to the temperature switch.
3. Place a suitable drip pan below the sensor to capture any coolant that may spill out during removal and installation.
4. Using a suitable wrench or equivalent, remove the switch from the engine. Remove the washer from the switch and discard.
   To install:
5. Install the temperature switch, using a new washer and tighten to 15–18 ft. lbs. (19–23 Nm).
6. Fasten the wire harness to the rear of the charge sensor.
7. Connect the negative battery cable.

Intake Air Temperature Sensor

OPERATION

The intake air temperature sensor, mounted in the intake air tube to the airflow meter and throttle body assembly, changes resistance in response to changes in intake air temperature. The resistance will decrease as the air temperature increased, and will increase as the air temperature decrease. The sensor provides a signal to the electronic control module of incoming air temperature. This information is used to adjust the injector pulse width and in turn the air/fuel ratio.

TESTING

1. Remove the intake air temperature sensor from the intake tube on the vehicle.
2. Using a hair dryer with adjustable temperature controls, start on the lowest setting and measure the sensor resistance with a multimeter. Record each reading. Do not place the hair dryer directly in front of the sensor. Make sure there is at least a 12 in. (30cm) gap between the sensor and hair dryer.
3. After the reading has been recorded, adjust the temperature controls of the hair dryer to increase the heat, and point at the sensor. Continue this through the entire heat range of the hair dryer, recording each reading.
4. If the sensor is working correctly, as the heat from the hair dryer increased, the resistance recorded from the sensor should have decreased. If the multimeter reading did not decrease, or decreased, then stopped decreasing, replace the sensor.

REMOVAL & INSTALLATION

▶ **See Figure 28**

➡ **When the battery cable has been disconnected and reconnected, some abnormal drive symptoms may occur while the powertrain control**

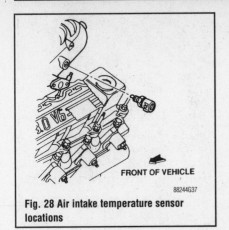

Fig. 28 Air intake temperature sensor locations

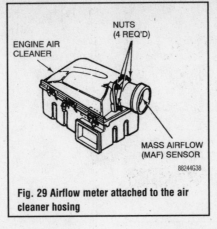

Fig. 29 Airflow meter attached to the air cleaner hosing

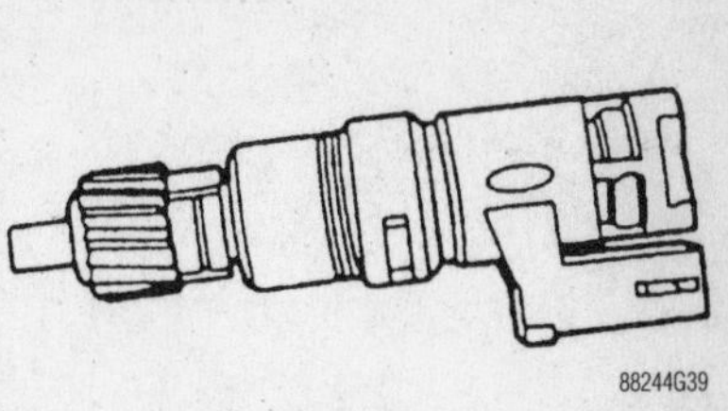

Fig. 30 Vehicle speed sensor and gear

module relearns its adaptive strategy. The vehicle may need to be driven 10 miles (16 km) or more to relearn the adaptive strategy.

1. Disconnect the negative battery cable.
2. Access the intake air temperature sensor on the side of the intake air tube, and unfasten the wire harness attached to the sensor.
3. Using a suitable wrench, remove the sensor from the intake tube.

To install:

4. Screw the intake air temperature sensor into the intake tube and secure in place with a suitable wrench.
5. Attach the wire harness to the temperature sensor.
6. Connect the negative battery cable.
7. Road test the vehicle.

Airflow Meter Sensor

OPERATION

▶ See Figure 29

The air flow sensor, mounted on the outside of the air cleaner assembly, uses a hot wire sensing element to measure the amount of air entering the engine. Air passing over the hot wire causes the wire to cool, which in turn creates an analog signal which is relayed to the electronic control unit where a intake mass air calculation is made. The electronic control module uses this information to determine the required fuel injector pulse width in order to provided the optimum air/fuel ratio.

TESTING

➡The airflow sensor electronics module and body are calibrated as a unit and must be tested as a complete assembly.

1. With the key **OFF**, check and make sure all engine control components are installed.
2. Unfasten the airflow sensor harness and connect a breakout box to the sensor. Connect the wire harness to the breakout box.
3. With the wheels blocked, start the vehicle and place in **PARK** or **NEUTRAL**. Allow the vehicle to reach normal operating temperature.
4. Using a multimeter, measure the voltage between test pin 14 at the breakout box, and the positive terminal of the battery or starter solenoid.
5. If the sensor is working correctly, at idle, the voltage reading should be 0.6–0.7 volts.
6. If the reading is below 0.6, perform the same test while applying throttle. If the voltage is below 0.8 volts while at throttle, replace the airflow sensor.

REMOVAL & INSTALLATION

➡When the battery cable has been disconnected and reconnected, some abnormal drive symptoms may occur while the powertrain control module relearns its adaptive strategy. The vehicle may need to be driven 10 miles (16 km) or more to relearn the adaptive strategy.

1. Disconnect the negative battery cable.
2. Unfasten the wire harness attached to the airflow sensor.
3. Loosen the air cleaner outlet tube clamp at the airflow sensor. Remove the outlet tube from the airflow sensor.
4. Remove the four retainer screws securing the airflow sensor to the air cleaner housing.
5. Remove the airflow sensor from the air cleaner. Remove and discard the gasket between the air cleaner and airflow sensor.

To install:

6. Remove all gasket from both mating surfaces.
7. Position the airflow sensor and new gasket to the air cleaner and secure in place with the retainer screws. Tighten the retainer screws to 88 inch lbs. (10 Nm).
8. Install the inlet tube to the airflow sensor and tighten the clamp to 18–27 inch lbs. (2–3 Nm).
9. Fasten the wire harness to the airflow sensor.
10. Connect the negative battery cable.
11. Road test the vehicle.

Vehicle Speed Sensor

OPERATION

▶ See Figure 30

The vehicle speed sensor, mounted to the speedometer cable at the transmission assembly, is a magnetic pickup that sends a signal to the electronic control module of the vehicle's speed. The electronic module uses this information to control transmission shift patterns.

The vehicle speed sensor is also used to send a speed signal to the speed control servo of the cruise control system.

TESTING

1. Place a drip pan below the speed sensor on the transmission body to catch any spilled fluid.
2. With the key in the **ON** position, use a multimeter and check for voltage at the sensor. If the voltage reading is less than 10.5 volts check the wire harness for a possible short. If there is no voltage, check the fuse box for a blown fuse.
3. Disconnect the speedometer cable from the speed sensor.
4. Disconnect the speed sensor from the transmission body.
5. Connect a multimeter to the speed sensor terminals and rotate the gear. If the resistance is between 190–250 ohms, the sensor is functioning correctly. If the reading is above or below the specified level, replace the switch.

REMOVAL & INSTALLATION

▶ See Figures 31, 32 and 33

➡When the battery cable has been disconnected and reconnected, some abnormal drive symptoms may occur while the powertrain control module relearns its adaptive strategy. The vehicle may need to be driven 10 miles (16 km) or more to relearn the adaptive strategy.

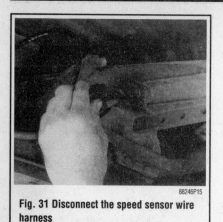

Fig. 31 Disconnect the speed sensor wire harness

Fig. 32 Remove the speed sensor retainer bolt

Fig. 33 Slide the speed sensor out of the transmission body

1. Disconnect the negative battery cable.
2. Unfasten the wire harness from the speed sensor.
3. Unfasten the speedometer cable from the speed sensor.
4. Place a drip pan below the speed sensor to catch any spilled fluid.
5. Remove the speed sensor from the transmission body by removing the retainer bolt, and removing the speed sensor from the transmission body.
6. Insert the speed sensor into the transmission body and secure I n place with the retainer bolt.
7. Connect the speedometer cable and speed sensor harness to the sensor assembly.
8. Connect the negative battery cable.
9. Check the transmission fluid level and add fluid if needed.

Throttle Position Sensor (TPS)

OPERATION

The throttle position sensor, mounted to the throttle body assembly, is a potentiometer type sender which provides a signal to the electronic control module that is related to the relative throttle plate position. As the throttle plate moves in relation to driving conditions, a signal is sent to the control unit which adjusts the injector pulse width and air/fuel ratio. As the throttle plate is opened further, more air is taken into the combustion chambers, and as a result the relative fuel demand of the engine changes. The throttle position sensor relays this information to the control unit which in alters the fuel amount.

TESTING

▶ See Figure 34

1. Visually inspect the throttle linkage and throttle for binding and sticking.
2. With the key in the **ON** position, use a multimeter and test for voltage at the two outside wires of the harness. Voltage should be between 4–6 volts. If

there is no voltage present, check the wire harness for a break, or the fuse box for a blown fuse.
3. Connect a breakout box between the powertrain control module and the powertrain control module wire harness.
4. Start the engine and allow to reach normal operating temperature. Record the voltage between the signal and return terminals at the breakout box while slowly opening the throttle plate. Depending on the throttle plate position, the voltage will be between 0.17–0.49 volts. If the voltage level is below or above the specified amount, replace the switch.

REMOVAL & INSTALLATION

▶ See Figures 35 and 36

➡When the battery cable has been disconnected and reconnected, some abnormal drive symptoms may occur while the powertrain control module relearns its adaptive strategy. The vehicle may need to be driven 10 miles (16 km) or more to relearn the adaptive strategy.

1. Disconnect the negative battery cable.
2. Unfasten the throttle position sensor electrical connector from the side of the throttle body assembly.
3. Scribe alignment marks on the throttle body and TPS sensor to indicate proper alignment during installation.
4. Remove the screws retaining the TPS electrical connector to the air throttle body.
5. Remove the TPS and gasket from the throttle body. Remove any gasket material from the mating surfaces.
   To install:
6. If installing a new TPS switch, compare the replacement sensor with the original, then scribe an alignment mark on the new sensor in the same area as the old one for proper alignment.
7. Place the TPS and new gasket on the throttle body, making sure the rotary tangs on the sensor are aligned with the throttle shaft blade. Slide the rotary tangs into position over the throttle shaft blade, then rotate the throttle position sensor CLOCKWISE ONLY to the alignment marks made earlier.

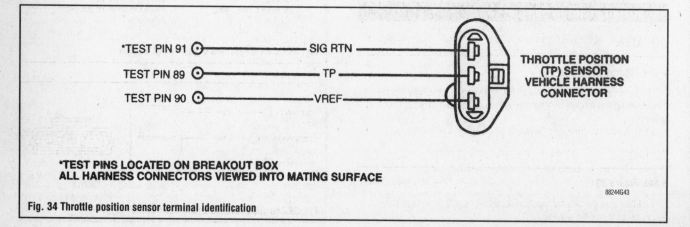

*TEST PIN 91 — SIG RTN
TEST PIN 89 — TP
TEST PIN 90 — VREF

THROTTLE POSITION (TP) SENSOR VEHICLE HARNESS CONNECTOR

***TEST PINS LOCATED ON BREAKOUT BOX
ALL HARNESS CONNECTORS VIEWED INTO MATING SURFACE**

Fig. 34 Throttle position sensor terminal identification

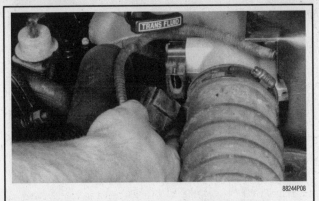

Fig. 35 Unfasten the wire harness from the position sensor

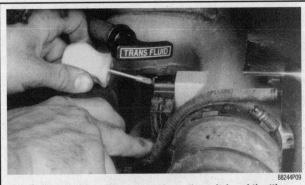

Fig. 36 After scribing alignment marks on the switch and throttle body, remove the retainer bolts

※※ CAUTION

Failure to install the TPS in this manner may result in excessive idle speeds.

8. Once the scribe marks are aligned, install the TPS retaining screws and tighten them to 11–16 inch lbs. (14–21 Nm).
9. Fasten the TPS electrical connector.
10. Connect the negative battery cable.
11. Start the engine, and check the idle speed. If installed correctly, the idle speed should be within specification.

➥Adjustment of the throttle position sensor requires the use of expensive test equipment that is not available to the do-it-yourself market. If adjustment is required, it should be performed by a qualified technician with the proper training and equipment to diagnose and repair the EEC-IV engine control system.

Camshaft Position Sensor

OPERATION

◆ See Figures 37 and 38

The camshaft position sensor relays the relative camshaft position to the powertrain control module for determining the position and stroke of the No. 1 cylinder.

This information is required for proper fuel injection functioning.

TESTING

◆ See Figure 39

1. Make sure the camshaft position sensor harness is connected to the sensor. Inspect the wire for any breaks.

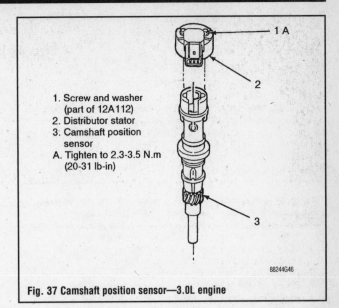

1. Screw and washer (part of 12A112)
2. Distributor stator
3. Camshaft position sensor
A. Tighten to 2.3-3.5 N.m (20-31 lb-in)

Fig. 37 Camshaft position sensor—3.0L engine

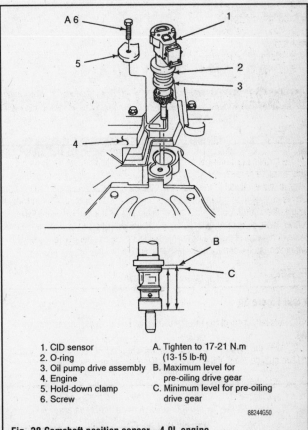

1. CID sensor
2. O-ring
3. Oil pump drive assembly
4. Engine
5. Hold-down clamp
6. Screw

A. Tighten to 17-21 N.m (13-15 lb-ft)
B. Maximum level for pre-oiling drive gear
C. Minimum level for pre-oiling drive gear

Fig. 38 Camshaft position sensor—4.0L engine

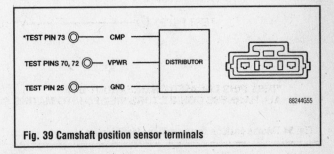

Fig. 39 Camshaft position sensor terminals

2. Turn the key to the **ON** position.

3. Disconnect the wire harness from the sensor. And test for current between the center terminal and the negative terminal of the battery. Voltage should register greater than 10.5 volts. If there is no current check the fuse box for a blown fuse, or a broken wire in the harness.

4. Connect a breakout box between the powertrain control module and control module wire harness.

5. Start the engine and allow it to reach normal operating temperature.

6. Record the voltage between the sensor and vehicle ground at different idle speeds. If the voltage varies more than 0.1 volts the sensor is functioning correctly.

REMOVAL & INSTALLATION

➡When the battery cable has been disconnected and reconnected, some abnormal drive symptoms may occur while the powertrain control module relearns its adaptive strategy. The vehicle may need to be driven 10 miles (16 km) or more to relearn the adaptive strategy.

1. Disconnect the negative battery cable.

2. Set engine cylinder No. 1 to top dead center of the compression stroke. Scribe an alignment mark on the sensor and engine block for proper sensor alignment during installation.

3. Unfasten the harness attached to the camshaft position sensor.

4. Remove the retainer bolt secure the position sensor in place. Lift the sensor out of the engine.

To install:

5. Slide the camshaft position sensor into place, making sure the alignment mark on the sensor aligns with the mark on the engine.

6. Install the retainer bolt and tighten to 13–15 ft. lbs. (17–19 Nm).

7. Fasten the wire harness to the position sensor.

8. Connect the negative battery cable.

9. Start the vehicle and check for proper vehicle operation.

Crankshaft Position Sensor

OPERATION

▶ **See Figures 40 and 41**

The crankshaft position sensor is a variable reluctance sensor which is used to inform the powertrain control module when the No.1 piston is at top dead center. This information is used by the powertrain control module controlling and adjusting ignition and fuel injector timing.

The crankshaft position sensor is non-adjustable. It is triggered by a 36 toothed wheel on the crankshaft vibration damper and pulley. This toothed wheel is minus one tooth which serves as a reference mark for top dead center by PCM.

REMOVAL & INSTALLATION

➡When the battery cable has been disconnected and reconnected, some abnormal drive symptoms may occur while the powertrain control module relearns its adaptive strategy. The vehicle may need to be driven 10 miles (16 km) or more to relearn the adaptive strategy.

1. Disconnect the negative battery cable,

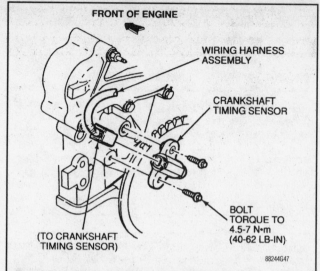

Fig. 40 Crankshaft position sensor—3.0L engine

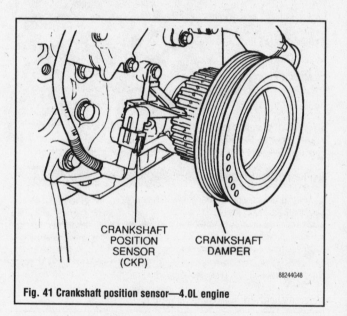

Fig. 41 Crankshaft position sensor—4.0L engine

2. Unfasten the wire harness attached to the crankshaft position sensor.

3. Remove the retainer bolts securing the sensor to the engine block.

4. Remove the crankshaft position sensor from the engine.

To install:

5. Position the crankshaft position sensor to the engine block and install the retainer bolts. On 3.0L engines, tighten the bolts to 35–62 inch lbs. (4–7 Nm). On 4.0L engines, tighten the bolts to 80–106 inch lbs. (9–12 Nm).

6. Fasten the wire harness to the position sensor.

7. Connect the negative battery cable.

TROUBLE CODES—EEC-IV

General Information

POWERTRAIN CONTROL MODULE

One part of the PCM is devoted to monitoring both input and output functions within the system. This ability forms the core of the self-diagnostic system. If a problem is detected within a circuit, the controller will recognize the fault, assign it an identification code, and store the code in a memory section. Depending on the year and model, the fault code(s) may be represented by two or three-digit numbers. The stored code(s) may be retrieved during diagnosis.

While the EEC-IV system is capable of recognizing many internal faults, certain faults will not be recognized. Because the computer system sees only electrical signals, it cannot sense or react to mechanical or vacuum faults affecting engine operation. Some of these faults may affect another component which will set a code. For example, the PCM monitors the output signal to the fuel injectors, but cannot detect a partially clogged injector. As long as the output driver responds correctly, the computer will read the system as functioning correctly. However, the improper flow of fuel may result in a lean mixture. This would, in turn, be detected by the oxygen sensor and noticed as a constantly lean signal by the PCM. Once the signal falls outside the pre-programmed limits, the engine control assembly would notice the fault and set an identification code.

Failure Mode Effects Management (FMEM)

The PCM contains back-up programs which allow the engine to operate if a sensor signal is lost. If a sensor input is seen to be out of range—either high or low—the FMEM program is used. The processor substitutes a fixed value for the missing sensor signal. The engine will continue to operate, although performance and driveability may be noticeably reduced. This function of the controller is sometimes referred to as the limp-in or fail-safe mode. If the missing sensor signal is restored, the FMEM system immediately returns the system to normal operation. The dashboard warning lamp will be lit when FMEM is in effect.

Hardware Limited Operation Strategy (HLOS)

This mode is only used if the fault is too extreme for the FMEM circuit to handle. In this mode, the processor has ceased all computation and control; the entire system is run on fixed values. The vehicle may be operated but performance and driveability will be greatly reduced. The fixed or default settings provide minimal calibration, allowing the vehicle to be carefully driven in for service. The dashboard warning lamp will be lit when HLOS is engaged. Codes cannot be read while the system is operating in this mode.

MALFUNCTION INDICATOR LAMP (MIL)

The CHECK ENGINE or SERVICE ENGINE SOON dashboard warning lamp is referred to as the Malfunction Indicator Lamp (MIL). The lamp is connected to the engine control assembly and will alert the driver to certain malfunctions within the EEC-IV system. When the lamp is lit, the PCM has detected a fault and stored an identity code in memory. The engine control system will usually enter either FMEM or HLOS mode and driveability will be impaired.

The light will stay on as long as the fault causing it is present. Should the fault self-correct, the MIL will extinguish but the stored code will remain in memory.

Under normal operating conditions, the MIL should light briefly when the ignition key is turned **ON**. As soon as the PCM receives a signal that the engine is cranking, the lamp will be extinguished. The dash warning lamp should remain out during the entire operating cycle.

HAND-HELD SCAN TOOLS

Although stored codes may be read through the flashing of the CHECK ENGINE or SERVICE ENGINE SOON lamp, the use of hand-held scan tools such as Ford's Self-Test Automatic Readout (STAR) tester or the second generation SUPER STAR II tester or their equivalent is highly recommended. There are many manufacturers of these tools; the purchaser must be certain that the tool is proper for the intended use.

The scan tool allows any stored faults to be read from the engine controller memory. Use of the scan tool provides additional data during troubleshooting,

but does not eliminate the use of the charts. The scan tool makes collecting information easier, but the data must be correctly interpreted by an operator familiar with the system.

ELECTRICAL TOOLS

The most commonly required electrical diagnostic tool is the Digital Multimeter, allowing voltage, ohmage (resistance) and amperage to be read by one instrument. Many of the diagnostic charts require the use of a volt or ohmmeter during diagnosis.

The multimeter must be a high impedance unit, with 10 megohms of impedance in the voltmeter. This type of meter will not place an additional load on the circuit it is testing; this is extremely important in low voltage circuits. The multimeter must be of high quality in all respects. It should be handled carefully and protected from impact or damage. Replace the batteries frequently in the unit.

Additionally, an analog (needle type) voltmeter may be used to read stored fault codes if the STAR tester is not available. The codes are transmitted as visible needle sweeps on the face of the instrument.

Almost all diagnostic procedures will require the use of a Breakout Box, a device which connects into the EEC-IV harness and provides testing ports for the 60 wires in the harness. Direct testing of the harness connectors at the terminals or by backprobing is not recommended; damage to the wiring and terminals is almost certain to occur.

Other necessary tools include a quality tachometer with inductive (clip-on) pickup, a fuel pressure gauge with system adapters and a vacuum gauge with an auxiliary source of vacuum.

Reading Codes

Diagnosis of a driveability problem requires attention to detail and following the diagnostic procedures in the correct order. Resist the temptation to begin extensive testing before completing the preliminary diagnostic steps. The preliminary or visual inspection must be completed in detail before diagnosis begins. In many cases this will shorten diagnostic time and often cure the problem without electronic testing.

VISUAL INSPECTION

This is possibly the most critical step of diagnosis. A detailed examination of all connectors, wiring and vacuum hoses can often lead to a repair without further diagnosis. Performance of this step relies on the skill of the technician performing it; a careful inspector will check the undersides of hoses as well as the integrity of hard-to-reach hoses blocked by the air cleaner or other components. Wiring should be checked carefully for any sign of strain, burning, crimping or terminal pull-out from a connector.

Checking connectors at components or in harnesses is required; usually, pushing them together will reveal a loose fit. Pay particular attention to ground circuits, making sure they are not loose or corroded. Remember to inspect connectors and hose fittings at components not mounted on the engine, such as the evaporative canister or relays mounted on the fender aprons. Any component or wiring in the vicinity of a fluid leak or spillage should be given extra attention during inspection.

Additionally, inspect maintenance items such as belt condition and tension, battery charge and condition and the radiator cap carefully. Any of these very simple items may affect the system enough to set a fault.

ELECTRONIC TESTING

If a code was set before a problem self-corrected (such as a momentarily loose connector), the code will be erased if the problem does not reoccur within 80 warm-up cycles. Codes will be output and displayed as numbers on the hand-held scan tool, such as 23. If the codes are being read through the dashboard warning lamp, the codes will be displayed as groups of flashes separated by pauses. Code 23 would be shown as two flashes, a pause and three more flashes. A longer pause will occur between codes. If the codes are being read on an analog voltmeter, the needle sweeps indicate the code digits in the same manner as the lamp flashes.

In all cases, the codes 11 or 111 are used to indicate PASS during testing. Note that the PASS code may appear, followed by other stored codes. These are codes from the continuous memory and may indicate intermittent faults, even though the system does not presently contain the fault. The PASS designation only indicates the system passes all internal tests at the moment.

Key On Engine Off (KOEO) Test

▶ **See Figures 42 and 43**

1. Connect the scan tool to the self-test connectors. Make certain the test button is unlatched or up.
2. Start the engine and run it until normal operating temperature is reached.
3. Turn the engine **OFF** for 10 seconds.
4. Activate the test button on the STAR tester.
5. Turn the ignition switch **ON** but do not start the engine.
6. The KOEO codes will be transmitted. Six to nine seconds after the last KOEO code, a single separator pulse will be transmitted. Six to nine seconds after this pulse, the codes from the Continuous Memory will be transmitted.
7. Record all service codes displayed. Do not depress the throttle on gasoline engines during the test.

Key On Engine Running (KOER) Test

▶ **See Figures 42 and 44**

1. Make certain the self-test button is released or de-activated on the STAR tester.

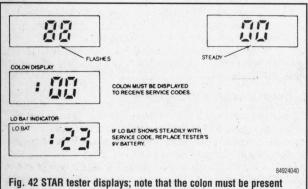

Fig. 42 STAR tester displays; note that the colon must be present before codes can be received

2. Start the engine and run it at 2000 rpm for two minutes. This action warms up the oxygen sensor.
3. Turn the ignition switch **OFF** for 10 seconds.
4. Activate or latch the self-test button on the scan tool.
5. Start the engine. The engine identification code will be transmitted. This is a single digit number representing ½ the number of cylinders in a gasoline engine. On the STAR tester, this number may appear with a zero, such as 20 = 2. For 7.3L diesel engines, the ID code is 5. The code is used to confirm that the correct processor is installed and that the self-test has begun.
6. If the vehicle is equipped with a Brake On/Off (BOO) switch, the brake pedal must be depressed and released after the ID code is transmitted.
7. If the vehicle is equipped with a Power Steering Pressure Switch (PSPS), the steering wheel must be turned at least ½ turn and released within 2 seconds after the engine ID code is transmitted.
8. Certain Ford vehicles will display a Dynamic Response code 6–20 seconds after the engine ID code. This will appear as one pulse on a meter or as a 10 on the STAR tester. When this code appears, briefly take the engine to wide open throttle. This allows the system to test the throttle position, MAF and MAP sensors.
9. All relevant codes will be displayed and should be recorded. Remember that the codes refer only to faults present during this test cycle. Codes stored in Continuous Memory are not displayed in this test mode.
10. Do not depress the throttle during testing unless a dynamic response code is displayed.

Reading Codes With Analog Voltmeter

▶ **See Figures 45 and 46**

In the absence of a scan tool, an analog voltmeter may be used to retrieve stored fault codes. Set the meter range to read DC 0–15 volts. Connect the + lead of the meter to the battery positive terminal and connect the − lead of the meter to the self-test output pin of the diagnostic connector.

Follow the directions given previously for performing the KOEO and KOER tests. To activate the tests, use a jumper wire to connect the signal return pin on the diagnostic connector to the self-test input connector. The self-test input line is the separate wire and connector with or near the diagnostic connector.

The codes will be transmitted as groups of needle sweeps. This method may be used to read either 2 or 3-digit codes. The Continuous Memory codes are separated from the KOEO codes by 6 seconds, a single sweep and another 6 second delay.

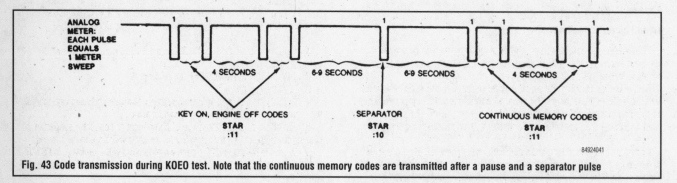

Fig. 43 Code transmission during KOEO test. Note that the continuous memory codes are transmitted after a pause and a separator pulse

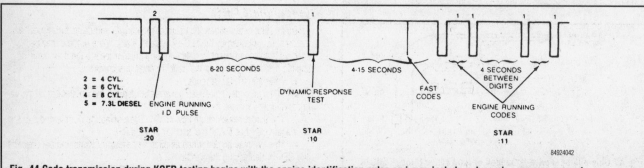

Fig. 44 Code transmission during KOER testing begins with the engine identification pulse and may include a dynamic response prompt

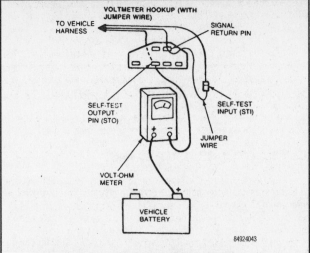

Fig. 45 Correct hookup to read codes with a voltmeter

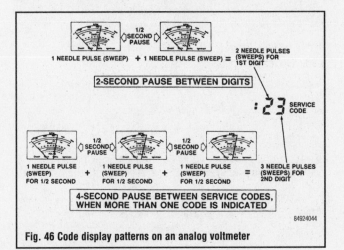

Fig. 46 Code display patterns on an analog voltmeter

Reading Codes With MIL

▶ See Figures 47 and 48

The Malfunction Indicator Lamp on the dashboard may also be used to retrieve the stored codes. This method displays only the stored codes and does not allow for any system investigation.

Follow the directions given previously for performing the KOEO and KOER tests. To activate the tests, use a jumper wire to connect the signal return pin on the diagnostic connector to the self-test input connector. The self-test input line is the separate wire and connector with or near the diagnostic connector.

Codes are transmitted by place value with a pause between the digits; Code 32 would be sent as 3 flashes, a pause and 2 flashes. A slightly longer pause divides codes from each other. Be ready to count and record codes; the only way to repeat a code is to re-cycle the system. This method may be used to read

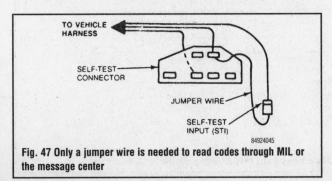

Fig. 47 Only a jumper wire is needed to read codes through MIL or the message center

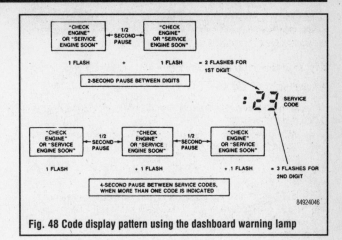

Fig. 48 Code display pattern using the dashboard warning lamp

either 2 or 3-digit codes. The Continuous Memory codes are separated from the KOEO codes by 6 seconds, a single flash and another 6 second delay.

To perform the KOER test:
1. Hold in all 3 buttons, start the engine and release the buttons.
2. Press the SELECT or GAUGE SELECT button 3 times. The message **dealer 4** should appear at the bottom of the message panel.
3. Initiate the test by using a jumper wire to connect the signal return pin on the diagnostic connector to the self-test input connector. The self-test input line is the separate wire and connector with or near the diagnostic connector.
4. The stored codes will be output to the vehicle display.
5. To exit the test, turn the ignition switch **OFF** and disconnect the jumper wire.

Other Test Modes

CONTINUOUS MONITOR OR WIGGLE TEST

Once entered, this mode allows the operator to attempt to recreate intermittent faults by wiggling or tapping components, wiring or connectors. The test may be performed during either KOEO or KOER procedures. The test requires the use of either an analog voltmeter or a hand-held scan tool.

To enter the continuous monitor mode during KOEO testing, turn the ignition switch **ON**. Activate the test, wait 10 seconds, then deactivate and reactivate the test; the system will enter the continuous monitor mode. Tap, move or wiggle the harness, component or connector suspected of causing the problem; if a fault is detected, the code will store in the memory. When the fault occurs, the dash warning lamp will illuminate, the STAR tester will light a red indicator (and possibly beep) and the analog meter needle will sweep once.

To enter this mode in the KOER test:
1. Start the engine and run it at 2000 rpm for two minutes. This action warms up the oxygen sensor.
2. Turn the ignition switch **OFF** for 10 seconds.
3. Start the engine.
4. Activate the test, wait 10 seconds, then deactivate and reactivate the test; the system will enter the continuous monitor mode.
5. Tap, move or wiggle the harness, component or connector suspected of causing the problem; if a fault is detected, the code will store in the memory.
6. When the fault occurs, the dash warning lamp will illuminate, the STAR tester will light a red indicator (and possibly beep) and the analog meter needle will sweep once.

OUTPUT STATE CHECK

This testing mode allows the operator to energize and de-energize most of the outputs controlled by the EEC-IV system. Many of the outputs may be checked at the component by listening for a click or feeling the item move or engage by a hand placed on the case. To enter this check:
1. Enter the KOEO test mode.
2. When all codes have been transmitted, depress the accelerator all the way to the floor and release it.
3. The output actuators are now all ON. Depressing the throttle pedal to the floor again switches the all the actuator outputs OFF.
4. This test may be performed as often as necessary, switching between ON and OFF by depressing the throttle.
5. Exit the test by turning the ignition switch **OFF**, disconnecting the jumper at the diagnostic connector or releasing the test button on the scan tool.

Clearing Codes

CONTINUOUS MEMORY CODES

These codes are retained in memory for 80 warm-up cycles. To clear the codes for the purposes of testing or confirming repair, perform the KOEO test. When the fault codes begin to be displayed, de-activate the test by either disconnecting the jumper wire (meter, MIL or message center) or releasing the test button on the hand scanner. Stopping the test during code transmission will erase the Continuous Memory. Do not disconnect the negative battery cable to clear these codes; the Keep Alive memory will be cleared and a new code, 19, will be stored for loss of PCM power.

KEEP ALIVE MEMORY

The Keep Alive Memory (KAM) contains the adaptive factors used by the processor to compensate for component tolerances and wear. It should not be routinely cleared during diagnosis. If an emissions related part is replaced during repair, the KAM must be cleared. Failure to clear the KAM may cause severe

OBD-I DIAGNOSTIC TROUBLE CODE (DTC) APPLICATIONS

DTC	Applicable System or Component
2-Digit Trouble Codes	
11	System pass
12	RPM unable to achieve upper test limit
13	RPM unable to achieve lower test limit
14	PIP circuit failure
15	PCM Keep Alive Memory (KAM) and/or Read Only Memory (ROM) test failed
16	Idle too low to perform EGO test
18	SPOUT circuit open or grounded, spark angle word failure, or IDA circuit failure
19	PCM internal voltage failure
21	ECT out of self-test range
23	TP sensor out of self-test range
24	IAT sensor out of self-test range
25	Knock not sensed during dynamic test
26	MAF out of self-test range
29	Insufficient input from VSS
31	PFE, EVP or EVR circuit below minimum voltage
32	EVP voltage below closed limit
33	EGR valve opening not detected
34	EVP voltage above closed limit
35	PFE or EVP circuit above maximum voltage
41	HEGO sensor circuit indicates system lean, or no HEGO switching detected (right)
42	HEGO sensor circuit indicates system rich (right)
44	Thermactor air system inoperative (right)
45	Thermactor air upstream during self-test
46	Thermactor air not bypassed during self-test
51	ECT or IAT reads -40°F, or circuit open
53	TP sensor circuit above maximum voltage
54	IAT sensor circuit open
56	MAF circuit above maximum voltage
61	ECT reads 254°F, or circuit is grounded
63	TP sensor circuit below minimum voltage
64	IAT sensor input below test minimum, or grounded
66	MAF sensor input below test minimum, or grounded
67	Neutral/Drive switch open, or A/C is on
74	Brake On/Off (BOO) switch failure, or not actuated
75	BOO switch circuit closed, or PCM input open
77	No Wide Open Throttle (WOT) seen in self-test, or operator error
79	A/C or defroster on during the self-test
81	Air management 2 circuit failure
84	EGR vacuum solenoid circuit failure
85	Canister purge solenoid circuit failure
87	Fuel pump primary circuit failure
91	HEGO sensor circuit indicates system lean, or no HEGO switching detected (left)
92	HEGO sensor circuit indicates system rich (left)
94	Thermactor air system inoperative (left)
95	Fuel pump secondary circuit failure, PCM to ground
96	Fuel pump secondary circuit failure, battery to PCM
98	Hard fault present

OBD-I DIAGNOSTIC TROUBLE CODE (DTC) APPLICATIONS

DTC	Applicable System or Component
3-Digit Trouble Codes	
111	System pass
112	IAT sensor circuit grounded or reads 254°F
113	IAT sensor circuit open, or reads -40°F
114	IAT outside test limits during KOEO test
116	ECT outside test limits during KOEO test
117	ECT sensor circuit grounded
118	ECT sensor circuit above maximum voltage, or reads -40°F
121	Closed throttle voltage higher or lower than expected
122	TP sensor circuit below minimum voltage
123	TP sensor circuit above maximum voltage
124	TP sensor voltage higher than expected, but with specified range
125	TP sensor voltage lower than expected, but with specified range
129	Insufficient MAF sensor change during Dynamic Response test
136	HEGO shows system always lean (left)
137	HEGO shows system always rich (left)
139	No HEGO switching (left)
144	No HEGO switching (right)
157	MAF sensor circuit below minimum voltage
158	MAF sensor circuit above maximum voltage
159	MAF sensor higher or lower than expected during KOEO test
167	Insufficient TP sensor change during Dynamic Response test
172	No HEGO switching detected, indicates lean (right)
173	HEGO shows system always rich (rear) or no HEGO switching detected, indicates rich
174	HEGO switching time is slow (right)
175	No HEGO switching, system at adaptive limit (left)
177	HEGO shows system always lean (left)
178	HEGO switching time is slow (left)
179	System at lean adaptive limit at part throttle, system rich (right)
181	System at rich adaptive limit at part throttle, system rich (right)
182	System at lean adaptive limit at idle, system rich (right)
183	System at rich adaptive limit at idle, system rich (right)
184	MAF higher than expected
185	MAF lower than expected
186	Injector pulse width higher than expected
187	Injector pulse width lower than expected
188	System at lean adaptive limit at part throttle, system rich (left)
189	System at rich adaptive limit at part throttle, system rich (left)
191	System at lean adaptive limit at idle, system rich (left)
192	System at rich adaptive limit at idle, system rich (left)
211	PIP circuit fault
212	Loss of IDM input to PCM or SPOUT circuit grounded
213	SPOUT circuit open
311	Thermactor air system inoperative (right)
313	Thermactor air not bypassed during self-test
314	Thermactor air system inoperative (left)
327	EVP or DPFE circuit below minimum voltage
328	EGR closed voltage lower than expected

89684C02

OBD-I DIAGNOSTIC TROUBLE CODE (DTC) APPLICATIONS

DTC	Applicable System or Component
3-Digit Trouble Codes (continued)	
332	Insufficient EGR flow detected
334	EGR closed voltage higher than expected
337	EVP or DPFE circuit above maximum voltage
452	Insufficient input from VSS
511	EEC processor ROM test failed
512	Keep Alive Memory test failed
513	Failure in EEC processor internal voltage
522	Vehicle not in Park or Neutral during KOEO test
539	A/C or defroster on during KOEO test
542	Fuel pump secondary circuit failure, PCM to ground
543	Fuel pump secondary circuit failure, battery to PCM
552	Air management 1 circuit failed
556	Fuel pump primary circuit failure
558	EGR vacuum regulator circuit failure
565	Canister purge circuit failure
998	Hard fault present

89684C03

driveability problems since the correction factor for the old component will be applied to the new component.

To clear the Keep Alive Memory, disconnect the negative battery cable for at least 5 minutes. After the memory is cleared and the battery reconnected, the vehicle must be driven at least 10 miles (16 km) so that the processor may relearn the needed correction factors. The distance to be driven depends on the engine and vehicle, but all drives should include steady-throttle cruise on open roads. Certain driveability problems may be noted during the drive because the adaptive factors are not yet functioning.

TROUBLE CODES—EEC-V

General Information

ON BOARD DIAGNOSTICS (OBD) II

➡**The 1986–95 Ford vehicles covered by this manual employ the fourth generation Electronic Engine Control system, commonly designated EEC-IV, to manage fuel, ignition and emissions on vehicle engines. All 1996–97 vehicles covered by this manual will be equipped with EEC-V.**

Ford developed the EEC-V system in response to the increased diagnostic requirements for the California Air Resource Board. The regulations developed by the Environmental Protection Agency are designated as the OBD II system.

The On Board Diagnostics (OBD) II system is similar to the OBD I system, but not identical. The OBD I requires that the Malfunction Indicator Lamp (MIL) illuminates to inform the driver when an emissions component or monitored system fails. The MIL also lights up to indicate when the Powertrain Control Module (PCM) is operating in Hardware Limited Operation Strategy (HLOS).

The EEC-V is an evolutionary development from the EEC-IV. None of the components involved are actually new, only the applications have changed.

The only component that has been added is another heated Oxygen sensor (HO$_2$S located behind the catalyst). These downstream sensors are called the Catalyst Efficiency Monitor Sensors (CEMS). This means that there are four sensors on models so equipped, instead of two.

POWERTRAIN CONTROL MODULE (PCM)

➡**PCM's for EEC-IV systems use a 60-pin connector. For the EEC-V PCM, a 104-pin connector is used.**

As with the EEC-IV system, the PCM is given responsibility for the operation of the emission control devices, cooling fans, ignition and advance and in some cases, automatic transmission functions. Because the EEC system oversees both the ignition timing and the fuel injector operation, a precise air/fuel ratio will be maintained under all operating conditions. The PCM is a microprocessor or small computer which receives electrical inputs from several sensors, switches and relays on and around the engine.

Based on combinations of these inputs, the PCM controls outputs to various devices concerned with engine operation and emissions. The engine control assembly relies on the signals to form a correct picture of current vehicle operation. If any of the input signals is incorrect, the PCM reacts to what ever picture is painted for it. For example, if the coolant temperature sensor is inaccurate and reads too low, the PCM may see a picture of the engine never warming up. Consequently, the engine settings will be maintained as if the engine were cold. Because so many inputs can affect one output, correct diagnostic procedures are essential on these systems.

One part of the PCM is devoted to monitoring both input and output functions within the system. This ability forms the core of the self-diagnostic system. If a problem is detected within a circuit, the controller will recognize the fault, assign it an identification code, and store the code in a memory section. The fault codes may be retrieved during diagnosis.

While the EEC system is capable of recognizing many internal faults, certain faults will not be recognized. Because the computer system sees only electrical signals, it cannot sense or react to mechanical or vacuum faults affecting engine operation. Some of these faults may affect another component which will set a code. For example, the PCM monitors the output signal to the fuel injectors, but cannot detect a partially clogged injector. As long as the output driver responds correctly, the computer will read the system as functioning correctly. However, the improper flow of fuel may result in a lean mixture. This would, in turn, be detected by the oxygen sensor and noticed as a constantly lean signal by the PCM. Once the signal falls outside the pre-programmed limits, the engine control assembly would notice the fault and set an identification code.

Additionally, the EEC system employs adaptive fuel logic. This process is used to compensate for normal wear and variability within the fuel system. Once the engine enters steady-state operation, the engine control assembly watches the oxygen sensor signal for a bias or tendency to run slightly rich or lean. If such a bias is detected, the adaptive logic corrects the fuel delivery to bring the air/fuel mixture towards a centered or 14.7:1 ratio. This compensating shift is stored in a non-volatile memory which is retained by battery power even with the ignition switched off. The correction factor is then available the next time the vehicle is operated.

➡**If the battery cable(s) is disconnected for longer than 5 minutes, the adaptive fuel factor will be lost. After repair it will be necessary to drive the car at least 10 miles (16 km) to allow the processor to relearn the correct factors. The driving period should include steady-throttle open road driving if possible. During the drive, the vehicle may exhibit drive-ability symptoms not noticed before. These symptoms should clear as the PCM computes the correction factor.**

Failure Mode Effects Management (FMEM)

The engine controller assembly contains back-up programs which allow the engine to operate if a sensor signal is lost. If a sensor input is seen to be out of range—either high or low—the FMEM program is used. The processor substitutes a fixed value for the missing sensor signal. The engine will continue to operate, although performance and driveability may be noticeably reduced. This function of the controller is sometimes referred to as the limp-in or fail-safe mode. If the missing sensor signal is restored, the FMEM system immediately returns the system to normal operation. The dashboard warning lamp will be lit when FMEM is in effect.

Hardware Limited Operation Strategy (HLOS)

This mode is only used if the fault is too extreme for the FMEM circuit to handle. In this mode, the processor has ceased all computation and control; the entire system is run on fixed values. The vehicle may be operated but performance and driveability will be greatly reduced. The fixed or default settings provide minimal calibration, allowing the vehicle to be carefully driven in for service. The dashboard warning lamp will be lit when HLOS is engaged. Codes cannot be read while the system is operating in this mode.

Data Link Connector (DLC)

The DLC for the EEC-V system is located in the passenger's compartment of the vehicle, attached to the instrument panel, and is accessible from the driver's seat.

The DLC is rectangular in design and capable of allowing access to 16 terminals. The connector has keying features that allow easy connection. The test equipment and the DLC have a latching feature to ensure a good mated connection.

Reading Codes

The EEC-V (OBD II) codes differ from the 2 or 3-digit codes of the (former) EEC-IV system in that they are accompanied by a letter prefix before a 4-digit number. Example: P0102 would indicate a Mass Air Flow (MAF) Sensor circuit (low input).

➡**The number of digits used in the OBD II codes, along with the letter prefix makes flash diagnosis all but impossible, so no provision has been made in OBD II systems to read codes in any other way than with a scan tool.**

When diagnosing the OBD II EEC-V system, the New Generation Star (NGS) tester or generic scan tool may be used to retrieve codes, view the system operating specifications or test the system components. There are also several other pieces of equipment which may be used for diagnosis purposes.

- •. Vacuum pressure gauge and pump
- Tach/Dwell Volt/Ohmmeter tester
- 104-pin Breakout Box
- Multimeter with a 10 megaohm impedance
- Distributorless ignition system tester
- Constant control relay modular tester
- Tachometer adapter
- Fuel pressure gauge
- Timing light
- Test light (non-powered)

Clearing Codes

PCM RESET

The PCM reset mode allows the scan tool to clear any emission related diagnostic information from the PCM. When resetting the PCM, a DTC P1000 will be stored until all OBD II system monitors or components have been tested to satisfy a trip without any other faults occurring.

The following items occur when the PCM Reset is performed:
- The DTC is cleared
- The freeze frame data is cleared
- The oxygen sensor test data is cleared
- The status of the OBD II system monitors is reset
- A DTC P1000 code is set

PCM fault codes may be cleared by using the scan tool or disconnecting the negative battery cable for a minimum of 15 seconds.

KEEP ALIVE MEMORY (KAM) RESET

The Keep Alive Memory (KAM) contains the adaptive factors used by the processor to compensate for component tolerances and wear. It should not be routinely cleared during diagnosis. If and emissions related part is replaced during repair, the KAM must be cleared. Failure to clear the KAM may cause severe driveability problems, since the correction factor for the old component will be applied to the new component.

To clear the KAM disconnect the negative battery cable for at least 5 minuets. After the memory is cleared and the battery is reconnected, the vehicle must be driven a couple of miles so that the PCM may relearn the needed correction factors. The distance to be driven depends on the engine and vehicle, but all drives should include steady throttle cruise on the open roads. Certain driveability problems may be noted during the drive because the adaptive factors are not yet functioning.

Test Equipment

The Ford EEC-V system will requires the use of a 104-pin Brake Out Box (BOB) to be used for diagnosis. The 104-pin BOB is used to test circuits exactly as the 60-pin BOB is used on the EEC-IV. Another piece of test equipment is the STAR (NSG) tester. This tester may be used on OBD I also.

TESTING

These test procedures listed below are for a generic scan tool in the enhanced diagnostic test mode. Only the manufacturer has the STAR tool. Your local jobber should have a generic tool available.

When performing these tests, always do a visual check and preparation of the vehicle first.
- Inspect the air cleaner and inlet ducting.
- Check all of the engine hoses for damages, leaks, cracks, proper routing etc.
- Check the EEC system wiring harness for good connections, bent or broken pins, corrosion, loose wiring etc.
- Check the engine coolant for proper levels and mixture.
- Check the PCM, sensors and actuators for any damages.
- Check the transmission fluid level and quality.
- Make any necessary repairs before proceeding with testing.
- Check the vehicle for safety such as the parking brake must be on. Wheels blocked, etc.

- Turn off all lights, radios, blower switches etc.
- Bring the engine up to operating temperature before running a quick test.

Key On Engine Off (KOEO)

A series of characters must be entered into the scan tool to perform this test. The codes are listed below and must be entered as such to perform the test correctly. See the manufacture of the scan tool for any additional instructions.
1. Perform the necessary vehicle preparation and visual inspection.
2. Connect the scan tool to the DLC.
3. Turn the ignition to the **ON** position but DO NOT start the engine.
4. Verify that the scan tool is connected and communicating correctly by entering the OBD II system readiness test. All scan tools are required to automatically enter this test once communication is established between the tool and the PCM.
5. Enter the following strings of information to initiate the KOEO self-test.
6. Enter the four strings separately and in the order shown. All of the string ID numbers must match in the order shown:
   a. 04, 31, 21, C4 103381, 9E 00 445443287329 20 8042 20 8062 20 8082 A851 FF, 2E
   b. 03, 32, 22FF, C4 10220202, 9E 00 434E54 20 8061 A961 00 04, EA
   c. 02, 32, 21, C4 10328100, 9E 00 574149 54 20 8081 A181 61 03, 5E
   d. 01, 32, 21, C4 103181, 9E 00 53544155254 20 8081 A 181 00 02, 54
7. Turn the ignition **OFF** to end the test cycle.

Key On Engine Running (KOER)

A series of characters must be entered into the scan tool to perform this test. The codes are listed below and must be entered as such to perform the test correctly. See the manufacture of the scan tool for any additional instructions.
1. Perform the necessary vehicle preparation and visual inspection.
2. Connect the scan tool to the DLC.
3. Turn the ignition to the **ON** position and start the engine.
4. Verify that the scan tool is connected and communicating correctly by entering the OBD II system readiness test. All scan tools are required to automatically enter this test once communication is established between the tool and the PCM.
5. Enter the following strings of information to initiate the KOEO self-test.

➡**After the test begins, cycle BOO, 4X4 and Transmission Control (TCS) switches, if equipped.**

6. Enter the four strings separately and in the order shown. All of the string ID numbers must match in the order shown:
   a. 08, 31, 21, C4103382, 9E 00 445443287329 20 8042 20 8062 20 8082 A851 FF, 33
   b. 07, 32, 22FF, C410220202, 9E 00 434E54 20 8061 A961 00 08, F2
   c. 06, 32, 21, C4 10328200, 9E 00 574149 54 20 8081 A181 61 07, 67
   d. 05, 32, 21, C4 103182, 9E 00 5354415254 20 8081 A181 00 06, 5D
7. Turn the ignition **OFF** to end the test cycle.

Continuous Memory Self-Test

1. Perform the necessary vehicle preparation and visual inspection.
2. Connect the scan tool to the DLC.
3. Turn the key to the **ON** position or start the vehicle.
4. See the manufacture's instructions to retrieve the DTC's.
5. When finished, turn the ignition **OFF**.
6. Disconnect the scan tool from the vehicle.

Accessing All Continuous Memory DTC's

1. Perform the necessary vehicle preparation and visual inspection.
2. Connect the scan tool to the DLC.
3. Turn the key to the **ON** position or start the vehicle. This may depend on the pinpoint manual instructions for the type of data requested.
4. Verify the tool is connected properly and communicating.
5. Enter the following string of characters to retrieve all the continuous DTC's (DTC CNT):
   - 09, 2C, 21, C4 10 13,, 9E 00 44 54 43 20 43 4E 54 20 8B 44, B2
6. The scan tool will display all the continuous DTC's.

4-22 DRIVEABILITY AND EMISSION CONTROLS

OBD-II DIAGNOSTIC TROUBLE CODE (DTC) APPLICATIONS

DTC	Applicable System or Component
	Constant Memory Trouble Codes
P0102	MAF sensor reference signal voltage too low
P0103	MAF sensor reference signal too high
P0112	IAT or ECT intermittent fault
P0113	IAT or ECT intermittent fault
P0117	IAT or ECT intermittent fault
P0118	IAT or ECT intermittent fault
P0121	TP sensor fault
P0122	TP sensor reference signal voltage too low
P0123	TP sensor reference signal voltage too high
P0125	ECT sensor fault
P0131	Heated Oxygen Sensor (HO2S) produced negative reference signal voltage
P0133	Fuel control system fault
P0135	HO2S circuit shorted to ground, open or shorted to VPWR circuit
P0136	HO2S fault
P0141	HO2S circuit shorted to ground, open or shorted to VPWR circuit
P0151	Heated Oxygen Sensor (HO2S) produced negative reference signal voltage
P0153	Fuel control system fault
P0155	HO2S circuit shorted to ground, open or shorted to VPWR circuit
P0156	HO2S fault
P0161	HO2S circuit shorted to ground, open or shorted to VPWR circuit
P0171	Air/fuel ratio is too lean or rich for PCM to correct
P0172	Air/fuel ratio is too lean or rich for PCM to correct
P0174	Air/fuel ratio is too lean or rich for PCM to correct
P0175	Air/fuel ratio is too lean or rich for PCM to correct
P0222	Traction Control (TC) system fault
P0223	TC system TP-B circuit voltage fault
P0230	Fuel pump primary circuit fault
P0231	Fuel pump relay and system fault
P0232	Fuel pump relay and system fault
P0300	Ignition engine speed input circuit fault
P0301	Misfire detection monitor and/or circuit fault
P0302	Misfire detection monitor and/or circuit fault
P0303	Misfire detection monitor and/or circuit fault
P0304	Misfire detection monitor and/or circuit fault
P0305	Misfire detection monitor and/or circuit fault
P0306	Misfire detection monitor and/or circuit fault
P0307	Misfire detection monitor and/or circuit fault
P0308	Misfire detection monitor and/or circuit fault
P0320	Ignition engine speed input circuit fault
P0325	Knock Sensor (KS) and/or circuit fault
P0326	Knock Sensor (KS) and/or circuit fault
P0330	Knock Sensor (KS) and/or circuit fault
P0331	Knock Sensor (KS) and/or circuit fault
P0340	Camshaft Position (CMP) sensor and/or circuit fault
P0350	Ignition coil primary circuit fault
P0351	Ignition coil primary circuit fault
P0352	Ignition coil primary circuit fault
P0353	Ignition coil primary circuit fault

89684C04

OBD-II DIAGNOSTIC TROUBLE CODE (DTC) APPLICATIONS

DTC	Applicable System or Component
	Constant Memory Trouble Codes (continued)
P0354	Ignition coil primary circuit fault
P0401	Insufficient EGR flow detected
P0402	EGR flow at idle fault
P0411	Electric air pump hose fault
P0412	Secondary Air Injection (AIR) system fault
P0413	AIR injection VPWR circuit voltage fault
P0414	AIR injection VPWR circuit voltage fault
P0416	AIR injection VPWR circuit voltage fault
P0417	AIR injection VPWR circuit voltage fault
P0420	Catalyst efficiency monitor and/or exhaust system fault
P0430	Catalyst efficiency monitor and/or exhaust system fault
P0442	Evaporative Emission (EVAP) system leak detected
P0443	Intermittent EVAP canister purge valve fault
P0446	EVAP system Fuel Tank Pressure (FTP) sensor fault
P0452	FTP sensor circuit input signal too low
P0453	FTP sensor circuit input signal too high
P0455	Evaporative Emission (EVAP) system leak detected
P0460	Fuel level input circuit fault
P0500	Vehicle Speed Sensor (VSS) and/or circuit fault
P0501	Vehicle Speed Sensor (VSS) and/or circuit fault
P0503	Intermittent VSS and/or circuit fault
P0552	Power Steering Pressure (PSP) sensor and/or circuit fault
P0553	Power Steering Pressure (PSP) sensor and/or circuit fault
P0703	BOO switch input signal fault
P0704	CPP or PNP switch fault, or CPP or PNP switch voltage is too high or open when it should be low or closed
P0707	Manual transmission fault
P0708	Manual transmission fault
P0712	Manual transmission fault
P0713	Manual transmission fault
P0715	Manual transmission fault
P0720	Manual transmission fault
P0721	Manual transmission fault
P0731	Manual transmission fault
P0732	Manual transmission fault
P0733	Manual transmission fault
P0734	Manual transmission fault
P0735	Manual transmission fault
P0736	Manual transmission fault
P0741	Manual transmission fault
P0743	Manual transmission fault
P0746	Manual transmission fault
P0750	Manual transmission fault
P0751	Manual transmission fault
P0755	Manual transmission fault
P0756	Manual transmission fault
P0760	Manual transmission fault
P0761	Manual transmission fault
P0765	Manual transmission fault

89684C05

OBD-II DIAGNOSTIC TROUBLE CODE (DTC) APPLICATIONS

DTC	Applicable System or Component
	Constant Memory Trouble Codes (continued)
P0781	Manual transmission fault
P0782	Manual transmission fault
P0783	Manual transmission fault
P0784	Manual transmission fault
P1000	All OBD-II monitors not yet successfully tested
P1100	MAF sensor reference signal voltage out of specifications
P1112	IAT or ECT intermittent fault
P1117	IAT or ECT intermittent fault
P1120	TP sensor reference voltage out of specifications
P1121	TP sensor reference signal inconsistent with MAF sensor reference signal
P1125	TP sensor reference voltage out of specifications
P1130	HO2S fault
P1131	HO2S fault
P1132	HO2S fault
P1150	HO2S fault
P1151	HO2S fault
P1152	HO2S fault
P1220	TC system series throttle system fault
P1224	Series throttle assembly fault
P1232	Low speed fuel pump primary circuit fault
P1233	Fuel pump driver module and/or system circuit fault
P1234	Fuel pump driver module and/or system circuit fault
P1235	Fuel pump circuit, fuel pump driver module or PCM fault
P1236	Fuel pump circuit, fuel pump driver module or PCM fault
P1237	Fuel pump driver module circuit fault
P1238	Fuel pump driver module circuit fault
P1260	Anti-theft system detected a break-in
P1270	Engine and/or vehicle speed exceeded calibrated limits during vehicle operation
P1285	Engine overheat condition was sensed by PCM
P1289	Intermittent CHT sensor and/or circuit fault
P1290	Intermittent CHT sensor and/or circuit fault
P1299	Engine overheat condition was sensed by PCM
P1309	CMP sensor output signal fault
P1400	Exhaust Gas Recirculation (EGR) system fault
P1401	EVP sensor signal voltage fault
P1405	Upstream pressure hose connection fault
P1406	Downstream pressure hose connection fault
P1409	EGR vacuum regulator solenoid fault
P1411	AIR injection is not being diverted when requested
P1413	AIR injection solid state relay voltage fault
P1414	AIR injection EAIR monitor circuit fault
P1442	Evaporative Emission (EVAP) system leak detected
P1443	Evaporative purge flow sensor fault
P1444	PF circuit input signal too low
P1445	PF circuit input signal too high
P1450	EVAP system unable to bleed fuel tank vacuum fault
P1451	EVAP system Canister Vent (CV) solenoid fault
P1452	EVAP system unable to bleed fuel tank vacuum fault

OBD-II DIAGNOSTIC TROUBLE CODE (DTC) APPLICATIONS

DTC	Applicable System or Component
	Constant Memory Trouble Codes (continued)
P1455	EVAP system fault
P1460	Wide Open Throttle A/C (WAC) circuit fault occurred during vehicle operation
P1461	Air Conditioning Pressure (ACP) sensor and/or circuit fault
P1462	ACP sensor reference signal too low
P1463	ACP sensor did not detect a pressure change in A/C system when activated
P1469	Frequent A/C compressor clutch cycling detected
P1474	Fan control circuit failure detected during vehicle operation
P1479	Fan control circuit failure detected during vehicle operation
P1483	Power-to-cooling fan circuit exceeded normal current draw when fan was activated
P1484	Variable load control module (VLCM) and/or circuit fault
P1500	Intermittent VSS reference signal fault
P1504	Idle Air Control (IAC) valve and/or circuit fault
P1505	IAC valve and/or circuit fault
P1506	IAC valve overspeed fault
P1507	Idle Air Control (IAC) valve and/or circuit fault
P1512	Intake Manifold Runner Control (IMRC) fault
P1513	Intake Manifold Runner Control (IMRC) fault
P1516	Intake Manifold Runner Control (IMRC) fault
P1517	Intake Manifold Runner Control (IMRC) fault
P1518	Intake Manifold Runner Control (IMRC) fault
P1519	Intake Manifold Runner Control (IMRC) fault
P1520	Intake Manifold Runner Control (IMRC) fault
P1530	Power-to-A/C clutch circuit open or short to power
P1537	Intake Manifold Runner Control (IMRC) fault
P1538	Intake Manifold Runner Control (IMRC) fault
P1539	Power-to-A/C clutch circuit exceeded normal current draw when A/C was activated
P1549	IMT valve and/or circuit fault
P1550	Power Steering Pressure (PSP) sensor and/or circuit fault
P1625	Open battery supply voltage to VLCM fan or A/C circuit detected
P1626	Open battery supply voltage to VLCM fan or A/C circuit detected
P1651	Power Steering Pressure (PSP) switch and/or circuit fault
P1701	Manual transmission fault
P1714	Manual transmission fault
P1715	Manual transmission fault
P1716	Manual transmission fault
P1717	Manual transmission fault
P1719	Manual transmission fault
P1728	Manual transmission fault
P1741	Manual transmission fault
P1742	Manual transmission fault
P1743	Manual transmission fault
P1744	Manual transmission fault
P1746	Manual transmission fault
P1747	Manual transmission fault
P1749	Manual transmission fault
P1751	Manual transmission fault
P1754	Manual transmission fault
P1756	Manual transmission fault

89684C06

89684C07

OBD-II DIAGNOSTIC TROUBLE CODE (DTC) APPLICATIONS

DTC	Applicable System or Component
Constant Memory Trouble Codes (continued)	
P1760	Manual transmission fault
P1761	Manual transmission fault
P1762	Manual transmission fault
P1767	Manual transmission fault
P1783	Manual transmission fault
P1784	Manual transmission fault
P1785	Manual transmission fault
P1786	Manual transmission fault
P1787	Manual transmission fault
P1788	Manual transmission fault
P1789	Manual transmission fault
U1020	Manual transmission fault
U1021	PCM-to-VLCM two-way communication fault
U1039	Manual transmission fault
U1051	Manual transmission fault
U1073	PCM-to-VLCM two-way communication fault
U1135	Manual transmission fault
U1256	PCM-to-VLCM two-way communication fault
U1451	Manual transmission fault
Key On, Engine Off (KOEO) Trouble Codes	
135P0	HO2S circuit shorted to ground, open or shorted to VPWR circuit
P0103	MAF sensor reference signal too high
P0112	IAT or ECT sensor reference signal voltage too low
P0113	IAT or ECT sensor reference signal voltage too high
P0117	Cylinder Head Temperature (CHT) sensor and/or circuit fault
P0118	IAT or ECT sensor reference signal voltage too high
P0122	TP sensor reference signal voltage too low
P0123	TP sensor reference signal voltage too high
P0141	HO2S circuit shorted to ground, open or shorted to VPWR circuit
P0155	HO2S circuit shorted to ground, open or shorted to VPWR circuit
P0161	HO2S circuit shorted to ground, open or shorted to VPWR circuit
P0222	Traction Control (TC) system fault
P0223	TC system TP-B circuit voltage fault
P0230	Fuel pump relay fault
P0231	Fuel pump secondary circuit fault
P0232	Fuel pump FPM circuit voltage too high
P0411	Electric air pump hose fault
P0412	Secondary Air Injection (AIR) system fault
P0413	AIR injection VPWR circuit voltage fault
P0414	AIR injection VPWR circuit voltage fault
P0416	AIR injection VPWR circuit voltage fault
P0417	AIR injection VPWR circuit voltage fault
P0443	Evaporative Emission (EVAP) system fault
P0452	FTP sensor circuit input signal too low
P0453	FTP sensor circuit input signal too high
P0460	Fuel level input circuit fault
P0603	Keep Alive Power (KAPWR) circuit and/or PCM fault
P0605	Defective PCM; replace the PCM

OBD-II DIAGNOSTIC TROUBLE CODE (DTC) APPLICATIONS

DTC	Applicable System or Component
Key On, Engine Off (KOEO) Trouble Codes (continued)	
P0704	CPP or PNP switch fault, or CPP or PNP switch voltage is too high or open when it should be low or closed
P0705	Manual transmission fault
P0712	Manual transmission fault
P0713	Manual transmission fault
P0743	Manual transmission fault
P0750	Manual transmission fault
P0755	Manual transmission fault
P0760	Manual transmission fault
P1000	DTC 1000 should be ignored; continue with other codes
P1101	Manifold Air Flow (MAF) sensor output voltage fault
P1116	Intake Air Temperature (IAT) or Engine Coolant Temperature (ECT) sensor fault
P1120	TP sensor reference voltage out of specifications
P1124	Throttle Position (TP) reference voltage out of specifications
P1151	HO2S fault
P1220	TC system series throttle system fault
P1224	Series throttle assembly fault
P1232	Low speed fuel pump primary circuit fault
P1233	Fuel pump driver module and/or system circuit fault
P1234	Fuel pump driver module and/or system circuit fault
P1235	Fuel pump circuit, fuel pump driver module or PCM fault
P1236	Fuel pump circuit, fuel pump driver module or PCM fault
P1237	Fuel pump driver module circuit fault
P1238	Fuel pump driver module circuit fault
P1288	Cylinder Head Temperature (CHT) sensor fault
P1289	CHT sensor reference signal too high
P1290	CHT sensor reference signal too low
P1390	Octane Adjust (OCT ADJ) system fault
P1400	Exhaust Gas Recirculation (EGR) system fault
P1401	EVP sensor signal voltage fault
P1409	EGR vacuum regulator solenoid fault
P1411	AIR injection is not being diverted when requested
P1413	AIR injection solid state relay voltage fault
P1414	AIR injection EAIR monitor circuit fault
P1451	EVAP system Canister Vent (CV) solenoid fault
P1460	Wide Open Throttle A/C (WAC) circuit fault
P1461	Air Conditioning Pressure (ACP) sensor and/or circuit fault
P1462	ACP sensor reference signal too low
P1464	ACCS input signal too high
P1473	Power-to-cooling fan circuit open or short to power
P1474	Fan control relay and/or circuit fault
P1479	Fan control relay and/or circuit fault
P1483	Power-to-cooling fan circuit exceeded normal current draw when fan was activated
P1484	Variable load control module (VLCM) and/or circuit fault
P1504	Idle Air Control (IAC) valve and/or circuit fault
P1505	IAC valve and/or circuit fault
P1516	Intake Manifold Runner Control (IMRC) fault
P1517	Intake Manifold Runner Control (IMRC) fault
P1518	Intake Manifold Runner Control (IMRC) fault

89684C08

89684C09

OBD-II DIAGNOSTIC TROUBLE CODE (DTC) APPLICATIONS

DTC	Applicable System or Component
Key On, Engine Off (KOEO) Trouble Codes (continued)	
P1519	Intake Manifold Runner Control (IMRC) fault
P1520	Intake Manifold Runner Control (IMRC) fault
P1530	Power-to-A/C clutch circuit open or short to power
P1537	Intake Manifold Runner Control (IMRC) fault
P1538	Intake Manifold Runner Control (IMRC) fault
P1539	Power-to-A/C clutch circuit exceeded normal current draw when A/C was activated
P1549	IMT valve and/or circuit fault
P1625	Battery voltage to VLCM fan or A/C circuit not detected
P1626	Battery voltage to VLCM fan or A/C circuit not detected
P1650	Power Steering Pressure (PSP) switch and/or circuit fault
P1703	Signal from Brake On/Off (BOO) switch detected when brake pedal is not applied
P1705	Manual transmission fault
P1709	Park/Neutral Position (PNP)/Clutch Pedal Position (CPP) switches and/or circuit fault
P1711	Manual transmission fault
P1746	Manual transmission fault
P1747	Manual transmission fault
P1754	Manual transmission fault
P1760	Manual transmission fault
P1767	Manual transmission fault
P1788	Manual transmission fault
P1789	Manual transmission fault
U1021	PCM-to-VLCM two-way communication fault
U1073	PCM-to-VLCM two-way communication fault
U1256	PCM-to-VLCM two-way communication fault

89684C10

VACUUM DIAGRAMS

♦ **See Figure 49**

Following are vacuum diagrams for most of the engine and emissions package combinations covered by this manual. Because vacuum circuits will vary based on various engine and vehicle options, always refer first to the vehicle emission control information label, if present. Should the label be missing, or should vehicle be equipped with a different engine from the vehicle's original equipment, refer to the diagrams below for the same or similar configuration.

If you wish to obtain a replacement emissions label, most manufacturers make the labels available for purchase. The labels can usually be ordered from a local dealer.

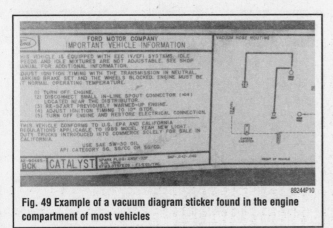

Fig. 49 Example of a vacuum diagram sticker found in the engine compartment of most vehicles

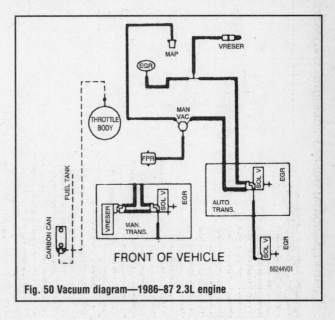

Fig. 50 Vacuum diagram—1986–87 2.3L engine

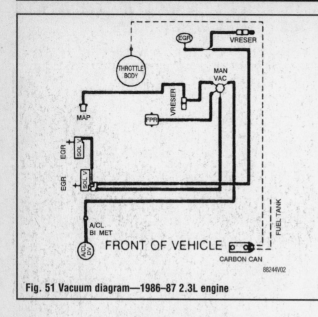

Fig. 51 Vacuum diagram—1986–87 2.3L engine

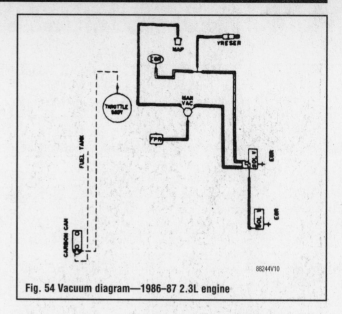

Fig. 54 Vacuum diagram—1986–87 2.3L engine

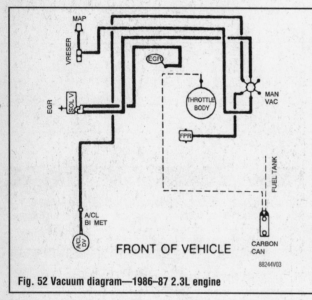

Fig. 52 Vacuum diagram—1986–87 2.3L engine

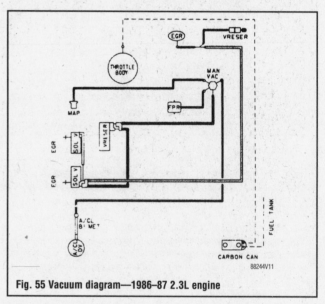

Fig. 55 Vacuum diagram—1986–87 2.3L engine

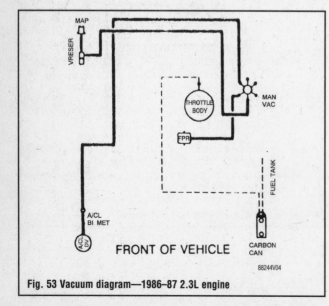

Fig. 53 Vacuum diagram—1986–87 2.3L engine

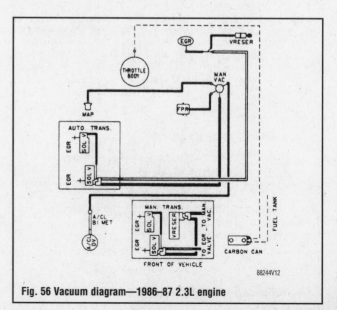

Fig. 56 Vacuum diagram—1986–87 2.3L engine

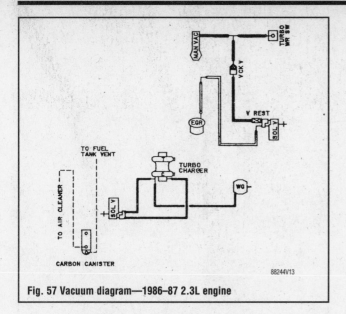

Fig. 57 Vacuum diagram—1986–87 2.3L engine

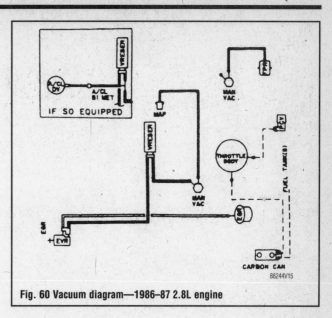

Fig. 60 Vacuum diagram—1986–87 2.8L engine

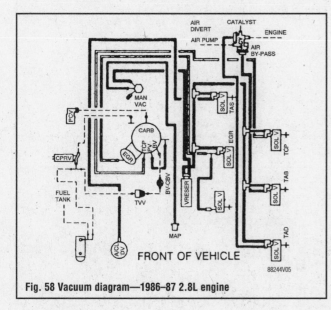

Fig. 58 Vacuum diagram—1986–87 2.8L engine

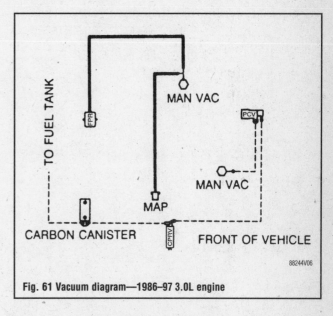

Fig. 61 Vacuum diagram—1986–97 3.0L engine

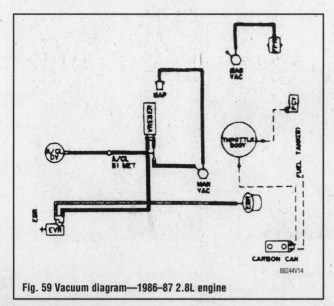

Fig. 59 Vacuum diagram—1986–87 2.8L engine

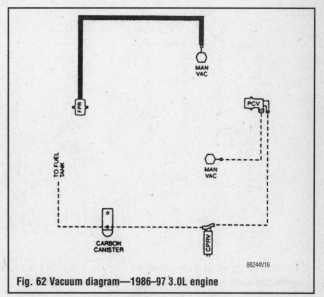

Fig. 62 Vacuum diagram—1986–97 3.0L engine

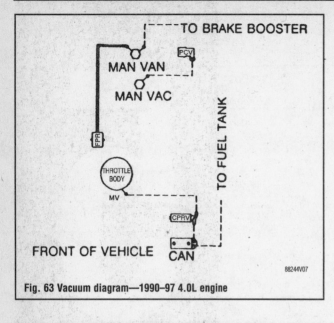

Fig. 63 Vacuum diagram—1990–97 4.0L engine

88244V07

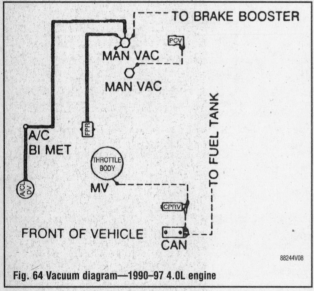

Fig. 64 Vacuum diagram—1990–97 4.0L engine

88244V08

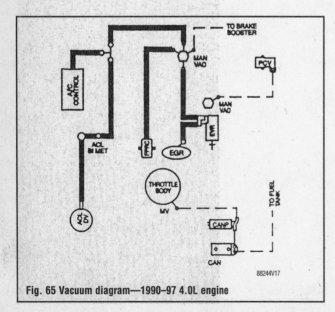

Fig. 65 Vacuum diagram—1990–97 4.0L engine

88244V17

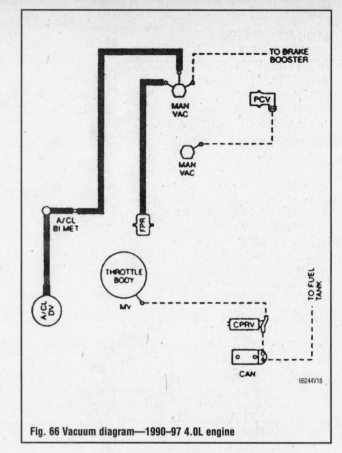

Fig. 66 Vacuum diagram—1990–97 4.0L engine

88244V18

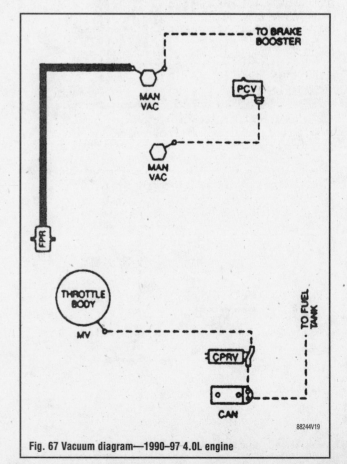

Fig. 67 Vacuum diagram—1990–97 4.0L engine

88244V19

5

FUEL SYSTEM

BASIC FUEL SYSTEM DIAGNOSIS

▶ See Figure 1

When there is a problem starting or driving a vehicle, two of the most important checks involve the ignition and the fuel systems. The questions most mechanics attempt to answer first, "is there spark?" and "is there fuel?" will often lead to solving most basic problems. For ignition system diagnosis and testing, please refer to the information on engine electrical components and ignition systems found earlier in this manual. If the ignition system checks out (there is spark), then you must determine if the fuel system is operating properly (is there fuel?).

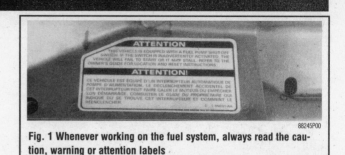

Fig. 1 Whenever working on the fuel system, always read the caution, warning or attention labels

FUEL LINES AND FITTINGS

Quick Connect Fuel Line Fittings

REMOVAL & INSTALLATION

➡**Quick Connect (push) type fuel line fittings must be disconnected using proper procedures or the fitting may be damaged. Two types of retainers are used on the push connect fittings. Line sizes of ⅜ in. and ⁵⁄₁₆ in. use a "hairpin" clip retainer. ¼ in. line connectors use a "duck bill" clip retainer. In addition, some engines use spring lock connections secured by a garter spring which requires a special tool (T81P-19623-G or equivalent) for removal.**

Hairpin Clip

▶ See Figure 2

1. Clean all dirt and/or grease from the fitting. Spread the two clip legs about ⅛ in. (3mm) each to disengage from the fitting, then pull the clip outward from the fitting. Use finger pressure only, do not use any tools.
2. Grasp the fitting and hose assembly and pull away from the steel line. Twist the fitting and hose assembly slightly while pulling, if necessary, when a sticking condition exists.
   To install:
3. Inspect the hairpin clip for damage, replace the clip if necessary. Reinstall the clip in position on the fitting.
4. Inspect the fitting and inside of the connector to insure freedom of dirt or obstruction. Install fitting into the connector and push together. A click will be heard when the hairpin snaps into proper connection. Pull on the line to insure full engagement.

Duck Bill Clip

▶ See Figure 2

Special tools are available to remove the retaining clips (Ford Tool No. T82L-9500-AH or equivalent).

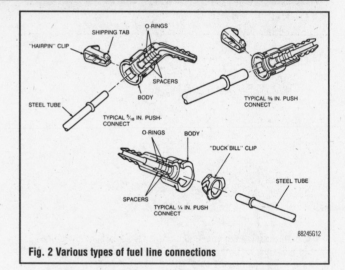

Fig. 2 Various types of fuel line connections

1. Align the slot on the push connector removal tool with either tab on the retaining clip.
2. Pull the line from the connector.
3. If the removal tool is not available, use a pair of narrow 6 in. (152mm) channel lock pliers with a jaw width of 0.2 in. (5mm) or less. Align the jaws of the pliers with the openings of the fitting case and compress the part of the retaining clip that engages the case. Compressing the retaining clip will release the fitting which may be pulled from the connector. Both sides of the clip must be compressed at the same time to disengage.
4. Inspect the retaining clip, fitting end and connector. Replace the clip if any damage is apparent.
   To install:
5. Push the line into the steel connector until a click is heard, indicting the clip is in place. Pull on the line to check engagement.

CARBURETED FUEL SYSTEM

Mechanical Fuel Pump

▶ See Figure 3

The fuel pump is bolted to the lower left side of the cylinder block. It is mechanically operated by an eccentric on the camshaft which drives a pushrod. The fuel pump cannot be disassembled for repairs and must be replaced if testing indicates it is not within performance specifications.

✳✳ CAUTION

When working near the fuel system, take precautions to avoid the risk of fire. Do not smoke or allow any open flame nearby. Have a fire extinguisher in close proximity.

REMOVAL & INSTALLATION

▶ See Figure 4

1. Disconnect the negative battery cable.
2. Remove the fuel tank filler cap, to allow any pressure in the tank to escape.
3. Place a drip pan below the fuel pump to catch any spilled fuel.
4. Tag or mark the fuel lines to the pump.
5. Loosen the fuel line nut at the pump inlet and outlet, using a flare-end wrench or suitable open-ended wrench. Fuel will spill out of the connection when loosened.
6. Loosen the fuel pump mounting bolts approximately two turns. Apply force with your hand to loosen the fuel pump if the gasket is stuck. If excessive

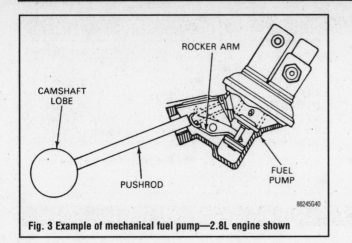

Fig. 3 Example of mechanical fuel pump—2.8L engine shown

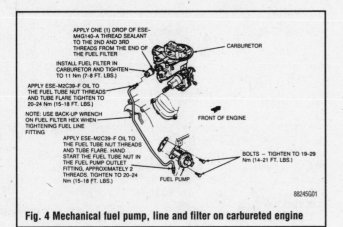

Fig. 4 Mechanical fuel pump, line and filter on carbureted engine

tension is on the pump, rotate the engine crankshaft pulley retainer bolt until the fuel pump cam lobe is near its low position.

7. Disconnect the fuel pump inlet and outlet lines using a suitable flare or opened-ended wrench.

8. Remove the fuel pump attaching bolts and remove the pump and gasket. Discard the old gasket.

9. Remove all gasket material from the engine and fuel pump mating surfaces.

To install:

10. Position the attaching bolts into the fuel pump and install a new gasket on the bolts. Position the fuel pump to the pushrod and the mounting pad on the engine. Turn the attaching bolts alternately and evenly. Tighten them to 14–21 ft. lbs. (19–29 Nm).

11. Connect and tighten the fuel outlet and inlet lines.

12. Connect the negative battery cable, and install fuel tank cap.

13. Start the engine and check all connections for fuel leaks. Stop the engine and check all fuel pump fuel line connections for fuel leaks by running a finger under the connections. Check for oil leaks at the fuel pump mounting pad.

TESTING

If a problem exists with the fuel pump, it normally will deliver either no fuel at all, or not enough to sustain high engine speeds or loads. When an engine has a lean (fuel starvation) condition, the fuel pump is often suspected as being the source of the problem, however similar symptoms will be present if the fuel filter is clogged or the fuel tank is plugged or restricted. It could also be a carburetor problem, kinked or plugged fuel line or a leaking fuel hose.

Before removing a suspect fuel pump:

1. Make sure there is fuel in the tank.
2. Replace the fuel filter to eliminate that possibility.
3. Check all rubber hoses from the fuel pump to the fuel tank for kinks or cracks.

4. With the engine idling, inspect all fuel hoses and lines for leaks in the lines or connections. Tighten loose connections.

5. Check the fuel pump outlet connection for leaks and tighten if required.

6. Inspect the fuel pump diaphragm crimp (the area where the stamped steel section is attached to the casting) and the breather hole(s) in the casting for evidence of fuel or oil leakage. Replace the fuel pump if leaking.

Capacity (Volume) Test

▶ See Figure 5

1. Remove the gas tank cap.
2. Remove the carburetor air cleaner.
3. Slowly disconnect the fuel line at the fuel filter. Use clean rags to catch any fuel spray. Exercise caution as the fuel line is pressurized and take precautions to avoid the risk of fire.

✳ CAUTION

The fuel system is under pressure. Release pressure slowly and contain spillage. Observe no smoking/no open flame precautions. Have a Class B-C (dry powder) fire extinguisher within arm's reach at all times.

4. Place a suitable non-breakable container (1 pint minimum capacity) at the end of the disconnected fuel line. A small piece of hose may be necessary on the fuel line end.

5. With the high tension wire removed from the coil, crank the engine ten revolutions to fill the fuel lines, then crank the engine again for 10 seconds and measure the fuel collected. The pump should deliver roughly ⅓ pint (0.16 liters) of fuel, minimum.

6. If the fuel flow is within specifications, perform a pressure test.

7. If the fuel flow is low, repeat the test using a remote vented can of gasoline. Remove the fuel pump inlet hose, then connect a length of fuel hose to the pump inlet and insert the other end into the remote gasoline can. If the fuel flow is now within specifications, the problem is a plugged in-tank filter or a leaking, kinked or plugged fuel line or hose. Make sure the fuel pump pushrod length is 6.10–6.14 in. (155–156mm); if short, replace the pushrod and install the fuel pump. If the fuel flow is still low, replace the fuel pump.

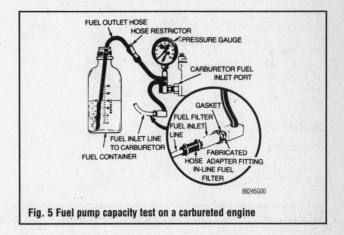

Fig. 5 Fuel pump capacity test on a carbureted engine

Pressure Test

1. Connect a 0–15 psi fuel pump pressure tester (Rotunda No. 059-00008 or equivalent) to the carburetor end of the fuel line.

✳ CAUTION

Observe the no smoking/no open flame precautions. Have a Class B-C (dry powder) fire extinguisher within arm's reach at all times.

2. Start the engine. It should be able to run for about 30 seconds on the fuel in the carburetor. Read the pressure on the gauge after about 10 seconds. It should be 4–6.5 psi (31–45 kPa).

3. If the pump pressure is too low or high, replace the fuel pump and retest.

4. Once all testing is complete, reconnect the fuel lines and remove the gauge.

Carburetor

◆ See Figures 6, 7 and 8

The only Aerostar models which are equipped with a carburetor are the vehicles with the 2.8L engine.

The Motorcraft Model 2150A 2-bbl feedback carburetor is used on the 2.8L (171 CID) engine. The feedback carburetor system uses a pulsing solenoid to introduce fresh air from the air cleaner into the idle and main system vacuum passages to lean the fuel and air mixture from the maximum rich condition (solenoid closed) to the maximum lean condition (solenoid open). The solenoid operates under the control of the EEC-IV system, described later in this section.

The 2150A carburetor uses an all electric choke system, consisting of the

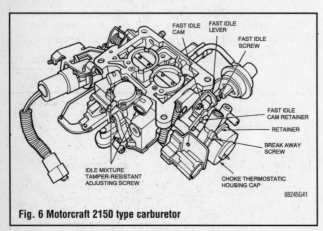

Fig. 6 Motorcraft 2150 type carburetor

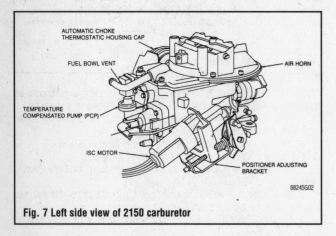

Fig. 7 Left side view of 2150 carburetor

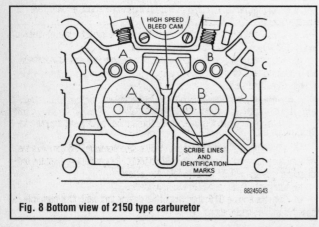

Fig. 8 Bottom view of 2150 type carburetor

choke pulldown diaphragm, choke housing and electric choke cap. The voltage applied to the choke cap is controlled by the EEC-IV computer through a "duty cycle" output, which varies between 0% (0 volts) and 100% (12 volts) to control choke operation. The tamper resistant choke cap retainer uses breakaway screws and is non-adjustable.

The fast idle speed at engine startup is controlled by the mechanical cam and adjustment screw. After startup, the cam moves out of the way, allowing the idle speed control (ISC) motor to control the idle speed. Both the kickdown and idle rpm are controlled by the EEC-IV system, eliminating the need for idle and fast idle speed adjustments. When the ignition is turned off (warm engine), the throttle rests against the curb idle screw stop to prevent run-on and then goes to maximum extension for preposition for the next engine start.

ADJUSTMENTS

Most carburetor adjustments are set at the factory and should require no further attention. Choke setting and idle speed specifications are provided on the Vehicle Emission Control Decal in the engine compartment or on the engine itself.

Accelerator Pump Stroke Adjustment

◆ See Figure 9

The accelerator pump stroke has been set at the factory for a particular engine application and should not be readjusted. If the stroke has been changed from the specified hole, reset to specifications by performing the following procedure:

1. Using a blunt tipped punch, remove the roll pin from the accelerator pump cover. Support the area under the roll pin when removing and be careful not to lose the pin.

2. Rotate the pump link and rod assembly until the keyed end of the assembly is aligned with the keyed hole in the pump over travel lever.

3. Reposition the rod and swivel assembly in the specified hole and reinstall the pump link in the accelerator pump cover. A service accelerator rod and swivel assembly is available (part no. 9F687) and must be used if replacement is necessary. Adjustment holes are not provided on the temperature compensated accelerator pump carburetor models.

4. Install the roll pin.

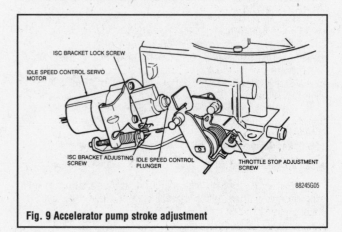

Fig. 9 Accelerator pump stroke adjustment

Dry Float Level Adjustment

◆ See Figure 10

The dry float level adjustment is a preliminary fuel level adjustment only. The final, wet level adjustment must be made after the carburetor is mounted on the engine.

1. Remove the air horn removed.

2. Raise the float and make sure the fuel inlet needle is seated correctly.

3. Check the distance between the top surface of the main body (gasket removed) and the top surface of the float for conformance. Depress the float tab lightly to seat the fuel inlet needle, if needed.

✳✳ CAUTION

Excessive pressure can damage the Viton® tip on the needle.

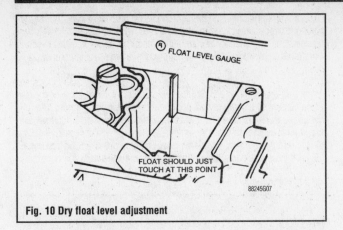

Fig. 10 Dry float level adjustment

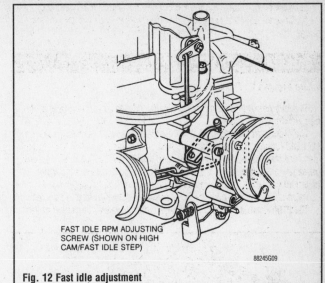

FAST IDLE RPM ADJUSTING
SCREW (SHOWN ON HIGH
CAM/FAST IDLE STEP)

Fig. 12 Fast idle adjustment

4. Take a measurement near the center of the float at a point ⅛ in. (3.2mm) from the free end of the float. If a cardboard float gauge is used, place the gauge in the corner of the enlarged end section of the fuel bowl. The gauge should touch the float near the end, but not on the end radius. If necessary, bend the tab on the float to bring the setting within the specified limits. This should provide the proper preliminary fuel level setting.

Wet Float Level Adjustment

▶ See Figure 11

1. With the vehicle level, engine warm and running, remove the air cleaner.
2. Insert fuel float level gauge T83L-9550-A, or equivalent, with the pointed end into the fuel bowl vent stack and rest the level across the other vent.
3. Siphon fuel into the sight tube and allow the fuel to reach a steady level. Take precautions to avoid the risk of fire. Do not smoke during this procedure.
4. Press down to level the gauge and read the fuel level on the sight tube. If the level is in the specified band, adjustment is not necessary. If the level is not correct, note the level on the sight and proceed to the next step.
5. Stop the engine and remove the choke link, air horn attaching screws, the vent hose and the air horn assembly.
6. Measure the vertical distance from the top of the machined surface of the main body to the level of the fuel in the fuel bowl.
7. With this measurement as a reference, bend the float tab up to raise the level or down to lower the level. Adjust to bring the fuel level to specifications.
8. Recheck the fuel level on the sight gauge. If satisfactory, install the remaining air horn screws. If not, repeat the adjustment procedure.
9. Install the choke link and check the choke plate to make sure its free.
10. Tighten the air horn screws. Install the carburetor vent (canister) hose, then check and adjust the curb idle speed. Install the air cleaner.

Idle Speed Adjustment

▶ See Figures 12 and 13

1. Warm up the engine in PARK or NEUTRAL until it reaches normal operating temperature. Set the parking brake and block the wheels. Make sure all accessories are turned off.

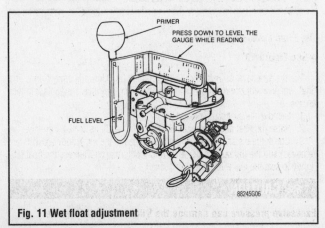

Fig. 11 Wet float adjustment

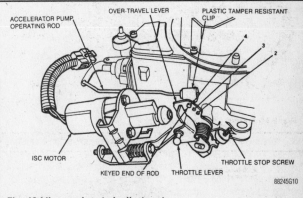

Fig. 13 Idle speed control adjustment

2. Remove the Air Charge Temperature (ACT) sensor and adapter from the air cleaner tray by removing the retaining clip. Leave the wiring harness connected.
3. Remove the air cleaner, then disconnect and plug the vacuum line at the cold weather duct and valve motor.
4. Turn the engine **OFF** and verify that the Idle Speed Control (ISC) plunger moves to its maximum extension within 10 seconds.
5. Disconnect and plug the EGR vacuum hose. Disconnect the idle speed control.
6. With the engine running, manually open the throttle and set the fast idle adjusting screw on the high cam.
7. Adjust the fast idle speed to the specification given on the underhood emission control sticker.
8. Open the throttle manually to release the fast idle cam, allowing the throttle lever to rest on the ISC plunger.
9. Loosen the ISC bracket lock screw, then adjust the ISC bracket screw to obtain 2,000 rpm. Tighten the bracket lock screw.
10. Reconnect the ISC motor connector. The engine rpm should automatically return to curb idle.
11. Simultaneously:
    a. manually hold the throttle above 1,000 rpm
    b. push the ISC plunger until it retracts fully
    c. after plunger retracts, release the throttle and quickly unplug the connection.
12. Adjust the anti-dieseling speed throttle stop screw to 750 rpm with the transmission (automatic or manual) in **NEUTRAL**. Be careful to adjust the anti-dieseling stop screw, NOT the curb idle stop screw.
13. Connect the ISC and EGR vacuum hoses.
14. Turn the engine **OFF**, then restart the engine and verify that curb idle speed is within specifications.

Mixture Adjustment

The fuel mixture is preset at the factory and computer controlled thereafter. No adjustments are possible without the use of propane enrichment equipment that is not readily available to the do-it-yourself market. All mixture adjustments should be performed at a qualified service facility to insure compliance with Federal and/or State Emission Control Standards.

REMOVAL & INSTALLATION

1. Disconnect the negative battery cable.
2. Remove the air cleaner.
3. Remove the throttle cable from the throttle lever.
4. Tag and disconnect all vacuum lines, emission hoses and electrical connections.
5. Disconnect the fuel line from the carburetor. Use a clean rag to catch any fuel spray and use a backup wrench or equivalent on the fuel filter to avoid twisting the line.
6. Remove the carburetor retaining nuts, then lift off the carburetor.
7. Remove the carburetor mounting gasket and spacer, if equipped.
8. Clean the gasket mating surfaces of the spacer and carburetor.

To install:

9. Position a new gasket on the spacer, if equipped, and install the carburetor. Secure the carburetor with the mounting nuts. To prevent leakage, distortion or damage to the carburetor body flange, snug the nuts then alternately tighten each nut in a crisscross pattern to 14–16 ft. lbs. (20–21 Nm).
10. Connect the fuel line and throttle cable.
11. Connect all emission lines, vacuum hoses and electrical connectors.
12. Start the engine and check the idle speeds (fast and curb). Refer to the underhood emission sticker for specifications.

OVERHAUL

Notes

➡ **All major and minor repair kits contain detailed instructions and illustrations. Refer to them for complete rebuilding instructions. To prevent damage to the throttle plates, make a stand using four bolts, eight flat washers and eight nuts. Place a washer and nut on the bolt, install through the carburetor base and secure with a nut.**

Generally, when a carburetor requires major service, a rebuilt unit may be purchased on an exchange basis, or a kit may be bought for overhauling the carburetor. The rebuild kit contains the necessary parts and some form of instructions for rebuilding. The instructions may vary between a simple exploded view and detailed step-by-step rebuilding instructions. Unless you are familiar with carburetor overhaul, the latter should be used.

There are some general overhaul procedures which should always be observed: Efficient carburetion depends greatly on careful cleaning and inspection during overhaul since dirt, gum, water, or varnish in or on the carburetor parts are often responsible for poor performance. Overhaul your carburetor in a clean, dust-free area. Carefully disassembly the carburetor, referring often to the exploded views. Keep all similar and look alike parts segregated during disassembly and cleaning to avoid accidental interchange during assembly. Make a note of all jet sizes.

When the carburetor is disassembled, wash all parts (except diaphragms, electric choke units. pump plunger, and any other plastic, leather, fiber, or rubber parts) in clean carburetor solvent. Do not leave parts in the solvent any longer than is necessary to sufficiently loosen the deposits. Excessive cleaning may remove the special finish from the float bowl and choke valve bodies, leaving these parts unfit for service. Rinse all parts in clean solvent and blow them dry with compressed air or allow them to air dry. Wipe clean all cork, plastic, leather, and fiber parts with a clean, lint free cloth.

Blow out all passages and jets with compressed air and be sure that there are no restrictions or blockages. Never use wire or similar tools to clean jets, fuel passages, or air bleeds. Clean all jets and valves separately to avoid accidental interchange.

Check all parts for wear or damage. If wear or damage is found, replace the defective parts. Especially check the following:
1. Check the float needle and seat for wear. If wear is found, replace the complete assembly.
2. Check the float hinge pin for wear and the float(s) for dents or distortion. Replace the float if fuel has leaked into it.

3. Check the throttle and choke shaft bores for wear or an out-of-round condition. Damage or wear to the throttle arm, shaft, shaft bore will often require replacement of the throttle body. These parts require a close tolerance; wear may allow air leakage, which could affect starting and idling.

➡ **Throttle shafts and bushings are usually not included in overhaul kits. They can be purchased separately.**

4. Inspect the idle mixture adjusting needles for burrs or grooves. Any such condition requires replacement of the needle, since you will not be able to obtain a satisfactory idle.
5. Test the accelerator pump check valves. They should pass air one way but not the other. Test for proper seating by blowing and sucking on the valve. Replace the valve if necessary. If the valve is satisfactory, wash the valve again to remove breath moisture.
6. Check the bowl cover for warped surfaces with a straightedge.
7. Closely inspect the valves and seats for wear and damage, replacing as necessary.
8. After the carburetor is assembled, check the choke valve for freedom of operation.

Carburetor overhaul kits are recommended for each overhaul. These kits contain all gaskets and new parts to replace those that deteriorate most rapidly. Failure to replace all parts supplied with the kit (especially gaskets) can result in poor performance later. Some carburetor manufacturers supply overhaul kits of three basic types: minor repair; major repair; and gasket kits. Basically, they contain the following:

Minor Repair Kits:
- All gaskets
- Float needle valve
- Volume control screw
- All diaphragms
- Spring for the pump diaphragm

Major Repair Kits:
- All jets and gaskets
- All diaphragms
- Float needle valve
- Volume control screw
- Pump ball valve
- Main jet carrier
- Float
- Other necessary items
- Some cover hold-down screws and washers

Gasket Kits:
- All gaskets

After cleaning and checking all components, reassemble the carburetor, using new parts and referring to the exploded view. When reassembling, make sure that all screws and jets are tight in their seats, but do not overtighten, as the tips will be distorted. Tighten all screws gradually, in rotation. Do not tighten needle valves into their seat; uneven jetting will result. Always use new gaskets. Be sure to adjust the float level when reassembling.

Disassembly

AIR HORN

➡ **The exterior of the carburetor should be cleaned with carburetor cleaner and the carburetor placed on a clean work surface, preferably a work stand.**

1. Remove the air cleaner anchor stud.
2. Remove the automatic choke control rod retainer.
3. Remove the air horn attaching bolts and washers. Don't lose the I.D. tag.
4. Remove the air horn and gasket.
5. Remove the screw securing the choke shaft lever to the choke shaft. Remove the choke control rod and plastic dust shield.
6. Remove the staking from the choke plate screws, remove the screws and slide the choke plate out the top of the air horn.

AUTOMATIC CHOKE

▶ **See Figure 14**

1. Remove the fast idle cam retainer.
2. Center-punch each breakaway screw securing the choke cap.

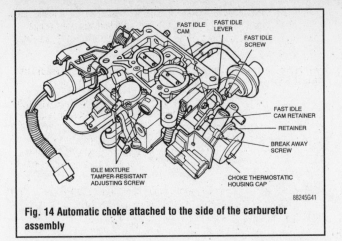

Fig. 14 Automatic choke attached to the side of the carburetor assembly

3. Using a ¼ inch drill bit, drill a recess in each screw, deep enough to remove the retainer from the cap.

➡️ If your carburetor is equipped with the large, tamper-proof choke cap retainer, skip Steps 4 and 5.

4. Use a flat, sharp chisel to remove the cap from the gasket.
5. Use a small pliers to remove the screw studs remaining in the choke housing.
6. Clean all gasket material from the cap and housing.

MAIN BODY

▸ See Figures 15 and 16

1. Pry the float shaft retainer from the fuel inlet seat.
2. Remove the float, float shaft retainer and inlet needle.
3. Remove the retainer, shaft and damper spring from the float lever.
4. Remove the needle seat, filter screen and main jets. There is a special wrench to aid in jet removal.
5. Remove the 2 booster venturi screws, booster venturi and metering rod assembly and gasket.
6. Remove the filter screen from the booster venturi screw.
7. Invert the main body and let the accelerator pump discharge weight and ball fall into your hand.
8. Remove the accelerator pump link and rod assembly.
9. Remove the accelerator pump cover attaching screws.
10. Remove the TCP valve and gasket.
11. Pull out the Elastomer® valve. If the valve tip breaks off during removal, make sure to remove the tip from the fuel bowl.

➡️ Whenever an Elastomer® valve is removed, it must be replaced!

12. Invert the main body and remove the enrichment valve cover and gasket.
13. Using a wrench or socket, remove the enrichment valve and gasket.
14. Support the area under the mixture screws and, using a pointed tool such as a sharp awl, tap each limiter plug forward to access the screws. Turn

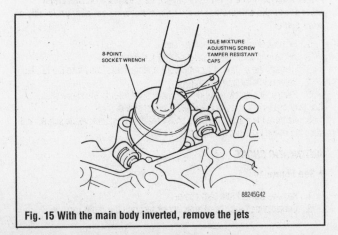

Fig. 15 With the main body inverted, remove the jets

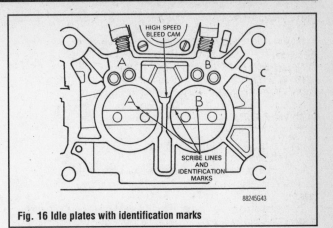

Fig. 16 Idle plates with identification marks

the screws inward slowly, counting the exact number of turns until seated. This will give you a reference for installing the screws. Now remove the screws and springs.

15. Remove the nut, washer and fast idle lever from the throttle shaft.
16. Remove the idle screw and retainer from the fast idle adjusting lever.
17. Remove the ISC motor.
18. Matchmark the throttle plates and shaft, and matchmark each plate and bore. File off the screw staking and remove the screws. Slide out the plates.
19. File off any burrs from the shaft.
20. Remove the 2 throttle position sensor screws and remove the sensor.
21. Slide the shaft from the main body.
22. Remove the 3 attaching screws and remove the duty cycle solenoid and gasket.
23. Clean all parts and inspect them for wear and/or damage.

Assembly

MAIN BODY

1. Slide the shaft into the main body. Rotate the shaft clockwise until the throttle lever clears the boss for the idle speed stop screw. Continue inserting the shaft into position, rotating it as necessary to properly position the cam.
2. Install the throttle plates. Loosely install new screws.
3. Close the throttle plate and hold the main body up to the light. Little or no light should show past the closed plates. Tap the plates lightly with a screwdriver handle to fully seat them. When fully seated, tighten the screws. Using a pair of diagonal cutters, crimp the exposed screw threads to lock them in place.
4. Install a new duty cycle solenoid gasket, solenoid and screws. Tighten the screws to 20–30 inch lbs. (2–3 Nm).
5. Install the throttle position sensor over the throttle shaft and flush with its mounting surface, with the sensor rotated counterclockwise as far as it will go. Rotate the sensor clockwise to line up the mounting holes and engage the sensor with the throttle shaft actuator pin. Install the screws and tighten them to 11–16 inch lbs. (1–2 Nm). Mount the sensor connector on the choke shield.
6. Install the fast idle lever on the throttle shaft.
7. Install the enrichment valve and new gasket. Tighten the valve to 9–10 ft. lbs. (11–13 Nm).
8. Install the enrichment valve cover and new gasket.
9. Install the mixture screws and springs. Turn the screws inward slowly, until seated, then, back them out the exact number of turns previously noted. If you somehow forgot the number of turns, back them out 1½ turns each.
10. Install the ISC motor.
11. Lubricate the tip of a new Elastomer® valve with polyethylene grease and insert the tip into the cavity of the accelerator pump center hole. Using a needlenose pliers, reach into the fuel bowl and grasp the tip. Pull the valve in until it seats in the pump cavity wall and cut off the tip forward of the retaining shoulder. Remove the tip remnant.
12. Install the accelerator pump diaphragm spring on the boss in the chamber. Insert the diaphragm in the cover, install the cover and screws. Tighten the left, longer, screws, but only finger tighten the right, shorter screws.
13. Install the accelerator pump link and rod assembly.
14. Position the booster assembly gasket and booster venturi. Drop the accelerator pump discharge ball fall into the passage in the main body. Using a flat punch, tap the ball against its seat, once. Drop the weight into position.

15. Install the filter screen onto the booster venturi screw. Tighten the screw to 65–85 inch lbs. (7–9 Nm).

16. Install the 2 booster venturi screws and metering rod assembly. Tighten the screws to 65–85 inch lbs. (7–9 Nm)

17. Install the needle seat, filter screen and main jets.

18. Install the inlet needle.

19. Install the retainer, shaft and damper spring into the float lever.

20. Install the float and float shaft retainer. Check the float setting.

21. Install the TCP valve and gasket. Tighten the screws to 19–24 inch lbs. (2–3 Nm).

AUTOMATIC CHOKE

1. Position the fast idle cam lever on the thermostatic choke shaft/lever assembly. The bottom of the fast idle cam lever adjusting screw must rest against the tang on the choke lever.

2. Insert the choke lever into the rear of the choke housing. Position the choke lever so that the hole in the lever is to the left side of the housing.

3. Install the fast idle cam rod on the fast idle cam lever. Place the fast idle cam on the fast idle cam rod and install the retainer.

4. Place the choke housing vacuum pickup port-to-main body gasket on the choke housing flange.

5. Position the choke housing on the main body and, at the same time, install the fast idle cam on the hub of the main body. Install the gasket and screws. Torque the screws to 13–20 inch lbs. (1–2 Nm).

6. Install the fast idle cam retainer.

➡Make certain that the bimetal spring tab is engaged in the slotted choke shaft lever.

7. Install the gasket, cap and retainer. If you are using break-away screws, tighten them until the heads break off.

AIR HORN

1. Position the choke shaft in the air horn.

2. Install the choke shaft lever to the choke shaft. Install the choke control rod and plastic dust shield.

3. Install the choke plate. Install the screws finger tight. Check the choke shaft and plate for binding. If any binding is detected, correct it. Hold the choke plate in the closed position, making sure it fits evenly against the air horn wall. Tighten the screws to 4–9 inch lbs. (0.4–1 Nm). Using a pair of angle cutters, crimp the exposed threaded ends of the screws to lock them in place.

4. Install the new air horn gasket.

5. Position the air horn on the main body, making sure that the choke plate rod fits through the seal and opening in the main body.

6. Connect the choke plate rod and automatic choke lever.

7. Install the air horn attaching bolts and washers, and the I.D. tag. Tighten the bolts to 27–37 inch lbs. (3–4 Nm).

8. Install the automatic choke control rod retainer.

9. Install the air cleaner anchor stud. Torque the stud to 5–7 ft. lbs. (6–9 Nm).

10. Perform all necessary adjustments.

FUEL INJECTION SYSTEM

General Information

▶ See Figure 17

The electronic fuel injection (MFI) system used on the 2.3L, 3.0L and 4.0L engines is classified as a multi-point, pulse time, speed density fuel delivery system which meters fuel into the intake air stream in accordance with engine demand through 4 or 6 injectors, depending on engine cylinder number, mounted on a tuned intake manifold.

The fuel injection system uses a high pressure, chassis or tank mounted electric fuel pump to deliver fuel from the tank to the fuel charging manifold assembly. The fuel charging manifold assembly incorporates electrically actuated fuel injectors directly above each of the engine's intake ports. The injectors, when energized, spray a metered quantity of fuel into the intake air stream. A constant pressure drop is maintained across the injector nozzles by a pressure regulator, connected in series with the fuel injectors and positioned downstream from them. Excess fuel supplied by the pump, but not required by the engine, passes through the regulator and returns to the fuel tank through a fuel return line.

On 4-cylinder engines, all injectors are energized simultaneously, once every crankshaft revolution. On 6-cylinder engines, the injectors are energized in two groups of three injectors, with each group activated once every other crankshaft revolution. The period of time that the injectors are energized (injector "on time" or "pulse width") is controlled by the computer. The input from various sensors is used to compute the required fuel flow rate necessary to maintain a prescribed air/fuel ratio.

✳✳ CAUTION

Fuel supply lines on vehicles with fuel injection will remain pressurized for long periods of time after engine shutdown. This fuel pressure must be relieved before any service procedures are attempted on the fuel system.

Relieving Fuel System Pressure

▶ See Figure 18

All fuel injected engines are equipped with a pressure relief valve located on the fuel supply manifold.

1. Remove the fuel tank cap.

2. Attach fuel pressure gauge T80L-9974-A, or equivalent, to the pressure relief valve to release the fuel pressure.

If a suitable pressure gauge is not available, disconnect the vacuum hose from the fuel pressure regulator and attach a hand vacuum pump. Apply 25 in.Hg (84 kPa) of vacuum to the regulator to vent the fuel system pressure into the fuel tank through the fuel return hose.

Fig. 17 Whenever working on the fuel system, always read the caution, warning or attention labels

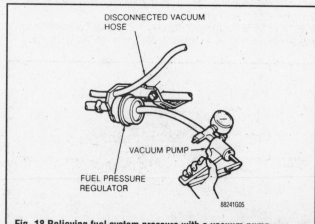

Fig. 18 Relieving fuel system pressure with a vacuum pump

➡This latter procedure will remove the fuel pressure from the lines, but not the fuel.

✳✳ CAUTION

The fuel system is under pressure. Release pressure slowly and contain any spillage. Use rags where needed to capture any spills Observe no smoking/no open flame precautions. Have a Class B-C (dry powder) fire extinguisher within arm's reach at all times.

Electric Fuel Pump

REMOVAL & INSTALLATION

2.3L Engine

◗ See Figure 19

The electric fuel pump is mounted on the chassis at the rear of the vehicle, in an assembly with the inline fuel filter.
1. Disconnect the negative battery cable.
2. Raise and support the vehicle safely on jackstands.
3. Locate the fuel pump which is mounted on the underbody, forward of the right rear wheel well.
4. Depressurize the fuel system.

✳✳ CAUTION

The fuel system is under pressure. Release pressure slowly and contain spillage. Observe no smoking/no open flame precautions. Have a Class B-C (dry powder) fire extinguisher within arm's reach at all times.

5. Place a drip pan below the filter to capture any spilled fuel.
6. Clean all dirt and/or grease from the fuel line fittings. "Quick Connect" fittings are used on all models equipped with a pressurized fuel system. These fittings must be disconnected using the proper procedure or the fittings may be damaged. Refer to the fuel line removal and installation procedures in this section.
7. Discard the fuel line retainer clips, and purchase new clips.
8. Remove the fuel filter and retainer from the metal mounting bracket.
9. Remove the fuel pump mounting bracket/pump assembly.
10. Remove the rubber insulator ring from the filter. Then remove the filter from the retainer assembly.

➡The direction of fuel flow (arrow on the filter) points to the open end of the retainer.

To install:
11. Place the new filter into the retainer with the flow arrow pointing toward the open end.
12. Position the pump/bracket assembly on the frame and tighten the mounting bolts.
13. Install the insulator ring. Replace the insulator(s) if the filter moves freely after installation of the retainer. Install the retainer on the metal bracket and tighten the mounting bolts.
14. Push the quick connect fittings onto the filter ends. Secure the fitting with the new retainer clips. A click will be heard when the hairpin clip snaps

into its proper position. Pull on the lines with moderate pressure to ensure proper connection.
15. Lower the vehicle.
16. Connect the negative battery cable.
17. Start the engine and check for fuel leaks.

3.0L and 4.0L Engines

◗ See Figure 20

The fuel pump for the 3.0L and 4.0L engines is part of the fuel gauge sender unit. To access this fuel pump the gas tank must be removed.
In the event the fuel sender or fuel pump fails, the entire unit must be removed and replaced.
1. Disconnect the negative battery cable.
2. Depressurize the fuel system and drain the fuel tank. Drain the gasoline into a suitable safety container and take precautions to avoid the risk of fire.

✳✳ CAUTION

The fuel system is under pressure. Release pressure slowly and contain any spillage. Observe no smoking/no open flame precautions. Have a Class B-C (dry powder) fire extinguisher within arm's reach at all times.

3. Loosen the gas tank filler pipe clamp.
4. Remove the bolt from the front strap and remove the gas tank front strap.
5. Remove the bolt from the rear strap and remove the gas tank rear strap.
6. Remove the fuel feed hose at the fuel gauge sender push connector.
7. Remove the fuel hose from the sender unit push connector.
8. Remove the fuel vapor hose from the vapor valve.
9. Slowly lower the fuel tank from the chassis.
10. Remove the shield from the fuel tank.
11. Remove any dirt from the fuel pump flange.
12. Turn the fuel pump locking ring counterclockwise to remove it. There are wrenches for this purpose, but you can loosen the ring by tapping it around with a wood dowel and plastic or rubber mallet.

✳✳ CAUTION

Never hammer on or near the fuel tank with metal tools! The risk of spark and explosion is always present!

13. Remove the fuel pump and bracket assembly. Discard the rubber O-ring.

✳✳ WARNING

Do not attempt to apply battery voltage to the pump to check its operation while removed from the vehicle. Running the pump dry will destroy it.

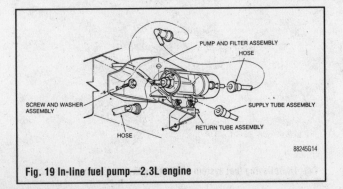

Fig. 19 In-line fuel pump—2.3L engine

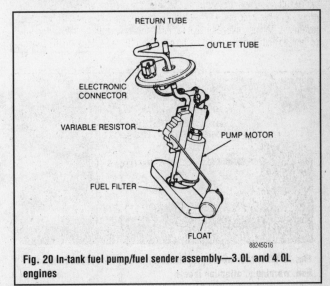

Fig. 20 In-tank fuel pump/fuel sender assembly—3.0L and 4.0L engines

To install:

14. Clean the around the fuel pump hole.
15. Coat the new O-ring with multi-purpose grease to hold it in place. Install the O-ring in the ring groove on the fuel pump.
16. Position the pump assembly in the tank making sure the keyways align and the seal ring remains stays in place.
17. Tighten the locking ring to 40–50 ft. lbs. (52–65 Nm).
18. Install the shield on to the fuel tank.
19. Raise the tank into position and support until all the straps are secured in place.
20. Connect the hoses and wires to the sender assembly.
21. Attach the rear strap to the vehicle.
22. Attach the front strap.
23. Install the fuel lines to the feed and return hoses at the fuel gauge sender push connector.
24. Install the filler pipe in position and tighten the filler pipe clamp.
25. Install the front and rear fuel tank mounting bolts and tighten them to 18–20 ft. lbs. for 1986–87 models; 35–45 ft. lbs. on 1988–90 models.
26. Connect the negative battery cable. Road test the vehicle.

Throttle Body

REMOVAL & INSTALLATION

2.3L Engine

▶ **See Figure 21**

1. Disconnect the negative battery cable.
2. Remove the throttle linkage shield.
3. Disconnect the throttle linkage and cruise control.
4. Unbolt the accelerator cable from the bracket.
5. Tag and disconnect the wiring at the throttle position sensor and air bypass valve.

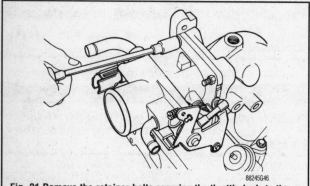

88245G46

Fig. 21 Remove the retainer bolts securing the throttle body to the intake manifold

6. Disconnect the air intake hose from the throttle body.
7. Disconnect the PCV and canister purge hoses.
8. Remove the 4 throttle body-to-upper intake manifold bolts and lift off the throttle body. Discard the gasket.
9. Clean all gasket material from the mating surfaces.

To install:

10. Position the throttle body and new gasket on the manifold. Hand start the bolts, then tighten them, evenly, to 15–25 ft. lbs. (19–32 Nm).
11. Connect the PCV and canister hoses.
12. Connect the air intake hose.
13. Connect the wiring to the throttle position sensor and air bypass valve.
14. Connect the throttle and cruise control linkages.
15. Connect the negative battery cable.

3.0L Engine

▶ **See Figures 22 thru 27**

The 3.0L throttle body is cast to the upper intake manifold assembly. To remove the throttle body, the entire upper intake manifold assembly must be removed.

1. Disconnecting the negative battery cable.
2. Remove the air cleaner outlet tube.
3. Remove the snow shield by removing the plastic retainer clips.
4. Tag and disconnect the vacuum and PCV hoses.
5. Disconnect and remove the accelerator and speed control cables (if equipped) from the accelerator mounting bracket and throttle lever.
6. Tag and disconnect the wiring harness at the throttle position sensor, air bypass valve and air charge temperature sensor.
7. Remove the retaining bolts and stud bolts and lift the throttle body assembly off the lower intake manifold.
8. Remove and discard the gasket. Clean all gasket material from the mating surfaces.

To install:

9. Install a new gasket on the lower intake manifold.
10. Install the air throttle body assembly on the lower intake manifold.
11. Install the bolts finger-tight, then tighten them evenly to 19 ft. lbs. (25 Nm).
12. Connect the wiring harness to the throttle position sensor, air charge temperature sensor and air bypass valve.
13. Install the accelerator cable and speed control cable, if equipped.
14. Install the vacuum hoses to the vacuum fittings, making sure the hoses are installed in their original locations.
15. Install the snow shield and air cleaner outlet tube.
16. Connect the negative battery cable.

4.0L Engine

1. Disconnect the negative battery cable.
2. Remove the air cleaner inlet tube.
3. Remove the snow shield.
4. Disconnect the throttle cable at the ball stud.
5. Unfasten the canister purge hose from under the throttle body.
6. Disconnect the wiring harness at the throttle position sensor.

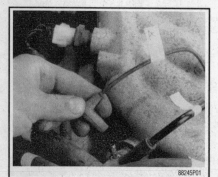

88245P01

Fig. 22 Tag and disconnect the vacuum lines attached to the manifold/throttle body assembly

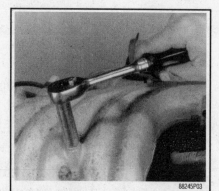

88245P03

Fig. 23 Loosen the manifold/throttle body retainer bolts

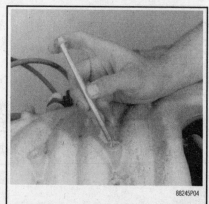

88245P04

Fig. 24 Lift the bolts out and place aside

Fig. 25 Remove and discard the gasket between the manifold sections

Fig. 26 Place rags in the intake chamber to prevent debris from falling in

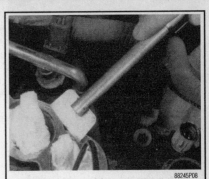

Fig. 27 With the chambers covered, clean any remaining gasket material from the mating surface

7. Remove the retaining bolts, then lift the throttle body assembly off the upper intake manifold.

8. Remove and discard the gasket.

To install:

9. Clean and inspect the mounting faces of the throttle body assembly and the upper intake manifold. Both surfaces must be clean and flat.

10. Install a new gasket on the manifold.

11. Install the air throttle body assembly on the intake manifold.

12. Install the bolts finger-tight, then tighten them evenly to 76–106 inch lbs. (8–12 Nm).

13. Fasten the wiring harness to the throttle position sensor.

14. Install the canister purge hose.

15. Install the snow shield and air cleaner outlet tube.

16. Connect the negative battery cable.

Fuel Injectors

REMOVAL & INSTALLATION

2.3L Engine

♦ See Figures 28 and 29

1. Disconnect the negative battery cable.

❊❊❊ CAUTION

Injectors and fuel rail must be handles with extreme care to prevent damage to sealing areas and sensitive fuel metering orifices.

2. Remove the fuel charging assembly from the vehicle and place on a clean flat surface.

3. Remove the fuel injector from the charging assembly by removing the injector retaining screw, then exerting a rotating pulling motion until the injector frees itself from the charging assembly.

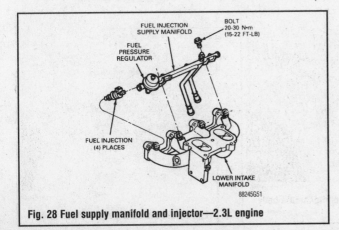

Fig. 28 Fuel supply manifold and injector—2.3L engine

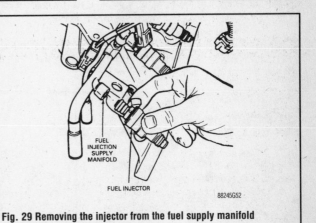

Fig. 29 Removing the injector from the fuel supply manifold

4. When the injector is removed, inspect the O-ring at both ends of the injector. If cracked or distorted, replace.

To install:

5. If installing new O-rings, lubricate the O-ring with light grade engine oil, and slide on to the injector.

6. If not already done, lubricate the injector O-rings with a light grade engine oil. Do not use silicone grease on the O-rings as it will clog the injectors.

7. Make sure the injector caps are clean and free of contamination. Install the injector by centering it in the charging assembly injector hole and applying a steady downward pressure with a slight rotational action. Make sure the injector is fully seated in the charging assembly hole. When fully seated, install the retainer screw.

8. When all the injectors are installed in the charging assembly, install the unit into the manifold as described in this section.

9. Connect the negative battery cable.

10. Build up fuel pressure by turning the ignition switch **ON** and **OFF** at least six times, leaving the ignition **ON** for at least five seconds each time. Check for fuel leaks.

11. Start the engine and allow it to reach normal operating temperature, then check for coolant leaks.

3.0L Engine

♦ See Figures 30, 31, 32, 33 and 34

1. Disconnect the negative battery cable.

2. Remove the fuel injectors from the intake manifold by lifting while gently rocking from side to side. Place all removed components on a clean surface to prevent contamination by dirt or grease.

❊❊❊ CAUTION

Injectors and fuel rail must be handles with extreme care to prevent damage to sealing areas and sensitive fuel metering orifices.

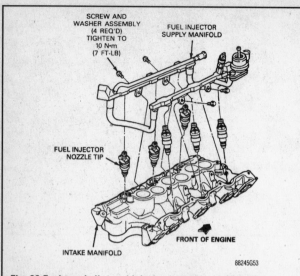

Fig. 30 Fuel supply line and injector assembly—3.0L engine

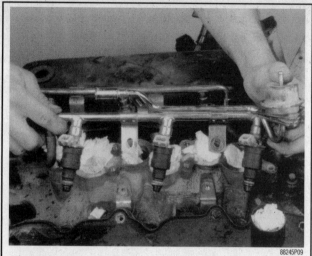

Fig. 31 With the fuel supply line removed from the engine, the injector are easily accessed

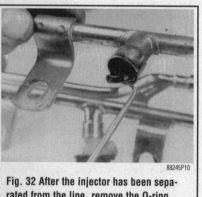

Fig. 32 After the injector has been separated from the line, remove the O-ring from the supply tube . . .

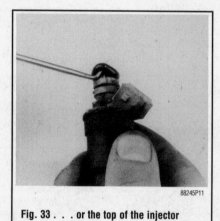

Fig. 33 . . . or the top of the injector

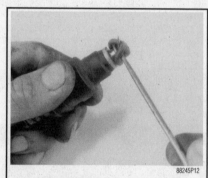

Fig. 34 Then remove the O-ring from the bottom of the injector. Discard all the O-rings

3. Remove the fuel injector retainer clip from the charging assembly, then exert a slight twisting/pulling motion and remove the injector.

4. Examine the injector O-rings for deterioration or damage and install new O-rings, if required (two per injector).

To install:

5. Make sure the injector caps are clean and free from contamination or damage.

6. If installing new O-rings, lubricate the O-rings with light engine, then slide on to the injector.

7. Lubricate all O-rings with clean engine oil, then install the injectors in the fuel rail using a light twisting/pushing motion. Secure the injector in the fuel rail with the retainer clip.

8. When all the injectors are installed in the fuel rail assembly, install the unit into the manifold as described in this section.

9. Connect the negative battery cable.

10. Build up fuel pressure by turning the ignition switch **ON** and **OFF** at least six times, leaving the ignition **ON** for at least five seconds each time. Check for fuel leaks.

11. Start the engine and allow it to reach normal operating temperature, then check for coolant leaks.

4.0L Engine

▶ See Figure 35

1. Disconnect the negative battery cable.

2. Remove the fuel injectors from the intake manifold by lifting while gently rocking from side to side. Place all removed components on a clean surface to prevent contamination by dirt or grease.

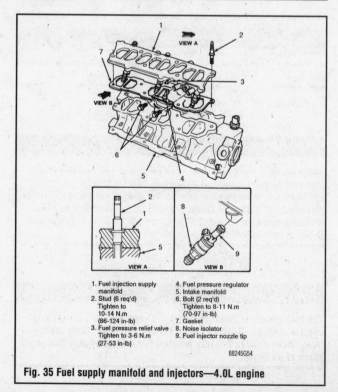

1. Fuel injection supply manifold
2. Stud (6 req'd) Tighten to 10-14 N.m (86-124 in-lb)
3. Fuel pressure relief valve Tighten to 3-6 N.m (27-53 in-lb)
4. Fuel pressure regulator
5. Intake manifold
6. Bolt (2 req'd) Tighten to 8-11 N.m (70-97 in-lb)
7. Gasket
8. Noise isolator
9. Fuel injector nozzle tip

Fig. 35 Fuel supply manifold and injectors—4.0L engine

※※ **CAUTION**

Injectors and fuel rail must be handles with extreme care to prevent damage to sealing areas and sensitive fuel metering orifices.

3. Remove the fuel injector from the charging assembly removing the retainer clip securing the injector to the fuel rail. After the clip is removed, exert a slight twisting/pulling motion and lift the injector away from the fuel rail.

4. Examine the injector O-rings for deterioration or damage and install new O-rings, if required (two per injector).

To install:

5. Make sure the injector caps are clean and free from contamination or damage.

6. If installing new O-rings, lubricate the O-rings with light engine, then slide on to the injector.

7. Lubricate all O-rings with clean engine oil, then install the injectors in the fuel rail using a light twisting/pushing motion. After the injector is positioned in the fuel rail, Secure in place with the injector retaining clip.

8. When all the injectors are installed in the fuel rail assembly, install the unit into the manifold as described in this section.

9. Connect the negative battery cable.

10. Build up fuel pressure by turning the ignition switch **ON** and **OFF** at least six times, leaving the ignition **ON** for at least five seconds each time. Check for fuel leaks.

11. Start the engine and allow it to reach normal operating temperature, then check for coolant leaks.

TESTING

Because the fuel injectors use a pulsed electrical signal, it is possible to test them for correct functioning.

Unfortunately, the equipment necessary to do this is beyond the budget of most weekend mechanics.

If you feel that one or more of the injectors are not functioning properly, it is recommended that the individual injectors, or the entire fuel supply manifold with the injectors be taken to an authorized dealer for testing.

Fuel Charging Assembly

The fuel charging assembly is referred to by many different names including fuel rail and fuel supply manifold. In either case, it still refers to the tubing system that delivers fuel to the individual injectors.

REMOVAL AND INSTALLATION

2.3L Engine

♦ **See Figure 36**

1. Drain the cooling system.

※※ **CAUTION**

When draining the coolant, keep in mind that cats and dogs are attracted to ethylene glycol antifreeze, and could drink any that is left in an uncovered container or in puddles on the ground. This will prove fatal in sufficient quantity. Always drain the coolant into a sealable container. Coolant should be reused unless it is contaminated or several years old.

2. Disconnect the negative battery cable.

3. Relieve the fuel system pressure as described in this section.

※※ **CAUTION**

The fuel system is under pressure. Release pressure slowly and contain spillage. Observe the no smoking/no open flame precautions. Have a Class B-C (dry powder) fire extinguisher within arm's reach at all times.

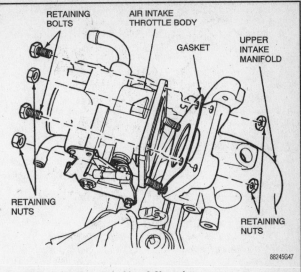

Fig. 36 Fuel charging assembly—2.3L engine

4. Tag and unfasten the electrical connectors to the throttle position sensor, knock sensor, air charge temperature sensor, coolant temperature sensor and the injector wiring harness.

5. Tag and disconnect the vacuum lines at the upper intake manifold vacuum tree, the EGR valve vacuum line and the fuel pressure regulator vacuum line.

6. Remove the plastic throttle linkage shield and disconnect the throttle linkage and speed control cable, if equipped. Unbolt the accelerator cable from the bracket and position out of the way.

7. Tag and disconnect the air intake hose, air bypass hose and crankcase vent hose.

8. Disconnect the PCV hose from the fitting on the underside of the upper intake manifold.

9. Loosen the hose clamp on the coolant bypass line at the lower intake manifold and disconnect the hose.

10. Disconnect the EGR tube from the EGR valve by removing the flange nut.

11. Remove the four upper intake manifold retaining nuts, then remove the upper intake manifold and throttle body assembly.

12. Unfasten the push connect fittings at the fuel supply manifold and fuel return lines, then disconnect the fuel return line from the fuel supply manifold.

13. Remove the engine oil dipstick bracket retaining bolt, then remove the bracket from the engine.

14. Tag and disconnect the electrical connectors from all four fuel injectors and move the harness aside.

15. Remove the two fuel supply manifold retaining bolt, then carefully remove the fuel supply manifold with the injectors attached. The injectors may be removed from the fuel supply manifold at this time by exerting a slight twisting/pulling motion.

16. Remove and discard the O-rings attached to each injector. Clean the gasket material from all mating surfaces.

To install:

17. Lubricate new injector O-rings with a light grade engine oil and install two on each injector. Do not use silicone grease on the O-rings as it will clog the injectors. Make sure the injector caps are clean and free of contamination.

18. Install the fuel injector supply manifold and injectors into the intake manifold. Make sure the injectors are seated completely.

19. Secure the fuel manifold assembly with the two retaining bolts. Tighten the retaining bolts to 15–22 ft. lbs. (20–30 Nm).

20. Fasten the four electrical connectors to the injectors.

21. Place a new gasket on the lower intake manifold, then place the upper intake manifold in position. Install the four retaining bolts and tighten them, to 15–22 ft. lbs. (20–30 Nm).

22. Install the engine oil dipstick tube and retainer bolt.

23. Connect the fuel supply and return fuel lines to the fuel supply manifold.

24. Connect the EGR tube to the EGR valve and tighten the fitting to 6–8.5 ft. lbs. (8–11.5 Nm).

25. Connect the coolant bypass line and tighten the clamp.

26. Connect the PCV system hose to the fitting on the underside of the upper intake manifold.

27. Install the upper intake manifold vacuum lines, being careful to install them in their original locations. Connect the vacuum lines to the EGR valve and fuel pressure regulator.

28. Hold the accelerator cable bracket in position on the upper intake manifold and install the retaining bolt. Tighten the bolt to 10–15 ft. lbs. (13–20 Nm).

29. Install the accelerator cable to the bracket.

30. If the throttle body was removed from the upper intake manifold, position a new gasket on the mounting flange and install the throttle body.

31. Connect the accelerator cable and speed control cable to the throttle body. Install the throttle linkage shield.

32. Fasten the electrical connectors to the throttle position sensor, knock sensor, air charge temperature sensor, coolant temperature sensor and injector wiring harness.

33. Connect the air intake hose, air bypass hose and crankcase vent hose.

34. Connect the negative battery cable.

35. Refill the cooling system.

36. Build up fuel pressure by turning the ignition switch **ON** and **OFF** at least six times, leaving the ignition **ON** for at least five seconds each time. Check for fuel leaks.

37. Start the engine and allow it to reach normal operating temperature, then check for coolant leaks.

3.0L Engine

▶ See Figures 37 thru 44

1. Disconnect the negative battery cable.

2. Remove the fuel cap to vent the fuel tank pressure. Depressurize the fuel system as described in this section.

✳✳ CAUTION

The fuel system is under pressure. Release pressure slowly and contain spillage. Observe no smoking/no open flame precautions.

Have a Class B-C (dry powder) fire extinguisher within arm's reach at all times.

3. Disconnect the push connect fitting at the fuel supply line.

4. Tad and disconnect the wiring harness at the throttle position sensor, air bypass valve and air charge temperature sensor.

5. Remove the air cleaner outlet tube between the air cleaner and throttle body by loosening the two clamps.

6. Remove the snow shield by removing the retaining nut on top of the shield and the two bolts on the side.

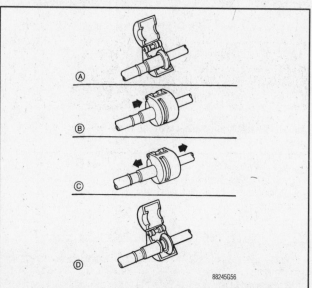

Fig. 37 Follow these diagrams to remove the spring lock connection

Fig. 38 Disconnect the wire harness attached to each injector

Fig. 39 Remove the retainer bolts securing the fuel charging line in place

Fig. 40 Remove the clip over the spring lock connection

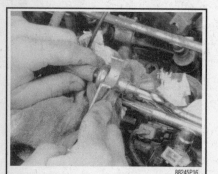

Fig. 41 Various tools can unfasten the spring lock connector, all work the same. Slide it into the spring . . .

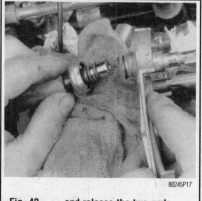

Fig. 42 . . . and release the two ends

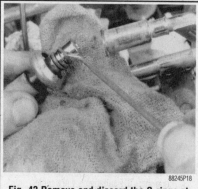

Fig. 43 Remove and discard the O-rings at one end of the connection

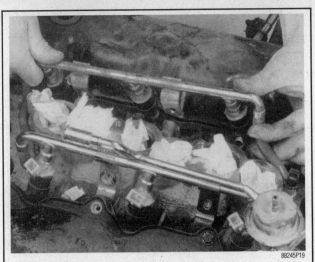

Fig. 44 Lift the charging assembly and injector out from the cylinder head

7. Tag and disconnect the vacuum hoses at the vacuum fittings on the intake manifold.

8. Disconnect and remove the accelerator and speed control cables (if equipped) from the accelerator mounting bracket and throttle lever.

9. Remove the transmission valve (TV) linkage from the throttle lever on automatic transmission equipped models.

10. Remove the intake retaining bolts and lift the air intake/throttle body assembly off the guide pins on the lower intake manifold and remove the assembly from the engine.

11. Remove and discard the gasket from the lower intake manifold assembly.

12. Carefully tag and disconnect the wiring harness from the fuel injectors.

13. Disconnect the vacuum line from the fuel pressure regulator.

14. Remove the fuel injector manifold retaining bolts, two on each side.

15. Carefully disengage the fuel rail assembly from the fuel injectors by lifting and gently rocking the rail.

16. Clean the gasket material from all the mating surfaces.

17. Inspect the condition of the sealing O-rings on the injectors. If cracked or torn, replace.

To install:

18. Carefully install the fuel rail assembly and injectors into the lower intake manifold, one side at a time, pushing down on the fuel rail to make sure the O-rings are seated.

19. Hold the fuel rail assembly in place and install the retaining bolts finger-tight. Tighten the retaining bolts to 6–8 ft. lbs. (8–12 Nm).

20. Connect the fuel supply and return lines.

21. Connect the fuel injector wiring harness at the injectors.

22. Connect the vacuum line to the fuel pressure regulator.

23. Clean and inspect the mounting faces of the air intake/throttle body assembly and the lower intake manifold. Both surfaces must be clean and flat.

24. Clean and oil the manifold stud threads.

25. Install a new gasket on the lower intake manifold.

26. Using the guide pins as locators, install the air intake/throttle body assembly to the lower intake manifold.

27. Install the stud bolt and retaining bolts finger-tight, then tighten them to 15–22 ft. lbs. (20–30 Nm) in the numbered sequence illustrated.

28. Connect the fuel supply and return lines to the fuel rail.

29. Connect the wiring harness to the throttle position sensor, air charge temperature sensor and air bypass valve.

30. Install the accelerator cable and speed control cable, if equipped.

31. Install the vacuum hoses to the vacuum fittings, making sure the hoses are installed in their original locations.

32. Install the throttle valve linkage to the throttle lever, if equipped with an automatic transmission.

33. Reconnect the negative battery cable.

34. Install the fuel tank cap.

35. Install the snow shield and air cleaner outlet tube.

36. Build up fuel pressure by turning the ignition switch **ON** and **OFF** at least six times, leaving the ignition **ON** for at least five seconds each time. Check for fuel leaks.

37. Start the engine and adjust the idle speed, if necessary.

4.0L Engine

♦ **See Figure 45**

1. Disconnect the negative battery cable.

2. Remove the air cleaner and intake duct.

3. Remove the weather shield.

4. Disconnect the throttle cable and bracket.

5. Tag and unfasten all vacuum lines connected to the manifold.

6. Tag and unfasten all electrical wires connected to the manifold assemblies.

7. Relieve the fuel system pressure.

✳✳ CAUTION

The fuel system is under pressure. Release pressure slowly and contain spillage. Observe no smoking/no open flame precautions. Have a Class B-C (dry powder) fire extinguisher within arm's reach at all times.

8. Tag and remove the spark plug wires.

9. Remove the ignition coil and bracket.

10. Remove the screws retaining the throttle body assembly to the upper manifold. Lift off the throttle body and discard the gasket.

11. Remove the attaching nuts and lift off the upper manifold.

12. Remove the rocker covers.

13. Disconnect the fuel supply line at the fuel manifold.

14. Disconnect the fuel return line at the pressure regulator as follows:

a. Disengage the locking tabs on the connector retainer and separate the retainer halves.

b. Check the visible, internal portion of the fitting for dirt. Clean the fitting thoroughly.

c. Push the fitting towards the regulator, insert the fingers on Fuel Line Coupling Key T90P-9550-A, or equivalent, into the slots in the coupling. Using the tool, pull the fitting from the regulator. The fitting should slide off easily, if properly disconnected.

15. Remove the Torx® head stud bolts retaining the manifold and remove the manifold.

16. Tag and remove the electrical harness connector from each injector.

17. Remove the retaining clip from each injector.

18. Grasp the injector body and pull upward while gently rocking the injector from side-to-side.

19. Remove the lower intake manifold bolts. Tap the manifold lightly with a plastic mallet and remove it.

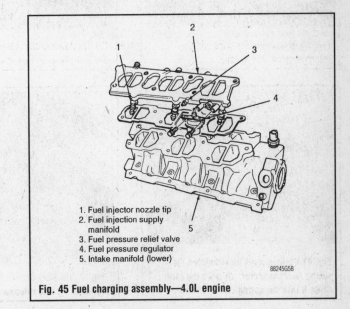

1. Fuel injector nozzle tip
2. Fuel injection supply manifold
3. Fuel pressure relief valve
4. Fuel pressure regulator
5. Intake manifold (lower)

Fig. 45 Fuel charging assembly—4.0L engine

20. Clean all mating surfaces of gasket material.
To install:
21. Apply RTV silicone gasket material at the junction points of the heads and manifold.

➡**This material will set within 15 minutes, depending on brand used, so work quickly!**

22. Install new manifold gaskets and again apply the RTV material.
23. Position the manifold and install the nuts hand-tight. Tighten the nuts to 18 ft. lbs. (23 Nm).
24. Once again, apply RTV material to the manifold/head joints.
25. Install the rocker covers.
26. Inspect the O-rings for each injector. There should be 2 for each. Replace them as required.
27. Inspect, and if necessary, replace the plastic cap covering the injector pintle. If there is no plastic cap, it may have fallen into the manifold.
28. Coat the O-rings or the injectors with 5W engine oil and push/twist each injector into the fuel manifold.
29. Install the retainers and electrical harness connectors.
30. Position the fuel supply manifold and press it down firmly until the injectors are fully seated in the fuel supply manifold and lower intake manifold.
31. Install the Torx® head bolts and tighten them to 7–10 ft. lbs. (9–13 Nm).
32. Install the fuel supply line and tighten the fitting to 15–18 ft. lbs. (19–23 Nm).
33. Install the fuel return line on the regulator by pushing it onto the fuel pressure regulator line of to the shoulder.

✳✳ WARNING

The connector should grip the line securely!

34. Install the connector retainer and snap the two halves of the retainer together.
35. Install the upper manifold. Tighten the nuts to 18 ft. lbs. (23 Nm).
36. Install the EDIS coil.

37. Connect the fuel and return lines.
38. Ensure that the mating surfaces of the throttle body and upper manifold are clean and free of gasket material.
39. Install a new gasket on the manifold and position the throttle body on the manifold. Tighten the bolts to 76–106 inch lbs. (8–12 Nm).
40. Connect all wires.
41. Connect all vacuum lines.
42. Connect the throttle linkage.
43. Install the weather shield.
44. Install the air cleaner and duct.
45. Fill and bleed the cooling system.
46. Connect the battery ground.
47. Run the engine and check for leaks.

Fuel Pressure Regulator

REMOVAL & INSTALLATION

▶ See Figures 46, 47, 48, 49 and 50

1. Disconnect the negative battery cable.
2. Depressurize the fuel system as described in this section.

✳✳ CAUTION

The fuel system is under pressure. Release pressure slowly and contain spillage. Observe the no smoking/no open flame precautions. Have a Class B-C (dry powder) fire extinguisher within arm's reach at all times.

3. Remove the vacuum and fuel lines at the pressure regulator.
4. Remove the three Allen retaining screws from the regulator housing.
5. Remove the pressure regulator assembly, gasket and O-ring. Discard the gasket and check the O-ring for signs of cracks or deterioration.

Fig. 46 Remove the vacuum line attached to the regulator—3.0L engine shown

Fig. 47 Remove the regulator retainer bolts—this regulator is secured with Allen head bolts

Fig. 48 Lift the regulator off the base

Fig. 49 Remove and discard the sealing gasket

Fig. 50 Also remove and discard the O-ring

6. Clean the gasket mating surfaces. If scraping is necessary, be careful not to damage the fuel pressure regulator or supply line gasket mating surfaces.

To install:

7. Lubricate the pressure regulator O-ring with light engine oil. Do not use silicone grease; it will clog the injectors.

8. Install the O-ring and a new gasket on the pressure regulator.

9. Install the pressure regulator on the fuel manifold and tighten the retaining screws to 27–40 inch lbs. (3–4 Nm).

10. Install the vacuum and fuel lines at the pressure regulator.

11. Connect the negative battery cable.

12. Build up fuel pressure by turning the ignition switch **ON** and **Off** at least six times, leaving the ignition **On** for at least five seconds each time. Check for fuel leaks.

13. Start the engine and allow it to reach normal operating temperature, then check for coolant leaks.

Pressure Relief Valve

REMOVAL & INSTALLATION

▶ **See Figure 51**

1. Disconnect the negative battery cable.
2. Relieve the fuel system pressure as described in this section.

❋ CAUTION

The fuel system is under pressure. Release pressure slowly and contain spillage. Observe the no smoking/no open flame precautions. Have a Class B-C (dry powder) fire extinguisher handy at all times.

3. Remove the pressure relief valve cap.
4. Using a suitable sized socket or wrench, loosen and remove the pressure relief valve from the mount on the fuel rail. Remove and discard the washer.

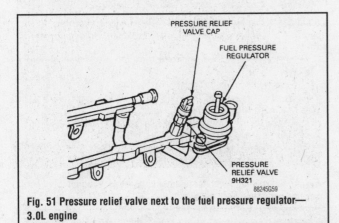

Fig. 51 Pressure relief valve next to the fuel pressure regulator—3.0L engine

FUEL TANK

Tank Assembly

REMOVAL & INSTALLATION

1. Disconnect the negative battery cable.
2. Depressurize the fuel system.

❋ CAUTION

The fuel system is under pressure. Release pressure slowly and contain spillage. Observe the no smoking/no open flame precautions. Have a Class B-C (dry powder) fire extinguisher handy at all times.

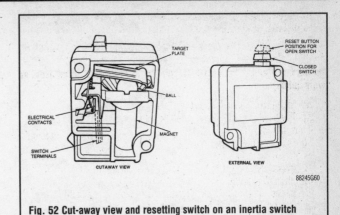

Fig. 52 Cut-away view and resetting switch on an inertia switch

To install:

5. Install the pressure relief valve and new washer into the fuel rail. Tighten the valve to 71 inch lbs. (8 Nm).

6. Install the pressure relief cap.

7. Connect the negative battery cable.

8. Build up fuel pressure by turning the ignition switch **ON** and **Off** at least six times, leaving the ignition **On** for at least five seconds each time. Check for fuel leaks.

9. Start the engine and allow it to reach normal operating temperature, then check for coolant leaks.

Inertia Fuel Shut-off Switch

The inertia switch shut off the fuel to the engine in the event of collision. once the shutoff switch has activated, it must be manually reset to start the engine.

RESETTING

▶ **See Figure 52**

To reset the inertia shutoff switch, access the switch at the right front kick panel and press and hold the button at the top of the switch. Continue to hold the reset button until it locks in place.

REMOVAL & INSTALLATION

1. Disconnect the negative battery cable.
2. Unfasten the wire harness at the bottom of the inertia switch.
3. Remove the retainer screws securing the inertia switch to the kick panel.

To install:

4. Position the inertia switch on the kick panel and secure in place with the retainer screws.

5. Fasten the wire harness to the bottom of the switch.

6. Connect the negative battery cable.

7. Start the vehicle and make sure the switch is not interrupting the fuel supply.

3. Raise and support the vehicle safely on jackstands.

4. Drain the fuel tank into a suitable gasoline approved safety container and take precautions to avoid the risk of fire.

5. Loosen the filler pipe clamp.

6. Place a floor jack or other suitable lifting device below the fuel tank.

7. Remove the bolt from the front strap and remove the front strap.

8. Remove the bolt from the rear strap and remove the rear strap.

9. Remove the fuel feed hose at the fuel gauge sender push connector.

10. Remove the fuel hose from the sender unit push connector.

11. Remove the fuel vapor hose from the vapor valve.

12. Lower the fuel tank from the chassis.

13. Remove the shield from the fuel tank.

Never hammer on or near the fuel tank with metal tools! The risk of spark and explosion is always present.

To install:
14. Raise the tank into position using a suitable lifting device.
15. Attach the rear strap to the vehicle.
16. Install the shield on the top of the fuel tank.
17. Position the tank to the vehicle and attach the front strap. do not torque the retainer bolt at this time.
18. Install the fuel lines to the feed and return hoses at the fuel gauge sender push connector.
19. Install the filler pipe in position and tighten the filler pipe clamp.
20. Install the rear strap and mounting bolt. Tighten the rear bolt and front strap retainer bolts to 18–20 ft. lbs. on 1986–87 models; 35–45 ft. lbs. on 1988–97 models.
21. Connect the negative battery cable.
22. Build up fuel pressure by turning the ignition switch **ON** and **Off** at least six times, leaving the ignition **ON** for at least five seconds each time. Check for fuel leaks.
23. Start the engine and allow it to reach normal operating temperature, then check for coolant leaks.

SENDING UNIT REPLACEMENT

▶ **See Figure 53**

The fuel tank level sending unit is incorporated into the fuel pump assembly for 1989 and later models. In the event the sending unit fails, the sending unit and pump must be replaced as a unit. The sending unit removal and installation procedure is the same for 1986–88 models as it is for 1989–97 models.
1. Disconnect the negative battery cable.
2. Depressurize the fuel system.

The fuel system is under pressure. Release pressure slowly and contain spillage. Observe the no smoking/no open flame precautions. Have a Class B-C (dry powder) fire extinguisher handy at all times.

3. Raise and safely support the vehicle on jackstands.
4. Loosen the gas tank filler pipe clamp.
5. Remove the bolt from the front strap and remove the gas tank front strap.
6. Remove the bolt from the rear strap and remove the gas tank rear strap.
7. Remove the fuel feed hose at the fuel gauge sender push connector.
8. Remove the fuel hose from the sender unit push connector.
9. Remove the fuel vapor hose from the vapor valve.
10. Slowly lower the fuel tank from the chassis.
11. Remove the shield from the fuel tank.
12. Remove any dirt from the fuel pump flange.
13. Turn the fuel pump locking ring counterclockwise to remove it. There are wrenches for this purpose, but you can loosen the ring by tapping it around with a wood dowel and plastic or rubber mallet.

Never hammer on or near the fuel tank with metal tools! The risk of spark and explosion is always present!

14. Remove the fuel pump and bracket assembly. Discard the rubber O-ring.

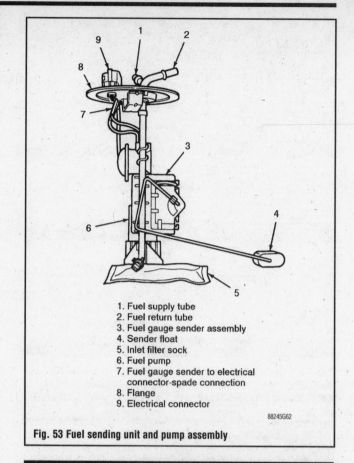

1. Fuel supply tube
2. Fuel return tube
3. Fuel gauge sender assembly
4. Sender float
5. Inlet filter sock
6. Fuel pump
7. Fuel gauge sender to electrical connector-spade connection
8. Flange
9. Electrical connector

88245G62

Fig. 53 Fuel sending unit and pump assembly

Do not attempt to apply battery voltage to the pump to check its operation while removed from the vehicle. Running the pump dry will destroy it.

To install:
15. Clean the around the fuel pump hole.
16. Coat the new O-ring with multi-purpose grease to hold it in place. Install the O-ring in the ring groove on the fuel pump.
17. Position the pump assembly in the tank making sure the keyways align and the seal ring remains stays in place.
18. Tighten the locking ring to 40–50 ft. lbs. (52–65 Nm).
19. Install the shield on to the fuel tank.
20. Raise the tank into position and support until all the straps are secured in place.
21. Connect the hoses and wires to the sender assembly.
22. Attach the rear strap to the vehicle.
23. Attach the front strap.
24. Install the fuel lines to the feed and return hoses at the fuel gauge sender push connector.
25. Install the filler pipe in position and tighten the filler pipe clamp.
26. Install the front and rear fuel tank mounting bolts and tighten them to 18–20 ft. lbs. for 1986–87 models; 35–45 ft. lbs. on 1988–90 models.
27. Connect the negative battery cable.
28. Build up fuel pressure by turning the ignition switch **ON** and **Off** at least six times, leaving the ignition **On** for at least five seconds each time. Check for fuel leaks.
29. Start the engine and allow it to reach normal operating temperature, then check for coolant leaks.

6

CHASSIS ELECTRICAL

UNDERSTANDING AND TROUBLESHOOTING ELECTRICAL SYSTEMS

Basic Electrical Theory

▶ See Figure 1

For any 12 volt, negative ground, electrical system to operate, the electricity must travel in a complete circuit. This simply means that current (power) from the positive (+) terminal of the battery must eventually return to the negative (-) terminal of the battery. Along the way, this current will travel through wires, fuses, switches and components. If, for any reason, the flow of current through the circuit is interrupted, the component fed by that circuit will cease to function properly.

Perhaps the easiest way to visualize a circuit is to think of connecting a light bulb (with two wires attached to it) to the battery—one wire attached to the negative (-) terminal of the battery and the other wire to the positive (+) terminal. With the two wires touching the battery terminals, the circuit would be complete and the light bulb would illuminate. Electricity would follow a path from the battery to the bulb and back to the battery. It's easy to see that with longer wires on our light bulb, it could be mounted anywhere. Further, one wire could be fitted with a switch so that the light could be turned on and off.

The normal automotive circuit differs from this simple example in two ways. First, instead of having a return wire from the bulb to the battery, the current travels through the frame of the vehicle. Since the negative (-) battery cable is attached to the frame (made of electrically conductive metal), the frame of the vehicle can serve as a ground wire to complete the circuit. Secondly, most automotive circuits contain multiple components which receive power from a single circuit. This lessens the amount of wire needed to power components on the vehicle.

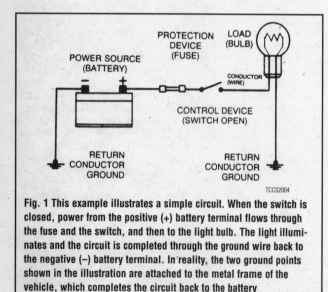

Fig. 1 This example illustrates a simple circuit. When the switch is closed, power from the positive (+) battery terminal flows through the fuse and the switch, and then to the light bulb. The light illuminates and the circuit is completed through the ground wire back to the negative (−) battery terminal. In reality, the two ground points shown in the illustration are attached to the metal frame of the vehicle, which completes the circuit back to the battery

HOW DOES ELECTRICITY WORK: THE WATER ANALOGY

Electricity is the flow of electrons—the subatomic particles that constitute the outer shell of an atom. Electrons spin in an orbit around the center core of an atom. The center core is comprised of protons (positive charge) and neutrons (neutral charge). Electrons have a negative charge and balance out the positive charge of the protons. When an outside force causes the number of electrons to unbalance the charge of the protons, the electrons will split off the atom and look for another atom to balance out. If this imbalance is kept up, electrons will continue to move and an electrical flow will exist.

Many people have been taught electrical theory using an analogy with water. In a comparison with water flowing through a pipe, the electrons would be the water and the wire is the pipe.

The flow of electricity can be measured much like the flow of water through a pipe. The unit of measurement used is amperes, frequently abbreviated as amps (a). You can compare amperage to the volume of water flowing through a pipe.

When connected to a circuit, an ammeter will measure the actual amount of current flowing through the circuit. When relatively few electrons flow through a circuit, the amperage is low. When many electrons flow, the amperage is high.

Water pressure is measured in units such as pounds per square inch (psi); The electrical pressure is measured in units called volts (v). When a voltmeter is connected to a circuit, it is measuring the electrical pressure.

The actual flow of electricity depends not only on voltage and amperage, but also on the resistance of the circuit. The higher the resistance, the higher the force necessary to push the current through the circuit. The standard unit for measuring resistance is an ohm. Resistance in a circuit varies depending on the amount and type of components used in the circuit. The main factors which determine resistance are:

• Material—some materials have more resistance than others. Those with high resistance are said to be insulators. Rubber materials (or rubber-like plastics) are some of the most common insulators used in vehicles as they have a very high resistance to electricity. Very low resistance materials are said to be conductors. Copper wire is among the best conductors. Silver is actually a superior conductor to copper and is used in some relay contacts, but its high cost prohibits its use as common wiring. Most automotive wiring is made of copper.

• Size—the larger the wire size being used, the less resistance the wire will have. This is why components which use large amounts of electricity usually have large wires supplying current to them.

• Length—for a given thickness of wire, the longer the wire, the greater the resistance. The shorter the wire, the less the resistance. When determining the proper wire for a circuit, both size and length must be considered to design a circuit that can handle the current needs of the component.

• Temperature—with many materials, the higher the temperature, the greater the resistance (positive temperature coefficient). Some materials exhibit the opposite trait of lower resistance with higher temperatures (negative temperature coefficient). These principles are used in many of the sensors on the engine.

OHM'S LAW

There is a direct relationship between current, voltage and resistance. The relationship between current, voltage and resistance can be summed up by a statement known as Ohm's law.

Voltage (E) is equal to amperage (I) times resistance ®: $E = I \times R$

Other forms of the formula are $R = E/I$ and $I = E/R$

In each of these formulas, E is the voltage in volts, I is the current in amps and R is the resistance in ohms. The basic point to remember is that as the resistance of a circuit goes up, the amount of current that flows in the circuit will go down, if voltage remains the same.

The amount of work that the electricity can perform is expressed as power. The unit of power is the watt (w). The relationship between power, voltage and current is expressed as:

Power (w) is equal to amperage (I) times voltage (E): $W = I \times E$

This is only true for direct current (DC) circuits; The alternating current formula is a tad different, but since the electrical circuits in most vehicles are DC type, we need not get into AC circuit theory.

Electrical Components

POWER SOURCE

Power is supplied to the vehicle by two devices: The battery and the alternator. The battery supplies electrical power during starting or during periods when the current demand of the vehicle's electrical system exceeds the output capacity of the alternator. The alternator supplies electrical current when the engine is running. Just not does the alternator supply the current needs of the vehicle, but it recharges the battery.

The Battery

In most modern vehicles, the battery is a lead/acid electrochemical device consisting of six 2 volt subsections (cells) connected in series, so that the unit is capable of producing approximately 12 volts of electrical pressure. Each sub-section consists of a series of positive and negative plates held a short distance apart in a solution of sulfuric acid and water.

The two types of plates are of dissimilar metals. This sets up a chemical reaction, and it is this reaction which produces current flow from the battery when its positive and negative terminals are connected to an electrical load . The power removed from the battery is replaced by the alternator, restoring the battery to its original chemical state.

The Alternator

On some vehicles there isn't an alternator, but a generator. The difference is that an alternator supplies alternating current which is then changed to direct current for use on the vehicle, while a generator produces direct current. Alternators tend to be more efficient and that is why they are used.

Alternators and generators are devices that consist of coils of wires wound together making big electromagnets. One group of coils spins within another set and the interaction of the magnetic fields causes a current to flow. This current is then drawn off the coils and fed into the vehicles electrical system.

GROUND

Two types of grounds are used in automotive electric circuits. Direct ground components are grounded to the frame through their mounting points. All other components use some sort of ground wire which is attached to the frame or chassis of the vehicle. The electrical current runs through the chassis of the vehicle and returns to the battery through the ground (-) cable; if you look, you'll see that the battery ground cable connects between the battery and the frame or chassis of the vehicle.

➡It should be noted that a good percentage of electrical problems can be traced to bad grounds.

PROTECTIVE DEVICES

▶ See Figure 2

It is possible for large surges of current to pass through the electrical system of your vehicle. If this surge of current were to reach the load in the circuit, the surge could burn it out or severely damage it. It can also overload the wiring, causing the harness to get hot and melt the insulation. To prevent this, fuses, circuit breakers and/or fusible links are connected into the supply wires of the electrical system. These items are nothing more than a built-in weak spot in the system. When an abnormal amount of current flows through the system, these protective devices work as follows to protect the circuit:

- Fuse—when an excessive electrical current passes through a fuse, the

fuse "blows" (the conductor melts) and opens the circuit, preventing the passage of current.
- Circuit Breaker—a circuit breaker is basically a self-repairing fuse. It will open the circuit in the same fashion as a fuse, but when the surge subsides, the circuit breaker can be reset and does not need replacement.
- Fusible Link—a fusible link (fuse link or main link) is a short length of special, high temperature insulated wire that acts as a fuse. When an excessive electrical current passes through a fusible link, the thin gauge wire inside the link melts, creating an intentional open to protect the circuit. To repair the circuit, the link must be replaced. Some newer type fusible links are housed in plug-in modules, which are simply replaced like a fuse, while older type fusible links must be cut and spliced if they melt. Since this link is very early in the electrical path, it's the first place to look if nothing on the vehicle works, yet the battery seems to be charged and is properly connected.

✳✳ CAUTION

Always replace fuses, circuit breakers and fusible links with identically rated components. Under no circumstances should a component of higher or lower amperage rating be substituted.

SWITCHES & RELAYS

▶ See Figures 3 and 4

Switches are used in electrical circuits to control the passage of current. The most common use is to open and close circuits between the battery and the various electric devices in the system. Switches are rated according to the amount of amperage they can handle. If a sufficient amperage rated switch is not used in a circuit, the switch could overload and cause damage.

Some electrical components which require a large amount of current to operate use a special switch called a relay. Since these circuits carry a large amount of current, the thickness of the wire in the circuit is also greater. If this large wire were connected from the load to the control switch, the switch would have to carry the high amperage load and the fairing or dash would be twice as large to accommodate the increased size of the wiring harness. To prevent these problems, a relay is used.

Relays are composed of a coil and a set of contacts. When the coil has a current passed though it, a magnetic field is formed and this field causes the contacts to move together, completing the circuit. Most relays are normally open, preventing current from passing through the circuit, but they can take any electrical form depending on the job they are intended to do. Relays can be considered "remote control switches." They allow a smaller current to operate devices that require higher amperages. When a small current operates the coil, a larger current is allowed to pass by the contacts. Some common circuits which may use relays are the horn, headlights, starter, electric fuel pump and other high draw circuits.

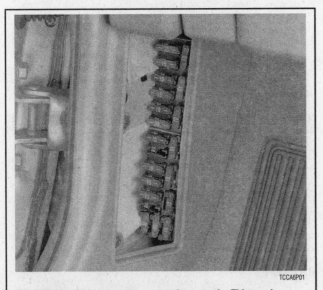

TCCA6P01

Fig. 2 Most vehicles use one or more fuse panels. This one is located on the driver's side kick panel

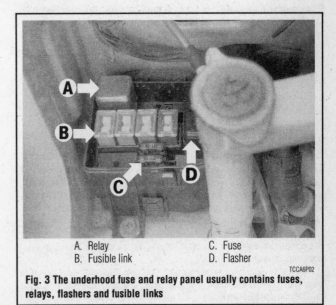

A. Relay
B. Fusible link
C. Fuse
D. Flasher

TCCA6P02

Fig. 3 The underhood fuse and relay panel usually contains fuses, relays, flashers and fusible links

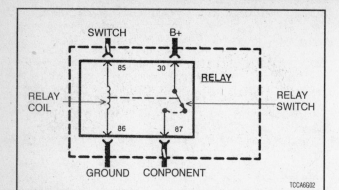

SWITCH   B+

RELAY

RELAY COIL

RELAY SWITCH

GROUND   CONPONENT

TCCA6G02

Fig. 4 Relays are composed of a coil and a switch. These two components are linked together so that when one operates, the other operates at the same time. The large wires in the circuit are connected from the battery to one side of the relay switch (B+) and from the opposite side of the relay switch to the load (component). Smaller wires are connected from the relay coil to the control switch for the circuit and from the opposite side of the relay coil to ground

LOAD

Every electrical circuit must include a "load" (something to use the electricity coming from the source). Without this load, the battery would attempt to deliver its entire power supply from one pole to another. This is called a "short circuit." All this electricity would take a short cut to ground and cause a great amount of damage to other components in the circuit by developing a tremendous amount of heat. This condition could develop sufficient heat to melt the insulation on all the surrounding wires and reduce a multiple wire cable to a lump of plastic and copper.

WIRING & HARNESSES

The average vehicle contains meters and meters of wiring, with hundreds of individual connections. To protect the many wires from damage and to keep them from becoming a confusing tangle, they are organized into bundles, enclosed in plastic or taped together and called wiring harnesses. Different harnesses serve different parts of the vehicle. Individual wires are color coded to help trace them through a harness where sections are hidden from view.

Automotive wiring or circuit conductors can be either single strand wire, multi-strand wire or printed circuitry. Single strand wire has a solid metal core and is usually used inside such components as alternators, motors, relays and other devices. Multi-strand wire has a core made of many small strands of wire twisted together into a single conductor. Most of the wiring in an automotive electrical system is made up of multi-strand wire, either as a single conductor or grouped together in a harness. All wiring is color coded on the insulator, either as a solid color or as a colored wire with an identification stripe. A printed circuit is a thin film of copper or other conductor that is printed on an insulator backing. Occasionally, a printed circuit is sandwiched between two sheets of plastic for more protection and flexibility. A complete printed circuit, consisting of conductors, insulating material and connectors for lamps or other components is called a printed circuit board. Printed circuitry is used in place of individual wires or harnesses in places where space is limited, such as behind instrument panels.

Since automotive electrical systems are very sensitive to changes in resistance, the selection of properly sized wires is critical when systems are repaired. A loose or corroded connection or a replacement wire that is too small for the circuit will add extra resistance and an additional voltage drop to the circuit.

The wire gauge number is an expression of the cross-section area of the conductor. Vehicles from countries that use the metric system will typically describe the wire size as its cross-sectional area in square millimeters. In this method, the larger the wire, the greater the number. Another common system for expressing wire size is the American Wire Gauge (AWG) system. As gauge number increases, area decreases and the wire becomes smaller. An 18 gauge wire is smaller than a 4 gauge wire. A wire with a higher gauge number will carry less current than a wire with a lower gauge number. Gauge wire size refers to

the size of the strands of the conductor, not the size of the complete wire with insulator. It is possible, therefore, to have two wires of the same gauge with different diameters because one may have thicker insulation than the other.

It is essential to understand how a circuit works before trying to figure out why it doesn't. An electrical schematic shows the electrical current paths when a circuit is operating properly. Schematics break the entire electrical system down into individual circuits. In a schematic, usually no attempt is made to represent wiring and components as they physically appear on the vehicle; switches and other components are shown as simply as possible. Face views of harness connectors show the cavity or terminal locations in all multi-pin connectors to help locate test points.

CONNECTORS

▶ **See Figures 5 and 6**

Three types of connectors are commonly used in automotive applications—weatherproof, molded and hard shell.

• Weatherproof—these connectors are most commonly used where the connector is exposed to the elements. Terminals are protected against moisture and dirt by sealing rings which provide a weathertight seal. All repairs require the use of a special terminal and the tool required to service it. Unlike standard blade type terminals, these weatherproof terminals cannot be straightened once they are bent. Make certain that the connectors are properly seated and all of the sealing rings are in place when connecting leads.

• Molded—these connectors require complete replacement of the connector if found to be defective. This means splicing a new connector assembly into

TCCA6P03

Fig. 5 Hard shell (left) and weatherproof (right) connectors have replaceable terminals

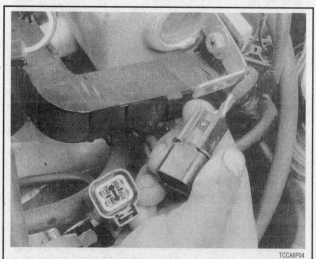

TCCA6P04

Fig. 6 Weatherproof connectors are most commonly used in the engine compartment or where the connector is exposed to the elements

the harness. All splices should be soldered to insure proper contact. Use care when probing the connections or replacing terminals in them, as it is possible to create a short circuit between opposite terminals. If this happens to the wrong terminal pair, it is possible to damage certain components. Always use jumper wires between connectors for circuit checking and NEVER probe through weatherproof seals.

• Hard Shell—unlike molded connectors, the terminal contacts in hard-shell connectors can be replaced. Replacement usually involves the use of a special terminal removal tool that depresses the locking tangs (barbs) on the connector terminal and allows the connector to be removed from the rear of the shell. The connector shell should be replaced if it shows any evidence of burning, melting, cracks, or breaks. Replace individual terminals that are burnt, corroded, distorted or loose.

Test Equipment

Pinpointing the exact cause of trouble in an electrical circuit is most times accomplished by the use of special test equipment. The following describes different types of commonly used test equipment and briefly explains how to use them in diagnosis. In addition to the information covered below, the tool manufacturer's instructions booklet (provided with the tester) should be read and clearly understood before attempting any test procedures.

JUMPER WIRES

✳✳ CAUTION

Never use jumper wires made from a thinner gauge wire than the circuit being tested. If the jumper wire is of too small a gauge, it may overheat and possibly melt. Never use jumpers to bypass high resistance loads in a circuit. Bypassing resistance, in effect, creates a short circuit. This may, in turn, cause damage and fire. Jumper wires should only be used to bypass lengths of wire or to simulate switches.

Jumper wires are simple, yet extremely valuable, pieces of test equipment. They are basically test wires which are used to bypass sections of a circuit. Although jumper wires can be purchased, they are usually fabricated from lengths of standard automotive wire and whatever type of connector (alligator clip, spade connector or pin connector) that is required for the particular application being tested. In cramped, hard-to-reach areas, it is advisable to have insulated boots over the jumper wire terminals in order to prevent accidental grounding. It is also advisable to include a standard automotive fuse in any jumper wire. This is commonly referred to as a "fused jumper". By inserting an in-line fuse holder between a set of test leads, a fused jumper wire can be used for bypassing open circuits. Use a 5 amp fuse to provide protection against voltage spikes.

Jumper wires are used primarily to locate open electrical circuits, on either the ground (-) side of the circuit or on the power (+) side. If an electrical component fails to operate, connect the jumper wire between the component and a good ground. If the component operates only with the jumper installed, the ground circuit is open. If the ground circuit is good, but the component does not operate, the circuit between the power feed and component may be open. By moving the jumper wire successively back from the component toward the power source, you can isolate the area of the circuit where the open is located. When the component stops functioning, or the power is cut off, the open is in the segment of wire between the jumper and the point previously tested.

You can sometimes connect the jumper wire directly from the battery to the "hot" terminal of the component, but first make sure the component uses 12 volts in operation. Some electrical components, such as fuel injectors or sensors, are designed to operate on about 4 to 5 volts, and running 12 volts directly to these components will cause damage.

TEST LIGHTS

▶ See Figure 7

The test light is used to check circuits and components while electrical current is flowing through them. It is used for voltage and ground tests. To use a 12 volt test light, connect the ground clip to a good ground and probe wherever necessary with the pick. The test light will illuminate when voltage is detected. This does not necessarily mean that 12 volts (or any particular amount of volt-

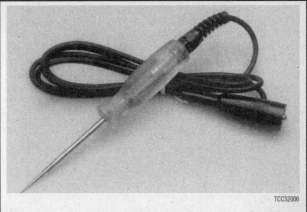

TCCS2006

Fig. 7 A 12 volt test light is used to detect the presence of voltage in a circuit

age) is present; it only means that some voltage is present. It is advisable before using the test light to touch its ground clip and probe across the battery posts or terminals to make sure the light is operating properly.

✳✳ WARNING

Do not use a test light to probe electronic ignition, spark plug or coil wires. Never use a pick-type test light to probe wiring on computer controlled systems unless specifically instructed to do so. Any wire insulation that is pierced by the test light probe should be taped and sealed with silicone after testing.

Like the jumper wire, the 12 volt test light is used to isolate opens in circuits. But, whereas the jumper wire is used to bypass the open to operate the load, the 12 volt test light is used to locate the presence of voltage in a circuit. If the test light illuminates, there is power up to that point in the circuit; if the test light does not illuminate, there is an open circuit (no power). Move the test light in successive steps back toward the power source until the light in the handle illuminates. The open is between the probe and a point which was previously probed.

The self-powered test light is similar in design to the 12 volt test light, but contains a 1.5 volt penlight battery in the handle. It is most often used in place of a multimeter to check for open or short circuits when power is isolated from the circuit (continuity test).

The battery in a self-powered test light does not provide much current. A weak battery may not provide enough power to illuminate the test light even when a complete circuit is made (especially if there is high resistance in the circuit). Always make sure that the test battery is strong. To check the battery, briefly touch the ground clip to the probe; if the light glows brightly, the battery is strong enough for testing.

➡ **A self-powered test light should not be used on any computer controlled system or component. The small amount of electricity transmitted by the test light is enough to damage many electronic automotive components.**

MULTIMETERS

Multimeters are an extremely useful tool for troubleshooting electrical problems. They can be purchased in either analog or digital form and have a price range to suit any budget. A multimeter is a voltmeter, ammeter and ohmmeter (along with other features) combined into one instrument. It is often used when testing solid state circuits because of its high input impedance (usually 10 megaohms or more). A brief description of the multimeter main test functions follows:

• Voltmeter—the voltmeter is used to measure voltage at any point in a circuit, or to measure the voltage drop across any part of a circuit. Voltmeters usually have various scales and a selector switch to allow the reading of different voltage ranges. The voltmeter has a positive and a negative lead. To avoid damage to the meter, always connect the negative lead to the negative (-) side of the circuit (to ground or nearest the ground side of the circuit) and connect the positive lead to the positive (+) side of the circuit (to the power source or the nearest power source). Note that the negative voltmeter lead will always be black and that the positive voltmeter will always be some color other than black (usually red).

• Ohmmeter—the ohmmeter is designed to read resistance (measured in ohms) in a circuit or component. Most ohmmeters will have a selector switch which permits the measurement of different ranges of resistance (usually the selector switch allows the multiplication of the meter reading by 10, 100, 1,000 and 10,000). Some ohmmeters are "auto-ranging" which means the meter itself will determine which scale to use. Since the meters are powered by an internal battery, the ohmmeter can be used like a self-powered test light. When the ohmmeter is connected, current from the ohmmeter flows through the circuit or component being tested. Since the ohmmeter's internal resistance and voltage are known values, the amount of current flow through the meter depends on the resistance of the circuit or component being tested. The ohmmeter can also be used to perform a continuity test for suspected open circuits. In using the meter for making continuity checks, do not be concerned with the actual resistance readings. Zero resistance, or any ohm reading, indicates continuity in the circuit. Infinite resistance indicates an opening in the circuit. A high resistance reading where there should be none indicates a problem in the circuit. Checks for short circuits are made in the same manner as checks for open circuits, except that the circuit must be isolated from both power and normal ground. Infinite resistance indicates no continuity, while zero resistance indicates a dead short.

❊❊ WARNING

Never use an ohmmeter to check the resistance of a component or wire while there is voltage applied to the circuit.

• Ammeter—an ammeter measures the amount of current flowing through a circuit in units called amperes or amps. At normal operating voltage, most circuits have a characteristic amount of amperes, called "current draw" which can be measured using an ammeter. By referring to a specified current draw rating, then measuring the amperes and comparing the two values, one can determine what is happening within the circuit to aid in diagnosis. An open circuit, for example, will not allow any current to flow, so the ammeter reading will be zero. A damaged component or circuit will have an increased current draw, so the reading will be high. The ammeter is always connected in series with the circuit being tested. All of the current that normally flows through the circuit must also flow through the ammeter; if there is any other path for the current to follow, the ammeter reading will not be accurate. The ammeter itself has very little resistance to current flow and, therefore, will not affect the circuit, but it will measure current draw only when the circuit is closed and electricity is flowing. Excessive current draw can blow fuses and drain the battery, while a reduced current draw can cause motors to run slowly, lights to dim and other components to not operate properly.

Troubleshooting Electrical Systems

When diagnosing a specific problem, organized troubleshooting is a must. The complexity of a modern automotive vehicle demands that you approach any problem in a logical, organized manner. There are certain troubleshooting techniques, however, which are standard:

• Establish when the problem occurs. Does the problem appear only under certain conditions? Were there any noises, odors or other unusual symptoms? Isolate the problem area. To do this, make some simple tests and observations, then eliminate the systems that are working properly. Check for obvious problems, such as broken wires and loose or dirty connections. Always check the obvious before assuming something complicated is the cause.

• Test for problems systematically to determine the cause once the problem area is isolated. Are all the components functioning properly? Is there power going to electrical switches and motors? Performing careful, systematic checks will often turn up most causes on the first inspection, without wasting time checking components that have little or no relationship to the problem.

• Test all repairs after the work is done to make sure that the problem is fixed. Some causes can be traced to more than one component, so a careful verification of repair work is important in order to pick up additional malfunctions that may cause a problem to reappear or a different problem to arise. A blown fuse, for example, is a simple problem that may require more than another fuse to repair. If you don't look for a problem that caused a fuse to blow, a shorted wire (for example) may go undetected.

Experience has shown that most problems tend to be the result of a fairly simple and obvious cause, such as loose or corroded connectors, bad grounds or damaged wire insulation which causes a short. This makes careful visual inspection of components during testing essential to quick and accurate troubleshooting.

Testing

OPEN CIRCUITS

♦ See Figure 8

This test already assumes the existence of an open in the circuit and it is used to help locate the open portion.

1. Isolate the circuit from power and ground.
2. Connect the self-powered test light or ohmmeter ground clip to the ground side of the circuit and probe sections of the circuit sequentially.
3. If the light is out or there is infinite resistance, the open is between the probe and the circuit ground.
4. If the light is on or the meter shows continuity, the open is between the probe and the end of the circuit toward the power source.

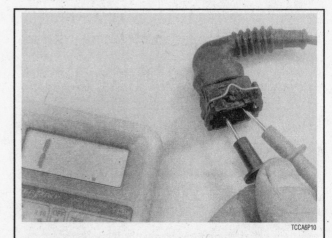

TCCA6P10

Fig. 8 The infinite reading on this multimeter indicates that the circuit is open

SHORT CIRCUITS

➡**Never use a self-powered test light to perform checks for opens or shorts when power is applied to the circuit under test. The test light can be damaged by outside power.**

1. Isolate the circuit from power and ground.
2. Connect the self-powered test light or ohmmeter ground clip to a good ground and probe any easy-to-reach point in the circuit.
3. If the light comes on or there is continuity, there is a short somewhere in the circuit.
4. To isolate the short, probe a test point at either end of the isolated circuit (the light should be on or the meter should indicate continuity).
5. Leave the test light probe engaged and sequentially open connectors or switches, remove parts, etc. until the light goes out or continuity is broken.
6. When the light goes out, the short is between the last two circuit components which were opened.

VOLTAGE

This test determines voltage available from the battery and should be the first step in any electrical troubleshooting procedure after visual inspection. Many electrical problems, especially on computer controlled systems, can be caused by a low state of charge in the battery. Excessive corrosion at the battery cable terminals can cause poor contact that will prevent proper charging and full battery current flow.

1. Set the voltmeter selector switch to the 20V position.
2. Connect the multimeter negative lead to the battery's negative (-) post or terminal and the positive lead to the battery's positive (+) post or terminal.
3. Turn the ignition switch **ON** to provide a load.
4. A well charged battery should register over 12 volts. If the meter reads below 11.5 volts, the battery power may be insufficient to operate the electrical system properly.

VOLTAGE DROP

▶ See Figure 9

When current flows through a load, the voltage beyond the load drops. This voltage drop is due to the resistance created by the load and also by small resistance created by corrosion at the connectors and damaged insulation on the wires. The maximum allowable voltage drop under load is critical, especially if there is more than one load in the circuit, since all voltage drops are cumulative.

1. Set the voltmeter selector switch to the 20 volt position.
2. Connect the multimeter negative lead to a good ground.
3. Operate the circuit and check the voltage prior to the first component (load).
4. There should be little or no voltage drop in the circuit prior to the first component. If a voltage drop exists, the wire or connectors in the circuit are suspect.
5. While operating the first component in the circuit, probe the ground side of the component with the positive meter lead and observe the voltage readings. A small voltage drop should be noticed. This voltage drop is caused by the resistance of the component.
6. Repeat the test for each component (load) down the circuit.
7. If a large voltage drop is noticed, the preceding component, wire or connector is suspect.

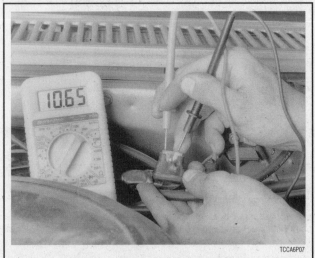

Fig. 9 This voltage drop test revealed high resistance (low voltage) in the circuit

RESISTANCE

▶ See Figures 10 and 11

※ WARNING

Never use an ohmmeter with power applied to the circuit. The ohmmeter is designed to operate on its own power supply. The normal 12 volt electrical system voltage could damage the meter!

1. Isolate the circuit from the vehicle's power source.
2. Ensure that the ignition key is **OFF** when disconnecting any components or the battery.
3. Where necessary, also isolate at least one side of the circuit to be checked, in order to avoid reading parallel resistance. Parallel circuit resistance will always give a lower reading than the actual resistance of either of the branches.
4. Connect the meter leads to both sides of the circuit (wire or component) and read the actual measured ohms on the meter scale. Make sure the selector switch is set to the proper ohm scale for the circuit being tested, to avoid misreading the ohmmeter test value.

Fig. 10 Checking the resistance of a coolant temperature sensor with an ohmmeter. Reading is 1.04 kilohms

Wire and Connector Repair

Almost anyone can replace damaged wires, as long as the proper tools and parts are available. Wire and terminals are available to fit almost any need. Even the specialized weatherproof, molded and hard shell connectors are now available from aftermarket suppliers.

Be sure the ends of all the wires are fitted with the proper terminal hardware and connectors. Wrapping a wire around a stud is never a permanent solution and will only cause trouble later. Replace wires one at a time to avoid confusion. Always route wires exactly the same as the factory.

➡**If connector repair is necessary, only attempt it if you have the proper tools. Weatherproof and hard shell connectors require special tools to release the pins inside the connector. Attempting to repair these connectors with conventional hand tools will damage them.**

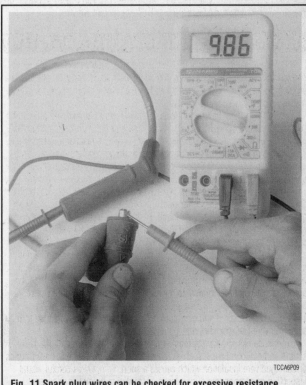

Fig. 11 Spark plug wires can be checked for excessive resistance using an ohmmeter

BATTERY CABLES

Disconnecting the Cables

When working on any electrical component on the vehicle, it is always a good idea to disconnect the negative (-) battery cable. This will prevent potential damage to many sensitive electrical components such as the Engine Control Module (ECM), radio, alternator, etc.

➡️**Any time you disengage the battery cables, it is recommended that you disconnect the negative (-) battery cable first. This will prevent you from accidentally grounding the positive (+) terminal to the body of the vehicle when disconnecting it, thereby preventing damage to the previously mentioned components.**

Before you disconnect the cable(s), first turn the ignition to the **OFF** position. This will prevent a draw on the battery which could cause arcing (electricity trying to ground itself to the body of a vehicle, just like a spark jumping the plug gap) and, of course, damaging some components such as the alternator diodes and any electronic control units.

When the battery cable(s) are reconnected (negative cable last), be sure to check that your lights, windshield wipers and other electrically operated safety components are all working correctly. If your vehicle contains an Electronically Tuned Radio (ETR), don't forget to also reset your radio stations. Ditto for the clock.

SUPPLEMENTAL RESTRAINT SYSTEM (SRS OR AIR BAG)

General Information

The Supplemental Restraint System (SRS or Air Bag), is designed to provide additional protection for the driver in addition to that which is provided by the use of a seat belt.

The system is made up of two basic systems. They are the air bag(s) and the electrical components made up of the impact sensors, backup power supply and electronic air bag diagnostic monitor assembly.

Special attention should always be applied when working on a vehicle equipped with an air bag. If for any reason the indicator light in the dash should come on, consult an authorized dealer immediately for complete diagnostic service.

SYSTEM OPERATION

The Supplemental Restraint System (SRS or Air Bag) provides increased protection for the driver and/or passenger in the event of an accident. The word "supplemental is key, as the air bag is designed to be used in addition to the seat belts. In the event of an accident, the air bag will be the most effective if the vehicle's occupants are held in position by the seat belts.

SYSTEM COMPONENTS

The air bag system consists of two subsystems: the air bag(s), and the electrical system, which includes the impact sensors and electronic diagnostic monitor.

➡️**For removal and installation procedures, refer to the Steering Wheel coverage in Section 8.**

Air Bag Module

▶ **See Figure 12**

The air bag module consists of the inflator, bag assembly, a mounting plate or housing, and a trim cover.

➡️**The air bag module components cannot be serviced. The air bag module is only serviced as a complete assembly.**

INFLATOR

Inside the inflator is an igniter. When two or more impact sensors detects a crash and the sensor contacts close, battery power flows to the igniter, which then converts the electrical energy to thermal (heat) energy, igniting the sodium azide/copper oxide gas inside the air bag. The combustion process produces nitrogen gas, which inflates the air bag.

AIR BAG

The air bag itself is constructed of neoprene coated nylon. Fill volume of the air bag is 2.3 cubic feet.

MOUNTING PLATE/HOUSING

A mounting plate and retainer attach and seal the air bag to the inflator. The mounting plate is used to attach the trim cover and to mount the entire module to the steering wheel or dash panel, depending on which side of the vehicle the air bag is mounted.

TRIM COVER

When the air bag is activated, tear seams molded into the trim cover separate to allow the air bag to inflate.

Diagnostic Monitor

The diagnostic monitor continually monitors all air bag system components and wiring connections for possible faults. If a fault is detected, a code will be displayed on the air bag warning light, located on the instrument cluster.

The diagnostic monitor illuminates the air bag light for approximately 6 seconds when the ignition switch is turned **ON**, then turns it off. This indicates that the air bag light is operational. If the air bag light does not illuminate, or if it stays on or flashes at any time, a fault has been detected by the diagnostic monitor.

Performing system diagnostics is the main purpose of the diagnostic monitor. The diagnostic monitor does not deploy the air bags in the event of a crash.

Sensors

▶ **See Figure 13**

The sensor is an electrical switch that reacts to impacts according to direction and force. It can discriminate between impacts that do or do not require air bag deployment. When an impact occurs that requires air bag deployment, the sensor contacts close and complete the electrical circuit necessary for system operation.

Four crash sensors are used on air bag equipped Aerostar vehicles: a dual crash and safing sensor located at the hood latch support, a crash sensor at each of the right and left fender aprons, and a safing sensor at the left-hand cowl side in the passenger compartment.

At least 2 crash sensors, one safing and one front, must be activated to inflate the air bag.

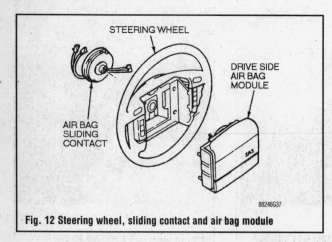

Fig. 12 Steering wheel, sliding contact and air bag module

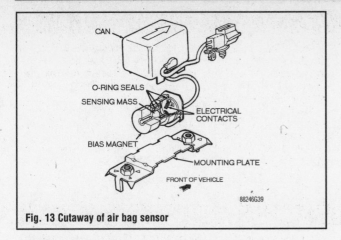

Fig. 13 Cutaway of air bag sensor

SERVICE PRECAUTIONS

• Always wear safety glasses when servicing an air bag vehicle, and when handling an air bag.

• Never attempt to service the steering wheel or steering column on an air bag equipped vehicle without first properly disarming the air bag system. The air bag system should be properly disarmed whenever ANY service procedure in this manual indicates that you should do so.

• When carrying a live air bag module, always make sure the bag and trim cover are pointed away from your body. In the unlikely event of an accidental deployment, the bag will then deploy with minimal chance of injury.

• When placing a live air bag on a bench or other surface, always face the bag and trim cover up, away from the surface. This will reduce the motion of the air bag if it is accidentally deployed.

• If you should come in contact with a deployed air bag, be advised that the air bag surface may contain deposits of sodium hydroxide, which is a product of the gas combustion and is irritating to the skin. Always wear gloves and safety glasses when handling a deployed air bag, and wash your hands with mild soap and water afterwards.

➡ **For removal and installation procedures, refer to the Steering Wheel coverage in Section 8.**

DISARMING THE SYSTEM

1. Disconnect the negative battery cable.
2. Disengage the electrical connector from the backup power supply.

➡ **The backup power supply allows air bag deployment if the battery or battery cables are damaged in an accident before the crash sensors close. The power supply is a capacitor that will leak down in approximately 15 minutes after the battery is disconnected, or in 1 minute if the battery positive cable is grounded. It is located in the instrument panel and is combined with the diagnostic monitor. The backup power supply must be disconnected before any air bag related service is performed.**

3. Remove the nut and washer assemblies retaining the driver air bag module to the steering wheel.
4. Disconnect the driver air bag module connector and attach a jumper wire to the air bag terminals on the clockspring.
5. Connect the backup power supply and negative battery cable.

REACTIVATING THE SYSTEM

➡ **For removal and installation procedures, refer to the Steering Wheel coverage in Section 8.**

1. Disconnect the negative battery cable and then the backup power supply.
2. Remove the jumper wire from the air bag terminals on the clockspring assembly and reconnect the air bag connector.
3. Position the air bag assembly.
4. Connect the backup power supply and negative battery cable. Verify that the air bag light illuminates when the ignition switch first is turned **ON**.

HEATING AND AIR CONDITIONING

Blower Motor

REMOVAL & INSTALLATION

▶ **See Figures 14, 15, 16, 17 and 18**

1. Disconnect the negative battery cable.
2. Remove the air cleaner or air inlet duct as necessary.
3. Remove the two screws attaching the vacuum reservoir to the blower assembly and remove the reservoir.
4. Disconnect the wire harness from the blower motor by pushing down on the plug tabs and pulling the connector off the motor.
5. Disconnect the blower motor cooling tube at the blower motor.

6. Remove the three screws attaching the blower motor and wheel to the heater blower assembly.
7. While holding the cooling tube aside, pull the blower motor and wheel from the heater blower assembly.
8. Remove the blower wheel hub clamp from the motor shaft, then pull the blower wheel from the motor shaft.
To install:
9. If the motor is being replaced, install the wheel on the new blower motor shaft and lock it in place with the hub clamp.
10. Glue a new motor housing gasket to the blower motor.
11. While holding the cooling tube aside, position the blower and wheel to the heater blower assembly. Install the three mounting screws.
12. Connect the blower motor cooling tube at the blower motor.
13. Fasten the wire harness connector at the blower motor.

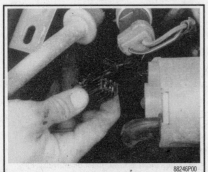

Fig. 14 Unfasten the wire harness from the rear of the blower motor

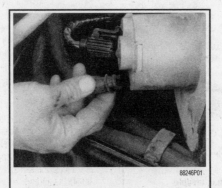

Fig. 15 Remove the rubber tube attached to the back of the motor housing

Fig. 16 Remove the retainer screws from the motor plate

Fig. 17 Separate the motor from the case

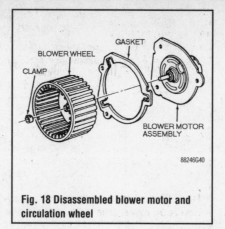

Fig. 18 Disassembled blower motor and circulation wheel

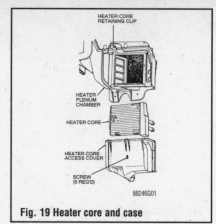

Fig. 19 Heater core and case

14. Install the vacuum reservoir on the bracket with two screws.
15. Install the air cleaner or air inlet duct assembly.
16. Connect the negative battery cable.
17. Test the heater/defroster to make sure the blower motor functions correctly.

Blower Motor Switch

REMOVAL & INSTALLATION

The blower motor switch is part of the heater control assembly, and cannot easily be separated. In the event the blower motor switch fails, the entire control assembly must be removed and replaced. Refer to the heater control procedure in this section for removal and installation instructions.

Heater Core

REMOVAL & INSTALLATION

▶ See Figure 19

1. Drain the cooling system antifreeze into a suitable container.

❊❊ CAUTION

When draining the coolant, keep in mind that cats and dogs are attracted to ethylene glycol antifreeze, and could drink any that is left in an uncovered container or in puddles on the ground. This will prove fatal in sufficient quantity. Always drain the coolant into a sealable container. Coolant should be reused unless it is contaminated or several years old.

2. Allow the engine to cool completely. Using a thick cloth for protection, carefully open the radiator cap or reservoir cap to allow any residual cooling system pressure to vent.
3. Disconnect the heater hoses from the heater core tubes using tool T85T-18539-AH or equivalent. Plug the heater hoses to prevent coolant loss during core removal.
4. Working in the passenger compartment, remove the six screws attach-

ing the heater core access cover to the plenum assembly. Remove the access cover.

5. Depress the retainer bracket at the top of the heater core and pull the heater core rearward and down, removing it from the plenum assembly.

❊❊ CAUTION

Some coolant will remain in the heater core. Exercise caution when removing and lay a protective cloth down to protect the interior of the vehicle during heater core removal.

To install:

6. Position the heater core and seal in the plenum assembly, snapping it into the retainer bracket at the top of the core.
7. Install the heater core access cover to the plenum assembly and secure it with the six screws.
8. Install the quick-connect heater hoses to the heater core tubes at the dash panel in the engine.
9. Fill the cooling system and bleed.
10. Start the engine, move the heater controls to the MAX HEAT position and check for leaks.

Air Conditioning Components

REMOVAL & INSTALLATION

Repair or service of air conditioning components is not covered by this manual, because of the risk of personal injury or death, and because of the legal ramifications of servicing these components without the proper EPA certification and experience. Cost, personal injury or death, environmental damage, and legal considerations (such as the fact that it is a federal crime to vent refrigerant into the atmosphere), dictate that the A/C components on your vehicle should be serviced only by a Motor Vehicle Air Conditioning (MVAC) trained, and EPA certified automotive technician.

➡If your vehicle's A/C system uses R-12 refrigerant and is in need of recharging, the A/C system can be converted over to R-134a refrigerant (less environmentally harmful and expensive). Refer to Section 1 for additional information on R-12 to R-134a conversions, and for additional considerations dealing with your vehicle's A/C system.

AUXILIARY HEATING AND AIR CONDITIONING SYSTEM

Blower Motor

REMOVAL & INSTALLATION

▶ See Figure 20

1. Disconnect the negative battery cable.
2. Remove the bench seat behind the driver's front seat. Refer to Section 10 for a detailed procedure.

3. Remove the service panel from the interior panel on the driver's side of the vehicle.
4. Remove the 3 retainer screws from the solenoid bracket.
5. Tag and disconnect the motor wiring.
6. Disconnect the cooling tube attached to the motor assembly.
7. Remove the mounting plate screws and separate the mounting plate from the motor assembly.

To install:

8. Attach the motor to the motor mounting plate and secure using the retainer screws. Tighten the screws to 13–17 inch lbs. (1–2 Nm).

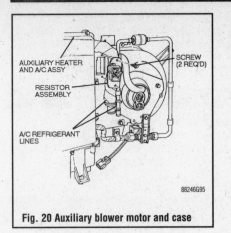

Fig. 20 Auxiliary blower motor and case

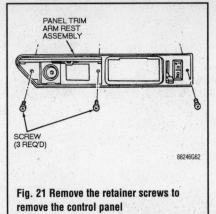

Fig. 21 Remove the retainer screws to remove the control panel

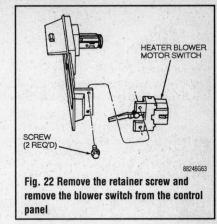

Fig. 22 Remove the retainer screw and remove the blower switch from the control panel

9. Attach the cooling tube to the motor.
10. Install the three solenoid retainer bracket screws. Tighten the screws to 13–17 inch lbs. (1–2 Nm).
11. Attach the wire harness to the motor.
12. Install the service panel and bench seat.
13. Connect the negative battery cable.
14. Check and make sure the blower motor function properly.

Heater Core

REMOVAL & INSTALLATION

1. Drain the cooling system into a suitable container.

❊❊ CAUTION

When draining the coolant, keep in mind that cats and dogs are attracted to ethylene glycol antifreeze, and could drink any that is left in an uncovered container or in puddles on the ground. This will prove fatal in sufficient quantity. Always drain the coolant into a sealable container. Coolant should be reused unless it is contaminated or several years old.

2. Remove the bench seat behind the driver's front seat. Refer to Section 10 for a detailed procedure.
3. Remove the service panel from the interior panel on the driver's side of the vehicle.
4. Unfasten the attaching screws and remove the floor duct by rotating it carefully downward.
5. Remove the heater core cover screws and lift out the cover.
6. Disconnect the heater hoses at the core tubes. Place rags below the core to catch any coolant which may spill out after the clamps are removed. Inspect the hose and replace if cracked or soft to the touch.
7. Slide the core and seal from the case. Remove the seal and discard.
To install:
8. Slide the heater core in to the case. Install a new seal around the edge of the case, then install the case cover.
9. Secure the case sections together by installing the retaining screws around the case edges.
10. Install and clamp the heater core hoses to the heater core tubes.
11. Install the floor duct and secure with screws.
12. Install the side service panel, followed by the rear bench seat.
13. Fill the cooling system and bleed.
14. Start the vehicle and allow to reach normal operating temperature. Turn the heat on and make sure it works properly.

Control Panel

The rear control panel of the auxiliary A/C and heating system is not a complete control assembly as compared to the panel in the dash. This panel consists only of a blower motor switch. The dash installed temperature panel controls all other auxiliary system functions.

The control panel for the auxiliary A/C and heating system is located on the driver's side panel behind the front driver's seat.

REMOVAL & INSTALLATION

▶ See Figure 21

1. Disconnect the negative battery cable.
2. Remove the ashtray from the assembly. Remove the three retainer screws securing the panel in place.
3. Slide the panel out enough to unfasten the blower switch wire harness and lighter wire harness.
To install:
4. Connect the lighter and blower switch harnesses to the control panel.
5. Position the control panel and secure in place using the retainer screws.
6. Install the ashtray.
7. Connect the negative battery cable.

Auxiliary Blower Motor Switch

REMOVAL & INSTALLATION

▶ See Figure 22

1. Disconnect the battery ground.
2. Using a small screwdriver behind the knob, apply pressure to the spring retainer and pull off the knob.
3. Remove the 3 screws securing the control panel in place, and remove the ashtray bezel.
4. Disconnect the wiring harness at the switch by lifting the locking tab.
5. Remove the 2 blower switch screws and lift out the switch.
To install:
6. Install the blower switch and secure in place with the two retainer screws.
7. Connect the wire harness to the rear of the switch.
8. Install the control panel and secure in position using the three retainer screws. Attach the ashtray bezel.
9. Install the knob to the blower switch.
10. Connect the negative battery cable. Make sure the blower works on all speeds.

Air Conditioning Components

REMOVAL & INSTALLATION

Repair or service of air conditioning components is not covered by this manual, because of the risk of personal injury or death, and because of the legal ramifications of servicing these components without the proper EPA certification and experience. Cost, personal injury or death, environmental damage, and legal considerations (such as the fact that it is a federal crime to vent refrigerant into the atmosphere), dictate that the A/C components on your vehicle should be serviced only by a Motor Vehicle Air Conditioning (MVAC) trained, and EPA certified automotive technician.

➡If your vehicle's A/C system uses R-12 refrigerant and is in need of recharging, the A/C system can be converted over to R-134a refrigerant (less environmentally harmful and expensive). Refer to Section 1 for additional information on R-12 to R-134a conversions, and for additional considerations dealing with your vehicle's A/C system.

CRUISE CONTROL

The cruise control system on the Aerostar consists of an operator control, servo or throttle actuator assembly, speed sensor, clutch (if equipped), brake and brake light switch, vacuum dump valve, amplifier module, and assorted wire harnesses and vacuum hoses. To activate the cruise control on these models, the engine must be running in a forward gear with the speed in excess of 30 mph (48 kph).

Control Switches

▶ See Figure 23

The cruise control switches for the vehicle can be found in the steering wheel. If for any reason one switch becomes defective, the entire switch assembly must be replaced.

REMOVAL & INSTALLATION

▶ See Figures 24 and 25

✳✳ CAUTION

On all models equipped with an Air Bag, follow the correct air bag disarming and arming procedures. Failure to follow these procedures may result in air bag deployment which could result in personal injury.

1. Disconnect the negative battery cable.
2. Disconnect the air bag back-up power supply, if equipped with an air bag.
3. Remove the nuts and washer securing the steering wheel pad or air bag pad, if so equipped, to the steering wheel. Remove the pad and place aside. If removing an air bag, place the air bag pad face down.
4. Unfasten the air bag electrical connector from the clockspring contact on the steering wheel, if equipped with an air bag.
5. Remove the air bag module from the steering wheel, if so equipped.
6. Unfasten the horn/speed control wire harness from the clockspring contact located at the upper center of the steering wheel.
7. Remove the retainer screws from the base of the speed control actuator switch panel.
8. Remove and discard the electrical tape from the wire connectors at each upper clip on the steering wheel. Unfasten the speed control harness at the untaped wire connectors and remove the switch panel.
To install:
9. Fasten the speed control switch panel harness to the connector at the upper clip on the steering wheel.

Once connected, wrap clean electrical tape over the connections.
10. Connect the horn/speed control wire harness to the clockspring contact on the steering wheel.
11. Install the air bag module in the steering wheel, if so equipped.
12. Install the steering wheel pad or air bag pad, if so equipped. Tighten the nuts to 35–53 inch lbs. (4–6 Nm).
13. Connect the negative battery cable and air bag power supply, if equipped with an air bag.
14. Road test the vehicle to make sure the control switches function properly.

Speed Sensor

REMOVAL & INSTALLATION

▶ See Figures 26, 27 and 28

The speed sensor is located on the transmission assembly on the driver's side of the vehicle.
1. Disconnect the negative battery cable.
2. Raise and support the front of the vehicle safely on jackstands. Place blocks behind the rear wheels to prevent vehicle movement.
3. Disconnect the wire harness attached to the speed sensor.
4. Disconnect the speedometer cable from the speed sensor.
5. Place a suitable drip pan below the speed sensor to catch any fluid which may spill out during removal and installation. Remove the retaining bolt and pull out the sensor. Discard the sealing O-ring around the assembly.
6. Remove the drive gear.
To install:
7. Install the drive gear to the speed sensor. Install a new O-ring coated with clean engine oil around the speed sensor assembly.
8. Install the speed sensor and tighten the connection.
9. Fasten the wire harness the speed sensor. Lower the vehicle.
10. Connect the negative battery cable. Check the transmission fluid level and add fluid if needed.
11. Road test the vehicle to make sure the cruise control system functions correctly.

Amplifier

REMOVAL & INSTALLATION

The amplifier is located below the Electronic Engine Control (EEC) module under the instrument panel, at the left end of the dashboard.

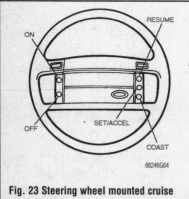

88246G64

Fig. 23 Steering wheel mounted cruise control switches

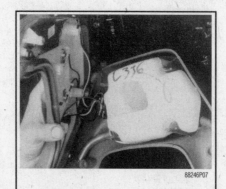

88246P07

Fig. 24 Lift the pad off to access the harness plug

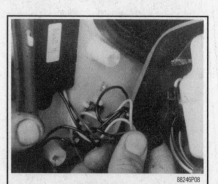

88246P08

Fig. 25 Unfasten the switch connection and remove the pad

Fig. 26 Unfasten the harness from the speed sensor

Fig. 27 Loosen the speed sensor retainer bolt. Notice the retainer clip at the end of the speedometer cable

Fig. 28 With the speedometer cable detached, remove the retainer bolt and slide out the speed sensor

1. Disconnect the negative battery cable.
2. Remove the retainer screws securing the panel below the steering column. Remove the panel and place aside.
3. Remove the 2 screws holding the amplifier to the EEC bracket.
4. Unplug the wiring at the amplifier assembly.

To install:
5. Fasten the wire harness to the amplifier assembly.
6. Position the amplifier to the EEC bracket and secure in place using the retainer screws.
7. Install the interior panel below the steering column and secure using the retainer screws.
8. Connect the negative battery cable.
9. Road test the vehicle to make sure the cruise control system functions correctly.

Servo

REMOVAL & INSTALLATION

1. Disconnect the negative battery cable.
2. From inside the vehicle, disconnect the control cable from the accelerator cable assembly.
3. From inside the engine compartment, tag and disconnect the vacuum hoses at the servo. Remove the wire harness attached to the servo.
4. Remove the 2 nuts retaining the servo to the bracket.
5. Remove the servo and speed control cable assembly.
6. Remove the 2 nuts holding the cable cover, then pull off the cover and disconnect the cable.

To install:
7. Connect the speed control cable to the servo assembly. Install the cable cover over the assembly and secure with the retainer nuts.
8. Position the servo assembly in the bracket and secure with the retainer nuts. Tighten the retainer nuts to 36–44 inch lbs. (4–5 Nm).
9. Install the vacuum hoses and wire harness to the servo assembly.
10. Connect the control cable to the accelerator cable.
11. Connect the negative battery cable.
12. Road test the vehicle to make sure the cruise control system functions correctly.

Actuator Cable

REMOVAL & INSTALLATION

♦ See Figures 29 and 30

1. Disconnect the actuator assembly from the servo body, then disconnect the actuator cable from the accelerator bracket and cable.
2. Remove the two nuts holding the actuator cable to the servo assembly.
3. Disconnect the cable from the servo clip.

To install:
4. Connect the actuator cable to the clip on the servo body.

Fig. 29 Unfasten the accelerator cable . . .

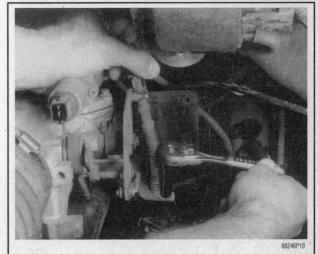
Fig. 30 . . . to access and remove the actuator cable. Remove the retainer screw and unfasten the bracket

5. Install the actuator cable to the servo assembly, securing in place with the two retainer nuts.
6. Connect the actuator cable to the accelerator bracket and cable. Connect the actuator assembly to the servo body.
7. Road test the vehicle to make sure the cruise control system functions correctly.

ADJUSTMENT

1. Remove the actuator cable retaining clip at the servo body.
2. Disengage the throttle positioner.
3. Run the engine at 2000 rpm for several minutes.
4. Pull on the cable to take up all slack.
5. While maintaining a slight tension on the cable, install the clip and snap it securely.

Brake Switch

REMOVAL & INSTALLATION

▶ See Figure 31

1. Disconnect the negative battery cable.
2. Unfasten the harness attached to the brake switch.
3. Remove the hairpin clip, then slide the switch, pushrod, nylon washer and bushing away from the pedal bracket.

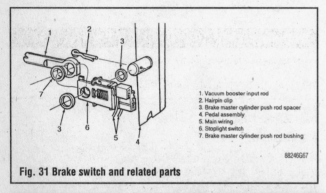

1. Vacuum booster input rod
2. Hairpin clip
3. Brake master cylinder push rod spacer
4. Pedal assembly
5. Main wiring
6. Stoplight switch
7. Brake master cylinder push rod bushing

88246G67

Fig. 31 Brake switch and related parts

4. Remove the washer, then slide the switch up and away.
To install:
5. Slide the switch down into position. Slide the washer over the front end of the switch.
6. Slide the bushing, nylon washer, pushrod and switch into the bracket and secure in place with the hairpin clip.
7. Fasten the wire harness to the brake switch.
8. Connect the negative battery cable.
9. Depress the brake pedal and make sure the rear brake lights work correctly. Road test the vehicle to make sure the cruise control system functions correctly.

Clutch Pedal Position Switch

REMOVAL & INSTALLATION

1. Disconnect the negative battery cable.
2. Unfasten the wire harness from the clutch switch.
3. Pull the clip away from the clutch pedal switch to separate it from the pin on the switch.
4. Rotate the clutch switch to expose the plastic cover.
5. Push the tabs together, allowing the cover to slide rearward, then separate it from the clutch switch.
6. Remove the clutch switch from the pushrod.
To install:
7. Install the clutch switch to the pushrod.
8. Install the switch cover, by pushing the tabs together and sliding the cover forward.
9. Rotate the switch into position.
10. Install the clutch switch to the locating pin clip.
11. Connect the wire harness to the switch.
12. Connect the negative battery cable.
13. Road test the vehicle to make sure the cruise control system functions correctly.

ENTERTAINMENT SYSTEMS

Radio

REMOVAL & INSTALLATION

1986–89 Models

▶ See Figures 32 thru 37

1. Disconnect the negative battery cable.
2. Remove the radio trim panel.
3. Remove the four screws at the sides of the radio which secure the mounting bracket assembly to the instrument panel.
4. Slide the radio out with the mounting and rear bracket attached.

5. Disconnect the antenna lead cable, speaker harness and power control harness from the radio.
6. Remove the nut and washer assembly attaching the radio rear support and ground cable on electronic radios.
7. Unfasten the screws and remove the mounting brackets from the radio.
To install:
8. Attach the rear support (and ground cable on electronic radios) with the nut and washer. Tighten the nut to 22–35 inch lbs. (2–4 Nm).
9. Install the mounting brackets to the radio and tighten the mounting screws to 9–12 inch lbs. (1–1.4 Nm).
10. Fasten the wiring connectors to the radio. Match the color of the harness to the color of the connector on the radio. Connect the antenna lead to the rear of the radio.
11. Position the radio with the mounting brackets to the instrument panel.

88246P09

Fig. 32 Remove the retainer screws at the base of the radio securing the trim panel in place

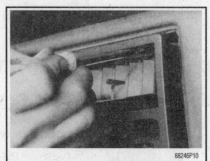

88246P10

Fig. 33 Some early models have retainer clips in the fresh air vents above the radio, which must be unfastened to remove the trim panel assembly

88246P11

Fig. 34 With the trim panel removed, unfasten the radio retainer screws at the sides of the radio

Fig. 35 Slide the radio out . . .

Fig. 36 . . . and unclip the wire harnesses attached to the rear of the radio

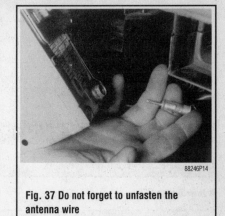

Fig. 37 Do not forget to unfasten the antenna wire

Make sure the hairpin area of the rear bracket is engaged to the instrument panel support.

12. Secure the radio and mounting brackets to the instrument panel with four screws. Make sure the mounting brackets are fully seated on the instrument panel.

13. Reconnect the battery ground cable.

1990–97 Models

▶ See Figure 38

➡To remove the radio in these vehicles, special radio removal tools T87P-19061A are required. If you do not have access to a pair of these, many automotive parts stores sell a similar tool which can be used. The radio cannot be removed without these tools.

1. Disconnect the negative battery cable.
2. Remove the radio trim panel.
3. Insert radio removal tools T87P-19061A or equivalent into the holes at both sides of the radio until they click in place. Pull evenly on the tools until the radio begins to slide out.
4. Slide the radio out with the mounting and rear bracket attached.
5. Disconnect the antenna lead cable, speaker harness, power control harness and, if equipped, the amplifier harness from the radio.
6. Remove the nut and washer assembly attaching the radio rear support (and ground cable on electronic radios).

To install:

7. Attach the rear support (and ground cable on electronic radios) with the nut and washer. Tighten the nut to 22–35 inch lb. (2–4 Nm).
8. Install the mounting brackets to the radio and tighten the mounting screws to 9–12 inch lb. (1–1.4 Nm).
9. Fasten the wiring connectors to the radio. Match the color of the harness to the color of the connector on the radio. Connect the antenna lead to the rear of the radio. Fasten the amplifier harness, if so equipped.
10. Position the radio with the mounting brackets to the instrument panel. Make sure the hairpin area of the rear bracket is engaged to the instrument panel support.

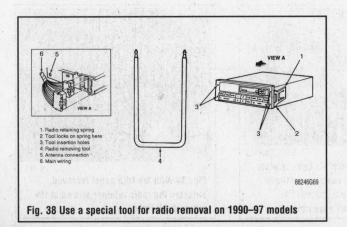

1. Radio retaining spring
2. Tool locks on spring here
3. Tool insertion holes
4. Radio removing tool
5. Antenna connection
6. Main wiring

Fig. 38 Use a special tool for radio removal on 1990–97 models

11. Secure the radio by pushing it in until the brackets at the side of the radio click into place.
12. Install the radio trim panel over the radio assembly.
13. Reconnect the battery ground cable.

Amplifier

➡The following procedures apply only to factory installed amplifiers.

REMOVAL & INSTALLATION

Dash Mounted Unit

▶ See Figure 39

1. Disconnect the negative battery cable.
2. From the bottom of the dash panel, on the driver's side, remove the 2 amplifier attaching screws from the lower instrument panel reinforcement.
3. Lower the amplifier and unplug the signal, power and speaker connectors.

To install:

4. Fasten the signal, power and speaker harnesses into the amplifier.
5. Secure the amplifier into position using the two retainer screws.
6. Connect the negative battery cable.
7. Turn the radio **ON** and make sure all the speakers produce a crisp, clear sound.

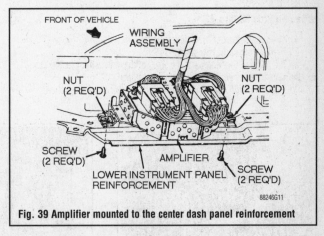

FRONT OF VEHICLE
WIRING ASSEMBLY
NUT (2 REQ'D)
NUT (2 REQ'D)
SCREW (2 REQ'D)
AMPLIFIER
LOWER INSTRUMENT PANEL REINFORCEMENT
SCREW (2 REQ'D)

Fig. 39 Amplifier mounted to the center dash panel reinforcement

Side Panel Mounted Unit

1. Disconnect the negative battery cable.
2. Remove the driver's side panel which runs from behind the front seat to the rear hatch of the vehicle.
3. With the panel removed, the amplifier is identified as a black or silver box in front of the rear tire. It will have three harnesses attached to it. Two are covered in black tape, while the third is gray in color.

4. Unfasten the three harnesses from the amplifier.
5. Remove the retainer screws securing the amplifier to the bracket.
6. Lower and remove the amplifier.

To install:

7. Fasten the signal, power and speaker harnesses into the amplifier.
8. Secure the amplifier into position using the retainer screws.
9. Install the side panel, making sure to use all the retainer screws removed earlier.
10. Connect the negative battery cable.
11. Turn the radio **ON** and make sure all the speakers produce a crisp, clear sound.

Graphic Equalizer

REMOVAL & INSTALLATION

1986–89 Models

▶ **See Figure 40**

1. Disconnect he negative battery cable.
2. Remove the trim panel around the equalizer assembly.
3. Remove the 4 equalizer attaching screws.
4. Slide the equalizer out from the dash panel.
5. Tag and unplug the connectors.
6. Remove the rear bracket and side brackets if you are installing a different unit.

To install:

7. Attach the rear and side brackets, if removed.
8. Attach the harnesses to the rear of the equalizer. Match the color of the harness to the color of the connector on the equalizer.
9. Slide the equalizer into the dash hole and secure in place using the retainer screws.
10. Install the dash trim panel around the equalizer.
11. Connect the negative battery cable.
12. Turn the radio **ON** and adjust the equalizer to make sure all the speakers produce a crisp, clear sound.

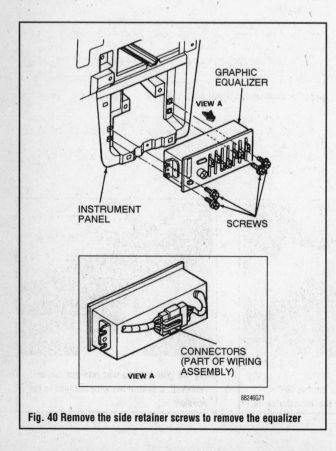

Fig. 40 Remove the side retainer screws to remove the equalizer

GRAPHIC EQUALIZER

VIEW A

INSTRUMENT PANEL

SCREWS

CONNECTORS (PART OF WIRING ASSEMBLY)

VIEW A

88246G71

1990–97 Models

➡**To remove the equalizer in these vehicles, a special pair of equalizer removal tools T87P-1906A or equivalent are required. If you do not have access to a pair of these, many automotive parts stores sell a similar tool which can be used. The equalizer cannot be removed without these tools.**

1. Disconnect he negative battery cable.
2. Remove the trim panel around the equalizer assembly.
3. Insert removal tools T87P-1906A or equivalent into the holes at either side of the equalizer until they click in place. Slowly pull on the tools until the equalizer begins to slide out.
4. Slide the equalizer out from the dash panel.
5. Tag and unplug the connectors.
6. Remove the rear bracket and side brackets if you are installing a different unit.

To install:

7. Attach the rear and side brackets, if removed.
8. Attach the harnesses to the rear of the equalizer. Match the color of the harness to the color of the connector on the equalizer.
9. Slide the equalizer into the dash hole and push in until the brackets at the side of the unit click in place.
10. Install the dash trim panel around the equalizer.
11. Connect the negative battery cable.
12. Turn the radio **ON** and adjust the equalizer to make sure all the speakers produce a crisp, clear sound.

Rear Radio Control Assembly

Some models equipped with a premium sound system and deluxe trim have an additional radio control panel mounted behind the driver's seat in the trim panel.

REMOVAL & INSTALLATION

➡**To remove the control assembly in these vehicles, a pair of special tools T87P-1906A or equivalent are required. If you do not have access to a pair of these, many automotive parts stores sell a similar tool which can be used. The control assembly cannot be removed without these tools.**

1. Disconnect the negative battery cable.
2. Insert removal tools T87P-19061A or equivalent into the holes at the side of the control assembly. Pull evenly on the tools until the control assembly begins to slide out.
3. Slide the control assembly out and unfasten the harness at the rear of the unit.
4. If installing a new unit, remove the brackets from the side of the control assembly.

To install:

5. Install the retainer brackets to the side of the replacement unit, using the screws removed from the original model.
6. Connect the wire harness to the back of the control assembly.
7. Slide the assembly into the hole in the side panel until the brackets in the side of the control unit click in place.
8. Connect the negative battery cable.
9. Turn the radio **ON** and, using the rear control panel, adjust the radio volume to make sure all the speaker produce a crisp clear sound.

Compact Disc Changer

Some Aerostar models equipped with the premium sound system have a compact disc changer mounted in the rear compartment on the passenger side.

REMOVAL & INSTALLATION

1. Disconnect the negative battery cable.
2. Remove the three front cradle screws followed by the three rear cradle screws.
3. Lift the cradle and CD player up, then remove the cradle retainer screws from the back of the CD player assembly.

4. Lift the CD player out of the cradle.
5. Unfasten the CD player data cable and power cable.
To install:
6. Connect the CD changer data power cable to the back of the changer assembly.
7. Slide the CD changer into the cradle assembly and secure the back of the assembly with the retainer screws.
8. Position the changer and cradle assembly to the floor of the vehicle and secure in place with the three floor retainer screws and three side retainer screws.
9. Connect the negative battery cable. Test the CD changer and make sure it functions correctly.

REMOVING A JAMMED CD CARTRIDGE

Occasionally the cartridge which holds the CD discs in the player unit gets caught in the unit and will not come out when the release bottom is pressed. Follow the proceeding steps to remove the cartridge.
1. Make sure that the radio is turned **OFF**.
2. Press the release button on the CD changer to make sure that power is getting to the unit. If the changer is working correctly, when you press the release button, the changer will attempt to eject the cartridge. If you do not hear any sound, check the fuse panel in the front of the vehicle to make sure a fuse has not blown.
3. To release the cartridge, insert a thin piece of plastic or cardboard the size of a credit card into the changer, between the top of the cartridge and the changer assembly.
4. Push the piece of plastic or cardboard in approximately 6–12 in. (15–30cm) until it catches the cartridge release mechanism in the changer. Slowly pull the piece of plastic or cardboard out with the cartridge.
5. Once the cartridge is removed, inspect it for any burrs around the cartridge, or any other obstruction that might prevent it from releasing. Replace the cartridge if needed.
6. If the cartridge appears good, insert the cartridge back into the changer and press the release button to eject it. If the cartridge will not release from the assembly, remove the cartridge again with the piece of plastic or cardboard, and have the changer repaired by an authorized dealer.

Speakers

REMOVAL & INSTALLATION

Dash Mounted Speakers

1986–89 MODELS

◆ **See Figures 41, 42 and 43**

1. Disconnect the negative battery cable.
2. Remove the instrument cluster housing. The instrument cluster does not have to be removed.

3. Remove the retaining screws securing the dash top panel.
4. Remove the retaining screws securing the speaker in place. Lift the speaker out to expose the wire harness.
5. Unfasten the harness from the back of the speaker. Inspect the speaker and replace if the paper cone is torn.
To install:
6. Connect the wire harness to the rear of the speaker.
7. Position the speaker in the dash panel and secure in place with the retainer screws.
8. Install the grille panel of the speaker.
9. Connect the negative battery cable. Turn the radio **ON** and make sure the speakers function properly.

1990–97 MODELS

1. Disconnect the negative battery cable.
2. Carefully pry up the speaker grille from the dash panel using a suitable prytool.
3. Remove the retaining screws securing the speaker in place. Lift the speaker out to expose the wire harness.
4. Unfasten the harness from the back of the speaker. Inspect the speaker and replace if the paper cone is torn.
To install:
5. Connect the wire harness to the rear of the speaker.
6. Position the speaker in the dash panel and secure in place with the retainer screws.
7. Install the grille panel of the speaker.
8. Connect the negative battery cable. Turn the radio **ON** and make sure the speakers function properly.

Door Mounted Speakers

1. Disconnect the negative battery cable.
2. Remove the door panel from the vehicle. Refer to Section 10 for the removal and installation procedure.
3. Remove the retaining screws securing the speaker in place. Lift the speaker out to expose the wire harness.
4. Unfasten the harness from the back of the speaker. Inspect the speaker and replace if the paper cone is torn.
To install:
5. Connect the wire harness to the rear of the speaker.
6. Position the speaker in place and secure with the retainer screws.
7. Install the door panel.
8. Connect the negative battery cable. Turn the radio **ON** and make sure the speakers function properly.

Side Panel Mounted Speakers

1. Disconnect the negative battery cable.
2. Carefully remove the side panel from the vehicle. Refer to Section 10 for the removal and installation procedure.
3. Remove the retaining screws securing the speaker in place. Lift the speaker out to expose the wire harness.

Fig. 41 Remove the retainer screws securing the top portion of the dash panel—1986 model shown

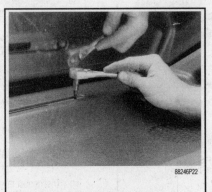
Fig. 42 Do not forget to remove the retainer screws inside the defroster vents

Fig. 43 With the speaker retainer screws removed, unfasten the wire harness to the speaker

4. Unfasten the harness from the back of the speaker. Inspect the speaker and replace if the paper cone is torn.

To install:

5. Connect the wire harness to the rear of the speaker.

6. Position the speaker in place and secure with the retainer screws.

7. Install the side panel into the vehicle.

8. Connect the negative battery cable. Turn the radio **ON** and make sure the speakers function properly.

Rear Hatch Mounted Speakers

▶ **See Figures 44 thru 50**

1. Disconnect the negative battery cable.

2. Open the rear hatch and support to prevent it from falling.

3. Remove the speaker panel from the hatch by removing the retainer screws from the hatch panel. Also remove the latch lift strap retainer screws. Remove the strap, followed by the panel and place them aside.

4. Remove the retaining screws securing the speaker in place. Support the speaker with one hand.

5. Lower the speaker and unfasten the wire connection.

6. Remove the speaker and inspect the speaker cone for any damage. Replace if needed.

To install:

7. Connect the wire harness to the speaker.

8. Position the speaker in place and secure using the retainer screws.

9. Install the rear hatch panel and secure the panel using the retainer screws.

10. Install the latch strap using the retainer screws.

11. Connect the negative battery cable. Turn the radio **ON** and make sure the speakers function properly.

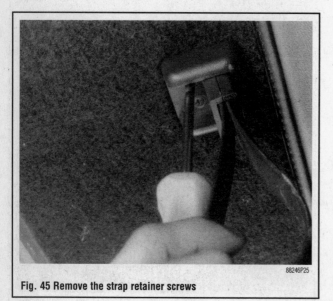

Fig. 44 Remove the rear hatch panel retainer screw

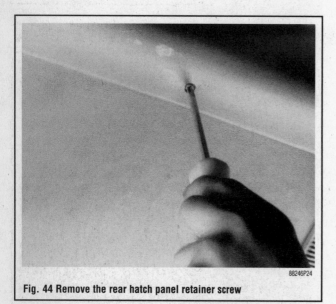

Fig. 45 Remove the strap retainer screws

Fig. 46 Unfasten the latch from the panel

Fig. 47 Lower the hatch panel

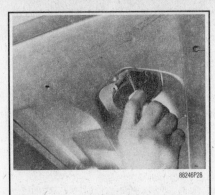

Fig. 48 Remove the speaker retainer screws

Fig. 49 Lower the speaker . . .

Fig. 50 . . . and unfasten the wire harness

WINDSHIELD WIPERS

Front Wiper Arm

REMOVAL & INSTALLATION

▶ See Figures 51, 52 and 53

1. Place the wiper arms in the parked position.
2. Raise the arm assembly up and away from the windshield.
3. Pull the slide latch away from the pivot shaft.
4. Support the arm and pull the assembly off the pivot. No tools should be needed.

To install:

5. Apply a light coating of grease to the wiper arm pivot shaft.
6. With the latch retracted, slide the wiper arm onto the pivot shaft. Press on the arm until the latch clicks into place on the shaft. Install the wiper arms so that, in the parked position, the distance between the center of the blade, where the blade attaches to the arm, and the top edge of the cowl grille is 2.3–3.4 in. (61–89mm) on either side.
7. Lower the arm onto the windshield, making sure it is even with the base of the glass.
8. Turn on the wipers and make sure the wiper pattern is satisfactory, and the wipers stop at the base of the glass.

Fig. 52 Lift the arm off the shaft

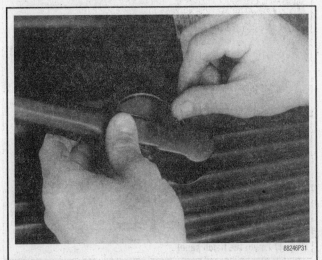

Fig. 51 While lifting the wiper arm, unfasten the latch on the wiper arm

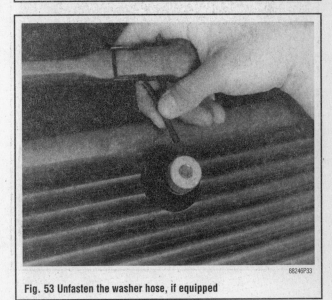

Fig. 53 Unfasten the washer hose, if equipped

Rear Wiper Arm

REMOVAL & INSTALLATION

▶ **See Figures 54 and 55**

1. Place the wiper arm in the parked position.
2. Raise the arm assembly up and away from the rear windshield.
3. Pull the slide latch away from the pivot shaft.
4. Support the arm and pull the assembly off the pivot. No tools should be needed.

To install:

5. Apply a light coating of grease to the wiper arm pivot shaft.
6. With the latch retracted, slide the wiper arm onto the pivot shaft. Press on the arm until the latch clicks into place on the shaft. Install the wiper arms so that, in the parked position, the point at which the arm attaches to the blade is 1 in. (26mm) above the lower glass weather seal.
7. Lower the arm onto the windshield, making sure it is even with the base of the glass.
8. Turn on the wipers and make sure the wiper pattern is satisfactory, and the wipers stop at the base of the glass.

Front Wiper Motor

REMOVAL & INSTALLATION

▶ **See Figures 56 thru 61**

1. Turn the wiper switch **ON**, then turn the ignition switch **ON** until the blades are in mid-pattern. Turn the ignition switch **OFF** to keep the blades in mid-pattern.
2. Disconnect the negative battery cable.
3. Unfasten the wiper motor wiring connector from inside the engine compartment.

4. Paint alignment matchmarks on the wiper arms, then remove both wiper arms.
5. Remove the cowl grille by removing the retainer screws securing the cowl into position.
6. Remove the linkage retaining clip and disassemble the linkage from the motor crank arm.
7. Support the wiper motor with one hand while removing the wiper motor retaining nuts.
8. Lower the motor. When it clears the mounting hole, remove the motor from the engine compartment.

To install:

9. Raise the motor into position with the pivot shaft protruding from the hole in the body. Secure the motor using the retainer nuts. Tighten the nuts to 60–85 inch lbs. (7–9 Nm).
10. Install the linkage and secure with the retainer clips.
11. Install the cowl grille using the retainer screws to secure.
12. Install the wiper arms, making sure the alignment is correct.
13. Fasten the wire harness to the wiper motor.
14. Connect the negative battery cable.
15. Test the wipers for correct operation.

Rear Wiper Motor

REMOVAL & INSTALLATION

▶ **See Figures 62, 63, 64 and 65**

1. Disconnect the negative battery cable.
2. Remove the wiper arm and blade from the vehicle.
3. Remove the motor shaft attaching nut and wedge block.
4. Remove the liftgate trim panel. See Section 10 for removal and installation procedures.
5. Unfasten the electrical connector from the motor. Remove the motor wiring pins from the inner panel, then remove the motor.

Fig. 54 While lifting up on the wiper arm, unfasten the latch

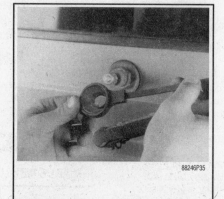

Fig. 55 Lift the wiper arm off the shaft

Fig. 56 Remove the cowl grille retainer plugs, or screws, depending on model year

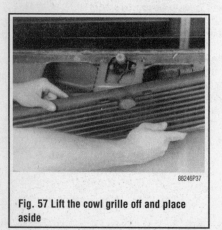

Fig. 57 Lift the cowl grille off and place aside

Fig. 58 Remove the retainer bolts from inside the cowl panel

Fig. 59 Unfasten the retainer bolts from the back of the cowl panel

Fig. 60 Remove the retainer clip securing the wiper linkage to the motor assembly

Fig. 61 Lift the motor out

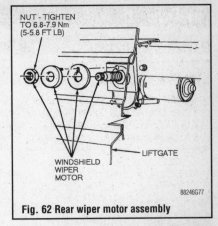

NUT - TIGHTEN TO 6.8-7.9 Nm (5-5.8 FT LB)

WINDSHIELD WIPER MOTOR

LIFTGATE

Fig. 62 Rear wiper motor assembly

Fig. 63 Remove the retainer nut from the motor shaft

Fig. 64 With the nut removed, lift off the first rubber seal . . .

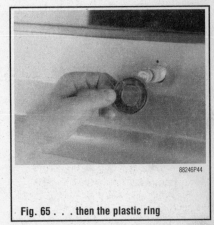

Fig. 65 . . . then the plastic ring

To install:

6. Place the motor into the liftgate so that the motor shaft protrudes through the opening in the outer panel.

7. Secure the motor to the liftgate inner panel by connecting the wiring pushpins in the holes provided.

8. Install the liftgate trim panel.

9. Install the wedge and attaching nut to the pivot shaft on the motor.

10. Load the articulating arm onto the drive pilot shaft. The wiper system must be in the rested position before the arm and blade is installed.

11. Locate the blade to the specified installation position.

12. Install the arm onto the pivot shaft after the articulating arm is in place with the slide latch in the unlocked position.

13. While applying a downward pressure on the arm head to insure full seating, raise the other end of the arm sufficiently to allow the latch to slide under the pivot shaft to the locked position. Use finger pressure only to slide the latch, then release the arm and blade against the rear window.

14. Connect the negative battery cable.

15. Test the rear wiper to make sure it functions properly.

Front Washer Motor

REMOVAL & INSTALLATION

1. Disconnect the negative battery cable.
2. Remove the washer reservoir and motor from the vehicle.

3. Using a small prytool, carefully pry up on the top of the motor until it clears the edge of the reservoir.

4. Pull the motor out of the reservoir.

To install:

5. Insert the end of the washer motor into the grommet in the reservoir.

6. Push the motor in until it locks into the tabs on the reservoir.

7. Install the reservoir and motor into the vehicle.

8. Check and add washer fluid if needed.

9. Test the washer nozzle to make sure it functions correctly.

Rear Washer Motor

REMOVAL & INSTALLATION

1. Disconnect the negative battery cable.

2. Remove the washer reservoir and motor from the vehicle.

3. Using a small prytool, carefully pry up on the top of the motor until it clears the edge of the reservoir.

4. Pull the motor out of the reservoir.

To install:

5. Insert the end of the washer motor into the grommet in the reservoir.

6. Push the motor in until it locks into the tabs on the reservoir.

7. Install the reservoir and motor into the vehicle.

8. Check and add washer fluid if needed.

9. Test the washer nozzle to make sure it functions correctly.

INSTRUMENTS AND SWITCHES

Instrument Cluster

✳✳ WARNING

Vinyl cleaners used on vehicle's interior surfaces can cause damage to the cluster lens, either through overspray or direct application. Take great pains to avoid spraying these cleaners on the lens! Clean the lens with glass cleaner only.

REMOVAL & INSTALLATION

Standard Cluster

▶ See Figures 66, 67, 68, 69 and 70

1. Disconnect the negative battery cable.
2. Remove the cluster housing-to-panel retaining screws and remove the cluster housing.
3. Remove the instrument cluster-to-panel retaining screws.
4. Lift the instrument cluster out slightly to gain access to the wire harness at the rear of the assembly.
5. Disconnect the wiring harness connectors from the printed circuit board.
6. Disengage the speedometer cable from the speedometer.
7. Remove the cluster by pulling it forward.

To install:

8. Apply a small amount of silicone dielectric compound (D7AZ-19A331-A or equivalent) in the drive hole of the speedometer head.
9. Position the cluster above the opening in the instrument panel.
10. Connect the speedometer cable to the speedometer head.
11. Connect the wiring harness connectors to the printed circuit board.
12. Position the cluster to the instrument panel and install the cluster-to-panel retaining screws.
13. Install the cluster housing to the panel.
14. Connect the battery ground cable.
15. Turn the ignition switch **ON** and check the operation of all gauges, lamps and signals.

Electronic Cluster

1. Disconnect the negative battery cable.
2. Remove the cluster housing-to-panel retaining screws and remove the cluster housing.
3. Remove the instrument cluster-to-panel retaining screws.
4. Pull the top of the cluster slightly toward the steering wheel.
5. Reach behind the cluster and unplug the three electrical connectors.
6. Swing the cluster out and remove it from the dash panel.

To install:

7. Insert the bottom of the cluster into the instrument panel alignment pins.
8. Plug in the three electrical connectors.
9. Seat the cluster and fasten the mounting screws.
10. Install the cluster housing to the panel.

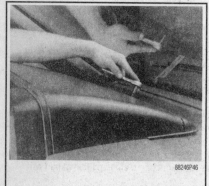

88246P46

Fig. 66 Remove the retainer screws securing the instrument cluster cover in place

88246P47

Fig. 67 Lift the cover off and place aside

88246P48

Fig. 68 Remove the lower instrument cluster retainer screws, located at both sides of the steering column

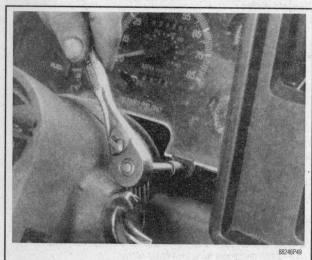

88246P49

Fig. 69 Using a suitable socket, remove the retainer screws from above the steering column

88246P50

Fig. 70 Remove the retainer screws securing the top of the instrument cluster

11. Connect the negative battery cable.

12. Turn the ignition switch **ON** and check cluster operation.

Speedometer

REMOVAL & INSTALLATION

Standard Model

1. Disconnect the negative battery cable.

2. Remove the cluster assembly from the vehicle and place on a clean, flat surface.

3. Remove the attaching screws and lift the lens from the cluster assembly.

4. Remove the retainer nuts from the voltmeter.

5. Remove the screw from the anti-slosh module and remove the module.

6. Remove the attaching screws and lift out the module.

7. Remove the screws retaining the gauges in place.

8. Using a pair of needlenose pliers, remove the gauge terminal clips by squeezing both ends of the clip and pushing it through the clip opening in the backplate.

9. Lift the bulbs and printed circuit board up, then lift the speedometer up and out of the instrument cluster.

To install:

10. With the bulbs and printed circuit board lifted up, slide the speedometer into position.

11. Position the circuit board to the instrument cluster assembly, and install the gauge terminal clips in place. Make sure that both tabs lock in place.

12. Install the gauges using the retainer screws.

13. Install the redundant module and anti-slosh module, and secure in place with the retainer screws.

14. Install the nuts on the voltmeter.

15. Attach the cluster lens and secure using the retaining screws.

16. Install the cluster assembly into the vehicle.

17. Connect the negative battery cable.

18. Test and make sure that all the gauges register, and all cluster bulbs function.

Electronic Model

1. Disconnect the negative battery cable.

2. Remove the cluster from the vehicle and place on a clean flat surface.

3. Remove the attaching screws and lift off the lens assembly.

4. Remove the attaching screws from the back of the speedometer gauge module.

5. Lift the flex circuit off the locator pins and remove the speedometer module.

To install:

6. Clean the face of the speedometer module with alcohol and a lint-free cloth.

7. Lift the flex circuit strip and insert the speedometer module.

8. Install the retainer screws to the module.

9. Install the cluster lens using the retainer screws.

10. Install the cluster into the vehicle.

11. Connect the negative battery cable.

12. Test the instrument cluster to make sure all gauges function correctly.

Tachometer

REMOVAL & INSTALLATION

Standard Model

1. Disconnect the negative battery cable.

2. Remove the cluster assembly from the vehicle and place on a clean flat surface.

3. Remove the attaching screws and lift the lens from the cluster assembly.

4. Remove the retainer nuts from the voltmeter.

5. Remove the screw from the anti-slosh module and remove the module.

6. Remove the attaching screws and lift out the redundant module.

7. Remove the screws retaining the gauges in place.

8. Using a pair of needlenose pliers, remove the gauge terminal clips by squeezing both ends of the clip and pushing it through the clip opening in the backplate.

9. Lift the bulbs and printed circuit board up, then lift the tachometer up and out of the instrument cluster.

To install:

10. With the bulbs and printed circuit board lifted up, slide the tachometer into position.

11. Position the circuit board to the instrument cluster assembly, and install the gauge terminal clips in place. Make sure that both tabs lock in place.

12. Install the gauges using the retainer screws.

13. Install the redundant module and anti-slosh module and secure in place with the retainer screws.

14. Install the nuts on the voltmeter.

15. Attach the cluster lens and secure using the retaining screws.

16. Install the cluster assembly into the vehicle.

17. Connect the negative battery cable.

18. Test and make sure that all the gauges register, and all cluster bulbs function.

Electronic Model

1. Disconnect the negative battery cable.

2. Remove the cluster from the vehicle and place on a clean, flat surface.

3. Remove the attaching screws and lift off the lens assembly.

4. Remove the attaching screws from the back of the tachometer module.

5. Lift the flex circuit off the locator pins and remove the tachometer module.

To install:

6. Clean the face of the tachometer module with alcohol and a lint-free cloth.

7. Lift the flex circuit strip and insert the tachometer module.

8. Install the retainer screws to the module.

9. Install the cluster lens using the retainer screws.

10. Install the cluster into the vehicle.

11. Connect the negative battery cable.

12. Test the instrument cluster to make sure all gauges function correctly.

Oil Pressure Gauge

➡The oil pressure gauge is installed into the instrument cluster with a second gauge that cannot be separated, usually a temperature gauge. In the event the fuel gauge needs replacing, the companion gauge will also have to be replaced.

REMOVAL & INSTALLATION

Standard Model

1. Disconnect the negative battery cable.

2. Remove the cluster assembly from the vehicle and place on a clean, flat surface.

3. Remove the attaching screws and lift the lens from the cluster assembly.

4. Remove the retainer nuts from the voltmeter.

5. Remove the screw from the anti-slosh module and remove the module.

6. Remove the attaching screws and lift out the redundant module.

7. Remove the screws retaining the gauges in place.

8. Using a pair of needlenose pliers, remove the gauge terminal clips by squeezing both ends of the clip and pushing it through the clip opening in the backplate.

9. Lift the bulbs and printed circuit board up, then lift the oil pressure and companion gauge assembly up and out of the instrument cluster.

To install:

10. With the bulbs and printed circuit board lifted up, slide the oil pressure and companion gauge and voltmeter into position.

11. Position the circuit board to the instrument cluster assembly, and install the gauge terminal clips in place. Make sure that both tabs lock in place.

12. Install the gauges using the retainer screws.

13. Install the redundant module and anti-slosh module, and secure in place with the retainer screws.

14. Install the nuts on the voltmeter.
15. Attach the cluster lens and secure using the retaining screws.
16. Install the cluster assembly into the vehicle.
17. Connect the negative battery cable.
18. Test and make sure that all the gauges register, and all cluster bulbs function.

Electronic Model

1. Disconnect the negative battery cable.
2. Remove the cluster from the vehicle and place on a clean flat surface.
3. Remove the attaching screws and lift off the lens assembly.
4. Remove the attaching screws from the back of the oil pressure gauge module.
5. Lift the flex circuit off the locator pins and remove the oil pressure module.

To install:
6. Clean the face of the oil pressure module with alcohol and a lint-free cloth.
7. Lift the flex circuit strip and insert the oil pressure module.
8. Install the retainer screws to the module.
9. Install the cluster lens using the retainer screws.
10. Install the cluster into the vehicle.
11. Connect the negative battery cable.
12. Test the instrument cluster to make sure all gauges function correctly.

Fuel Gauge

➡The fuel gauge is installed into the instrument cluster with a second gauge that cannot be separated, usually a voltmeter. In the event the fuel gauge needs replacing, the companion gauge will also have to be replaced.

REMOVAL & INSTALLATION

Standard Model

1. Disconnect the negative battery cable.
2. Remove the cluster assembly from the vehicle and place on a clean flat surface.
3. Remove the attaching screws and lift the lens from the cluster assembly.
4. Remove the retainer nuts from the voltmeter.
5. Remove the screw from the anti-slosh module and remove the module.
6. Remove the attaching screws and lift out the redundant module.
7. Remove the screws retaining the gauges in place.
8. Using a pair of needlenose pliers, remove the gauge terminal clips by squeezing both ends of the clip and pushing it through the clip opening in the backplate.
9. Lift the bulbs and printed circuit board up, then lift the fuel and companion gauge assembly up and out of the instrument cluster.

To install:
10. With the bulbs and printed circuit board lifted up, slide the fuel gauge and companion gauge into position.
11. Position the circuit board to the instrument cluster assembly, and install the gauge terminal clips in place. Make sure that both tabs lock in place.
12. Install the gauges using the retainer screws.
13. Install the redundant module and anti-slosh module, and secure in place with the retainer screws.
14. Install the nuts on the voltmeter.
15. Attach the cluster lens and secure using the retaining screws.
16. Install the cluster assembly into the vehicle.
17. Connect the negative battery cable.
18. Test and make sure that all the gauges register, and all cluster bulbs function.

Electronic Model

1. Disconnect the negative battery cable.
2. Remove the cluster from the vehicle and place on a clean, flat surface.

3. Remove the attaching screws and lift off the lens assembly.
4. Remove the attaching screws from the back of the fuel gauge module.
5. Lift the flex circuit off the locator pins and remove the fuel module.

To install:
6. Clean the face of the fuel module with alcohol and a lint-free cloth.
7. Lift the flex circuit strip and insert the fuel module.
8. Install the retainer screws to the module.
9. Install the cluster lens using the retainer screws.
10. Install the cluster into the vehicle.
11. Connect the negative battery cable.
12. Test the instrument cluster to make sure all gauge function correctly.

Temperature Gauge

➡The temperature gauge is installed into the instrument cluster with a second gauge that cannot be separated, usually an oil pressure gauge. In the event the fuel gauge needs replacing, the companion gauge will also have to be replaced.

REMOVAL & INSTALLATION

Standard Model

1. Disconnect the negative battery cable.
2. Remove the cluster assembly from the vehicle and place on a clean, flat surface.
3. Remove the attaching screws and lift the lens from the cluster assembly.
4. Remove the retainer nuts from the voltmeter.
5. Remove the screw from the anti-slosh module and remove the module.
6. Remove the attaching screws and lift out the redundant module.
7. Remove the screws retaining the gauges in place.
8. Using a pair of needlenose pliers, remove the gauge terminal clips by squeezing both ends of the clip and pushing it through the clip opening in the backplate.
9. Lift the bulbs and printed circuit board up, then lift the temperature and companion gauge assembly up and out of the instrument cluster.

To install:
10. With the bulbs and printed circuit board lifted up, slide the temperature and companion gauge assembly into position.
11. Position the circuit board to the instrument cluster assembly, and install the gauge terminal clips in place. Make sure that both tabs lock in place.
12. Install the gauges using the retainer screws.
13. Install the redundant module and anti-slosh module, and secure in place with the retainer screws.
14. Install the nuts on the voltmeter.
15. Attach the cluster lens and secure using the retaining screws.
16. Install the cluster assembly into the vehicle.
17. Connect the negative battery cable.
18. Test and make sure that all the gauges register, and all cluster bulbs function.

Electronic Model

1. Disconnect the negative battery cable.
2. Remove the cluster from the vehicle and place on a clean flat surface.
3. Remove the attaching screws and lift off the lens assembly.
4. Remove the attaching screws from the back of the temperature gauge module.
5. Lift the flex circuit off the locator pins and remove the temperature module.

To install:
6. Clean the face of the temperature module with alcohol and a lint-free cloth.
7. Lift the flex circuit strip and insert the temperature module.
8. Install the retainer screws to the module.
9. Install the cluster lens using the retainer screws.
10. Install the cluster into the vehicle.
11. Connect the negative battery cable.
12. Test the instrument cluster to make sure all gauges function correctly.

Voltmeter

➡The voltmeter is installed into the instrument cluster with a second gauge that cannot be separated, usually a fuel gauge. In the event the fuel gauge needs replacing, the companion gauge will also have to be replaced.

REMOVAL & INSTALLATION

Standard Model

1. Disconnect the negative battery cable.
2. Remove the cluster assembly from the vehicle and place on a clean, flat surface.
3. Remove the attaching screws and lift the lens from the cluster assembly.
4. Remove the retainer nuts from the voltmeter.
5. Remove the screw from the anti-slosh module and remove the module.
6. Remove the attaching screws and lift out the redundant module.
7. Remove the screws retaining the gauges in place.
8. Using a pair of needlenose pliers, remove the gauge terminal clips by squeezing both ends of the clip and pushing it through the clip opening in the backplate.
9. Lift the bulbs and printed circuit board up, then lift the voltmeter and companion gauge assembly up and out of the instrument cluster.

To install:

10. With the bulbs and printed circuit board lifted up, slide the voltmeter and companion gauge into position.
11. Position the circuit board to the instrument cluster assembly, and install the gauge terminal clips in place. Make sure that both tabs lock in place.
12. Install the gauges using the retainer screws.
13. Install the redundant module and anti-slosh module, and secure in place with the retainer screws.
14. Install the nuts on the voltmeter.
15. Attach the cluster lens and secure using the retaining screws.
16. Install the cluster assembly into the vehicle.
17. Connect the negative battery cable.
18. Test and make sure that all the gauges register, and all cluster bulbs function.

Electronic Model

1. Disconnect the negative battery cable.
2. Remove the cluster from the vehicle and place on a clean, flat surface.
3. Remove the attaching screws and lift off the lens assembly.
4. Remove the attaching screws from the back of the voltmeter module.
5. Lift the flex circuit off the locator pins and remove the voltmeter module.

To install:

6. Clean the face of the voltmeter module with alcohol and a lint-free cloth.
7. Lift the flex circuit strip and insert the voltmeter module.
8. Install the retainer screws to the module.
9. Install the cluster lens using the retainer screws.
10. Install the cluster into the vehicle.
11. Connect the negative battery cable.
12. Test the instrument cluster to make sure all gauges function correctly.

Front Wiper Switch

REMOVAL & INSTALLATION

♦ See Figure 71

The front wiper switch is integrated into the turn signal switch on the steering column. In the event the wiper switch fails, the entire switch will have to be replaced.

➡**The switch handle is an integral part of the switch.**

1. Disconnect the negative battery cable.
2. Remove the cluster finish panel assembly retaining screws.
3. Remove the left control pod assembly retaining screws.
4. Remove the wiring connector from the wiper switch.

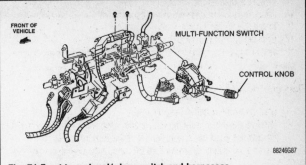

Fig. 71 Front turn signal/wiper switch and harnesses

5. Remove the two lamp switch-to-control pod retaining screws and remove the switch pod.

To install:

6. Insert the lamp switch-to-control pod retainer screws into the wiper switch and secure in place.
7. Install the wire harness to the wiper switch.
8. Attach the left control pod retainer screws.
9. Install the cluster finish trim panel using the retainer screws.
10. Connect the negative battery cable.
11. Test the wiper system to make sure it functions on all speeds and in all positions.

Rear Wiper Switch

REMOVAL & INSTALLATION

♦ See Figure 72

1. Disconnect the negative battery cable.
2. Remove the retainer screws from the center switch panel. Lift the panel out enough to reach the back of the switches.
3. Push the rear wiper/washer switch out.
4. Disconnect the wire harness from the wiper/washer switch.

To install:

5. Connect the wiper/washer wire harness to the rear of the switch.
6. Install the switch into the switch panel.
7. Secure the switch panel to the dash using the retainer screws.
8. Connect the negative battery cable.
9. Test the rear wiper/washer to make sure the system operates correctly.

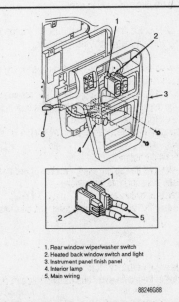

1. Rear window wiper/washer switch
2. Heated back window switch and light
3. Instrument panel finish panel
4. Interior lamp
5. Main wiring

Fig. 72 Rear defroster and wiper control switch in center trim panel

Headlight Switch

REMOVAL & INSTALLATION

▶ **See Figure 73**

1. Disconnect the negative battery cable.
2. Remove the retaining screws and lift off the cluster finish panel assembly.
3. Remove the left control pod assembly retaining screws.
4. Disconnect the wiring connector from the rear of the switch.
5. Remove the two lamp switch-to-control pod retaining screws and remove the switch.

To install:

6. Insert the lamp switch-to-control pod retainer screws into the headlight switch and secure in place.
7. Install the wire harness to the rear of the headlight switch.
8. Attach the left control pod retainer screws.
9. Install the cluster finish panel using the retainer screws.
10. Connect the negative battery cable.
11. Test the headlight switch to make sure all lights function.

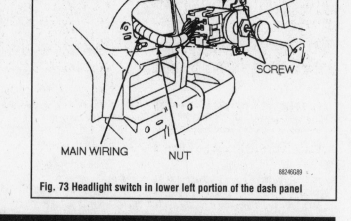

Fig. 73 Headlight switch in lower left portion of the dash panel

LIGHTING

Headlights

REMOVAL & INSTALLATION

Sealed Beam Type

▶ **See Figures 74, 75, 76, 77 and 78**

1. Disconnect the negative battery cable.
2. Remove the headlight trim bezel attaching screws and remove the headlight trim bezel around the headlight.
3. Remove the headlight retaining ring screws and remove the retaining ring. Do not disturb the adjusting screw settings.
4. Pull the headlight forward and disconnect the wiring harness from the back of the lamp, then remove the headlight from the vehicle.

To install:

5. Connect the wiring harness to the headlight and place the light in position, making sure the locating tabs on the rear of the lamp are fitted in the positioning slots.
6. Install the headlamp retaining ring.
7. Place the headlight trim bezel in position and install the retaining screws.
8. Connect the negative battery cable.
9. Turn **ON** the headlight switch to make sure all the lights work correctly.

Non-Sealed Beam Type

Most headlights today are of a non-sealed beam design, which means that if a light burns out, only the bulb has to be replaced. All Aerostar vehicles with this type of headlight use a 9004 type headlight bulb.

1. Disconnect the negative battery cable.
2. Remove the headlight trim bezel attaching screws and remove the headlight trim bezel around the headlight.
3. Remove the headlight retaining ring screws and remove the retaining ring. Do not disturb the adjusting screw settings.
4. Pull the headlight forward and disconnect the wiring harness from the back of the lamp, then remove the headlight from the vehicle.

To install:

5. Connect the wiring harness to the headlight and place the light in position, making sure the locating tabs on the rear of the lamp are fitted in the positioning slots.
6. Install the headlamp retaining ring.
7. Place the headlight trim in position and install the retaining screws.
8. Connect the negative battery cable.
9. Turn **ON** the headlight switch to make sure all the lights work correctly.

BULB REPLACEMENT

▶ **See Figure 79**

➡ The 9004 headlight bulb is a halogen type bulb. This type of bulb is very sensitive to oils on the glass lens. When removing or installing a

Fig. 74 Remove the retainer screws from the side of the headlight bezel

Fig. 75 Also remove the retainer screws from the front of the headlight bezel

Fig. 76 Remove the screws securing the trim ring around the headlight

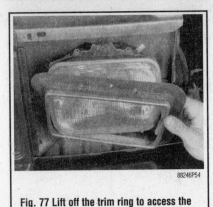

Fig. 77 Lift off the trim ring to access the headlight retainer ring

Fig. 78 With the retainer ring removed, lift out the headlight enough to unfasten the wire harness

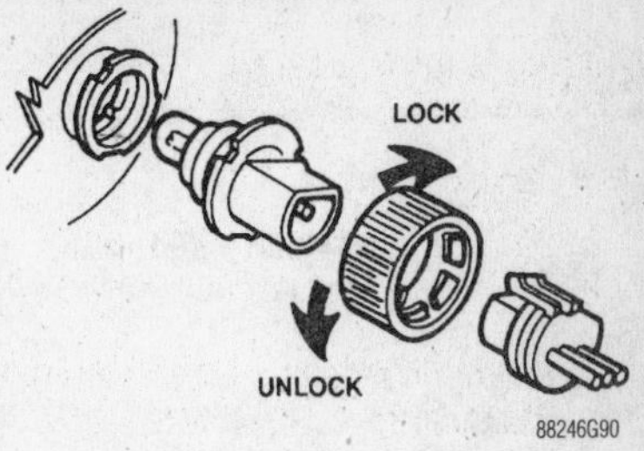

Fig. 79 Type 9004 headlight bulb, retainer ring and harness

type 9004 bulb, **NEVER** touch the lens, or bulb life will be severely reduced.

1. Disconnect the negative battery cable.
2. From inside the engine compartment, twist off the headlight bulb retainer ring and slide over the harness plug.
3. Grasp the base of the bulb and pull it out from the headlamp.
4. Unplug the bulb from the harness.

To install:

5. Grasp the base of the bulb with your hand. Plug the wire harness into the bulb.
6. Insert the bulb into the headlamp.
7. Twist the headlight bulb retainer ring on until it locks in place.
8. Connect the negative battery cable.
9. Turn **ON** the headlight switch to make sure all the lights work correctly.

AIMING

1. Park the vehicle on level ground, so that it is perpendicular to, and facing a flat wall about 25 ft. (7.6m) away.
2. Remove any stone shields and switch on the lights to low beam.
3. The horizontal distance between the light beams on the wall should be the same as between the headlights themselves.
4. The vertical height of the light beams above the ground should be 4 in. (10cm) less than the distance between the ground and the center of the lamp lenses for the lights.
5. If adjustment is needed, turn the adjusting screw on the headlight ring. Each headlight will have two adjusting screws. One will control the vertical

plain, and the other will control the horizontal plain. Adjust in small increments.

6. Test to make sure the lights work correctly, and the light pattern is even.

Signal and Marker Lights

REMOVAL & INSTALLATION

Front Turn Signal and Parking Light

▸ See Figures 80, 81, 82 and 83

1. Remove the screws securing the headlight trim bezel in place.
2. Pull the bezel out enough to access the lamp wire and plug.

➡The turn signal/parking light harness is the larger harness of the two installed to the bezel assembly.

3. Remove the lamp assembly by twisting counterclockwise and pulling out.
4. Depress and twist the bulb approximately ⅛ turn counterclockwise to remove from the socket.

To Install:

5. Install the bulb by inserting it into the light socket and twisting clockwise.
6. Install the light assembly into the bezel by inserting it into the hole and twisting clockwise slightly.
7. Install the trim bezel and secure with the retainer screws.
8. Test to make sure the lights work correctly.

Fig. 80 Remove the headlight bezel side retainer screws . . .

Fig. 81 . . . followed by the front retainer screws

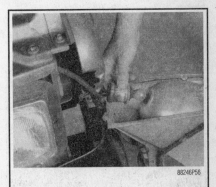

Fig. 82 Lift the bezel out and turn the socket base to remove the socket and bulb

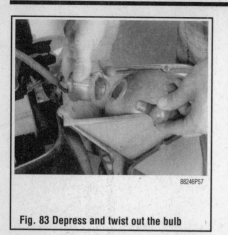

Fig. 83 Depress and twist out the bulb

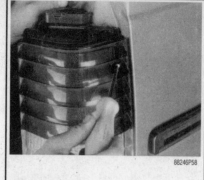

Fig. 84 Remove the tail lens retainer screws

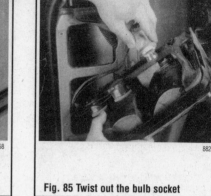

Fig. 85 Twist out the bulb socket

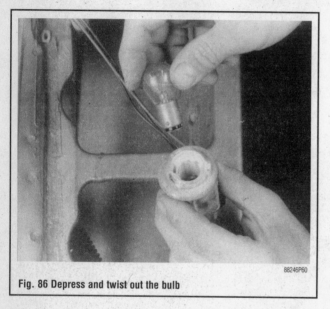

Fig. 86 Depress and twist out the bulb

Side Marker Light

1. Remove the screws securing the headlight trim bezel in place.
2. Pull the bezel out enough to access the lamp wire and plug.

➡ **The side marker harness is the smaller harness of the two installed to the bezel assembly.**

3. Remove the lamp assembly by twisting counterclockwise and pulling out.
4. Depress and twist the bulb approximately ¼ turn counterclockwise to remove from the socket.

To install:

5. Install the bulb by inserting it into the light socket and twisting clockwise.
6. Install the light assembly into the bezel by inserting it into the hole and twisting clockwise slightly.
7. Install the trim bezel and secure with the retainer screws.
8. Test to make sure the lights work correctly.

Rear Turn Signal, Brake and Parking Lights

▶ **See Figures 84, 85 and 86**

1. Remove the four screws retaining the lens assembly to the vehicle.
2. Remove the lamp assembly by grasping the base and twisting counterclockwise, then pulling it out from the lens assembly.
3. Remove the bulb socket from the lamp assembly, by pressing the bulb in, twisting it counterclockwise, then pulling it out.

To install:

4. Insert the replacement bulb into the socket, press down on it then twist clockwise into position.

5. Insert the bulb and socket assembly into the lens assembly and twist the socket clockwise to lock it in place.
6. Install the lens assembly to the vehicle and secure in place with the retainer screws.
7. Test to make sure the lights work correctly.

High-Mount Brake Light

LIFTGATE MOUNTED VERSION

▶ **See Figure 87**

1. Remove the retainer screws securing the lens assembly to the lamp housing.
2. Pull the lens assembly out of the lamp housing.
3. Pull the bulb straight out of the socket. This type of bulb does not have to be twisted out.

To install:

4. Insert a replacement bulb into the socket and press in place.
5. Attach the lens housing to the lamp assembly.
6. Secure the lamp and lens together with the retainer screws.
7. Test to make sure the lights work correctly.

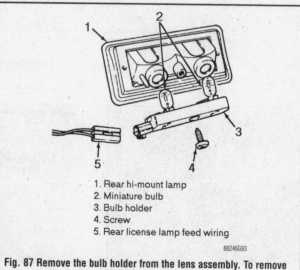

1. Rear hi-mount lamp
2. Miniature bulb
3. Bulb holder
4. Screw
5. Rear license lamp feed wiring

Fig. 87 Remove the bulb holder from the lens assembly. To remove a bulb, simply grasp the bulb and pull straight out

ROOF MOUNTED VERSION

1. Remove the interior light from the headliner.
2. Unfasten the brake light wire harness at the headliner.
3. Remove the retainer nuts securing the brake light to the roof of the vehicle.

4. Lift the brake light away from the vehicle.
5. Remove the retainer screws securing the lens to the lamp housing. Remove the lens.
6. Pull the bulb straight out of the socket. This type of bulb does not have to be twisted out.

To install:

7. Insert a replacement bulb in to the socket and press in place.
8. Secure the lamp and lens together with the retainer screws.
9. Position the brake light onto the roof of the vehicle.
10. Secure the brake light in place using the retainer nuts.
11. Fasten the brake light wire harness.
12. Install the interior light.
13. Test to make sure the lights work correctly.

Dome Light

▶ See Figures 88 and 89

1. Carefully snap the lens out of the lamp assembly by squeezing in on the sides of the lens.
2. Remove the bulb from the retainer clips.
3. To remove the lamp body, unfasten the retaining screws and carefully pry at each corner to remove the body from the clips.

To install:

4. If installing the lamp body, secure in place using the clips, then install the retainer screws.
5. Insert the bulb into the retainer clips, making sure the bulb is seated firmly in each contact point.
6. Snap the lens into place.
7. Test to make sure the light works correctly.

Cargo Lamp

1. Remove the lens by squeezing in on the sides of the lens.
2. Depress the bulb and rotate it counterclockwise to remove it.

To install:

3. Insert a replacement bulb. Depress the bulb and turn clockwise to lock it in place.
4. Install the lens.
5. Test to make sure the light works correctly.

License Plate Light

▶ See Figures 90, 91, 92 and 93

1. Remove the 2 screws retaining the lamp to the rear door panel.
2. Pull the lamp assembly out enough to remove the lenses and access the bulb.
3. Rotate the socket ¼ turn counterclockwise from the backside of the lamp.
4. Pull the bulb straight out from the socket. Twisting is not needed on these type bulbs.

To install:

5. Insert the bulb into the socket. Twisting is not needed on these type bulbs.
6. Insert the socket into the lamp, and rotate it clockwise to lock in place.
7. Position the lens to the door panel and secure using the retainer screws.
8. Test to make sure the lights work correctly.

Fig. 88 Remove the plastic cover over the interior light assembly

Fig. 89 Remove the interior bulb from the clips

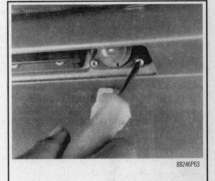

Fig. 90 Remove the retainer screws securing the lens in place

Fig. 91 Lower the lens and bulb assembly

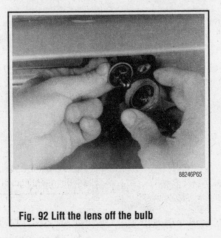

Fig. 92 Lift the lens off the bulb

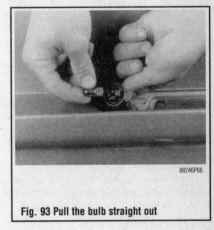

Fig. 93 Pull the bulb straight out

TRAILER WIRING

Wiring the vehicle for towing is fairly easy. There are a number of good wiring kits available and these should be used, rather than trying to design your own.

All trailers will need brake lights and turn signals, as well as tail lights and side marker lights. Most areas require extra marker lights for overwide trailers. Also, most areas have recently required back-up lights for trailers, and most trailer manufacturers have been building trailers with back-up lights for several years.

Additionally, some Class I, most Class II and just about all Class III trailers will have electric brakes. Add to this number an accessories wire, to operate trailer internal equipment or to charge the trailer's battery, and you can have as many as seven wires in the harness.

Determine the equipment on your trailer and buy the wiring kit necessary. The kit will contain all the wires needed, plus a plug adapter set which includes the female plug, mounted on the bumper or hitch, and the male plug, wired into, or plugged into the trailer harness.

When installing the kit, follow the manufacturer's instructions. The color coding of the wires is usually standard throughout the industry. One point to note: some domestic vehicles, and most imported vehicles, have separate turn signals. On most domestic vehicles, the brake lights and rear turn signals operate with the same bulb. For those vehicles without separate turn signals, you can purchase an isolation unit so that the brake lights won't blink whenever the turn signals are operated, or, you can go to your local electronics supply house and buy four diodes to wire in series with the brake and turn signal bulbs. Diodes will isolate the brake and turn signals. The choice is yours. The isolation units are simple and quick to install, but far more expensive than the diodes. The diodes, however, require more work to install properly, since they require the cutting of each bulb's wire and soldering in place of the diode.

One, final point: the best kits are those with a spring loaded cover on the vehicle-mounted socket. This cover prevents dirt and moisture from corroding the terminals. Never let the vehicle socket hang loosely; always mount it securely to the bumper or hitch.

CIRCUIT PROTECTION

Fuse Panel and Fuses

Most of the replaceable fuses for the electrical system are located on the fuse panel under the instrument panel, to the left of the steering column. In addition to the plastic fuses installed in the fuse box, there are one or more circuit breakers and a flasher relay.

For access to the fuse panel, remove the fasteners from the lower edge of the cover, then pull the cover downward until the spring clips disengage from the instrument panel. On the base models, the cover simply snaps on and off.

The locations of various fuses are illustrated in the owner's manual, and in some cases, on the cover of the fuse panel.

REPLACEMENT

▶ **See Figures 94, 95 and 96**

Fuses are replaced by simply pulling them out. A blown or open fuse can be seen as a break in the metal filament that runs between the blades. The fuse is made with a plastic body so the break can be clearly seen.

Fuses that open (blow) may be replaced, but will continue to open until the cause of the overload condition is corrected. If a fuse needs to be replaced, use only a new fuse rated according to the specifications and of the same amperage number as the one removed. At the time of manufacture, five spare fuses were located inside the fuse panel cover.

❊❊ CAUTION

Always replace a blown fuse or fuse link with the same rating as specified. Never replace a fuse with a higher amperage rating than the one removed, or severe wiring damage and a possible fire can result.

Fusible Links

A fusible link is a short length of Hypalon (high temperature) insulated wire, integral with the wiring harness, and should not be confused with standard wire. The fusible link is several wire gauges smaller than the circuit it protects, and is designed to melt and break the circuit should an overload occur. Under no circumstances should a fusible link be replaced with a standard length of wire.

The higher melting temperature properties and additional thickness of the Hypalon insulation will usually allow the undersized internal fuse wire to melt and disintegrate within the Hypalon casing with little damage to the high temperature insulation other than discoloration and/or bubbling of the insulation surface. In extreme cases of excessive circuit current, the insulation may separate after the fuse wire has disintegrated, however, the bare wire will seldom be exposed. If it becomes difficult to determine if the fuse link is burnt open, perform a continuity test. When heavy current flows, such as when a booster battery is connected incorrectly or when a short to ground occurs in the wiring harness, the fusible link burns out to protect the alternator and/or wiring.

Production fuse links have a flag molded on the wire or on the terminal insulator. Color identification of the flag or connector is Blue-20 gauge wire, Red-18 gauge wire, Yellow-17 gauge wire, Orange-16 gauge wire, and Green-14 gauge wire.

REPLACEMENT

To repair any blown fuse link use the following procedure:

1. Determine which circuit is damaged, its location and the cause of the open fuse link. If the damaged fuse link is one of three fed by a common No. 10 or 12 gauge feed wire, determine the specific affected circuit.

2. Disconnect the negative battery cable.

3. Cut the damaged fuse link from the wiring harness and discard it. If the fuse link is one of three circuits fed by a single feed wire, cut it out of the harness at each splice end and discard it.

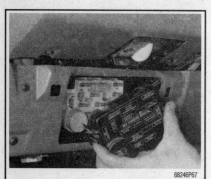

Fig. 94 Remove the cover over the fuse box. Notice that the cover identifies what the fuse protects

Fig. 95 The inside of the cover holds the spare fuses in place

Fig. 96 To remove a fuse, simply pull it straight out

4. Identify and procure the proper fuse link and butt connectors for attaching the fuse link in the harness.

5. To repair any fuse link in a 3-link group with one feed:

a. After cutting the open link out of the harness, cut each of the remaining undamaged fuse links close to the feed wire weld.

b. Strip approximately ½ in. (12.7mm) of insulation from the detached ends of the two good fuse links. Then insert two wire ends into one end of a butt connector, and carefully push one stripped end of the replacement fuse link into the same end of the butt connector. Crimp all three firmly together.

➥**Care must be taken when fitting the three fuse links into the butt connector, as the internal diameter is a snug fit for three wires. Make sure to use a proper crimping tool. Pliers, side cutters, etc. will not apply the proper crimp to retain the wires and withstand a pull test.**

c. After crimping the butt connector to the three fuse links, cut the weld portion from the feed wire and strip approximately ½ in. (12.7mm) of insulation from the cut end. Insert the stripped end into the open end of the butt connector and crimp very firmly.

d. To attach the remaining end of the replacement fuse link, strip approximately ½ in. (12.7mm) of insulation from the wire end of the circuit from which the blown fuse link was removed, and firmly crimp a butt connector to the stripped wire. Then, insert the end of the replacement link into the other end of the butt connector and crimp firmly.

e. Using rosin core solder with a consistency of 60 percent tin and 40 percent lead, solder the connectors and the wires at the repairs, and insulate with electrical tape.

6. To replace any fuse link on a single circuit in a harness, cut out the damaged portion, strip approximately ½ in. (12.7mm) of insulation from the two wire ends and attach the appropriate replacement fuse link to the stripped wire ends with two proper size butt connectors. Solder the connectors and wires, and insulate with tape.

7. To repair any fuse link which has an eyelet terminal on one end such as the charging circuit, cut off the open fuse link behind the weld, strip approximately ½ in. (13mm) of insulation from the cut end, and attach the appropriate new eyelet fuse link to the cut stripped wire with an appropriate size butt connector. Solder the connectors and wires at the repair, and insulate with tape.

8. Connect the negative battery cable to the battery and test the system for proper operation.

➥**Do not mistake a resistor wire for a fuse link. The resistor wire is generally longer and has print stating, "Resistor: don't cut or splice." When attaching a single No. 16, 17, 18 or 20 gauge fuse link to a heavy gauge wire, always double the stripped wire end of the fuse link before inserting and crimping it into the butt connector for positive wire retention.**

Circuit Breaker

Selected circuits, such as headlights and windshield wipers, are protected with circuit breakers. A circuit breaker is designed to stop current flow in case of a short circuit or overload. It will automatically restore current flow after a few seconds, but will again interrupt current flow if the overload or short circuit continues. This on/off cycle will continue as long as the overload or short circuit exists, except for the circuit breakers protecting the power door lock and power window circuits, which will not restore current flow until the overload is removed.

Flasher

Both the turn signal and hazard warning flashers are mounted on the fuse panel on the Aerostar. The turn signal flasher is mounted to the front of the fuse panel, and the hazard warning flasher is mounted on the rear of the fuse panel.

REPLACEMENT

To gain access to the flasher relays, remove the cover from the lower edge of the instrument panel. With the cover removed and the fuse panel exposed, the flasher relays are the round cylinders within the panel. To remove a relay, simple pull the relay out. When installing a relay, make sure the terminals on the relay line up with the terminals in the fuse panel.

WIRING DIAGRAMS

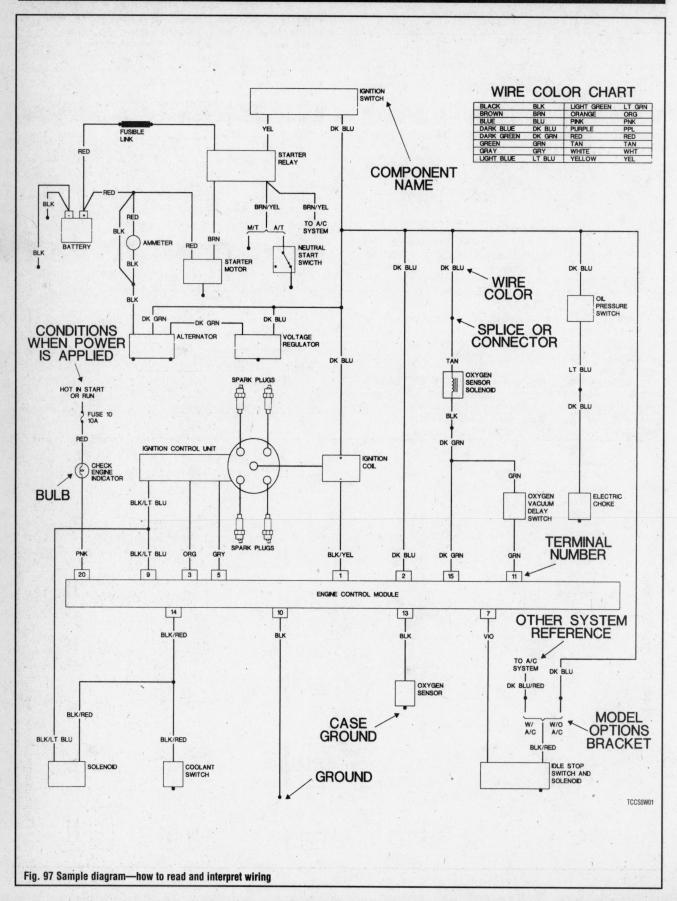

WIRE COLOR CHART

BLACK	BLK	LIGHT GREEN	LT GRN
BROWN	BRN	ORANGE	ORG
BLUE	BLU	PINK	PNK
DARK BLUE	DK BLU	PURPLE	PPL
DARK GREEN	DK GRN	RED	RED
GREEN	GRN	TAN	TAN
GRAY	GRY	WHITE	WHT
LIGHT BLUE	LT BLU	YELLOW	YEL

Fig. 97 Sample diagram—how to read and interpret wiring

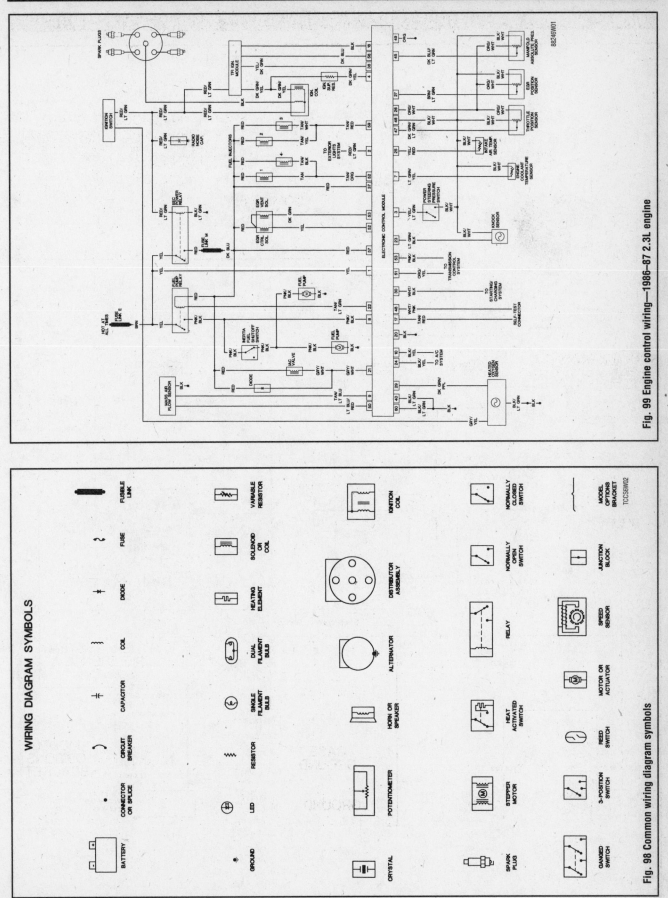

Fig. 99 Engine control wiring—1986-87 2.3L engine

Fig. 98 Common wiring diagram symbols

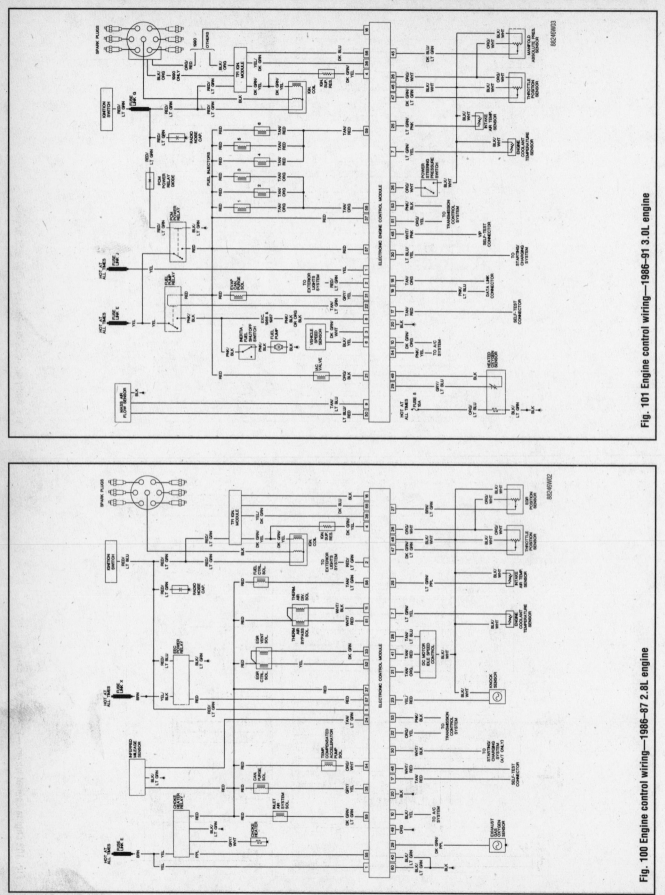

Fig. 101 Engine control wiring—1986-91 3.0L engine

Fig. 100 Engine control wiring—1986-87 2.8L engine

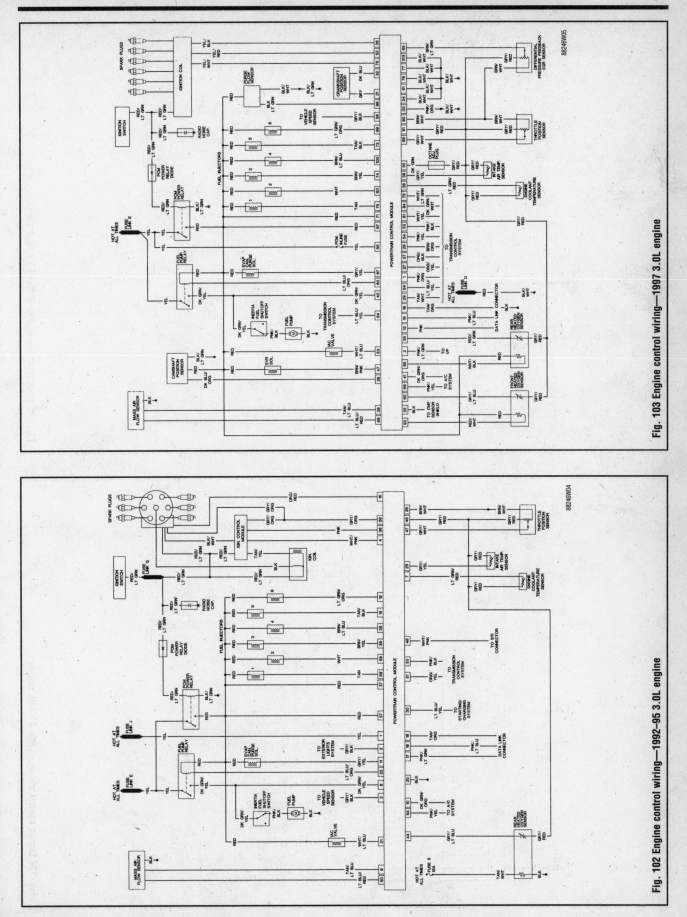

Fig. 103 Engine control wiring—1997 3.0L engine

Fig. 102 Engine control wiring—1992-95 3.0L engine

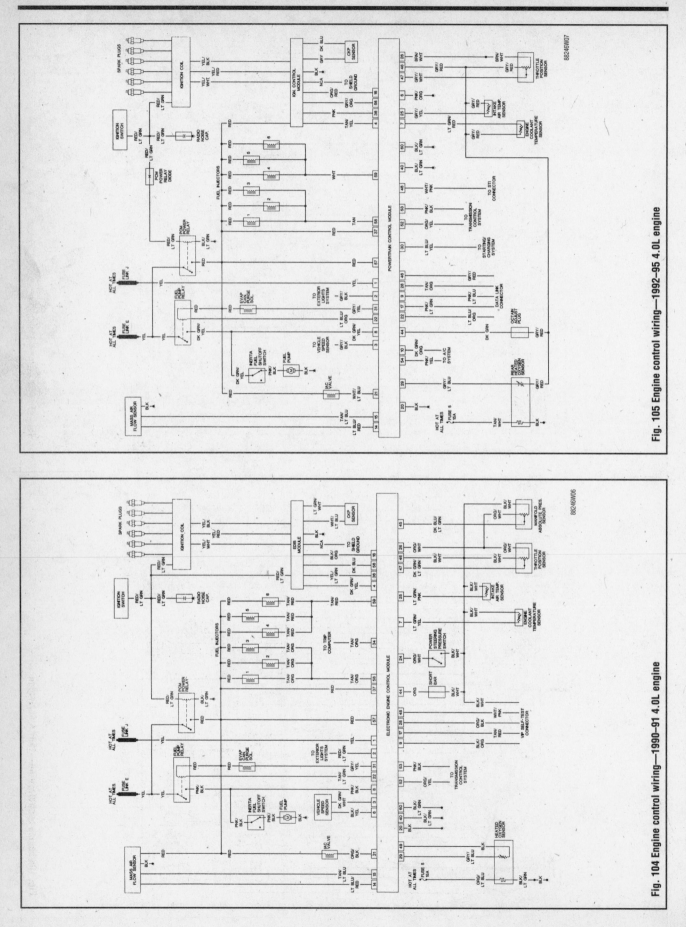

Fig. 105 Engine control wiring—1992–95 4.0L engine

Fig. 104 Engine control wiring—1990–91 4.0L engine

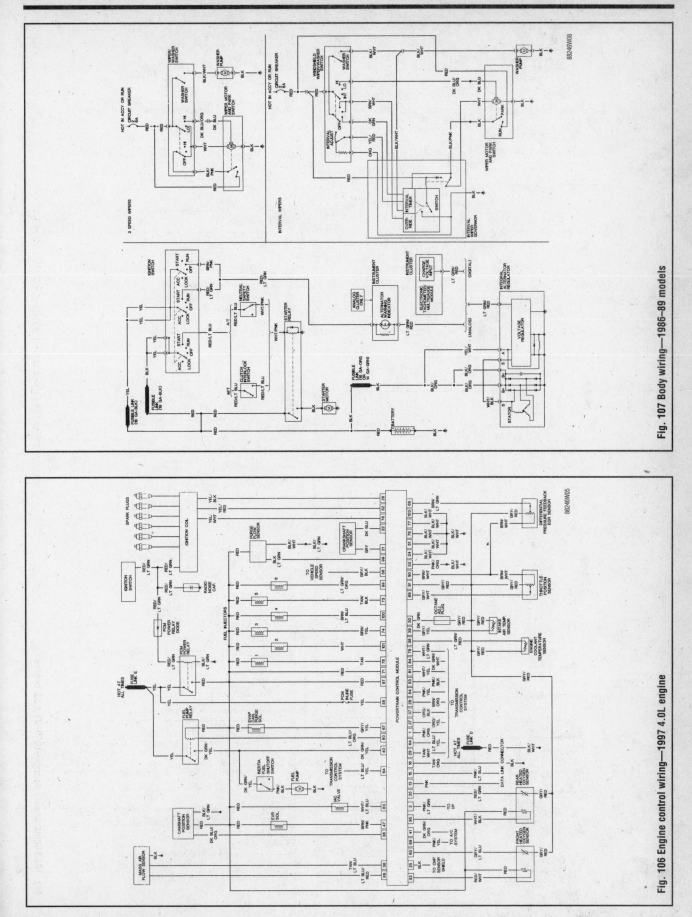

Fig. 107 Body wiring—1986-89 models

Fig. 106 Engine control wiring—1997 4.0L engine

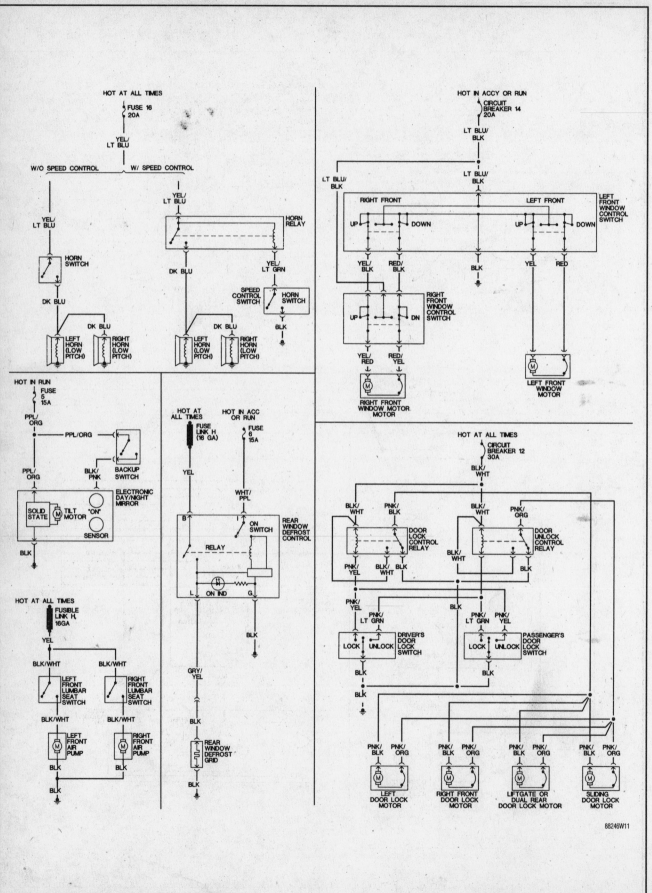

Fig. 108 Body wiring (continued)—1986–89 models

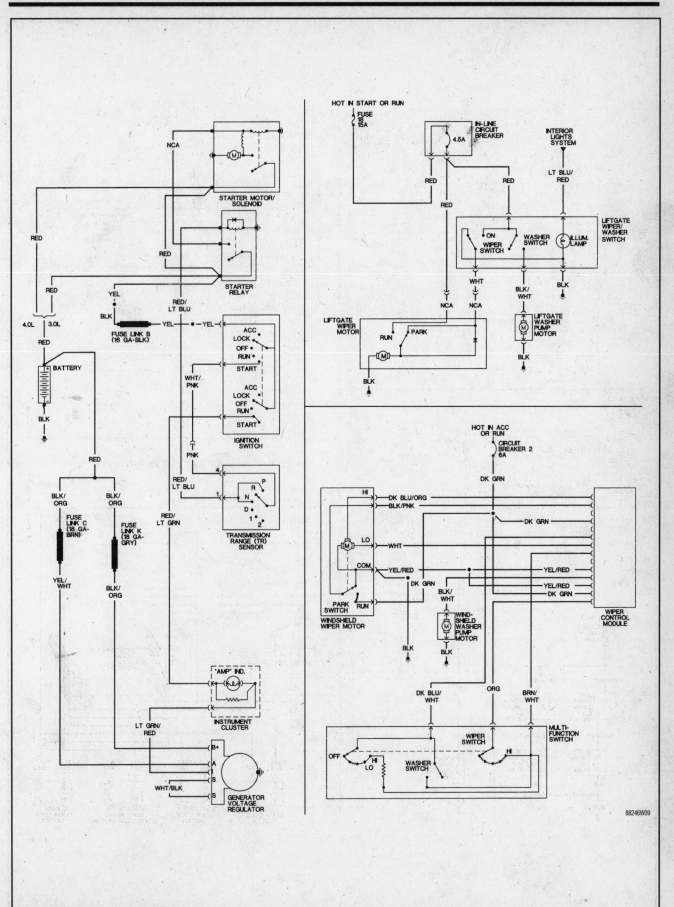

Fig. 109 Body wiring—1990-97 models

88246W09

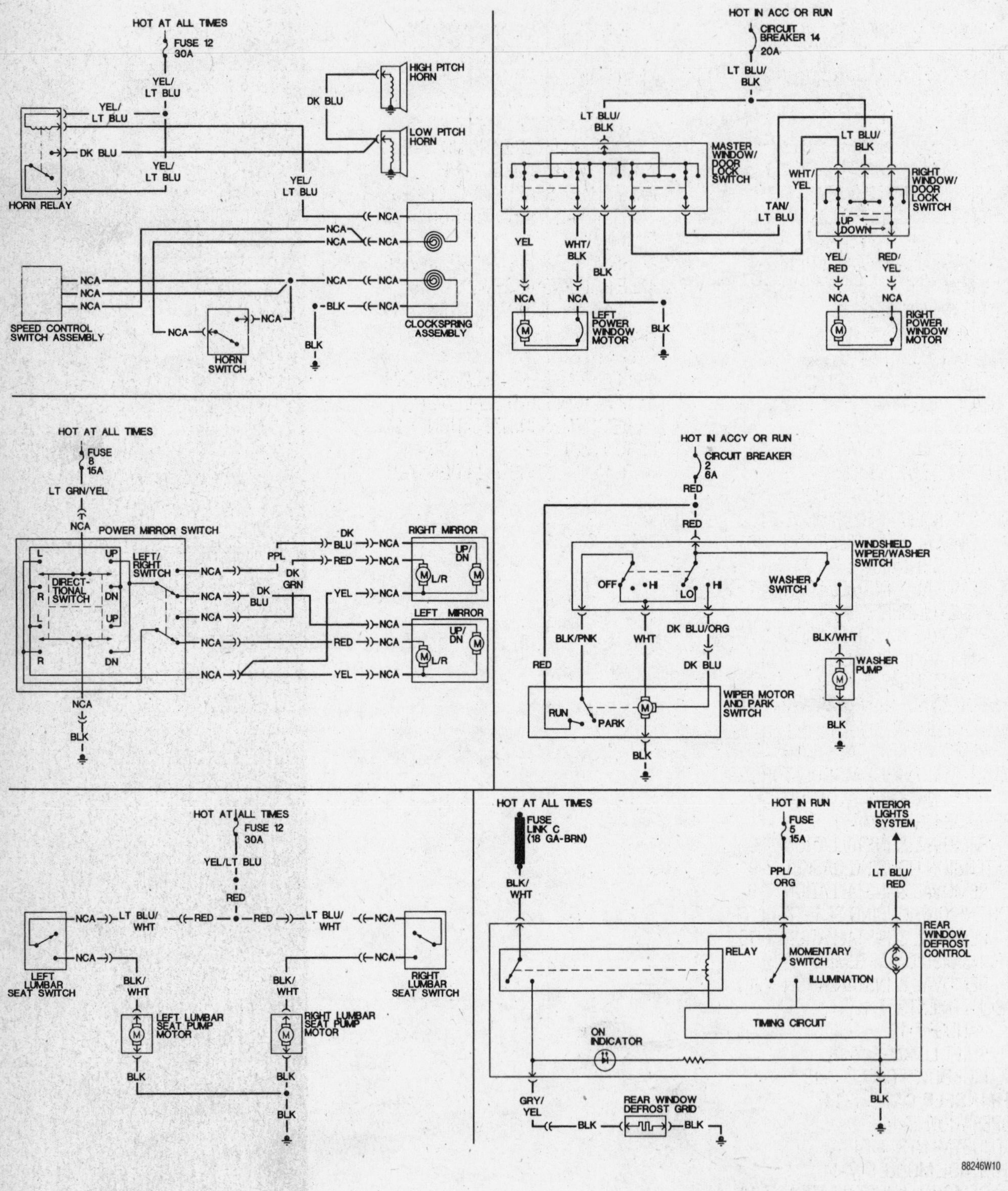

Fig. 110 Body wiring (continued)—1990–97 models

7

DRIVE TRAIN

MANUAL TRANSMISSION

Adjustments

SHIFT LINKAGE

1986–91 Models

▶ See Figure 1

Because this vehicle utilizes a direct control mechanism between the shifter and transmission gears, no linkage adjustment is necessary or possible. In the event it becomes hard to engage the shifter, inspect the shifter arm and or the remote shift adapter for any signs of bending.

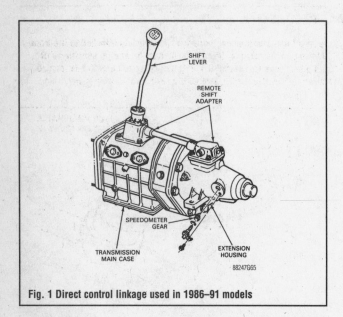

Fig. 1 Direct control linkage used in 1986–91 models

1992–97 Models

The M5OD transmission uses no linkage between the shifter and transmission. In this transmission, the shifter directly engages the selector forks. No linkage adjustment is necessary or possible. In the event the transmission becomes hard to engage, inspect the fluid level and or consult an authorized manual transmission mechanic.

CLUTCH SWITCH

▶ See Figure 2

The clutch switch, or 3-Function switch as it is called by Ford, is used to require the driver to depress the clutch pedal to the floor in order to start the vehicle. It also cuts off the speed control system when the clutch pedal is depressed. And finally, this switch provides a fuel control signal to the powertrain control module.

Because the clutch actuation system is hydraulically driven, and the clutch switch is an integral part of the clutch master cylinder, there is no clutch free-play, and no necessary clutch switch adjustment. If the hydraulic fluid level is properly maintained, the clutch system and switch should function correctly for many years.

Shift Handle

REMOVAL & INSTALLATION

1. With the emergency brake fully engaged, place the vehicle in NEUTRAL with blocks behind all four wheels to prevent any vehicle movement.

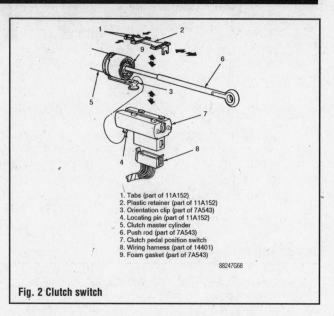

1. Tabs (part of 11A152)
2. Plastic retainer (part of 11A152)
3. Orientation clip (part of 7A543)
4. Locating pin (part of 11A152)
5. Clutch master cylinder
6. Push rod (part of 7A543)
7. Clutch pedal position switch
8. Wiring harness (part of 14401)
9. Foam gasket (part of 7A543)

88247G68

Fig. 2 Clutch switch

2. Remove the shift handle by grasping the handle and turning counter-clockwise.
   To install:
   If you are installing an aftermarket or other type shift handle, make sure that the handle hole diameter and thread pattern are similar to the shift rod width and thread pattern.
3. Install the handle by grasping the handle and turning clockwise until tight.
4. Before starting the vehicle, engage the clutch pedal and shift the transmission to make sure the handle does not move. If the handle has a shift pattern written on it, make sure the pattern is readable to the driver.

Shift Rod

REMOVAL & INSTALLATION

1986–91 Models

1. With the emergency brake fully engaged, place the vehicle in NEUTRAL with blocks behind all four wheels to prevent any vehicle movement.
2. Remove the necessary interior panels or components around the shifter rod and floor carpet around the shifter seal. Remove the rubber shifter boot to access the shifter seal plate attached to the floor of the vehicle.
3. Remove the bolts securing the shifter plate to the floor of the vehicle. Remove the plate to expose the top of the transmission and shifter.
4. Remove the four retainer bolts securing the shift rod to the transmission assembly. Lift the plate and shift rod out.
   To install:
5. Apply a multi-purpose long life grease to the ball end which installs into the transmission assembly.
6. Install the shift rod back into the transmission body and secure in place with the retainer bolts. Tighten the four retainer bolts to 6–9 ft. lbs. (8–12 Nm).
7. Install the extension housing seal to the floor and any other parts removed earlier.

1992–97 Models

▶ See Figure 3

1. With the emergency brake fully engaged, place the vehicle in NEUTRAL with blocks behind all four wheels to prevent any vehicle movement.
2. Remove the necessary interior panels or components around the shifter rod and floor carpet around the shifter seal. Remove the rubber shifter boot to access the shifter seal plate attached to the floor of the vehicle.

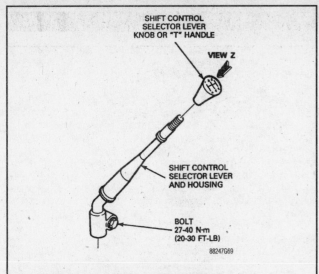

Fig. 3 Shift rod removed from the transmission rod

3. Remove the bolts securing the shifter plate to the floor of the vehicle. Remove the plate to expose the top of the transmission and shifter.

4. Loosen the retainer nut and bolt securing the shift rod to the transmission.

5. Lift the shift rod up and out.

To install:

6. Connect the shift rod on to the transmission rod with the groove in the shift rod aligned with the notch in the transmission rod.

7. Tighten the retainer nut and bolt to 12–15 ft. lbs. (16–19 Nm).

8. Install the extension housing seal to the floor and any other parts removed earlier.

Reverse Light Switch

REMOVAL & INSTALLATION

▶ See Figure 4

The reverse switch is accessed from under the vehicle on the driver's side.

➡On 1986–91 models, there are two switches attached to the transmission on the driver's side. One switch is the neutral sensing switch, the other is the reverse switch. The reverse switch is located lower than the neutral sensing switch and is closer to the engine block.

1. Disconnect the negative battery cable.

2. With the emergency brake fully engaged, place the vehicle in NEUTRAL with blocks behind the rear wheels to prevent any vehicle movement.

3. Raise the vehicle and safely support it on jackstands.

4. From underneath the vehicle, remove the wires attached to the reverse switch.

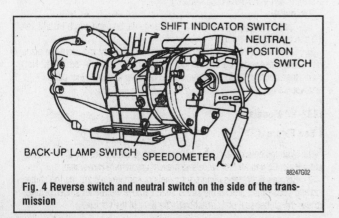

Fig. 4 Reverse switch and neutral switch on the side of the transmission

5. Place a drip pan of suitable size to catch any fluid which may spill while removing and installing the reverse switch. Using a suitable open-ended wrench or socket, remove the reverse switch. Remove the crush washer and discard.

To install:

6. Install the reverse switch into the hole using a new crush washer and tighten.

7. Connect the wire harness to the reverse switch.

8. Lower the vehicle and connect the negative battery cable. Check the fluid level and add fluid if needed.

9. Place the vehicle in reverse and have an assistant check to make sure the reverse light functions correctly.

Neutral Sensing Switch

REMOVAL & INSTALLATION

▶ See Figure 5

➡On all Aerostar models, there are two switches attached to the transmission on the driver's side. One switch is the neutral sensing switch, the other is the reverse switch. The neutral sensing switch is located above the reverse switch, toward the rear of the transmission.

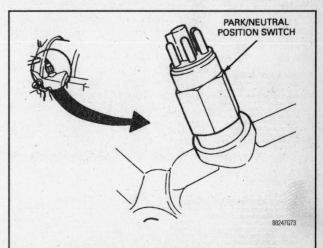

Fig. 5 Close-up of neutral switch on the side of the transmission

1. Disconnect the negative battery cable.

2. With the emergency brake fully engaged, place the vehicle in NEUTRAL with blocks behind the rear wheels to prevent any vehicle movement.

3. Raise the vehicle and safely support it on jackstands.

4. From underneath the vehicle, remove the wires attached to the neutral sensing switch.

5. Place a drip pan of suitable size to catch any fluid which may spill while removing and installing the switch. Using a suitable open-ended wrench or socket, remove the neutral sensing switch. Remove the crush washer and discard.

To install:

6. Install the neutral sensing switch into the hole using a new crush washer and tighten.

7. Connect the wire harness to the switch.

8. Lower the vehicle and connect the negative battery cable. Check the fluid level and add fluid if needed.

Extension Housing Seal

REMOVAL & INSTALLATION

▶ See Figure 6

➡This procedure can be completed with the transmission assembly bolted to the engine.

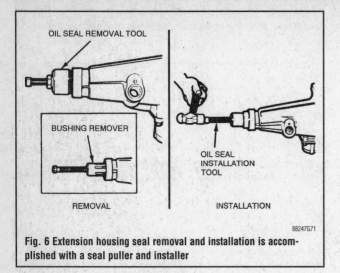

OIL SEAL REMOVAL TOOL

BUSHING REMOVER

REMOVAL

OIL SEAL INSTALLATION TOOL

INSTALLATION

88247G71

Fig. 6 Extension housing seal removal and installation is accomplished with a seal puller and installer

1. Disconnect the negative battery cable.
2. With the emergency brake fully engaged, place the vehicle in NEUTRAL with blocks behind the rear wheels to prevent any vehicle movement.
3. Raise the vehicle and safely support it on jackstands.
4. Scribe an alignment mark on the driveshaft and rear axle flange to index the driveline position for installation and balance purposes. Place a drip pan below the transmission where the driveshaft attaches to the transmission to catch any fluid which may spill out.
5. Remove the U-bolts and nuts from the rear axle flange, then remove the driveshaft. Cap the transmission extension housing to prevent lubricant leakage.
6. Remove the extension housing seal using seal remover T74P-77248-R or equivalent.
7. Loosen and remove the extension housing retainer bolts using a suitable socket or open-ended wrench.
8. Inspect the counterbore of the extension housing for burrs and remove if needed using an oilstone or equivalent.

To install:

➡The lube hole in the replacement seal must line up with the lube hole in the extension housing.

9. Install the replacement seal using bushing replacer T77L-7697-F or equivalent. Make sure that the lube holes align correctly. Install the seal until it bottoms in the extension housing.
10. Remove the cap from the extension housing, then install the driveshaft, making sure the marks scribed on the driveshaft and rear axle flange are in alignment. Install the U-bolts and nuts and tighten the nuts to 8–15 ft. lbs. (11–20 Nm).
11. Lower the vehicle and connect the negative battery cable. Check the transmission fluid level and add fluid if needed.

Transmission Assembly

REMOVAL & INSTALLATION

1986–91 Models

1. Disconnect the negative battery terminal.
2. Shift the transmission into NEUTRAL. Place blocks behind the rear wheels to prevent any movement.
3. Remove any interior components around the shift rod and handle to allow for working clearance.
4. Remove the shifter seal from inside the vehicle.
5. Remove the shift handle and lever assembly from the transmission remote shift rail adapter.
6. Raise the vehicle and support it safely on jackstands.
7. Tag and disconnect the starter cable and wires. Remove the starter retaining bolts and remove the starter.
8. Remove the clip retaining the tube to the hydraulic clutch slave cylinder.

Remove the tube and fitting from the slave cylinder, then cap the end of the tube and slave cylinder to prevent the entry of dirt, moisture or other contaminants into the hydraulic clutch system.

9. Tag and disconnect the back-up lamp switch and neutral sensing switch wires from the senders on the transmission. Remove the speedometer cable (conventional speedometer), or the electrical connector (electronic speedometer) from the fitting.
10. Scribe an alignment mark on the driveshaft and rear axle flange to index the driveline position for installation and balance purposes. Place a drip pan below the transmission where the driveshaft attaches to the transmission to catch any fluid which may spill out.
11. Remove the U-bolts and nuts from the rear axle flange, then remove the driveshaft. Cap the transmission extension housing to prevent lubricant leakage.
12. Place jackstands or other support devices under the engine block.
13. Remove the nuts retaining the insulator to the crossmember. Loosen the nut and washer assemblies attaching the front insulators to the crossmember brackets.
14. Position a transmission jack or equivalent under the transmission and slightly raise the transmission.
15. Remove the bolts retaining the clutch housing to the engine. Bring the transmission rearward to separate the clutch housing from the dowel pins in the rear of the engine block. Slowly lower the transmission from the vehicle.

➡If the transmission is to be removed from the vehicle for an extended period, support the rear of the engine with a safety stand and wood block.

To install:

16. Position the transmission on a suitable transmission jack or equivalent, then lift the transmission into position. Make sure the input shaft splines engage the pilot bearing in the flywheel. The clutch housing must be piloted onto the dowel pins in the engine block.

❊❊ WARNING

Do not force the transmission in or the dowel pins could be damaged.

17. Install the bolts retaining the clutch housing to the engine block. Tighten the bolts to 28–33 ft. lbs. (38–51 Nm). To avoid galvanic corrosion, only aluminum washers can be used to attach the housing to the engine.
18. If removed, position the insulator on the transmission, then install and tighten the bolts to 60–80 ft. lbs. (82–108 Nm).
19. Position the crossmember in the frame brackets, install the nuts and bolts, and partially tighten.
20. Lower the transmission so the insulator studs are piloted into the proper holes in the crossmember. Install and tighten the nuts to 71–94 ft. lbs. (97–127 Nm). Tighten the nut and washer assemblies attaching the front insulators to the frame brackets to 28–33 ft. lbs. (38–51 Nm).
21. The balance of the installation is the reverse of removal.
22. Connect the negative battery cable.
23. Check the transmission fluid level and add fluid if needed.
24. Bleed the hydraulic clutch system as described later in this section.

1992–97 Models

1. Disconnect the negative battery terminal.
2. Shift the transmission into NEUTRAL. Place blocks behind the rear wheels to prevent any movement.
3. Remove any interior components around the shift rod and handle to allow for working clearance.
4. Remove the shifter sealing plate from inside the vehicle.
5. Remove the shift handle and lever assembly from the transmission by loosening the nut and bolt securing the U-clamp around the shift rod.
6. Raise the vehicle and support it safely on jackstands.
7. Tag and disconnect the starter cable and wires. Remove the starter retaining bolts and remove the starter.
8. Remove the clip retaining the tube to the hydraulic clutch slave cylinder. Remove the tube and fitting from the slave cylinder, then cap the end of the tube and slave cylinder to prevent the entry of dirt, moisture or other contaminants into the hydraulic clutch system.
9. Tag and disconnect the back-up lamp switch from the sender on the transmission. Remove the speedometer cable from the fitting.

10. Scribe an alignment mark on the driveshaft and rear axle flange to index the driveline position for installation and balance purposes. Place a drip pan below the transmission where the driveshaft attaches to the transmission to catch any fluid which may spill out.

11. Remove the U-bolts and nuts from the rear axle flange, then remove the driveshaft. Cap the transmission extension housing to prevent lubricant leakage.

12. Place jackstands or other support devices under the engine block.

13. Remove the nuts retaining the insulator to the crossmember. Loosen the nut and washer assemblies attaching the front insulators to the crossmember brackets.

14. Position a transmission jack or equivalent under the transmission and slightly raise the transmission.

15. Remove the bolts retaining the clutch housing to the engine. Bring the transmission rearward to separate the clutch housing from the dowel pins in the rear of the engine block. Slowly lower the transmission from the vehicle.

➡**If the transmission is to be removed from the vehicle for an extended period, support the rear of the engine with a safety stand and wood block.**

To install:

16. Position the transmission on a suitable transmission jack or equivalent, then lift the transmission into position. Make sure the input shaft splines engage the pilot bearing into the flywheel. The clutch housing must be piloted in the dowel pins in the engine block.

✳✳ WARNING

Do not force the transmission in or the dowel pins could be damaged.

17. Install the bolts retaining the clutch housing to the engine block. Tighten the bolts to 28–33 ft. lbs. (38–51 Nm). To avoid galvanic corrosion, only aluminum washers can be used to attach the housing to the engine.

18. If removed, position the insulator on the transmission, then install and tighten the bolts to 60–80 ft. lbs. (82–108 Nm).

19. Position the crossmember in the frame brackets, install the nuts and bolts and partially tighten.

20. Lower the transmission so the insulator studs are piloted in the proper holes in the crossmember. Install and tighten the nuts to 71–94 ft. lbs. (97–127 Nm). Tighten the nut and washer assemblies attaching the front insulators to the frame brackets to 28–33 ft. lbs. (38–51 Nm).

21. The balance of the installation is the reverse of removal.

22. Connect the negative battery cable.

23. Check the transmission fluid level and add fluid if needed.

24. Bleed the hydraulic clutch system as described later in this section.

CLUTCH

✳✳ CAUTION

The clutch driven disc may contain asbestos, which has been determined to be a cancer causing agent. Never clean clutch surfaces with compressed air and avoid inhaling dust from any clutch surface. When cleaning clutch surfaces, use a commercially available brake cleaning fluid.

Adjustments

LINKAGE

Because the clutch system in the Aerostar is hydraulically driven, there is no clutch cable or linkage installed, and therefore no adjustments are needed.

In the event the clutch pedal develops a squeak or uneven feel when depressing, spray the pedal bushing assembly with a suitable penetrating oil and work the pedal back and forth.

PEDAL HEIGHT

Clutch pedal height is determined by the hydraulic pressure present in the clutch hydraulic system. There is no provision for pedal height adjustment.

If pedal height changes over a period of time, check the pedal assembly and make sure it is not bent. Also check the hydraulic fluid level and bleed the hydraulic system. Refer to the bleeding procedure in this section for an explanation on clutch bleeding.

It is not unusual for clutch pedal travel to increase as the clutch disc wears. In the event the clutch fails to engage, check the fluid level and bleed the hydraulic system before immediately assuming the clutch is worn and needs replacing.

FREE-PLAY

Because the clutch system in the Aerostar is hydraulically driven, clutch pedal free-play is controlled by the hydraulic fluid in the system and is not adjustable.

If the amount of free-play increases over time, inspect the fluid level and bleed the hydraulic system. Refer to the bleeding procedure in the section for an explanation on clutch hydraulic bleeding.

Driven Disc and Pressure Plate

REMOVAL & INSTALLATION

▶ **See Figures 7 and 8**

✳✳ CAUTION

The clutch driven disc may contain asbestos, which has been determined to be a cancer causing agent. Never clean clutch surfaces with compressed air and avoid inhaling dust from any clutch surface. When cleaning clutch surfaces, use a commercially available brake cleaning fluid.

1. Disconnect the negative battery cable.

2. Unfasten the clutch hydraulic system master cylinder from the clutch pedal and firewall.

3. Raise the vehicle and support it safely on jackstands.

4. Tag the starter wires and remove the starter from the vehicle.

5. Remove the hydraulic tube retainer clip at the slave cylinder. Remove the tube from the slave cylinder.

6. Remove the transmission/clutch housing from the vehicle.

7. Mark the assembled position of the pressure plate and cover to the flywheel for reassembly.

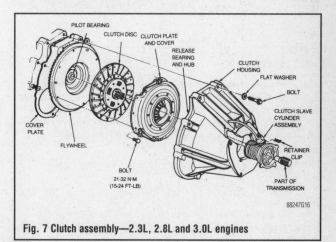

Fig. 7 Clutch assembly—2.3L, 2.8L and 3.0L engines

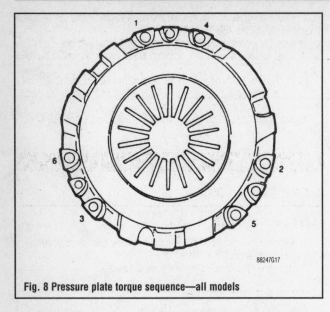

Fig. 8 Pressure plate torque sequence—all models

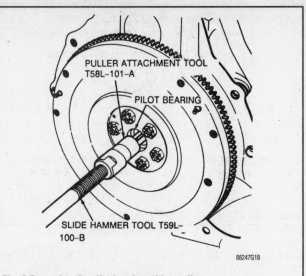

Fig. 9 Removing the pilot bearing with a puller

8. Loosen the pressure plate and cover attaching bolts evenly until the pressure plate springs are expanded, then remove the bolts completely.

9. Remove the pressure plate, cover assembly and clutch disc from the flywheel in order, and place aside.

10. Clean the pressure plate and flywheel surfaces with a suitable commercial alcohol base solvent to be sure that surfaces are free from any oil film. Do not use cleaners with a petroleum base and do not immerse the pressure plate in the solvent.

To install:

11. Position the clutch disc on the flywheel so that the clutch alignment tool (T74P-7137-K or equivalent) can enter the clutch pilot bearing and align the disc.

12. When installing the original pressure plate and cover assembly, align the assembly and flywheel according to the marks made during the removal procedure. Position the pressure plate and cover assembly on the flywheel, align the pressure plate and disc, and install the retaining bolts that fasten the assembly to the flywheel. Hand-tighten the bolts at first until all the bolts are installed, then tighten the bolts in a star pattern to 15–25 ft. lbs. (21–32 Nm). Remove the clutch pilot tool.

13. Install the transmission and clutch housing as outlined in this section. Use aluminum washers under the retaining bolt to prevent galvanic corrosion.

14. Install the clutch hydraulic tube to the slave cylinder, being careful not to damage the O-ring seal. Install the retainer clip.

15. Connect the hydraulic clutch master cylinder to the clutch pedal and to the dash panel.

16. Bleed the clutch system as described in this section.

17. Lower the vehicle and connect the negative battery cable.

Clutch Pilot Bearing

REMOVAL & INSTALLATION

♦ See Figures 9 and 10

➡A needle roller bearing assembly is used as a clutch pilot bearing. It is inserted directly into the engine flywheel. The needle bearing clutch pilot can only be installed with the seal end of the bearing facing the transmission. The bearing and seal are pre-greased and do not require additional lubrication. A new bearing seal must be installed whenever a bearing is removed.

1. Remove the transmission, clutch pressure plate and disc as described in this section.

2. Remove the pilot bearing using a slide hammer and adapter T58L 101 A or equivalent.

To install:

3. Coat the pilot bore in the crankshaft with a small quantity of multi-pur-

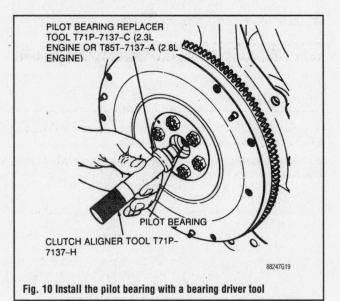

Fig. 10 Install the pilot bearing with a bearing driver tool

pose, longlife lubricant such as part number C1AZ 19590 A or equivalent. Avoid using too much lubricant as it may be thrown on the clutch disc when the clutch revolves.

4. Using the proper driver tool, carefully install the pilot bearing with the seal facing the transmission.

5. Install the clutch pressure plate, disc and transmission as described in this section. Be careful not to damage the bearing during transmission installation while the transmission input shaft is being inserted into the bearing.

Clutch Release Bearing

REMOVAL & INSTALLATION

♦ See Figure 11

1. Remove the clutch slave cylinder as described in this section.

2. Remove the release bearing from the clutch slave cylinder by carefully bending back the four symmetrical plastic retainers of the bearing carrier. Slide the bearing off the input shaft.

To install:

3. Lubricate the release bearing with multi-purpose, longlife lubricant (such as part number C1AZ 19590 B or equivalent). Fill the annular groove of the

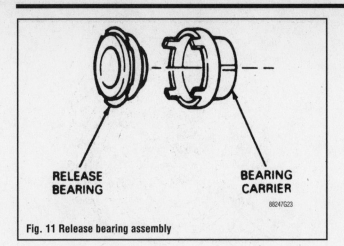

Fig. 11 Release bearing assembly

release bearing and apply a thin coat on the inside diameter of the release bearing.

4. Assemble the release bearing to the clutch slave cylinder by pushing the bearing into place while aligning the four symmetrical plastic retainers of the bearing carrier.

5. Install the clutch slave cylinder as described in this section.

Master Cylinder

▶ See Figure 12

REMOVAL & INSTALLATION

➡**Do not separate the clutch master cylinder from the reservoir unless individual component replacement is required.**

1. Remove as much hydraulic fluid from the clutch reservoir as possible using a turkey baster or other suitable tool.

2. Disconnect the clutch master cylinder/clutch switch pushrod from the clutch pedal assembly.

3. Slide the clutch reservoir out of the slots located in the electrical box cover, inside the engine compartment.

4. Place a suitable drip pan below the master cylinder to catch any fluid which may drip out during removal and installation.

5. On the clutch housing, remove the circlip retaining the hydraulic tube to the slave cylinder. Remove the tube and fitting, then plug both lines to prevent the entry of dirt, moisture or other contaminants into the hydraulic system.

6. Disconnect the tube from the clips on the underbody side rail.

7. Remove the bolts retaining the clutch master cylinder to the engine compartment. Remove the clutch master cylinder, reservoir and tube as an assembly.

To install:

8. Slide the clutch pedal pushrod through the hole in the engine compartment. Make sure it is located on the correct side of the clutch pedal.

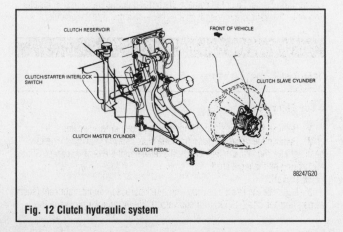

Fig. 12 Clutch hydraulic system

9. Place the master cylinder assembly in position, then install the bolts and tighten to 15–20 ft. lbs. (21–27 Nm).

10. Insert the tube in the routing clips on the underbody side rail.

11. Insert the tube and fitting in the clutch slave cylinder and install the circlip.

12. Position the clutch reservoir in the slots of the electrical box cover.

13. Install the retainer bushing in the clutch master cylinder pushrod, then install the retainer and pushrod on the clutch pedal shaft.

14. Add hydraulic fluid and bleed the clutch hydraulic system as described in this section.

Slave Cylinder

REMOVAL & INSTALLATION

▶ See Figures 13, 14, 15, 16 and 17

1. Remove as much hydraulic fluid from the clutch reservoir as possible using a turkey baster or other suitable tool.

2. Raise and safely support the vehicle on jackstands.

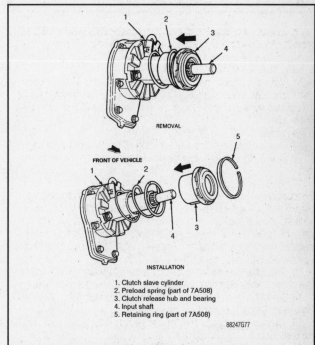

1. Clutch slave cylinder
2. Preload spring (part of 7A508)
3. Clutch release hub and bearing
4. Input shaft
5. Retaining ring (part of 7A508)

Fig. 13 Clutch slave cylinder assembly—1993 model shown

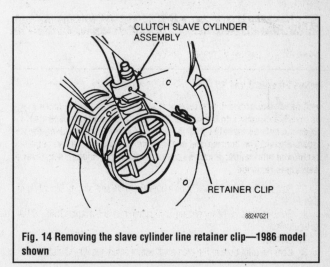

Fig. 14 Removing the slave cylinder line retainer clip—1986 model shown

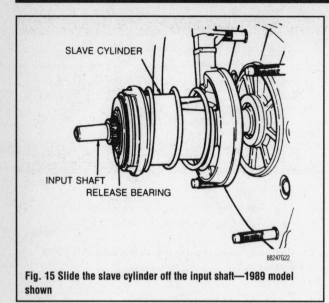

Fig. 15 Slide the slave cylinder off the input shaft—1989 model shown

SLAVE CYLINDER

INPUT SHAFT
RELEASE BEARING

88247G22

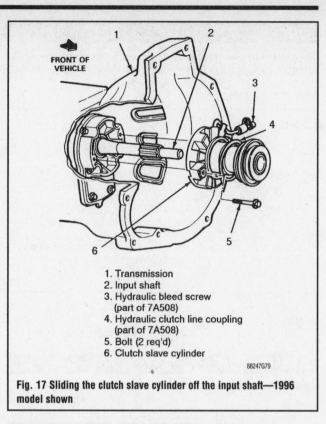

1. Transmission
2. Input shaft
3. Hydraulic bleed screw
   (part of 7A508)
4. Hydraulic clutch line coupling
   (part of 7A508)
5. Bolt (2 req'd)
6. Clutch slave cylinder

FRONT OF VEHICLE

88247G79

Fig. 17 Sliding the clutch slave cylinder off the input shaft—1996 model shown

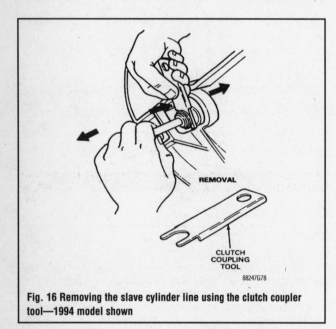

REMOVAL

CLUTCH COUPLING TOOL

88247G78

Fig. 16 Removing the slave cylinder line using the clutch coupler tool—1994 model shown

3. Place a suitable drip pan below the transmission and hydraulic line to catch any fluid which may drip out.

4. Disconnect the hydraulic line to the slave cylinder by removing the retainer clip, or using disconnect tool T88T-70522-A or equivalent.

5. Remove the transmission from the vehicle. Refer to the procedure in this section.

6. Working from inside the clutch housing, remove the clutch slave cylinder-to-transmission bolts and slide the slave cylinder off the transmission input shaft.

   To install:

7. Slide the slave cylinder onto the input shaft and position it in place. Secure using the retainer bolts, tightening them to 14–19 ft. lbs. (19–25 Nm).

8. Install the transmission as described in this section.

9. Connect the hydraulic line to the slave cylinder using tool T88T-70522-A or equivalent.

10. Lower the vehicle. Add hydraulic fluid and bleed the system as outlined in the procedure in this section.

HYDRAULIC CLUTCH SYSTEM BLEEDING

After any clutch hydraulic system work has been completed, or if air is trapped in the line, the system must be bled. The following procedure is used with the hydraulic system installed on the vehicle. The largest portion of the filling is carried out by gravity.

1. Clean all dirt and grease from around the reservoir cap.

2. Remove the cap and diaphragm and fill the reservoir to the top with approved DOT 3 or DOT 4 brake fluid.

3. To keep brake fluid from entering the clutch housing, place a suitable rubber tube of appropriate inside diameter from the bleed screw to a clear container with brake fluid filling the bottom ⅓ of the container. Make sure that the end of the tube is below the top level of the fluid.

4. Loosen the bleeder screw (located at the slave cylinder body) next to the inlet connection.

5. Fluid should now begin to flow from the master cylinder, down the tube and into the slave cylinder. The reservoir must be kept full at all times to insure that there will be no additional air drawn into the system.

6. Bubbles should appear at the bleeder screw outlet, indicating that air is being expelled. When the slave cylinder is full, a steady stream of fluid will come from the slave cylinder outlet. When no more bubbles emerge from the tube, tighten the bleeder screw.

7. Place the diaphragm and cap on the reservoir. The fluid in the reservoir should be level with the step or mark on the reservoir.

8. Have an assistant exert a light load on the clutch pedal, then slightly loosen the bleed screw. Maintain pressure until the pedal touches the floor, then tighten the bleed screw. Do not allow the clutch pedal to return until the bleed screw is tightened completely. Fluid and any air that is left should be expelled through the bleed port.

9. Refill the reservoir to the level at the step or fill mark. Install the diaphragm and cap. If evidence of air still exists, repeat Step 7.

10. The hydraulic system should now be fully bled and should properly release the clutch. Check the vehicle by starting, pushing the clutch pedal to the floor and placing the shift lever in REVERSE. There should be no grinding of gears with the clutch pedal within 0.50 in. (13mm). If there is gear clash, inspect the hydraulic system for air and repeat the bleeding procedure.

AUTOMATIC TRANSMISSION

Neutral Start Switch

REMOVAL & INSTALLATION

▶ **See Figure 18**

The neutral start switch is accessed from under the vehicle on the driver's side.
1. Disconnect the negative battery cable.
2. With the emergency brake fully engaged, place the vehicle in NEUTRAL with blocks behind the rear wheels to prevent any vehicle movement.
3. Raise the vehicle and safely support it on jackstands.
4. Tag and disconnect the neutral start switch electrical harness from the neutral start switch.
5. Remove the neutral start switch and O-ring using the neutral start switch socket tool T74P 77247 A, or equivalent. Discard the O-ring.

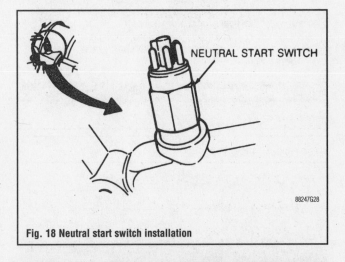

Fig. 18 Neutral start switch installation

✴✴ WARNING

Other tools could crush or puncture the walls of the switch.

To install:
6. Install the switch and new O-ring into the hole in the transmission assembly. Tighten the neutral start switch to 7–10 ft. lbs. (10–14 Nm).
7. Fasten the wire harness to the neutral start switch.
8. Lower the vehicle. Connect the negative battery cable.
9. Check the operation of the switch with the parking brake engaged. The engine should only start with the transmission in PARK or NEUTRAL.

Vacuum Control Modulator

REMOVAL & INSTALLATION

▶ **See Figure 19**

The vacuum control modulator is accessible from under the vehicle on the driver's side.
1. Disconnect the negative battery cable.
2. With the emergency brake fully engaged, place the vehicle in NEUTRAL with blocks behind the rear wheels to prevent any vehicle movement.
3. Raise the vehicle and safely support it on jackstands.
4. From underneath the vehicle, remove the vacuum hose attached to the vacuum assembly. Inspect the hose for cracks or tears and replace if needed.
5. Remove the vacuum diaphragm retainer bolt and clamp securing the assembly to the side of the transmission.

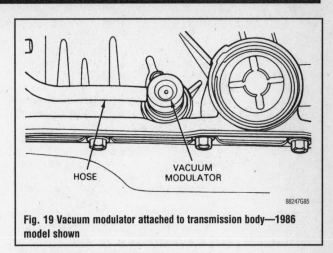

Fig. 19 Vacuum modulator attached to transmission body—1986 model shown

➡**Do not bend or pry the clamp during removal.**

6. Remove the vacuum control modulator and rod from the transmission body. If the assembly is difficult to remove, twist the modulator back and forth while carefully pulling it out.
7. Once removed, install the vacuum control rod back into the transmission assembly.
To install:
8. Apply a thin coat of oil around the edge of the vacuum control assembly and install into the transmission using a twisting back and forth motion.
9. Secure the vacuum assembly using the retainer bolt. Tighten the bolt to 80–106 inch lbs. (9–12 Nm).
10. Connect the vacuum hose to the control assembly.
11. Lower the vehicle and connect the negative battery cable.

Reverse Light Switch

REMOVAL & INSTALLATION

The reverse switch is accessed from under the vehicle on the driver's side.
1. Disconnect the negative battery cable.
2. With the emergency brake fully engaged, place the vehicle in NEUTRAL with blocks behind the rear wheels to prevent any vehicle movement.
3. Raise the vehicle and safely support it on jackstands.
4. From underneath the vehicle, remove the wires attached to the reverse switch.
5. Place a drip pan of suitable size to catch any fluid which may spill while removing and installing the reverse switch. Using a suitable open-ended wrench or socket, remove the reverse switch. Remove the crush washer and discard.
To install:
6. Install the reverse switch into the hole using a new crush washer and tighten.
7. Connect the wire harness to the reverse switch.
8. Lower the vehicle and connect the negative battery cable. Check the fluid level and add fluid if needed.
9. Place the vehicle in reverse and have an assistant check to make sure the reverse light functions correctly.

Extension Housing Gasket

REMOVAL & INSTALLATION

➡**This procedure can be completed with the transmission assembly bolted to the engine.**

1. Disconnect the negative battery cable.
2. With the emergency brake fully engaged, place the vehicle in NEUTRAL with blocks behind the rear wheels to prevent any vehicle movement.

3. Raise the vehicle and safely support it on jackstands.

4. From underneath the vehicle, tag and remove the wires attached to the reverse light switch neutral sensing switch, if equipped.

5. Place a drip pan of suitable size to catch any fluid which may spill while removing and installing the switch(es).

6. Scribe an alignment mark on the driveshaft and rear axle flange to index the driveline position for installation and balance purposes. Place a drip pan below the transmission where the driveshaft attaches to the transmission to catch any fluid which may spill out.

7. Remove the U-bolts and nuts from the rear axle flange, then remove the driveshaft. Cap the transmission extension housing to prevent lubricant leakage.

8. Place jackstands under the extension housing and remove the transmission mounting nuts and bolts.

9. Loosen and remove the extension housing retainer bolts using a suitable socket or open-ended wrench.

10. Carefully remove the extension housing from the vehicle.

11. Remove the extension housing gasket and clean all material from the mating surfaces.

To install:

12. Apply a light coating of petroleum jelly or equivalent to the extension housing seal, then position it on the transmission.

13. Slide the extension housing into position against the transmission making sure you do not distort the housing gasket. Install the retainer bolts and tighten to 27–38 ft. lbs. (36–52 Nm).

14. Remove the cap from the extension housing, then install the driveshaft, making sure the marks scribed on the driveshaft and rear axle flange are in alignment. Install the U-bolts and nuts and tighten the nuts to 8–15 ft. lbs. (11–20 Nm).

15. Install the transmission mounting nuts and bolts and tighten to 60–80 ft. lbs. (82–108 Nm).

16. Install the reverse light switch and neutral sensing switch, if equipped, into the hole using a new crush washer and tighten.

17. Connect the wire harness to the switch.

18. Lower the vehicle and connect the negative battery cable. Check the fluid level and add fluid if needed.

Extension Housing Seal

REMOVAL & INSTALLATION

▶ See Figure 20

➥This procedure can be completed with the transmission assembly bolted to the engine.

1. Disconnect the negative battery cable.

2. With the emergency brake fully engaged, place the vehicle in NEUTRAL with blocks behind the rear wheels to prevent any vehicle movement.

Fig. 20 Extension housing seal removal and installation

3. Raise the vehicle and safely support it on jackstands.

4. Scribe an alignment mark on the driveshaft and rear axle flange to index the driveline position for installation and balance purposes. Place a drip pan below the transmission where the driveshaft attaches to the transmission to catch any fluid which may spill out.

5. Remove the U-bolts and nuts from the rear axle flange, then remove the driveshaft. Cap the transmission extension housing to prevent lubricant leakage.

6. Remove the extension housing seal using seal remover T74P-77248-R or equivalent.

7. Loosen and remove the extension housing retainer bolts using a suitable socket or open-ended wrench.

8. Inspect the counterbore of the extension housing for burrs and remove if needed using an oilstone or equivalent.

To install:

➥The lube hole in the replacement seal must line up with the lube hole in the extension housing.

9. Install the replacement seal using bushing replacer T77L-7697-F or equivalent. Make sure that the lube holes align correctly. Install the seal until it bottoms out in the extension housing.

10. Remove the cap from the extension housing, then install the driveshaft, making sure the marks scribed on the driveshaft and rear axle flange are in alignment. Install the U-bolts and nuts and tighten the nuts to 8–15 ft. lbs. (11–20 Nm).

11. Lower the vehicle and connect the negative battery cable. Check the fluid level and add fluid if needed.

Transmission Assembly

REMOVAL & INSTALLATION

▶ See Figures 21 thru 26

1. Disconnect the negative battery cable.

2. Raise the vehicle and support it safely on jackstands.

3. Place a drain pan under the transmission. Starting at the rear and working toward the front, loosen the transmission pan attaching bolts and allow the fluid to drain. After the fluid is drained, install a bolt at each corner to temporarily retain the pan.

4. Remove the torque converter access cover and adapter plate bolts from the lower end of the converter housing.

5. Remove the four flywheel-to-converter attaching nuts by placing a 22mm socket and breaker bar on the crankshaft pulley attaching bolt. Rotate the pulley clockwise (as viewed from the front) to gain access to each of the nuts.

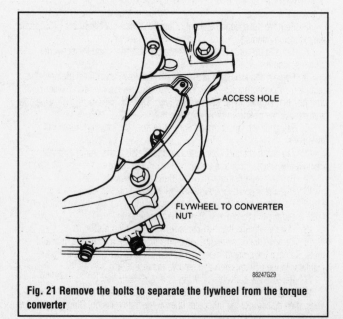

Fig. 21 Remove the bolts to separate the flywheel from the torque converter

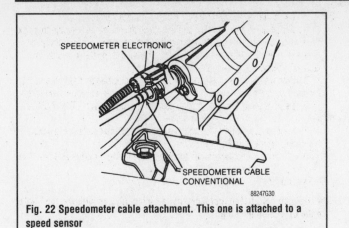

Fig. 22 Speedometer cable attachment. This one is attached to a speed sensor

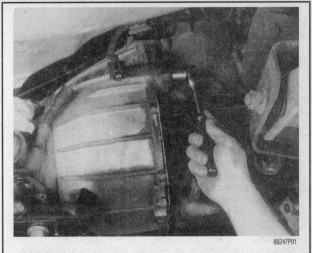

Fig. 24 Remove the retainer bolts securing the transmission to the engine block

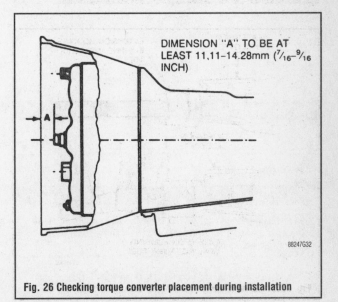

Fig. 23 Linkage and electrical connection at the transmission body

Fig. 25 Carefully separate the transmission

✳✳ WARNING

On belt driven overhead cam engines, never rotate the pulley counterclockwise under any circumstances!

6. Scribe an alignment mark to index the driveshaft to the rear axle flange. Remove the U-bolts and nuts retaining the driveshaft to the rear axle flange, then remove the driveshaft. Place a drip pan below the housing to catch any dripping fluid.

7. Remove the speedometer cable and/or vehicle speed sensor (VSS) from the extension housing.

8. Tag and disconnect the neutral start switch wires and the converter clutch solenoid.

9. Remove the kickdown cable from the upper selector lever. Remove the retaining circlip from the selector cable bracket, then remove the selector cable from the ball stud on the lower selector lever. Depress the tab on the retainer and remove the kickdown cable from the bracket.

10. Tag and disconnect the vacuum hose from the transmission vacuum modulator.

11. Tag and disconnect the relay to starter cable at the starter terminal. Remove the starter mounting bolts and the ground cable and remove the starter.

12. Remove the filler tube from the transmission.

13. Place jackstands or equivalent below the engine block.

14. Position a transmission jack or equivalent under the transmission and raise it slightly to take the weight off the crossmember.

15. Remove the insulator-to-crossmember retaining nuts.

16. Remove the crossmember-to-frame side support attaching nuts and bolts. Remove the crossmember. If required, remove the bolts retaining the insulator to the transmission and remove the insulator.

17. Remove the converter housing-to-engine fasteners.

18. Slightly lower the transmission jack to gain access to the oil cooler lines, then disconnect the oil cooler lines at the transmission. Plug all openings to prevent contamination by dirt or grease.

Fig. 26 Checking torque converter placement during installation

19. Slide the transmission toward the rear so it disengages from the dowel pins and the converter is disengaged from the flywheel. Carefully lower the transmission and remove it from the vehicle. Remove the torque converter by sliding it straight out from the transmission.

➡ **If the transmission is to be removed for an extended period of time, support the engine with a safety stand and wood block.**

To install:

20. Position the torque converter to the transmission, making sure the converter hub is fully engaged in the pump gear. Slowly rotate the torque converter while pressing inward until it seats completely. Make sure the torque converter rotates freely and does not bind up.

21. Place the transmission on a transmission jack or equivalent and secure.

22. Rotate the converter so that the drive studs are in alignment with the holes in the flexplate.

23. Lift the transmission into position enough to connect the oil cooler lines to the case.

24. Move the converter and transmission assembly forward into position, being careful not to damage the flexplate and converter pilot. The converter housing is piloted into position by the dowels in the rear of the engine block.

➡ **Do not allow the transmission to get into a nose-down position during installation as this may cause the converter to move forward and disengage from the pump gear. The converter must rest squarely against the flexplate. This indicates that the converter pilot is not binding in the engine crankshaft.**

25. Install the converter housing-to-engine attaching fasteners and tighten to 28–38 ft. lbs. (38–51 Nm).

26. If removed, position the insulator on the transmission, then install and tighten the retaining bolts to 60–80 ft. lbs. (82–108 Nm).

27. Position the crossmember in the brackets in the frame. The markings on the crossmember indicate the direction of installation. Install the nuts and bolts and tighten securely.

28. Slowly lower the transmission so the insulator studs are installed in the proper slots in the crossmember. Install the nuts and tighten them to 71–94 ft. lbs. (97–127 Nm). Remove the transmission jack.

29. Position the starter assembly on the converter housing. Install the ground cable and tighten the starter mounting bolts to 15–20 ft. lbs. (21–27 Nm). Connect the relay-to-starter cable and tighten the nut and washer.

30. Position a 22mm socket and breaker bar on the crankshaft pulley bolt, then rotate the pulley clockwise (as viewed from the front) to gain access to the converter-to-flexplate studs. Install the nut on each stud and tighten to 20–34 ft. lbs. (27–46 Nm).

✳✳ WARNING

On belt driven overhead camshaft engines, never rotate the pulley in a counterclockwise direction as viewed from the front.

31. Position the converter access cover and adapter plate on the converter housing, then install and tighten the attaching bolts to 12–16 ft. lbs. (16–22 Nm).

32. Install the driveshaft so that the index marks made earlier are in alignment. Install the U-bolts and tighten the nuts to 8–15 ft. lbs. (11–20 Nm).

33. The balance of installation is the reverse of removal.

Adjustments

BANDS

▸ **See Figures 27 and 28**

✳✳ WARNING

When adjusting the bands, do not allow the adjustment screw to back out. The band strut could fall into the transmission assembly and cause extensive damage.

➡ **When adjusting the bands, remove and discard the locknuts, and replace with new locknuts.**

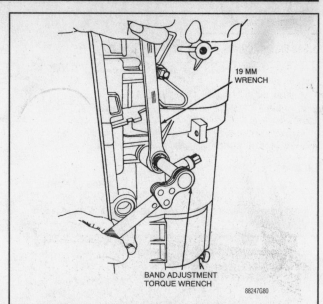

Fig. 27 Intermediate band adjustment. Notice that the adjuster is closer to the rear of the transmission

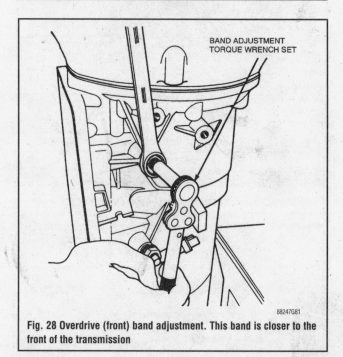

Fig. 28 Overdrive (front) band adjustment. This band is closer to the front of the transmission

There are two band adjusting screws located on the driver's side of the transmission assembly, accessible from under the vehicle. The overdrive (front) band is closer to the engine block; the intermediate band is farther back on the transmission toward the driveshaft.

1. Disconnect the negative battery cable.
2. Raise the vehicle and support it safely on jackstands.
3. Remove and discard the band locknut. Then loosen the band adjusting screw.
4. Apply petroleum jelly to the locknut seal, then install a new locknut and hand-tighten.
5. Tighten the band adjusting screw using a torque wrench to 10 ft. lbs. (14 Nm). Then loosen the adjusting screw two turns (2.5 turns for the intermediate band on 1997 models) and hold firmly.
6. Tighten the locknut to 35–45 ft. lbs. (47–61 Nm).
7. Lower the vehicle.

SHIFT LINKAGE

▶ **See Figures 29, 30 and 31**

1. Raise the vehicle and support it safely on jackstands. Set the parking brake firmly.
2. Place the shift lever in the OVERDRIVE position.
3. Working from under the vehicle, loosen the adjustment screw on the shift cable and remove the end fitting from the manual lever ball stud.
4. Place the manual lever in the OVERDRIVE position by moving the lever all the way rearward, then moving it three detents forward.
5. Connect the cable end fitting to the manual lever.

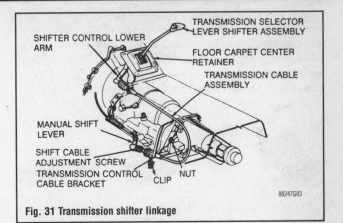

Fig. 31 Transmission shifter linkage

➡ Too much pressure on the arm can move the shifter to the DRIVE position. Apply pressure only until the resistance of the detent nib is felt.

6. Tighten the adjustment screw to 45–60 inch lbs. (5–7 Nm). After adjustment, check for proper PARK engagement. The control lever must move to the right when engaged in PARK. Check the transmission control lever in all detent positions with the engine running to insure correct detent/transmission action and readjust if required.

KICKDOWN CABLE

▶ **See Figures 32 and 33**

The self-adjusting kickdown cable is attached to the accelerator pedal near the accelerator cable. The kickdown cable is routed from the transmission through the dash to the accelerator pedal. A self-adjuster mechanism is located in the engine compartment at the inlet for the cable on the dash.

The kickdown cable is self-adjusting over a tolerance range of 1 in. (25mm). If the cable requires readjustment, reset the cable by depressing the semi-circular metal tab on the self-adjuster mechanism and pulling the cable forward (toward the front of the van) to the "zero" position setting. The cable will then automatically readjust to the proper length when kicked down.

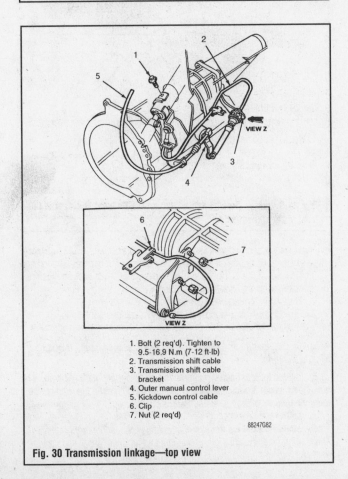

1. Bolt (2 req'd). Tighten to 9.5–16.9 N.m (7–12 ft-lb)
2. Transmission shift cable
3. Transmission shift cable bracket
4. Outer manual control lever
5. Kickdown control cable
6. Clip
7. Nut (2 req'd)

Fig. 30 Transmission linkage—top view

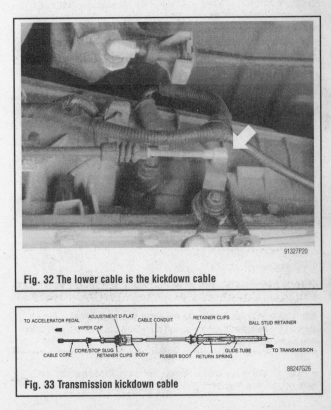

Fig. 32 The lower cable is the kickdown cable

Fig. 33 Transmission kickdown cable

Fig. 29 Transmission linkage attached to the driver's side of the transmission body—1989 model shown

TRANSFER CASE

Operation

The front drive axle for the Electronic Four-Wheel Drive (E-4WD) is a Dana model 28-2 assembly. The axle assembly contains a spiral bevel gear in which the centerline of the drive pinion is mounted on the centerline of the ring gear. The carrier assembly is aluminum and is mounted to the sub-frame assembly. Differential bearing adjustment is accomplished with shims placed between the bearings and differential case.

Adjustments

The electronic four wheel drive equipped Aerostar vehicle has all wheel drive torque available on a full time basis. The control module located under the driver's seat senses wheel slippage and locks the interaxle differential as needed through the use of an electromagnetic clutch. This is an automatic feature, needing no driver input.

Because the functioning of this all wheel drive feature is automatic, there are no adjustments needed or possible to this system.

Control Module

REMOVAL & INSTALLATION

The control module is located under the driver's seat of the vehicle.
1. Disconnect the negative battery cable.
2. Remove the driver's seat from the vehicle by removing the four seat retainer nuts and bolts. If the seat is equipped with power functions, the wire harness to the seat will have to be unfastened to remove the seat completely.
3. Remove the trim panel securing the carpet in position at the base of the door jam.
4. Lift the carpet up and remove the retaining screws securing the control module to the floor of the vehicle.
5. Unfasten the wire harness attached to the control module and remove the module.

To install:
6. Fasten the wire harness to the control module. If the connector does not fit easily, remove and try again. Do not force the connector in.
7. Position the control module under the carpet and secure in place using the retainer screws.
8. Install the door jam trim panel over the carpet using the retaining screws.
9. Install the seat into position using the retainer nuts and bolts. If the seat is equipped with power options, connect the wire harness to the seat.
10. Connect the negative battery cable.

Rear Output Shaft Seal

REMOVAL & INSTALLATION

▶ See Figures 34 and 35

1. Raise the vehicle and support it safely with jackstands.

➡**Mark the driveshaft and flanges so they can be reassembled in their original position.**

2. Place a suitable drain pan below the transfer case where it connects to the rear driveshaft. Loosen and remove the retainer bolts securing the rear driveshaft to the rear axle. Separate the driveshaft from the transfer case and place aside.
3. Use seal remover T74P-77248-A or equivalent to remove the seal from the transfer case. Discard the seal.
4. Inspect the counterbore of the transfer case for any burrs and clean, if needed, with an oilstone.

To install:
5. Lubricate the new seal with Mercon® type transmission fluid.
6. Install the seal in the transfer case so that the hole in the bottom of the seal is at the 6 o'clock position.

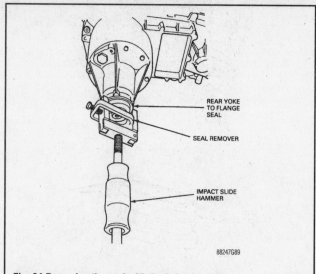

Fig. 34 Removing the seal with the help of a puller

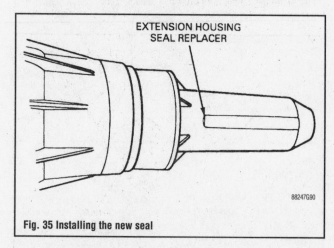

Fig. 35 Installing the new seal

7. Use seal replacer T61-1L-7657-A or equivalent to install the seal into the transfer case. Install until the seal bottoms out in the transfer case.
8. Install the rear driveshaft.
9. Lower the vehicle and add fluid to the transfer case, if needed.

Front Output Shaft Seal

REMOVAL & INSTALLATION

▶ See Figures 36 and 37

1. Raise the vehicle and support it safely with jackstands.
2. Place a suitable drain pan under the transfer case.
3. Remove the transfer case drain plug and drain the fluid from the assembly.

➡**Mark the driveshaft and flanges so they can be reassembled in their original position.**

4. Place a suitable drain pan below the transfer case where it connects to the front driveshaft. Loosen and remove the retainer bolts securing the front driveshaft to the front axle assembly. Separate the driveshaft from the transfer case and place aside.
5. Remove the locknut from the front output shaft using locknut wrench T90T-7127-E or equivalent. Hold the nut and turn the splines of the output shaft to remove the nut.

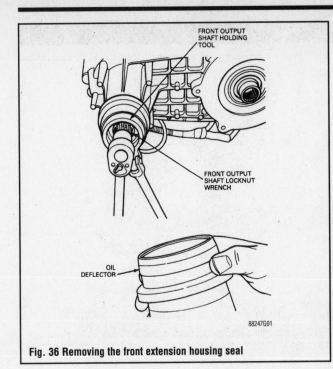

Fig. 36 Removing the front extension housing seal

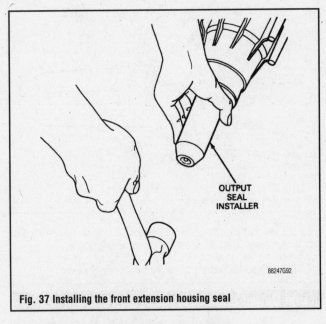

Fig. 37 Installing the front extension housing seal

6. Remove the deflector from the front output shaft.

7. Remove the steel bushing from the shaft assembly.

8. Use seal remover T90T-1175-AC or equivalent to remove the front output shaft seal.

9. Inspect the counterbore of the transfer case for any burrs and clean, if needed, with an oilstone.

To install:

10. Lubricate the new seal with Mercon® type transmission fluid.

11. Install the seal in the transfer case using seal replacer T90T-7127-D or equivalent. Install until the seal bottoms out in the transfer case.

12. Install the steel bushing on the output shaft with the inner diameter O-ring groove toward the O-ring in the seal.

13. Install the deflector to the assembly.

14. Apply Loctite® to the locknut. Use shaft holder tool T90T-7127-F or

equivalent and locknut wrench T90T-7127-E or equivalent to install the locknut. Tighten the locknut to 115–165 ft. lbs. (156–224 Nm).

15. Install the front driveshaft.

16. Lower the vehicle and add fluid to the transfer case.

Transfer Case Assembly

REMOVAL & INSTALLATION

▶ **See Figure 38**

1. Disconnect the negative battery cable.

2. Raise the vehicle and support it safely with jackstands.

3. Place a suitable drain pan under the transfer case and drain plug.

4. Remove the transfer case drain plug and drain the fluid from the assembly.

5. Tag and disconnect the transfer case control harness from the side of the assembly.

➡ **Mark the driveshaft and flanges so they can be reassembled in their original position.**

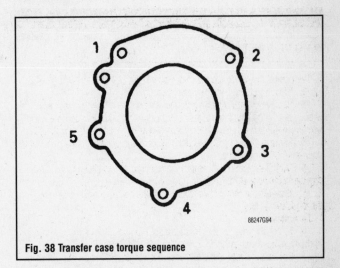

Fig. 38 Transfer case torque sequence

6. Disconnect the front driveshaft from the shaft flange.

7. Remove the bolts that connect the inboard halfshaft flange to the axle shaft. Wire the halfshafts to the body, maintaining a level position.

8. Place a suitable drain pan below the transfer case where it connects to the rear driveshaft. Loosen and remove the retainer bolts securing the rear driveshaft to the rear axle. Separate the driveshaft from the transfer case and place aside.

9. Support the assembly with a transmission jack or equivalent, then remove the locknuts and bolts that connect the transfer case to the extension housing.

10. Lower the hoist and slide the transfer case away from the extension housing. Remove all gasket material from the mating surfaces.

To install:

11. Using a new extension housing gasket, position the gasket between the transfer case and extension housing.

12. Raise the transfer case assembly into position with a hoist or equivalent and insert the retainer bolts. Apply Loctite® and tighten the bolts to 25–34 ft. lbs. (34–46 Nm).

13. The balance of the installation is the reverse of removal, however, note the following torque specs:

- Rear driveshaft retainer bolts– 61–87 ft. lbs. (83–118 Nm).
- Inboard halfshaft flange bolts– 26 ft. lbs. (35 Nm).
- Front driveshaft retainer bolts– 22–30 ft. lbs. (30–40 Nm).

DRIVELINE

Front Driveshaft and U-Joints

▶ See Figures 39 and 40

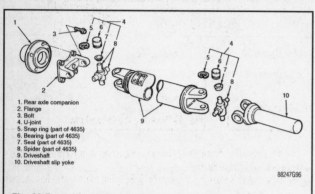

1. Rear axle companion
2. Flange
3. Bolt
4. U-joint
5. Snap ring (part of 4635)
6. Bearing (part of 4635)
7. Seal (part of 4635)
8. Spider (part of 4635)
9. Driveshaft
10. Driveshaft slip yoke

88247G96

Fig. 39 Front driveshaft assembly—4-wheel drive version

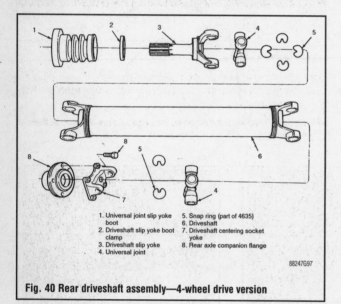

1. Universal joint slip yoke boot
2. Driveshaft slip yoke boot clamp
3. Driveshaft slip yoke
4. Universal joint
5. Snap ring (part of 4635)
6. Driveshaft
7. Driveshaft centering socket yoke
8. Rear axle companion flange

88247G97

Fig. 40 Rear driveshaft assembly—4-wheel drive version

REMOVAL & INSTALLATION

▶ See Figures 41 and 42

1. Raise the vehicle and support it safely with jackstands.
2. Place a suitable drain pan under the transfer case and driveshaft to catch any fluid that may drip out.

➡ Mark the driveshaft and flanges so they can be reassembled in their original position.

3. Remove the driveshaft slip yoke boot clamp using a wire cutter or equivalent. Discard the clamp.
4. Remove the bolts securing the driveshaft to the front axle. Slide the driveshaft out from the transfer case. When removed, note the wide-tooth spline on the driveshaft. During installation, this spline must align correctly with the corresponding opening in the transfer case.

To install:

5. Apply a light coating of grease to the splines of the driveshaft.
6. Slide the driveshaft into the transfer case, making sure the wide-tooth spline slides into the corresponding groove in the transfer case.
7. Position and connect the driveshaft to the front axle using the retainer bolts. Tighten the bolts to 22–30 ft. lbs. (30–41 Nm).

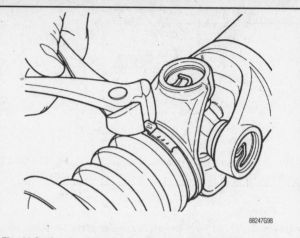

Fig. 41 Cutting the clamp around the boot at the front of the drive-shaft

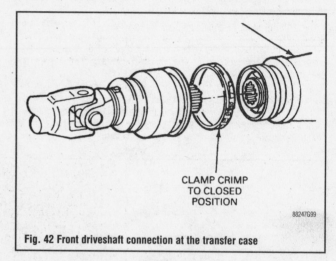

CLAMP CRIMP TO CLOSED POSITION

88247G99

Fig. 42 Front driveshaft connection at the transfer case

8. Slide the slip yoke boot over the lip on the transfer case, and secure in place using a new clamp.
9. Lower the vehicle.

U-JOINT REPLACEMENT

▶ See Figures 43, 44 and 45

1. Remove the driveshaft from the vehicle and place on a clean surface.

※※ WARNING

Do not clamp any driveshaft into a vise. In addition to driveshaft tube failure, the balance of the driveshaft could be affected, causing damage to the vehicle under driving conditions.

2. Mark the position of the U-joint components in relation to the driveshaft. To maintain proper driveshaft balance, these components must be installed in the same location.
3. Clamp U-joint tool T74P-4635-C or equivalent into a vise.
4. Remove the snaprings from the U-joint bearing caps.
5. Position the slip yoke of the U-joint in the clamp tool and press out the bearing.
6. Remove the slip yoke from the clamp tool, then rotate it 180° and position in the vise. Press the bearing to remove the spider. Remove the yoke from the spider.
7. Remove the remaining bearing in the same manner.

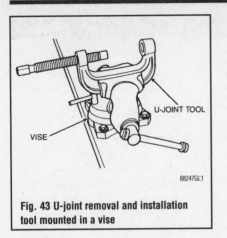

Fig. 43 U-joint removal and installation tool mounted in a vise

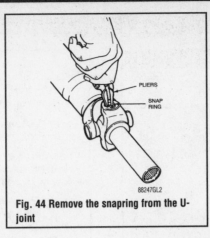

Fig. 44 Remove the snapring from the U-joint

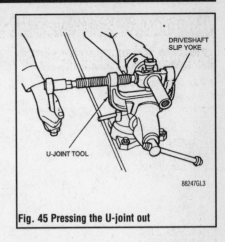

Fig. 45 Pressing the U-joint out

To install:

➡ **Universal joint kits are to be installed as a complete kit. Never mix components from other U-joints**

8. Start a new bearing cup into the yoke of the driveshaft.

9. Position the spider in the driveshaft yoke and press the bearing ¼ in. (6.3mm) below the yoke surface using the clamp.

10. Remove the driveshaft from the clamp, and install a snapring over the new bearing.

11. Start a new bearing cup in the opposite yoke. Place the assembly in the clamp and press the bearing in place. When complete, install another snapring over this bearing to lock in place.

12. Install the remaining bearing in the same manner. Make sure to install a snapring after each bearing has been pressed in place.

13. Before installing the driveshaft into the vehicle, make sure the U-joint rotates in all directions easily. If the joint binds, use a plastic-faced hammer and tap on the driveshaft yoke-side of the joint to seat the bearing.

14. If the driveshaft is equipped with a grease fitting, apply a premium long life grease to the joint assembly.

15. Install the driveshaft into the vehicle. Refer to the procedure in this section.

Rear Driveshaft and U-Joints

REMOVAL & INSTALLATION

▶ **See Figures 46 thru 52**

1. Raise the vehicle and support it safely with jackstands.

2. Place a suitable drain pan under the transfer case and driveshaft to catch any fluid that may drip out.

➡ **Mark the driveshaft and flanges so they can be reassembled in their original position.**

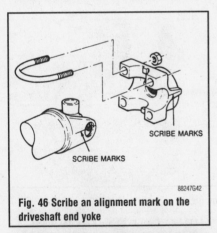

Fig. 46 Scribe an alignment mark on the driveshaft end yoke

Fig. 47 Remove the retainer nuts securing the U-bolt around the U-joint

Fig. 48 Slide the U-bolt out as far as it will go

Fig. 49 When both U-bolts are loosened, the shaft will move enough to completely remove the U-bolt

Fig. 50 Lower the driveshaft

Fig. 51 If you are not removing a U-joint, tape around the joint to protect it while removing the shaft

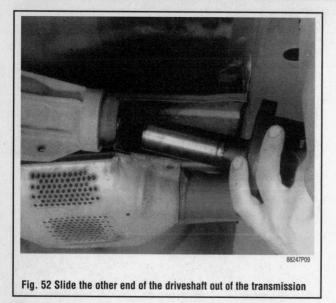

Fig. 52 Slide the other end of the driveshaft out of the transmission

3. Remove the bolts securing the driveshaft to the rear axle flange.

➡**Do not allow the driveshaft to hang free. Support the driveshaft during removal.**

4. Slide the driveshaft out from the transfer case until it clears the extension housing. Plug the extension housing hole to prevent fluid leakage.

To install:

5. Apply a light coating of grease to the splines of the driveshaft.
6. Slide the driveshaft into the transfer case.
7. Position and connect the driveshaft to the front axle using the retainer bolts. Tighten the bolts to 65–87 ft. lbs. (88–119 Nm).
8. Lower the vehicle. Check the transfer case fluid level and add if needed.

U-JOINT REPLACEMENT

Refer to Front Driveshaft U-Joint Replacement in this Section.

DRIVESHAFT BALANCING

▶ **See Figures 53, 54 and 55**

If after servicing one or more driveshafts, the vehicle vibrates or shakes, the driveshaft(s) may have to be removed and balanced.

➡**Before taking the time to balance the driveshaft, remove it from the vehicle, rotate it 180° and reinstall it. In some cases this may solve the problem. In the event it does not, then the driveshaft must be balanced.**

To balance the driveshaft, proceed as follows:
1. Raise both the front and rear of the vehicle and support safely with jackstands. Make sure that all the wheels are off the ground and can rotate freely.
2. Remove the wheels and tires. If equipped with drum brakes, install the lug nuts to hold the drums in place.
3. Start the vehicle and place in gear. Bring the engine speed up until the shaking or vibration begins. Record this speed.
4. Locate the heavy side of the rear of the driveshaft and scribe a mark on that side.
5. Install two screw-type hose clamps on the rear of the driveshaft with the screw head 180° from the heavy side (scribe mark) of the driveshaft.
6. Run the vehicle again up to the speed at which the vibration began. If the vibration is still present, rotate the clamps an additional 45° from their original position.
7. Run the vehicle up to the speed at which the vibration began. If the vibration is still present, rotate the clamps again, in small increments.
8. With the installation of the clamps, the vibration level should decrease. In the event the vibration is not totally eliminated, locate the heavy side of the front of the driveshaft and use two clamps there to reduce the vibration.
9. When the vibration is totally eliminated, install the wheels and tires, then lower the vehicle.

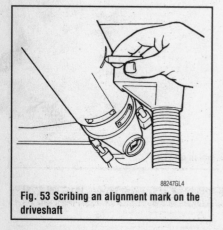

Fig. 53 Scribing an alignment mark on the driveshaft

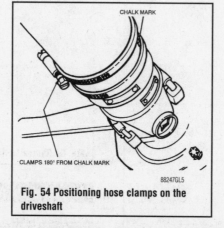

Fig. 54 Positioning hose clamps on the driveshaft

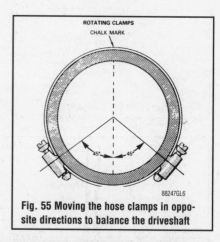

Fig. 55 Moving the hose clamps in opposite directions to balance the driveshaft

FRONT DRIVE AXLE

▶ **See Figure 56**

Axle Shaft, Bearing and Seal

REMOVAL & INSTALLATION

▶ **See Figure 57**

1. Raise the vehicle and support safely with jackstands.
2. Place a floor jack or equivalent under the axle and remove the axle assembly from the vehicle. Refer to the procedure in this section.

3. Place the axle on a clean surface.
4. Remove the cover plate, and drain the lubricant into a suitable container. Mount the axle assembly into a secure holding fixture.
5. Rotate the axle shafts so the open side of the snapring is visible. Remove the snaprings using care not to damage them.
6. Remove the axle shaft(s) from the axle housing.
7. Remove the oil seal and caged needle bearings using a slide hammer and collet T50T-100-A and D80L-100-T, or equivalent pulling fixture. When removed, discard the seal and bearing.
8. Inspect the counterbore for burrs. Use an oilstone, if needed, to remove any marks.

To install:

9. Make sure the bearing bore is free from nicks and burrs. Install the needle bearing using bearing installer T83T-1244-A or equivalent. Drive in the bearing until seated fully.

10. Coat the new seal with multi-purpose lubricant and drive the seal into the bore using seal installer T90T-3110-A or equivalent.

✳✳ WARNING

Replace the axle snaprings if any damage or looseness is evident. If the snapring fails during operation, personal injury may result!

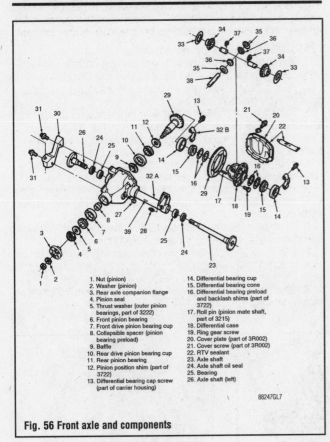

1. Nut (pinion)
2. Washer (pinion)
3. Rear axle companion flange
4. Pinion seal
5. Thrust washer (outer pinion bearings, part of 3222)
6. Front pinion bearing
7. Front drive pinion bearing cup
8. Collapsible spacer (pinion bearing preload)
9. Baffle
10. Rear drive pinion bearing cup
11. Rear pinion bearing
12. Pinion position shim (part of 3722)
13. Differential bearing cap screw (part of carrier housing)
14. Differential bearing cup
15. Differential bearing cone
16. Differential bearing preload and backlash shims (part of 3722)
17. Roll pin (pinion mate shaft, part of 3215)
18. Differential case
19. Ring gear screw
20. Cover plate (part of 3R002)
21. Cover screw (part of 3R002)
22. RTV sealant
23. Axle shaft
24. Axle shaft oil seal
25. Bearing
26. Axle shaft (left)

88247GL7

Fig. 56 Front axle and components

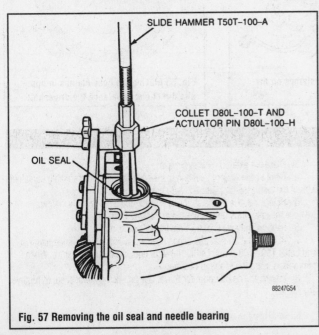

Fig. 57 Removing the oil seal and needle bearing

11. Install the axle shafts and drive the snapring into the axle grooves. Do not drive the snapring using the center of the ring. Use a suitable tool against the notches on the side of the snapring. Replace any snapring that is damaged.

12. Apply RTV gasket sealer to the cover plate and install. Tighten the cover bolts to 25 ft. lbs. (34 Nm).

13. Refill the axle assembly with Hypoid gear lubricant.

14. Install the axle assembly into the vehicle.

15. Lower the vehicle.

Pinion Seal

REMOVAL & INSTALLATION

▶ **See Figure 58**

1. Remove the driveshaft using the procedure outlined in this section.

2. While holding the companion flange with tool T78P-4851-A or equivalent, remove the pinion nut and washer.

3. Remove the flange and oil seal from the carrier using a seal puller T90T-1175-AC and slide hammer or equivalent. Discard the seal.

4. Inspect the counterbore of the burrs and clean with an oilstone if needed.

To install:

5. Lubricate the new seal using light oil, then install the seal using seal installer T71T-3010-R or equivalent.

6. Install the companion flange, washer and nut. Tighten the nut to 140–275 ft. lbs. (190–373 Nm).

7. Install the driveshaft as outlined in this section.

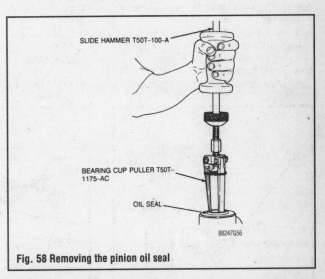

Fig. 58 Removing the pinion oil seal

Axle Housing Assembly

REMOVAL & INSTALLATION

1. Disconnect the negative battery cable.

2. Raise the vehicle and support safely with jackstands.

3. Remove the front wheels and tires.

4. Mark the driveshaft flanges so they can be reinstalled their original position. Then disconnect the front driveshaft from the front axle flanges.

5. Remove the bolts connect the halfshafts to the axle shaft and housing. Wire the halfshafts to the body.

6. Disconnect the vent hose.

7. Support the axle housing with a suitable floor jack or hoist.

8. Remove the locknuts that connect the axle mounting bracket to the vehicle crossmember.

9. Lower the jack or hoist and remove the axle assembly from the vehicle.

To install:

10. Using Loctite® on the retainer bolts, attach the axle mounting bracket to the axle housing and tighten to 80 ft. lbs. (108 Nm).

11. Raise the axle into position under the vehicle, and insert the axle mounting hardware through the mounting bracket. Using Loctite®, tighten the nuts to 85 ft. lbs. (115 Nm).

12. Attach the vent hose, and reconnect the halfshafts to the axle housing. Tighten the halfshaft bolts to 26 ft. lbs. (35 Nm).

13. Install the driveshaft and tighten the bolts to 26 ft. lbs. (35 Nm).

14. Install the front wheels and tires. Lower the vehicle and connect the negative battery cable.

REAR AXLE

▶ See Figure 59

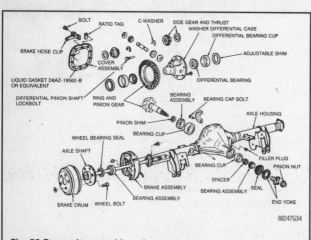

Fig. 59 Rear axle assembly and components

Axle Shaft

REMOVAL & INSTALLATION

▶ See Figures 60, 61, 62, 63 and 64

1. Raise the vehicle and support safely on jackstands.
2. Remove the rear wheels and brake drums.

✷✷ CAUTION

Brake shoes may contain asbestos, which has been determined to be a cancer causing agent. Never clean the brake surfaces with compressed air and avoid inhaling any dust from any brake surface. When cleaning brake surfaces, use a commercially available brake cleaning fluid.

3. Clean all dirt and grease from the area of the carrier cover with a wire brush and/or cloth.

4. Drain the rear axle lubricant into a suitable container by removing the housing cover.

Fig. 60 With the fluid drained and the cover removed, the rear axle gears are clearly visible

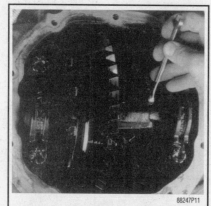

Fig. 61 Remove the retainer bolt securing the pinion shaft—3.45:1 ratio axle shown

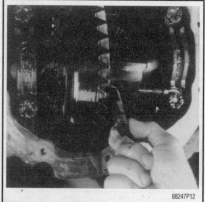

Fig. 62 Slide the pinion shaft out—3.45:1 ratio axle shown

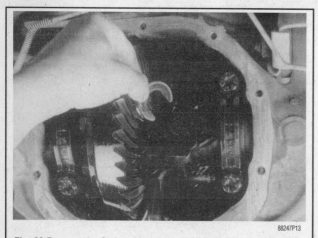

Fig. 63 Remove the C-clamp from the gear assembly—3.45:1 ratio axle shown

Fig. 64 Slide the axle shaft out

5. For 3.45:1 ratio axles, remove the differential pinion shaft lockbolt, then slide out the differential pinion shaft. The pinion gears may be left in place. Once the axle shafts are removed, reinstall the pinion shaft and lockbolt.

6. For 3.45:1 ratio axles, push the flanged end of the axle shafts toward the center of the vehicle and remove the C-lockwasher from the button end of the axle shaft.

7. For 3.45:1 ratio axles, remove the axle shaft from the housing, being careful not to damage the oil seal.

8. For 3.73:1 and 4.10:1 ratio axles, remove the pinion shaft lockbolt.

9. For 3.73:1 and 4.10:1 ratio axles, place your hand behind the differential case and push out the pinion shaft until the step on the shaft contacts the ring gear.

10. For 3.73:1 and 4.10:1 ratio axles, remove the C-lockwasher from the axle shafts.

11. For 3.73:1 and 4.10:1 ratio axles, remove the axle shafts from the housing, being careful not to damage the oil seal.

To install:

12. On 3.73:1 and 4.10:1 ratio axles, make sure the differential pinion shaft step contacts the ring gear before sliding the axle shaft into the axle housing. Start the splines into the side gear and push firmly until the button end of the axle shaft can be seen in the differential case.

✳✳ CAUTION

Care must be taken so as not to let the axle shaft splines damage the oil seal or wheel bearing assembly.

13. Install the C-lockwasher on the button end of the axle shaft splines, the pull the shaft outboard until the shaft splines engage and the C-lockwasher seats in the counterbore of the differential side gear.

14. Position the differential pinion shaft through the case and pinion gears, aligning the hole in the shaft with the lockscrew hole. Install the lockbolt and tighten to 15–22 ft. lbs. (21–29 Nm).

15. Apply a continuous bead of silicone rubber sealant to the carrier casting face. Make sure the machined surface on both cover and carrier are clean before applying sealer.

16. Install the cover and tighten the cover bolts to 15–20 ft. lbs. (21–27 Nm), except the ratio tag bolt, which is tightened to 15–25 ft. lbs. (30–34 Nm).

➡ **The cover assembly must be installed within 15 minutes of application of the sealer or new sealer must be applied.**

17. Install the wheels and tires. Lower the vehicle.

18. Add lubricant until it is about ½ in. (13mm) below the bottom of the filler hole in the running position. Install the filler plug and tighten it to 15–30 ft. lbs. (20–41 Nm).

Axle Bearing and Seal

REMOVAL & INSTALLATION

▶ **See Figure 65**

1. Remove the axle shaft as described in this section.

2. Insert an axle bearing remover tool T85L-1225-AH or equivalent attached to a slide hammer into the bore and position it behind the bearing to the tangs on the bearing outer race. Remove the bearing and seal as a unit with the slide hammer.

To install:

3. Lubricate the new bearing with rear axle lubricant and install the bearing into the housing bore using bearing replacer tool T78P-1225-A, or equivalent.

4. Apply multipurpose, long-life grease between the lips of the axle shaft seal.

5. Install a new axle shaft seal using seal replacer tool T78P-1177-A, or equivalent.

✳✳ WARNING

Installation of the bearing or seal assembly without the proper tool may result in an early bearing or seal failure. If the seal becomes cocked in the bore during installation, remove it and install a new one.

6. Install the axle shaft as described in this section.

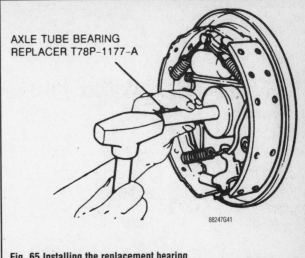

Fig. 65 Installing the replacement bearing

Pinion Seal

REMOVAL & INSTALLATION

▶ **See Figures 66, 67, 68, 69 and 70**

➡ **Replacement of the pinion oil seal involves removal and installation of only the pinion nut and the axle end yoke. However, this operation disturbs the pinion bearing preload, and this preload must be carefully reset during assembly.**

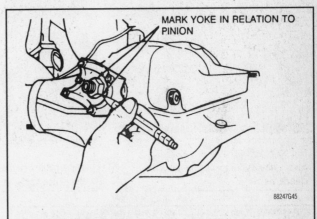

Fig. 66 Scribe an alignment mark on the end yoke

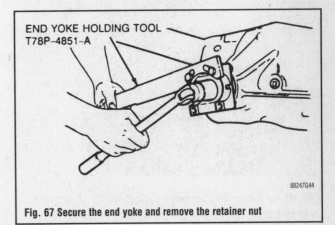

Fig. 67 Secure the end yoke and remove the retainer nut

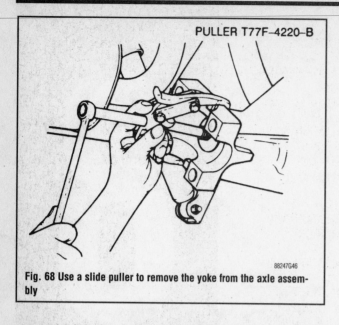

Fig. 68 Use a slide puller to remove the yoke from the axle assembly

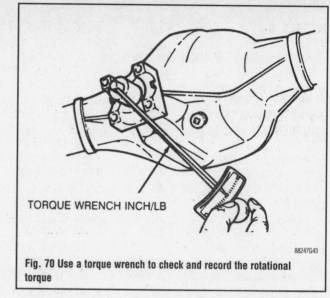

Fig. 70 Use a torque wrench to check and record the rotational torque

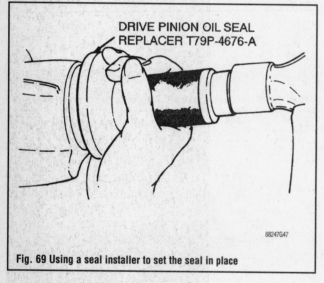

Fig. 69 Using a seal installer to set the seal in place

1. Raise the vehicle and support safely on jackstands.
2. Remove the rear wheels and tires.
3. Scribe alignment marks on the driveshaft end and the axle end yoke to insure proper driveshaft positioning during assembly.
4. Place a suitable drip pan below the axle housing to catch any spilled fluid.
5. Disconnect the driveshaft from the rear axle end yoke and remove the driveshaft from the transmission extension housing. Cap or plug the transmission extension housing to prevent oil leakage.
6. Install an inch pound torque wrench on the pinion nut, then record the torque required to maintain rotation of the pinion gear through several revolutions.
7. While holding the end yoke with holding tool T78P-4851-A, or equivalent, remove the pinion nut using a suitable socket on a breaker bar or equivalent. Clean the area around the oil seal and place a drain pan under the yoke to catch any fluid leakage.
8. Mark the axle yoke in relation to the pinion shaft so the flange can be installed in the same position.
9. Use a suitable puller tool to remove the axle end yoke from the pinion shaft.

10. Remove the pinion seal with a small prytool or other suitable tool and discard the seal.
11. Check the splines on the pinion shaft to make sure they are free from burrs or any other damage. If burrs are noted, remove them by using a fine crocus cloth, working in a rotational pattern.
To install:
12. Apply multi-purpose, long-life grease between the lips of the pinion seal.
13. Install the seal using seal replacer tool T79P-4676-A or equivalent. Place the seal on the tool, then drive it into position on the pinion.

❊❊ WARNING

Installation of the pinion seal without the proper tool may result in early seal failure. If the seal becomes cocked during installation, remove it and install a new seal. Never hammer on a seal metal casing.

14. Check the seal surface of the yoke for scratches, nicks or a groove around the diameter. If any of these conditions exist, replace the yoke. Apply a small amount of lubricant to the end yoke splines, then align the mark on the end yoke with the mark on the pinion shaft and install the yoke.

➡**The companion shaft must never be hammered on or installed with power tools.**

15. Wipe the pinion clean.
16. Install a new nut and spacer on the pinion shaft, then hold the end yoke and tighten the nut while rotating the pinion occasionally to insure proper bearing seating. In addition, take frequent pinion bearing torque preload readings with the inch pound torque wrench until the original recorded rotational torque reading is obtained or to 8–14 inch lbs. (1–2 Nm).

➡**Under no circumstances should the pinion nut be backed off to reduce preload. If reduced preload is required, a new collapsible pinion spacer and pinion nut must be installed.**

17. Remove the cap or plug from the extension housing and install the front of the driveshaft on the transmission output shaft. Connect the rear end of the driveshaft to the axle end yoke, aligning the scribe marks made earlier. Tighten the four nuts to 70–95 ft. lbs. (95–128 Nm).
18. Install the wheels and tires. Lower the vehicle.
19. Remove the filler plug and add hypoid gear lubricant until it is about ½ in. (13mm) below the bottom of the filler hole in the running position. Install the filler plug and tighten it to 15–30 ft. lbs. (20–41 Nm).

8

SUSPENSION AND STEERING

WHEELS

Wheel Assembly

REMOVAL & INSTALLATION

▶ See Figure 1

1. Apply the vehicle parking brake and block the opposite wheel.
2. If equipped with an automatic transmission, place the selector lever in **P**; with a manual transmission, position the shifter in Reverse.
3. If equipped, remove the wheel cover or hub cap.
4. Break loose the lug nuts. If a nut is stuck, never use heat to loosen it otherwise damage to the wheel and bearings may occur. If the nuts are seized, one or two heavy hammer blows directly on the end of the bolt head usually loosens the rust. Be careful as continued pounding will likely damage the brake drum or rotor.
5. Raise the vehicle until the tire is clear of the ground. Support the vehicle safely using jackstands.
6. Remove the lug nuts, then remove the tire and wheel assembly.

To install:

7. Make sure the wheel and hub mating surfaces, as well as the wheel lug studs, are clean and free of all foreign material. Always remove rust from the wheel mounting surfaces and the brake rotors/drums. Failure to do so may cause the lug nuts to loosen in service.
8. Position the wheel on the hub or drum and hand-tighten the lug nuts. Make sure that the coned ends of the lug nuts face inward.
9. Tighten all the lug nuts, in a crisscross or star pattern, until they are snug.
10. Remove the supports, if any, and lower the vehicle. Tighten the lug nuts, in a crisscross or star pattern. Always use a torque wrench to achieve the proper lug nut torque value and to prevent stretching the wheel studs.
11. Repeat the torque pattern to assure proper wheel tightening.
12. If equipped, install the hub cab or wheel cover.

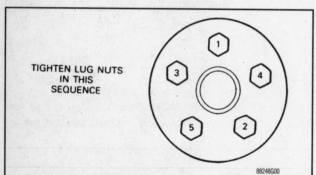

Fig. 1 Make certain to tighten the lug nuts in a crisscross or star pattern to ensure proper mounting of the wheel to the hub or drum of the vehicle

INSPECTION

Check the wheels for any damage. They must be replaced if they are bent, dented, heavily rusted, have elongated bolt holes, or have excessive lateral or radial run-out. Wheels with excessive run-out may cause a high-speed vehicle vibration.

Replacement wheels must be of the same load capacity, diameter, width, off-set and mounting configuration as the original wheels. Using the wrong wheels may affect wheel bearing life, ground and tire clearance, or speedometer and odometer calibrations.

Wheel Lug Studs

REPLACEMENT

Front Wheel

▶ See Figure 2

1. Raise and safely support the vehicle on jackstands.
2. Remove the wheel and tire assembly as described earlier in this section.
3. Remove the front brake rotor. For more details, refer to Section 9.
4. Position the rotor in a press so that the pressure applied by the ram is not directly exerted on the rotor surface. Press the old stud from the rotor.
5. Discard the old lug stud.

To install:

6. Position a new stud in the rotor hole. Align the serrations of the new stud with the serration marks from the old stud. With a hammer, lightly tap the stud until the serrations on the stud are started in the hole.

➡**Make sure that the stud is not installed in an off-center position in the rotor hub.**

7. Position the rotor in a press so that the rotor is supported on the wheel mounting flange. Allow enough clearance for the stud to pass completely through the hole. Do not apply ram pressure directly on the rotor surface.
8. Press the stud into the rotor until it is flush against the inner surface of the rotor hub.
9. Install the rotor onto the vehicle. For more details, refer to Section 9 of this manual.
10. Install the wheel and tire as described earlier in this section.

Rear Wheel

▶ See Figures 3, 4 and 5

✳ WARNING

Never use a hammer to remove the wheel lug stud. Damage to the axle shaft flange or bearing may result.

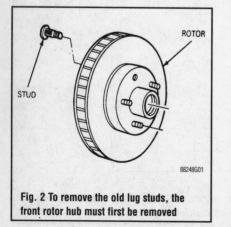

Fig. 2 To remove the old lug studs, the front rotor hub must first be removed

Fig. 3 The rear brake drum slides off of the rear wheel lug studs—do not use a hammer to drive the old studs out of the axle flange

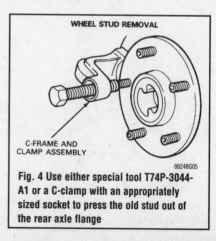

Fig. 4 Use either special tool T74P-3044-A1 or a C-clamp with an appropriately sized socket to press the old stud out of the rear axle flange

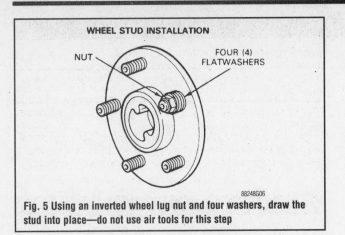

Fig. 5 Using an inverted wheel lug nut and four washers, draw the stud into place—do not use air tools for this step

1. Raise and safely support the vehicle on jackstands.
2. Remove the wheel and tire assembly as described earlier in this section.
3. Remove the brake drum from the axle shaft studs.

4. Using C-Frame and Clamp Tool T74P-3044-A1 or equivalent, press the stud from its seat in the axle flange. The stud may also be removed by pressing it out using an appropriately sized socket and C-clamp. Discard the old stud.

To install:

5. Insert the new stud into the hole in the flange. Rotate the stud slowly. Make sure that the serrations are aligned with those made by the original stud.
6. Place four flat washers over the outer end of the stud and thread the wheel lug nut with the flat side against the washers.
7. Tighten the wheel lug nut until the stud head seats against the back side of the flange.

✶✶ WARNING

Do not use air tools as the serrations may be stripped from the stud.

8. Remove the lug nut and washers from the newly installed stud.
9. Install the brake drum. For more information, refer to Section 9.
10. Install the tire and wheel assembly, as described earlier in this section.
11. Lower the vehicle.

2-WHEEL DRIVE FRONT SUSPENSION

▶ See Figure 6

The front suspension on rear wheel drive models is a short/long arm suspension system with helical coil springs. It consists of spindles, steering knuckles, upper and lower control arms with integral ball joints and bushings, adjustment shims, coil springs, shock absorbers and a stabilizer bar. The springs are computer-selected based on vehicle options.

The critical joint in the front chassis area includes the front crossmember, longitudinal side member, and upper control arm. Whenever this joint is loosened or removed (including engine service) it is imperative that new fasteners or cleaned and lubricated present fasteners be installed with the proper installation torque at this critical joint.

Coil Springs

REMOVAL & INSTALLATION

▶ See Figures 7, 8 and 9

1. Place the steering wheel and front wheels in the centered (straight ahead) position.

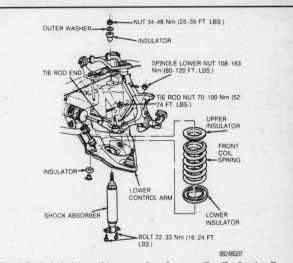

Fig. 7 Exploded view and torque values for mounting the front coil spring

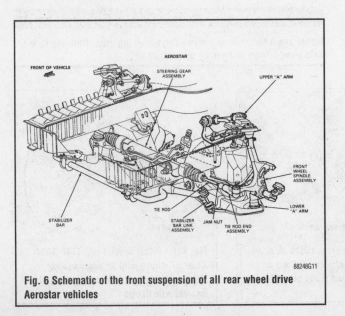

Fig. 6 Schematic of the front suspension of all rear wheel drive Aerostar vehicles

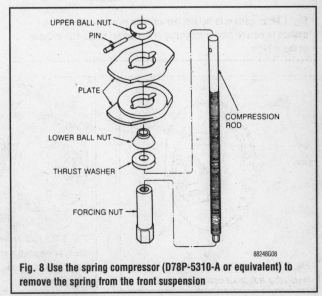

Fig. 8 Use the spring compressor (D78P-5310-A or equivalent) to remove the spring from the front suspension

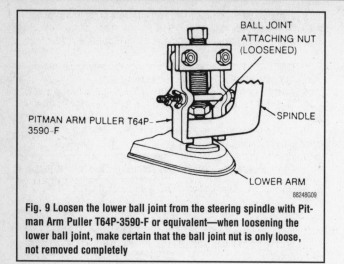

BALL JOINT ATTACHING NUT (LOOSENED)

PITMAN ARM PULLER T64P-3590-F

SPINDLE

LOWER ARM

88248G09

Fig. 9 Loosen the lower ball joint from the steering spindle with Pitman Arm Puller T64P-3590-F or equivalent—when loosening the lower ball joint, make certain that the ball joint nut is only loose, not removed completely

→Whenever the steering linkage is disconnected, the steering system must be centered prior to beginning any work.

2. Raise the van and support it safely on jackstands. Place the jackstands beneath the frame at the jacking pads.

3. Remove the tire and wheel assemblies, as described earlier in this section.

4. Disconnect the stabilizer bar link bolt from the lower control arm.

5. Remove the two bolts attaching the shock absorber to the lower arm assembly.

6. Remove the upper nut and washer retaining the shock absorber and remove the shock absorber from the vehicle.

7. Using spring compressor tool D78P-5310-A or equivalent, install one plate with the pivot ball seat facing downward into the coils of the spring. Rotate the plate so that it is flush with the upper surface of the lower arm.

8. Install the other plate with the pivot ball seat facing upward into the coils of the spring, so that the nut rests in the upper plate.

9. Insert the compression rod into the opening in the lower arm, through the upper and lower plate and upper ball nut. Insert the securing pin through the upper ball nut and compression rod. This pin can only be inserted one way into the upper ball nut because of a stepped hole design.

10. With the upper ball nut secured, turn the upper plate so that it walks up the coil until it contacts the upper spring seat, then back it off ½ turn.

11. Install the lower ball nut and thrust washer on the compression rod, then screw on the forcing nut. Tighten the forcing nut until the spring is compressed enough so that it is free in its seat.

12. Loosen the two lower arm pivot bolts. Remove the cotter pin and loosen, but not remove the nut attaching the lower ball joint to the spindle. Using Pitman arm puller T64P-3590-F, or equivalent, loosen the lower ball joint.

13. Remove the puller tool.

14. Support the lower control arm with a hydraulic jack, then remove the ball joint nut. Slowly lower the control arm and remove the coil spring.

Handle the coil spring with care. A compressed coil spring has enough stored energy to be dangerous if suddenly released. Mount the spring securely in a vise and slowly loosen the spring compressor if the spring is being replaced.

15. If the coil spring is being replaced, measure the compressed length of the old spring and mark the position of the compressor plates on the old spring with chalk. Remove the spring compressor from the old spring carefully.

To install:

16. Install the spring compressor on the new spring, placing the compressor plates in the same position as marked on the old spring. Make sure the upper ball nut securing pin is installed properly, then compress the new spring to the compressed length of the old spring.

17. Position the coil spring assembly into the lower control arm.

18. Place a hydraulic jack under the lower control arm and slowly raise it into position. Reconnect the ball joint and install the nut. Tighten the ball joint castle nut to 80–120 ft. lbs. (108–163 Nm) and install a new cotter pin. The nut may be tightened slightly to align the cotter pin hole, but not loosened.

19. Slowly release the spring compressor and remove it from the coil spring.

20. Reconnect the steering center link to the Pitman arm.

21. Install the shock absorber.

22. Reconnect the stabilizer bar link bolt to the lower control arm. Tighten the nuts to 9–12 ft. lbs. (12–16 Nm).

23. Lower the vehicle. Although this procedure should not disturb any alignment settings, anytime the front end is disassembled for service, the alignment should be checked.

Shock Absorber

REMOVAL & INSTALLATION

♦ See Figures 7, 10, 11, 12 and 13

The low pressure gas shock absorbers are charged with nitrogen gas to 135 psi (930 kPa). Do not attempt to open, puncture or apply heat to the shock absorbers.

1. Raise the vehicle and support it safely on jackstands.

2. Remove the nut and washer retaining the shock absorber to the coil spring upper bracket.

3. Remove the two bolts retaining the shock absorber to the bottom of the lower control arm.

4. Remove the shock absorber through the lower control arm.

5. If necessary, purge the new shock absorber of air by extending and compressing it several times before installation.

To install:

6. Position the shock absorber up into the coil spring.

7. Install the upper shock absorber mounting nut finger-tight.

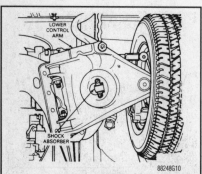

LOWER CONTROL ARM

SHOCK ABSORBER

88248G10

Fig. 10 There are only three nuts securing the shock absorber in the vehicle—one on the top and two on the bottom

88248P17

Fig. 11 When removing the shock, support the lower control arm with a hydraulic floor jack

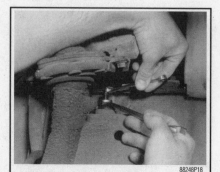

88248P18

Fig. 12 Using two wrenches, remove the shock absorber upper retaining nut, then . . .

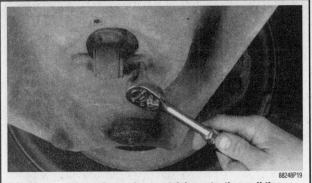

Fig. 13 . . . remove the two lower retaining nuts, then pull the shock down and out of the front coil spring

8. Install the two lower nuts to 16–24 ft. lbs. (22–33 Nm).
9. Tighten the upper retaining nut to 25–35 ft. lbs. (34–48 Nm).
10. Lower the vehicle.

Upper Ball Joint

INSPECTION

1. Raise the vehicle by placing a hydraulic floor jack under the lower control arm.
2. Have an assistant grasp the top and bottom of the tire and move the wheel in and out.
3. As the wheel is being moved, observe the upper control arm where the spindle attaches to it. Any movement between the upper part of the spindle and the upper ball joint indicates a worn ball joint which must be replaced.

➠During this check, the lower ball joint will be unloaded and may move; this is normal and not an indication of a worn ball joint. Also, do not mistake a loose wheel bearing for a defective ball joint.

REMOVAL & INSTALLATION

▶ See Figures 14, 15, 16, 17 and 18

➠Ford Motor Company recommends replacement of the upper control arm and ball joint as an assembly, rather than replacement of the ball joint alone. However, aftermarket ball joints are available. The following procedure is for replacement of the ball joint only. See the Upper Control Arm removal and installation procedure for complete assembly replacement.

1. Raise the van and support it safely with jackstands placed under the frame lifting pads. Allow the front wheels to fall to their full down position.
2. Remove the front wheels.

3. Place a hydraulic floor jack under the lower control arm and raise the jack until it just contacts the arm.
4. Drill a ⅛ in. (3mm) hole completely through each ball joint attaching rivet.
5. Use a chisel to cut the head off of each rivet, then drive them from the upper control arm with a suitable small drift or blunt punch.
6. Raise the lower control arm about 6 in. (15cm) with the hydraulic jack.
7. Remove the pinch nut and bolt holding the ball joint stud from the spindle.
8. Using a suitable tool, loosen the ball joint stud from the spindle, then remove the ball joint from the upper arm.

To install:
9. Clean all metal burrs from the upper arm and install a new ball joint, using the service part nuts and bolts to attach the ball joint to the upper arm. Do not attempt to rivet the ball joint again once it has been removed.
10. Attach the ball joint stud to the spindle, then install the pinch bolt and nut and tighten to 27–37 ft. lbs. (36–50 Nm).
11. Install the tire and wheel assemblies as described earlier in this section.
12. Remove the hydraulic jack and lower the van. Have the front end alignment checked.

Lower Ball Joint

INSPECTION

1. Position a floor jack under the lower control arm and jack the vehicle up far enough for the tire to clear the ground.

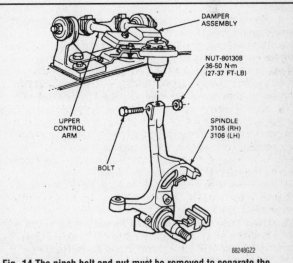

Fig. 14 The pinch bolt and nut must be removed to separate the upper ball joint from the spindle

Fig. 15 Support the lower control arm and remove the front brake line-to-upper control arm retaining bolt

Fig. 16 Remove the upper ball joint pinch nut, then . . .

Fig. 17 . . . drive the pinch bolt out of the steering knuckle with a drift or punch

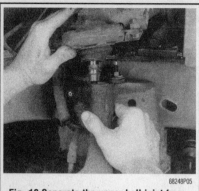

Fig. 18 Separate the upper ball joint from the steering knuckle

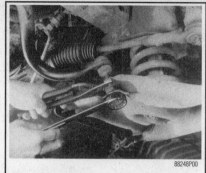

Fig. 19 To separate the lower control arm from the stabilizer end link, first loosen the end link nut . . .

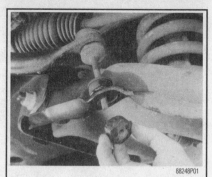

Fig. 20 . . . then remove the stabilizer nut, bushings and end link from the stabilizer bar

2. Grasp the lower edge of the tire and move the wheel in and out. While the wheel is being moved, observe the lower spindle jaw and the lower control arm. A 1/32 in. (0.8mm) or greater movement between the lower control arm and the lower spindle jaw indicates the lower ball joint must be replaced.

3. Inspect the rubber bushings at the lower control arm attachment points for wear or looseness. Repair or replace the parts if any damage is found.

REMOVAL & INSTALLATION

➡The manufacturer recommends that the lower control arm and ball joint should be replaced as an assembly.

The lower ball joint is pressed into the lower control arm. Although Ford recommends replacing the lower arm and ball joint together, the old ball joint can also be pressed out and the new one pressed in. Refer to the lower control arm removal procedures to remove the lower control arm. Once the lower control arm is removed, the ball joint may be pressed out.

Front Stabilizer Bar

REMOVAL AND INSTALLATION

▶ See Figures 19 and 20

1. Raise the van and support it safely on jackstands.
2. Loosen and remove the nuts retaining the stabilizer bar to the lower control arm link on each side.
3. Remove the insulators and disconnect the stabilizer bar from the links.
4. If required, remove the nuts retaining the links to the lower control arm, then remove the insulators and links.
5. Remove the bolts retaining the bar mounting bracket to the frame and remove the stabilizer bar. If required, remove the insulators from the stabilizer bar.

To install:
6. If the stabilizer bar insulators are being replaced, install them on the stabilizer bar. Place the bar, insulators and mounting bracket in position on the frame and install the retaining bolts. Tighten the retaining bolts to 16–24 ft. lbs. (22–33 Nm).
7. If removed, connect the link and insulators to the lower control arm. Install and tighten the nuts to 12–18 ft. lbs. (16–24 Nm).
8. Connect the links and insulators to the stabilizer bar, then install and tighten the nuts to 12–18 ft. lbs. (16–24 Nm).
9. Once all mounting nuts are tightened, lower the vehicle.

Upper Control Arm

REMOVAL & INSTALLATION

▶ See Figure 21

1. Place the steering wheel and front tires in the centered (straight ahead) position.

➡Anytime the steering linkage is disconnected from the spindle, the steering system must be centered before beginning the service procedure.

2. Raise the van and support it safely with jackstands placed under the frame lifting pads. A hydraulic floor jack should be placed under the control arm to raise and lower the arm during coil spring removal. Make sure the van is supported securely on the jackstands and only work on one side at a time.

➡NEVER service both front suspension assemblies at the same time.

3. Remove the spindle, as described in this section.
4. Remove the bolt retaining the cowl drain bracket and bolt retainer plate, then remove the bracket and plate.
5. Matchmark the position of the control arm mounting brackets on the flat plate.
6. Remove the bolt and washer retaining the front mounting bracket to the flat plate.
7. From beneath the rail, remove the three nuts from the bolts retaining the two upper control arm mounting brackets to the body rail.
8. Remove the three long bolts retaining the mounting brackets to the body rail by rotating the upper control arm out of position in order to remove the bolts. Remove the upper control arm, upper ball joint and mounting bracket assembly, and the flat plate from the van.
9. If necessary, remove the damper assembly from the upper control arm by removing the three retaining bolts.
10. Inspect the upper and/or lower ball joint boot seal and replace if necessary.
11. If required to service the upper control arm and upper ball joint assembly or the mounting brackets and adjusting arm assembly, remove the nuts retaining the upper control arm to the adjusting arm. Note the **exact** position and number of shims on each control arm stud. These shims control caster and camber. Remove the upper control arm from the adjusting arm.

➡The adjusting arm and mounting brackets are serviced as an assembly, Ford recommends that the upper control arm and upper ball joint also be serviced as an assembly; however, aftermarket ball joint kits are available.

To install:
12. Install the upper control arm in the adjusting arm. Install the shims on the control arm studs with the same number of shims in the exact position as

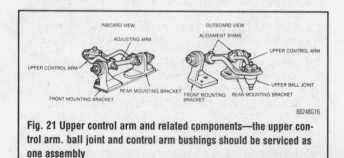

Fig. 21 Upper control arm and related components—the upper control arm. ball joint and control arm bushings should be serviced as one assembly

marked during removal. Install and tighten the nuts retaining the shims to the control arm.

13. If removed, install the damper assembly to the upper control arm. Tighten the damper retaining bolts to 22–29 ft. lbs. (30–39 Nm).

14. Place the flat plate for the mounting brackets in position on the body rail, then install and tighten the bolts to 10–14 ft. lbs. (14–18 Nm).

15. Place the mounting brackets and upper control arm assembly in position on the flat plate.

16. Install the three long bolts and washers retaining the mounting brackets to the body rail. Rotate or rock the upper control arm and mounting bracket assembly until the bolt heads rest against the mounting bracket and the studs extend through the body rail.

17. Move the mounting brackets into the position marked on the flat plate during removal.

18. Install and tighten the nuts and washers retaining the mounting bracket bolts to the body rail to 135–142 ft. lbs. (175–185 Nm) for the front bolt, and 145–152 ft. lbs. (188–198 Nm) for the center and rear bolts on 1986–90 models, and to 145–152 ft. lbs. (188–198 Nm) for 1991–97 models. Make sure the mounting brackets do not move from the marked position on the flat plate to minimize corrections.

✳✳ WARNING

The torque required for the mounting bracket-to-body rail nuts and bolts is critical. Be precise when tightening to the specified torque and use an accurate torque wrench. Tighten with one smooth motion rather than short jerks.

19. Install and tighten the bolt retaining the front mounting bracket to the flat plate to 35–47 ft. lbs. (47–64 Nm).

20. Place the bolt retainer plate and cowl drain bracket in position on the mounting bracket and flat plate assembly, then install and tighten the bolt to 10–14 ft. lbs. (14–18 Nm).

21. Install the spindle as described later in this section.

22. Have the front end aligned by a professional automotive mechanic.

CONTROL ARM BUSHING REPLACEMENT

The manufacturer recommends that the lower control arm, bushings and ball joints be replaced together as one assembly. Therefore, separate control arm bushing removal procedures are not necessary.

Lower Control Arm

REMOVAL & INSTALLATION

1. Place the steering wheel and front wheels in the centered (straight ahead) position.

➡Anytime the steering linkage is disconnected from the spindle, the steering system must be centered before beginning the service procedure.

2. Raise the van and support it safely with jackstands placed under the frame lifting pads. A hydraulic floor jack should be placed under the control arm to raise and lower the arm during coil spring removal. Make sure the van is supported securely on the jackstands and only work on one side at a time.

3. Remove the coil spring as described earlier in this section.

4. Remove the bolts and nuts retaining the lower control arm to the crossmember and remove the lower control arm from the frame.

5. If new control arm bushings or ball joints are necessary, replace the entire lower control arm assembly.

To install:

6. Position the new lower control arm assembly to the frame crossmember and install the retaining bolts in the proper direction as illustrated. Temporarily snug the bolts, but do not tighten to specifications.

7. If the old crossmember is being installed, inspect the lower ball joint boot and replace it if necessary.

8. Install the coil spring as previously described.

9. Install the front tire and wheel assemblies.

10. Lower the van so it rests in the normal ride position on a level surface.

11. Tighten the lower control arm-to-crossmember mounting bolts to 187–260 ft. lbs. (254–352 Nm) for 1986–90 models, and to 100–140 ft. lbs. (136–190 Nm) for 1991–97 models.

12. Have the front end alignment checked.

Knuckle and Spindle

REMOVAL & INSTALLATION

◗ **See Figures 22, 23 and 24**

➡Ford Motor Company refers to the entire knuckle and spindle assembly as a spindle.

1. Place the steering wheel and front tires in the centered (straight ahead) position.

➡Anytime the steering linkage is disconnected from the spindle, the steering system must be centered before beginning the service procedure.

2. Raise the van and support it safely with jackstands placed under the frame lifting pads. A hydraulic floor jack should be placed under the control arm to raise and lower the arm during coil spring removal. Make sure the van is supported securely on the jackstands and only work on one side at a time. Never service both front suspension assemblies at the same time.

3. Remove the front tire and wheel assemblies.

4. Remove the caliper, rotor and dust shield from the spindle. For more information, refer to Section 9.

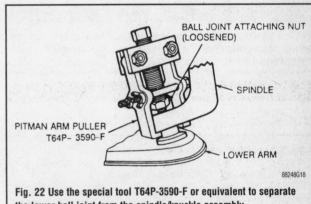

Fig. 22 Use the special tool T64P-3590-F or equivalent to separate the lower ball joint from the spindle/knuckle assembly

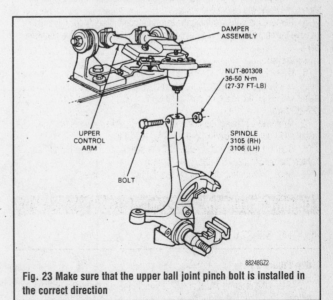

Fig. 23 Make sure that the upper ball joint pinch bolt is installed in the correct direction

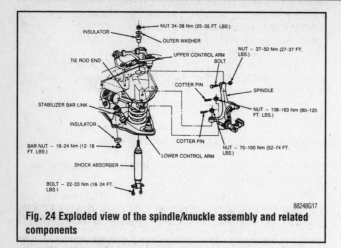

Fig. 24 Exploded view of the spindle/knuckle assembly and related components

5. Remove the cotter pin and nut retaining the tie rod end to the spindle's lower arm. Disconnect the tie rod end with a suitable Pitman arm puller such as tool T64P–3590–F or equivalent.

6. Support the lower control arm with a hydraulic floor jack. Make sure the jack pad securely contacts the control arm. Remove the cotter pin, then loosen the nut retaining the spindle to the lower control arm ball joint. Disconnect the lower ball joint from the spindle using the same Pitman arm puller used earlier, then remove the tool and ball joint retaining nut.

7. Slowly lower the jack under the control arm until the ball joint is disengaged from the spindle.

✱✱✱ CAUTION

Use extreme caution when lowering the lower control arm. The coil spring may quickly expand with dangerous force. Never lower the control arm quickly.

8. Remove the bolt and nut retaining the spindle to the upper control arm ball joint, then remove the spindle from the van.

To install:

9. Position the spindle upper arm on the upper ball joint. Install the nut and bolt and tighten to 27–37 ft. lbs. (37–50 Nm). Inspect the upper and lower ball joint boot seals for damage and replace if necessary.

10. Position the spindle lower arm over the ball joint stud, then **slowly** raise the lower control arm with the hydraulic jack until the ball joint stud extends through the spindle arm and is seated in the spindle. Install the ball joint castle nut and tighten it to 80–120 ft. lbs. (108–163 Nm), then install a new cotter pin. The castle nut may be tightened slightly to align the castellations with the cotter pin hole, but under no circumstances loosen the nut to align.

11. Connect the tie rod end to the spindle arm. Firmly seat the tie rod end stud into the tapered hole to prevent rotation while tightening the castellated nut. Tighten the tie rod nut to 52–74 ft. lbs. (70–100 Nm), then install a new cotter pin. The castle nut may be tightened slightly to align the castellations with the cotter pin hole, but under no circumstances loosen the nut to align.

12. Install the dust shield, rotor and caliper as described in Section 9.
13. Install the front wheels.
14. Lower the vehicle.

Front Hub and Wheel Bearings

REMOVAL & INSTALLATION

▶ See Figures 25, 26, 27 and 28

If wheel bearing adjustment will not eliminate looseness or rough and noisy operation, the hub and bearings should be cleaned, inspected and repacked with lithium base wheel bearing grease. If the bearing cups or the cone and roller assemblies are worn or damaged, they must be replaced as follows:

➡Sodium based grease is not compatible with lithium based grease and the two should not be mixed. Do not lubricate the front and/or rear wheel bearings without first identifying the type of grease being used. Use of incompatible wheel bearing lubricant could result in premature lubricant breakdown and subsequent bearing damage.

1. Raise the van until the tire clears the ground. Install a jackstand for safety, then remove the front tire.

2. Remove the brake caliper from the spindle as described in Section 9, then wire it to the underbody. Do not let the caliper hang by the brake hose.

3. Remove the grease cup from the hub. Remove the cotter pin, castellated retainer, adjusting nut and flat washer from the spindle. Remove the outer bearing cone and roller assembly.

4. Pull the hub and rotor assembly off the spindle.

5. Place the hub and rotor on a clean workbench, with the back side facing up, and remove the grease seal using a suitable seal remover or small prybar. Discard the grease seal.

6. Remove the inner bearing cone and roller assembly from the hub.

7. Clean the inner and outer bearing cups with solvent. Inspect the cups for scratches, pits, excessive wear and other damage. If the cups are worn or damaged, remove them with a bearing cup puller (T77F–1102–A or equivalent) as illustrated.

8. Wipe all old lubricant from the spindle and the inside of the hub with a clean rag. Cover the spindle and brush all loose dirt and dust from the dust shield. Remove the cover cloth carefully to prevent dirt from falling on the spindle.

To install:

9. If the inner or outer bearing cups were removed, install replacement cups using a suitable driver tool (T80T–4000–W or equivalent) and bearing cup replacer. Make sure the cups are seated properly in the hub and not cocked in the bore.

10. Thoroughly clean all old grease from the surrounding surfaces.

11. Pack the bearing and cone assemblies with suitable wheel bearing grease using a bearing packer tool. If a packer tool is not available, work as much grease as possible between the rollers and cages, then grease the cone surfaces.

12. Place the inner bearing cone and roller assembly in the inner cup. Apply a light film of grease to the lips of a new grease seal and install the seal with an

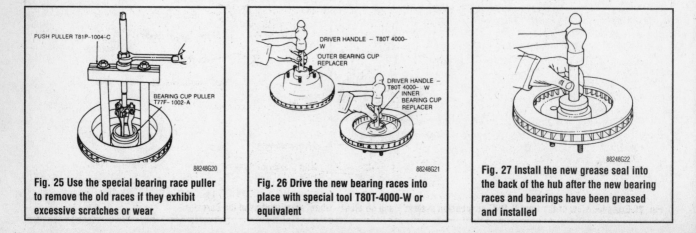

Fig. 25 Use the special bearing race puller to remove the old races if they exhibit excessive scratches or wear

Fig. 26 Drive the new bearing races into place with special tool T80T-4000-W or equivalent

Fig. 27 Install the new grease seal into the back of the hub after the new bearing races and bearings have been greased and installed

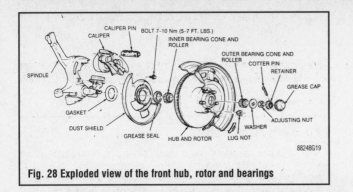

Fig. 28 Exploded view of the front hub, rotor and bearings

appropriate driver tool as illustrated. Make sure the grease seal is properly seated and not cocked in the bore.

13. Install the hub and rotor assembly on the spindle. Keep the hub centered on the spindle to prevent damage to the retainer and the spindle threads.

14. Install the outer bearing cone and roller assembly (after being fully greased) and the flat washer on the spindle, then install the adjusting nut finger-tight. Adjust the wheel bearing. For more details, refer to Section 1.

15. Install the caliper onto the spindle. For more information, refer to Section 9.

16. Install the front wheel, then lower the van and tighten the lug nuts to 85–115 ft. lbs. (115–155 Nm). Install the wheel cover.

17. Repeat steps 1–16 for the other front wheel if needed.

18. Before moving the van, pump the brake pedal several times to restore normal brake travel.

ALL WHEEL DRIVE FRONT SUSPENSION

▶ See Figure 29

The E-4WD front suspension is a short/long arm suspension system with helical coil springs. It consists of spindles, upper and lower control arms with integral ball joints and bushings, adjustment shims, coil springs, shock absorbers and a stabilizer bar. The springs are computer-selected based on the vehicle options.

The lower control arm is attached to the engine crossmember through the pivot bushings and to the spindles through the ball joint assembly. The lower arms provide support for the coil springs and attachments for the shock absorber and stabilizer bar.

The upper control arm assembly is attached to the top of the front longitudinal side member. The upper arm assembly is attached to the spindle at the upper ball joint and is anchored to the body using three primary crossmember bolts as well as one additional bolt and washer assembly.

The shock absorbers are telescopic, direct-action design. They are nonadjustable units and must be replaced as complete assemblies.

The front stabilizer bar is fastened to the front of the frame and to the lower control arm. The stabilizer bar is standard equipment on all Aerostar models.

Each front wheel is bolted to a hub assembly. There are two opposed tapered roller bearings (inner and outer) with grease retainer seals (inner and outer) encased in one single cup or cartridge. Unlike four-wheel drive wheel hubs, the all-wheel drive hubs are always engaged to the front drive axle and cannot be manually disengaged.

Coil Spring

REMOVAL & INSTALLATION

▶ See Figures 30, 31, 32 and 33

1. Place the steering wheel and front tires in the centered (straight ahead) position. Anytime the steering linkage is disconnected from the spindle, the steering system must be centered prior to beginning any suspension work.

2. Raise the van and support it safely on jackstands. Place the jackstands beneath the frame at the jacking pads.

3. Remove the wheel/tire assemblies from the front of the vehicle.

4. Disconnect the stabilizer bar link bolt from the lower control arm.

5. Remove the shock absorber, as described later in this section.

6. Remove the steering center link from the Pitman arm.

7. Using spring compressor tool D78P–5310–A or equivalent, install one plate with the pivot ball seat facing downward into the coils of the spring. Rotate the plate so that it is flush with the upper surface of the lower arm.

8. Install the other plate with the pivot ball seat facing upward into the coils of the spring, so that the nut rests in the upper plate.

9. Insert the compression rod into the opening in the lower arm, through the upper and lower plate and upper ball nut. Insert the securing pin through

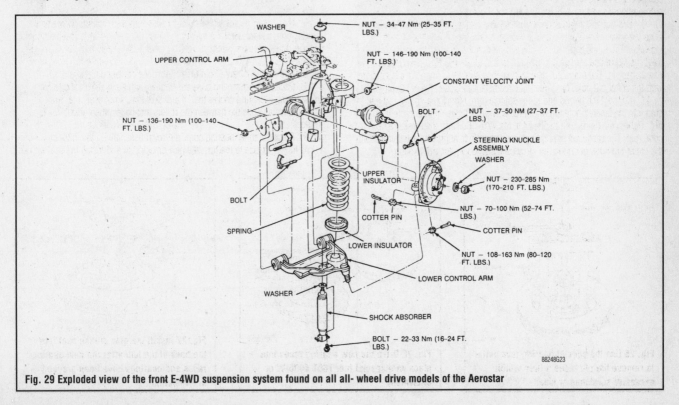

Fig. 29 Exploded view of the front E-4WD suspension system found on all all-wheel drive models of the Aerostar

the upper ball nut and compression rod. This pin can only be inserted one way into the upper ball nut because of a stepped hole design.

10. With the upper ball nut secured, turn the upper plate so that it walks up the coil until it contacts the upper spring seat, then back it off ½ turn.

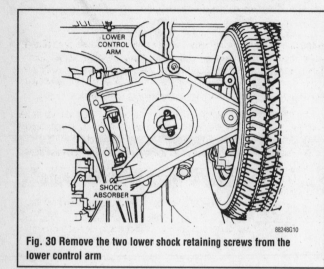

Fig. 30 Remove the two lower shock retaining screws from the lower control arm

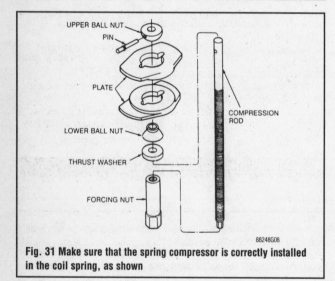

Fig. 31 Make sure that the spring compressor is correctly installed in the coil spring, as shown

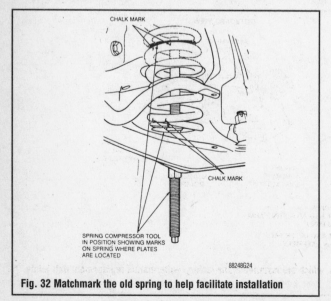

Fig. 32 Matchmark the old spring to help facilitate installation

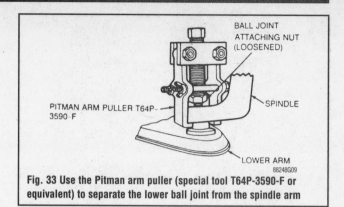

Fig. 33 Use the Pitman arm puller (special tool T64P-3590-F or equivalent) to separate the lower ball joint from the spindle arm

11. Install the lower ball nut and thrust washer on the compression rod, then screw on the forcing nut. Tighten the forcing nut until the spring is compressed enough so that it is free in its seat.

12. Loosen the two lower arm pivot bolts. Remove the cotter pin and loosen, but do not remove the nut attaching the lower ball joint to the spindle. Using Pitman arm puller T64P–3590–F, or equivalent, loosen the lower ball joint.

13. Remove the puller tool from the lower ball joint.

14. Support the lower control arm with a hydraulic jack, then remove the ball joint nut. Slowly lower the control arm and remove the coil spring.

❋❋ CAUTION

Handle the coil spring with care. A compressed coil spring has enough stored energy to be dangerous if suddenly released. Mount the spring securely in a vise and slowly loosen the spring compressor if the spring is being replaced.

15. If the coil spring is being replaced, measure the compressed length of the old spring and mark the position of the compressor plates on the old spring with chalk. Remove the spring compressor from the old spring carefully.

To install:

16. Install the spring compressor on the new spring, placing the compressor plates in the same position as marked on the old spring. Make sure the upper ball nut securing pin is installed properly, then compress the new spring to the compressed length of the old spring.

17. Position the coil spring assembly into the lower control arm.

18. Place a hydraulic jack under the lower control arm and slowly raise it into position. Reconnect the ball joint and install the nut. Tighten the ball joint castle nut to 80–120 ft. lbs. (108–163 Nm) for 1986–90 models; and to 59–81 ft. lbs. (80–110 Nm) for 1991–97 models, then install a new cotter pin. The nut may be tightened slightly to align the cotter pin hole, but not loosened.

19. Slowly release the spring compressor and remove it from the coil spring.

20. Reconnect the steering center link to the Pitman arm.

21. Install the shock absorber, as described later in this section.

22. Reconnect the stabilizer bar link bolt to the lower control arm. Tighten the stabilizer link nut to 6–9 ft. lbs. (8–12 Nm).

23. Install the tire and wheel assemblies.

24. Lower the vehicle. Although this procedure should not disturb any alignment settings, anytime the front end is disassembled for service, the alignment should be checked.

25. With the front of the vehicle resting on the ground, tighten the two lower control arm-to-crossmember bolts to 100–140 ft. lbs. (136–190 Nm).

Shock Absorber

REMOVAL & INSTALLATION

▶ See Figure 34

❋❋ WARNING

The low pressure gas shock absorbers are charged with nitrogen gas to 135 psi (930 kPa). Do not attempt to open, puncture or apply heat to the shock absorbers.

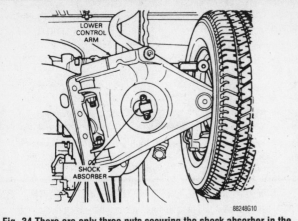

Fig. 34 There are only three nuts securing the shock absorber in the vehicle—one on the top and two on the bottom

1. Raise the vehicle and support it safely on jackstands.
2. Remove the nut and washer retaining the shock absorber to the coil spring upper bracket.
3. Remove the two bolts retaining the shock absorber to the bottom of the lower control arm.
4. Remove the shock absorber through the lower control arm.
5. If necessary, purge the new shock absorber of air by extending and compressing it several times before installation.

To install:
6. Position the shock absorber up into the coil spring.
7. Install the upper shock absorber mounting nut finger-tight.
8. Install the two lower nuts to 16–24 ft. lbs. (22–33 Nm).
9. Tighten the upper retaining nut to 25–35 ft. lbs. (34–48 Nm).
10. Lower the vehicle.

Upper Ball Joint

INSPECTION

1. Raise the vehicle by placing a hydraulic floor jack under the lower control arm.
2. Have an assistant grasp the top and bottom of the tire and move the wheel in and out.
3. As the wheel is being moved, observe the upper control arm where the spindle attaches to it. Any movement between the upper part of the spindle and the upper ball joint indicates a worn ball joint which must be replaced.

→During this check, the lower ball joint will be unloaded and may move; this is normal and not an indication of a worn ball joint. Also, do not mistake a loose wheel bearing for a defective ball joint.

REMOVAL & INSTALLATION

♦ **See Figure 35**

→The manufacturer recommends replacement of the upper control arm and ball joint as an assembly, rather than replacement of the ball joint alone. However, aftermarket ball joints are available. The following procedure is for replacement of the ball joint only. Refer to the Upper Control Arm procedures for complete assembly replacement.

1. Raise the van and support it safely with jackstands placed under the frame lifting pads. Allow the front wheels to fall to their fully extended (down) position.
2. Remove the front wheel/tire assemblies from the vehicle.
3. Place a hydraulic floor jack under the lower control arm and raise the jack until it just contacts the arm.
4. Drill a ⅛ in. (3mm) hole completely through each upper ball joint attaching rivet.
5. Use a chisel to cut the head off of each rivet, then drive them from the upper control arm with a suitable small drift or blunt punch.
6. Raise the lower control arm about 6 in. (15cm) with the hydraulic jack.
7. Remove the pinch nut and bolt holding the ball joint stud to the spindle/knuckle.
8. Using a suitable tool, loosen the ball joint stud from the spindle and remove the ball joint from the upper arm. Make sure to support the knuckle to keep it from tipping excessively and possibly damaging the brake hose.

To install:
9. Clean all metal burrs from the upper arm and install a new ball joint, using the service part nuts and bolts to attach the ball joint to the upper arm. Do not attempt to rivet the ball joint again once it has been removed.
10. Attach the ball joint stud to the spindle, then install the pinch bolt and nut and tighten to 27–37 ft. lbs. (37–50 Nm).
11. Remove the hydraulic jack, then install the front wheel/tire assemblies. Lower the van and have the front end alignment checked by a professional automotive mechanic.

Lower Ball Joint

INSPECTION

1. Position a floor jack under the lower control arm and jack the vehicle up far enough for the tire to clear the ground.
2. Grasp the lower edge of the tire and move the wheel in and out. While the wheel is being moved, observe the lower spindle jaw and the lower control arm.

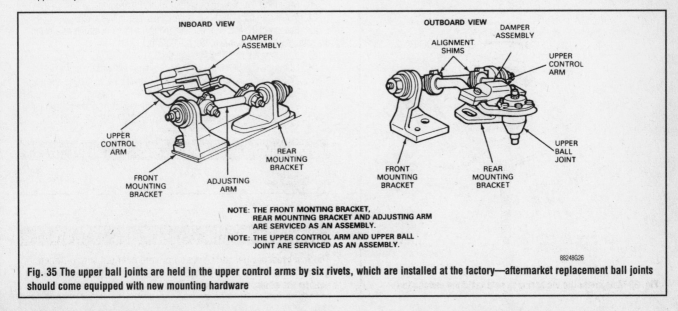

Fig. 35 The upper ball joints are held in the upper control arms by six rivets, which are installed at the factory—aftermarket replacement ball joints should come equipped with new mounting hardware

A 1/32 in. (0.8mm) or greater movement between the lower control arm and the lower spindle jaw indicates the lower ball joint must be replaced.

3. Inspect the rubber bushings at the lower control arm attachment points for wear or looseness. Repair or replace the parts if any damage is found.

REMOVAL & INSTALLATION

The manufacturer recommends servicing the lower ball joint and lower control arm as one assembly. The lower ball joint is pressed into the lower control arm. The lower ball joint can, however, be replaced separately by pressing the old ball joint out and pressing a new one in. Refer to the lower control arm procedures to remove the lower control arm and to service the lower ball joints.

Stabilizer Bar

REMOVAL & INSTALLATION

1. Raise the van and support it safely on jackstands.
2. Loosen and remove the nuts retaining the stabilizer bar to the lower control arm link on each side, then remove the insulators and disconnect the bar from the links.
3. If required, remove the nuts retaining the links to the lower control arm, then remove the insulators and links.
4. Remove the bolts retaining the bar mounting bracket to the frame and remove the stabilizer bar. If required, remove the insulators from the stabilizer bar.
   To install:
5. If the stabilizer bar insulators are being replaced, install them on the stabilizer bar. Place the bar, insulators and mounting bracket in position on the frame and install the retaining bolts. Tighten the retaining bolts to 16–24 ft. lbs. (22–33 Nm).
6. If applicable, connect the link and insulators to the lower control arm. Install and tighten the nut to 12–18 ft. lbs. (16–24 Nm) for 1986–90 models, and to 6–9 ft. lbs. (8–12 Nm) for 1991–97 models.
7. Connect the links and insulators to the stabilizer bar, then install and tighten the nuts to 12–18 ft. lbs. (16–24 Nm) for 1986–90 models, and to 6–9 ft. lbs. (8–12 Nm) for 1991–97 models.
8. Lower the vehicle.

Upper Control Arm

REMOVAL & INSTALLATION

♦ **See Figure 36**

1. Place the steering wheel and front tires in the centered (straight ahead) position.

➡**Anytime the steering linkage is disconnected from the spindle, the steering system must be centered before beginning the service procedure.**

2. Raise the van and support it safely with jackstands placed under the frame lifting pads. A hydraulic floor jack should be placed under the control arm to raise and lower the arm during coil spring removal. Make sure the van is supported securely on the jackstands and only work on one side at a time. Never service both front suspension assemblies at the same time.

✳✳ WARNING

When servicing any component in the upper control arm and ball joint system, only work on one side of the vehicle is at a time. Never service both sides at the same time.

3. Remove the front wheel and tire assemblies from the front of the vehicle.
4. Remove the upper ball joint-to-spindle bolt and nut. Disengage the upper ball joint from the spindle. When disconnecting the upper ball joint-to-spindle connection, use a floor jack to support the lower control arm. If the lower control arm is not supported, the spring may jump out of its seat, causing possible physical injury or component damage.
5. Remove the bolt retainer plate screw. Remove the plate.
6. Matchmark the position of the control arm mounting brackets on the flat plate.
7. Remove the bolt and washer retaining the front mounting bracket to the flat plate.
8. From beneath the rail, remove the three nuts from the bolts retaining the two upper control arm mounting brackets to the body rail.
9. Remove the three long bolts retaining the mounting brackets to the body rail by rotating the upper control arm out of position in order to remove the bolts. Remove the upper control arm, upper ball joint and mounting bracket assembly, and the flat plate from the van.
10. Inspect the upper and/or lower ball joint boot seal, and replace if necessary.
11. If required to service the upper control arm and upper ball joint assembly, or the mounting brackets and adjusting arm assembly, remove the nuts retaining the upper control arm to the adjusting arm. Note the **exact** position and number of shims on each control arm stud. These shims control caster and camber. Remove the upper control arm from the adjusting arm.

➡**The adjusting arm and mounting brackets are serviced as an assembly. Ford recommends that the upper control arm and upper ball joint also be serviced as an assembly; however, aftermarket ball joint kits are available.**

12. If necessary, remove the damper assembly from the upper control arm by removing the three retaining bolts.

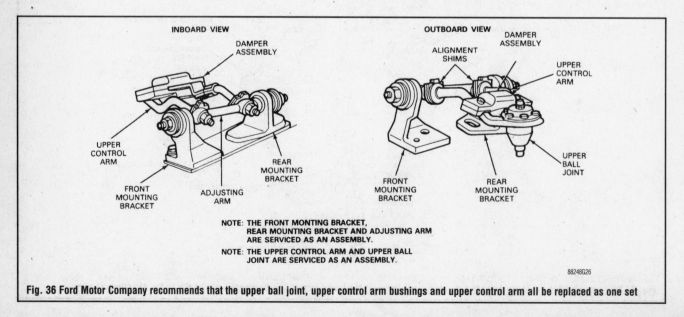

INBOARD VIEW

OUTBOARD VIEW

NOTE: THE FRONT MONTING BRACKET, REAR MOUNTING BRACKET AND ADJUSTING ARM ARE SERVICED AS AN ASSEMBLY.

NOTE: THE UPPER CONTROL ARM AND UPPER BALL JOINT ARE SERVICED AS AN ASSEMBLY.

88248G26

Fig. 36 Ford Motor Company recommends that the upper ball joint, upper control arm bushings and upper control arm all be replaced as one set

To install:

13. If removed, install the upper control arm in the adjusting arm. Install the shims on the control arm studs with the same number of shims in the exact position as marked during removal. Install and tighten the nuts retaining the shims to the control arm.

14. Place the flat plate for the mounting brackets in position on the body rail, then install and tighten the bolts to 10–14 ft. lbs. (14–18 Nm).

15. Place the mounting brackets and upper control arm assembly in position on the flat plate.

16. Install the three long bolts and washers retaining the mounting brackets to the body rail. Rotate or rock the upper control arm and mounting bracket assembly until the bolt heads rest against the mounting bracket and the studs extend through the body rail.

✳✳ WARNING

The torque required for the mounting bracket-to-body rail nuts and bolts is critical. Be precise when tightening to the specified torque and use an accurate torque wrench. Torque with one, smooth motion rather than short jerks.

17. Move the mounting brackets into the position marked on the flat plate during removal. Install and tighten the nuts and washers retaining the mounting bracket bolts to the body rail to the following specifications:
   a. 1986–90 models—135–142 ft. lbs. (175–185 Nm) for the front bolt, and 145–152 ft. lbs. (188–198 Nm) for the center and rear bolts.
   b. 1991–97 models—all three bolts to 145–152 ft. lbs. (188–198 Nm).

➡**Make sure the mounting brackets do not move from the marked position on the flat plate to minimize corrections.**

18. Install and tighten the smaller bolt retaining the front mounting bracket to the flat plate to 35–47 ft. lbs. (47–64 Nm).

19. Place the bolt retainer plate and cowl drain bracket in position on the mounting bracket and flat plate assembly, then install and tighten the bolt to 10–14 ft. lbs. (14–18 Nm).

20. Install the upper ball joint stud to the upper spindle/knuckle arm. Install and tighten the pinch bolt and nut to 27–37 ft. lbs. (37–50 Nm).

21. Install the tire/wheel assemblies.

22. Have the front end aligned. Caster and camber are adjusted by adding or removing shims.

CONTROL ARM BUSHING REPLACEMENT

The upper control arm bushings are integral to the upper control arm itself. These bushings are not replaceable, so the entire control arm assembly must be replaced as a set.

Lower Control Arm

REMOVAL & INSTALLATION

♦ **See Figure 37**

1. Place the steering wheel and front wheels in the centered (straight ahead) position.

➡**Anytime the steering linkage is disconnected from the spindle, the steering system must be centered before beginning the service procedure.**

2. Raise the van and support it safely with jackstands placed under the frame lifting pads. A hydraulic floor jack should be placed under the control arm to raise and lower the arm during coil spring removal. Make sure the van is supported securely on the jackstands and only work on one side at a time.

3. Remove the front wheel/tire assemblies from the van.

4. Remove the front stabilizer bar and end link from the lower control arm, as described earlier in this section.

5. Remove the coil spring as described earlier in this section.

6. Remove the bolts and nuts retaining the lower control arm to the crossmember and remove the lower control arm from the frame.

7. If new control arm bushings or ball joints are necessary, replace the entire lower control arm assembly.

To install:

8. Position the new lower control arm assembly to the frame crossmember, then install the retaining bolts in the proper direction as illustrated. Temporarily snug the bolts, but do not tighten to the full torque specifications yet.

9. Inspect the lower ball joint boot and replace it if necessary.

10. Install the coil spring as described earlier in this section.

11. Install the stabilizer bar and end links as described earlier in this section.

12. Install the front wheels and tires to the van.

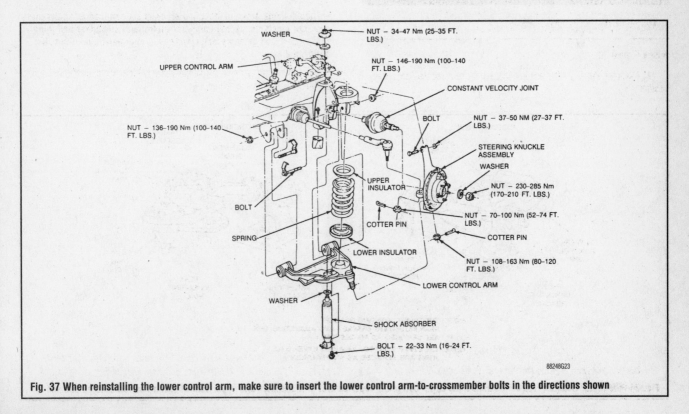

Fig. 37 When reinstalling the lower control arm, make sure to insert the lower control arm-to-crossmember bolts in the directions shown

13. Lower the van so that it rests in the normal ride position on a level surface.

14. Tighten the lower control arm-to-crossmember mounting bolts to 187–260 ft. lbs. (254–352 Nm) for 1986–90 models, and to 100–140 ft. lbs. (136–190 Nm) for 1991–97 models.

Knuckle and Spindle

REMOVAL & INSTALLATION

▶ See Figure 38

1. Place the steering wheel and front tires in the centered (straight ahead) position.

➡Any time the steering linkage is disconnected from the spindle, the steering system must be centered before beginning the service procedure.

2. Remove the front wheel covers, if necessary.

3. Remove the center hub nut and washer.

4. Raise the van, but do not yet support it on jackstands. Be very careful when the vehicle is lifted without being supported by jackstands.

5. Remove the spring tension from the upper and lower control arms. Support the lower control arm with jackstands, then lower the vehicle so that the spring is partially compressed enough to take the tension out of the spring **OR** compress the spring using a spring compressor tool until all spring tension is removed from the control arms. Once the correct height of the van is reached, support the vehicle frame with a second set of jackstands. The lower control arm is supported with one jackstands while the van is supported by jackstands on the frame; this positions the lower control arm in the proper position for knuckle and spindle service.

6. Remove the caliper, rotor and dust shield from the spindle. For more information, refer to Section 9.

7. Remove the cotter pin and nut retaining the tie rod end to the spindle's lower arm. Disconnect the tie rod end with a suitable Pitman arm puller such as tool T64P-3590-F or equivalent.

8. Install a hub remover/installer T81P-1104 (A, B and C adapters are needed) or equivalent. Free the hub, bearing and knuckle assembly from the halfshaft by pushing the outer CV joint shaft until it releases from the assembly.

9. If a spring compressor was utilized in Step 5, perform the following:

a. Support the lower control arm with a hydraulic floor jack. Make sure the jack pad securely contacts the control arm. Remove the cotter pin, then loosen the nut retaining the spindle to the lower control arm ball joint. Disconnect the lower ball joint from the spindle using the same Pitman arm puller used in Step 5, then remove the tool and ball joint retaining nut.

b. Slowly lower the jack under the control arm until the ball joint is disengaged from the spindle.

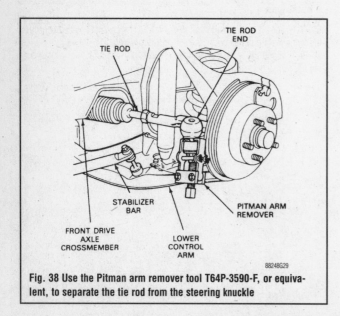

Fig. 38 Use the Pitman arm remover tool T64P-3590-F, or equivalent, to separate the tie rod from the steering knuckle

Use extreme caution when lowering the lower control arm. The coil spring may quickly expand with dangerous force. Never lower the control arm quickly.

c. Remove the bolt and nut retaining the spindle to the upper control arm ball joint, then remove the spindle from the van.

10. If the van was lowered in order to remove the spring tension in Step 5, perform the following steps:

a. Remove the retaining nut and bolt, then push up on the upper control arm until the ball joint stud is clear of the steering knuckle.

b. Remove the cotter pin and nut from the lower ball joint, then, using the Pitman Arm Puller T64P-3590-F or equivalent, remove the ball joint stud from the knuckle.

c. Remove the knuckle from the vehicle.

To install:

11. Position the steering knuckle on the CV-joint shaft. Check to see if the CV-joint shaft splines are in proper mesh.

12. Position the spindle's upper arm on the upper ball joint. Install and tighten the nut and bolt to 27–37 ft. lbs. (37–50 Nm). Inspect the upper and lower ball joint boot seals for damage and replace if necessary.

13. Position the spindle's lower arm over the lower ball joint stud, then **slowly** lift the lower control arm until the ball joint stud extends through the spindle arm and is seated in the spindle. Install the ball joint castle nut and tighten it to 80–120 ft. lbs. (108–163 Nm) for 1986–90 models, and to 59–81 ft. lbs. (80–110 Nm) for 1991–97 models. Install a new cotter pin through the castle nut. The castle nut may be tightened slightly to align the castellations with the cotter pin hole, but under no circumstances loosen the nut to align them.

14. Connect the tie rod end to the spindle arm. Firmly seat the tie rod end stud into the tapered hole to prevent rotation while tightening the castellated nut. Torque the tie rod nut to 52–74 ft. lbs. (70–100 Nm), then install a new cotter pin. The castle nut may be tightened slightly to align the castellations with the cotter pin hole, but under no circumstances loosen the nut to align.

15. Install the rotor and caliper. For more information, refer to Section 9.

16. Install the front tires, then tighten the lug nuts to 85–115 ft. lbs. (116–155 Nm).

17. Lower the vehicle.

18. Tighten the center hub nut to 170–210 ft. lbs. (230–285 Nm).

19. Install the wheel covers.

Front Hub and Wheel Bearing

REMOVAL & INSTALLATION

▶ See Figure 39

➡The front wheel bearing/hub assembly is non-serviceable and non-adjustable. The assembly has to be replaced as a complete unit.

1. Raise the vehicle and safely support it with jackstands.

2. Remove the front wheels.

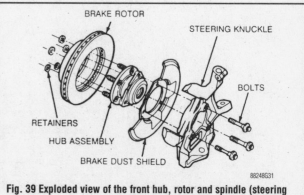

Fig. 39 Exploded view of the front hub, rotor and spindle (steering knuckle) mounting—the bearing/hub assembly is not serviceable, so the entire assembly should be replaced

3. Remove the brake caliper and rotor. For more information, refer to Section 9.

4. Remove the three bolts retaining the hub/bearing assembly to the spindle, then remove the hub/bearing assembly from the spindle.

To install:

5. Install the hub/bearing assembly to the steering knuckle, then tighten the three retaining bolts to 65 ft. lbs. (88 Nm).

6. Install the brake rotor and caliper. For more information, refer to Section 9.

7. Install the front wheels.

8. Lower the vehicle.

Front End Alignment

If the tires are worn unevenly, if the vehicle is not stable on the highway, or if the handling seems uneven in spirited driving, wheel alignment should be checked. If an alignment problem is suspected, first check tire inflation and look for other possible causes such as worn suspension and steering components, accident damage or unmatched tires. Repairs may be necessary before the wheels can be properly aligned. Wheel alignment requires sophisticated equipment and can only be performed at a properly equipped shop.

CASTER

Wheel alignment is defined by three different adjustments in three planes. Looking at the vehicle from the side, caster angle describes the steering axis rather than a wheel angle. The spindle (steering knuckle) is attached to the strut at the top and the control arm at the bottom. The wheel pivots around the line between these points to steer the vehicle. When the upper point is tilted back, this is described as positive caster. Having a positive caster tends to make the wheels self-centering, increasing directional stability. Excessive positive caster makes the wheels hard to steer, while an uneven caster will cause a pull to one side. Caster and camber are adjusted with shims and are closely interrelated; refer to the following camber procedure for caster adjustment.

CAMBER

Looking at the wheels from the front of the vehicle, camber adjustment is the tilt of the wheel. When the wheel is tilted in at the top, this is negative camber.

In a turn, a slight amount of negative camber helps maximize contact of the outside tire with the road. Too much negative camber makes the vehicle unstable in a straight line.

Caster and camber adjustment is provided by shims on the upper control arm. The two different shims initially provided from the assembly plant include one 2mm thickness and one 6mm thickness, for a total shim stack thickness of 8mm at each leg of the upper control arm. These shims are added, removed, or switched from the front and rear legs of the upper control arms as required to adjust the front end alignment.

Camber adjustment is obtained by removing or adding an equal number of shims to the front and rear leg of the wire arm. Caster adjustment is obtained by removing shims from the front leg and installing them on the rear leg, and vice-versa. If the same amount is switched from one leg to the other, caster will be changed but camber will not be affected. If unequal amounts are removed and added to the front and rear legs, both caster and camber will be changed.

TOE-IN

Looking down at the wheels from above the vehicle, toe alignment is the distance between the front of the wheels relative to the distance between the back of the wheels. If the wheels are closer at the front, they are said to be toed-in or to have a negative toe. A small amount of negative toe enhances directional stability and provides a smoother ride on the highway. On most front wheel drive vehicles, standard toe adjustment is either zero or slightly positive. When power is applied to the front wheels, they tend to toe-in naturally.

Toe-in should only be checked and adjusted after the caster and camber have been adjusted to specifications. Caster and camber adjustments change the position of the steering arms, thus affecting toe. Toe is defined as the difference between measurements taken between the front and rear of the tires. Positive toe or toe-in occurs when the front of the tires are pointed inboard of the rear of the tires. Negative toe or toe-out occurs when the front of the tires are pointed outboard of the rear of the tires. The toe specification is designed to provide optimum vehicle handling and tire life under a variety of driving and load carrying conditions.

➡**All wheel alignment adjustments and readings must be performed on an alignment rack level to within ¹⁄₁₆ in. (1.5mm) side-to-side and front-to-rear. Refer all alignment checks and adjustments to a qualified repair shop.**

REAR SUSPENSION

♦ **See Figure 40**

The Aerostar rear suspension is a coil spring type system. It supports and links the rear axle to the frame with one upper control arm and two lower control arms. The rear suspension uses low pressure gas shock absorbers, of the telescopic double acting type.

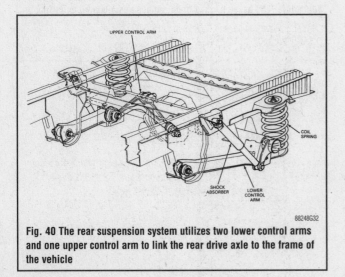

Fig. 40 The rear suspension system utilizes two lower control arms and one upper control arm to link the rear drive axle to the frame of the vehicle

Coil Springs

REMOVAL & INSTALLATION

♦ **See Figure 41**

1. Raise the vehicle and support it safely with jackstands placed beneath the frame rear lift points or under the rear bumper support brackets.

2. Support the rear axle assembly by placing a hydraulic floor jack under the differential housing.

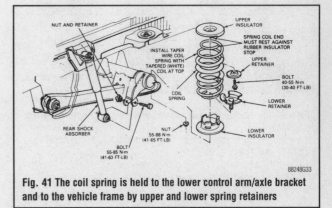

Fig. 41 The coil spring is held to the lower control arm/axle bracket and to the vehicle frame by upper and lower spring retainers

3. Remove the nut and bolt retaining the shock absorber to the axle mount on the lower control arm. Disconnect the shock absorber from the axle bracket.

4. Carefully lower the rear axle until the coil springs are no longer under compression.

5. Remove the nut securing the lower retainer and spring to the control arm.

6. Remove the bolt securing the upper retainer and spring to the frame.

7. Remove the spring and retainers, then remove the upper and lower insulators.

To install:

8. Before installing the spring, first make sure the axle is in the lowered (spring unloaded) position. Place the lower insulator on the control arm and the upper insulator at the top of the spring.

9. Install the coil spring in position between the control arm and vehicle frame. The small diameter, tapered coils (white colored) must face upward.

10. Install the upper retainer and bolt, then tighten the bolt to 30–40 ft. lbs. (40–55 Nm).

11. Install the lower retainer and nut, then tighten the nut to 41–65 ft. lbs. (55–88 Nm).

12. Raise the axle to the normal ride position with the hydraulic floor jack.

13. Position the shock absorber in the axle bracket, then install the bolt so the head is positioned outboard of the bracket. Install the nut and tighten it to 41–65 ft. lbs. (55–88 Nm).

14. Remove the jackstands and lower the vehicle.

Shock Absorber

REMOVAL & INSTALLATION

▶ **See Figures 42 thru 47**

❊❊ CAUTION

The low pressure gas shock absorbers are charged with 135 psi (930 kPa) of nitrogen gas. Do not attempt to open or heat the shock absorbers.

1. Raise the van and support it safely on jackstands. Place the jackstands under the axle to take the load off of the shock absorbers.

2. Remove the shock absorber lower attaching bolt and nut, then swing the lower end free of the mounting bracket on the axle housing.

3. Remove the attaching bolt and washer from the upper mounting bracket, then remove the shock absorber from the vehicle.

To install:

4. Position the upper end of the shock absorber in the upper mounting bracket, then install and tighten the upper nut and washer to 25–35 ft. lbs. (38–48 Nm) for 1986–90 models, and to 41–63 ft. lbs. (55–85 Nm) for 1991–97 models.

5. Pivot the lower end of the shock absorber into the lower bracket. Install the lower bolt and nut to 41–65 ft. lbs. (55–88 Nm).

6. Lower the vehicle.

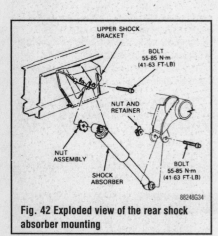

Fig. 42 Exploded view of the rear shock absorber mounting

Fig. 43 Before removing the rear shock absorber, support the rear axle with a hydraulic floor jack

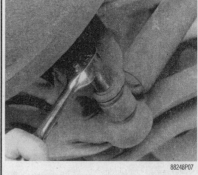

Fig. 44 Loosen the lower shock absorber mounting bolt, then . . .

Fig. 45 . . . remove the bolt, washer and nut

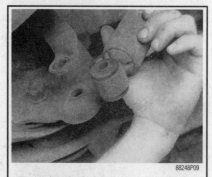

Fig. 46 Swing the lower end of the shock absorber out of the shock mounting bracket

Fig. 47 Remove the upper shock absorber mounting bolt, then remove the shock absorber from the vehicle

Control Arms/Links

REMOVAL & INSTALLATION

Lower Control Arm

▶ See Figure 48

1. Raise the vehicle and support it safely with jackstands placed beneath the frame rear lift points or under the rear bumper support brackets.

2. Remove the rear wheel(s).

3. Support the rear axle assembly at a normal ride height level by placing a hydraulic floor jack under the differential housing.

4. Remove the nut and bolt retaining the shock absorber to the axle mount on the lower control arm. Disconnect the shock absorber from the axle bracket.

5. Carefully lower the rear axle until the coil springs are no longer under compression.

6. Remove the nut retaining the lower retainer and spring to the control arm, then remove the spring insulator from the arm.

7. Remove the bolt and nut retaining the lower control arm to the axle housing.

8. Remove the nut and bolt retaining the lower control arm to the vehicle frame bracket, then remove the lower control arm from the vehicle.

To install:

9. Position the lower arm in the frame bracket. Install the bolt so that the head is inboard on the frame bracket. Install the nut but do not tighten at this time.

10. Position the lower control arm in the bracket on the axle housing. Install the bolt so the head is inboard on the axle bracket. Install the nut but do not tighten at this time.

11. Install the insulator on the lower control arm.

12. With the axle in the lowered (spring unloaded) position, install the coil spring and lower retainer on the lower control arm.

13. Install the nut attaching the retainer and spring to the lower control arm. Tighten the nut to 41–65 ft. lbs. (55–88 Nm).

14. Raise the axle to the normal load position, then tighten the nut and bolt retaining the lower control arm to the axle housing to 100–145 ft. lbs. (135–197 Nm) for 1986–90 models, and to 95–130 ft. lbs. (129–177 Nm) for 1991–97 models. Tighten the nut and bolt retaining the lower control arm to the frame bracket to 100–145 ft. lbs. (135–197 Nm) for 1986–90 models, and to 95–130 ft. lbs. (129–177 Nm) for 1991–97 models.

15. Position the shock absorber in the lower axle mounting bracket, then install the bolt so that the head is outboard of the axle bracket. Install the nut and tighten it to 41–65 ft. lbs. (55–88 Nm).

16. Install the wheel(s).

17. Remove the jackstands and lower the vehicle.

Upper Control Arm

▶ See Figures 49 and 50

1. Raise the vehicle and support it safely with jackstands placed beneath the frame rear lift points or under the rear bumper support brackets.

2. Support the rear axle assembly at a normal ride height level by placing a hydraulic floor jack under the differential housing.

3. Remove the nut and bolt retaining the shock absorber to the axle mount on the lower control arm. Disconnect the shock absorber from the axle bracket.

4. Carefully lower the rear axle until the coil springs are no longer under compression.

➡ To ease control arm removal, follow the next three steps in the exact sequence. If the left bracket attachments are loosened prior to disengaging the arm from the right bracket, the decompressed left bushing will force the arm against the right hand bracket and make removal difficult.

5. Remove the upper control arm-to-rear axle bolt and nut. Disconnect the upper control arm from the axle. Scribe a mark aligning the position of the cam adjuster in the axle bushing. The cam adjuster controls the rear axle pinion angle for driveline angularity.

6. Remove the bolt and nut retaining the upper control arm to the right frame bracket. Rotate the arm to disengage it from the body bracket.

7. Remove the nut and washer retaining the upper control arm to the left frame bracket. Remove the outer insulator and spacer, then remove the control arm from the bracket. Remove the inner insulator and washer from the control arm stud.

To install:

8. Position the washer and inner insulator on the control arm stud. Install the control arm so the stud extends through the left frame bracket. Install the spacer and outer insulator over the stud, then install the nut and washer assembly and tighten until snug. Do not tighten to specified torque at this time.

9. Position the upper control arm in the right frame bracket, then install the bolt and nut and tighten until snug. Do not tighten to specified torque at this time.

10. Making sure the scribe marks on the cam adjuster and axle bushing are in alignment, connect the upper control arm to the axle. Install the nut and bolt and tighten until snug. Do not tighten to specified torque at this time.

11. Raise the axle to the normal ride position.

12. Position the shock absorber in the lower mounting bracket, then install the bolt so the head is outboard of the axle bracket. Install the nut and tighten to 41–65 ft. lbs. (55–88 Nm).

13. With the axle in the normal ride position, tighten all upper control arm fasteners to the specified torque. Tighten the nut and washer assembly retaining the control arm to the left frame bracket to 60–100 ft. lbs. (81–135 Nm). Tighten the nut and bolt retaining the control arm to the right frame bracket to 100–145 ft. lbs. (135–197 Nm) for 1986–90 models, and to 92–133 ft. lbs. (125–170

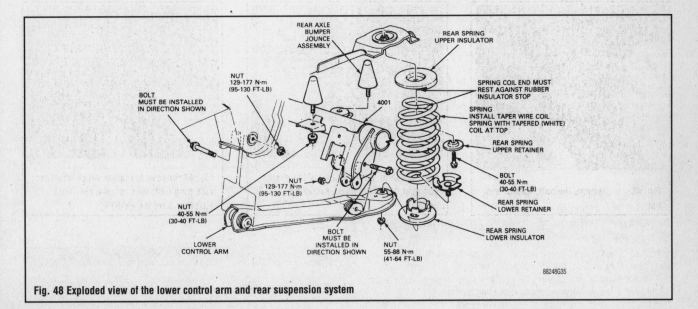

Fig. 48 Exploded view of the lower control arm and rear suspension system

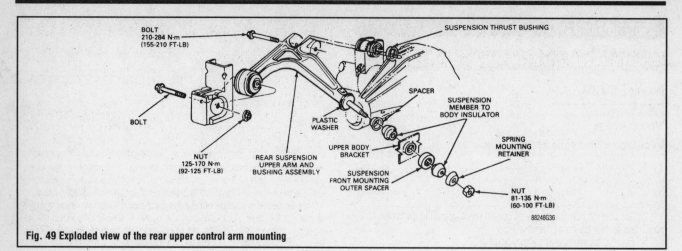

Fig. 49 Exploded view of the rear upper control arm mounting

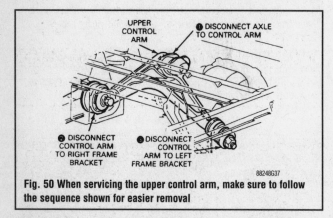

Fig. 50 When servicing the upper control arm, make sure to follow the sequence shown for easier removal

Nm) for 1991–97 models. Tighten the nut and bolt retaining the control arm to the axle to 100–145 ft. lbs. (135–197 Nm) for 1986–90 models, and to 155–210 ft. lbs. (210–284 Nm) for 1991–97 models.

14. Remove the jackstands and lower the vehicle.

Rear Wheel Bearings

REPLACEMENT

♦ **See Figures 51 and 52**

The rear wheel bearing is pressed into the outer axle tube housing. A grease seal is pressed into the tube over the bearing. The axle shaft is retained in the carrier assembly by a C-clip in the differential case. When the C-clip is removed, the axle shaft can be removed from the axle tube.

1. Remove the rear axle shaft. For more information, refer to Section 7.
2. Insert a rear axle bearing remover T85L-1225-AH and an impact slide hammer T50T-100-A, or equivalents, into the axle bore. Position it behind the rear wheel bearing so that the tangs on the tool engage the bearing outer race. Remove the rear wheel bearing and inner wheel bearing oil seal as a unit, using the impact slide hammer.

To install:

3. Lubricate the new rear wheel bearing with rear axle lubricant, then install it into the housing bore using an axle tube bearing replacer T78P-1225-A, or equivalent.
4. Apply premium long-life grease XG-1-C or equivalent between the lips of the inner wheel bearing oil seal.

❊❊ WARNING

Installation of the rear wheel bearing or inner wheel bearing oil seal assembly without the proper tool may result in premature failure. If the inner wheel bearing oil seal becomes cocked in the bore during installation, remove it and install a new one.

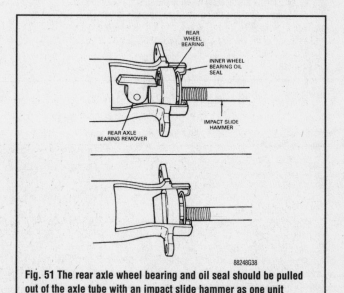

Fig. 51 The rear axle wheel bearing and oil seal should be pulled out of the axle tube with an impact slide hammer as one unit

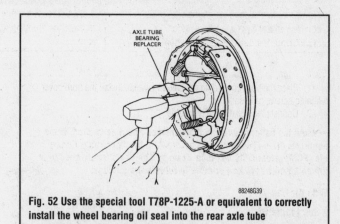

Fig. 52 Use the special tool T78P-1225-A or equivalent to correctly install the wheel bearing oil seal into the rear axle tube

5. Install a new inner wheel bearing oil seal using an axle tube seal replacer tool T78P-1177-A or equivalent, as shown in the accompanying illustration.
6. Install the rear axle shaft. For more information, refer to Section 7 in this manual.

Rear End Alignment

The rear suspension systems of the Aerostar models are not adjustable and, therefore, do not require alignments.

STEERING

Steering Wheel

REMOVAL & INSTALLATION

Without Air Bag

▶ **See Figures 53, 54 and 55**

1. Center the front wheels to the straight-ahead position.
2. Disconnect the negative battery cable.
3. Remove the steering wheel horn cover by removing the screws from the spokes and lifting the horn cover off of the steering wheel.
4. Separate the horn switch/speed control wires by pulling the connectors apart, then remove the horn cover assembly.
5. Remove the steering wheel attaching bolt.
6. Matchmark the steering wheel to the steering column shaft.
7. Using a suitable steering wheel puller, such as tool T67L–3600–A or equivalent, remove the steering wheel from the upper steering shaft. Do not strike the end of the steering column upper shaft with a hammer or steering shaft bearing damage will occur.

To install:

8. Install the steering wheel onto the steering column so that the scribe marks align.
9. Install the steering wheel retaining bolt to 23–33 ft. lbs. (31–45 Nm).
10. Attach the horn switch/speed control wires to the horn cover.

4. Disconnect the air bag wiring harness from the air bag module, then remove the module from the wheel.
5. Separate the speed control wires by pulling the connectors apart, if so equipped.
6. Remove the steering wheel attaching bolt.
7. Using a suitable steering wheel puller, such as tool T67L-3600-A or equivalent, remove the steering wheel from the upper steering shaft. Route the contact assembly wiring harness through the steering wheel as the wheel is lifted off of the shaft. Do not strike the end of the steering column upper shaft with a hammer otherwise the steering shaft bearing will be damaged.

To install:

8. Make sure that the vehicle's front wheels are pointing straight ahead.
9. Route the contact assembly wiring harness through the steering wheel opening at the three o'clock position, then position the steering wheel on the steering column shaft. The steering wheel and shaft alignment marks should be aligned, Make certain that the air bag module wiring harness is not pinched.
10. Install a new steering wheel retaining bolt to 23–33 ft. lbs. (31–45 Nm).
11. Attach the speed control wire to the wheel, then snap the connector assembly into the steering wheel clip.

✳✳ WARNING

Be sure that the wiring does not get trapped between the steering wheel and contact assembly.

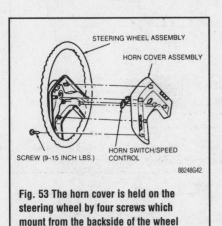

Fig. 53 The horn cover is held on the steering wheel by four screws which mount from the backside of the wheel

Fig. 54 After removing the horn cover, remove the steering wheel retaining bolt, then . . .

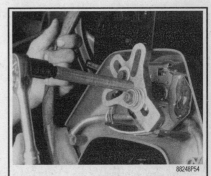

Fig. 55 . . . use a steering wheel puller to remove the steering wheel from the steering column

11. Place the horn cover onto the steering wheel. Install the horn cover retaining screws until snug.
12. Connect the negative battery cable.

➡ **When the battery has been disconnected and reconnected, some abnormal drive symptoms may occur while the Powertrain Control Module (PCM) relearns its adaptive strategy. The vehicle may need to be driven 10 miles (16 km) or more to relearn the strategy.**

With Air Bag

▶ **See Figure 56**

1. Center the front wheels to the straight-ahead position.
2. Disconnect the negative battery cable and air bag backup power supply. For more information, refer to Section 6.

✳✳ WARNING

The back-up power supply must be disconnected before any air bag component is serviced.

3. Remove the four air bag module retaining nuts, then lift the air bag module off of the steering wheel.

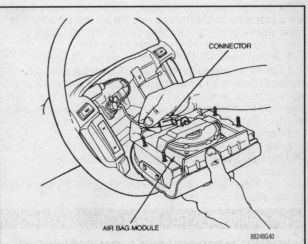

Fig. 56 Before lifting the air bag module completely away from the steering wheel, make sure to disconnect the air bag system wiring harness from the module

12. Connect the air bag wiring harness to the air bag module, then install the module onto the steering wheel. Tighten the module retaining nuts to 3–4 ft. lbs. (4–6 Nm).

13. Connect the air bag backup power supply and negative battery cable. Verify the air bag warning indicator in the instrument panel.

➡When the battery has been disconnected and reconnected, some abnormal drive symptoms may occur while the Powertrain Control Module (PCM) relearns its adaptive strategy. The vehicle may need to be driven 10 miles (16 km) or more to relearn the strategy.

Turn Signal (Combination) Switch

REMOVAL & INSTALLATION

1986–91 Models

▶ See Figure 57

1. Disconnect the negative battery cable.
2. Remove the steering wheel as described earlier in this section. If equipped with tilt column, remove the upper extension shroud by squeezing it at the six and twelve o'clock positions and popping it free of the retaining plate at the three o'clock position.
3. Remove the two trim shroud halves from the steering column by removing the attaching screws.
4. Remove the turn signal switch lever by grasping the lever and using a pulling/twisting motion of the hand while pulling the lever straight out from the switch.
5. If so equipped, peel back the foam sight shield from the turn signal switch.
6. Disconnect the two turn signal switch electrical connectors.
7. Remove the two self-tapping screws attaching the turn signal switch to the lock cylinder housing, then disengage the switch from the housing.

To install:
8. To install, first align the turn signal switch mounting holes with the corresponding holes in the lock cylinder housing and install the two self-tapping screws. Tighten the screws until snug.
9. Position the foam sight shield to the turn signal switch.
10. For 1986–91 models, install the turn signal switch lever into the switch manually by aligning the key on the lever with the keyway in the switch and by pushing the lever toward the switch until fully engaged.
11. Connect the turn signal switch electrical connectors, then install the steering column shrouds.
12. Install the steering wheel as described earlier in this section.
13. Connect the negative battery cable.

1992–97 Models

▶ See Figures 58 and 59

1. Make sure that the vehicle's front wheels are in the straight-ahead position and the steering column shaft alignment mark is at the 12 o'clock position.
2. Disconnect battery ground cable and, if applicable, the air bag backup power supply. For more information and service precautions, refer to Section 6.

➡Before servicing the air bag module, refer to the Supplemental Restraint System (SRS) service precautions in Section 6 of this manual.

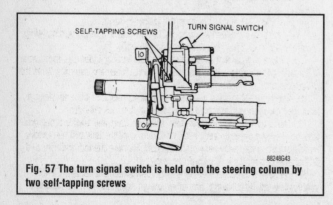

Fig. 57 The turn signal switch is held onto the steering column by two self-tapping screws

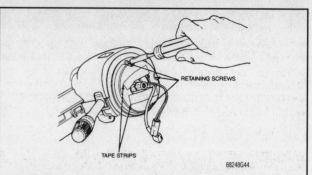

Fig. 58 Use two strips of tape on the contact assembly to keep it from rotating after removal—vehicles equipped with Supplemental Restraint System (SRS)

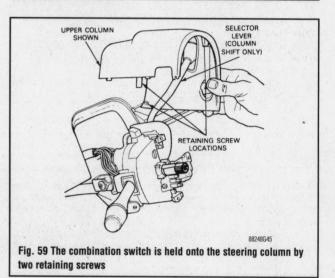

Fig. 59 The combination switch is held onto the steering column by two retaining screws

3. Remove the steering wheel as described earlier in this section.
4. Remove the right and left mouldings from the instrument panel by pulling the panels up and snapping them out of the retainer.
5. Remove the instrument panel lower trim panel and lower steering column shroud.
6. For vehicles equipped with air bags, perform the following steps:
   a. Disconnect the air bag contact assembly wiring harness.
   b. Apply two strips of tape across the contact assembly stator and rotor to prevent accidental rotation.
   c. Remove the three contact assembly retaining screws, then pull the contact assembly off of the steering column shaft.
7. Unplug the two combination switch electrical connectors from the combination switch.
8. Remove the two combination switch retaining screws, then lift the switch off of the steering column.

To install:
9. Position the combination switch onto the steering column.
10. Attach the two combination switch electrical connectors to the switch, then install the two switch retaining screws until snug.
11. For vehicles equipped with air bags, perform the following steps:
   a. Make sure that the vehicle's front wheels are still pointing to the front and that the steering column shaft alignment mark is at the 12 o'clock position.
   b. Align the contact assembly to the column shaft and mounting bosses. Slide the contact assembly onto the steering column shaft.
   c. Install the three contact retaining screws until snug. Remove the tape strips.
   d. Route the contact assembly wiring harness down the steering column, then attach the electrical harness connectors.

➡If a new contact assembly is being installed, remove the plastic lock mechanism after the contact is secured to the steering column.

12. Install the lower shroud and the instrument panel cover.
13. Install the steering wheel as described earlier in this section.
14. If applicable, connect the air bag backup power supply.
15. Connect the negative battery cable.

➡ **When the battery has been disconnected and reconnected, some abnormal drive symptoms may occur while the Powertrain Control Module (PCM) relearns its adaptive strategy. The vehicle may need to be driven 10 miles (16 km) or more to relearn the strategy.**

16. Verify that the air bag warning indicator illuminates and functions correctly.

Ignition Switch

REMOVAL & INSTALLATION

▶ **See Figures 60 and 61**

1. Rotate the lock cylinder key to the LOCK position and disconnect the negative battery cable.
2. For 1986–91 models with tilt columns, remove the upper extension shroud by squeezing it at the six and twelve o'clock positions and popping it free of the retaining plate at the three o'clock position.
3. Remove the two trim shroud halves by removing the two attaching screws.
4. Detach the ignition switch electrical connector.
5. For 1986–91 models, drill out the break-off head bolts connecting the switch to the lock cylinder housing with a ⅛ in. (3mm) drill, then remove the two bolts using an EX-3 screw extractor tool or equivalent screw extractor.
6. For 1992–97 models, remove the two retaining screws from the ignition switch.
7. Disengage the ignition switch from the actuator pin and remove the switch.

To install:

8. Rotate the ignition key to the RUN position (approximately 90° clockwise from LOCK).
9. Install the replacement switch by aligning the holes on the switch casting base with the holes in the lock cylinder housing. Note that the replacement switch

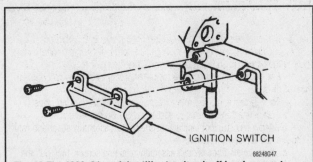

88248G47

Fig. 60 The 1986–91 models utilize two break-off head screws to hold the ignition switch to the steering column

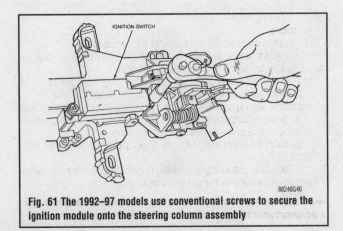

88248G46

Fig. 61 The 1992–97 models use conventional screws to secure the ignition module onto the steering column assembly

is provided in the RUN position. Minor movement of the lock cylinder to align the actuator pin with the U-shaped slot in the switch carrier may be necessary.

10. Install new break-off head bolts and tighten until the heads shear off.
11. Attach the electrical connector to the ignition switch.
12. Connect the negative battery terminal, then check the ignition switch for proper operation in all modes. If correct, install the steering column shrouds.

Ignition Lock Cylinder

REMOVAL & INSTALLATION

Operational Lock Cylinders

▶ **See Figures 62 and 63**

➡ **The following procedure pertains to vehicles that have functional lock cylinders and ignition keys.**

1. Disconnect the negative battery cable.
2. For 1986–91 models, remove the trim shroud, then remove the electrical connector from the key warning switch.
3. Turn the lock cylinder to the RUN position.
4. Place a ⅛ in. (3mm) diameter pin or small drift punch in the hole located at 4 o'clock and 1¼ in. (32mm) from the outer edge of the lock cylinder housing. Depress the retaining pin and pull out the lock cylinder.

To install:

5. On 1986–91 models, prior to installing the lock cylinder, lubricate the cylinder cavity, including the drive gear with lock lubricant D8AZ-19587-A or equivalent.
6. Turn the lock cylinder to the RUN position, depress the retaining pin, and insert it into the lock cylinder housing. Make sure the cylinder is fully seated and aligned into the interlocking washer before turning the key to the OFF position. This action will permit the cylinder retaining pin to extend into the hole in the lock cylinder housing.
7. Using the ignition key, rotate the lock cylinder to insure correct mechanical operation in all positions. Install the electrical connector onto the key warning switch.
8. Connect the negative battery cable, then check for proper ignition functions and verify that the column is locked in the LOCK position. Install the trim shrouds.

➡ **When the battery has been disconnected and reconnected, some abnormal drive symptoms may occur while the Powertrain Control Module (PCM) relearns its adaptive strategy. The vehicle may need to be driven 10 miles (16 km) or more to relearn the strategy.**

Non-Operational Lock Cylinders

▶ **See Figure 64**

➡ **The following procedure applies to vehicles where the ignition lock is inoperative and the lock cylinder cannot be rotated due to a lost or broken ignition key.**

1. Disconnect the negative battery cable.
2. Remove the horn cover (or air bag module) and the steering wheel, as described earlier in this section.
3. Remove the trim shrouds and the connector from the key warning switch.
4. For 1986–91 models, perform the following steps:
   a. Use a ⅛ in. (3mm) diameter drill to drill out the retaining pin, being careful not to drill any deeper than ½ in. (13mm).
   b. Place a chisel at the base of the ignition lock cylinder cap, then use a hammer to strike the chisel with sharp blows to break the cap away from the lock cylinder.
5. For 1992–97 models, use a pair of locking pliers, or the equivalent, to twist the lock cylinder cap until it separates from the lock cylinder.
6. Using a ⅜ in. (10mm) diameter drill, drill down the middle of the ignition lock key slot approximately 1¾ in. (45mm) until the lock cylinder breaks loose from the break-away base of the cylinder. Remove the lock cylinder and drill shavings from the lock cylinder housing.
7. Remove the retainer, washer and ignition switch and actuator. Thoroughly clean all drill shavings and other foreign materials from the casting.

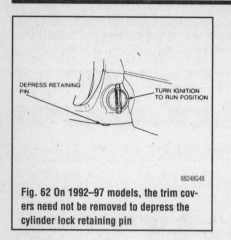

Fig. 62 On 1992–97 models, the trim covers need not be removed to depress the cylinder lock retaining pin

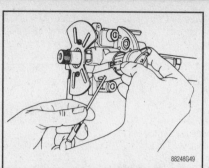

Fig. 63 Remove the lock cylinder by pushing the retaining pin in with a drift or punch and pulling the cylinder out of its bore

Fig. 64 Remove the snapring, washer and drive gear, then clean the components of any metal shavings before replacing the lock cylinder

8. Carefully inspect the lock cylinder housing for damage from the removal operation. If any damage is apparent, the housing must be replaced.

To install:

9. Position the lock drive gear in the base of the lock cylinder housing in the same position as noted during the removal procedure. The position of the lock drive gear is correct if the last tooth on the drive gear meshes with the last tooth on the rack. Verify correct gear to rack alignment by inserting a flat bladed screwdriver in the recess of the gear and rotating it to the full counterclockwise position. After verification, rotate the drive gear back to the original removal position. Install the washer and retainer. Note that the flats in the recess of the drive gear align with the flats in the washer.

10. Install the ignition lock cylinder as described in the previous procedure.
11. Connect the key warning switch wire, then install the shroud.
12. Install the steering wheel and horn cover or air bag module.
13. Connect the negative battery cable.
14. Check for proper ignition and accessory operation and verify that the column locks in the LOCK position.

➡ When the battery has been disconnected and reconnected, some abnormal drive symptoms may occur while the Powertrain Control Module (PCM) relearns its adaptive strategy. The vehicle may need to be driven 10 miles (16 km) or more to relearn the strategy.

Steering Linkage

REMOVAL & INSTALLATION

Outer Tie Rod End

♦ **See Figures 65 thru 70**

1. Position the front wheels so that they point straight ahead.
2. Mark the tie rod end jam nut on the tie rod threads for installation purposes.

Fig. 65 To remove the tie rod ends, first slightly loosen the tie rod jam nut, then . . .

Fig. 66 . . . remove the cotter pin retaining the tie rod castle nut

Fig. 67 Loosen, then remove the tie rod end castle nut

Fig. 68 Using a Pitman arm puller, or equivalent, separate the tie rod end from the steering knuckle

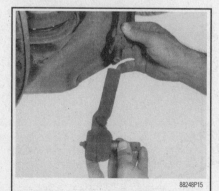

Fig. 69 Unthread the tie rod from the rack and pinion steering gear rod, then . . .

Fig. 70 . . . measure the length of the exposed threads to help facilitate installation of the new tie rod ends

3. Remove and discard the cotter pin from the lower tie rod joint stud, then remove the nut.

4. Separate the tie rod ends from the spindle arms using remover tool T64P-3590-F, or the equivalent.

5. Hold the tie rod end with a wrench and loosen the tie rod jam nut.

6. Grip the inner tie rod with locking pliers, then remove the tie rod end. Note the number of turns required to remove the tie rod end.

To install:

7. Thread the new outer tie rod onto the inner tie rod the same number of turns recorded during removal. Snug the jam nut against the outer tie rod end in the position marked prior to removal, then tighten the jam nut to 35–60 ft. lbs. (48–68 Nm).

8. With the steering gear, steering wheel and front wheels in the centered position, attach the tie rod ends to the spindle arms. Install the nuts and tighten them to 52–73 ft. lbs. (70–100 Nm). Install a new cotter pin. If required, advance the castle nut to the next castellation if the hole in the nut and stud do not line up. Do not loosen the nuts to line up the cotter pin hole.

➡**Make sure the tie rod ball studs are seated in the spindle tapers to prevent rotation while tightening the nut.**

9. Have the front end alignment checked at a qualified service shop.

Power Rack and Pinion

REMOVAL & INSTALLATION

1986–90 Models

▶ **See Figure 71**

1. Start the engine, then rotate the steering gear from lock to lock (entire gear travel) and record the number of steering wheel rotations. Divide the number of steering wheel rotations by two to get the required number of turns to place the steering wheel in the centered (straight ahead) position. From one lock position, rotate the steering wheel the required number of turns to center the steering rack.

2. Stop the engine, then disconnect the negative battery cable.

3. Turn the ignition switch to the **ON** position, then raise the vehicle and support it safely.

4. Remove the bolt retaining the lower intermediate steering column shaft to the steering gear, then disconnect the shaft from the gear.

5. Disconnect the pressure and return lines from the steering gear valve housing. Plug the lines and ports in the steering gear valve housing to prevent the entry of dirt into the system.

6. Remove and discard the cotter pin retaining the nut to the tie rod ends. Remove the nut, then separate the tie rod ends from the spindle arms using remover tool T64P-3590-F, or equivalent.

7. Support the steering gear and remove the two nuts, bolts and washers retaining the gear to the crossmember. Remove the gear and, if required, remove the front and rear insulators from the gear housing.

To install:

8. Install the insulators in the gear housing, if removed. The rubber insulators must be pushed completely inside the gear housing before the gear is

installed against the crossmember. No gap is allowed between the insulator and the face of the rear boss. Use rubber lubricant or soapy water to facilitate installation of the insulators in the gear housing.

9. Position the steering gear on the crossmember, then install the nuts, bolts and washers. Tighten the nuts to 65–90 ft. lbs. (88–122 Nm).

10. Connect the pressure and return lines to the appropriate ports on the steering gear valve housing, then tighten the fittings to 10–15 ft. lbs. (15–20 Nm). The fitting design allows the hoses to swivel when properly tightened. Do not attempt to eliminate this looseness by overtightening or damage to the fittings will occur.

11. With the steering gear, steering wheel and front wheels in the centered position, attach the tie rod ends to the spindle arms. Install the nuts and tighten them to 52–73 ft. lbs. (70–100 Nm). If required, advance the castle nuts to the next castellation and install new cotter pins. Do not loosen the nuts to line up the cotter pin hole.

➡**Make sure the tie rod ball studs are seated in the spindle tapers to prevent rotation while tightening the nut.**

12. Connect the steering column intermediate shaft to the gear pinion, then install the bolt and tighten it to 30–42 ft. lbs. (41–57 Nm).

13. Lower the vehicle and turn the ignition key to the **OFF** position, then connect the negative battery cable.

14. Check the power steering fluid level in the pump and top off as required.

15. Have the front end alignment checked at a qualified service shop.

1991–97 Models

TWO WHEEL DRIVE VEHICLES

▶ **See Figures 72 thru 79**

1. Turn the ignition key to the **OFF** position.

2. On vehicles equipped with automatic transmissions, position the transmission selector in PARK and set the hand brake.

3. For vehicles equipped with manual transmissions, put the gear shift lever in reverse and set the hand brake.

4. Raise and safely support the front of the vehicle on jackstands.

5. Remove the front wheels.

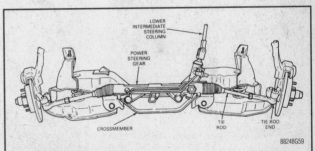

Fig. 72 The power steering rack and pinion assembly is mounted to the front crossmember by two bolts—1991–97 rear wheel drive models

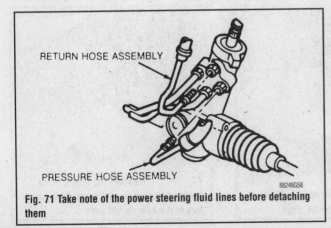

Fig. 71 Take note of the power steering fluid lines before detaching them

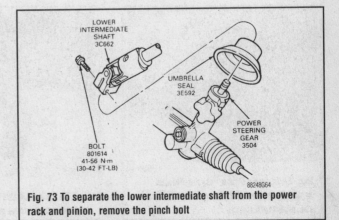

Fig. 73 To separate the lower intermediate shaft from the power rack and pinion, remove the pinch bolt

6. Remove the lower intermediate steering column shaft retaining bolt from the steering gear.

7. Disconnect the shaft from the steering gear.

8. Unscrew the quick connect fitting for the power steering pressure and return lines at the rack and pinion steering gear valve housing.

➡ **Do not remove the right and left transfer tube fitting.**

9. Plug the ends of the fluid lines removed from the steering gear and the ports in the steering gear valve housing to prevent damage and entry of dirt.

10. Remove and discard the cotter pin retaining the tie rod end.

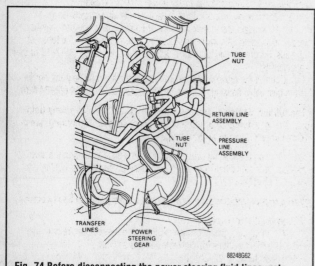

Fig. 74 Before disconnecting the power steering fluid lines, note which line goes to which valve connection

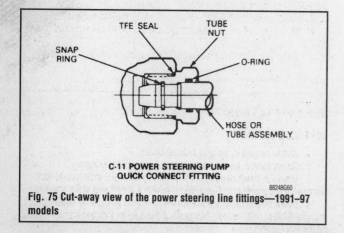

C-11 POWER STEERING PUMP QUICK CONNECT FITTING

Fig. 75 Cut-away view of the power steering line fittings—1991–97 models

11. Remove the tie rod nut.

12. Separate the steering tie rod ends from the spindle using a Pitman arm puller T64P-3590-F or equivalent.

13. Support the steering gear and remove the two nuts, bolts, and washer assemblies retaining the steering gear to the vehicle crossmember.

14. Remove the steering gear from the vehicle. If required, remove the front and rear insulators from the gear housing.

To install:

15. If removed, install the insulators into the steering gear housing.

➡ **The larger end of the inner sleeve faces the rear of the vehicle and contacts the crossmember.**

16. Push the insulators in until there is no space between the lip on the insulator and edge of the steering gear housing.

17. Position the steering gear on the crossmember. Install the nuts, bolts and washers retaining the gear to the crossmember. Tighten the nuts to 80–105 ft. lbs. (108–142 Nm).

18. Unplug the power steering fluid lines and steering gear valve housing.

19. If required, replace the TFE seal on the power steering pressure and return line quick connect fitting. Install a new seal as follows:

a. Unscrew the tube nut, then replace the plastic seal washer.

b. To facilitate assembly of the new TFE seal, a tapered shaft may be required to stretch the washer so that it may be slipped over the tube nut threads. Recommended tools are D90P-3517-A2 and D90P-3517-A3 or their equivalents.

20. Connect the pressure and return lines to the appropriate ports on the steering gear valve housing. Tighten the fittings to 20–25 ft. lbs. (27–34 Nm).

➡ **The fittings' design allows the hoses to swivel when properly tightened. Do not attempt to eliminate looseness by over-tightening, since this can cause damage to the fittings.**

21. With the steering gear, steering wheel and front wheels in the straight ahead position, attach the tie rod ends to the spindle arms. Tighten the tie rod nuts to 52–73 ft. lbs. (70–100 Nm).

SEAL INSTALLATION TOOLS D90P-3517-A2 AND D90P-3517-A3 OR EQUIVALENT

Fig. 76 A tool, such as the one shown, is extremely helpful in installing a new TFE seal

Fig. 77 To remove the rack and pinion assembly, first disconnect the intermediate shaft from the gear, . . .

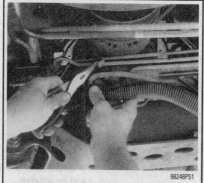

Fig. 78 . . . detach the power steering line clips and attached lines, then . . .

Fig. 79 . . . remove the steering gear-to-crossmember bolts

➡ **Make sure that the tie rod end ball studs are seated in the tapered spindle holes to prevent rotation while tightening the nut.**

22. If necessary, advance the tie rod nuts to the next slot, then install a new cotter pin.

23. Position the steering column lower intermediate shaft over the steering gear input shaft spline and dust seal. Replace the pinch bolt and tighten it to 30–42 ft. lbs. (41–56 Nm).

➡ **Verify that no rotation from the straight ahead position has occurred.**

24. Install the front wheels.

25. Lower the vehicle.

26. Refill the power steering pump reservoir with the proper fluid.

27. Purge air from the power steering system. Verify the absence of any unusual power steering noise.

28. Have the front end aligned by a qualified automotive mechanic.

29. Make sure that the power steering system operates correctly and is not leaking.

30. Check and adjust the fluid level in the power steering pump reservoir.

ALL WHEEL DRIVE VEHICLES

1. Start the engine, then rotate the steering gear from lock to lock (entire gear travel) and record the number of steering wheel rotations. Divide the number of steering wheel rotations by two to get the required number of turns to place the steering wheel in the centered (straight ahead) position. From one lock position, rotate the steering wheel the required number of turns to center the steering rack.

➡ **Verify that the front wheels and steering wheel are in the straight ahead position.**

2. Stop the engine, then disconnect the negative battery cable.

3. On automatic transmissions, put the transmission selector in PARK and set the hand brake.

4. On manual transmissions, put the gear shift lever in Reverse and set the hand brake.

5. Remove the front hub caps.

6. Remove the hub nut and washer.

7. Raise the vehicle and support it safely on jackstands.

8. Remove the front wheels.

9. Remove the bolt retaining the lower intermediate steering column shaft to the steering gear, then disconnect the shaft from the gear.

10. Disconnect the pressure and return lines from the steering gear valve housing. Plug the lines and ports in the steering gear valve housing to prevent the entry of dirt into the system.

11. Remove both steering knuckles, as described earlier in this section.

12. Remove both lower control arms, as described earlier in this section.

13. Remove the five nuts from the forward edge of the crossmember lower plate assembly.

14. Remove the nut from the driver side rear edge of the crossmember lower plate assembly.

15. Remove the two bolts from the center and passenger side rear edge of the crossmember lower plate assembly.

16. Remove the lower plate.

17. While supporting the steering gear, remove the two bolts and spacers retaining the steering gear to the crossmember.

18. Remove the power steering rack and pinion gear from the vehicle.

To install:

19. If removed, install the insulators into the steering gear housing.

➡ **The larger end of the inner sleeve faces the rear of the vehicle and contacts the crossmember.**

20. Push the insulators in until there is no space between the lip on the insulator and edge of the steering gear housing.

21. Position the steering gear on the crossmember. Install the nuts, bolts and washers retaining the gear to the crossmember. Tighten the nuts to 61–82 ft. lbs. (83–111 Nm).

22. Install the crossmember lower plate by inserting the studs on the plate through the front edge of the crossmember.

23. Install the two bolts in the center and passenger side of the crossmember lower plate assembly. Tighten the nuts to 35–47 ft. lbs. (47–64 Nm).

24. Install the nut on the stud located at the driver side rear edge of the crossmember lower plate assembly. Tighten it to 22–30 ft. lbs. (30–41 Nm).

25. Install the five nuts on the studs at the forward edge of the crossmember lower plate assembly. Tighten these nuts also to 22–30 ft. lbs. (30–41 Nm).

26. Install both front lower control arms, as described earlier in this section.

27. Install both steering knuckles, as described earlier in this section.

➡ **Make sure that the steering gear and front wheels are in the straight ahead position before attaching the tie rod ends to the steering knuckles. Make sure that the tie rod end ball studs are seated in the tapered spindle holes to prevent rotation while tightening the nut.**

28. Unplug the power steering fluid lines and steering gear valve housing.

29. If required, replace the TFE seal on the power steering pressure and return line quick connect fitting. Install a new seal as follows:

    a. Unscrew the tube nut, then replace the plastic seal washer.

    b. To facilitate assembly of the new TFE seal, a tapered shaft may be required to stretch the washer so that it may be slipped over the tube nut threads. Recommended tools are D90P-3517-A2 and D90P-3517-A3 or their equivalents.

30. Connect the pressure and return lines to the appropriate ports on the steering gear valve housing. Tighten the fittings to 20–25 ft. lbs. (27–34 Nm).

➡ **The fittings' design allows the hoses to swivel when properly tightened. Do not attempt to eliminate looseness by over-tightening, since this can cause damage to the fittings.**

31. Position the steering column lower intermediate shaft over the steering gear input shaft spline and dust seal. Replace the pinch bolt and tighten it to 30–42 ft. lbs. (41–56 Nm).

➡ **Verify that no rotation from the straight ahead position has occurred.**

32. Install the front wheels.

33. Install the hub nuts and washers. For more information, refer to the steering knuckle procedure located earlier in this section.

34. Install the front hub caps.

35. Lower the vehicle.

36. Refill the power steering pump reservoir with the proper fluid.

37. Purge air from the power steering system. Verify the absence of any unusual power steering noise.

38. Have the front end aligned by a qualified automotive mechanic.

39. Make sure that the power steering system operates correctly and is not leaking.

40. Check and adjust the fluid level in the power steering pump reservoir.

ADJUSTMENTS

Rack Yoke Plug Preload

1986–90 MODELS

1. Attach the gear to a proper holding device.

2. Do not remove the external pressure lines unless necessary.

3. Drain the power steering fluid by rotating the input shaft lock-to-lock twice using the proper tool. Cover the ports with a shop towel while draining.

4. Insert an inch lb. torque wrench with a maximum capacity of 30–60 ft. lbs. (41–81 Nm) into the tool, then position the adapter tool and torque wrench on the input shaft splines.

5. Loosen the yoke plug locknut, using the proper tool

6. Loosen the yoke plug with an appropriate socket.

7. Rotate the input shaft so the rack is in the center of travel by counting the number of complete revolutions of the input shaft and dividing by two.

8. Tighten the yoke plug to 45–50 inch lbs. (5–6 Nm).

➡ **Clean the threads of the yoke plug prior to tightening to prevent a false reading.**

9. Back off the yoke plug approximately ⅛ turn (44° minimum to 54° maximum) until the torque required to initiate and sustain rotation of the input shaft is 7–18 inch lbs. (1–2 Nm).

10. Install the proper tool to hold the yoke plug locknut. While holding the yoke plug, tighten the locknut 44–66 ft. lbs. (61–89 Nm).

➡ **Do not allow the yoke plug to move while tightening or the preload will be affected.**

11. Recheck the input shaft torque after tightening the locknut.

Power Steering Pump

REMOVAL & INSTALLATION

➡An identification tag is attached to the power steering pump reservoir. The top line of this tag indicates the basic model number (HBC) and the suffix. Always use these tags when requesting service parts as there may be slight differences in internal components.

2.3L Engine

▶ See Figures 80 and 81

1. Drain the power steering fluid from the pump by disconnecting the fluid return hose at the reservoir and draining the fluid into a suitable container.
2. Remove the pressure hose from the pump. If required, disconnect and remove the power steering pressure switch from the fitting on the gear assembly. Detach the electrical connector from the switch and unscrew the switch from the fitting.
3. Loosen the pivot bolt and adjusting bolt on the alternator bracket to release belt tension, then remove the drive belt from the power steering pump pulley.
4. Install a steering pump pulley remover tool (T69L-10300-B or equivalent) on the pulley. Hold the pump and rotate the tool nut counterclockwise to remove the pulley. Do not apply in-and-out pressure on the pump shaft or the internal thrust areas will be damaged.
5. Remove the bolts attaching the pump to the bracket, then remove the pump from the vehicle.

To install:
6. Position the pump on the bracket, then install the bolts to 30–45 ft. lbs. (41–61 Nm).
7. Install a power steering pump pulley installer tool (T65P-3A733-C or equivalent), then press the pulley onto the pump shaft. The pull-off groove must face the front of the vehicle and the pulley must be pressed on the shaft until flush with a tolerance of 0.010 in. (0.25.4cm).

2. Remove the pressure hose from the pump fitting by unscrewing the hose swivel nut.
3. Remove the accessory drive belt. For more details, refer to Section 1.
4. Remove the oil dipstick tube.
5. If equipped, remove the power steering pump support.
6. Install a steering pump pulley remover tool (T69L-10300-B or equivalent) on the pulley. Hold the pump and rotate the tool nut counterclockwise to remove the pulley. Do not apply in-and-out pressure on the pump shaft or the internal thrust areas will be damaged.

✳✳ WARNING

Do not apply pressure on the power steering pump rotor shaft. Pressure will damage internal thrust areas of the power steering pump.

7. Remove the bolts attaching the pump to the A/C compressor mounting bracket, then remove the pump.

To install:
8. Position the new pump on the A/C compressor mounting bracket, then install the bolts to 35–45 ft. lbs. (47–61 Nm). Position the support on the A/C compressor mounting bracket, then install the mounting bolts to 35–45 ft. lbs. (47–61 Nm).

➡The fore/aft location of the power steering pump pulley on the steering pump rotor shaft is critical. Incorrect belt alignment may cause drive belt squeal or chirp. Make sure pull-off groove on the power steering pump pulley is facing front and flush with the end of the shaft to within 0.010 in. (0.25.4cm).

9. Install a power steering pump pulley replacer tool (T65P-3A733-C or equivalent) and press the pulley onto the pump shaft.
10. Install the accessory drive belt. For more information, refer to Section 1.
11. Install the power steering pump support, if removed.
12. Install the oil dipstick tube.
13. Install the pressure hose tube nut and new Teflon® washer into the

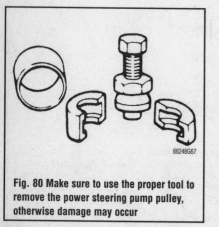

Fig. 80 Make sure to use the proper tool to remove the power steering pump pulley, otherwise damage may occur

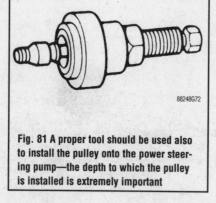

Fig. 81 A proper tool should be used also to install the pulley onto the power steering pump—the depth to which the pulley is installed is extremely important

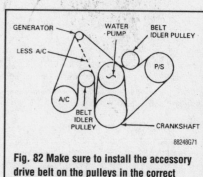

Fig. 82 Make sure to install the accessory drive belt on the pulleys in the correct order, otherwise a component may inadvertently be turned backwards—3.0L engines with A/C

8. Position the belt on the pulley, then place a 1 in. wrench on the alternator boss and lift up on the alternator until the specified belt tension is read on a suitable belt tension gauge. Tighten the adjustment bolt to 24–40 ft. lbs. (33–54 Nm) and the pivot bolt to 45–57 ft. lbs. (61–78 Nm). For more information regarding tightening the accessory drive belts, refer to Section 1.
9. Install the pressure hose to the pump fitting. If removed, install the power steering pressure switch on the gear assembly and connect the wires.
10. Connect the return hose to the pump and tighten the clamp.
11. Fill the reservoir with specified power steering fluid, then start the engine and turn the steering wheel from stop to stop to remove any air from the system.
12. Check the system for leaks.

2.8L, 3.0L and 4.0L Engines

▶ See Figures 80 thru 85

1. Drain the power steering fluid from the pump by disconnecting the fluid return hose at the reservoir and draining the fluid into a suitable container.

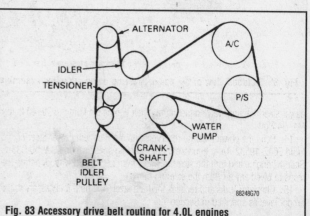

Fig. 83 Accessory drive belt routing for 4.0L engines

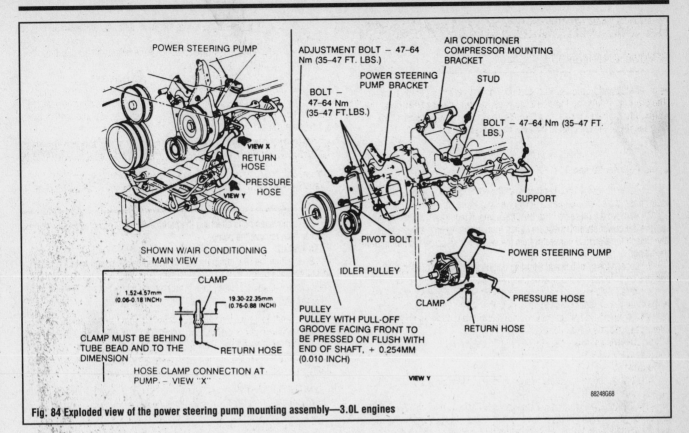

Fig. 84 Exploded view of the power steering pump mounting assembly—3.0L engines

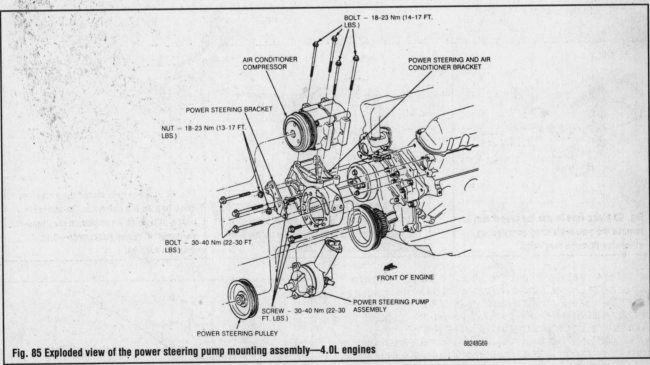

Fig. 85 Exploded view of the power steering pump mounting assembly—4.0L engines

power steering pump valve outlet fitting, then tighten the fitting to 30–40 ft. lbs. (41–54 Nm).

14. Refill the power steering reservoir with the Premium Power Steering Fluid E6AZ-19582-AA or equivalent fluid meeting specification ESW-M2C33-F. Start the engine and turn the steering wheel from left to right without hitting the stops to bleed any air from the steering pump.

15. Check for leaks and recheck the fluid level. Add fluid if necessary to the proper level as specified in Section 1.

BLEEDING

To bleed the air out of the power steering pump and system, first make sure that the power steering reservoir is adequately full. If the level is low, fill the power steering reservoir with the Premium Power Steering Fluid E6AZ-19582-AA or equivalent fluid meeting specification ESW-M2C33-F. Start the engine and turn the steering wheel from left to right without hitting the stops to bleed any air from the steering pump. Check for leaks and recheck the fluid level. Add fluid if necessary to the proper level as specified in Section 1.

TORQUE SPECIFICATIONS

Component	Ft. Lbs.	Nm
Front Suspension—Rear Wheel Drive Models		
Crossmember bolt retainer plate screw	10-14	14-48
Crossmember-to-frame rail bolts	145-195	196-264
Damper assembly retainer bolts	22-29	30-39
Jounce bumper-to-frame bolt	25-34	34-46
Lower control arm-to-No. 1 crossmember nut and bolt	100-140 ①	136-190
Rebound bumper-to-frame bolt	15-21	20-28
Shock absorber-to-lower control arm bolts	17-24	23-32
Shock absorber-to-upper spring seat nut	25-34	34-46
Spindle-to-lower ball joint nut	83-113 ②	113-153
Spindle-to-upper ball joint nut	27-37 ②	36-50
Stabilizer bar mounting bracket-to-frame rail bolts	16-24	22-33
Stabilizer link-to-lower control arm nut	71-106 inch lbs.	8-12
Stabilizer link-to-stabilizer bar nut	71-106 inch lbs.	8-12
Tie rod end-to-spindle arm nut	52-74 ②	70-100
Upper control arm bracket-to-body rail bolts	35-46	47-63
Upper control arm-to-adjusting arm nuts	70-100	95-135
Wheel lug nuts	100	135
Front Suspension—All Wheel Drive Models		
Bolt retainer bracket-to-frame screw	10-14	14-19
Crossmember-to-frame rail bolts	145-195	196-264
Damper bolts	22-29	30-39
Front mounting bracket bolt	35-47	47-64
Hub nut	170-210	230-285
Jounce bumper-to-frame bolt	24-33	32-45
Lower control arm-to-No. 1 crossmember nut and bolt	100-140 ①	136-190
Shock absorber-to-lower control arm bolts	16-24	22-33
Shock absorber-to-upper spring seat nut	25-35	34-47
Spindle-to-lower ball joint nut	59-81 ②	80-110
Spindle-to-upper ball joint nut	27-37	37-50
Stabilizer bar mounting bracket-to-frame rail bolts	16-24	22-33
Stabilizer link-to-lower control arm nut	53-80 inch lbs.	8-12
Stabilizer link-to-stabilizer bar nut	53-80 inch lbs.	8-12
Tie rod end-to-spindle arm nut	52-74 ②	70-100
Upper control arm-to-adjusting arm nuts	70-700	95-135
Rear Suspension		
Lower control arm-to-axle nut and bolt	95-130 ③	129-177
Rear spring lower retainer nut	45-60	60-80
Rear spring upper retainer bolt	30-40	40-55
Rear suspension arm-to-axle housing bolt	155-210 ③	210-284
Rear suspension arm-to-left frame bracket	64-88 ③	87-119
Rear suspension arm-to-right frame bracket	92-125 ③	125-170
Rear suspension lower arm-to-frame bracket nut and bolt	95-130 ③	129-177
Shock absorber-to-lower bracket nut	45-60	60-80
Shock absorber-to-upper bracket bolt	45-60	60-80

91328C01

TORQUE SPECIFICATIONS

Component	Ft. Lbs.	Nm
Steering		
Power steering hose fitting	22-30	30-40
Power steering pump valve housing bolts	30-45	42-62
Selector shaft adjuster nut	35-45	48-61
Selector shaft cover bolts	32-40	43-54
Steering column intermediate shaft connecting bolts	30-42 ①	41-57
Steering column mounting nuts	88-115 inch lbs.	13-17
Steering gear bearing cap	50	67
Steering gear locknut	30-40	40-55
Steering gear mounting bolts—AWD models	61-82	83-111
Steering gear mounting bolts—RWD models	80-105	108-142
Steering wheel nut	23-33	31-45
Tie rod jam nut	35-50	48-68

Notes:
① Tighten to the specified value with the vehicle in the normal ride position with all other fasteners already tightened to specification.
② Tighten to the specified value, then advance the nut to the next castellation in order to install a new cotter pin, if necessary.
③ The rear axle must be in teh normal ride position when tightening.

91328C02

9

BRAKES

BRAKE OPERATING SYSTEM

Brake Light Switch

REMOVAL & INSTALLATION

1. Disconnect the wires to the stop light switch located below the instrument panel.

➡**The locking tab must be lifted before the connector can be removed.**

2. Detach the wiring harness from the stop light switch at the connector.
3. Remove the hairpin clip, slide the stop light switch, pushrod, nylon washer and bushing away from the brake pedal.

➡**It is necessary to remove the vacuum booster input rod and one bushing spacer washer from the brake pedal pin.**

4. Remove the washer and the stop light switch by sliding the switch up or down.

To install:

5. Position the stop light switch so that the U-shaped side is nearest the brake pedal and directly over/under the pin. Then slide the stop light switch up/down trapping the vacuum booster input rod and bushing between the switch side plates.
6. Push the switch and pushrod assembly firmly toward the brake pedal arm.

❋❋ CAUTION

When assembling, do not substitute other types of pin clips. Use only factory supplied hairpin clips.

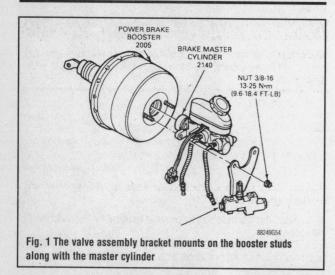

Fig. 1 The valve assembly bracket mounts on the booster studs along with the master cylinder

7. Assemble the outside white plastic washer to the pin, then install the hairpin clip to hold the entire assembly.

❋❋ CAUTION

Stop light switch wire harness must have sufficient length to travel with the switch during the full stroke of the brake pedal. If the wire length is too short, reroute or repair the harness as required.

8. Assemble the connector to the stop light switch.
9. Check the stop light switch for proper operation.

Master Cylinder

REMOVAL & INSTALLATION

▶ **See Figures 1, 2, 3, 4 and 5**

➡**Care should be employed when removing the brake master cylinder to not scratch the exposed primary piston.**

1. Disconnect the negative battery cable.
2. Detach the wiring harness from the low fluid level warning switch in the brake master cylinder reservoir, if equipped.
3. Detach the brake warning lamp connector from the master cylinder.
4. If equipped, disconnect the brake pressure differential valve warning lamp switch from the combination valve.
5. Disconnect the hydraulic lines from the brake master cylinder. Plug the hydraulic brake fluid lines to keep dirt, water or other contaminants from entering the system.

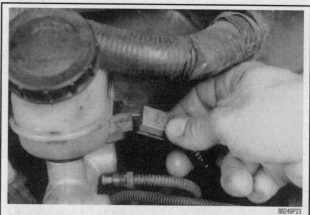

Fig. 2 Detach the low fluid level warning switch electrical connector from the master cylinder, . . .

Fig. 3 . . . then remove as much brake fluid from the master cylinder as possible

Fig. 4 Using a flare nut wrench, disconnect the hydraulic brake system lines from the master cylinder

Fig. 5 Remove the two master cylinder-to-brake booster nuts, then remove the cylinder from the vehicle

6. Remove the nuts retaining the master cylinder and bracket holder to the brake power booster, then remove the master cylinder from the vehicle by pulling it straight forward.

To install:

7. Before installing the master cylinder, adjust the booster assembly pushrod as described earlier in this section.

➥**DO NOT assemble the brake master cylinder to the power brake booster without the square section interface seal.**

8. Position the master cylinder assembly over the booster pushrod and onto the two power booster studs. Install the attaching nuts to 12–20 ft. lbs. (17–27 Nm).
9. Reattach the various wiring connectors.
10. Remove the hydraulic fluid line plugs.
11. Loosely connect the hydraulic brake system lines to the master cylinder. Fill the master cylinder reservoir with DOT 3 brake fluid to the FILL line on the side of the master cylinder. Bleed the air from the master cylinder and the entire hydraulic system. For more details on bleeding the hydraulic system and master cylinder, refer to the bleeding procedures located later in this section.
12. Tighten all hydraulic lines.
13. Make sure the master cylinder reservoir is filled to the proper level, then install the cap diaphragm.

Power Brake Booster

REMOVAL & INSTALLATION

This procedure allows the removal and installation of the power brake booster without disconnecting any brake fluid lines, thereby avoiding the necessity of bleeding the brake system. If the removal of the master cylinder is desired, refer to the procedure located earlier in this section.

1. Disconnect the negative battery cable.
2. Detach the brake warning lamp connector.
3. Support the master cylinder from underneath with a prop or using a similar method.
4. Remove the nuts retaining the master cylinder to the brake booster. Do not remove, or even loosen, the brake fluid lines from the master cylinder. Allow the master cylinder to temporarily remain seated on the booster while removing the remaining components.
5. Loosen the clamp that secures the manifold vacuum hose to the booster check valve, then remove the hose. Remove the booster check valve from the booster only if a new booster will be installed.
6. From inside the vehicle, for vehicles equipped with a pushrod mounted brake light switch, remove the hairpin retainer, then slide the brake light switch, pushrod, spacers and bushing off the brake pedal arm.
7. Remove the nuts that hold the booster to the firewall.
8. Pull the master cylinder off the brake power booster enough to remove the booster from the firewall. Make sure that the master cylinder will be supported adequately while the booster is out of the vehicle.

To install:

➥**Check the pushrod extension as described earlier in this section, before installing the master cylinder onto the booster.**

9. Mount the booster assembly on the engine side of the firewall by sliding the bracket mounting bolts and valve operating rod in through the holes in the dash panel.
10. From inside the van, install the booster retaining nuts.
11. Position the master cylinder on the booster assembly, install the retaining nuts, and remove the prop from underneath the master cylinder.
12. Install the booster check valve. Connect the manifold vacuum hose to the booster check valve and secure it with a clamp.
13. From inside the van on vehicles equipped with the pushrod mounted stop lamp switch, install the bushing and position the switch on the end of the

pushrod. Then install the switch and rod on the pedal arm, along with the spacers on each side, and secure with the hairpin retainer.
14. Connect the stop lamp switch wiring.
15. Start the engine and check the brake operation.

ADJUSTMENTS

Pushrod

For the pushrod adjustment procedure refer to the brake pedal adjustment procedures located at the beginning of this section.

Bleeding the Brake System

▶ **See Figures 6, 7, 8 and 9**

➥**For vehicles equipped with ABS systems, refer to the section of each particular ABS system for the brake bleeding procedure.**

When any part of the hydraulic system has been disconnected for repair or replacement, air may get into the lines and cause a spongy pedal action. This requires the bleeding of the hydraulic system after it has been properly connected to be sure all air is expelled from the brake cylinders and lines.

Always bleed the master cylinder (when necessary) before any of the wheels. Bleed one brake cylinder at a time. Start bleeding on the right rear brake, then the left rear. Proceed to the right front brake, then the left front. Keep the reservoir filled with brake fluid during the bleeding operation.

1. Bleed the longest line first.
2. On the master cylinder, wrap a cloth around the tubing below the fitting and loosen the hydraulic line nut at the master cylinder.
3. Push the brake pedal down slowly by hand to the floor. This will force air trapped in the master cylinder to escape at the fitting.
4. Hold the pedal down and tighten the fitting. Release the brake pedal.

➥**Do not release the brake pedal until the fitting is tightened or air will re-enter the master cylinder.**

5. Repeat this procedure until air ceases to escape at the fitting and the brake pedal is firm.
6. Place a box wrench on the bleeder fitting on the brake wheel cylinder or caliper next to be bled. Attach a rubber drain tube to the bleeder fitting.

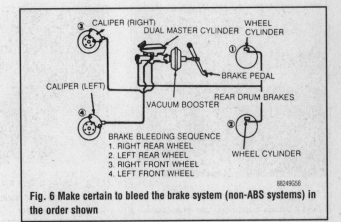

Fig. 6 Make certain to bleed the brake system (non-ABS systems) in the order shown

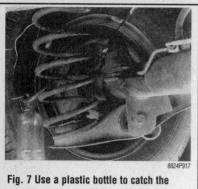

Fig. 7 Use a plastic bottle to catch the expelled brake fluid from a plastic tube installed over the bleeder valve

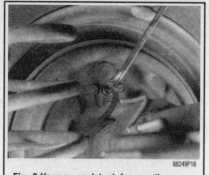

Fig. 8 Have an assistant depress the pedal, then loosen the bleeder until fluid flows from the valve

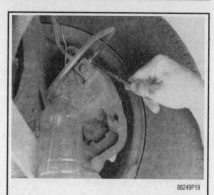

Fig. 9 Perform the same bleeding procedure to the front brake calipers as well

➡Make sure the end of the tube fits snugly around the bleeder fitting.

7. Submerge the free end of the tube in a container partially filled with clean brake fluid. Loosen the bleeder fitting approximately ¾ of a turn.

8. Slowly push the brake pedal all the way down. Close the bleeder fitting, then return the brake pedal to the fully released position. Repeat this procedure until air bubbles no longer appear at the submerged end of the bleeder tube.

9. When the fluid is completely free of air bubbles, close the bleeder fitting and remove the bleeder tube.

10. Repeat this procedure at the brake wheel cylinder or caliper on the opposite side. Refill the master cylinder reservoir after each wheel cylinder is bled.

11. When the bleeding operation is complete, fill the master cylinder to the maximum level line on the reservoir.

FRONT DISC BRAKES

✳✳ CAUTION

Brake pads may contain asbestos, which has been determined to be a cancer causing agent. Never clean the brake surfaces with compressed air! Avoid inhaling any dust from any brake surface! When cleaning brake surfaces, use a commercially available brake cleaning fluid.

Brake Pads

REMOVAL & INSTALLATION

▶ See Figures 10 thru 17

➡Always replace both disc pad assemblies on the front or rear of a vehicle (both front wheels or both rear wheels). Never service only one wheel.

1. To avoid fluid overflow when the caliper piston is pressured into the caliper cylinder bores, siphon or remove part of the brake fluid out of the larger master cylinder reservoir (connected to the front disc brakes). Discard the removed fluid.

✳✳ CAUTION

System contamination may result if anything other than a clean device is used to remove fluid from the brake master cylinder.

2. Raise and safely support the front end on jackstands.
3. Remove the front wheel(s).
4. Remove the front brake calipers as described later in this section.

➡Make sure to support the brake caliper with strong cord or wire from the vehicle body or frame rail if it is not going to be completely removed from the vehicle.

5. Compress the anti-rattle clips and remove the inner brake pad from the caliper.

6. Press each ear of the outer shoe away from the caliper, then slide the torque buttons out of the retention notches.

To install:

7. Place a new anti-rattle clip on the lower end of the inner pad. Be sure the tabs on the clip are positioned properly and the clip is fully seated.

8. Position the inner pad and anti-rattle clip tab against the pad abutment and the loop type spring away from the rotor. Compress the anti-rattle clip and slide the upper end of the pad into position on the brake caliper.

Fig. 10 Use a C-clamp to depress the piston so the torque buttons on the pads to clear the caliper

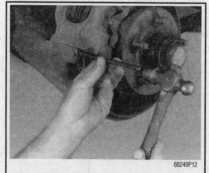

Fig. 11 Use a punch and hammer to tap the retaining pins out of the caliper and spindle channels, then . . .

Fig. 12 . . . pull the caliper off of the front rotor

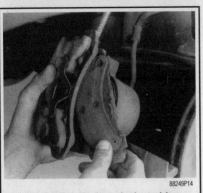

Fig. 13 Remove the inner brake pad from the brake caliper, then . . .

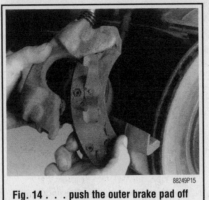

Fig. 14 . . . push the outer brake pad off of the brake caliper

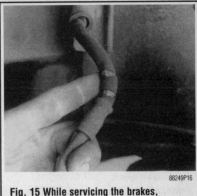

Fig. 15 While servicing the brakes, inspect the rubber brake hoses for damage

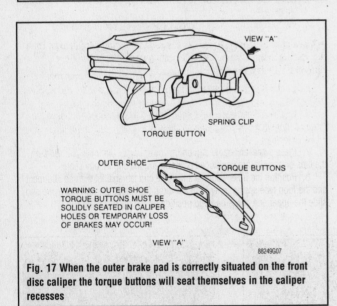

Fig. 16 Make sure to install the inner brake pad in the orientation as shown

Fig. 17 When the outer brake pad is correctly situated on the front disc caliper the torque buttons will seat themselves in the caliper recesses

9. Install the outer pad, making sure the torque buttons on the pad spring clip are seated solidly in the matching holes of the caliper.

10. Install the caliper on the rotor, making sure the mounting surfaces are free of dirt. Lubricate the caliper sliding grooves with disc brake caliper grease, or the equivalent. For more details, refer to the procedure later in this section.

11. If removed, install the brake hose to the caliper.

12. Bleed the brakes as described earlier in this section.

13. Install the wheel and tire assemblies. Tighten the lug nuts to 85–115 ft. lbs. (116–156 Nm).

14. Remove the jackstands and lower the vehicle. Check the brake fluid level and fill as necessary. Check the brakes for proper operation.

INSPECTION

Replace the front pads when the pad thickness is at the minimum thickness recommended by Ford Motor Co., which is $\frac{1}{16}$ in. (1.5mm), or at the minimum allowed by the applicable state or local motor vehicle inspection code, whichever is greater. Pad thickness may be checked by removing the wheel, then looking through the inspection port in the caliper assembly at the outer edge of the brake pad.

Front Caliper

REMOVAL & INSTALLATION

▸ See Figures 18 thru 23

➡Always replace all disc pad assemblies on an axle. Never service one wheel only.

1. To avoid fluid overflow when the caliper piston is pressured into the caliper cylinder bores, siphon or remove part of the brake fluid out of the larger master cylinder reservoir (connected to the front disc brakes). Discard the removed fluid.

❄❄ CAUTION

System contamination may result if anything other than a clean device is used to remove brake fluid from the master cylinder.

2. Raise and safely support the front end on jackstands.
3. Remove the front wheel(s).

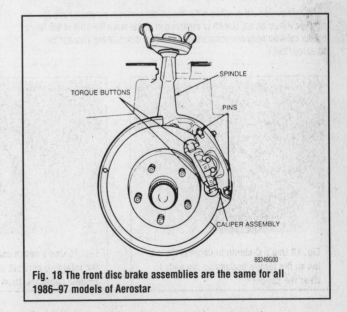

Fig. 18 The front disc brake assemblies are the same for all 1986–97 models of Aerostar

Do not position the C-clamp on the brake shoe hold-down spring. Also, do not compress the wheel cylinder piston further than is required to disengage the torque buttons from the front disc brake caliper. Damage to the brake shoe hold-down spring will result. Replace the shoe if the brake shoe hold-down spring is bent or damaged.

4. Use an 8 in. (20cm) C-clamp to move the wheel cylinder piston back into its bore as follows:

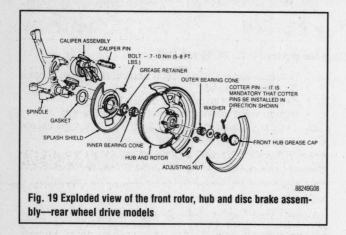

Fig. 19 Exploded view of the front rotor, hub and disc brake assembly—rear wheel drive models

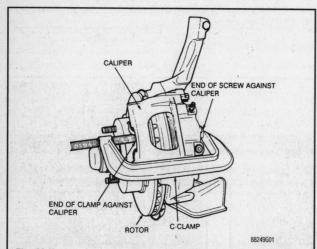

Fig. 20 Use an eight inch (20cm) C-clamp (positioned as shown) to depress the caliper piston until the torque buttons are clear of the caliper body

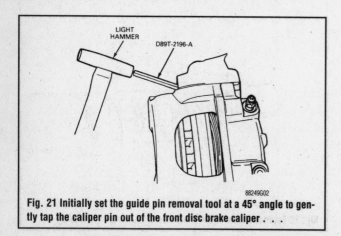

Fig. 21 Initially set the guide pin removal tool at a 45° angle to gently tap the caliper pin out of the front disc brake caliper . . .

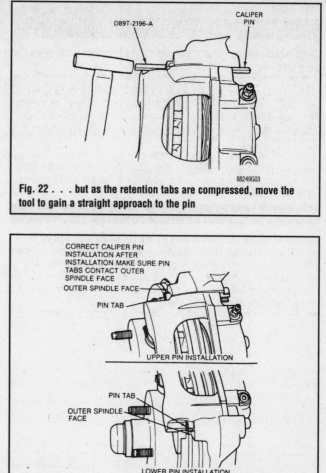

Fig. 22 . . . but as the retention tabs are compressed, move the tool to gain a straight approach to the pin

Fig. 23 For correct installation, the guide pins should be positioned as shown

a. Place the head of the C-clamp against the front disc brake caliper, and the screw end of the clamp against the outer shoe below the spring clip.
b. Tighten the clamp until the torque buttons just clear the caliper (about ⅛ in. or 3mm).
c. Remove the C-clamp from the caliper.

➡Do not use a screwdriver or similar tool to pry the piston away from the rotor.

5. Clean excess dirt from the area around the pin tabs.
6. Using the Caliper Pin Remover D89T-2196-A or equivalent and a light hammer, drive the caliper pin from the front disc brake caliper as follows:
a. Position the notched end of the tool against the caliper pin (retention tab half), at a 45° angle from the pin retention tabs.
b. Tap the tool with the hammer to compress the retention tabs.
c. As the retention tabs are compressed, move the tool to gain a straight approach to the pin. Continue tapping to drive the pin through the caliper/spindle groove.

➡Never reuse caliper pins. Always install new pins whenever a caliper is removed.

7. Repeat the same caliper pin removal procedure for the lower pin.
8. Remove the caliper from the rotor. If the caliper is to be completely removed for service, remove the brake hose from the caliper, otherwise wire the caliper so that it hangs from the vehicle body. Make sure that there is no stress placed on the brake fluid line while it is hanging.

➡Do not let the caliper hang from the brake hose.

9. At this point the brake pads may be removed from the caliper.

To install:

✳✳ CAUTION

Never attempt to bottom out the wheel cylinder piston with the outer shoe installed.

10. The brake caliper piston must be "bottomed out" when installing new pads. Be sure that enough fluid has been removed from the brake master cylinder to prevent fluid overflow. Bottom out the wheel cylinder piston with an 8 in. (20cm) C-clamp using a worn-out inner shoe or a block of wood to push against the brake caliper piston.
11. Install new brake pads, if necessary.
12. Install the caliper on the rotor, making sure the mounting surfaces are free of dirt. Lubricate the caliper sliding grooves with disc brake caliper grease, or the equivalent.

✳✳ CAUTION

Be sure to install the caliper pins so the retention tabs will be in contact with the front wheel spindle, not the front disc brake caliper. When the upper pin is properly positioned, the retention tabs will be at the top, against the front wheel spindle. When the lower pin is properly positioned, the retention tab will be at the bottom, also in contact with the front wheel spindle.

13. From the caliper outboard side, position the pin between the caliper and spindle grooves. The pin must be positioned so the tabs will be installed against the spindle outer face (inward).

➡Never reuse caliper pins. Always install new pins whenever a caliper is removed.

14. Tap the pin on the outboard end with a hammer. Continue tapping the pin inward until the retention tabs on the sides of the pin contact the spindle face. Repeat this procedure for the lower pin.

➡During the installation procedure do not allow the tabs of the caliper pin to be tapped too far into the spindle groove. If this happens it will be necessary to tap the other end of the caliper pin until the tabs snap into place. The tabs on each end of the caliper pin must be free to catch on the spindle face.

15. If removed, install the brake hose to the caliper.
16. Bleed the brakes as described earlier in this section.
17. Install the wheel and tire assemblies. Tighten the lug nuts to 85–115 ft. lbs. (116–156 Nm).
18. Remove the jackstands and lower the vehicle. Check the brake fluid level and fill as necessary. Check the brakes for proper operation.

CALIPER OVERHAUL

◆ See Figures 24, 25, 26, 27 and 28

1. Remove the front disc brake caliper as described earlier in this section.
2. Disconnect the brake hose.
3. Clean the exterior of the caliper with denatured alcohol.
4. Remove the plug from the caliper inlet port and drain the fluid.
5. Air pressure is necessary to remove the piston. Apply air to the inlet port slowly and carefully until the piston pops out of its bore.

✳✳ CAUTION

If high pressure air is applied the piston will pop out with considerable force and cause damage or injury. It's a good idea to cushion the piston with a thick shop rag placed across from it in the caliper.

6. If the piston jams, release the air pressure and tap sharply on the piston end with a soft hammer. Reapply air pressure.
7. When the piston is out, Remove the boot from the piston and the seal from the bore.

Fig. 24 Use air pressure to push the piston from the caliper—use a piece of wood to prevent damage

Fig. 25 Remove the brake caliper piston from the piston, then . . .

Fig. 26 . . . remove the piston boot and . . .

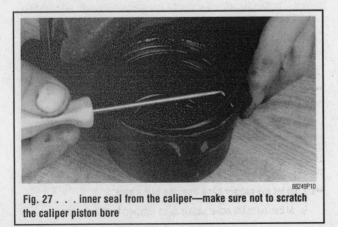
Fig. 27 . . . inner seal from the caliper—make sure not to scratch the caliper piston bore

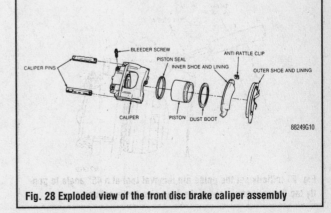
Fig. 28 Exploded view of the front disc brake caliper assembly

To assemble:

8. Clean the housing and piston with denatured alcohol. Dry with compressed air.

9. Lubricate the new piston seal, boot and piston with clean brake fluid, and assemble them in the caliper.

10. The dust boot can be worked in with the fingers and the piston should be pressed straight in until it bottoms. Be careful to avoid cocking the piston in the bore.

11. A C-clamp may be necessary to bottom the piston.

12. Install the caliper as described above.

Brake Disc (Rotor)

REMOVAL & INSTALLATION

♦ **See Figures 19 and 29 thru 35**

1. Raise and support the front end on jackstands.
2. Remove the wheel.
3. Remove the caliper assembly as described earlier in this section.
4. For 4-wheel drive models, follow the procedure given under hub and wheel bearing removal in Section 7 for models with manual and automatic locking hubs.
5. For 2-wheel drive vans:
   a. Remove the grease cup from the hub.
   b. Remove the cotter pin, castellated retainer, adjusting nut and flat washer from the spindle.
   c. Remove the outer bearing cone and roller assembly.
   d. Pull the hub and rotor assembly off the spindle.

To install:

➡New rotor assemblies come protected with an anti-rust coating which should be removed with denatured alcohol or degreaser. New hubs must be packed with EP wheel bearing grease. If the old rotors are to be reused, check them for cracks, grooves or waviness. Rotors that aren't too badly scored or grooved can be resurfaced by most automotive shops. Minimum rotor thickness should be stamped on the rotor. If refinishing exceeds that, the rotor will have to be replaced.

6. For rear wheel drive models, perform the following steps:
   a. Install the hub and rotor assembly on the spindle. Keep the hub centered on the spindle to prevent damage to the retainer and the spindle threads.
   b. Install the outer bearing cone and roller assembly and the flat washer on the spindle, then install the adjusting nut finger tight. Adjust the wheel bearing(s) as described in Section 8.
7. For all wheel drive vehicles, refer to the front hub procedure located in Section 7.
8. Install the caliper to the spindle as described in Section 8.
9. Install the front tire(s), then lower the van and tighten the lugnuts to 85–115 ft. lbs. (115–155 Nm). Install the wheel cover.

Fig. 29 After removing the front wheel, remove the dust cap from the brake rotor/hub

Fig. 30 Remove the old cotter pin, then . . .

Fig. 31 . . . pull the castellated retainer from the spindle

Fig. 32 Remove the retaining nut and . . .

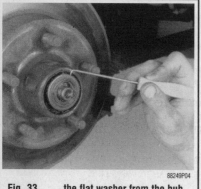
Fig. 33 . . . the flat washer from the hub assembly

Fig. 34 Remove the outer hub bearings, then . . .

Fig. 35 . . . pull the rotor off the spindle, without sliding the inner bearings across the spindle threads

10. Before moving the van, pump the brake pedal several times to restore normal brake travel.

✳✳ CAUTION

After 500 miles of driving, re-tighten the wheel lugnuts to 85–115 ft. lbs. (115–155 Nm). If this is not done, the wheel may come off.

INSPECTION

The brake rotor should be checked for scratches, scoring and cracks. If any cracks, or excessive scoring and scratches are found, the rotor must be replaced with a new one.

Smaller scratches and scoring will be removed when the rotor is refinished. Check the rotor for runout as follows:

1. First eliminate the wheel bearing end-play by tightening the adjusting nut to specifications. Check to ensure that the front disc brake rotor can still be rotated,

2. Clamp a dial indicator to the spindle knuckle assembly so that the stylus contacts the rotor approximately 1 in. (25.4mm) from the outer edge.

3. Rotate the rotor one turn (360°) and take an indicator reading. If the reading exceeds 0.003 in. (0.08mm) total lateral runout, replace or resurface the front disc brake rotor.

Rotor Refinishing

The rotor should be refinished to remove scoring, out-of-round, and runout. Use a disc brake lathe to resurface the rotors.

✳✳ CAUTION

Always resurface both rotors so braking friction will be equal for both wheels. NEVER resurface just one rotor!

The minimum overall thickness specifications shown on the rotor allows for a 0.030 in. (0.8mm) machining cut plus 0.030 in. (0.8mm) for additional wear. If the thickness falls below the minimum, the rotor must be replaced.

REAR DRUM BRAKES

✳✳ CAUTION

Brake shoes may contain asbestos, which has been determined to be a cancer causing agent. Never clean the brake surfaces with compressed air! Avoid inhaling any dust from any brake surface! When cleaning brake surfaces, use a commercially available brake cleaning fluid.

Brake Drums

REMOVAL & INSTALLATION

1. Block both front wheels so that the vehicle will not roll when raised.
2. Raise and support the rear of the van safely on jackstands.
3. Remove the rear wheel(s).
4. Remove the 3 retaining nuts, then pull the brake drum off of the lug studs. It may be necessary to back off the brake shoe adjustment in order to remove the brake drum. This is may be necessary since the brake drum may be grooved or worn from being in service for an extended period of time.

To install:

5. Before installing a new brake drum, be sure to remove any protective coating with carburetor degreaser.

6. Slide the brake drum onto the lug studs, then adjust the brakes as described earlier in this section.

7. Install the rear wheel(s).
8. Lower the vehicle.
9. Remove the wheel blocks.

INSPECTION

After the brake drum has been removed from the vehicle, it should be inspected for runout, severe scoring, cracks, and the proper inside diameter.

Minor scores on a brake drum can be removed with fine emery cloth, provided that all grit is removed from the drum before it is installed on the vehicle.

A badly scored, rough, or out-of-round (runout) drum can be ground or turned on a brake drum lathe. Do not remove any more material from the drum than is necessary to provide a smooth surface for the brake shoe to contact. The maximum diameter of the braking surface is shown on the inside of each brake drum. Brake drums that exceed the maximum braking surface diameter shown on the brake drum, either through wear or refinishing, must be replaced, since the drum loses its ability to dissipate heat, created by the friction between the brake drum and brake shoes, when the outside wall of the brake drum reaches a certain thickness (thinner than the original thickness). Also the brake drum will have more tendency to warp and/or crack.

The maximum braking surface diameter specification, which is shown on each drum, allows for a 0.060 in. (1.5mm) machining or cut over the original nominal drum diameter plus 0.030 in. (0.8mm) additional wear before reaching the diameter at which the drum must be discarded. Use a brake drum micrometer to measure the inside diameter of the brake drums.

Brake Shoes

INSPECTION

1. Raise and support the rear of the vehicle. Make certain to block the front wheels to keep the vehicle from rolling. Do not apply the parking brake, otherwise the rear drums will not be able to be removed.

2. Remove the rear wheels.

3. Pull the rear brake drums off of the lug studs. It may be necessary to loosen the brake shoes, as described earlier in this section in the brake adjustment procedure.

4. Inspect the brake shoe linings for any damage which could affect the functioning of the rear brakes, such as cracking or chipping of the brake shoe lining material.

✳✳ CAUTION

If a worn lining is not replaced, the brake drum may become severely damaged. Always replace the primary and secondary brake shoe lining assemblies on both rear brake assemblies at the same time.

5. Replace the brake shoes if they are worn to within ⅟₃₂ (0.79.4cm) of any rivet head, or when the lining is soaked with brake fluid, oil or grease.

6. If the brake drum and linings are in good condition, install the wheel and brake drum. The condition of the brake drum and shoe linings of the opposite wheel will usually be about the same as the wheel removed. It is a good idea, however, to check the other wheel anyhow.

7. Lower the vehicle and remove the blocks from the front wheels.

REMOVAL & INSTALLATION

▶ **See Figures 36 thru 52**

1. Raise and support the rear end on jackstands.
2. Remove the wheel and brake drum from the side to be worked on.

➡**If you have never replaced the brakes on a vehicle before and you are not too familiar with the procedures involved, only disassemble and assemble one side at a time, leaving the other side intact as a reference during reassembly.**

3. Install a clamp over the ends of the wheel cylinder to prevent the pistons of the wheel cylinder from coming out, causing loss of fluid and much grief.

4. Contract the brake shoes by pulling the self-adjusting lever away from

the star wheel adjustment screw, then turn the star wheel up and back until the pivot nut is drawn onto the star wheel as far as it will come.

5. Pull the adjusting lever, cable and automatic adjuster spring down and toward the rear to unhook the pivot hook from the large hole in the secondary shoe web. Do not attempt to pry the pivot hook from the hole.

6. Remove the automatic adjuster spring and the adjuster lever.

7. Remove the secondary shoe-to-anchor spring with a brake tool.

➡ Brake tools are very common implements and are available at auto parts stores.

8. Remove the primary shoe-to-anchor spring and unhook the cable anchor. Remove the anchor pin plate, if so equipped.

9. Remove the cable guide from the secondary shoe.

10. Remove the shoe hold-down springs, shoes, adjusting screw, pivot nut, and socket. Note the color and position of each hold-down spring for assembly. To remove the hold-down springs, reach behind the brake backing plate and place one finger on the end of one of the brake hold-down spring mounting pins. Using a pair of pliers, grasp the washer type retainer on top of the hold-down spring that corresponds to the pin that you are holding. Push down on the pliers and turn them 90° to align the slot in the washer with the head on the

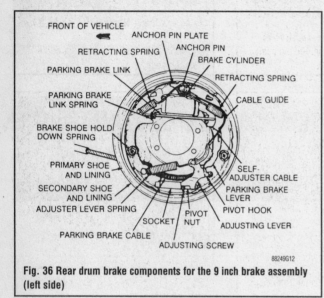

Fig. 36 Rear drum brake components for the 9 inch brake assembly (left side)

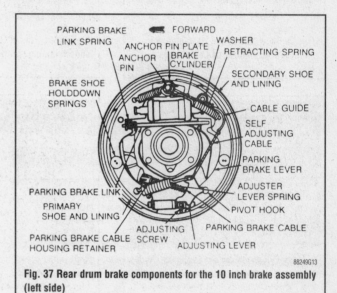

Fig. 37 Rear drum brake components for the 10 inch brake assembly (left side)

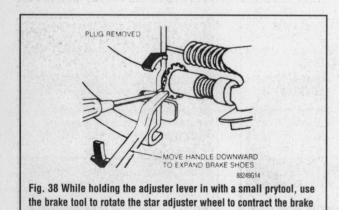

Fig. 38 While holding the adjuster lever in with a small prytool, use the brake tool to rotate the star adjuster wheel to contract the brake shoes

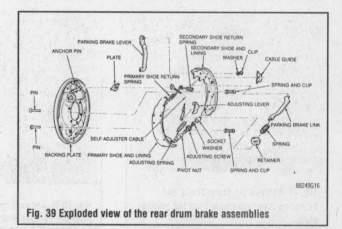

Fig. 39 Exploded view of the rear drum brake assemblies

Fig. 40 Remove the rear wheels to gain access to the rear brake assemblies

Fig. 41 Pull the rear brake drum off of the lug studs—the brake shoes may need to be adjusted down

Fig. 42 Use brake cleaner to remove the dust from the brake assemblies—NEVER use compressed air

Fig. 43 Once the brake dust is removed, the brake assemblies can be disassembled

Fig. 44 Disconnect the two upper brake shoe retaining springs from the top post, then . . .

Fig. 45 . . . detach the retaining cable from the post

Fig. 46 Remove the brake shoe retaining bracket from the top post as well

Fig. 47 Remove the brake shoe-to-backing plate retaining springs and . . .

Fig. 48 . . . and make sure to remove the rear mounting pins

Fig. 49 Remove the brake shoes and adjusting lever assembly from the backing plate

Fig. 50 Disconnect the parking brake cable from the parking brake lever, then . . .

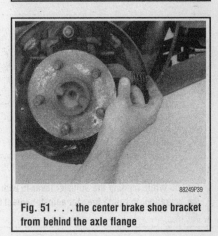
Fig. 51 . . . the center brake shoe bracket from behind the axle flange

spring mounting pin. Remove the spring and washer retainer and repeat this operation on the hold-down spring on the other shoe.

11. Remove the parking brake link and spring. Disconnect the parking brake cable from the parking brake lever.

12. After removing the rear brake secondary shoe. On 9 in. (23cm) brakes remove the parking brake lever from the shoe. On 10 in. (25.4cm) brakes disassemble the parking brake lever from the shoe by removing the retaining clip and spring washer.

To install:

13. Assemble the parking brake lever to the secondary shoe, and on 10 in. (25.4cm) brakes secure it with the spring washer and retaining clip.

14. Apply a light coating of Lubriplate® at the points where the brake shoes contact the backing plate.

15. Position the brake shoes on the backing plate, and install the hold-down spring pins, springs, and spring washer type retainers. Install the parking brake link, spring and washer. Connect the parking brake cable to the parking brake lever.

16. Install the anchor pin plate, and place the cable anchor over the anchor pin with the crimped side toward the backing plate.

➡The primary brake shoe is the shoe with the smallest amount of friction surface and the secondary shoe has the larger friction surface. Always make sure the primary shoe is facing forward and the secondary is facing rearward after installation.

17. Install the primary shoe-to-anchor spring with the brake tool.

18. Install the cable guide on the secondary shoe web with the flanged holes fitted into the hole in the secondary shoe web. Thread the cable around the cable guide groove.

19. Install the secondary shoe-to-anchor (long) spring. Be sure that the cable end is not cocked or binding on the anchor pin when installed. All of the parts should be flat on the anchor pin. Remove the wheel cylinder piston clamp.

20. Apply Lubriplate® to the threads and the socket end of the adjusting star wheel screw. Turn the adjusting screw into the adjusting pivot nut to the limit of the threads and then back off ½ turn.

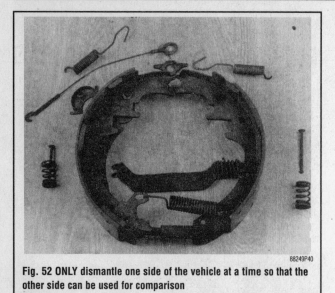

Fig. 52 ONLY dismantle one side of the vehicle at a time so that the other side can be used for comparison

✳✳ CAUTION

Interchanging the brake shoe adjusting screw assembles from one side of the vehicle to the other would cause the brake shoes to retract rather than expand each time the automatic adjusting mechanism operates. To prevent this, the socket end of the adjusting screw is stamped with an "R" or an "L" for RIGHT or LEFT. The adjusting pivot nuts can be distinguished by the number of lines machined around the body of the nut; one line indicates left hand nut and two lines indicates a right hand nut.

21. Place the adjusting socket on the screw and install this assembly between the shoe ends with the adjusting screw nearest to the secondary shoe.

22. Place the cable hook into the hole in the adjusting lever from the backing plate side. The adjusting levers are stamped with an **R** (right), or an **L** (left), to indicate their installation on the right or left hand brake assembly.

23. Position the hooked end of the adjuster spring in the primary shoe web and connect the loop end of the spring to the adjuster lever hole.

24. Pull the adjuster lever, cable and automatic adjuster spring down toward the rear to engage the pivot hook in the large hole in the secondary shoe web.

25. After installation, check the action of the adjuster by pulling the section of the cable between the cable guide and the adjusting lever toward the secondary shoe web far enough to lift the lever past a tooth on the adjusting screw star wheel. The lever should snap into position behind the next tooth, and release of the cable should cause the adjuster spring to return the lever to its original position. This return action of the lever will turn the adjusting screw star wheel one tooth. The lever should contact the adjusting screw star wheel one tooth above the center line of the adjusting screw.

26. If the automatic adjusting mechanism does not perform properly, check the following:

a. Check the cable end fittings. The cable ends should fill or extend slightly beyond the crimped section of the fittings. If this is not the case, replace the cable.

b. Check the cable guide for damage. The cable groove should be parallel to the shoe web, and the body of the guide should lie flat against the web. Replace the cable guide if this is not so.

c. Check the pivot hook on the lever. The hook surfaces should be square with the body on the lever for proper pivoting. Repair or replace the hook as necessary.

d. Make sure that the adjusting screw star wheel is properly seated in the notch in the shoe web.

27. Install the rear brake drum onto the lug studs.

28. Install the rear wheel.

29. Lower the vehicle.

ADJUSTMENT

Rear drum brakes are adjusted automatically by alternately driving the vehicle forward and reverse, and applying the brakes firmly. Brake adjustment occurs during reverse stops only.

Manual brake adjustment is required only after the brake shoes have been replaced, or if the brake shoe adjusting lever kit has malfunctioned and was replaced. Perform the manual adjustment with the brake drums removed, using the Brake Adjustment Gauge D81L-1103-A or equivalent and the following procedure:

Brake Drums Removed

◆ See Figures 53, 54 and 55

➡When adjusting the rear brake shoes, check the parking brake rear cable and conduit for proper adjustment. Make sure the equalizer operates freely.

1. Raise the vehicle and safely support it on jackstands.
2. Remove the rear wheels.
3. Remove the brake drum as described later in this section.
4. Clean the brake components with a brake parts cleaner. Never use air to blow the brake parts clean.
5. Carefully remove the brake shoe hold-down spring. Using sandpaper, clean the shoe-to-backing plate contact points while holding the shoe away from the brake backing plate.
6. Check the brake backing plate for damage. If any damage is found, it must be replaced. If no damage is found, apply a small amount of Disc Brake Caliper Slide Grease D7AZ-19590-A, or equivalent to the points where the shoes touch the brake backing plate. Be careful not to get the lubricant on the linings.
7. Reinstall the brake shoe hold-down spring.
8. Using the Brake Adjustment Gauge D81L-1103-A or equivalent adjust to the inside diameter of the drum braking surface.
9. Position the opposite side of the tool over the brake shoes. Adjust the shoes until they touch the gauge. The gauge contact points on the shoes must be parallel to the vehicle with the center line through the center of the axis.

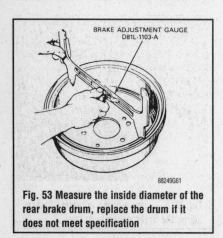

Fig. 53 Measure the inside diameter of the rear brake drum, replace the drum if it does not meet specification

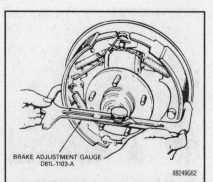

Fig. 54 Flip the tool over and measure the brake shoes—adjust the brake shoes until they touch the inside edges of the tool

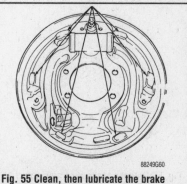

Fig. 55 Clean, then lubricate the brake shoe-to-braking plate contact points with brake grease

10. Hold the brake shoe adjusting lever kit out of engagement while rotating the adjusting star wheel of the adjuster cylinder. Make sure that the star wheel turns freely.

11. If necessary, remove the adjuster for disassembly and cleaning. Lubricate the adjusting screw threads and pilot end with a thin, uniform coating of the disc brake grease.

12. Install the brake drums. Install the retaining nuts, then tighten securely.

13. Install the wheels.

14. Lower the vehicle.

15. Complete the adjustment by sharply applying the brakes several times while driving the vehicle alternately in forward and reverse.

16. After adjusting the brake shoes, check the brake operation by making several stops while driving forward.

Brake Drums Installed

▶ See Figures 56, 57 and 58

Adjust the single anchor brake by turning the adjusting screw (part of the brake shoe adjusting screw nut) located between the lower ends of the brake shoes as follows:

1. Place the transmission in Neutral. Raise and safely support the rear of the vehicle on jackstands.

2. Remove the cover from the adjusting hole at the bottom of the backside of the brake backing plate, then turn the adjusting star wheel with a brake tool inside the hole to expand the brake shoes until they drag against the brake drum and lock the brake drum.

3. When the shoes are against the brake drum, loosen the adjusting star wheel and additional 10–12 notches so that the brake drum rotates freely without drag.

4. If the brake drum does not rotate freely, remove the wheel and brake drum. Clean the brake components with a brake parts cleaner. Do not use air to blow the brakes clean.

   a. Carefully remove the brake shoe hold-down spring. Using sandpaper, clean the shoe-to-backing plate contact points while holding the shoe away from the brake backing plate.

   b. Check the brake backing plate for damage. If any damage is found, it must be replaced. If no damage is found, apply a small amount of Disc Brake Caliper Slide Grease D7AZ-19590-A, or equivalent to the points where the shoes touch the brake backing plate. Be careful not to get the lubricant on the linings.

   c. Reinstall the brake shoe hold-down spring.

   d. Install the wheel and brake drum.

5. Install the adjusting hole cover on the brake backing plate.

6. Check and adjust the other rear wheel.

7. Apply the brakes. If the pedal travels more than halfway to the floor, there is too much clearance between the brake shoes and the brake drums. Repeat Steps 2 and 3 of this procedure.

✳✳ CAUTION

Perform the road test only when the brakes will apply and the vehicle can be safely stopped.

8. When the rear brake shoes have been properly adjusted, lower the vehicle. Road test the brakes to ensure proper operation.

Wheel Cylinders

REMOVAL & INSTALLATION

▶ See Figure 59

1. Block the front wheels of the vehicle.

2. Raise and support the rear of the vehicle on jackstands.

3. Remove the wheel and drum.

4. Remove the rear brake shoe assemblies.

5. Disconnect the brake line at the fitting on the brake backing plate. It is a good idea to use a flare nut wrench to keep the flare nut from "rounding out" when being loosened.

6. Remove the screws that hold the wheel cylinder to the backing plate, then pull the cylinder off of the brake shoe backing plate.

To install:

7. Clean the backing plate with brake parts cleaner.

8. Position the new rear brake wheel cylinder onto the brake backing plate.

9. Install the wheel cylinder retaining nuts onto the wheel cylinder studs until snug.

10. Install the rear brake shoe assemblies, as described earlier in this section.

11. Install the rear drums and wheels.

12. Bleed the brake system.

13. Lower the rear of the vehicle, then remove the front wheel blocks.

OVERHAUL

▶ See Figures 60 thru 69

Wheel cylinder overhaul kits may be available, but often at little or no savings over a reconditioned wheel cylinder. It often makes sense with these components to substitute a new or reconditioned part instead of attempting an overhaul.

If no replacement is available, or you would prefer to overhaul your wheel cylinders, the following procedure may be used. When rebuilding and installing wheel cylinders, avoid getting any contaminants into the system. Always use clean, new, high quality brake fluid. If dirty or improper fluid has been used, it will be necessary to drain the entire system, flush the system with proper brake fluid, replace all rubber components, then refill and bleed the system.

1. Remove the wheel cylinder from the vehicle and place on a clean workbench.

2. First remove and discard the old rubber boots, then withdraw the pistons. Piston cylinders are equipped with seals and a spring assembly, all located behind the pistons in the cylinder bore.

3. Remove the remaining inner components, seals and spring assembly. Compressed air may be useful in removing these components. If no compressed air is available, be VERY careful not to score the wheel cylinder bore when removing parts from it. Discard all components for which replacements were supplied in the rebuild kit.

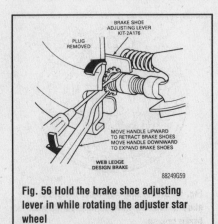

Fig. 56 Hold the brake shoe adjusting lever in while rotating the adjuster star wheel

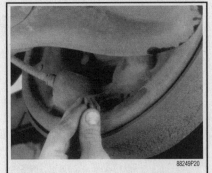

Fig. 57 To gain access to the drum brake adjusting wheel, remove the adjustment hole plug, then . . .

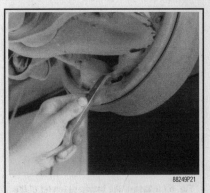

Fig. 58 . . . use a brake adjusting tool to adjust the brake shoes in or out

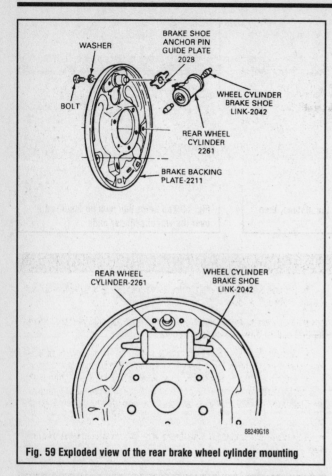

Fig. 59 Exploded view of the rear brake wheel cylinder mounting

4. Wash the cylinder and metal parts in denatured alcohol or clean brake fluid.

✳✳ WARNING

Never use a mineral-based solvent such as gasoline, kerosene or paint thinner for cleaning purposes. These solvents will swell rubber components and quickly deteriorate them.

5. Allow the parts to air dry or use compressed air. Do not use rags for cleaning, since lint will remain in the cylinder bore.
6. Inspect the piston and replace it if it shows scratches.
7. Lubricate the cylinder bore and seals using clean brake fluid.
8. Position the spring assembly.
9. Install the inner seals, then the pistons.
10. Insert the new boots into the counterbores by hand. Do not lubricate the boots.
11. Install the wheel cylinder.

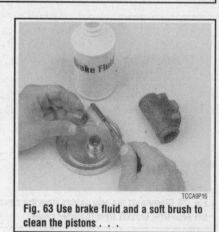

Fig. 60 Remove the outer boots from the wheel cylinder

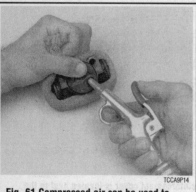

Fig. 61 Compressed air can be used to remove the pistons and seals

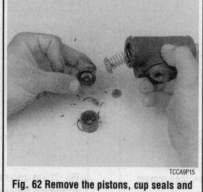

Fig. 62 Remove the pistons, cup seals and spring from the cylinder

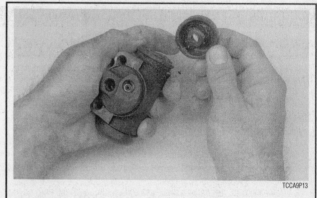

Fig. 63 Use brake fluid and a soft brush to clean the pistons . . .

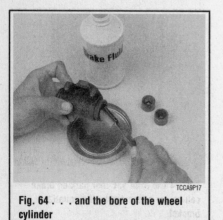

Fig. 64 . . . and the bore of the wheel cylinder

Fig. 65 Once cleaned and inspected, the wheel cylinder is ready for assembly

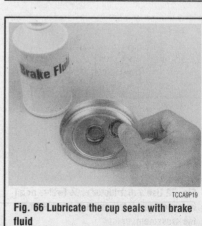

Fig. 66 Lubricate the cup seals with brake fluid

Fig. 67 Install the spring, then the cup seals in the bore

Fig. 68 Lightly lubricate the pistons, then install them

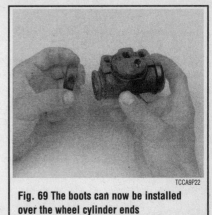

Fig. 69 The boots can now be installed over the wheel cylinder ends

PARKING BRAKE

Cables

REMOVAL & INSTALLATION

Front Cable

▶ **See Figures 70, 71, 72, 73 and 74**

1. Place the control in the released position and insert the lock pin in the control assembly. Refer to the tension release procedure located earlier in this section.

2. Disconnect the rear parking brake cables from the equalizer. Remove the equalizer from the front cable.

3. Remove the bolts retaining the cover from the underbody reinforcement bracket. Remove the cover.

➡ **It may be necessary to loosen the fuel tank straps and partially lower the fuel tank to gain access to the cover.**

4. Remove the cable anchor pin from the pivot hole in the control assembly ratchet plate. Guide the front cable from the control assembly.

5. Insert a ½ in. box end twelve point wrench over the front fitting of the front cable. Push the wrench onto the cable retainer fitting in the crossmember. Compress the retainer fingers and push the retainer rearward through the hole.

➡ **Ford recommends using a distributor lock bolt wrench for the above step.**

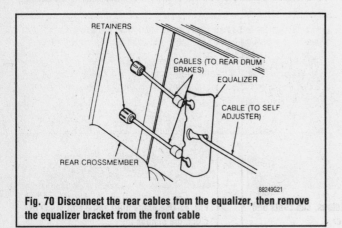

Fig. 70 Disconnect the rear cables from the equalizer, then remove the equalizer bracket from the front cable

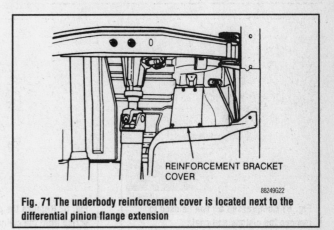

Fig. 71 The underbody reinforcement cover is located next to the differential pinion flange extension

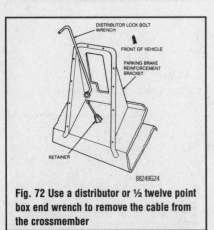

Fig. 72 Use a distributor or ½ twelve point box end wrench to remove the cable from the crossmember

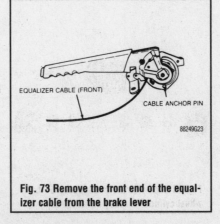

Fig. 73 Remove the front end of the equalizer cable from the brake lever

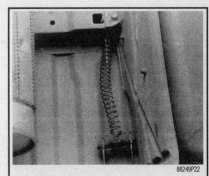

Fig. 74 The front and rear parking brake cables are connected by the equalizer bracket

6. Compress the retainer fingers on the rear crossmember and remove the retainer from the crossmember. Pull the cable ends through the crossmembers and remove the cable.

To install:

7. Feed the cables through both the holes in both crossmembers. Push the retainers through the holes so the fingers expand over each hole.

8. Route the cable around the control assembly pulley and insert the cable anchor pin in the pivot hole in the ratchet plate.

9. Connect the equalizer to the front and rear cables.

10. Remove the lock pin from the control assembly to apply cable tension.

11. Position the cover on the reinforcement bracket. Install and tighten the bolts after visually checking to be sure the front cable is attached to the control.

12. Position the boot over the control. Install and tighten the screws.

13. Apply and release the control. Make sure the rear brakes are applied and released.

Rear Cables (Equalizer-To-Drum)

▶ **See Figures 75 and 76**

1. Place the control in the released position and insert the lock pin in the control assembly. Refer to Tension Release procedure.

2. Raise the vehicle and remove the hub cap, wheel and tire, and brake drum.

3. Disconnect the rear parking brake cables from the equalizer.

4. Compress the retainer fingers on the rear crossmember and remove the cable retainer from the rear crossmember. Remove the cable from the crossmember and from the bracket on the frame.

5. On the wheel side of the backing plate, compress the retainer fingers so the retainer passes through the hole in the backing plate.

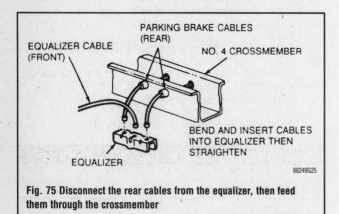

Fig. 75 Disconnect the rear cables from the equalizer, then feed them through the crossmember

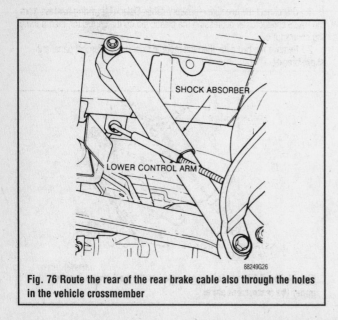

Fig. 76 Route the rear of the rear brake cable also through the holes in the vehicle crossmember

6. Lift the cable out of the slot in the parking brake lever (attached to the brake secondary shoe) and remove the cable through the backing plate hole.

To install:

7. Route the cable through the hole in the backing plate. Insert the cable anchor behind the slot in the parking brake lever. Make sure the cable is securely engaged in the parking brake lever so the cable return spring is holding the cable in the parking brake lever.

8. Push the retainer through the hole in the backing plate so the retainer fingers engage the backing plate.

9. Route the cable through the bracket on the frame and through the hole in the crossmember.

10. Push the retainer through the hole in the crossmember so the retainer fingers engage the crossmember.

11. Connect the rear cable to the equalizer.

12. Remove the lock pin from the control assembly to apply cable tension.

13. Apply and release the control assembly several times. May sure the drum brakes apply and release.

ADJUSTMENTS

The parking brake system is self adjusting and requires no adjustment, however if any component in the parking brake system requires servicing (or removing the rear axle), the cable tension must be released. After servicing is completed, the cables are connected to the equalizer and tension is reset.

Cable Tension Release

▶ **See Figure 77**

1. Place the parking brake control in the "released" position.

2. Insert a steel pin through the pawl lock-out pin hole. The pin must be inserted from the inboard side of the parking brake control (larger hole) at a slightly upward and forward angle, then swept downward and rearward to displace the self-adjusting pawl. This locks out the self-adjusting pawl.

3. Raise the vehicle on a hoist and have an assistant remain in the vehicle to perform Step 4.

➡**Be careful not to damage the plastic coating on the cable strand. Remove the parking brake rear cable and conduits from the parking brake cable bracket.**

4. Have the assistant pull rearward on the parking brake cable bracket or parking brake rear cable and conduit about 1–2½ in. (25–60mm) to rotate the self-adjuster reel backward.

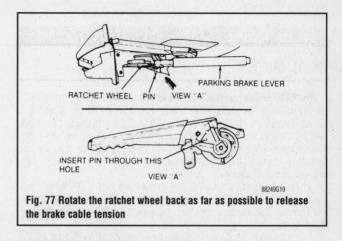

Fig. 77 Rotate the ratchet wheel back as far as possible to release the brake cable tension

Resetting Cable Tension

▶ **See Figure 77**

1. Make sure the parking brake cables are connected to the equalizer.

2. Remove the steel pin from the holes in the control assembly being careful to keep fingers out of the way. This restores tension to the cables. Apply and release the parking brakes several times to set cable tension.

Brake Lever

REMOVAL & INSTALLATION

1. Remove the front and inboard rear screws attaching the boot to the floor. Pivot the boot back on the hinge and remove the two rear screws and remove the boot.

2. Place the control in the released position and insert the lock pin in the control assembly.

3. Remove the cable anchor pin from the pivot hole in the control assembly ratchet plate and guide the equalizer cable from the control assembly.

4. Remove the bolts retaining the control assembly to the floor panel. Remove the control assembly to the floor panel and remove the control assembly.

REAR ANTI-LOCK BRAKE SYSTEM (RABS)

General Information

The 1990–92 Aerostar vehicles may be equipped with Rear Anti-lock Brake System (RABS). The system continually monitors rear wheel speed with a sensor mounted on the rear axle. If rear wheel lockup is sensed, the RABS module activates the electro-hydraulic valve causing the isolation valve to close. With the valve closed, the rear wheel cylinders are isolated from the master cylinder and pressure can not increase. If the rate of deceleration is still too great, the module will energize the dump solenoid with a series of rapid pulses to bleed off rear brake fluid.

Component Location

• The RABS module is mounted on the driver's side of the wheelhouse under the instrument panel

• The dual solenoid electro-hydraulic valve is located on the fender apron below the master cylinder

• The speed sensor and excitor ring is located in the rear differential housing

• The RABS diagnostic connector is located on the main wire bundle inside the driver's side of the van under the dash slightly rearward of the No. 53 pin connector

• The yellow ANTI-LOCK warning light is in the instrument panel

• The diode/resistor element is located about 3 in. (76mm) left of the instrument cluster connector in the cluster wiring harness

• The sensor test connector with cap is located forward of the No. 53 pin connector on the left fender apron

System Testing

SYSTEM SELF TEST

The RABS module performs system tests and self-tests during start up and normal operation. The valve, sensor and fluid level circuits are monitored for proper operation. If a fault is found, the RABS will be deactivated and the REAR ANTI-LOCK light will be lit until the ignition is turned off. When the light is lit, the diagnostic flashout code may be obtained. Under normal operation, the light will stay on for about 2 seconds while the ignition switch is in the ON position and will go out shortly after.

A flash code may be obtained only when the yellow light is ON. Before reading the code, drive the vehicle to a level area and place the shift lever in the PARK or NEUTRAL position. Keep the vehicle ignition ON. **To obtain the flash code:**

1. Locate the RABS diagnostic connector (orange/black wire) and attach a jumper wire to it and ground it to the chassis.

2. Quickly remove the ground. When the ground is made and then removed, the RABS light will begin to flash.

3. The code consists of a number of short flashes and ends with a long flash. Count the short flashes and include the following long flash in the count to obtain the code number. Example: three short and one long flash indicates a Code 4. The code will continue until the ignition is turned OFF.

To install:

❊❊ CAUTION

Do NOT remove the steel lock pin from the control assembly until the equalizer cable is reconnected to the control assembly.

5. Route the cable around the control assembly pulley and insert the cable anchor pin in the pivot hole in the ratchet plate.

6. Position the control assembly with the cable attached to it on the floor panel and tighten the retaining bolts.

7. Remove the lock pin from the control assembly to reset the cable tension.

8. Position the boot over the assembly and tighten the screws.

9. Apply and release the control several times. Make sure the parking brakes are applied and released and not dragging. Check to see if the brake warning light is working properly.

Diagnostic Codes

• Diagnostic code 2—Open isolate circuit
• Diagnostic code 3—Open dump circuit
• Diagnostic code 4—RABS Valve switch closed or open dump valve
• Diagnostic code 5—System dumps too many times in 2WD)2WD and 4WD vehicles), condition occurs while making normal or hard stops. Rear brake may lock.
• Diagnostic code 6—Sensor signal rapidly cuts in and out, condition only occurs while driving
• Diagnostic code 7—No isolate valve self test
• Diagnostic code 8—No dump valve self test
• Diagnostic code 9—High sensor resistance
• Diagnostic code 10—Low sensor resistance
• Diagnostic code 11—Stop lamp switch circuit defective, condition indicated only when driving above 35 mph (56 km/h)
• Diagnostic code 12—Low brake fluid level detected during anti-lock stop
• Diagnostic code 13—Speed processor check
• Diagnostic code 14—Program check
• Diagnostic code 15—Memory failure
• Diagnostic code 16—16 or more flashes should not occur

RABS Module

REMOVAL & INSTALLATION

▶ See Figure 78

1. Disconnect the negative (-) battery cable. Detach the wiring harness from the RABS connector by depressing the plastic tab on the connector, then pulling the connector off.

2. Remove the two nuts, then the module from the instrument panel anti-shake bracket.

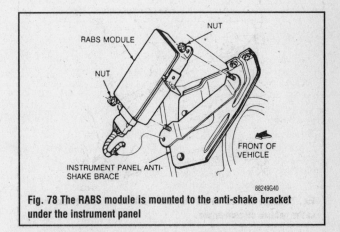

Fig. 78 The RABS module is mounted to the anti-shake bracket under the instrument panel

To install:

3. Position the module onto the anti-rattle bracket, then install the retaining nuts until snug.

4. Attach the electrical connectors to the RABS module.

5. Connect the negative battery cable.

Speed Sensor

REMOVAL & INSTALLATION

▶ **See Figure 79**

1. Disconnect the negative (-) battery cable.
2. Detach the speed sensor connector at the rear differential.
3. Remove the sensor hold-down bolt, then remove the sensor.
4. Clean the axle mounting surface using care not to get any dirt in the axle housing.
5. Inspect and clean the magnetized sensor pole piece.

To install:

6. Lubricate the new O-ring on the sensor with new motor oil, then install the sensor.

7. Tighten the retaining bolt to 30 ft. lbs. (40 Nm).

8. Reattach the wiring harness connector. Connect the negative battery cable.

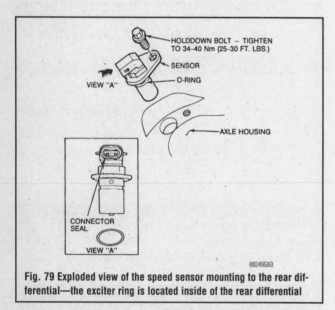

Fig. 79 Exploded view of the speed sensor mounting to the rear differential—the exciter ring is located inside of the rear differential

Electro-Hydraulic Valve

REMOVAL & INSTALLATION

▶ **See Figure 80**

1. Disconnect the negative (-) battery cable.
2. Detach the valve wiring harness connectors from the valve.
3. Disconnect the two brake lines from the valve. Plug the disconnected brake lines to keep dirt or contaminants from entering the system.
4. Remove the retaining screw, then remove the valve assembly from the fender apron.

To install:

5. Position the electro-hydraulic valve onto the inner fender. Install the retaining screw to 40 inch lbs. (5 Nm).

6. Reattach the wiring harness connectors to the valve.

7. Connect the negative battery cable.

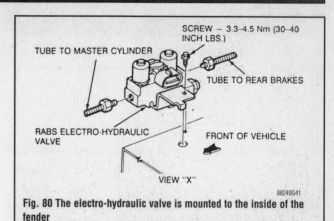

Fig. 80 The electro-hydraulic valve is mounted to the inside of the fender

Excitor Ring

INSPECTION

1. Remove the speed sensor as described earlier in this section.

2. View the exciter ring through the sensor hole. Rotate the rear axle and check the exciter ring teeth for damage or breakage. Dented or broken teeth could cause the RABS system to function when not required.

REMOVAL & INSTALLATION

To service the exciter ring, the differential case must be removed from the axle housing, and the exciter ring pressed off the case. This procedure requires specialized tools and specific knowledge of differential assemblies. Have the exciter ring removed by a reputable automotive technician.

Bleeding the ABS System

When any part of the hydraulic system has been disconnected for repair or replacement, air may get into the lines and cause spongy pedal action. This requires bleeding of the hydraulic system after it has been properly connected to be sure all air is expelled from the brake cylinder s and lines. The ABS hydraulic system must be bled with an Anti-lock Brake Adapter T90P-50-ALA and Jumper T93T-50-ALA, or equivalent. If these tools are not used, air will be trapped in the HCU which eventually leads to a spongy brake pedal.

➡**The ABS system must be bled in two steps.**

1. Disconnect the 40-pin plug from the Electronic Control Unit (ECU) and install the anti-lock brake adapter to the wire harness 40-pin plug.

2. Place the bleed/harness in the bleed position.

3. Turn the ignition switch **ON**. At this time point the red OFF indicator should turn on.

4. Push the motor button on the adapter down. This starts the pump motor. The red OFF indicator turns off and the green ON indicator turns on. The pump motor will run for 60 seconds. once the motor button is pushed (the button need not be held depressed). If the pump motor is to be turned off for any reason before this 60 seconds has elapsed, push the abort button and the pump motor will turn off.

5. After the first 20 seconds have passed, push and hold the valve button for 20 seconds. This bleeds any trapped air from the brake master cylinder and HCU.

6. The pump continues to run for an additional 20 seconds after the valve button is released.

7. Bleed the brake lines in the following order:
   a. Right rear.
   b. Left front.
   c. Left rear.
   d. Right front.

REAR ANTI-LOCK BRAKE SYSTEM II (RABS II)

General Information

The Rear Anti-Lock Brake System II (RABS II) continually monitors rear wheel speed with a sensor mounted on the rear axle housing while the brakes are applied. When the teeth on the speed sensor ring, mounted on the ring gear, pass the sensor pole piece, an AC voltage is induced in the sensor circuit with a frequency proportional to the average rear wheel speed. In the event of an impending lockup condition during braking, the Anti-Lock Electronic Control Unit modulates the hydraulic pressure to the rear brake drums. This inhibits rear wheel lockup.

Component Locations

• The Anti-Lock Electronic Control Unit is mounted on the driver's side of the wheelhouse under the instrument panel
• The dual solenoid electro-hydraulic valve is located on the fender apron below the master cylinder
• The speed sensor and excitor ring is located in the rear differential housing
• The RABS diagnostic connector is located on the main wire bundle inside the driver's side of the van under the dash slightly rearward of the No. 53 pin connector
• The yellow ANTI-LOCK warning light is in the instrument panel
• The diode/resistor element is located about 3 in. (76mm) left of the instrument cluster connector in the cluster wiring harness
• The sensor test connector with cap is located forward of the No. 53 pin connector on the left fender apron

Testing

SYSTEM SELF TEST

The RABS II module performs system tests and self-tests during start up and normal operation. The valve, sensor and fluid level circuits are monitored for proper operation. If a fault is found, the RABS II will be deactivated and the REAR ANTI-LOCK light will be lit until the ignition is turned off. When the light is lit, the diagnostic flashout code may be obtained. Under normal operation, the light will stay on for about 2 seconds while the ignition switch is in the ON position and will go out shortly after.

A flash code may be obtained only when the yellow light is ON. Before reading the code, drive the vehicle to a level area and place the shift lever in the PARK or NEUTRAL position. Keep the vehicle ignition ON.

To obtain flash codes:

➡**Verify that the ignition switch is in the RUN position (the engine does not need to be running).**

1. Locate the black RABS II diagnostic connector. The diagnostic connector has two mating halves (one of which has a black/orange wire connected to it).
2. Some models were built with locking terminals in the diagnostic connector, making it difficult to disconnect the two mating halves. Use the following procedure if the model is equipped with this particular type of connector:
    a. Lift the latch on the female housing to disengage the locking mechanism.
    b. Attempt to separate the two connector halves until the terminals lock.
    c. On the top portion of the connector housing, opposite from the mounting tabs, there is a small hole. Insert a narrow scribe tool into the hole until it stops.
    d. Separate the two connector housing halves by pushing the tool handle toward the black/orange wire.
3. Attach one end of a jumper wire to the black with orange stripe wire side of the diagnostic connector. Momentarily ground the opposite end of the jumper wire by connecting it to a good chassis ground for 1–2 seconds.
4. Grounding the wire thus should start the REAR ABS lamp flashing. If the light does not start flashing, perform the diagnostic tests.

✱✱ CAUTION

Care must be taken to connect only the black/orange stripe wire to the ground. Attaching the mating connector wire to ground will result in a blown fuse.

5. The code consists of a number of short flashes and ends with a long flash. Count the short flashes and include the following long flash in the count to obtain the code number. Example: three short and one long flash indicates a Code 4. The code will continue until the ignition is turned OFF.

Diagnostic Codes

• Diagnostic code 2—Open RABS isolation solenoid circuit
• Diagnostic code 3—Open RABS dump solenoid circuit
• Diagnostic code 4—Open/grounded RABS valve reset circuit
• Diagnostic code 5—Excessive dump solenoid activity
• Diagnostic code 6—Erratic speed sensor circuit
• Diagnostic code 7—No isolation solenoid during self test
• Diagnostic code 8—No dump solenoid during self test
• Diagnostic code 9—High speed sensor resistance
• Diagnostic code 10—Low speed sensor resistance
• Diagnostic code 11—Stop lamp circuit always closed
• Diagnostic code 12—Loss of brake fluid during anti-lock stop
• Diagnostic code 13—Anti-lock electrical control unit failure
• Diagnostic code 16—16 or more flashes should not occur

Anti-Lock Electronic Control Unit

REMOVAL & INSTALLATION

▶ **See Figure 81**

1. Disconnect the negative (-) battery cable. Detach the wiring harness connector from the anti-lock electronic control unit module by depressing the plastic tab on the connector, then pulling the connector off.
2. Remove the two nuts, then the unit from the instrument panel anti-shake bracket.

    To install:
3. Position the electronic unit onto the anti-rattle bracket, then install the retaining nuts until snug.
4. Attach the electrical connectors to the Anti-Lock Electronic Control Unit.
5. Connect the negative battery cable.

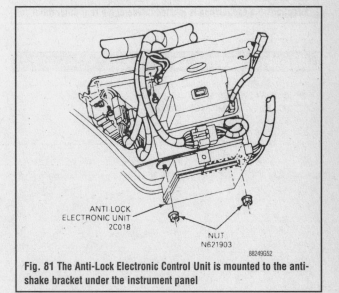

Fig. 81 The Anti-Lock Electronic Control Unit is mounted to the anti-shake bracket under the instrument panel

Anti-lock Brake Control Module

REMOVAL & INSTALLATION

1. Disconnect and plug the anti-lock brake control module and rear brake tube attached to the anti-lock brake control module.
2. Detach the wiring harness connector from the anti-lock brake control module.
3. Remove the screw which retains the anti-lock brake control module to the fender apron. Remove the anti-lock brake control module.
   To install:
4. Position the anti-lock brake control module on the fender apron. Install the retaining screw to 30–40 inch lbs. (3–4 Nm).
5. Attach the wiring harness connector to the anti-lock brake control module.

✳✳ CAUTION

Do not over-tighten the fittings.

6. Connect the rear brake tube to the anti-lock brake control module, then tighten as follows:
   a. ½–20 threaded fittings use 10–17 ft. lbs. (14–23 Nm).
   b. ⁷⁄₁₆–24 and ⅜–24 threaded fittings use 10–15 ft. lbs. (14–20 Nm).
7. Bleed the brake system as described earlier in this section.

Speed Sensor

REMOVAL & INSTALLATION

▶ **See Figure 82**

1. Disconnect the negative (-) battery cable.
2. Detach the speed sensor connector at the rear differential.
3. Remove the sensor hold-down bolt, then remove the sensor.
4. Clean the axle mounting surface using care not to get any dirt in the axle housing.
5. Inspect and clean the magnetized sensor pole piece.
   To install:
6. Lubricate the new O-ring on the sensor with new motor oil, then install the sensor.
7. Tighten the retaining bolt to 25–30 ft. lbs. (34–40 Nm).
8. Reattach the wiring harness connector. Connect the negative battery cable.

Excitor Ring

INSPECTION

1. Remove the speed sensor as described earlier in this section.
2. View the excitor ring through the sensor hole. Rotate the rear axle and check the excitor ring teeth for damage or breakage. Dented or broken teeth could cause the RABS system to function when not required.

REMOVAL & INSTALLATION

To service the excitor ring, the differential case must be removed from the axle housing, and the excitor ring pressed off the case. This procedure requires

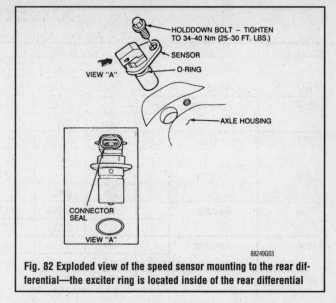

Fig. 82 Exploded view of the speed sensor mounting to the rear differential—the exciter ring is located inside of the rear differential

specialized tools and specific knowledge of differential assemblies. Have the excitor ring removed by a reputable automotive technician.

Bleeding the ABS System

When any part of the hydraulic system has been disconnected for repair or replacement, air may get into the lines and cause spongy pedal action. This requires bleeding of the hydraulic system after it has been properly connected to be sure all air is expelled from the brake cylinders and lines. The ABS hydraulic system must be bled with an Anti-lock Brake Adapter T90P-50-ALA and Jumper T93T-50-ALA, or equivalent. If these tools are not used, air will be trapped in the HCU which eventually leads to a spongy brake pedal.

➡**The ABS system must be bled in two steps.**

1. Disconnect the 40-pin plug from the Electronic Control Unit (ECU) and install the anti-lock brake adapter to the wire harness 40-pin plug.
2. Place the bleed/harness in the bleed position.
3. Turn the ignition switch **ON**. At this time point the red OFF indicator should turn on.
4. Push the motor button on the adapter down. This starts the pump motor. The red OFF indicator turns off and the green ON indicator turns on. The pump motor will run for 60 seconds. once the motor button is pushed (the button need not be held depressed). If the pump motor is to be turned off for any reason before this 60 seconds has elapsed, push the abort button and the pump motor will turn off.
5. After the first 20 seconds have passed, push and hold the valve button for 20 seconds. This bleeds any trapped air from the brake master cylinder and HCU.
6. The pump continues to run for an additional 20 seconds after the valve button is released.
7. Bleed the brake lines in the following order:
   a. Right rear.
   b. Left front.
   c. Left rear.
   d. Right front.

BRAKE SPECIFICATIONS
All measurements in inches unless noted

Year	Model		Master Cylinder Bore	Front Brake Disc			Rear Brake Drum Diameter			Minimum Lining Thickness	
				Original Thickness	Minimum Thickness	Maximum Runout	Original Inside Diameter	Max. Wear Limit	Maximum Machine Diameter	Front	Rear
1986	Aerostar	①	NA	0.850	0.810	0.003	9.00	9.09	9.06	0.030	0.030
		②	NA	0.850	0.810	0.003	10.00	10.09	10.06	0.030	0.030
1987	Aerostar	①	NA	0.850	0.810	0.003	9.00	9.09	9.06	0.030	0.030
		②	NA	0.850	0.810	0.003	10.00	10.09	10.06	0.030	0.030
1988	Aerostar	①	NA	0.850	0.810	0.003	9.00	9.09	9.06	0.030	0.030
		②	NA	0.850	0.810	0.003	10.00	10.09	10.06	0.030	0.030
1989	Aerostar	①	NA	0.850	0.810	0.003	9.00	9.09	9.06	0.030	0.030
		②	NA	0.850	0.810	0.003	10.00	10.09	10.06	0.030	0.030
1990	Aerostar	①	NA	0.850	0.810	0.003	9.00	9.09	9.06	0.030	0.030
		②	NA	0.850	0.810	0.003	10.00	10.09	10.06	0.030	0.030
1991	Aerostar	①	NA	0.850	0.810	0.003	9.00	9.09	9.06	0.030	0.030
		②	NA	0.850	0.810	0.003	10.00	10.09	10.06	0.030	0.030
1992	Aerostar	①	NA	0.850	0.810	0.003	9.00	9.09	9.06	0.030	0.030
		②	NA	0.850	0.810	0.003	10.00	10.09	10.06	0.030	0.030
1993	Aerostar	①	NA	0.850	0.810	0.003	9.00	9.09	9.06	0.030	0.030
		②	NA	0.850	0.810	0.003	10.00	10.09	10.06	0.030	0.030
1994	Aerostar	①	0.938	0.850	0.810	0.003	9.00	9.09	9.06	0.030	0.030
		②	0.938	0.850	0.810	0.003	10.00	10.09	10.06	0.030	0.030
1995	Aerostar	①	0.938	0.850	0.810	0.003	9.00	9.09	9.06	0.030	0.030
		②	0.938	0.850	0.810	0.003	10.00	10.09	10.06	0.030	0.030
1996	Aerostar	①	0.938	0.850	0.810	0.003	9.00	9.09	9.06	0.030	0.030
		②	0.938	0.850	0.810	0.003	10.00	10.09	10.06	0.030	0.030
1997	Aerostar	①	0.938	0.850	0.810	0.003	9.00	9.09	9.06	0.030	0.030
		②	0.938	0.850	0.810	0.003	10.00	10.09	10.06	0.030	0.030

Note: NA - Not Available
① With 9 inch brakes
② With 10 inch brakes

91329C01

Troubleshooting the Brake System

Problem	Cause	Solution
Low brake pedal (excessive pedal travel required for braking action.)	• Excessive clearance between rear linings and drums caused by inoperative automatic adjusters	• Make 10 to 15 alternate forward and reverse brake stops to adjust brakes. If brake pedal does not come up, repair or replace adjuster parts as necessary.
	• Worn rear brakelining	• Inspect and replace lining if worn beyond minimum thickness specification
	• Bent, distorted brakeshoes, front or rear	• Replace brakeshoes in axle sets
	• Air in hydraulic system	• Remove air from system. Refer to Brake Bleeding.
Low brake pedal (pedal may go to floor with steady pressure applied.)	• Fluid leak in hydraulic system	• Fill master cylinder to fill line; have helper apply brakes and check calipers, wheel cylinders, differential valve, tubes, hoses and fittings for leaks. Repair or replace as necessary.
	• Air in hydraulic system	• Remove air from system. Refer to Brake Bleeding.
	• Incorrect or non-recommended brake fluid (fluid evaporates at below normal temp).	• Flush hydraulic system with clean brake fluid. Refill with correct-type fluid.
	• Master cylinder piston seals worn, or master cylinder bore is scored, worn or corroded	• Repair or replace master cylinder
Low brake pedal (pedal goes to floor on first application—o.k. on subsequent applications.)	• Disc brake pads sticking on abutment surfaces of anchor plate. Caused by a build-up of dirt, rust, or corrosion on abutment surfaces	• Clean abutment surfaces
Fading brake pedal (pedal height decreases with steady pressure applied.)	• Fluid leak in hydraulic system	• Fill master cylinder reservoirs to fill mark, have helper apply brakes, check calipers, wheel cylinders, differential valve, tubes, hoses, and fittings for fluid leaks. Repair or replace parts as necessary.
	• Master cylinder piston seals worn, or master cylinder bore is scored, worn or corroded	• Repair or replace master cylinder
Decreasing brake pedal travel (pedal travel required for braking action decreases and may be accompanied by a hard pedal.)	• Caliper or wheel cylinder pistons sticking or seized	• Repair or replace the calipers, or wheel cylinders
	• Master cylinder compensator ports blocked (preventing fluid return to reservoirs) or pistons sticking or seized in master cylinder bore	• Repair or replace the master cylinder
	• Power brake unit binding internally	• Test unit according to the following procedure: (a) Shift transmission into neutral and start engine (b) Increase engine speed to 1500 rpm, close throttle and fully depress brake pedal (c) Slow release brake pedal and stop engine (d) Have helper remove vacuum check valve and hose from power unit. Observe for backward movement of brake pedal. (e) If the pedal moves backward, the power unit has an internal bind—replace power unit

TCCA9C01

Troubleshooting the Brake System (cont.)

Problem	Cause	Solution
Spongy brake pedal (pedal has abnormally soft, springy, spongy feel when depressed.)	• Air in hydraulic system	• Remove air from system. Refer to Brake Bleeding.
	• Brakeshoes bent or distorted	• Replace brakeshoes
	• Brakelining not yet seated with drums and rotors	• Burnish brakes
	• Rear drum brakes not properly adjusted	• Adjust brakes
Hard brake pedal (excessive pedal pressure required to stop vehicle. May be accompanied by brake fade.)	• Loose or leaking power brake unit vacuum hose	• Tighten connections or replace leaking hose
	• Incorrect or poor quality brakelining	• Replace with lining in axle sets
	• Bent, broken, distorted brakeshoes	• Replace brakeshoes
	• Calipers binding or dragging on mounting pins. Rear brakeshoes dragging on support plate.	• Replace brake mounting pins and bushings. Clean rust or burrs from rear brake support plate ledges and lubricate ledges with molydisulfide grease. NOTE: If ledges are deeply grooved or scored, do not attempt to sand or grind them smooth—replace brake support plate.
	• Caliper, wheel cylinder, or master cylinder pistons sticking or seized	• Repair or replace parts as necessary
	• Power brake unit vacuum check valve malfunction	• Test valve according to the following procedure: (a) Start engine, increase engine speed to 1500 rpm, close throttle and immediately stop engine (b) Wait at least 90 seconds then depress brake pedal (c) If brakes are not vacuum assisted for 2 or more applications, check valve is faulty
	• Power brake unit has internal bind	• Test unit according to the following procedure: (a) With engine stopped, apply brakes several times to exhaust all vacuum in system (b) Shift transmission into neutral, depress brake pedal and start engine (c) If pedal height decreases with foot pressure and less pressure is required to hold pedal in applied position, power unit vacuum system is operating normally. Test power unit. If power unit exhibits a bind condition, replace the power unit.
	• Master cylinder compensator ports (at bottom of reservoirs) blocked by dirt, scale, rust, or have small burrs (blocked ports prevent fluid return to reservoirs).	• Repair or replace master cylinder. CAUTION: Do not attempt to clean blocked ports with wire, pencils, or similar implements. Use compressed air only.
	• Brake hoses, tubes, fittings clogged or restricted	• Use compressed air to check or unclog parts. Replace any damaged parts.
	• Brake fluid contaminated with improper fluids (motor oil, transmission fluid, causing rubber components to swell and stick in bores	• Replace all rubber components, combination valve and hoses. Flush entire brake system with DOT 3 brake fluid or equivalent.
	• Low engine vacuum	• Adjust or repair engine

TCCA9C02

10

BODY AND TRIM

EXTERIOR

Doors

ADJUSTMENT

Front

1. Determine which hinge bolts must be loosened to move the door in the desired direction.
2. Loosen the bolts just enough to permit movement of the door with a padded pry bar or equivalent.
3. Move the door as necessary for the proper fit, then tighten the hinge bolts to 18–25 ft. lbs. (24–34 Nm).
4. Check the striker plate alignment for proper door engagement.

Sliding Door

The sliding door latch is located at the rear of the door. When the door is pushed forward to close, the latch engages the striker, which will position the rear of the sliding door flush to the body. There are two wedges located on the front of the sliding door which fit into two slots located on the B pillar. These wedges must enter the two slots to assure a proper fit and closed position for the front of the sliding door.

➡For proper sliding door operation it is critical that the two wedges on the front face of the sliding door fit smoothly into the two wedge pockets located in the B pillar. If performing any of the following adjustments, re-alignment of the to wedge-to-wedge pockets may be necessary.

IN OR OUT—FRONT UPPER

➡Support the sliding door so that no up or down movement is made to the door during this adjustment.

To adjust the front upper edge of the sliding door, loosen the two nuts retaining the body side door bracket assembly to the upper guide roller assembly, in or out as required to obtain a flush fit of the door to the body. The upper guide roller assembly rides freely within the upper track on the body. The bracket assembly and upper guide do not support the sliding door.

IN OR OUT—FRONT LOWER

The lower edge of the sliding door is adjusted by loosening the adjusting nut on the lower guide assembly and moving the door in or out as required to obtain a flush fit. The lower guide vertical roller is a load bearing roller and should roll easily within the lower track as the sliding door is opened or closed.

STRIKER REAR LATCH

Adjusting the striker in or out will position the rear edge of the sliding door as required to obtain the proper fit to the body.

➡The striker adjusts in or out only. Up and down adjustment is obtained with the rear hinge and lower front guide.

FORE OR AFT

To adjust the sliding door fore and aft, the three bolts retaining the center door hinge to the door may be loosened and the hinge adjusted fore and aft as required.

➡Some up and down adjustments may be obtained from the center hinge by moving the center hinge strap up or down as desired, prior to securing the retainer bolts. The vertical hinge rollers within the body center track assembly must be parallel to the top of the track and maintain a minimum clearance of 0.040 in. (1mm) from the top of the track for smooth operation.

Hood

REMOVAL & INSTALLATION

▶ **See Figures 1, 2, 3 and 4**

1. Disconnect the negative (-) battery cable.
2. Open, then prop the hood in the upright position.
3. Cover all body panels with an old blanket or similar piece of cloth to protect them against scratches in the paint or on the windshield.
4. Separate any electrical connectors from the hood wiring to the main engine compartment wiring (such as the underhood lamp wiring).
5. Using white paint or a grease pencil, matchmark the hood hinge locations in respect to the hood. This will make installation and alignment much easier.
6. With an assistant, hold the hood while removing the hood hinge-to-hood attaching bolts.
7. Lift the hood off of the vehicle.

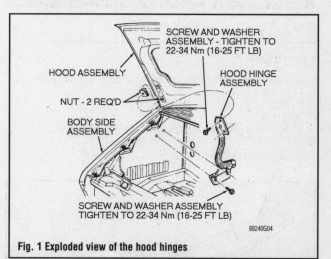

Fig. 1 Exploded view of the hood hinges

Fig. 2 To remove the hood, first detach all electrical wiring connectors from the hood

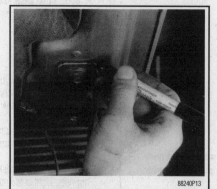

Fig. 3 Outline the hood hinge to help facilitate installation of the hood

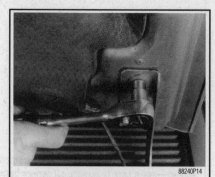

Fig. 4 Have an assistant hold the hood while loosening the hinge bolts, then lift the hood off the vehicle

To install:

8. With an assistant's help, hold the hood in position so that the hood and hinge bolt holes are aligned, then install the hinge-to-hood bolts finger-tight.

9. Move the hood until the matchmarks made earlier are aligned, then tighten the hood-to-hinge bolts to 16–25 ft. lbs. (22–34 Nm).

10. Carefully close the hood and check the alignment.

ALIGNMENT

The hood should be aligned so that the gap between the hood and the side fenders is uniform around the entire circumference. The hood should also sit flush with the surrounding body panels. If the hood is out of alignment, loosen the hood-to-hinge bolts, then move the hood in the desired direction. Tighten the hood-to-hinge bolts, then recheck the hood alignment. To raise and lower the hood, either loosen the hinge-to-body bolts or adjust the front rubber snubber to the desired height.

Rear Hatch

ALIGNMENT

The hatch can be adjusted side-to-side and up-and-down by loosening the hinge-to-header attaching nut. Adding spacers permits in or out adjustments as required. The hatch should be adjusted for an even and parallel fit with the door opening. Tighten the nuts to 13–20 ft. lbs. (17–27 Nm).

The striker assembly can be moved ⅛ in. (4mm) radially (side-to-side/back and forth) as necessary. Tighten the striker to 30–40 ft. lbs. (41–55 Nm).

Grille

REMOVAL & INSTALLATION

▶ **See Figure 5**

1. Open the hood, then remove the retaining screws from the radiator grille.
2. Remove the grille from the vehicle.
To install:
3. Position the grille in place, then install the retaining screws until snug.
4. Close the hood.

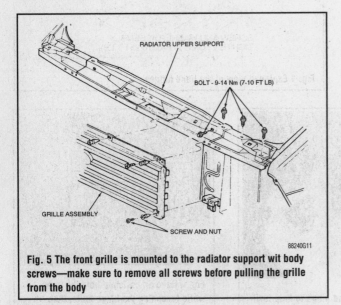

Fig. 5 The front grille is mounted to the radiator support wit body screws—make sure to remove all screws before pulling the grille from the body

Outside Mirrors

REMOVAL & INSTALLATION

Manual Mirror

▶ **See Figure 6**

1. Remove the front door interior trim panel as described later in this section.
2. With the window in the down position, remove the two mirror attaching nuts.
3. Remove the outside rear view mirror from the door.
To install:

➡**When installing the outside rear view mirror, make certain that the gasket is installed between the outside rear view mirror and door.**

4. Position the gasket and mirror on the outside of the door.
5. Install the two retaining nuts, then tighten them to 24–39 inch lbs. (3–5 Nm).
6. Install the interior door trim panel.

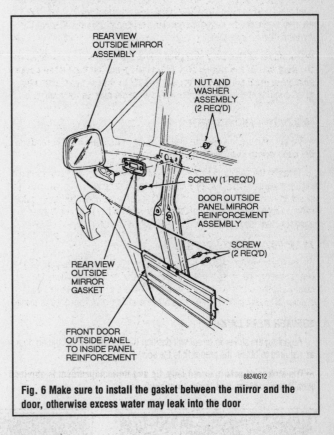

Fig. 6 Make sure to install the gasket between the mirror and the door, otherwise excess water may leak into the door

Power Mirror

▶ **See Figure 7**

1. Disconnect the negative battery cable.
2. Remove the door trim panel as outlined later in this section.
3. With the window in the down position, remove the two mirror retaining nuts.
4. Detach the electrical connector.
5. Remove the mirror assembly from the outside of the vehicle.
To install:
6. Position the gasket and mirror onto the door, then install the two retaining nuts. Tighten the nuts to 41 inch lbs. (5 Nm).

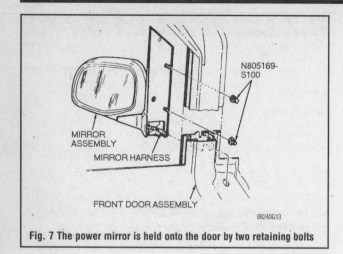

Fig. 7 The power mirror is held onto the door by two retaining bolts

7. Attach the mirror wiring harness connectors.
8. Connect the negative battery cable and check the operation of the mirror.
9. Install the door trim panel.

➡When the battery has been disconnected and reconnected, some abnormal drive symptoms may occur while the Powertrain Control Module (PCM) relearns its adaptive strategy. The vehicle may need to be driven 10 miles (16 km) or more to relearn the strategy.

INTERIOR

Instrument Panel and Pad

REMOVAL & INSTALLATION

▶ See Figures 8, 9, 10 and 11

1. Disconnect the negative battery cable.
2. Detach the wiring connector from the instrument panel, located in the engine compartment, by loosening the bolt and separating the connector halves.
3. Remove the left and right windshield inside mouldings.
4. Remove the defroster grille.
5. Remove the glove compartment door finish panel.
6. Remove the instrument panel steering column cover.
7. Remove the four bolts attaching the steering column lower reinforcement. Remove the reinforcement.
8. Remove the right and left cowl side panels.
9. Remove the two nuts retaining the hood latch control handle and cable assembly to the left cowl side. Remove the control handle and cable assembly, then reinstall the nuts to hold the bracket and relay in place.
10. Detach the wiring on the left cowl side panel and, if equipped, the vacuum hose harness connector. The number and location of the connectors may vary depending on optional equipment.

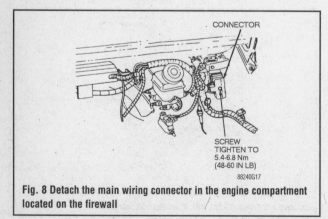

Fig. 8 Detach the main wiring connector in the engine compartment located on the firewall

Antenna

REMOVAL & INSTALLATION

1. Disconnect the negative battery cable.
2. Remove the necessary components to gain access to the rear of the radio and to the top of the heater unit under the dashboard.
3. Disconnect the antenna lead-in cable from the radio body or from the antenna base.
4. Disengage the cable from the retainers along the top of the heater case.
5. Remove the antenna mast from the antenna base.
6. Unsnap the cap from the antenna base and remove.
7. Remove the three antenna base attaching screws and remove the antenna from the vehicle.
To install:
8. Place the gasket on the cowl panel, then insert the antenna lead and base.
9. Install the three base screws, then snap the cap onto the base.
10. Install the antenna mast to the antenna base.
11. Route the antenna lead along the retainers on the heater case.
12. Reconnect the lead to the radio and install any components which were removed to access the radio and heater unit.
13. Connect the negative battery cable.

➡When the battery has been disconnected and reconnected, some abnormal drive symptoms may occur while the Powertrain Control Module (PCM) relearns its adaptive strategy. The vehicle may need to be driven 10 miles (16 km) or more to relearn the strategy.

11. Detach the brake light switch wiring connector. Detach the clutch pedal position switch on manual transmission equipped vehicles. For more information, refer to Section 7.
12. Remove the steering column-to-extension shaft pinch bolt. Compress the extension shaft toward the engine, then separate from the column U-joint.
13. Detach the transmission control selector indicator from the steering column.
14. Disconnect the wiring from the windshield wiper intermittent control

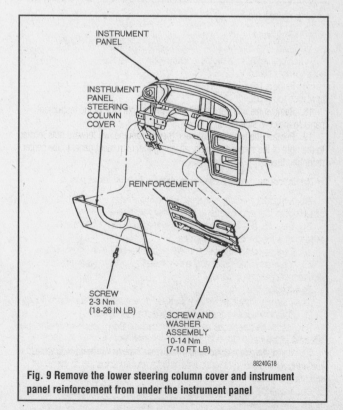

Fig. 9 Remove the lower steering column cover and instrument panel reinforcement from under the instrument panel

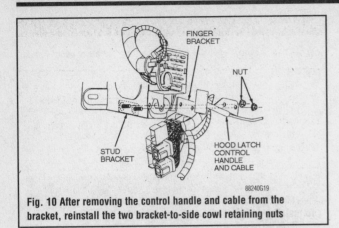

Fig. 10 After removing the control handle and cable from the bracket, reinstall the two bracket-to-side cowl retaining nuts

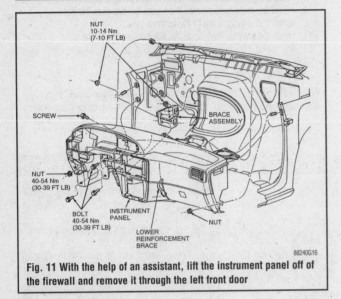

Fig. 11 With the help of an assistant, lift the instrument panel off of the firewall and remove it through the left front door

module and, if equipped, the wiring from the low oil level relay. Both are located to the right of the steering column.

15. Disconnect the radio antenna lead-in cable at the right cowl side panel.

16. Disconnect the heater temperature cable. If equipped, detach the vacuum hose harness connector.

17. Remove the five screws attaching the top of the instrument panel to the cowl side top panel.

18. Remove the one nut attaching the lower right side of the instrument panel to the cowl side panel.

19. Remove the two rearward nuts, then loosen the two forward nuts located to the right of the steering column, attaching the instrument panel to the center mounting bracket.

➡ **The following removal steps require the help of an assistant.**

20. Support the instrument panel. Remove the three bolts and one nut attaching the instrument panel to the left cowl side panel.

21. Carefully pull the instrument panel rearward, then disconnect any remaining wires or other components.

22. Carefully remove the instrument panel through the left front door.

23. If replacing the instrument panel, transfer all the components to the replacement instrument panel.

To install:

24. Carefully install the instrument panel through the left front door.

25. Carefully position the instrument panel on the firewall.

26. Install the three bolts and one nut attaching the instrument panel to the left cowl side panel.

27. Install the two rearward nuts, then install the two forward nuts located to the right of the steering column, attaching the instrument panel to the center mounting bracket.

28. Install the one nut attaching the lower right side of the instrument panel to the cowl side panel.

29. Install the five screws attaching the top of the instrument panel to the cowl side top panel.

30. Attach the heater temperature cable. If equipped, attach the vacuum hose harness connector.

31. Attach the radio antenna lead-in cable at the right cowl side panel.

32. Attach the wiring to the windshield wiper intermittent control module and, if equipped, the wiring to the low oil level relay. Both are located to the right of the steering column.

33. Attach the transmission control selector indicator to the steering column.

34. Install the extension shaft to the steering column U-joint. Install the steering column-to-extension shaft pinch bolt.

35. Attach the brake light switch wiring connector. Attach the clutch pedal position switch on manual transmission equipped vehicles. For more information, refer to Section 7.

36. Attach the wiring on the left cowl side panel and, if equipped, the vacuum hose harness connector. The number and location of the connectors may vary depending on optional equipment.

37. Remove the two nuts retaining the hood latch control handle and cable assembly to the left cowl side, install the control handle and cable assembly, then reinstall the nuts.

38. Install the right and left cowl side panels.

39. Install the four bolts attaching the steering column lower reinforcement. Install the reinforcement.

40. Install the instrument panel steering column cover.

41. Install the glove compartment door finish panel.

42. Install the defroster grille.

43. Install the left and right windshield inside mouldings.

44. Attach the wiring connector for the instrument panel located, in the engine compartment. Install the bolt, then tighten until snug.

45. Connect the negative battery cable.

Floor Console

REMOVAL & INSTALLATION

◆ **See Figure 12**

1. Open the cassette door, then remove the tape cartridge container.
2. Remove the two nuts and washers from the container opening.

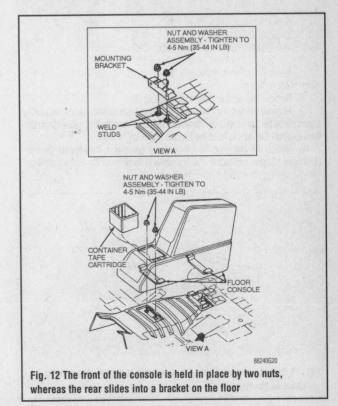

Fig. 12 The front of the console is held in place by two nuts, whereas the rear slides into a bracket on the floor

3. Lift the console assembly up over the two weld screws. Move the console rearward approximately 2 in. (51mm), then lift up on the console assembly.

To install:

4. Place the console assembly approximately 2 in. (51mm) rearward of the console panel rear mounting bracket. Push the console forward and, at the same time, lift the front of the console. Place the front over the two weld screws.

5. Install the two nuts and washers onto the weld screws retaining the console in place.

6. Install the tape cartridge container.

Door Panels

REMOVAL & INSTALLATION

Front Doors

MODELS WITH OPTIONAL TRIM PACKAGE

♦ See Figures 13 thru 22

1. Remove the screw retaining the front door trim finish panel to the door inner panel.

2. Remove the screws retaining the front door trim panel moulding assembly to the door inner panel.

3. Remove the screw retaining the door window regulator handle and remove the handle and washer.

4. At each plastic clip location, carefully pry the trim panel away from the door inner panel (upward to clear the door release handle, and door lock control), then remove the trim panel.

➡The manufacturer recommends making a special push pin removal tool, shown in the illustration to complete Step 4.

➡Do not use the trim panel to pull the clips from the inner panel holes.

To install:

5. Replace bent or broken trim clips as necessary.

6. Position the door panel onto the door so that the plastic retainer clips line up with the holes in the door. Push the door panel until the plastic retainers are secured in the door.

7. Install the door window regulator handle and washer onto the door, then install the retaining screw.

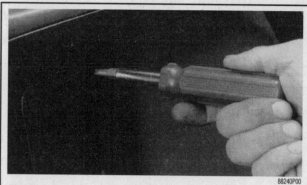

Fig. 13 Remove the window switch panel by removing the retaining screws

Fig. 14 Pull the switch panel out the mounting hole, . . .

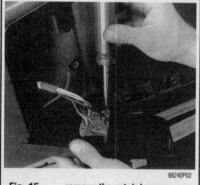

Fig. 15 . . . remove the retaining screws, then . . .

Fig. 16 . . . remove the switch assembly from the panel

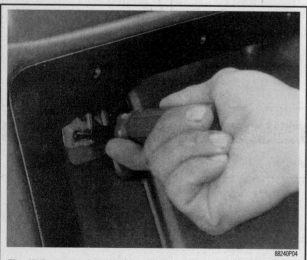

Fig. 17 Remove the door panel retaining screws from through the window switch panel hole

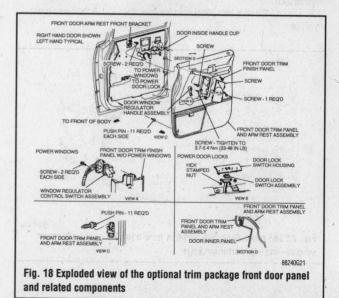

Fig. 18 Exploded view of the optional trim package front door panel and related components

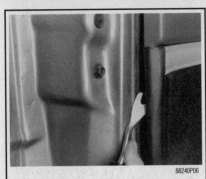

Fig. 19 Where the retaining pins are located, gently pry the door trim panel off of the door

Fig. 20 Lift the door trim panel off the door, then . . .

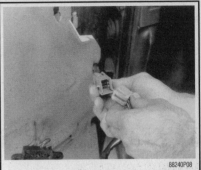

Fig. 21 . . . detach any electrical wiring harness connectors from the door trim panel

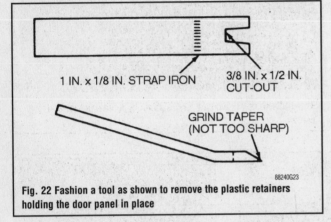

1 IN. x 1/8 IN. STRAP IRON

3/8 IN. x 1/2 IN. CUT-OUT

GRIND TAPER (NOT TOO SHARP)

Fig. 22 Fashion a tool as shown to remove the plastic retainers holding the door panel in place

8. Install the screws retaining the front door trim panel moulding assembly to the door inner panel.

9. Install the screw retaining the front door trim finish panel to the door inner panel.

MODELS WITH STANDARD TRIM PACKAGE

▶ See Figure 23

1. Remove the door trim panel retaining screws.
2. Pull the trim panel away from the door.

To install:

3. Position the door trim panel onto the door, then install the seven retaining screws.

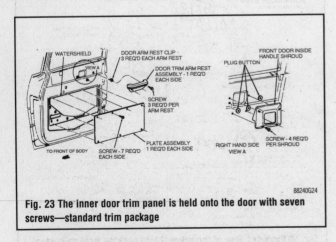

WATERSHIELD

VIEW A

DOOR ARM REST CLIP 3 REQ'D EACH ARM REST

DOOR TRIM ARM REST ASSEMBLY - 1 REQ'D EACH SIDE

SCREW 3 REQ'D PER ARM REST

FRONT DOOR INSIDE HANDLE SHROUD

PLUG BUTTON

PLATE ASSEMBLY 1 REQ'D EACH SIDE

TO FRONT OF BODY

SCREW - 7 REQ'D EACH SIDE

RIGHT HAND SIDE VIEW A

SCREW - 4 REQ'D PER SHROUD

Fig. 23 The inner door trim panel is held onto the door with seven screws—standard trim package

Sliding Door Trim Panel

MODELS WITH OPTIONAL TRIM PACKAGE

▶ See Figure 24

1. Remove the screws retaining the sliding door garnish moulding to the sliding door inner panel, then remove the garnish panel.
2. Remove the screws retaining the sliding door trim panel to the sliding door inner panel, then remove the trim panel. Remove the screw at the ashtray bezel.

To install:

3. Install the ashtray trim bezel, then install the retaining screw until snug.
4. Position the trim panel onto the sliding door. Secure the trim panel onto the door with the retaining screws.
5. Install the trim garnish panel. Secure it in place with the attaching screws.

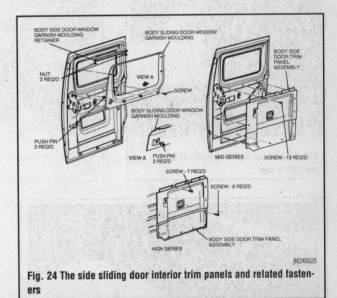

BODY SIDE DOOR WINDOW GARNISH MOULDING RETAINER

BODY SLIDING DOOR WINDOW GARNISH MOULDING

BODY SIDE DOOR TRIM PANEL ASSEMBLY

NUT 2 REQ'D

VIEW A

SCREW

BODY SLIDING DOOR WINDOW GARNISH MOULDING

PUSH PIN 2 REQ'D

VIEW A PUSH PIN 2 REQ'D

MID-SERIES

SCREW - 13 REQ'D

SCREW - 7 REQ'D

SCREW - 6 REQ'D

HIGH SERIES

BODY SIDE DOOR TRIM PANEL ASSEMBLY

Fig. 24 The side sliding door interior trim panels and related fasteners

Interior Trim Panels

REMOVAL & INSTALLATION

▶ See Figure 25

The interior trim panels are either held on with screws (vehicles with base trim option) or with plastic push pins, which snap into holes in the metal body panels behind the trim panels (vehicles with custom trim option).

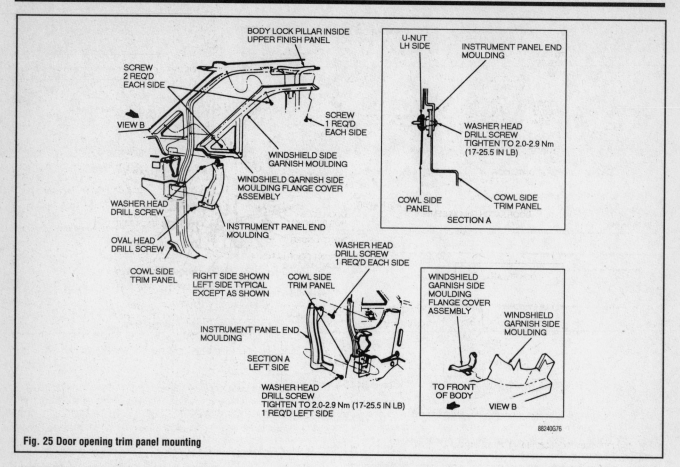

Fig. 25 Door opening trim panel mounting

1. Remove any peripheral trim pieces covering the edges of the trim panel to be removed.
2. Before removing the trim panel, locate all retaining screws (these usually are not hidden from view).
3. Remove all of the trim panel retaining screws.
4. Gently pull the trim panel from the body panel. If the trim panel resists being removed, there may be trim panel retaining push pins.
5. Use a wooden stick or trim tool to gently pry the trim panel away from the body panel at each push pin.

➡ **Do not pull on the trim panel itself to pry the push pins out of their retaining holes.**

6. Pull the trim panel away from the body, then check the back of the trim panel for any wiring or other components which may still be attached to the trim panel.
7. Remove the trim panel from the vehicle.

To install:
8. Attach any wiring or other components detached during removal.
9. Position the trim panel onto the body panel so that the push pins and body retaining holes align.
10. Push the trim panel in until the push pins snap in place.
11. Install any retaining screws, then install any trim pieces.

Door Locks

REMOVAL & INSTALLATION

Front

▶ **See Figure 26**

1. Remove the trim panel and water shield from the door.
2. Remove the remote control assembly and disconnect the rod.
3. Disconnect the pushbutton rod and handle rod from the latch.
4. Remove the lock assembly attaching screws and remove the lock from the door.

To install:
5. Install the rod retaining clips in the new lock assembly. The remote control rod, lock cylinder rod, and the anti-theft shield should be attached to the lock before installation.
6. Position the lock in the door, then install and securely tighten the lock retaining screws.
7. Connect the rods to the handle, lock cylinder and the remote control.
8. Connect the handle rod and pushbutton rod to the lock, and check the operation of the lock.
9. Install the water shield and trim panel to the door.

Sliding Door

▶ **See Figure 27**

1. Remove the sliding door panels, water shield and access hole cover plates.
2. Unlatch the sliding door.
3. Remove the actuator rod retainer from the center door retainer hole.
4. Disconnect the rear door lock actuator rod from the remote control assembly.
5. Open the door enough to gain access to the three lock retainer bolts attaching the rear lock to the sliding door, and remove the bolts.
6. Remove the sliding door rear lock with the remote control actuator rod attached to the lock.

To install:
7. Install the sliding door rear lock with the remote control actuator rod attached to the lock.
8. Open the door enough to gain access to the three lock retainer bolts attaching the rear lock to the sliding door, then install the bolts. Do not tighten the three lock retainer bolts more than 6–10 ft. lbs. (8–14 Nm).
9. Connect the rear door lock actuator rod to the remote control assembly.
10. Install the actuator rod retainer to the center door retainer hole.
11. Latch the sliding door.
12. Install the sliding door panels, water shield and access hole cover plates.

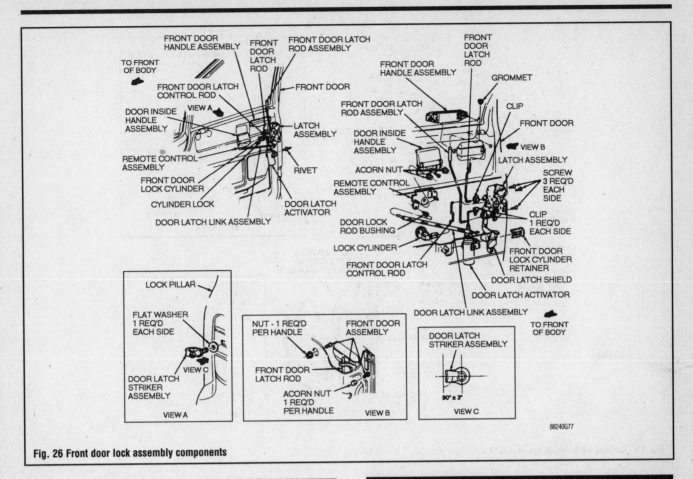

Fig. 26 Front door lock assembly components

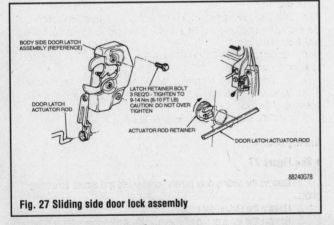

Fig. 27 Sliding side door lock assembly

Hatch Lock

REMOVAL & INSTALLATION

▶ See Figures 28, 29, 30 and 31

1. Open the hatch, then remove the hatch door trim panel and handle, if so equipped.
2. Disconnect the latch release rod from the control assembly.
3. Remove the three latch retaining screws, then remove the luggage compartment door lock mechanism cover and latch from the liftgate.
4. On vehicles equipped with a Hatch Ajar warning signal, pull the latch slightly away from the liftgate, then disconnect the electrical wire harness from the latch.

To install:

5. Attach the electrical Hatch Ajar warning wire harness to the latch.

Fig. 28 Remove the retaining screws from the rear panel of the hatch lock assembly

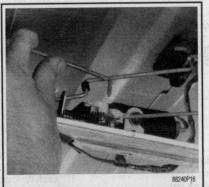

Fig. 29 Disconnect the attaching rod from the latch mechanism, then . . .

Fig. 30 . . . remove the hatch panel and latch mechanism from the hatch

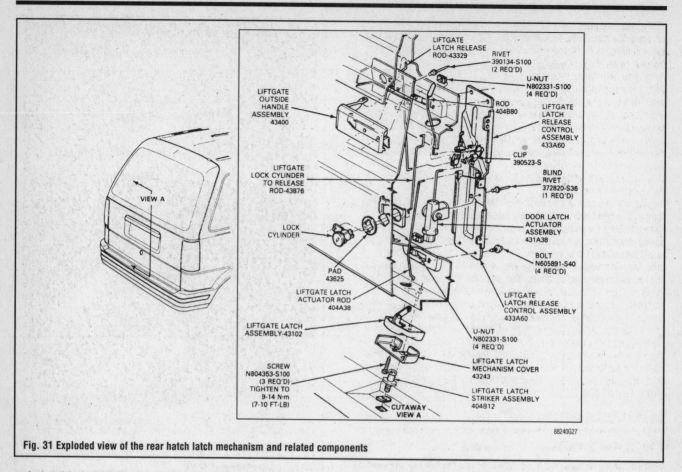

Fig. 31 Exploded view of the rear hatch latch mechanism and related components

6. Install the latch into the door. Install the luggage compartment door lock mechanism cover, then install and tighten the three latch retaining screws to 36–70 inch lbs. (4–8 Nm).

7. Attach the hatch latch release rod to the control assembly.

8. Install the hatch door trim panel and handle, if so equipped. Close the hatch.

Electric Window Motor

REMOVAL & INSTALLATION

▶ See Figure 32

1. Disconnect the battery ground cable.
2. Remove the interior door trim panel.
3. Detach the electric window motor wire from the wire harness connector.
4. Using a ½ in. (13mm) diameter drill bit, drill two holes in the door inner panel at the drill dimples located opposite the two unexposed motor drive retainer screws.

➡Check inside the door to make sure that electrical wires are not in line with the holes to be drilled in the door inner panel.

5. Remove the three motor mount retainer bolts using the two drilled holes and the larger hole to access the bolt heads.

6. Push the motor toward the outside sheet metal to disengage the motor and drive from the regulator gear. After the motor and drive are disengaged, prop the window in the full UP position.

7. Remove the motor and drive from inside the door.

To install:

8. Install the motor and drive into the door.

9. Make sure that the window is in the full UP position. Push the motor to engage the motor and drive onto the regulator gear.

10. Install the three motor mount retainer bolts using the two drilled holes and the larger hole to access the bolt heads.

11. Attach the electric window motor wire to the wire harness connector.

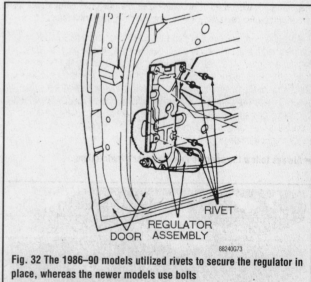

Fig. 32 The 1986–90 models utilized rivets to secure the regulator in place, whereas the newer models use bolts

12. Install the interior door trim panel.
13. Connect the battery ground cable.

Windshield and Fixed Glass

REMOVAL & INSTALLATION

If your windshield, or other fixed window, is cracked or chipped, you may decide to replace it with a new one yourself. However, there are two main reasons why replacement windshields and other window glass should be installed only by a professional automotive glass technician: safety and cost.

The most important reason a professional should install automotive glass is for safety. The glass in the vehicle, especially the windshield, is designed with safety in mind in case of a collision. The windshield is specially manufactured from two panes of specially-tempered glass with a thin layer of transparent plastic between them. This construction allows the glass to "give" in the event that a part of your body hits the windshield during the collision, and prevents the glass from shattering, which could cause lacerations, blinding and other harm to passengers of the vehicle. The other fixed windows are designed to be tempered so that if they break during a collision, they shatter in such a way that there are no large pointed glass pieces. The professional automotive glass technician knows how to install the glass in a vehicle so that it will function optimally during a collision. Without the proper experience, knowledge and tools, installing a piece of automotive glass yourself could lead to additional harm if an accident should ever occur.

Cost is also a factor when deciding to install automotive glass yourself. Performing this could cost you much more than a professional may charge for the same job. Since the windshield is designed to break under stress, an often life saving characteristic, windshields tend to break VERY easily when an inexperienced person attempts to install one. Do-it-yourselfers buying two, three or even four windshields from a salvage yard because they have broken them during installation are common stories. Also, since the automotive glass is designed to prevent the outside elements from entering your vehicle, improper installation can lead to water and air leaks. Annoying whining noises at highway speeds from air leaks or inside body panel rusting from water leaks can add to your stress level and subtract from your wallet. After buying two or three windshields, installing them and ending up with a leak that produces a noise while driving and water damage during rainstorms, the cost of having a professional do it correctly the first time may be much more alluring. We here at Chilton, therefore, advise that you have a professional automotive glass technician service any broken glass on your vehicle.

WINDSHIELD CHIP REPAIR

▶ **See Figures 33 and 34**

➡**Check with your state and local authorities on the laws for state safety inspection. Some states or municipalities may not allow chip repair as a viable option for correcting stone damage to your windshield.**

Although severely cracked or damaged windshields must be replaced, there is something that you can do to prolong or even prevent the need for replacement of a chipped windshield. There are many companies which offer windshield chip repair products, such as Loctite's® Bullseye windshield repair kit. These kits usually consist of a syringe, pedestal and a sealing adhesive. The syringe is mounted on the pedestal and is used to create a vacuum which pulls the plastic layer against the glass. This helps make the chip transparent. The adhesive is then injected which seals the chip and helps to prevent further stress cracks from developing

➡**Always follow the specific manufacturer's instructions.**

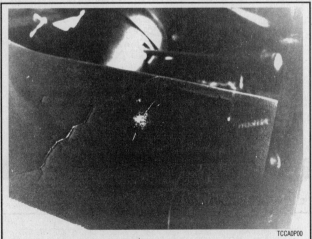

Fig. 33 Small chips on your windshield can be fixed with an after-market repair kit, such as the one from Loctite

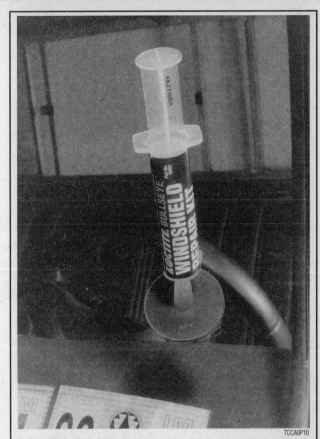

Fig. 34 Most kits us a self-stick applicator and syringe to inject the adhesive into the chip or crack

Inside Rear View Mirror

REPLACEMENT

1. Locate and mark the location of the inside rear view mirror bracket on the outside surface of the windshield glass with a wax pencil.

2. If the clear vinyl wafer remained on the windshield glass, apply low heat with a heat gun until the wafer softens. Peel the vinyl wafer from the windshield glass, taking care not to scratch or mar the windshield glass surface.

3. Thoroughly clean the inside of the windshield glass with mild abrasive cleaning powder and a clean cloth saturated in alcohol to remove the old adhesive. Then, use a paper towel to remove all cleaner from the windshield glass. Do not contaminate the clean area. Roughen the bonding surface of the inside rear view mirror bracket with fine grit sandpaper. Wipe the surface clean with a paper towel soaked in alcohol. Do not contaminate the cleaned bracket.

4. If the vinyl wafer is still adhered to the inside rear view mirror bracket, apply low heat with a heat gun until the wafer softens, then peel it off.

5. Use fine grit sandpaper on the inside rear view mirror bracket to lightly scuff the surface. Wipe it clean with an alcohol moistened cloth.

6. Using the applicator, apply a generous amount of Rear View Mirror Adhesive D9AZ-19554-CA or equivalent to the bonding surface of the inside rear view mirror bracket and windshield glass. Allow the adhesive material to dry for three minutes. DO NOT TOUCH THE MOUNTING SURFACE.

7. Apply two drops of Rear View Mirror Adhesive or equivalent to the mounting surface of the inside rear view mirror bracket. Using a clean toothpick or wooden match, quickly spread the adhesive evenly over the mounting surface of the mirror bracket.

8. Quickly position the mirror bracket onto the windshield glass, using the locator marked on the outside of the windshield glass. The ⅜ in. (9.5mm) circular depression in the bracket must be down and toward the inside of the passenger compartment. Press the mirror bracket against the windshield glass for about one minute.

9. Allow the adhesive to set for five minutes. Then, remove any excess adhesive material from the windshield glass with an alcohol dampened rag.

Seats

REMOVAL & INSTALLATION

Front

1. Remove the support insulator screw and insulator.
2. Remove the support-to-floor pan attaching bolts and seat belt bolt.

3. With an assistant, remove the seat assembly from the vehicle.
4. To remove the seat supports, place the assembly on a bench, disconnect the latch tie rod and remove the four seat support-to-seat track nuts.

To install:

5. Position the seat tracks to the seat cushion, then tighten the attaching bolts to 18 ft. lbs. (24 Nm).
6. Connect the latch tie rod.
7. With an assistant, position the seat assembly into the vehicle and install the mounting bolts. Tighten the mounting bolts to 20 ft. lbs. (27 Nm). Install the seat belt bolt.
8. Place the seat insulator on the rear inboard support foot and install the retaining screw.

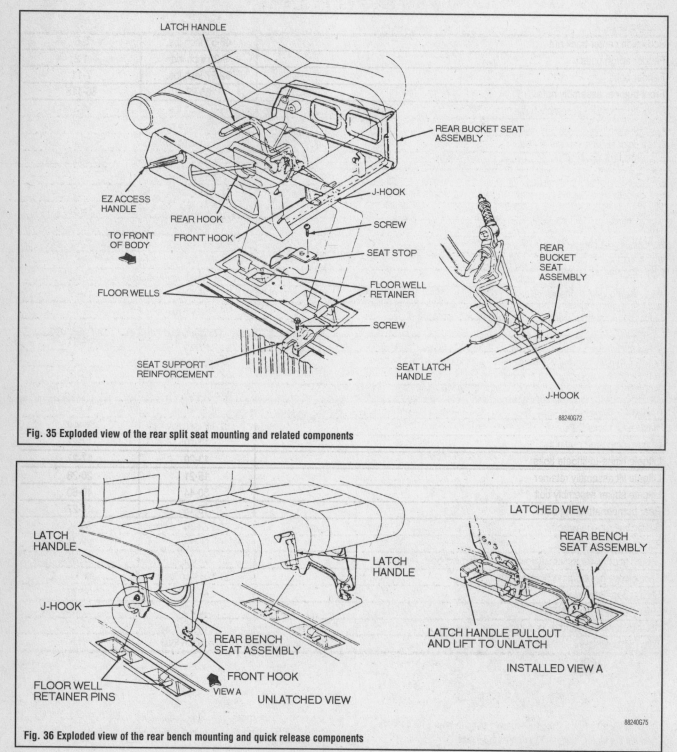

Fig. 35 Exploded view of the rear split seat mounting and related components

Fig. 36 Exploded view of the rear bench mounting and quick release components

Rear

◆ **See Figures 35 and 36**

1. Rotate the latch handles upward simultaneously.
2. Lift the rear of the seat, causing the seat to rotate about the forward attachment until the seat latches are clear of the rear floor attachments.
3. With an assistant, pull the seat rearward to disengage it from the front floor pins.

To install:

➡Care should be taken when storing seats out of the vehicle, so the latches are not damaged.

4. Lift the seat assembly into the vehicle and engage the front hooks into the front floor well retaining pins.
5. Lower the rear of the seat into engagement with the floor well rear retainer pin. The latches should rotate downward as the seat is lowered into position. Make sure the handles are in the latched position and the seat is fully secured.

TORQUE SPECIFICATIONS

Component	Ft. Lbs.	Nm
Body side center track nut	48-53 inch lbs.	5-6
Fender apron bolts	9-20 inch lbs.	1-2
Fender bolts	62-97 inch lbs.	7-11
Front bumper assembly nuts	65-87	88-118
Front bumper trim assembly bolts	40-53 inch lbs.	4-6
Front bumper trim assembly shoulder bolt	62-88 inch lbs.	9-14
Front door equalizer bracket nuts	62-88 inch lbs.	9-14
Front door galss stabilizer attaching screws	62-88 inch lbs.	9-14
Front door glass run attaching bolts	53-88 inch lbs.	7-14
Front door guide-to-glass bracket	53-88 inch lbs.	7-14
Front door hinge-to-body bolts	18-26	25-35
Front door hinge-to-body nuts	18-26	25-35
Front door regulator inner panel bolts	62-88 inch lbs.	9-14
Front door regulator motor and drive bolts	35-62 inch lbs.	5-9
Front seat shoulder safety belt bolt	22-30	30-40
Front seat support-to-floorpan bolts	14-20	19-27
Grille moulding screw	14-17 inch lbs.	1-2
Hinge-to-hood bolts	16-25	22-34
Hood hinge-to-body bolts	16-25	22-34
Hood latch bolt	62-88 inch lbs.	9-14
Hood latch handle nuts	71-88 inch lbs.	10-14
Hood support rod bolt	62-88 inch lbs.	9-14
Instrument panel bolts	30-39	40-54
Instrument panel nuts	62-88 inch lbs.	10-14
Liftgate hinge-to-body nuts	13-20	17-27
Liftgate hinge-to-liftgate bolts	13-20	17-27
Liftgate lift assembly retainer	15-21	20-28
Liftgate striker assembly bolt	30-44	40-60
Rear bumper attaching bolts	13-19	17-27
Safety belt attaching bolts	22-30	30-40
Sliding door bracket bolt	16-25	22-34
Sliding door guide assembly lower reinforcement bolt	16-25	22-34
Sliding door guide upper bracket nuts	80-124 inch lbs.	9-14
Sliding door latch striker	40-52	54-71
Sliding door-to-hinge bolts	13-15	17-20
Splash shield nuts and bolts	13-20	17-27
Trim panel screws	15-19 inch lbs.	1-2

91320C01

AIR/FUEL RATIO: The ratio of air-to-gasoline by weight in the fuel mixture drawn into the engine.

AIR INJECTION: One method of reducing harmful exhaust emissions by injecting air into each of the exhaust ports of an engine. The fresh air entering the hot exhaust manifold causes any remaining fuel to be burned before it can exit the tailpipe.

ALTERNATOR: A device used for converting mechanical energy into electrical energy.

AMMETER: An instrument, calibrated in amperes, used to measure the flow of an electrical current in a circuit. Ammeters are always connected in series with the circuit being tested.

AMPERE: The rate of flow of electrical current present when one volt of electrical pressure is applied against one ohm of electrical resistance.

ANALOG COMPUTER: Any microprocessor that uses similar (analogous) electrical signals to make its calculations.

ARMATURE: A laminated, soft iron core wrapped by a wire that converts electrical energy to mechanical energy as in a motor or relay. When rotated in a magnetic field, it changes mechanical energy into electrical energy as in a generator.

ATMOSPHERIC PRESSURE: The pressure on the Earth's surface caused by the weight of the air in the atmosphere. At sea level, this pressure is 14.7 psi at 32°F (101 kPa at 0°C).

ATOMIZATION: The breaking down of a liquid into a fine mist that can be suspended in air.

AXIAL PLAY: Movement parallel to a shaft or bearing bore.

BACKFIRE: The sudden combustion of gases in the intake or exhaust system that results in a loud explosion.

BACKLASH: The clearance or play between two parts, such as meshed gears.

BACKPRESSURE: Restrictions in the exhaust system that slow the exit of exhaust gases from the combustion chamber.

BAKELITE: A heat resistant, plastic insulator material commonly used in printed circuit boards and transistorized components.

BALL BEARING: A bearing made up of hardened inner and outer races between which hardened steel balls roll.

BALLAST RESISTOR: A resistor in the primary ignition circuit that lowers voltage after the engine is started to reduce wear on ignition components.

BEARING: A friction reducing, supportive device usually located between a stationary part and a moving part.

BIMETAL TEMPERATURE SENSOR: Any sensor or switch made of two dissimilar types of metal that bend when heated or cooled due to the different expansion rates of the alloys. These types of sensors usually function as an on/off switch.

BLOWBY: Combustion gases, composed of water vapor and unburned fuel, that leak past the piston rings into the crankcase during normal engine operation. These gases are removed by the PCV system to prevent the buildup of harmful acids in the crankcase.

BRAKE PAD: A brake shoe and lining assembly used with disc brakes.

BRAKE SHOE: The backing for the brake lining. The term is, however, usually applied to the assembly of the brake backing and lining.

BUSHING: A liner, usually removable, for a bearing; an anti-friction liner used in place of a bearing.

CALIPER: A hydraulically activated device in a disc brake system, which is mounted straddling the brake rotor (disc). The caliper contains at least one piston and two brake pads. Hydraulic pressure on the piston(s) forces the pads against the rotor.

CAMSHAFT: A shaft in the engine on which are the lobes (cams) which operate the valves. The camshaft is driven by the crankshaft, via a belt, chain or gears, at one half the crankshaft speed.

CAPACITOR: A device which stores an electrical charge.

CARBON MONOXIDE (CO): A colorless, odorless gas given off as a normal byproduct of combustion. It is poisonous and extremely dangerous in confined areas, building up slowly to toxic levels without warning if adequate ventilation is not available.

CARBURETOR: A device, usually mounted on the intake manifold of an engine, which mixes the air and fuel in the proper proportion to allow even combustion.

CATALYTIC CONVERTER: A device installed in the exhaust system, like a muffler, that converts harmful byproducts of combustion into carbon dioxide and water vapor by means of a heat-producing chemical reaction.

CENTRIFUGAL ADVANCE: A mechanical method of advancing the spark timing by using flyweights in the distributor that react to centrifugal force generated by the distributor shaft rotation.

CHECK VALVE: Any one-way valve installed to permit the flow of air, fuel or vacuum in one direction only.

CHOKE: A device, usually a moveable valve, placed in the intake path of a carburetor to restrict the flow of air.

CIRCUIT: Any unbroken path through which an electrical current can flow. Also used to describe fuel flow in some instances.

CIRCUIT BREAKER: A switch which protects an electrical circuit from overload by opening the circuit when the current flow exceeds a predetermined level. Some circuit breakers must be reset manually, while most reset automatically.

COIL (IGNITION): A transformer in the ignition circuit which steps up the voltage provided to the spark plugs.

COMBINATION MANIFOLD: An assembly which includes both the intake and exhaust manifolds in one casting.

COMBINATION VALVE: A device used in some fuel systems that routes fuel vapors to a charcoal storage canister instead of venting them into the atmosphere. The valve relieves fuel tank pressure and allows fresh air into the tank as the fuel level drops to prevent a vapor lock situation.

COMPRESSION RATIO: The comparison of the total volume of the cylinder and combustion chamber with the piston at BDC and the piston at TDC.

CONDENSER: 1. An electrical device which acts to store an electrical charge, preventing voltage surges. 2. A radiator-like device in the air conditioning system in which refrigerant gas condenses into a liquid, giving off heat.

CONDUCTOR: Any material through which an electrical current can be transmitted easily.

CONTINUITY: Continuous or complete circuit. Can be checked with an ohmmeter.

COUNTERSHAFT: An intermediate shaft which is rotated by a mainshaft and transmits, in turn, that rotation to a working part.

CRANKCASE: The lower part of an engine in which the crankshaft and related parts operate.

CRANKSHAFT: The main driving shaft of an engine which receives reciprocating motion from the pistons and converts it to rotary motion.

CYLINDER: In an engine, the round hole in the engine block in which the piston(s) ride.

CYLINDER BLOCK: The main structural member of an engine in which is found the cylinders, crankshaft and other principal parts.

CYLINDER HEAD: The detachable portion of the engine, usually fastened to the top of the cylinder block and containing all or most of the combustion chambers. On overhead valve engines, it contains the valves and their operating parts. On overhead cam engines, it contains the camshaft as well.

DEAD CENTER: The extreme top or bottom of the piston stroke.

DETONATION: An unwanted explosion of the air/fuel mixture in the combustion chamber caused by excess heat and compression, advanced timing, or an overly lean mixture. Also referred to as "ping".

DIAPHRAGM: A thin, flexible wall separating two cavities, such as in a vacuum advance unit.

DIESELING: A condition in which hot spots in the combustion chamber cause the engine to run on after the key is turned off.

DIFFERENTIAL: A geared assembly which allows the transmission of motion between drive axles, giving one axle the ability to turn faster than the other.

DIODE: An electrical device that will allow current to flow in one direction only.

DISC BRAKE: A hydraulic braking assembly consisting of a brake disc, or rotor, mounted on an axle, and a caliper assembly containing, usually two brake pads which are activated by hydraulic pressure. The pads are forced against the sides of the disc, creating friction which slows the vehicle.

DISTRIBUTOR: A mechanically driven device on an engine which is responsible for electrically firing the spark plug at a predetermined point of the piston stroke.

DOWEL PIN: A pin, inserted in mating holes in two different parts allowing those parts to maintain a fixed relationship.

DRUM BRAKE: A braking system which consists of two brake shoes and one or two wheel cylinders, mounted on a fixed backing plate, and a brake drum, mounted on an axle, which revolves around the assembly.

DWELL: The rate, measured in degrees of shaft rotation, at which an electrical circuit cycles on and off.

ELECTRONIC CONTROL UNIT (ECU): Ignition module, module, amplifier or igniter. See Module for definition.

ELECTRONIC IGNITION: A system in which the timing and firing of the spark plugs is controlled by an electronic control unit, usually called a module. These systems have no points or condenser.

END-PLAY: The measured amount of axial movement in a shaft.

ENGINE: A device that converts heat into mechanical energy.

EXHAUST MANIFOLD: A set of cast passages or pipes which conduct exhaust gases from the engine.

FEELER GAUGE: A blade, usually metal, or precisely predetermined thickness, used to measure the clearance between two parts.

FIRING ORDER: The order in which combustion occurs in the cylinders of an engine. Also the order in which spark is distributed to the plugs by the distributor.

FLOODING: The presence of too much fuel in the intake manifold and combustion chamber which prevents the air/fuel mixture from firing, thereby causing a no-start situation.

FLYWHEEL: A disc shaped part bolted to the rear end of the crankshaft. Around the outer perimeter is affixed the ring gear. The starter drive engages the ring gear, turning the flywheel, which rotates the crankshaft, imparting the initial starting motion to the engine.

FOOT POUND (ft. lbs. or sometimes, ft.lb.): The amount of energy or work needed to raise an item weighing one pound, a distance of one foot.

FUSE: A protective device in a circuit which prevents circuit overload by breaking the circuit when a specific amperage is present. The device is constructed around a strip or wire of a lower amperage rating than the circuit it is designed to protect. When an amperage higher than that stamped on the fuse is present in the circuit, the strip or wire melts, opening the circuit.

GEAR RATIO: The ratio between the number of teeth on meshing gears.

GENERATOR: A device which converts mechanical energy into electrical energy.

HEAT RANGE: The measure of a spark plug's ability to dissipate heat from its firing end. The higher the heat range, the hotter the plug fires.

HUB: The center part of a wheel or gear.

HYDROCARBON (HC): Any chemical compound made up of hydrogen and carbon. A major pollutant formed by the engine as a byproduct of combustion.

HYDROMETER: An instrument used to measure the specific gravity of a solution.

INCH POUND (inch lbs.; sometimes in.lb. or in. lbs.): One twelfth of a foot pound.

INDUCTION: A means of transferring electrical energy in the form of a magnetic field. Principle used in the ignition coil to increase voltage.

INJECTOR: A device which receives metered fuel under relatively low pressure and is activated to inject the fuel into the engine under relatively high pressure at a predetermined time.

INPUT SHAFT: The shaft to which torque is applied, usually carrying the driving gear or gears.

INTAKE MANIFOLD: A casting of passages or pipes used to conduct air or a fuel/air mixture to the cylinders.

JOURNAL: The bearing surface within which a shaft operates.

KEY: A small block usually fitted in a notch between a shaft and a hub to prevent slippage of the two parts.

MANIFOLD: A casting of passages or set of pipes which connect the cylinders to an inlet or outlet source.

MANIFOLD VACUUM: Low pressure in an engine intake manifold formed just below the throttle plates. Manifold vacuum is highest at idle and drops under acceleration.

MASTER CYLINDER: The primary fluid pressurizing device in a hydraulic system. In automotive use, it is found in brake and hydraulic clutch systems and is pedal activated, either directly or, in a power brake system, through the power booster.

MODULE: Electronic control unit, amplifier or igniter of solid state or integrated design which controls the current flow in the ignition primary circuit based on input from the pick-up coil. When the module opens the primary circuit, high secondary voltage is induced in the coil.

NEEDLE BEARING: A bearing which consists of a number (usually a large number) of long, thin rollers.

OHM: (Ω) The unit used to measure the resistance of conductor-to-electrical flow. One ohm is the amount of resistance that limits current flow to one ampere in a circuit with one volt of pressure.

OHMMETER: An instrument used for measuring the resistance, in ohms, in an electrical circuit.

OUTPUT SHAFT: The shaft which transmits torque from a device, such as a transmission.

OVERDRIVE: A gear assembly which produces more shaft revolutions than that transmitted to it.

OVERHEAD CAMSHAFT (OHC): An engine configuration in which the camshaft is mounted on top of the cylinder head and operates the valve either directly or by means of rocker arms.

OVERHEAD VALVE (OHV): An engine configuration in which all of the valves are located in the cylinder head and the camshaft is located in the cylinder block. The camshaft operates the valves via lifters and pushrods.

OXIDES OF NITROGEN (NOx): Chemical compounds of nitrogen produced as a byproduct of combustion. They combine with hydrocarbons to produce smog.

OXYGEN SENSOR: Use with the feedback system to sense the presence of oxygen in the exhaust gas and signal the computer which can reference the voltage signal to an air/fuel ratio.

PINION: The smaller of two meshing gears.

PISTON RING: An open-ended ring with fits into a groove on the outer diameter of the piston. Its chief function is to form a seal between the piston and cylinder wall. Most automotive pistons have three rings: two for compression sealing; one for oil sealing.

PRELOAD: A predetermined load placed on a bearing during assembly or by adjustment.

PRIMARY CIRCUIT: the low voltage side of the ignition system which consists of the ignition switch, ballast resistor or resistance wire, bypass, coil, electronic control unit and pick-up coil as well as the connecting wires and harnesses.

PRESS FIT: The mating of two parts under pressure, due to the inner diameter of one being smaller than the outer diameter of the other, or vice versa; an interference fit.

RACE: The surface on the inner or outer ring of a bearing on which the balls, needles or rollers move.

REGULATOR: A device which maintains the amperage and/or voltage levels of a circuit at predetermined values.

RELAY: A switch which automatically opens and/or closes a circuit.

RESISTANCE: The opposition to the flow of current through a circuit or electrical device, and is measured in ohms. Resistance is equal to the voltage divided by the amperage.

RESISTOR: A device, usually made of wire, which offers a preset amount of resistance in an electrical circuit.

RING GEAR: The name given to a ring-shaped gear attached to a differential case, or affixed to a flywheel or as part of a planetary gear set.

ROLLER BEARING: A bearing made up of hardened inner and outer races between which hardened steel rollers move.

ROTOR: 1. The disc-shaped part of a disc brake assembly, upon which the brake pads bear; also called, brake disc. 2. The device mounted atop the distributor shaft, which passes current to the distributor cap tower contacts.

SECONDARY CIRCUIT: The high voltage side of the ignition system, usually above 20,000 volts. The secondary includes the ignition coil, coil wire, distributor cap and rotor, spark plug wires and spark plugs.

SENDING UNIT: A mechanical, electrical, hydraulic or electro-magnetic device which transmits information to a gauge.

SENSOR: Any device designed to measure engine operating conditions or ambient pressures and temperatures. Usually electronic in nature and designed to send a voltage signal to an on-board computer, some sensors may operate as a simple on/off switch or they may provide a variable voltage signal (like a potentiometer) as conditions or measured parameters change.

SHIM: Spacers of precise, predetermined thickness used between parts to establish a proper working relationship.

SLAVE CYLINDER: In automotive use, a device in the hydraulic clutch system which is activated by hydraulic force, disengaging the clutch.

SOLENOID: A coil used to produce a magnetic field, the effect of which is to produce work.

SPARK PLUG: A device screwed into the combustion chamber of a spark ignition engine. The basic construction is a conductive core inside of a ceramic insulator, mounted in an outer conductive base. An electrical charge from the spark plug wire travels along the conductive core and jumps a preset air gap to a grounding point or points at the end of the conductive base. The resultant spark ignites the fuel/air mixture in the combustion chamber.

SPLINES: Ridges machined or cast onto the outer diameter of a shaft or inner diameter of a bore to enable parts to mate without rotation.

TACHOMETER: A device used to measure the rotary speed of an engine, shaft, gear, etc., usually in rotations per minute.

THERMOSTAT: A valve, located in the cooling system of an engine, which is closed when cold and opens gradually in response to engine heating, controlling the temperature of the coolant and rate of coolant flow.

TOP DEAD CENTER (TDC): The point at which the piston reaches the top of its travel on the compression stroke.

TORQUE: The twisting force applied to an object.

TORQUE CONVERTER: A turbine used to transmit power from a driving member to a driven member via hydraulic action, providing changes in drive ratio and torque. In automotive use, it links the driveplate at the rear of the engine to the automatic transmission.

TRANSDUCER: A device used to change a force into an electrical signal.

TRANSISTOR: A semi-conductor component which can be actuated by a small voltage to perform an electrical switching function.

TUNE-UP: A regular maintenance function, usually associated with the replacement and adjustment of parts and components in the electrical and fuel systems of a vehicle for the purpose of attaining optimum performance.

TURBOCHARGER: An exhaust driven pump which compresses intake air and forces it into the combustion chambers at higher than atmospheric pressures. The increased air pressure allows more fuel to be burned and results in increased horsepower being produced.

VACUUM ADVANCE: A device which advances the ignition timing in response to increased engine vacuum.

VACUUM GAUGE: An instrument used to measure the presence of vacuum in a chamber.

VALVE: A device which control the pressure, direction of flow or rate of flow of a liquid or gas.

VALVE CLEARANCE: The measured gap between the end of the valve stem and the rocker arm, cam lobe or follower that activates the valve.

VISCOSITY: The rating of a liquid's internal resistance to flow.

VOLTMETER: An instrument used for measuring electrical force in units called volts. Voltmeters are always connected parallel with the circuit being tested.

WHEEL CYLINDER: Found in the automotive drum brake assembly, it is a device, actuated by hydraulic pressure, which, through internal pistons, pushes the brake shoes outward against the drums.

MASTER
INDEX